U^{the}nofficial Guide®to

Bed & Breakfasts and Country Inns in the Southwest

Other Unofficial Guides

the Unofficial Guide® to

Bed & Breakfasts and Country Inns in the Southwest

1st Edition

Joel Grossman

Wiley Publishing, Inc.

Please note that prices fluctuate in the course of time, and travel information changes under the impact of many factors that influence the travel industry. We therefore suggest that you write or call ahead for confirmation when making your travel plans. Every effort has been made to ensure the accuracy of information throughout this book, and the contents of this publication are believed correct at the time of printing. Nevertheless, the publishers cannot accept responsibility for errors or omissions or for changes in details given in this guide or for the consequences of any reliance on the information provided by the same. Assessments of attractions and so forth are based upon the author's own experience, and therefore, descriptions given in this guide necessarily contain an element of subjective opinion, which may not reflect the publisher's opinion or dictate a reader's own experience on another occasion. Readers are invited to write the publisher with ideas, comments, and suggestions for future editions.

Published by:

Wiley Publishing, Inc.
909 Third Avenue
New York, NY 10022

Produced by Menasha Ridge Press
COVER DESIGN BY MICHAEL J. FREELAND
INTERIOR DESIGN BY MICHELE LASEAU
ILLUSTRATIONS BY RASHELL SMITH, SHELLEY NORRIS, KELLY HARDESTY,
  BETTY SCHULTE, CLINT LAHNEN, BRENT SAVAGE, AND KARL BRANDT

For information on our other products and services or to obtain technical support, please contact our Customer Care Department within the U.S. at (800) 762-2974, outside the U.S. at (317) 572-3993, or fax (317) 572-4002

Wiley also publishes its books in a variety of electronic formats. Some content that appears in print may not be available in electronic formats.

ISBN 0-7645-6501-X

ISSN 1537-8128

Manufactured in the United States of America

5   4   3   2   1

Contents

List of Maps

About the Author

Joel Grossman, a Los Angeles native and full-time freelance writer since 1979, has written everything from hotel reviews and gardening articles to computer history and science stories. He has written about Santa Monica's Big Blue Bus, rattlesnakes, and Southern California's science and technology pioneers for the *Los Angeles Times* Magazine. Many travel agents and corporate travel planners have used his anonymous Star Service hotel reviews for locations such as Africa, Tahiti, New Zealand, London, and the United States. Pasadena's Caltech University has published his work on solar sailing and computer history. Encyclopedia Brittanica published his article on invading insects in their 2001 science annual. That article was the result of his studying enough entomology at the University of California, Berkeley to get a job advising farmers on how to cut their pesticide use, which led to Grossman's further writing about the subject for magazines as varied as *Terra* (Los Angeles County Natural History Museum), *Rodale's Organic Gardening, Fine Gardening, Flower & Garden, The New Farm, Environmental Action, The World & I,* and *Agrichemical Age.* Then, an editor said, "If you can write about agriculture and bugs, you can write about anything." Alas, when a writing teacher said that full-time freelancing was possible for those who could write ten pages a day, the world beyond bugs and farm fields proved too big and alluring to do anything else but wander in and write. An interest in photography—useful for illustrating magazine articles—led to Grossman also taking photos to help this book's illustrators.

Acknowledgments

The Southwest, particularly when Texas is included, is a huge chunk of real estate. Even though I logged 20,000 miles on the roads of Arizona, Nevada, Utah, New Mexico, and Texas, it's inevitable that some places slipped through the cracks. To those bed-and-breakfasts missed or in the Appendix only, I beg forgiveness and understanding for the trials of working alone in an immense landscape, where it was sometimes hundreds of miles to the next stopping place. There are so many people to thank, and so little space. Know that those glasses of icewater on those 100°+ desert days and those cups of coffee and snacks offered to this weary wandering writer were all deeply appreciated as genuine acts of human kindness. Memories of the conversations and good moments, however fleeting, brought smiles to my soul during the interminable hours hunched up at the computer deciphering my notes. To better understand this vast region has been an immense privilege. The only way to say thank you to so many—outside of a laundry list of names—is in the writing itself, in each and every introduction and bed-and-breakfast profile. So, consider this book my thank-you note for all the help. Hopefully, we will all share and extend the good memories again another time.

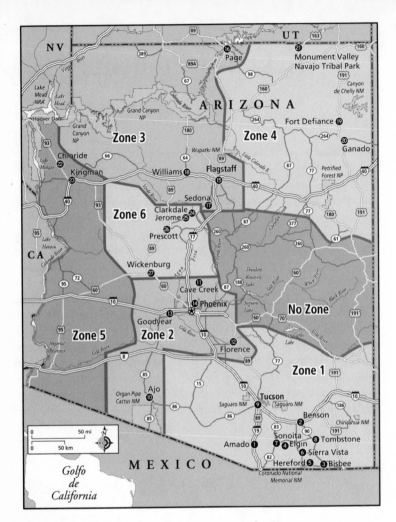

Arizona Properties by Zone and City

Arizona Properties by Zone and City *(continued)*

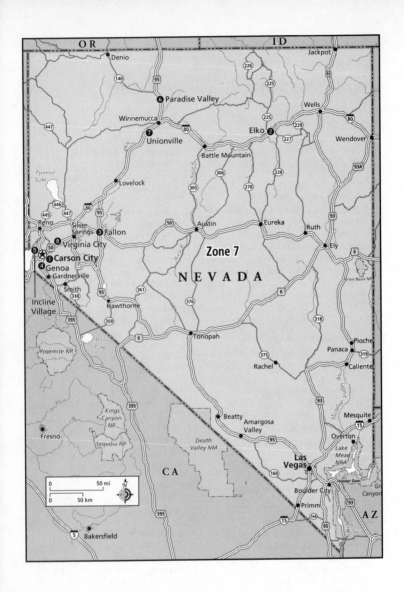

Nevada Properties by Zone and City

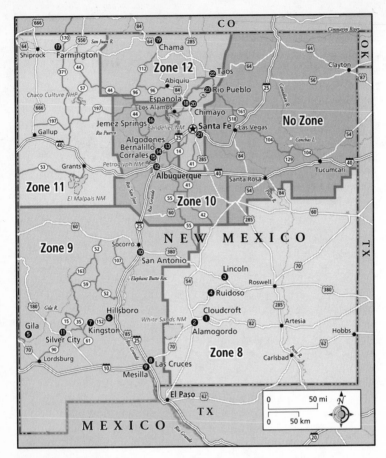

New Mexico Properties by Zone and City

New Mexico Properties by Zone and City
(continued)

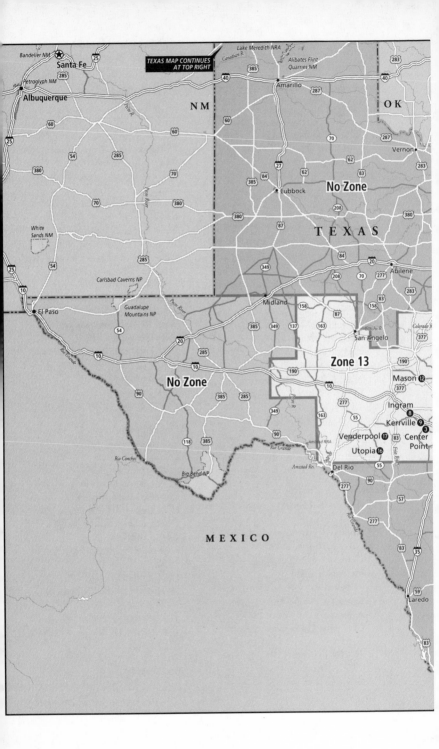

TEXAS MAP CONTINUES
AT TOP RIGHT

Bandelier NM

Santa Fe

Petroglyph NM

Albuquerque

Lake Meredith NRA

Alibates Flint
Quarries NM

Amarillo

NM

OK

Vernon

No Zone

TEXAS

White
Sands NM

Lubbock

Carlsbad Caverns NP

Abilene

Guadalupe
Mountains NP

El Paso

Pecos River

Midland

San Angelo

Colorado R.

Zone 13

Mason

Ingram

Kerrville

Center
Point

No Zone

Vanderpool

Utopia

Amistad NRA

Big Bend NP

Del Rio

Rio Conchos

Amistad Res.

Rio Grande

MEXICO

Laredo

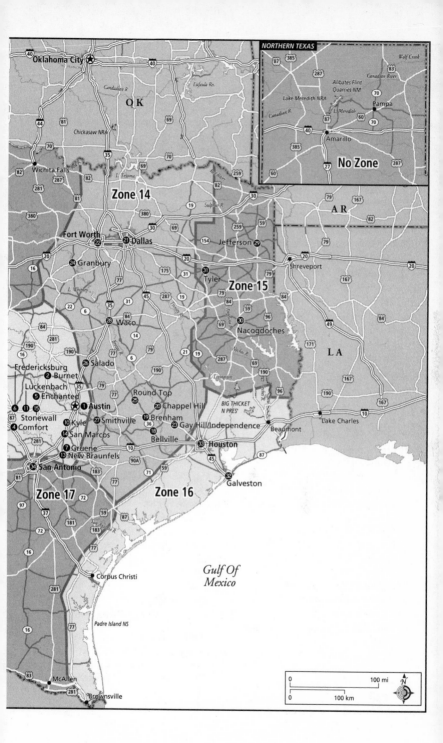

Texas Properties by Zone and City

Texas Properties by Zone and City *(continued)*

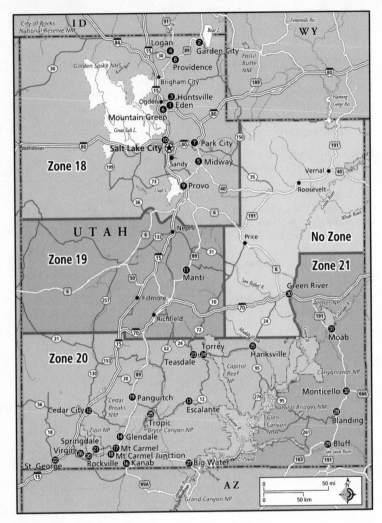

Utah Properties by Zone and City

Utah Properties by Zone and City *(continued)*

Mini Indexes

5-STAR PROPERTIES

Arizona

Agave Grove Bed and Breakfast
Adobe Village Graham Inn
Bed & Breakfast at Saddlerock Ranch
Canyon Villa Inn
Casa de San Pedro
Crickethead Inn
Flying Eagle Bed & Breakfast
Hacienda del Desierto
The Royal Elizabeth Bed and
   Breakfast Inn
Sheridan House Inn
Skywatcher's Inn
Terry Ranch Bed & Breakfast

New Mexico

Bottger-Koch Mansion Bed &
   Breakfast
Casa de las Chimeneas Bed &
   Breakfast Inn
Casa Europa
The Don Gaspar Compound Inn
Good Life Inn
Hacienda Manzanal
La Hacienda Grande
Los Poblanos Inn

Yours Truly Bed and Breakfast

Texas

Ant Street Inn
Carriage House Inn/Ranch House
Inn
Hidden Oaks Bed & Breakfast
The Inn Above Onion Creek
Kiepersol Estates Bed and Breakfast
Mariposa Ranch
Noble Inns: Jackson House (JH) &
   Pancoast Carriage House (PCH)
The Orchard Inn
Runnymede Country Inn
Texas Ranch Life

Utah

Baker House Bed & Breakfast
The Big Yellow Inn Bed & Breakfast
Blue Boar Inn
Desert Hills Bed & Breakfast
Dream Keeper Inn
Greene Gate Village
The Mayor's House Bed & Breakfast
Rodgers House Bed & Breakfast Inn
Seven Wives Inn

BED-AND-BREWS

Texas

Fredericksburg Bed & Brew

BOAT-AND-BREAKFASTS

Texas

Stacia Leigh Bed & Breakfast Aboard the Chryseis

BUDGET ACCOMMODATIONS (at least 1 room $75 or less)

Arizona

Agave Grove Bed and Breakfast

Birch Tree Inn
Bisbee Grand Hotel

BUDGET ACCOMMODATIONS (at least 1 room $75 or less) *(continued)*

BUDGET ACCOMMODATIONS (at least I room $75 or less) *(continued)*

New Mexico *(continued)*
Madeleine Inn
Meson de Mesilla
Old Taos Guesthouse Bed and
   Breakfast
Parlor Car Bed & Breakfast
Rancho Arriba Bed and Breakfast
Silver River Adobe Inn
Stewart House Bed & Breakfast
T.R.H. Smith Mansion Bed &
   Breakfast

Texas
1st Bed and Breakfast in Texas—
   Pride House
Austin Folk House Bed and Breakfast
Inn at Salado
Mason Square/Red Door B&B
Old Mulberry Inn Bed & Breakfast
Tin Star Ranch
Willow Creek Ranch

DINNER SERVED

Arizona
Albers House
Apple Orchard Inn Bed & Breakfast
Boots & Saddles
Briar Wreath Inn Bed & Breakfast
Full Circle Ranch
Ghost City Inn B&B
Goat Springs Hospitality
Guest House Inn
Hassayampa Inn
Sheridan House Inn
Sled Dog Inn
Tombstone Boarding House
Tse Li Gah Sinil' Hospitality

Nevada
Gold Hill Hotel
Old Pioneer Garden Country Inn

New Mexico
Bear Mountain Lodge
Casa Blanca Inn
Casa de las Chimeneas Bed &
   Breakfast Inn
Casa de Patron B&B Inn
Casa del Granjero
Casitas de Gila Guesthouses
The Dancing Bear Bed and Breakfast
Devonshire Adobe Inn Ltd Bed and
   Breakfast

Dobson House Solar Earth Ship
Enchanted Villa Bed and Breakfast
Good Life Inn
Grant Corner Inn
Hacienda Rancho de Chimayo
La Hacienda Grande
The Lodge
Meson de Mesilla
Rancho Arriba Bed and Breakfast
Riverdancer Inn

Texas
Angel Arbor Bed & Breakfast Inn
Azalea Plantation
Etta's Place
Far View—A Bed & Breakfast Estate
Fredericksburg Bed & Brew
Full Moon Inn
Governors' Inn
Hotel St. Germain
Inn Above Onion Creek
Inn at Salado
Kiepersol Estates Bed and Breakfast
Mariposa Ranch
Murski Homestead B&B
Patrician Bed & Breakfast Inn
Pine Creek Lodge
Rose Hill Manor
Southern House
Texas Ranch Life

DINNER SERVED (continued)

Utah

Anton Boxrud Bed & Breakfast
Bankurz Hatt
Blue Boar Inn
Cali Cochitta
Greene Gate Village
Historic Manti House Inn
Inn on the Creek
Legacy Inn Bed & Breakfast &
  Gift Shop
Muley Twist Inn
Seven Wives Inn
Yardley Inn & Spa
Zion Waterside Lodge

FAMILY-ORIENTED

Arizona

Aspen Inn Bed & Breakfast
Briar Patch Inn
Cactus Quail Bed and Breakfast
Canyon Colors Bed and Breakfast
Car-Mars's Southwest Bed &
  Breakfast
Coyote Crossing
Cozy Cactus Bed & Breakfast
Inn at Castle Rock
Jeremiah Inn Bed and Breakfast, Ltd.
Lake Mary Bed & Breakfast
Lynx Creek Farm B&B
Prescott Pines Inn Bed & Breakfast)
Priscilla's Bed and Breakfast
Sled Dog Inn

Nevada

1906 House
Deer Run Ranch Bed & Breakfast
Gold Hill Hotel
Old Pioneer Garden Country Inn
The Crooked House

New Mexico

Adobe Abode
Casa de Patron B&B Inn
Casitas de Gila Guesthouses
Don Gaspar Compound Inn
Enchanted Villa Bed and Breakfast)
Happy Trails
Old Taos Guesthouse
San Geronimo Lodge

Texas

O'Casey's Bed and Breakfast
River Oaks Lodge
Texas Ranch Life
Willow Creek Ranch

Utah

Eagle Feather Inn
Francisco's Farm Bed & Breakfast
Grayson Country Inn
Legacy Inn Bed & Breakfast &
  Gift Shop
Pioneer House Inn
Rainbow Country Bed & Breakfast
Rocky Top Ranch Bed and Breakfast
Saltair Bed and Breakfast
Snowberry Inn Bed & Breakfast
Zion Waterside Lodge

FARM, RANCH, OR RURAL SETTINGS

Arizona

Andora Crossing
Cactus Quail Bed and Breakfast
Car-Mars's Southwest Bed &
  Breakfast
Casa de San Pedro

FARM, RANCH, OR RURAL SETTINGS *(continued)*

Arizona *(continued)*

Country Gardens Bed and Breakfast
Coyote Crossing
Crickethead Inn
Desert Dove Bed & Breakfast
Fall Inn to Nature
Flying Eagle Bed & Breakfast
Full Circle Ranch
Goat Springs Hospitality
Hacienda del Desierto
Hacienda del Rey Bed & Breakfast
Indian Springs Ranch Bed and
  Breakfast
Inn at Rancho Sonora
Lake Mary Bed & Breakfast
Lynx Creek Farm B&B
Rainbow's End Bed and Breakfast
Ramsey Canyon Inn
Rancho Milagro Bed & Breakfast
Skywatcher's Inn
Stone Flower Bed & Breakfast
Tse Li Gah Sinil' Hospitality
Visit the Hogan

Nevada

Deer Run Ranch Bed & Breakfast
Old Pioneer Garden Country Inn
Stonehouse Country Inn
Wild Rose Inn

New Mexico

Adobe & Pines Inn
Alma del Monte Spirit of the
  Mountain
Bear Mountain Lodge
Black Range Lodge
Casa Blanca Bed and Breakfast
Casa de Alegria Bed and Breakfast
Casa de Patron B&B Inn
Casa del Rio
Casa Escondida Bed and Breakfast
Casa Europa
Casitas de Gila Guesthouses
  Cottages

Cottonwood Inn
Dancing Bear Bed and Breakfast
Desert Willow Bed and Breakfast
Dobson House Solar Earth Ship
Dragonfly Journeys
Enchanted Villa Bed and Breakfast
Good Life Inn
Hacienda Manzanal
Hacienda Rancho de Chimayo
Hacienda Vargas Bed and
  Breakfast Inn
Happy Trails
Inn on the Rio
La Hacienda Grande
Little Tree Bed & Breakfast
Los Poblanos Inn
Old Taos Guesthouse
Rancho Arriba Bed and Breakfast
Riverdancer Inn
Salsa del Salto Bed & Breakfast Inn
San Geronimo Lodge
Stewart House Bed & Breakfast
Yours Truly Bed and Breakfast

Texas

Ab Butler's Dogtrot at Triple Creek
Airy Mount Inn
Bluebird Hill Bed & Breakfast
Browning Plantation
Chuck Wagon Inn
Full Moon Inn
Heart of my Heart Ranch
Inn Above Onion Creek
Kiepersol Estates
Lamb's Rest Inn
Lazy Oak Bed and Breakfast
Mariposa Ranch
Murski Homestead
Old Home Place Guest Ranch
Orchard Inn
Outpost @ Cedar Creek
Palo Alto Creek Farm
Pine Creek Lodge
River Oaks Lodge

GROUPS/CONFERENCES/WEDDINGS EASILY ACCOMMODATED
(continued)

Texas (continued)
Browning Plantation
Carrington's Bluff
Crystal River Inn
Etta's Place
Far View—A Bed & Breakfast Estate
Full Moon Inn
Governors' Inn
Gruene Mansion Inn
Hidden Oaks Bed & Breakfast
Hoffman Haus
Hotel St. Germain
Inn Above Onion Creek
Inn at Salado
Kiepersol Estates Bed and Breakfast
Mariposa Ranch
Outpost @ Cedar Creek
Patrician Bed & Breakfast Inn
Pine Creek Lodge

Rockin River Inn
Runnymede Country Inn
Stacia Leigh Bed & Breakfast Aboard
   the Chryseis
Texas Ranch Life
Tin Star Ranch
Willow Creek Ranch

Utah
Greene Gate Village
Grist Mill Inn Bed & Breakfast
Historic Manti House Inn
Inn on Capitol Hill
Inn on the Creek
Logan House Inn and Conference
Center
Peery Hotel
Providence Inn
Zion Waterside Lodge

HISTORIC

Arizona
Bisbee Grand Hotel
Buford House Bed & Breakfast
Casa Alegre
Elysian Grove Market Bed &
   Breakfast Inn
Ghost City Inn B&B
Guest House Inn
Hassayampa Inn
Hotel Brunswick
Hotel La More/The Bisbee Inn
Inn at Castle Rock
The Red Garter Bed and Bakery
Royal Elizabeth Bed and Breakfast Inn
School House Inn
Surgeon's House

Nevada
1906 House
Chollar Mansion

Gold Hill Hotel
Old Pioneer Garden Country Inn

New Mexico
Black Range Lodge
Casa de Patron B&B Inn
Casa del Granjero
Cottages
Don Gaspar Compound Inn
Hacienda Antigua
Hacienda del Sol
Hacienda Rancho de Chimayo
Hacienda Vargas Bed and
   Breakfast Inn
Inn on the Rio
La Dona Luz Inn
La Hacienda Grande
La Posada de Taos
Laughing Horse Inn
Los Poblanos Inn
Willows Inn Bed and Breakfast

HISTORIC (continued)

Texas

1st Bed and Breakfast in Texas—
  Pride House
Airy Mount Inn
Ant Street Inn
Beckmann Inn and Carriage House
Bonner Garden Bed & Breakfast
Browning Plantation
Far View—A Bed & Breakfast Estate
Fredericksburg Bed & Brew
Full Moon Inn
Gruene Mansion Inn
Hotel St. Germain
Inn at Salado
The Katy House Bed & Breakfast
Magnolia House
Mariposa Ranch
Meyer Bed & Breakfast on Cypress
  Creek
Nutt House Hotel
Oge House Inn on the Riverwalk
Palo Alto Creek Farm

Riverwalk Inn
Riverwalk Vista
Stacia Leigh Bed & Breakfast Aboard
  the Chryseis

Utah

1904 Imperial Hotel
Armstrong Mansion Bed and
  Breakfast
Bankurz Hatt
Greene Gate Village
Grist Mill Inn Bed & Breakfast
Historic Manti House Inn
Inn on Capitol Hill
Peery Hotel
Providence Inn
Quicksand and Cactus Bed &
  Breakfast
Red Brick Inn of Panguitch
Seven Wives Inn
Viola's Garden Bed and Breakfast
Washington School Inn

HORSES WELCOME

Arizona

Amado Territory Inn
Full Circle Ranch
Indian Springs Ranch Bed and
  Breakfast
Rainbow's End Bed and Breakfast
Rancho Milagro Bed & Breakfast

Nevada

Old Pioneer Garden Country Inn
Stonehouse Country Inn

New Mexico

Adobe & Pines Inn
Bear Mountain Lodge

Casa del Granjero
Casa Europa
Hacienda Vargas Bed and
  Breakfast Inn
Happy Trails

Texas

Old Home Place Guest Ranch
Texas Ranch Life

Utah

Canyon Livery Bed & Breakfast
Francisco's Farm Bed & Breakfast
Hubbard House
Rocky Top Ranch Bed and Breakfast

MOUNTAIN SETTING

Arizona

Adobe Village Graham Inn
Agave Grove Bed and Breakfast

Alma de Sedona Inn
Apple Orchard Inn Bed & Breakfast
Bed & Breakfast at Saddlerock Ranch

MOUNTAIN SETTING *(continued)*

MOUNTAIN SETTING (continued)

Utah (continued)
  SkyRidge
  Snow Family Guest Ranch Bed &
    Breakfast

Snowberry Inn Bed & Breakfast
Stone Canyon Inn
Washington School Inn
Zion Waterside Lodge

NO CREDIT CARDS

Arizona
  Andora Crossing
  Bed & Breakfast at Saddlerock Ranch
  Chez Rina
  Crickethead Inn
  Elysian Grove Market Bed &
    Breakfast Inn
  Goat Springs Hospitality
  Hacienda Alta Bed and Breakfast
  Indian Springs Ranch Bed and
    Breakfast
  Lantern Light Inn Bed & Breakfast
  Rainbow's End Bed and Breakfast
  Rancho Milagro Bed & Breakfast
  Tse Li Gah Sinil' Hospitality
  Visit the Hogan

Nevada
  1906 House
  Chollar Mansion

Old Pioneer Garden Country Inn
Stonehouse Country Inn

New Mexico
  Dobson House Solar Earth Ship
  Enchanted Villa Bed and Breakfast
  Potteries Bed & Breakfast

Texas
  Bluebird Hill Bed & Breakfast
  Rockin River Inn
  Texas Stagecoach Inn
  Willow Creek Ranch

Utah
  Bullberry Inn Bed & Breakfast
  Hummingbird Inn Bed & Breakfast
  Rocky Top Ranch Bed and Breakfast

OBSERVATORY-AND-BREAKFAST

Arizona
  Skywatcher's Inn

PETS PERMITTED

Arizona
  Cottages at Prescott Country Inn
  Bed & Breakfast
  Goat Springs Hospitality
  Hotel La More/The Bisbee Inn
  Inn at Castle Rock
  Inn at Rancho Sonora
  Lynx Creek Farm B&B

Sled Dog Inn
Surgeon's House
Tombstone Boarding House

Nevada
  The Crooked House
  Gold Hill Hotel
  Old Pioneer Garden Country Inn
  Once Upon a Time Bed and Breakfast

PETS PERMITTED *(continued)*

New Mexico

Adobe & Pines Inn
Alexander's Inn
American Artists Gallery House Bed
  & Breakfast
Apple Tree Bed & Breakfast Inn
Black Range Lodge
Casa Blanca Bed and Breakfast
Casa del Granjero
Casa Encantada Bed & Breakfast Inn
Casa Escondida Bed and Breakfast
Casa Europa
Hacienda Antigua
Hacienda Nicholas
Hacienda Vargas Bed and Breakfast
  Inn
Happy Trails
Inn of the Arts Bed & Breakfast
Inn on the Rio
Jazz Inn Bed & Breakfast
La Dona Luz Inn
La Hacienda Grande
Laughing Horse Inn
Little Tree Bed & Breakfast
The Lodge
Old Taos Guesthouse Bed and
  Breakfast
San Geronimo Lodge
Silver River Adobe Inn
T.R.H. Smith Mansion Bed & Breakfast

Water Street Inn Bed & Breakfast
Yours Truly Bed and Breakfast

Texas

Austin Folk House Bed and Breakfast
Brook House Bed & Breakfast
Carrington's Bluff
Etta's Place
Full Moon Inn
Governors' Inn
Hoffman Haus
Hotel St. Germain
The Katy House Bed & Breakfast
O'Casey's Bed and Breakfast
Old Home Place Guest Ranch
Patrician Bed & Breakfast Inn
Rockin River Inn
Ruckman Haus Bed & Breakfast
Tin Star Ranch

Utah

An Olde Penny Farthing Inn Bed &
  Breakfast
Eagle Feather Inn
Francisco's Farm Bed & Breakfast
Hubbard House
Rainbow Country Bed & Breakfast
Red Brick Inn of Panguitch
Rocky Top Ranch Bed and Breakfast
Saltair Bed and Breakfast
Snowberry Inn Bed & Breakfast

ROMANTIC

Arizona

Adobe Village Graham Inn
Albers House
Apple Orchard Inn Bed & Breakfast
Briar Wreath Inn Bed & Breakfast
Canyon Villa Inn
Coyote Crossing
Creekside Inn at Sedona
Hacienda del Desierto
Maricopa Manor Bed and Breakfast
  Inn

Sheridan House Inn
Wishing Well Bed & Breakfast

Nevada

Deer Run Ranch Bed & Breakfast

New Mexico

Bottger-Koch Mansion Bed &
  Breakfast
Casa de las Chimeneas Bed &
  Breakfast Inn

ROMANTIC (continued)

New Mexico (continued)
Casa Europa
Cottages
Don Gaspar Compound Inn
Good Life Inn
Los Poblanos Inn

Texas
Carriage House Inn/Ranch House Inn
Heart of my Heart Ranch
Hotel St. Germain
Inn Above Onion Creek
Kiepersol Estates Bed and Breakfast
Lamb's Rest Inn
Mariposa Ranch
Noble Inns
Oge House Inn on the Riverwalk

Palo Alto Creek Farm
Riverwalk Inn
Stacia Leigh Bed & Breakfast Aboard
   the Chryseis

Utah
Angel House Inn
Anniversary Inn South Temple
Armstrong Mansion Bed and
   Breakfast
Eagle's Nest Bed & Breakfast
Seven Wives Inn
SkyRidge
Stone Canyon Inn
Sunflower Hill Bed & Breakfast Inn
Valley House Inn
Washington School Inn

RUSTIC

Arizona
Andora Crossing
Goat Springs Hospitality
Rainbow's End Bed and Breakfast
Ramsey Canyon Inn
Sled Dog Inn
Tse Li Gah Sinil' Hospitality
Visit the Hogan

Nevada
Old Pioneer Garden Country Inn)

New Mexico
Black Range Lodge
Casa Blanca Bed and Breakfast
Casa del Rio
Laughing Horse Inn
The Lodge

Rancho Arriba Bed and Breakfast
Silver River Adobe Inn

Texas
Ab Butler's Dogtrot at Triple Creek
Airy Mount Inn
Chuck Wagon Inn
Murski Homestead
Outpost @ Cedar Creek
Riverwalk Inn

Utah
Cali Cochitta
Muley Twist Inn
Panguitch Anglers Fly Shop and Inn
Rocky Top Ranch Bed and Breakfast
Snowberry Inn Bed & Breakfast
Zion Waterside Lodge

SOLO-ORIENTED

Arizona
Agave Grove Bed and Breakfast
Buford House Bed & Breakfast

Casa Alegre
Congenial Quail Bed & Breakfast
Crickethead Inn

SOLO-ORIENTED (continued)

Arizona (continued)
Hacienda Bed & Breakfast
Lantern Light Inn Bed & Breakfast
Rainbow's End Bed and Breakfast
Ramsey Canyon Inn
Skywatcher's Inn

Nevada
Once Upon a Time Bed and Breakfast
Wild Rose Inn

New Mexico
Alexander's Inn
American Artists Gallery House Bed
   & Breakfast
Bear Mountain Lodge
Casa Blanca Inn
Casa de Alegria Bed and Breakfast
Casa del Granjero
Cinnamon Morning Bed & Breakfast
Cottonwood Inn
Dancing Bear Bed and Breakfast
Hacienda Antigua
Hacienda Manzanal
Hacienda Nicholas
Inn on the Rio
Jazz Inn Bed & Breakfast
La Hacienda Grande
Laughing Horse Inn
Little Tree Bed & Breakfast
Rancho Arriba Bed and Breakfast
Silver River Adobe Inn
Spencer House Bed & Breakfast Inn
Water Street Inn Bed & Breakfast
Yours Truly Bed and Breakfast

Texas
1st Bed and Breakfast in Texas—
   Pride House
Airy Mount Inn
Amelia's Place
Austin Folk House

Beckmann Inn and Carriage House
Bonner Garden Bed & Breakfast
Brook House Bed & Breakfast
Browning Plantation
Carrington's Bluff
Chuck Wagon Inn
Governors' Inn
Hidden Oaks Bed & Breakfast
Ingleside Bed and Breakfast
Inn at Salado
The Katy House Bed & Breakfast
Lazy Oak Bed and Breakfast
Old Mulberry Inn
Orchard Inn
Patrician Bed & Breakfast Inn
Queen Anne Bed & Breakfast
River Run Bed & Breakfast Inn
Riverwalk Vista
Rockin River Inn
Ruckman Haus Bed & Breakfast
Runnymede Country Inn
Steamboat Inn
Texas Stagecoach Inn
Texas White House Bed & Breakfast

Utah
Anton Boxrud Bed & Breakfast
Brigham Street Inn
Desert Hills Bed & Breakfast
Grist Mill Inn Bed & Breakfast
Harvest House Bed & Breakfast at
   Zion
Historic Smith Hotel Bed & Breakfast
   LLC
Hubbard House
Muley Twist Inn
Old Miner's Lodge
An Olde Penny Farthing Inn
Red Brick Inn of Panguitch
Rodgers House Bed & Breakfast Inn

SMOKING PERMITTED

Arizona
Goat Springs Hospitality
Hassayampa Inn

Nevada
Gold Hill Hotel

New Mexico
Enchanted Villa Bed and Breakfast

Texas
Amelia's Place

SWIMMING POOL

Arizona
Adobe Village Graham Inn
Agave Grove Bed and Breakfast
Alma de Sedona Inn
Bed & Breakfast at Saddlerock Ranch
Canyon Colors Bed and Breakfast
Canyon Villa Inn
Car-Mars's Southwest Bed & Breakfast
Casa Alegre
Casa Luna Bed and Breakfast
Coyote Crossing
Full Circle Ranch
Hacienda Bed & Breakfast
Indian Springs Ranch Bed and Breakfast
Inn at Rancho Sonora
Jeremiah Inn Bed and Breakfast
Lodge at Sedona
Maricopa Manor Bed and Breakfast Inn
Royal Elizabeth Bed and Breakfast Inn

New Mexico
Hacienda Antigua
Happy Trails
Inn on the Rio
The Lodge
Meson de Mesilla

Salsa del Salto Bed & Breakfast Inn
San Geronimo Lodge
Willows Inn Bed and Breakfast

Texas
Bonner Garden Bed & Breakfast
Browning Plantation
Far View—A Bed & Breakfast Estate
Heart of my Heart Ranch
Inn Above Onion Creek
Lamb's Rest Inn
Meyer Bed & Breakfast on Cypress Creek
Noble Inns: Pancoast Carriage House
Old Home Place Guest Ranch
Pine Creek Lodge
Rockin River Inn
Runnymede Country Inn
Willow Creek Ranch

Utah
Arrowhead Bed & Breakfast
Dream Keeper Inn
Greene Gate Village
Inn on the Creek
Mayor's House Bed & Breakfast
Seven Wives Inn
Snow Family Guest Ranch Bed & Breakfast

THREE OR FEWER ROOMS

Arizona
Cactus Quail Bed and Breakfast
Canyon Colors Bed and Breakfast

Desert Dove Bed & Breakfast
Goat Springs Hospitality
Hacienda Alta Bed and Breakfast

THREE OR FEWER ROOMS *(continued)*

Arizona *(continued)*
Hacienda del Rey Bed & Breakfast
Rancho Milagro Bed & Breakfast
Tse Li Gah Sinil' Hospitality
Visit the Hogan

Nevada
Deer Run Ranch Bed & Breakfast
Once Upon a Time Bed and Breakfast

New Mexico
Casa Blanca Bed and Breakfast
Desert Willow Bed and Breakfast
Dobson House Solar Earth Ship
Dragonfly Journeys
Good Life Inn
Happy Trails
Parlor Car Bed & Breakfast
Potteries Bed & Breakfast
Rancho Arriba Bed and Breakfast
Silver River Adobe Inn

Texas
Ab Butler's Dogtrot at Triple Creek
Airy Mount Inn
Bluebird Hill Bed & Breakfast
Corner Cottage
Haussegen
Murski Homestead B&B
Palo Alto Creek Farm
Southern House

Utah
DreamKatchers' Bed & Breakfast
Eagle Feather Inn
Francisco's Farm Bed & Breakfast
Joy's Bed & Breakfast
Quicksand and Cactus Bed & Breakfast
Rocky Top Ranch Bed and Breakfast
Valley House Inn

TWENTY OR MORE ROOMS

Arizona
Casa Benavides Bed and Breakfast Inn
Gruene Mansion Inn
Hotel Brunswick
Hotel La More/The Bisbee Inn

Utah
Inn on the Creek
Peery Hotel

WATERSIDE SETTING (including creeks)

Arizona
Amado Territory Inn
Briar Patch Inn
Casa de San Pedro
Creekside Inn at Sedona
Deer Run Ranch Bed & Breakfast
Inn on Oak Creek
Ramsey Canyon Inn

New Mexico
Casa del Rio
Casitas de Gila Guesthouses
Dancing Bear Bed and Breakfast

Desert Willow Bed and Breakfast
Dragonfly Journeys
Los Poblanos Inn
Silver River Adobe Inn

Texas
Ab Butler's Dogtrot at Triple Creek
Beckmann Inn and Carriage House
Corner Cottage
Full Moon Inn
Heart of my Heart Ranch
Kiepersol Estates
Lamb's Rest Inn

WATERSIDE SETTING (including creeks)

Texas (continued)
Meyer Bed & Breakfast on Cypress
  Creek
Oge House Inn on the Riverwalk
Orchard Inn
Pine Creek Lodge
River Oaks Lodge
River Run Bed & Breakfast Inn
Riverwalk Inn
Riverwalk Vista
Rockin River Inn

Stacia Leigh Bed & Breakfast Aboard
  the Chryseis
Texas Ranch Life
Texas Stagecoach Inn
Willow Creek Ranch

Utah
Panguitch Anglers Fly Shop and Inn
Snow Family Guest Ranch Bed &
Breakfast
Zion Waterside Lodge

Introduction

How Come "Unofficial"?

The book in your hands is part of a unique travel and lifestyle guidebook series begun in 1985 with *The Unofficial Guide to Walt Disney World.* That guide, a comprehensive, behind-the-scenes, hands-on prescription for getting the most out of a complex amusement park facility, spawned a series of like titles: *The Unofficial Guide to Chicago, The Unofficial Guide to New Orleans,* and so on. Today, dozens of *Unofficial Guides* help millions of savvy readers navigate some of the world's more complex destinations and situations.

The *Unofficial Guides to Bed-and-Breakfasts and Country Inns* continue the tradition of insightful, incisive, cut-to-the-chase information, presented in an accessible, easy-to-use format. Unlike in some popular books, no property can pay to be included—those reviewed are solely our choice. And we don't simply rehash the promotional language of these establishments. We visit the good, the bad, and the quirky. We finger the linens, chat with the guests, and sample the scones. We screen hundreds of lodgings, affirming or debunking the acclaimed, discovering or rejecting the new and the obscure. In the end, we present detailed profiles of the lodgings we feel represent the best of the best, select lodgings representing a broad range of prices and styles within each geographic region.

We also include introductions for each state and zone to give you an idea of the nearby general attractions. Area maps with the properties listed by city help you pinpoint your general destination. And detailed mini-indexes help you look up properties by categories and lead you to places that best fit your needs.

With *The Unofficial Guides to Bed-and-Breakfasts and Country Inns,* we strive to help you find the perfect lodging for every trip. This guide is unofficial because we answer to no one but you.

Letters, Comments, and Questions from Readers

We expect to learn from our mistakes, as well as from the input of our readers, and to improve with each book and edition. Many of those who use the

Unofficial Guides write to us to ask questions, make comments, or share their own discoveries and lessons learned. We appreciate all such input, both positive and critical, and encourage our readers to continue writing. Readers' comments and observations will contribute immeasurably to the improvement of revised editions of the *Unofficial Guides.*

How to Write the Author
Joel Grossman
*The Unofficial Guide to Bed-and-Breakfasts
   and Country Inns in the Southwest*
P.O. Box 43673
Birmingham, AL 35243

Be an Unofficial Correspondent
Look out for new or special properties not profiled in this book. If you provide us with five new lodgings that we choose to visit and write about in the next edition, we'll credit you and send a copy when the edition is published. That's reason enough to get out and explore the vastness of the Southwest.

When you write, be sure to put your return address on your letter as well as on the envelope—they may get separated. And remember, our work takes us out of the office for long periods of research, so forgive us if our response is delayed.

What Makes It a Bed-and-Breakfast?
Comparing the stale, sterile atmosphere of most hotels and motels to the typical bed-and-breakfast experience—cozy guest room, intimate parlor, friendly hosts, fresh-baked cookies, not to mention a delicious breakfast— why stay anywhere other than a bed-and-breakfast? But this isn't a promotional piece for the bed-and-breakfast life. Bed-and-breakfasts are not hotels. Here are some of the differences:

A bed-and-breakfast or small inn, as we define it, is a small property (about 3 to 25 guest rooms, with a few exceptions) with hosts around, a distinct personality, individually decorated rooms, and breakfast included in the price (again, with a few exceptions). Many of these smaller properties have owners living right there; at others, the owners are nearby, a phone call away.

Recently, the bed-and-breakfast and small inn trade has taken off—with mixed results. This growth has taken place on both fronts: the low and high ends. As bed-and-breakfasts gain popularity, anyone with a spare bedroom can pop an ad in the Yellow Pages for "Billy's Bedroom B&B." These enterprises generally lack professionalism, don't keep regular hours or days of operation, are often unlicensed, and were avoided in this guide.

On the other end of the spectrum are luxury premises with more amenities than the finest hotels. Whether historic homes or lodgings built to be bed-and-breakfasts or inns, interiors are posh, baths are private and en suite, and breakfasts are gourmet affairs. In-room whirlpool tubs and fireplaces are the norm, and extras range from in-room refrigerators (perhaps stocked with champagne) to complimentary high tea to free use of state-of-the-art recreational equipment to . . . the list goes on! (One longtime innkeeper, whose historic home was tidily and humbly maintained by hours of elbow grease and common sense, dubbed this new state of affairs "the amenities war.")

The result is an industry in which a simple homestay bed-and-breakfast with a shared bath and common rooms can be a budget experience, while a new, upscale bed-and-breakfast can be the luxury venue of a lifetime.

Who Stays at Bed-and-Breakfasts?

American travelers are finally catching on to what Europeans have known for a long time. Maybe it's a backlash against a cookie-cutter, strip-mall landscape, or a longing for a past that maybe never was. Maybe it's a need for simple pleasures in a world over-the-top with theme parks and high-tech wonders. Who can say for sure?

The bed-and-breakfast trade has grown so large that it includes niches catering to virtually every need: some bed-and-breakfasts and small inns are equipped to help travelers conduct business, others provide turn-down service and fresh flowers by the honeymooners' canopied bed, and still others offer amenities for reunions or conferences. Whatever your needs, there is a bed-and-breakfast or small inn tailored to your expectations. The challenge, and one this guide was designed to help you meet, is sifting through the choices until you find the perfect place.

Romantics

More and more, properties are establishing at least one room or suite with fireplace, whirlpool, canopied king, and the trappings of romance. Theme rooms can also be especially fun for fantasizing. Always check out the privacy factor. Sometimes a property that caters to families has a carriage house in the back or a top-floor room away from the others. If an inn allows children under 16, don't be surprised if it's noisy; look for ones that are for older children or adults only.

Families

Face it, Moms and Dads: rumpled surroundings will sometimes have to be accepted where children are welcome. You may have to give up pristine decor and breakfast tea served in bone china for the relaxed, informal mood, but on the upside, you won't have to worry as much about Anna or Sam knocking over the Wedgwood collection on the sideboard.

When an establishment says "Yes" to kids, that usually means a really kid-friendly place. Check the age restrictions. If your children are under-aged but well-behaved, let the host know; often they will make exceptions. (But be sure it's true—other guests are counting on it.) On the flip side, honeymooners or other folks who might prefer common areas free of crayons, and breakfasts without sugar-frosted confetti, may want to look elsewhere.

Many bed-and-breakfasts with cottages, cabins, or accommodations that really separate guests are perfect for families with trouble-free infants and well-behaved kids. This gives parents with good intentions an alternative to "sweating-it-out" in case easy-going Timmy decides to break a tooth and cries through the night.

Generally, bed-and-breakfasts are not ideal for high-action kids. But if your children enjoy games, puzzles, books, a chance for quiet pleasures, and meeting others; if they don't need TVs; and if they can be counted on to be thoughtful and follow instructions ("whisper before 9 a.m.," "don't put your feet on the table"), you and your kids can have a wonderful experience together—and so can the rest of the guests.

Business Travelers

For individual business travelers, bed-and-breakfasts and small inns are becoming much more savvy at anticipating your needs, but in differing degrees. While phone lines and data ports are fairly common, they vary from one bed-and-breakfast to another. Some say they offer data ports when in fact they have two phone jacks in every room but only one phone line servicing the entire property. This can be fine for a three-room inn in the off-season, but if you're trying to conduct business, look for properties with private lines and/or dedicated data ports. If in doubt, ask. Rooms are often available with desks, but these also vary, particularly in surface area and quality of lighting. If this is an important feature, ask for specifics and make sure you secure a room with a desk when you reserve.

Some establishments even offer couriers, secretarial support, and laundry services. And for business travelers who don't have time to take advantage of a leisurely and sumptuous breakfast, the hosts often provide an early-morning alternative, sometimes continental, sometimes full.

Finally, there are intangibles to consider. After the sterile atmosphere of the trade show, meeting hall, or boardroom, a small inn with a host and a plate of cookies and a personal dinner recommendation can be nice to come home to. The atmosphere is also a plus for business meetings or seminars. The relaxed surroundings are quite conducive to easygoing give and take. During the week when guest rooms are often available, some bed-and-breakfasts and small inns are usually eager to host business groups. Discounts are often included and special services such as catering and equipment are offered if you rent the entire property. But forget weekends; these properties are still tourist oriented.

Independents

If you are on your own, small lodgings are ideal. Look for a place with single rates, and even if a special rate isn't listed, you can often negotiate a small discount. If you want some interaction, just sit in the parlor, lounge, or common rooms, and talk to people before meals. Most of the time if you're friendly and interested, you'll get an invite to join someone at a table. You could talk to the innkeepers about this even before you arrive, and they might fix you up with friendly folks. (And if you are traveling with others, invite a single to join you.) As for breakfast, communal tables are perfect for singles. Note our profiles to choose properties with that in mind.

Groups

Whether you are part of a wedding, reunion, or just a group of people who want to travel together, an inn or bed-and-breakfast is a delightful place to stay. The atmosphere is special, your needs are taken care of in a personal way, the grounds are most often spacious and lovely, and in the evening you can all retire in close proximity. It's especially fun when you take over the whole place—so you may want to choose an especially small property if that's your goal.

Those with Special Needs

Look in our profiles for mention of disabled facilities or access. Then call for details to determine just how extensive the accessibility is. Remember also that some of these houses are quite old, and owners of a small bed-and-breakfast will not have a team of accessibility experts on retainer—so be specific with your questions. If doorways must be a certain width to accommodate a wheelchair or walker, know how many inches before you call; if stairs are difficult for Great Aunt Mary Ann, don't neglect to find out how many are present outside, as well as inside. And if a property that seems otherwise special doesn't seem to have facilities, perhaps you can patch things together, such as a room on the first floor. Realistically, though, some historic properties were built with many stairs and are situated on hilltops or in rural terrain, so you will have to choose very carefully.

If you suffer from allergies or aversions, talk this over when you book. A good innkeeper will make every attempt to accommodate you. As for food, if you request a special meal and give enough notice, you can often get what you like. That's one of the joys of a small, personalized property.

You and Your Hosts

Hosts are the heart of your small inn or bed-and-breakfast experience and color all aspects of the stay. They can make or break a property, and sometimes an unassuming place will be the most memorable of all because of the care and warmth of the hosts. Typically, they are well versed in navigating the area and can be a wealth of "insider information" on restaurants, sightseeing, and the like.

While many—most, in these guides—hosts live on the premises, they often have designed or remodeled their building so that their living quarters are separate. Guests often have their own living room, den, parlor, and sitting room; you may be sharing with other guests, but not so much with your hosts. The degree of interaction between host families and guests varies greatly; we try to give a feel for the extremes in the introduction to each profile. In most cases, hosts are accessible but not intrusive; they will swing through the common areas and chat a bit, but are sensitive to guests' need for privacy. Sometimes hosts are in another building altogether; in the other extreme, you intimately share living space with your hosts. This intimate, old-style bed-and-breakfast arrangement is called a "homestay." We try to note this.

In short, most bed-and-breakfast hosts are quite gracious in accommodating travelers' needs, and many are underpinning their unique small lodging with policies and amenities from hotel-style lodgings. But bed-and-breakfasts and small inns are not the Sheraton, and being cognizant of the differences can make your experience more pleasant.

Planning Your Visit

When You Choose

If you're not sure where you want to travel, browse through our listings. Maybe something in an introduction or a description of a property will spark your interest.

If you know you are going to a certain location, note the properties in that zone, and then read the entries. You can also call for brochures or take a further look at websites, especially to see rooms or to book directly.

WEBSITES

bbchannel.com	bbinternet.com	bbonline.com
bnbcity.com	bnbinns.com	epicurious.com
getawayguides.com	innbook.com	inns.com
innsandouts.com	innsnorthamerica.com	johansens.com
relaischateaux.fr/[name of inn]	travel.com/accom/bb/usa	travelguide.com
trip.com	triple1.com	virtualcities.com

When You Book

Small properties usually require booking on your own. Some travel agents will help, but they may charge a fee, because many small properties don't give travel agents commissions. The fastest, easiest ways to book are through the Internet or a reservation service, but if you have special needs or questions, we suggest contacting properties directly to get exactly what you want.

Ask about any special needs or requirements, and make sure your requests are clear. Most of these properties are not designed for people in wheelchairs, so be sure to ask ahead of time if you need that accessibility. Specify what's important to you—privacy, king-size bed, fireplace, tub versus shower, view or first-floor access. A host won't necessarily know what you want, so make sure you decide what is important—writing it down will help you remember. Note the room you want by name, or ask for the "best" room if you're not sure. Remember to ask about parking conditions—does the property have off-street parking or will you have to find a place on the street? And if air-conditioning is a must for you, always inquire—some bed-and-breakfasts do not have it.

Verify prices, conditions, and any factors or amenities that are important to you. The best time to call is in the early afternoon, before new guests arrive for the day and when hosts have the most free time. Book as soon as possible; for weekends and holidays, preferred properties could be filled a year or more in advance.

A Word about Negotiating Rates

Negotiating a good rate can be more straightforward at a bed-and-breakfast than at a hotel. For starters, the person on the other end of the line will probably be the owner and will have the authority to offer you a discount. Second, the bed-and-breakfast owner has a smaller number of rooms and guests to keep track of than a hotel manager and won't have to do a lot of checking to know whether something is available. Also, because the number of rooms is small, each room is more important. In a bed-and-breakfast with four rooms, the rental of each room increases the occupancy rate by 25%.

To get the best rate, just ask. If the owner expects a full house, you'll probably get a direct and honest "no deal." On the other hand, if there are rooms and you are sensitive about price, chances are you'll get a break. In either event, be polite and don't make unreasonable requests. If you are overbearing or contentious on the phone, the proprietor may suddenly discover no rooms available.

Some Considerations

Like snowflakes, no two bed-and-breakfasts are alike. Some are housed in historic homes or other buildings (churches, schoolhouses, miner's hotels, and more). Some are humble and cozy, some are grand and opulent. Some are all in one building, while others are scattered amongst individual, free-standing units. Some offer a breakfast over which you'll want to linger for hours, and others…well, others make a darn good muffin. Bed-and-breakfasts are less predictable than hotels and motels but can be much more interesting. A few bed-and-breakfast aficionados have discovered that "interesting" sometimes comes at a price. This guide takes the "scary" out of "interesting" and presents only places that meet a certain standard of cleanliness, predictability, and amenities. However, there are certain questions and issues common to bed-and-breakfasts and small inns that first-time visitors should consider:

Choosing Your Room

Check out your room before lugging your luggage (not having elevators is usually part of the charm). This is standard procedure at small properties and saves time and trouble should you prefer another room. When a guest room has an open door, it usually means the proud innkeeper wants you to peek. You may just find a room that you like better than the one you are assigned, and it may be available, so ask.

Bathrooms

Americans are picky about their potties. While the traditional bed-and-breakfast set-up involved several bedrooms sharing a bath, this is becoming less common. Even venerable Victorians are being remodeled to include private baths. In fact, many bed-and-breakfasts offer ultra-luxurious bath facilities, including whirlpool tubs, dual vanities, and so forth. Our advice is not to reject shared bath facilities out of hand, as these can be excellent values. Do check the bedroom-to-bath ratio, however. Two rooms sharing a bath can be excellent; three or more can be problematic with a full house.

Security

Many bed-and-breakfasts have property locks and room locks as sophisti-cated as hotels and motels. Others do not. For the most part, inns with three stars or more have quality locks throughout the premises. (Many with lower rankings do as well.) Very often, bed-and-breakfasts will leave the key in the room or in the door if you choose to use one. Beyond locks, most bed-and-breakfasts provide an additional measure of security in that they are small properties, generally in a residential district, and typically with live-in hosts on the premises.

Privacy

At a hotel, you can take your key and hole up in solitude for the duration of your stay. It's a little harder at a bed-and-breakfast, especially if you take part in a family-style breakfast (although many inns offer the option of an early continental breakfast if you're pressed for time or feeling antisocial, and some offer en suite breakfast service). Most bed-and-breakfast hosts we've met are very sensitive to guests' needs for privacy and seem to have a knack for being as helpful or as unobtrusive as you wish. If privacy is hard to achieve at a given property, we've noted that in the profile.

Autonomy

Most bed-and-breakfasts provide a key to the front door and/or an unlocked front door certain hours of the day. While you might be staying in a family-style atmosphere, you are seldom subject to rules such as a curfew. (A few properties request that guests be in by a specific time; these policies are noted and rare.) Some places have "quiet hours," usually from about 10 or 11 p.m. until about 7 a.m. Such policies tend to be in place when properties lack sufficient sound insulation and are noted in the profile. Generally, higher ratings tend to correspond with better sound insulation.

What the Ratings Mean

We have organized this book so that you can get a quick idea of each property by checking out the ratings, reading the information at the beginning of each entry and then, if you're interested, reading the more detailed overview of each property. Obviously ratings are subjective, and people of good faith (and good taste) can and do differ. But you'll get a good, relative idea, and the ability to quickly compare properties.

Overall Rating The overall ratings are represented by stars, which range in number from one to five and represent our opinion of the quality of the property as a whole. It corresponds something like this:

★★★★★	The Best
★★★★½	Excellent
★★★★	Very Good
★★★½	Good
★★★	Good enough
★★½	Fair
★★	Not so good
★½	Barely Acceptable
★	Unacceptable

The overall rating for the bed-and-breakfast or small inn experience takes into account all factors of the property, including guest rooms and public rooms, food, facilities, grounds, maintenance, hosts, and something we'll call "specialness," for lack of a better phrase. Many times it involves the personalities and personal touches of the hosts.

Some properties have fairly equal star levels for all of these things, but most have some qualities that are better than others. Also, large, ambitious properties that serve dinner would tend to have a slightly higher star rating for the same level of qualities than a smaller property (the difference, say, between a great novel and a great short story; the larger it is the harder it is to pull off, hence the greater the appreciation). Yet a small property can earn five stars with a huge dose of "specialness."

Overall ratings and room quality ratings do not always correspond. While guest rooms may be spectacular, the rest of the inn may be average, or vice versa. Generally, though, we've found through the years that a property is usually consistently good or bad throughout.

Room Quality Rating   The quality ratings, also given on a five-star scale, represent our opinion of the quality of the guest rooms and bathrooms only. For the room quality ratings we factored in view, size, closet space, bedding, seating, desks, lighting, soundproofing, comfort, style, privacy, decor, "taste," and other intangibles. A really great private bathroom with a claw-foot tub and antique table might bring up the rating of an otherwise average room. Conversely, poor maintenance or lack of good lighting will lower the rating of a spacious, well-decorated room. Sometimes a few rooms are really special while others are standard, and we have averaged these where possible. It's difficult to codify this, but all factors are weighed, and the ratings seem to come up easily.

Value Rating   The value ratings—also expressed using a one-to-five -star scale—are a combination of the overall and room quality ratings, divided by the cost of an average guest room. They are an indication rather than a scientific formulation—a general idea of value for money. If getting a good deal means the most to you, choose a property by looking at the value rating. Otherwise, the overall and room quality ratings are better indicators of a satisfying experience. A five-star value, A room quality, overall five-star inn or bed-and-breakfast would be ideal, but most often, you'll find a three-star value, and you are getting your money's worth. If a wonderful property is fairly priced, it may only get a three-star value rating, but you still might prefer the experience to an average property that gets a five-star value rating.

Price   Our price range is the lowest-priced room to the highest-priced room in regular season. The range does not usually include specially priced times such as holidays and low season. The room rate is based on double occupancy and assumes breakfast is included. It does not assume that other meals are included in the rate. However, be sure to check the inn's Food & Drink category. Lodgings where MAP, which stands for the hotel industry's standard Modified American Plan, is applicable offer breakfast and dinner in the room rate. Unless specifically noted, prices quoted in the profiles do not include gratuities or state and local taxes, which can be fairly steep. Gratuities are optional; use your own discretion. Prices change constantly, so check before booking.

The Profiles Clarified

The bulk of information about properties is straightforward, but much of it is in abbreviated style, so the following clarifications may help. They are arranged in the order they appear in the profile format. Many of the properties have similar names. Town names, too, can be strikingly similar. Make sure you don't confuse properties or town names when selecting an inn.

Location

First, check the map for location. Our directions are designed to give you a general idea of the property's location. For more complete directions, call the property or check its website.

Building

This category denotes the design and architecture of the building. Many of the properties in the *Unofficial Guides* are historically and architecturally interesting. Here are a few architectural terms you may want to brush up on, in no particular order: Colonial, Craftsman, Queen Anne, Princess Anne, Cape Cod, Hand-hewn Log, Foursquare, Art Deco, Georgian, Victorian, Arts and Crafts, Ranch, Farmhouse, Gabled, Boarding House, Miner's Hotel, Teepee, Duncan Phyfe accessories, Sandstone, Timber Sided, Bunkhouse, Carriage House, Chalet, William Morris wallpaper, Sheepherder's Wagon, Eastlake, Greek Revival, Edwardian, claw-foot tub, pedestal sink, and many more. The more you know the jargon, the better you can select the property you want.

Food & Drink

For food and drink, we offer a taste of the inn or bed-and-breakfast, so to speak. Most properties go all out to fill you up at breakfast, so that you could easily skip lunch (factor that into the value). In some areas, however, the tourist board regulates that properties can only serve a continental breakfast without a hot dish. Note whether we state "gourmet breakfast," if that experience is paramount. In most cases, a bed-and-breakfast breakfast—even a continental—tends to include more homemade items, greater selection, and greater care in presentation.

In this category, what we call "specialties" are really typical dishes, which may not always be served, but should give you a good idea of the cuisine. Very few bed-and-breakfasts and inns do not include the breakfast in the price. However, it is almost always offered as an option.

Many inns and bed-and-breakfasts offer afternoon tea, snacks, sherry, or pre-dinner wine and after-dinner desert. Note that if an inn offers meals to the public as well as guests, the atmosphere becomes less personal. Also, if MAP is noted in this category, it means the inn offers meals other than breakfast as part of the room rate.

Some inns provide alcoholic beverages to guests, some forbid consumption of alcohol—either extreme is noted in the inn's profile. The norm is that alcohol consumption is a private matter, and guests may bring and consume their own, if they do so respectfully. Glassware is generally provided. Bed-and-breakfasts are not well suited to drunkenness and partying.

A diet and a bed-and-breakfast or small inn go together about as well as a haystack and a lighted match. Come prepared to eat. Some bed-and-breakfasts will serve dinner on request, and we included that info when it was available.

Most bed-and-breakfasts are sensitive to dietary needs and preferences but need to be warned of this in advance. When you make your reservation, be sure to explain if you are diabetic, wheat- or dairy-intolerant, or vegetarian/vegan, or otherwise restricted. Many proprietors pride themselves on accommodating difficult diets.

Recreation

We do not usually spell out whether the activities noted in the format are on-site. With some exceptions, assume that golf, tennis, fishing, canoeing, skiing, and the like are not on-site (since these are small properties, not resorts). Assume that games and smaller recreational activities are on the property. But there are some exceptions, so ask.

Amenities & Services

These blend a bit. Generally, amenities include extras such as swimming pools and games, and services cover perks such as business support and air conditioning. Business travelers should note if any services are mentioned, and if there are public rooms, group discounts, and so forth to back them up. Almost all bed-and-breakfasts and inns can provide advice regarding touring, restaurants, and local activities; many keep maps, local menus and brochures on hand.

Deposit

Be pretty confident that you will indeed be staying at a particular bed-and-breakfast when you make a reservation. The more popular the property, usually the more deposit you'll have to put down, and the further ahead. Many cancellation policies are very strict, and many innkeepers are recommending that guests purchase travelers insurance in case there is an unforeseen circumstance. When canceling after the site's noted policy, most will still refund, less a fee, if the room is re-rented. Check back on this.

Discounts

Discounts may extend to singles, long-stay guests, kids, seniors, packages, and groups. Even though discounts may not be listed in the text, it doesn't hurt to ask, as these sorts of things can be flexible in small establishments, midweek, off-season, last-minute, and when innkeepers may want to fill their rooms. This category also includes a dollar figure for additional persons sharing a room (beyond the two included in the basic rate).

Credit Cards

For those properties that do accept credit cards (we note those that do not), we've listed credit cards accepted with the following codes:

V	VISA	MC	MasterCard
AE	American Express	D	Discover
DC	Diner's Club International	CB	Carte Blanche

Check-In/Out

As small operators, most bed-and-breakfast hosts need to know approximately when you'll be arriving. Many have check-in periods (specified in the profiles) during which the hosts or staff will be available to greet you. Most can accommodate arrival beyond their stated check-in period but need to be advised so they can arrange to get a key to you. Think about it—they have to buy groceries and go to the kids' soccer games just like you. And they have to sleep sometime. Don't show up at 11:30 p.m. and expect a smiling bellhop—the same person who lets you in is probably going to be up at 5 or 6 a.m. slicing mushrooms for your omelet!

Check-in times are often flexible, but, as with any commercial lodging, check-out times can be critical, as the innkeeper must prepare your room for incoming guests. If you need to stay longer, just ask. Sometimes a host will let you leave your bags and enjoy the common areas after check-out, as long as you vacate your room. Please take cancellation policies seriously. A "no-show" is not a cancellation! If an establishment has a seven-day, or 72-hour, or whatever cancellation policy, you are expected to call and cancel your reservation prior to that time, or you could be liable for up to the full amount of your reserved stay. After all, a four-unit bed-and-breakfast has lost 25% of its revenue if you arbitrarily decide not to show up.

Smoking

We've indicated in the inn's profile if smoking is banned outright or if it is OK to smoke outside, but ask your hosts before you light up. Be mindful, too, of how you dispose of the butts—when you flick them into a nearby shrub, it's likely that your hosts, not some sanitation team, will be plucking them out next week.

Pets

We have not mentioned most of the inn-house pets in the profiles, as this situation changes even more frequently than most items. Many properties have pets on the premises. Don't assume that because an establishment does not allow guests to bring pets that pets aren't present. Dogs and cats and birds (and horses, pigs, goats, llamas, etc.) are often around. If you foresee a problem with this, be sure to clarify "how around," before booking. If properties allow pets, we have noted this, but most do not. And if you can't bear to leave your own beloved Fido or Miss Kitty for long periods, and want to stay in an inn that does not allow them, good innkeepers often know of reputable boarding facilities nearby.

Open

Properties often claim they are open all year, but they can close at any time—at the last minute for personal reasons or if business is slow. Similarly, properties that close during parts of the year may open specially for groups. If you can get a bunch of family or friends together, it's a great way to stay at popular inns and bed-and-breakfasts that would be otherwise hard to book. And remember, in low-season things slow down, dinners may not be served, and even when some properties are "open," they may be half-closed.

An Important Note

Facts and situations change constantly in the small-lodging business. Innkeepers get divorced, prices go up, puppies arrive, chefs quit in the middle of a stew, and rooms get redecorated, upgraded, and incorporated. So use this format as a means to get a good overall idea of the property, and then inquire when you book about the specific details that matter most. Changes will definitely occur, so check to be sure.

Making the Most of Your Stay

Once you're settled in, it's a good idea to scope out the entire place, or you may not realize until too late that your favorite book was on the shelf, or that an old-fashioned swing would have swung you into the moonlight on a warm evening. If you are alone in the inn, it can feel like the property is yours (and that, in fact, is a good reason to go midweek or off-season). Take advantage of the charms of these lodgings: the fireplace, the piano, other guests, the gardens. What makes an inn or bed-and-breakfast experience an integral part of a trip are moments that become cherished memories.

Did you love it? You can perhaps duplicate in your daily life some of the touches that made the experience special, whether it was warm towels, an early weekend breakfast by candlelight, fancy snacks in the afternoon or a special recipe for stuffed French toast. Hosts usually enjoy sharing ideas and recipes. You can also make small "bed-and-breakfast" type changes at your own home that may make all of the difference in your world—a small rose in a vase, a new throw rug, a handmade quilt from a local craft fair—or really splurge and install a whirlpool tub with waterfall faucet!

These small lodgings are stress-busters, far away from sitcoms and the media mania of the day. They are cozy places to settle into and curl up with a book, a honey, or a dream. Or, if you must, a laptop and a cell phone.

Gathering Information

While each zone has a brief introduction, and each profile lists nearby attractions, this book in no way purports to be a guidebook to the southwestern United States.

In addition to consulting one or more of the many useful Southwest guidebooks on the market, we suggest turning to the Internet and to your prospective bed-and-breakfast hosts as sources of information. Don't abuse your hosts, but they can (a) steer you to some good phone numbers and other resources, and (b) perhaps mail you a flyer or two about local sites and happenings with your reservation confirmation.

Some of the bed-and-breakfasts profiled in this guide have links from their websites to other websites of interest in their region.

Bed-and-Breakfasts on the Internet

The World Wide Web is full of websites for bed-and-breakfasts and small inns. It's full of booking services and tourism information sites that link you to home pages and listings for bed-and-breakfasts and small inns. Once you link up to one of the thousands of bed-and-breakfast or small inn websites, you can revel in detailed descriptions and click your way through colored photographs until your head spins (believe us, we know). If you see something you like, you can, in some cases, submit a reservation request on-line, or e-mail the hosts directly for a little cyberchat about your specific needs.

There's no denying that the Internet is a great resource for travelers in general, and for bed-and-breakfast/small inn seekers in particular. The problem comes in sorting the wheat from the chaff and in remembering that a great website does not necessarily equal a great lodging experience. (Think about it: do you want your bed-and-breakfast host spending his time whipping up omelets and cruising the local farmer's market or sitting in front of a computer until 3 a.m. in his underwear scanning photos of his backyard gazebo?)

Out-of-date information is another serious problem with Internet listings. We found many Southwest databases and Internet Yellow Page listings that showed us hundreds of inns, conveniently separated into geographic areas. Too good to be true, right? Calling the telephone numbers, we discovered that over half the listings were defunct. Many others were the scary type of bed-and-breakfast we're trying to avoid—the "let's-rent-Cindy's-room-while-she's-at-college" type.

Arizona

Arizona packs an amazing array of activities and sights into its mountains, valleys, and deserts. The 277-mile-long Grand Canyon, carved by the Colorado River, is an international attraction. The nearest bed-and-breakfasts to Grand Canyon National Park are over an hour away along historic Route 66 in Williams and in the pine forest–surrounded railroad town of Flagstaff. An hour south of Flagstaff are oak forests and Sedona, a New Age haven with expensive art galleries and red rock formations.

East of the Grand Canyon are the Navajo and Hopi Nations, where finding a bed-and-breakfast becomes much more difficult, though a few Native Americans open their hogans to visitors. Sleeping bags laid out on sheepskins in mud-floor hogans may seem a bit campground-like, but the cultural rewards of Indian Country can often be expanded to include a sweat lodge or storytelling session with the elders.

West of the Grand Canyon, along the California and Nevada borders, is Arizona's Western border. The Colorado River and Lake Mead National Recreation Area are water playgrounds. Summer temperatures are blisteringly hot, which is fine for cacti, rattlesnakes, and farming cotton, lettuce, and cantaloupes. Mild winter temperatures lure in hundreds of thousands of wintering snowbird RVs, but bed-and-breakfasts are almost nonexistent in the area.

Central Territory cities like Jerome and Prescott and high country cities like Pinetop-Lakeside offer desert dwellers high-elevation respite from the extreme summer heat. The high country is best known for its camping and outdoor water activities, and its few bed-and-breakfasts go their own way outside the state bed-and-breakfast association's inspection system. Jerome, a 5,000-foot-elevation terraced copper mining town where the police chief owns a bed-and-breakfast and drives a Harley, is reached via twisty mountain roads. Prescott (pronounced press-kit), a former territorial capitol still surrounded by pine forests and mountains, mixes cowboy art, summer horse racing, and weekend events on the town square.

   Phoenix, the major city in the Valley of the Sun and a snowbird winter favorite, is no stranger to summer days above 110° F. Though an hour to the south, Tucson, whose 100–200 bed-and-breakfasts are the most in Arizona, is typically about 10° cooler than Phoenix. Further south into Old West Country and the San Pedro River Valley around Tombstone and Bisbee, summer temperatures moderate even more, which works out well for the start of bird-watching season.

FOR MORE INFORMATION

Arizona's Best Bed & Breakfasts Directory. Lists inspected members of the Arizona Association of Bed & Breakfasts, P.O. Box 22086, Flagstaff, AZ 86002. Call toll-free (800) 284-2589; www.arizona-bed-breakfast.com

Arizona Journeys (published annually). Arizona Office of Tourism, 2702 N. Third St., Suite 4015, Phoenix, AZ 85004. Phone (602) 230-7733; arizonaguide.com

AZ Tourist News (complimentary monthly newspaper). 58 E. 5th St., Tucson, AZ 85705. Phone (520) 620-0567 or toll-free (800) 462-8705; www.aztourist.com

Discover Navajo: The Official Navajo Nation Visitor Guide. Navajo Tourism, P.O. Box 663, Window Rock, AZ 86515. Phone (520) 871-6436

Old West Country

Part of Mexico until the 1854 Gadsden Purchase, Tucson and its 400,000 people are the metropolitan center of southern Arizona's Old West Country. Sprawling Tucson is a desert valley ringed by mountain ranges like the Tucsons, Rincons, and Santa Catalinas. Coyote, quail, pig-like javelina, rattlesnakes, saguaros, ocotillos, and ironwood trees share this northernmost portion of the Sonoran Desert, which extends across the border into northern Mexico.

The annual February gem show is Tucson's big event, and bed-and-breakfasts book full several months in advance. Major league baseball's spring training Cactus League is shared with Phoenix to the north. From May until July 4, Tucson has dry heat. Then come two months of summer monsoons. By October the heat dissipates, and snowbirds begin their annual migration into the RV campgrounds lining Interstate 10.

South of I-10, in the San Pedro Riparian National Conservation Area, bird-watching is a major pursuit, particularly in spring and late summer. Bed-and-breakfasts near the Coronado National Memorial in Hereford/ Palominas and Ramsey Canyon cater to bird-watching groups seeking species ranging from large cranes to tiny, iridescent migratory hummingbirds. Benson's telescope-equipped bed-and-breakfast entices lovers of heavenly bodies for all-night gazing sessions and astronomy lessons.

South of Benson, Kartchner Caverns State Park requires advance reservations to tour the recently discovered colorful limestone caves. Tombstone is where Wyatt Earp and his brothers joined Doc Holliday to gun down the Clantons and McLaurys at the O.K. Corral. Tombstone residents claim that ghosts dressed in Old West garb and walking the wooden sidewalks haunt the whole town. Bisbee, an old mountainside copper mining town, owes its historic preservation to 1960s and 1970s hippies who moved in and became artists, carpenters, and electricians.

AMADO TERRITORY INN, Amado

OVERALL ★★★★ | QUALITY ★★★½ | VALUE ★★★★ | PRICE RANGE $90–$135
($350 FOR HOUSE)

Located halfway between Tucson and Mexico near migratory bird refuges, this is a popular group retreat for birders, church groups, weddings, and family reunions. The huge main lounge has green wood ceilings, leather seating, and large windows looking out over a seasonal creek, the large Jackie Parker Ranch, and the more distant Santa Rita Mountains. Views are equally impressive from the glass dining atrium and are shared from the patios of east-facing upper rooms that look down on the tops of mesquite trees in the garden. An absence of phones and TVs reinforces the notion of a retreat, though it may feel a bit too motel-like for some individuals. A cafe serving Greek and nouveau Southwestern fare adds convenience to the location.

SETTING & FACILITIES

Location 35 mi. south of Tucson on Interstate 19 at Exit 48 **Near** Tubac, Tumacacori National Historical Park, San Xavier Mission, Madera Canyon, Nogales, Buenos Aires National Wildlife Refuge **Building** Old West territorial style, 2 stories, built in 1997 **Grounds** 17 acres w/ paths, gardens, small waterfalls, a fish/frog pond, putting green, plant nursery **Public Space** Lounge w/ fireplace, dining atrium **Food & Drink** Full breakfast; Mon. & Tues. high tea; cafe serves all meals **Recreation** Bird-watching, horse riding (arranged), golf, fishing **Amenities & Services** Meetings & weddings (200 seated; 300 standing), stage, dance floor, banquet rooms, catering, bonfire, wellness center w/ massage & aromatherapy, gem store

ACCOMMODATIONS

Units 9 guest rooms, 1 2-BR house **All** Wood floor, ceiling fan, metalwork mirror, ranch brand on door **Some** Handicap-accessible (1), balcony (2), patio (2), pedestal sink **Bed & Bath** Kings, queens, twins; all private baths; house has 2 baths w/ tubs **Favorites** Oasis house w/ 2 BRs, full kitchen, fireplace, wood furnishings, large walk-in closet, brick patio **Comfort & Decor** Interior hallways with rugs covering wood floors open onto spare white-walled rooms with minimal Southwest decor and baths with wood walls.

RATES, RESERVATIONS, & RESTRICTIONS

Deposit Credit card; refund if canceled 14 days prior to scheduled arrival **Discounts** AAA, AARP, airline, corp.; golf packages; group rental of whole inn and house **Credit Cards** AE, MC, V, D **Check-In/Out** 3 p.m./11 a.m. **Smoking** No **Pets** No (on-site boarding available for pets & horses) **Kids** Over age 12 welcome **No-Nos** N/A **Minimum Stay** None **Open** All year **Host** Betty Hilton, P.O. Box 81, Amado 85645 **Phone** (520) 398-8684 or toll-free (888) 398-8684 **Fax** (520) 398-8186 **E-mail** info@amado-territory-inn.com **Web** www.amado-territory-inn.com

SKYWATCHER'S INN, Benson

OVERALL ★★★★★ | QUALITY ★★★★½ | VALUE ★★★★★ | PRICE RANGE $75–$110

Started as the small hilltop Vega-Bray Observatory, the luxurious living quarters with sumptuous purple and gold living room carpets and drapes were built so astronomers would not face a sleepy-eyed drive back to Tucson after a night of stargazing. The menagerie of telescopes includes a 20-inch scope with CCD camera imaging. Astronomers (optional) need to be booked along with rooms and work with any skill level. Guests are greeted by their private astronomer, who devises a viewing and lesson plan for each night, typically starting with basics in the Rolloff room (roof rolls off). The media room has comfortable black leather seating, a big-screen TV, surround sound, a wood ceiling fan, and *Star Trek* cabinet. Breakfast in the solarium overlooks the Serenity Ranch pond and riverfront cattle pasture.

SETTING & FACILITIES

Location 45 mi. SE of Tucson; from I-10 east of Benson, go east on frontage road from Exit 306 (Pomerene), cross RR tracks, & take Airport Rd. 1.9 mi. to Astronomers Lane (dirt road) **Near** Kartchner Caverns, Tombstone, Dragoon Mountains, Willcox **Building** Modern hilltop ranch house w/ telescope domes **Grounds** Narrow hilltop w/ outdoor sitting areas; extends downhill to pond & pastures along San Pedro River **Public Space** Sunrise-facing LR w/ fireplace, breakfast solarium, formal DR, media room, full kitchen, laundry; telescope rooms **Food & Drink** Full breakfast; afternoon/evening cookies and beverages **Recreation** Astronomy, fishing (pond w/ catfish, bass), boating, San Pedro River nature trail **Amenities & Services** Internet access, computers, telescopes, astronomy lessons ($95/4 hours), fishing equipment, row & paddle boats, outdoor grills

ACCOMMODATIONS

Units 4 **All** TV/VCR, sitting area **Some** Murphy beds, handicap accessible **Bed & Bath** Queens (3), double (1) plus double & queen sofa beds; Jacuzzi tub (1), tub (2), all private baths. **Favorites** Galaxy room has double Murphy bed, double sofa bed, planet wallpaper, & block glass bath; handicap-accessible Egyptian room has Jacuzzi tub, marble & block glass walk-in double shower, & connects with Astronomers Studio to form a suite **Comfort & Decor** Varies from Egyptian in Egyptian room to pastel florals in Garden room to outer space in Galaxy room.

RATES, RESERVATIONS, & RESTRICTIONS

Deposit Lenient cancellation policy when related to overcast skies ruining astronomical viewing **Discounts** Groups; 10% off stays over 4 days **Credit Cards** MC, V **Check-In/Out** 3–6 p.m./11 a.m. **Smoking** Smoking porch **Pets** Not encouraged (host has small outdoor dog) **Kids** Yes **No-Nos** N/A **Minimum Stay** None **Open** All year **Host** Cleo Douglas, C/O 5655 N. Via Umbrosa, Tucson 85750 **Phone** (520) 615-3886 **Fax** (520) 615-3886 **E-mail** vegasky@mindspring.com **Web** www.communiverse.com/skywatcher

THE BISBEE GRAND HOTEL, Bisbee

OVERALL ★★★½ | QUALITY ★★★½ | VALUE ★★★★ | PRICE RANGE $72–$150

This former hotel for traveling mining executives—which claims an upstairs female and a downstairs male ghost—has gone all out in creatively decorating theme rooms. Cowboy lovers can soak in a double Jacuzzi while admiring John Wayne and Hopalong Cassidy posters and sleep in a covered wagon in the Hollywood Western Suite. The Captain's Suite satisfies yearnings for the sea. The new Hacienda Room has a Native American cliff-dwelling theme. Bird and rose wallpaper and stuffed tropical birds, including an oversized raven in the bath, decorate the Bird Room. The Old West bar is a popular hangout, where locals enjoy ribbing the owner about all the "fufu" in the rooms.

SETTING & FACILITIES
Location Town center, 61 Main St. **Near** Tombstone, ghost towns, Kartchner Caverns **Building** Renovated 1906 Old West Victorian-style hotel **Grounds** Opens onto street w/ shops & galleries **Public Space** Bar w/ pool table, electric darts, fireplace, TV **Food & Drink** Full breakfast buffet; Old Western-style saloon **Recreation** Golf, bird-watching **Amenities & Services** Travel agent commissions

ACCOMMODATIONS
Units 8 guest rooms, 7 suites **All** Ceiling fans, sitting areas **Some** Sink, TV **Bed & Bath** Kings, queens, doubles; all private baths, tubs (5), Jacuzzis (2). **Favorites** Victorian Suite w/ French doors to sitting room, fireplace, red velvet, chandelier over canopied king bed, & swinging saloon-style door to bath w/ claw-foot tub; Oriental Suite w/ carved wood wedding bed inlaid w/ glass pictures, gold & black boat wall scene, peacock bath decor **Comfort & Decor** Early 1900s period feel with antiques and widely varying room themes, for example, Hollywood movie Westerns, nautical.

RATES, RESERVATIONS, & RESTRICTIONS
Deposit 1 night or 50% of total if over 3 nights; 48-hour cancellation for full refund minus $15 fee **Discounts** Weekday corp. & gov't **Credit Cards** MC, V, D **Check-In/Out** After 1 p.m./11 a.m. **Smoking** No **Pets** No **Kids** Yes **No-Nos** N/A **Minimum Stay** None **Open** All year **Host** Bill Thomas, P.O. Box 825, Bisbee 85603 **Phone** (520) 432-5900 or toll-free (800) 421-1909 **Fax** (520) 432-5900 **E-mail** BisbeeGrandHotel@msn.com **Web** www.bisbeegrandhotel.com

HOTEL LA MORE/THE BISBEE INN, Bisbee

OVERALL ★★★ | QUALITY ★★★½ | VALUE ★★★★ | PRICE RANGE $55–$80 ($120–$165 SUITES)

Deeply steeped in local history, going back to the early 1900s when mining, a stock exchange, and an electric trolley line made Bisbee the largest town between St. Louis and San Francisco, the bed-and-breakfast is perched on steep Chihuahua Hill overlooking Brewery Gulch, hillside homes, and the old town below. Next door are Arizona's oldest apartment building, the 1914 Brook, and the expertly restored Hotel La More Saloon (originally a mercantile store, then a mechanic's garage with bays) that doubles as an art display venue and weekend jazz and live entertainment club. The Copper Queen Mine Tour, mining museum, fine restaurants, and funky arts and crafts shops are a short jaunt downhill.

SETTING & FACILITIES
Location From corner of Naco Rd. & OK St., go uphill to 45 OK St. **Near** Tombstone, ghost towns, Kartchner Caverns **Building** Recently renovated 1916 frontier mining town hotel w/ suites in adjacent 1905 brick annex **Grounds** Opens onto narrow hillside street overlooking town **Public Space** TV room, restaurant, saloon next door **Food & Drink** Full breakfast; restaurant offers other meals and catering; saloon **Recreation** Golf, bird-watching **Amenities & Services** Weddings, meetings, lunches

ACCOMMODATIONS
Units 20 guest rooms, 3 suites **All** Pedestal sink **Some** Fax/modem hookup, queen sleeper sofa **Bed & Bath** Kings (3), queens (4), full doubles & twins; kings & queens in 1- and 2-BR suites; 19 private baths, 4 shared baths. **Favorites** Upstairs (30 outside wooden stairs) suites have full kitchen, LR w/ TV/VCR, phone w/ modem hookup, queen sleeper sofa, shower/tub (2), private yard **Comfort & Decor** Early 1900s antique furniture from original hotel, hand-sewn quilts, wallpaper, carpets, and wood molding set period mood.

RATES, RESERVATIONS, & RESTRICTIONS
Deposit Standard hotel booking procedures **Discounts** Seniors, students, 3 or more nights (except weekends, holidays), whole hotel group rentals **Credit Cards** AE, MC, V, D **Check-In/Out** 3–9 p.m./11 a.m. **Smoking** No (front porch benches only) **Pets** Yes (if well behaved; deposit required) **Kids** Yes (if well behaved & accompanied by an adult at all times; under age 2 no charge & free playpen) **No-Nos** N/A **Minimum Stay** None **Open** All year **Host** Kathleen Anderson, P.O. Box 1855, Bisbee 85603 **Phone** (520) 432-5131 or toll-free (888) 432-5131 **Fax** (520) 432-5343 **E-mail** bisbeeinn@hotmail.com **Web** www.hotellamore.com; www.bisbeeinn.com

THE INN AT CASTLE ROCK, Bisbee

OVERALL ★★★½ | QUALITY ★★★½ | VALUE ★★★★ | PRICE RANGE $59–$87

An 1890s boarding house for affluent single miners and then a 1940s apartment building, this three-story red-and-white structure with green-and-yellow accents became the 1970s fantasy canvas of the late Jim Babcock, the proprietress's father, whose murals and paintings grace the inside. Old silver mine tunnels that filled with spring water (once the town water supply) are now patio and hillside goldfish ponds. Rooms like Last Chance and

Crying Shame celebrate local mines, whereas Victoria is papered in Victorian sheet music covers. The 1960s-style parlor celebrates Bisbee's postmining hippie heritage with a painted ceiling, crash-pad sofas, Chinese lanterns, and map wallpaper. The Bisbee Repertory Theater, which anchors Main Street's shops and galleries, is three doors away.

SETTING & FACILITIES
Location Follow Main St. past the shops & galleries to where the street curves & the name changes to (112) Tombstone Canyon Rd. **Near** Tombstone, ghost towns, Kartchner Caverns **Building** Restored 3-story 1890s hillside miners' boarding house w/ eclectic, slightly Victorian facade **Grounds** An acre of hillside gardens w/ trails, fruit trees, ivy, sitting areas, 3 small fishponds, patio **Public Space** Parlor w/ fireplace, games, & TV; atrium & garden patio w/ pay phone **Food & Drink** Full breakfast on patio or in DR; fruit & yogurt pancakes a specialty; event catering **Recreation** Golf, bird-watching **Amenities & Services** Weddings and special events in small conference rooms and gardens

ACCOMMODATIONS
Units 15 **All** No phones or TVs **Some** Private entrances **Bed & Bath** Kings, queens, singles, doubles in varying combinations; all private baths, some tubs. **Favorites** Sultan's Harem has cloth tapestry ceiling; King Richard has king bed & small room w/ single bed built into rock hillside & opening onto porch; Return to Paradise has balcony entrance & side room with 1 double & 2 single beds for families **Comfort & Decor** Eclectic and extremely varied rooms range from cliff-dwelling murals to old map and sheet music wallpapers.

RATES, RESERVATIONS, & RESTRICTIONS
Deposit Credit card or personal check; at least 1 day's notice of cancellation **Discounts** Groups **Credit Cards** AE, MC, V, D, DC **Check-In/Out** After 2 p.m./11 a.m. **Smoking** OK on patio, porches, garden **Pets** Yes ($10/night) **Kids** Yes **No-Nos** N/A **Minimum Stay** None **Open** All year **Host** Jeannene Babcock, P.O. Box 1161, Bisbee 85603 **Phone** (520) 432-4449 or (520) 432-7195 or toll-free (800) 566-4449 **Fax** (520) 432-7868 **E-mail** mail@theinn.org **Web** www.theinn.org

SCHOOL HOUSE INN, Bisbee

OVERALL ★★★★ | QUALITY ★★★★ | VALUE ★★★★ | PRICE RANGE $60–$90

Those yearning for their good old elementary school days can check in at the School House Inn, which is in a residential section of old Bisbee, about a mile from shops, galleries and restaurants. If numbers are tormenting, you might want to bypass the Math Room and try the History or Art Rooms. The Principal's Office retains the original architecture, adding a queen and two single beds, and the Reading and Writing Rooms have kings. The hosts, one a former teacher, live on-premises in the Teachers' Lounge. All in all, a comfortable choice for school nostalgia buffs visiting this former mining boom town.

SETTING & FACILITIES
Location Corner of Pace & Tombstone Canyon **Near** Tombstone, ghost towns, Kartchner Caverns **Building** Restored 2-story 1918 elementary school **Grounds** 0.5 acre includes parking lot above city park (former school playground) **Public Space** Upper balcony, family room **Food & Drink** Full breakfast on patio or in family room **Recreation** Golf, bird-watching **Amenities & Services** Soda machine, telescope

ACCOMMODATIONS
Units 6 guest rooms & 3 2-BR suites **All** Sitting area, writing desk, ceiling fan, clock **Some** Handicap-accessible **Bed & Bath** Kings, queens, doubles; all private baths, tubs only, except shower/tubs in suites **Favorites** Music Room has double bed, rattan sitting area, hill views; Geography Room has globe in corner sitting area & copper map above bed **Comfort & Decor** School memorabilia in hallways and school subject themes like reading, writing, and arithmetic in each room.

RATES, RESERVATIONS, & RESTRICTIONS
Deposit 48-hour cancellation notice required **Discounts** Business groups, seminars, retreats **Credit Cards** AE, MC, V, D, DC **Check-In/Out** 3–5 p.m./11 a.m. **Smoking** Patio and balcony only **Pets** No **Kids** Over age 14 **No-Nos** N/A **Minimum Stay** None **Open** All year **Hosts** Jeff & Bobby Blankenbeckler, P.O. Box 32, Bisbee 85603 **Phone** (520) 432-2996 or toll-free (800) 537-4333 **Fax** N/A **E-mail** N/A **Web** www.bestinns. net/usa/az/school.html

RANCHO MILAGRO BED & BREAKFAST, Elgin

OVERALL ★★★★ | QUALITY ★★★★ | VALUE ★★★★ | PRICE RANGE $125

Situated on 5,300-foot-elevation grasslands that are a virtual yucca forest, Rancho Milagro gets daily breezes and stays about 15° F cooler in summer than Tucson, with the same mild winters and an occasional light snow. A wing of guest rooms with private entrances and porches looks out on the 35,000-acre Babacomeri Ranch. The Huachuca, Santa Rita, and Whetstone Mountains frame the distance, with cattle and horse pastures and Bureau of Land Management land with antelopes in the foreground. Neighbors are few and far between, and the night sky is clear enough for telescopes, making is a real retreat. A simple and relaxing place.

SETTING & FACILITIES
Location 9 mi. SE of Sonoita: go 5 mi. SE from Sonoita on AZ 83, then east on Elgin Rd. for 4 mi. and straight on Camino del Corral (dirt road) where Elgin Rd. curves left **Near** Wineries, migratory bird refuges, Kartchner Caverns, Parker Canyon, Tombstone, Bisbee **Building** 1996 ranch house **Grounds** 80 acres of grasslands w/ cattle & horse pasture **Public Space** Guests share patio but not main house w/ hosts **Food & Drink** Cont'l breakfast on patio **Recreation** Bird-watching, horse riding **Amenities & Services** Phone, 4-stall stable for horses

ACCOMMODATIONS

Units 3 **All** Cable TV/VCR, ceiling fan, wood-burning stove, private entrance, front porch, horseshoe key ring **Some** Connecting rooms (2) **Bed & Bath** King (1) and queens (2); all private baths, spa jet tubs **Favorites** Connecting queen-bed rooms make a good family suite **Comfort & Decor** White walls, cement floor, viga beam ceiling, wood furniture, wicker rocking chair, Mexican tile baths with horseshoe towel racks.

RATES, RESERVATIONS, & RESTRICTIONS

Deposit 1 night deposit; refunded less $15 if cancellation 7 days before scheduled arrival **Discounts** None **Credit Cards** None (cash or check only) **Check-In/Out** 2 p.m./11 a.m. **Smoking** No **Pets** No (horses welcome) **Kids** Not recommended **No-Nos** N/A **Minimum Stay** 2 nights **Open** All year **Hosts** Karen Leonard & Michael Johnson, P.O. Box 981, Sonoita 85637 **Phone** (520) 455-0381 **Fax** N/A **E-mail** info@ranchomilagrobb.com **Web** www.ranchomilagrobb.com

CASA DE SAN PEDRO, Hereford/Palominas

OVERALL ★★★★★ | QUALITY ★★★★½ | VALUE ★★★★ | PRICE RANGE $100–$139

An ecologically conscious property boasting one of the region's first commercial evaporative fields, this high (4,000-foot elevation) Sonoran Desert bed-and-breakfast has a gate to adjacent Bureau of Land Management lands with a Clovis mammoth site and bird-rich San Pedro River trails. Warblers in spring, and sparrows, raptors, and sandhill cranes in winter, draw birders. JB's Bright Spot in Palominas serves up good ribs, and fine restaurants like Le Chene are within 20 minutes in historic Bisbee. The host, a former hotel executive chef, specializes in pies and cobblers, which are available from afternoon to evening. Many guests spend mornings relaxing and reading around a courtyard with a fountain, roses, pomegranates, boxwood, and lantana or by a pond with dragonflies.

SETTING & FACILITIES

Location From Sierra Vista, go SE on AZ 92 for 18.5 mi.; between mileposts 339 & 340 go north 2 mi. on Palominas Rd., then east 2 mi. on Waters Rd. to S. Yell Lane **Near** Coronado National Memorial, San Pedro Riparian National Conservation Area, Bisbee, Tombstone **Building** Mid-1990s Territorial-style hacienda w/ fountain in central courtyard **Grounds** 10 acres, includes ponds, sheltered river overlook w/ barbecue, trails into BLM and riparian lands **Public Space** Lounge w/ large view windows, LR w/ wildlife views, DR, guest services room **Food & Drink** Full breakfast; pies, snacks, & beverages available all day; catering for groups; special dietary needs **Recreation** Bird-watching, horse riding **Amenities & Services** Guest services room w/ laundry, microwave, fridge stocked w/ beverages; gift shop; binoculars, telescope, computerized bird identification

ACCOMMODATIONS

Units 10 **All** Ceiling fan & climate control, Fernando Salgado Mexican village painting, private entrance **Some** Allergy-free & handicap-accessible rooms **Bed & Bath** Kings & doubles; all private baths **Favorites** Room 3 w/ its denim bedspreads & dark woods **Comfort & Decor** Spanish-Mexican with clean white walls, hand-carved Mexican furniture, and baths with saltillo tile floors and painted tile sinks.

RATES, RESERVATIONS, & RESTRICTIONS

Deposit Cash or credit card; cancellation fee charged **Discounts** Groups, off-season, stays of 5 or more days **Credit Cards** AE, MC, V, D **Check-In/Out** 4–6 p.m./11 a.m. **Smoking** No **Pets** No **Kids** Age 12 and older **No-Nos** N/A **Minimum Stay** May be required **Open** All year **Host** Craig Anderson, 8933 S. Yell Lane, Hereford 85615 **Phone** (520) 366-1300 or toll-free (800) 588-6468 **Fax** (520) 366-1300 **E-mail** casadesanpedro@naturesinn.com **Web** www.naturesinn.com

RAMSEY CANYON INN, Sierra Vista

OVERALL ★★★ | QUALITY ★★★★ | VALUE ★★★★ | PRICE RANGE $121–$145

Managed by the Nature Conservancy for its 90-year-old owner, who lives in an adjacent house and planted a now seven-decade-old giant sequoia on the property from her honeymoon trip, this bed-and-breakfast is for bird-watching. Birders flock here from March to May and again in August for the return of the migrating birds. Art on the walls, much of it for sale, revolves around Ramsey Canyon's 14 species of hummingbirds. Ramsey Creek cuts through the property, which is planted with apricot, peach, plum, pear, and other fruit trees. Indoors, the comfortable great room with its fireplace and wildlife references and the kitchen with its freshly baked fruit pies and shelves of antique products are the chief attractions.

SETTING & FACILITIES

Location 90 mi. SE of Tucson; from AZ 92, 6 mi. south of Sierra Vista, go west on Ramsey Canyon Rd. to the end **Near** Ramsey Canyon, Arizona Folklore Preserve, Parker Canyon Lake, Coronado National Memorial **Building** Stone & wood former warehouse converted to B&B in 1960s **Grounds** Dirt paths, fountain, benches, fruit trees, creek, nature preserve **Public Space** LR, DR/kitchen **Food & Drink** Full breakfast served family-style; homemade pies & beverages in afternoon **Recreation** Bird-watching **Amenities & Services** Museum, gift shop, nature preserve

ACCOMMODATIONS

Units 6 guest rooms, plus 2-unit duplex w/ full kitchen (no breakfast) **All** Sitting room, ceiling fan **Some** Private patio (1) **Bed & Bath** King (1), queens (3), two doubles (2); duplex has queens & sleeper sofa; all private baths, tubs (2) **Favorites** Costa's w/ king bed and private patio is largest; Blue-throated has double beds, orchard view, & creek sounds **Comfort & Decor** All rooms have varied decor, antiques, and hummingbird pictures.

RATES, RESERVATIONS, & RESTRICTIONS

Deposit 50% of total bill, refundable minus $25 fee if cancellation is 14 days prior to scheduled arrival **Discounts** Groups **Credit Cards** MC, V **Check-In/Out** 3–5 p.m./11 a.m. **Smoking** No **Pets** No **Kids** Under age 16 in duplex only **No-Nos** N/A **Minimum Stay** 2 nights **Open** All year (except Wed. & Thurs. of Thanksgiving and Christmas Eve and Day) **Host** Kathy Kay, 29 Ramsey Canyon Rd., Hereford 85615 **Phone** (520) 378-1010 **Fax** (520) 803-0819 **E-mail** lodging@theriver.com **Web** www.ramseycanyoninn.com

RAINBOW'S END BED & BREAKFAST, Sonoita

OVERALL ★★★★ | QUALITY ★★★★ | VALUE ★★★★ | PRICE RANGE $90

One of the few bed-and-breakfasts boarding horses, this horse breeding ranch with riding trails into Coronado National Forest was the proprietors' dream at the end of the rainbow. Large porches with wrought iron and carved wood horse benches are situated at the front and back to watch sunrises and sunsets and gaze at owls, birds, and bunnies in the surrounding hills and horse pastures. Electric fences and the possibility of spooking breeding horses preclude young children and pets. The decor is woodsy with antiques and a distinct cowboy and horse feel. Guests are within minutes (via scenic roads) of wineries, caverns, birding areas, and historic towns like Bisbee and Tombstone. But many come just for the peace and quiet.

SETTING & FACILITIES

Location 45 mi. SE of Tucson on AZ 83, 0.7 mi. east of the intersections of AZ 82 & 83 **Near** Wineries, county fairgrounds, Fort Huachuca, Tombstone, Bisbee, Patagonia Lake State Park, Nogales, Kartchner Caverns **Building** Recently remodeled 1960s ranch manager's house; owners live in separate historic ranch house **Grounds** 64 acres with stables, pastures, & grassland plateaus opening onto public lands with rolling hills **Public Space** LR, kitchen, front & back porches **Food & Drink** Self-help cont'l breakfast left in fridge for guests; snacks & beverages available throughout day **Recreation** Horse riding (must provide own horse), bird-watching **Amenities & Services** Horse boarding ($15; extra for grass hay, bedding); shared kitchen

ACCOMMODATIONS

Units 4 All Central AC & heating, radio/alarm clock **Some** N/A **Bed & Bath** Kings (2), 2 singles (1), single and queen (1); all private baths, tubs (3) **Favorites** Room 3, w/ bright yellows, cowboy & Chinese horse posters **Comfort & Decor** Carved wood doors, living room rock fireplace with green and white tiles, horse and cowboy art, tiled baths.

RATES, RESERVATIONS, & RESTRICTIONS

Deposit 1 night's deposit; refund minus $15 fee if cancellation within 14 days of scheduled arrival **Discounts** None **Credit Cards** None **Check-In/Out** 3–6 p.m./11 a.m. **Smoking** No **Pets** No (only horses w/ current coggins and health certificate) **Kids** Age 12 or older

No-Nos Spooking the horses **Minimum Stay** None **Open** All year **Hosts** Elen & Charlie Kentnor, 3088 AZ 83, P.O. Box 717, Sonoita 85637 **Phone** (520) 455-0202 **Fax** (520) 455-0303 **E-mail** elenkentnor@compuserve.com **Web** www.gaitedmountainhorses.com

THE BUFORD HOUSE BED & BREAKFAST, Tombstone

OVERALL ★★★ | QUALITY ★★★½ | VALUE ★★★★ | PRICE RANGE $65–$95

Featured on the History Channel's "Haunted Tombstone," Buford House was built in the 1880s by mining engineer George Buford, whose modus operandi was building homes as boarding houses and selling them at a profit when he moved on to the next mine. Keeping the original historic structure means sinks in rooms and three rooms sharing two hallway baths, which become private when the bed-and-breakfast is not full. The older architecture, specifically the adobe mud insulated from newer walls by air pockets, creaks from wind currents, adding to the haunted mystique. Purported spirits include a benign cat ghost leaving behind paw prints in bedspreads. More unsettling ghosts visit the host family, who are an invaluable and enriching fount of local history.

SETTING & FACILITIES
Location 4 blocks from center of town **Near** Bisbee, ghost towns, Kartchner Caverns **Building** 1880s Sonoran adobe (stucco added by later owner) w/ Territorial wraparound porch **Grounds** 5 city lots w/ small garden, barbecue area, fenced open space for owners' dogs **Public Space** LR w/ fireplace, DR, upstairs patio **Food & Drink** Full breakfast in DR **Recreation** Exploring ghost towns **Amenities & Services** TV/VCR in LR

ACCOMMODATIONS
Units 5 units, 4 upstairs and 1 downstairs **All** Sink, AC, carpets **Some** Ceiling fan **Bed & Bath** Queens, doubles; 3 upper rooms share 2 baths; 2 private baths, 2 shared, sunken tubs (2) **Favorites** Garden room w/ full double bed, gas log fireplace, sunken tiled tub, & private door opening to downstairs patio w/ koi pond fed by small watercourse **Comfort & Decor** Victorian antiques and sinks in rooms are part of 1880s original boarding house feel; two rifles mounted in dining room are Old West vintage.

RATES, RESERVATIONS, & RESTRICTIONS
Deposit Negotiated individually **Discounts** None **Credit Cards** AE **Check-In/Out** 3 p.m./noon **Smoking** Outside **Pets** No (owner has 2 outdoor dogs & cat) **Kids** Yes **No-Nos** N/A **Minimum Stay** None **Open** All year **Hosts** Ruth & Richard Allen, 113 E. Stafford St., Tombstone 85638 **Phone** (520) 457-3969 **Fax** N/A **E-mail** N/A **Web** N/A

PRISCILLA'S BED & BREAKFAST, Tombstone

OVERALL ★★★ | QUALITY ★★★ | VALUE ★★★★ | PRICE RANGE $45–$69

The second bed-and-breakfast to open in Tombstone's modern era is on a quiet street with a fountain, trees, and large lawn beckoning invitingly from behind a white picket fence. Like the Buford House, keeping the building in its original state, with the original wood and gas light fixtures, has meant sinks and vanities in the upstairs Primrose, Rose, and Violet Rooms, which share a hall bath. Europeans adapt better than Americans do to shared baths, but this arrangement is actually an authentic replication of being a visitor during Tombstone's early days, when Wyatt Earp and his brothers ran the town.

SETTING & FACILITIES
Location 2 blocks from OK Corral and Allen Street **Near** Bisbee, ghost towns, Kartchner Caverns **Building** 1904 country Victorian **Grounds** White picket fence encloses 5 city lots w/ lawns and gardens **Public Space** Downstairs parlor **Food & Drink** Full breakfast **Recreation** Exploring Tombstone & area ghost towns **Amenities & Services** TV in LR

ACCOMMODATIONS
Units 4 guest rooms, 1 downstairs and 3 upstairs **All** Early 1900s antiques, lace curtains, sink & vanity in room **Some** TV (1) **Bed & Bath** Double & single beds; 1 private bath, 3 rooms share upstairs bath **Favorites** Downstairs 2-room suite w/ a double & 2 single beds, shower/tub, & TV is great for families **Comfort & Decor** Lace curtains and Victorian antiques are the motif.

RATES, RESERVATIONS, & RESTRICTIONS
Deposit Encouraged **Discounts** Whole house rentals **Credit Cards** AE, MC, V, DC, CB **Check-In/Out** Customized **Smoking** No (outside only) **Pets** Small dogs (owner is allergic to cats) **Kids** Yes **No-Nos** N/A **Minimum Stay** No **Open** All year **Hosts** Barbara & Larry Gray, 101 N. Third St., Tombstone 85638 **Phone** (520) 457-3844 **Fax** N/A **E-mail** priscilla@tombstone1880.com **Web** tombstone1880.com/priscilla

TOMBSTONE BOARDING HOUSE, *Tombstone*

OVERALL ★★★½ | QUALITY ★★★½ | VALUE ★★★★ | PRICE RANGE $60–$80

Tombstone's first bed-and-breakfast and still the best, the Boarding House belies its name with private baths, gourmet dinners, and Sunday champagne brunch in the intimate Lamplight Room (two rooms, each with four tables). Vegetarians will appreciate the host's husband's Mexican restaurant, Don Teodoro's, on the next block (15 N. 4th Street), where Buddhists from the monastery in nearby St. David head to break their fasts. Ghosts have been sighted in the Green and White Rooms, but local residents say the whole town is full of ghosts, and they learn to live with them. The Blue Room has the only king bed and a bath with pinstripe wallpaper and makeup lights, and no ghost sightings yet.

SETTING & FACILITIES
Location 2 blocks from center, corner of 4th & Stafford **Near** Bisbee, ghost towns, Kartchner Caverns **Building** 1880 adobe rooming house and banker's house remodeled

& enlarged by 1930s artist **Grounds** White picket fence surrounds 6 city lots of land, 1/3 occupied by B&B **Public Space** Front porch for afternoon sitting **Food & Drink** Full breakfast in Lamplight Room; afternoon refreshments; dinner, Sun. champagne brunch available **Recreation** Exploring Tombstone and area ghost towns **Amenities & Services** Private parties in Lamplight Room

ACCOMMODATIONS

Units 5 guest rooms, 1 cabin **All** Private entrance, ceiling fan **Some** Sink in BR **Bed & Bath** King (1), queens (2), doubles (2), double and twin (1); all private baths, 2 claw-foot shower/tubs. **Favorites** Cabin has double & 30-inch bed, TV, fridge, coffeemaker, & is good for longer stays; White Room is smallest, has Jimmy Clanton ghost sightings; Green Room has huge corner-view windows & sighting of a ghost walking in door and out back wall **Comfort & Decor** 1880s ambience created via antiques and period wallpaper.

RATES, RESERVATIONS, & RESTRICTIONS

Deposit Full amount; full refund minus $10 for cancellations over 7 days prior to arrival date **Discounts** Groups **Credit Cards** AE, MC, V, D **Check-In/Out** 3–6 p.m./11 a.m. **Smoking** No **Pets** Yes (must obtain advance permission; no pets left alone in rooms; owner has 3 Dalmatians outside) **Kids** Yes (if well behaved) **No-Nos** N/A **Minimum Stay** None **Open** All year **Host** Shirley Villarin, 108 N. 4th St., Tombstone 85638 **Phone** (520) 457-3716 or toll-free (877) 225-1319 **Fax** (520) 457-3038 **E-mail** N/A **Web** N/A

AGAVE GROVE BED & BREAKFAST, Tucson

OVERALL ★★★★ | QUALITY ★★★★½ | VALUE ★★★★ | PRICE RANGE $60–$175

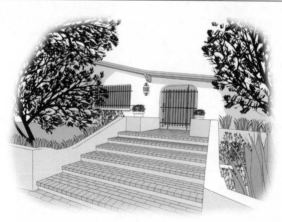

With a coyote den and an acre left wild for quail half a mile from major thoroughfares and within five miles of 50 restaurants, Agave Grove captures the best of nature and civilization. The front yard is a virtual botanical garden with several varieties of mesquite, palo verde, agave, prickly pear, cholla, and ocotillo. Harried professionals who want some nature without being too far from all Tucson has to offer find this thick-walled, mountain-view estate a perfect spot for privacy and relaxation. There are better spots for pure nature experiences and places more in the heart of the city, but few get the blend so right.

SETTING & FACILITIES

Location I mi. north of city limits, south of Orange Blvd. and east of La Cholla Blvd. **Near** Foothills Mall, parks, mountains, museums **Building** 1976 Southwest hacienda-style ranch estate **Grounds** 2.5 acres w/ large circular driveway, desert gardens, pool, & citrus trees **Public Space** Patio, entertainment LR, sunken quiet LR, DR **Food & Drink** Full breakfast on brick patio, DR, or in room; fruit-filled Dutch pancakes a favorite; caters to special diets w/ advance notice **Recreation** Golf, tennis, jogging, biking **Amenities & Services** Pool, Jacuzzi, pool table, TV/VCR, putting green, covered parking, receptions & special events (parking for 30 cars)

ACCOMMODATIONS

Units 4 guest rooms, including 2 2-room suites **All** Phone (shared line), cable TV, clock radio, thermostat, private entrance **Some** Ceiling fan (3), fridge and microwave (2 suites), handicap-accessible (I) **Bed & Bath** Kings & queens; all private baths, some Jacuzzis & sunken tubs **Favorites** Eastlake Suite has queen, Chicago Victorian antiques, wrought-iron table & chairs, & private arched spa room w/ separate bath for romantic getaways; Sonoran Desert Suite is ADA compliant w/ king, king sleeper sofa, & optional cots for families **Comfort & Decor** White walls, patchwork quilts, light Southwestern or wicker and beach motif.

RATES, RESERVATIONS, & RESTRICTIONS

Deposit 50%; all refundable minus $20 fee within 14 days or applicable to rebooking if less than 14 days **Discounts** Multiple rooms, promotional programs **Credit Cards** AE, MC, V, D **Check-In/Out** Customizable **Smoking** Designated outside areas **Pets** No (boarding kennel 2 mi. away; $4–$8/night) **Kids** Yes (in suite) **No-Nos** N/A **Minimum Stay** 2 nights holidays, special event weekends **Open** All year **Hosts** Denise & John Kiber, 800 W. Panorama Rd., Tucson 85704 **Phone** (520) 797-3400 or toll-free (888) 822-4283 **Fax** (520) 797-0980 **E-mail** agavebb@azstarnet.com **Web** www.bbonline.com/az/agave

THE CACTUS QUAIL BED & BREAKFAST, *Tucson*

OVERALL ★★★★ | QUALITY ★★★★ | VALUE ★★★★ | PRICE RANGE $109–$139

From the backyard spa under mesquite trees near the horse corral, this desert retreat merges into government lands with hiking trails into the Santa Catalina Mountains. Wildlife is abundant, particularly coyote, javelina, rabbits, and quail. Guests like to relax with a drink on the back patio and watch the mountains change from white to blue to purple to pink at sunset. The living room has a fireplace, Southwestern wood furnishings, saltillo tiles, ceiling fan, large view windows, and cabinets of gifts for sale. The Don West mural,

"Waiting for Pancho Villa to Return at Night," occupies three walls and the ceiling of the Hacienda Room, which also has pueblo logs sticking out of the wall. Another room mural portrays Mexican, Pueblo, and cowboy cultures.

SETTING & FACILITIES

Location From AZ 77 (N. Oracle Rd.) north of Oro Valley and Catalina State Park, go east on Mountainaire Dr. to Dust Devil Dr. **Near** Catalina State Park, Biosphere 2 **Building** 1970s Southwest ranch-style house **Grounds** 5 acres of desert merge from backyard patio into Coronado National Forest and Catalina State Park **Public Space** Living room w/ gift cabinets & closets (jewelry, tapes, CDs, & clothing for sale), DR, patio **Food & Drink** Full breakfast in DR; blueberry blue corn buttermilk pancakes w/ Mexican baked banana & breakfast burros w/ chorizo are favorites; snacks in buffet area **Recreation** Golf, back yard hiking trails **Amenities & Services** Kitchen to cook lunch or dinner, hot tub

ACCOMMODATIONS

Units 3 **All** TV/VCR, coffeemaker, fridge, iron, hand-painted carved wood armoires **Some** Bose radio (2), mural (2), loft (1) **Bed & Bath** California kings, futon in loft; 1 private bath, 2 rooms share bath w/ tub (rented together at discount to families & people who know each other) **Favorites** Bunkhouse has views of mesquite trees, ladder to loft that kids like, white walls w/ cowboy pictures, metal cattle sculpture, cowboy lamps, tile shower **Comfort & Decor** Metal sculpture, carved wood, Mexican tiles, and bright ceramic sinks contribute to strong Southwestern motif.

RATES, RESERVATIONS, & RESTRICTIONS

Deposit Credit card; 7-day cancellation notice **Discounts** Whole house, multiple rooms, 7 nights pay for 6 **Credit Cards** AE, MC, V, D, DC **Check-In/Out** 4–6 p.m./11 a.m.-noon **Smoking** Outside only **Pets** No (owner has 2 cats, 3 dogs, 5 horses) **Kids** Yes **No-Nos** N/A **Minimum Stay** None **Open** All year **Hosts** Marty & Sue Higbee, 14000 N. Dust Devil Dr., Tucson 85739 **Phone** (520) 825-6767 or toll-free (888) 825-6767 **Fax** (520) 825-4101 **E-mail** spectacularviews@cactusquail.com **Web** www.cactusquail.com

CAR-MARS'S SOUTHWEST BED & BREAKFAST, Tucson

OVERALL ★★★★ | QUALITY ★★★★ | VALUE ★★★★ | PRICE RANGE $65–$125

A spacious orange ranch house with lots of small, easily missed steps up and down, Car-Mar's offers ample comforts, not the least of which is the 24-hour swimming pool and a bath amenity basket that can hold its own with the finest hotels. The two smallest rooms (all are named after daughters), the dusty rose–colored Cynthia's and the peach-and-white Pamela's with its saguaro (cactus) rib door, share a bath and are usually rented together by families. Both kids and adults like writing their comments and drawing pictures on the dining room walls, a piece of spontaneous wall art that the hostess nurtures and treasures.

SETTING & FACILITIES
Location South Tucson, near intersection of AZ 86 (Ajo Hwy.) & Kinney Rd. **Near** Airport, Saguaro National Park West, Desert Museum, Old Tucson Studios, San Xavier Mission **Building** 1980 Territorial ranch house **Grounds** 7 acres w/ pool & patio usable **Public Space** LR, DR, TV room, patio w/ picnic tables **Food & Drink** Full breakfast in DR **Recreation** Golf **Amenities & Services** Pool, Jacuzzi, outdoor fireplace

ACCOMMODATIONS
Units 4 **All** Robes, hair dryer, big bath amenity basket, ice bucket, ceiling fan, central AC/heat **Some** TVs (2), microwave, fridge, private patio **Bed & Bath** Queens; 2 private baths, 1 shared bath, some tubs **Favorites** Lorree's Room opens onto patio and pool, has armoire w/ TV/VCR, carpet & saltillo tile floor, saguaro rib shower, fireplace seating; Rocio's Room has saguaro rib ceiling, glass door to private patio w/ fire chimney, & shower w/ block glass & stained-glass saguaro scene **Comfort & Decor** Saguaro rib furnishings, Indian art, and saltillo tiles of the Southwest dominate over stained glass and Victorian antiques.

RATES, RESERVATIONS, & RESTRICTIONS
Deposit 50% at booking and 50% 15 days before arrival; refund minus $25 fee for cancellations under 15 days in advance, otherwise refund only if room re-rented **Discounts** Whole house rentals **Credit Cards** MC, V **Check-In/Out** 4–6 p.m./11 a.m. **Smoking** No **Pets** No (inquire for exceptions; owner's schnauzer allowed inside) **Kids** Yes **No-Nos** N/A **Minimum Stay** None **Open** All year **Host** Carole Martinez, 6766 W. Oklahoma St., Tucson 85746 **Phone** (520) 578-1730 or toll-free (888) 578-1730 **Fax** (520) 578-7272 **E-mail** carmarbb@aol.com **Web** members.aol.com/carmarbb

CASA ALEGRE, *Tucson*

OVERALL ★★★★ | QUALITY ★★★★ | VALUE ★★★★★ | PRICE RANGE $80–$135

Located in the West University Historic Neighborhood near the 4th Avenue business district, Casa Alegre is a good choice for those wanting Tucson's urban hub rather than desert scenery. The hostess teaches a bed-and-breakfast course at Pima Community College and knows how to make the most of her historic Craftsman building and two city lots. Expansions include the Mexican casita, a little stand-alone house with its own kitchen, along with a pool, hot tub, and gardens behind the main house. Those wanting to be closer to the University of Arizona should consider the Peppertree or Catalina Park (see Appendix), whereas the Royal Elizabeth is the unchallenged Convention Center favorite.

SETTING & FACILITIES
Location From I-10, take Speedway Blvd. exit east for 1 mi. to corner of 5th Ave. **Near** Museums, medical center, university, parks, downtown **Building** 1915 Arts & Crafts bungalow **Grounds** Double city lot w/ patio, pool, & gardens **Public Space** LR w/ leaded

glass, stencils, dark wood cabinetry, & lava fireplace; back room w/ wind instruments hanging on walls is patio entrance **Food & Drink** Full breakfast in sun room w/ 1920s stained glass; afternoon tea & cookies; stocked fridge near pool **Recreation** Golf **Amenities & Services** Pool, hot tub, off-street parking

ACCOMMODATIONS

Units 6 **All** Original octagon floor tiles in baths **Some** Fridge (2), hardwood floors, carpets **Bed & Bath** Queens; all private baths, 2 w/ separate tubs **Favorites** Saguaro Room at back of inn has fireplace, lots of windows, pine furniture; Rose Quartz room contains hostess's father's mining engineer memorabilia; Hacienda Room has hand-carved padre bed, 1920s Mexican armoire, & fridge **Comfort & Decor** Varies widely from florals in Garden Room and Victorian in Amethyst Room to Mexican in Casita.

RATES, RESERVATIONS, & RESTRICTIONS

Deposit Full amount; cancellation within 14 days for full refund, otherwise forfeit 1 night or half total amount **Discounts** Weekly, corp., senior **Credit Cards** MC, V, D **Check-In/Out** 4–6 p.m./11 a.m. **Smoking** Outdoor patio, porch only **Pets** No (owner's cat stays outside) **Kids** Yes (well-behaved, under adult supervision) **No-Nos** N/A **Minimum Stay** No **Open** All year **Host** Phyllis Florek, 316 E. Speedway Blvd., Tucson 85705 **Phone** (520) 628-1800 or toll-free (800) 628-5654 **Fax** (520) 792-1880 **E-mail** info@casaalegreinn.com **Web** www.casaalegreinn.com

CASA LUNA BED & BREAKFAST, Tucson

OVERALL ★★★★ | QUALITY ★★★★ | VALUE ★★★★ | PRICE RANGE $95–$250

Popular with businessmen for its no-frills approach, plain white walls, good beds, and dirt roads for morning walks, Casa Luna customizes to the point where businesses rent it out for a month at a time and use the kitchen and barbecue to cook their own dinners poolside. A wash runs along one side, coyotes howl at night, and quail and rabbits are common. The Mesquite Room downstairs (you can hear walking upstairs) has its own separate parking area, twin beds convertible to a king, a full-size hide-a-bed, wrought iron, and wicker. Rooms opening directly onto the great room are also popular with families and individuals.

SETTING & FACILITIES

Location Near intersection of N. Alvernon Way & E. River Rd. **Near** Shopping malls, parks, Sabino Canyon **Building** 1974 version of a Tuscan-era villa, w/ guest house added in 1995 **Grounds** 2.5 acres bordering wash, w/ patio, small waterfall, & pond by hot tub & pool **Public Space** Great room w/ fireplace, kitchenette, dishwasher, satellite TV, stereo, deck **Food & Drink** Cont'l-plus buffet breakfast served in great room or poolside; barbecue, kitchenette for self-cooking **Recreation** Golf, tennis **Amenities & Services** Poolside weddings

ACCOMMODATIONS

Units 4 guest rooms in stand-alone guest house. **All** Private entrance, ceiling fan, TV, hair dryer, robes **Some** CD clock **Bed & Bath** Kings, queens, or twins; all private baths, I Jacuzzi tub. **Favorites** Willow Room in main house is villa-like w/ private balcony, Jacuzzi tub, pastel accents; Palo Verde has king bed & huge block glass shower **Comfort & Decor** No frills, just plain white walls, some white wicker, and wood.

RATES, RESERVATIONS, & RESTRICTIONS

Deposit Whole amount (under 3 nights) or 50% (longer stays); refunds negotiated individually **Discounts** Whole house rentals **Credit Cards** AE, MC, V, D **Check-In/Out** 4–6 p.m./noon **Smoking** No **Pets** No **Kids** Yes (must know how to swim) **No-Nos** N/A **Minimum Stay** None **Open** All year **Hosts** Katie Grundy & Elizabeth Magoon, 4210 N. Saranac Dr., Tucson 85718 **Phone** (520) 577-4943 or toll-free (888) 482-7925 **Fax** (520) 615-5097 **E-mail** casaluna@casa-luna.com **Web** www.casa-luna.com

THE CONGENIAL QUAIL BED & BREAKFAST, Tucson

OVERALL ★★★★ | QUALITY ★★★★ | VALUE ★★★★ | PRICE RANGE $80–$145

When two English teachers specializing in American literature set up a bed-and-breakfast, book themes inevitably follow. The smallest room, the Little Golden Classic, celebrates Little Golden Books and the hosts' childhood paintings. It works well for families with kids, because it shares a Mexican-tiled bath with the American Homestead (current American fiction), which has the hosts' New York heirloom Cushman peg-assembled furniture and family pictures. Good food goes with good literature. So the hostess collects mesquite beans, pineapple guava, herbs, and prickly pear from the yard for jam, syrup, and nopales (cactus) and eggs, which are served up on a 1940s baked enamel dinette set on the Indiana breakfast porch.

SETTING & FACILITIES

Location NW of intersection of Prince Rd. & 1st Ave. **Near** Tucson Mall, parks, galleries, museums, university **Building** 1940 ranch house w/ 1950 guest house **Grounds** 3 acres w/ herb & desert gardens, wild quail, & rabbits **Public Space** LR, DR, kitchen, game room w/ music & TV/VCR **Food & Drink** Full breakfast on Hoosier breakfast porch or outside; 24-hour coffee/tea in kitchen **Recreation** Golf, Rillito Downs horse racing **Amenities & Services** 25-jet hot tub seats 6

ACCOMMODATIONS

Units 4 **All** Fresh flowers, robes, T-shirts, ceiling fan, clock radio, reading lights **Some** Stereos, handicap-accessible (1) **Bed & Bath** Kings, queens, singles in varying combinations; 2 private baths, 1 shared bath, baths w/ Mexican tiles, some tubs **Favorites** Casita Sonora is 600 sq. ft. w/ large porch, Mexican fireplace, Hispanic art, Southwestern literature, ADA bath, festive tropical feel; Castaway Cottage has Caribbean art, sponged peach wall w/ blue accents, book nook w/ sci fi and fantasy, sitting area, Talavera tile bath, 2d door opening to hammock between mesquite trees **Comfort & Decor** Varies from room to room, with books tied to room theme.

RATES, RESERVATIONS, & RESTRICTIONS

Deposit Credit card, cash or check; 14-day cancellation for refund **Discounts** Ask **Credit Cards** AE, MC, V **Check-In/Out** 3 p.m./none **Smoking** No **Pets** No (2 resident cats) **Kids** Yes **No-Nos** N/A **Minimum Stay** 2 nights Sept.–May, weekends Feb.–April **Open** All year **Hosts** Laurie & Bob Haskett, 4267 N. Fourth St., Tucson 85705 **Phone** (520) 887-9487 or toll-free (800) 895-2047 **Fax** N/A **E-mail** congenialquail@hotmail.com **Web** www.bbonline.com/az/quail

COYOTE CROSSING, Tucson

OVERALL ★★★★½ | QUALITY ★★★★½ | VALUE ★★★★★ | PRICE RANGE $75–$125

A short distance down a dirt road marked by metal-sculpted howling coyotes, Coyote Crossing is located at a natural coyote crossing with plenty of cottontail rabbits and doves among the saguaros. The Roadrunner's Delight and Jack Rabbit's Hideaway can connect into a suite for families on one side of the house, leaving Coyote's Lair and Quail's Nest private for couples on the other side of the living room. The Cactus Wren's Hollow breakfast room looks out on citrus trees, and the poolside mountain panorama includes the distant lights of Tucson at night. The hostess crafts unique gift items like crocheted hot sauce bottle serapes and little children's toys.

SETTING & FACILITIES

Location Marana, NW of Tucson, near intersection of N. Cortaro & W. Ina Rds. **Near** Picture Rocks, Saguaro National Park West, Desert Museum **Building** 1964–65 Mexican adobe hacienda-style ranch house **Grounds** 5 acres w/ citrus, pool, & plenty of cactus & wildlife **Public Space** LR w/ fireplace & music, DR, poolside patio **Food & Drink** Cont'l-plus breakfast in DR **Recreation** Golf, horse riding **Amenities & Services** Heated pool, Jacuzzi, data port

ACCOMMODATIONS

Units 4 guest rooms, 2 combine into suite **All** Private entrance, robes, AC/heat, ceiling fan, cable TV, fridge, coffeemaker, hair dryer, hypoallergenic soap **Some** Microwave (1) **Bed & Bath** Kings w/ single-bed options; all private baths, 1 Jacuzzi tub **Favorites** Coyote's Lair is largest, w/ sitting area, desk, mountain views, 2-person Jacuzzi, microwave, 2d door opening onto patio/pool **Comfort & Decor** Clean and spare white walls with desert and Western art, cactus wallpaper, abundant amenities.

RATES, RESERVATIONS, & RESTRICTIONS

Deposit Credit card; full refund if cancel 7 days in advance and room is re-rented, otherwise may get credit toward future stay **Discounts** Longer stays **Credit Cards** AE, MC, V **Check-In/Out** 3–6 p.m./11 a.m. **Smoking** No **Pets** No **Kids** Age 6 and older **No-Nos** N/A **Minimum Stay** 2 nights Oct. 1–May 31 **Open** 11 months (closed July) **Hosts** Sylvia & Tom Kleinschmidt, 6985 N. Camino Verde, Tucson 85743 **Phone** (520) 744-3285 or toll-free (877) 740-3200 **Fax** (520) 744-5161 **E-mail** info@coyotecrossingbb.com **Web** www.coyotecrossingbb.com

CRICKETHEAD INN, *Tucson*

OVERALL ★★★★★ | QUALITY ★★★★½ | VALUE ★★★★★ | PRICE RANGE $75–$85

A Volkswagen hubcap with a smiling face hidden in the desert brush along the bumpy dirt entrance road foreshadows a giant saguaro with outstretched arms standing by a welcome sign. A weathered Deco-era airport limo rusts alongside a caboose (the owner's former home) and boxcar scrap metal workshop used to fashion the giant red-eyed cricket head assemblage near a gate opened by a giant wrench. The back porch is more like an African game lodge with a small goldfish waterhole frequented by javelina, birds, and the occasional big cat. The backyard of saguaro, cholla, octotillo, and ironwood opens onto a wash and national park land, which the agile can hike by slipping through the barbed wire.

SETTING & FACILITIES
Location Saguaro National Park West, NW of Tucson; from I-10 go west on W. Ina Rd., then south on N. Wade Rd., which becomes W. Picture Rocks Rd. **Near** Picture Rocks, Saguaro National Park Red Hills Visitor Center, Desert Museum **Building** Eclectic Arizona hacienda blends Mexican brick & the funky South Pacific **Grounds** Several acres of native desert stretch from back porch to desert wash where barbed wire marks north boundary of Saguaro National Park West; front has funky sculptural assemblages, old mining equipment, vehicles, & railroad cars **Public Space** Great room w/ big glass windows, colored lights, high beamed ceiling w/ fan, dark carved woods, batik fabrics, & Indonesian puppets; kitchen w/ DR; back porch adjacent to garden & waterhole **Food & Drink** Full breakfast in DR; common stove & fridge for guest use **Recreation** Bird & wildlife watching, horse riding **Amenities & Services** Big-screen TV, game-watching at waterhole, South Pacific fabrics & puppets for sale

ACCOMMODATIONS
Units 3 guest rooms, plus 2-room stand-alone casita **All** Ceiling fan, porch w/ seating **Some** Music boom box (casita) **Bed & Bath** Queens, doubles; all private baths, tub in casita. **Favorites** Cardinal room is a corner w/ the most light, Mexican fish mirror, & purple accents; Casita has carved wood bed w/ full canopy, fireplace, Indonesian masks, Sea of Cortés tile scene in bath **Comfort & Decor** Stained glass, carved and painted dark woods, and batik fabrics lend a touch of the exotic South Seas that is harmoniously blended with Mexican fired bricks and furnishings.

RATES, RESERVATIONS, & RESTRICTIONS
Deposit Half amount of stay; refund if cancellation 2 weeks or more before scheduled arrival **Discounts** Groups, week or longer stays, special occasion gifts **Credit Cards** None (cash or checks only) **Check-In/Out** 3:30–6 p.m./11 a.m. **Smoking** On private porches only **Pets** No **Kids** Ask **No-Nos** Moderate quiet is requested **Minimum Stay** 2 nights **Open** Most of year (may close in June, July) **Host** Mike Lord, 9480 W. Picture Rocks Rd., Tucson 85743 **Phone** (520) 682-7126 **Fax** (520) 682-7126 **E-mail** N/A **Web** N/A

DESERT DOVE BED & BREAKFAST, Tucson

OVERALL ★★★★ | QUALITY ★★★★ | VALUE ★★★★ | PRICE RANGE $90–$97

Ecologically designed on an east–west axis for solar heating and cooling effects by the hosts' architect son, Desert Dove is well positioned for those wanting to hike or bike into Saguaro National Park East, as well as for watching sunrises and sunsets. Environmental concerns extend inside, so carpeted areas are minimal, pets are prohibited, air and water is purified, and a wood-burning stove is used for cooking, which should help those with allergies and chemical sensitivities. Walls are thick adobe. Business travelers appreciate the combination of desert quiet, modem-friendliness, and closeness to downtown. Honeymooners also like the privacy, and Tucson's E. Tanque Verde Road restaurant row is nearby.

SETTING & FACILITIES
Location 0. 3 mi. from Saguaro National Park East, in foothills of Rincon Mountains **Near** Park Place mall, Pima Air & Space Museum, Colossal Cave, Kartchner Caverns **Building** 1997 solar adobe **Grounds** 4 acres w/ plenty of outdoor seating & a saguaro rib shelter **Public Space** Living room w/ open-truss high ceiling & skylights, multipurpose room w/ microwave, fridge, iron, table **Food & Drink** Full breakfast in DR or patio; afternoon snacks **Recreation** Bird-watching, biking, hiking **Amenities & Services** Hydrotherapy spa, hallway phone

ACCOMMODATIONS
Units 2 **All** Private entrance, ceiling fan, central AC, robes, hair dryers, clock radio, data port **Some** Bath skylight **Bed & Bath** Queen beds; private baths. **Favorites** Antique Garden room has Catalina Mountain views **Comfort & Decor** Colored polished concrete floor squares, white wicker desks and chairs, country antiques, some adobe brick walls.

RATES, RESERVATIONS, & RESTRICTIONS
Deposit I night or 50% (4 nights or more); refund if cancellation over 7 days before scheduled arrival, otherwise refund only if room re-rented (also credit toward another date) **Discounts** N/A **Credit Cards** AE, MC, V, D **Check-In/Out** 3–5 p.m./I I a.m. **Smoking** No **Pets** No **Kids** No **No-Nos** N/A **Minimum Stay** None **Open** All year **Hosts** Harvey & Betty Ros, 11707 E. Spanish Trail, Tucson 85730 **Phone** (520) 722-6879 or toll-free (877) 722-6879 **Fax** N/A **E-mail** info@desertdovebb.com **Web** www. desertdovebb.com

ELYSIAN GROVE MARKET BED & BREAKFAST INN, Tucson

OVERALL ★★★★ | QUALITY ★★★½ | VALUE ★★★★ | PRICE RANGE $85

A favorite of housekeeping magazines for its kitchen—an old meat locker with the original heavy freezer door done up in blues, reds, and yellows and recycled galvanized duct countertops—the Market's saltillo tile floors, adobe seating areas, and fresco walls are true to the Mexican roots of the surrounding nineteenth-century barrio neighborhood. The large living room with its descending staircase and local Mexican-influenced paintings, including Aryen Hart's mylar and colored inks on steel, also attracts film-makers (e.g. *Boys on the Side*). Mexican food a short stroll away ranges from no-frills Sonoran at El Minuto (in the same family since 1936) to the more nouvelle Barrio Grill.

SETTING & FACILITIES

Location Barrio Historic District, downtown; from Congress St. go south on Stone Ave. & west on Simpson St. **Near** Museums, schools, parks, convention center **Building** 1920s corner barrio grocery store **Grounds** Large backyard garden area w/ fountains, chess set, mesquite, prickly pear, & tree lights at night **Public Space** Front room is extremely large, has fireplace, large paintings, descending staircase **Food & Drink** Breakfast on old Mexican table in front room **Recreation** Golf **Amenities & Services** Weddings in yard

ACCOMMODATIONS

Units 4 guest rooms, also rented as 2 2-BR apartment suites w/ shared LR **All** No frills, no phones, no TVs **Some** Front & back doors **Bed & Bath** Queen (1), doubles, singles, roll-a-ways; each pair of rooms shares a bath **Favorites** Small upstairs loft w/ French doors opening onto garden is where owner likes to stay; downstairs old wine cellar is more spacious, has adobe seating areas built into wall & can hold enough beds for 5 people to sleep **Comfort & Decor** Pension style from hostess's Latin American travels includes antique, brass, and four-poster beds; pedestal sinks and pull-chain toilets; saltillo tile floors; and fresco-painted walls.

RATES, RESERVATIONS, & RESTRICTIONS

Deposit 50% when booking; refund if re-rented (sometimes gives credit toward another date) **Discounts** None **Credit Cards** None (cash and checks only) **Check-In/Out** 3–6 p.m./11 a.m. **Smoking** No **Pets** Flexible (need to ask; owner has cat) **Kids** Yes **No-Nos** N/A **Minimum Stay** None **Open** All year **Host** Deborah LaChapelle, 400 West Simpson St., Tucson 85701 **Phone** (520) 628-1522 **Fax** N/A **E-mail** N/A **Web** www.bbonline.com/az/elysiangrove

HACIENDA BED & BREAKFAST, *Tucson*

OVERALL ★★★★ | QUALITY ★★★½ | VALUE ★★★★ | PRICE RANGE $75–$125

Thick block walls keep out the commuter noise on busy Grant St., except for the upstairs patios during rush hour, in this hypoallergenic (filtered water; Pine-Sol & vinegar for cleaning) no-frills combination of two town-houses. The backyard is an urban oasis with a swimming pool and barbe-cue. The location is convenient to downtown, all the shopping malls, and restaurants for those wanting the best of urban Tucson. The Hacienda also borders Tucson's East Side, making it a good point for excursions north up Catalina Highway into the Santa Catalina Mountains and Mt. Lemmon, as well as southeast on the Old Spanish Trail to Saguaro National Park East.

SETTING & FACILITIES

Location Grant Rd. just east of Craycroft Rd. **Near** Shopping malls, parks, medical centers, Sabino Canyon, Tanque Verde restaurant row **Building** 2 1968 contemporary townhouses w/ Spanish arches **Grounds** Back yard patio & pool **Public Space** 2 LRs w/ sliding glass doors to patio, 1 w/ player piano, videos, & games, the other w/ a floating hardwood dance floor **Food & Drink** Full breakfast; afternoon tea; evening snacks; barbecue on patio for guest use; dietary restrictions met w/ advance notice **Recreation** Golf, tennis, jogging **Amenities & Services** Exercise room w/ TV, treadmill, Stairmaster, free weights; sparkling cider & nuts for special occasions w/ advance notice

ACCOMMODATIONS

Units 6 All Cable TV/VCR, fridge, robes, mirrored closets, coffeemaker, phone, hair dryer, ceiling fan, off-street parking **Some** Microwaves (2), sitting areas (4 uppers), desks (5), private entrance **Bed & Bath** Kings, queens, twins, hide-a-beds; all private baths, tubs, jetted tubs (2) **Favorites** Desert Rose has skylight above queen and hide-a-bed, large walk-in closet, marble jetted tub; Teal Garden is handicap-accessible, w/ queen & full-size sleeper sofa, microwave, garden wallpaper, private entrance to covered parking in back; Summer Flowers has jetted tub in middle of room, is a favorite of newlyweds **Comfort & Decor** White walls, no frills, but a variety of framed art.

RATES, RESERVATIONS, & RESTRICTIONS

Deposit 1 night or 50% (4 nights or more); refund minus $10 fee if canceled 14 days prior to scheduled arrival or room is re-rented **Discounts** 25% June, July, Aug.; 10% AAA, corp., senior **Credit Cards** AE, MC, V, D, DC **Check-In/Out** 3–6 p.m./11 a.m. **Smoking** No **Pets** No **Kids** Yes (well behaved) **No-Nos** N/A **Minimum Stay** None **Open** All year **Hosts** Fred & Barbara Shamseldin, 5704 E. Grant, Tucson 85712 **Phone** (520) 290-2224 or toll-free (888) 236-4421 **Fax** (520) 721-9066 **E-mail** info@tucsonhacienda.com **Web** www.tucsonhacienda.com

HACIENDA DEL DESIERTO, Tucson

OVERALL ★★★★★ | QUALITY ★★★★★ | VALUE ★★★★★ | PRICE RANGE
$125–$175

Designed like an old stagecoach stop, two big wooden doors open from the dirt frontage road into a walled brick courtyard with ample flowers (provided hungry javelinas are kept out) and a yucca-shaped copper fountain. The Great Room lives up to its name with skylights, a huge teepee-like fireplace, saltillo floor tiles, and beams and planks salvaged from the old St. Mary's Hospital. Extensive brick patios in back are great for sitting, though the Saguaro Cactus Trail leads from here into the park. However, the rooms are impressive enough that it is tempting to stay inside and not venture beyond the private porches.

SETTING & FACILITIES

Location East Side of Tucson; from Old Spanish Trail, go west on Camino del Desierto **Near** Saguaro National Park East, Colossal Cave, Pima Air & Space Museum **Building** 1970s Territorial style hacienda w/ Mexican courtyard **Grounds** 16 acres of desert w/ extensive patios & porches & a pond to lure wildlife **Public Space** Great room, front courtyard gardens, back patios **Food & Drink** Cont'l-plus breakfast in Mexican courtyard, DR, or patio; cookies & cold drinks on arrival **Recreation** Golf, bird- & wildlife-watching **Amenities & Services** Hydrotherapy spa

ACCOMMODATIONS

Units 4 **All** Private entrance, sitting area, robes, slippers, phone (party line), data port, coffeemaker, hair dryer, alarm clock, TV/VCR, ceiling fan, antique stove **Some** Kitchenettes (3), laundry (1), private patio & barbecue (3) **Bed & Bath** Kings (2), queens (2), twins & hide-a-bed (2d) beds; all private baths, Jacuzzi tub (1), tubs (2), bath amenity basket **Favorites** Casita has saguaro rib ceiling, stained glass, LR with saltillo tile floor, full kitchen, washer & dryer, 2 BRs, patio w/ barbecue, private spa; Galleria has 2 large purple, salmon, & white sponge-painted rooms; Rose Room has king & queen beds, sitting area, desert-view porch w/ barbecue, full fridge, shower only; Patio Suite has queen, LR double hide-a-bed, skylight in bath, courtyard view **Comfort & Decor** Spanish-Mexican style with arches, saltillo tile floors, decorative tiles, sponge-painted walls, unique headboards, antique gas and wood-burning stoves.

RATES, RESERVATIONS, & RESTRICTIONS

Deposit 1 night or 1/3 total (whichever is greater); refund minus $20 if cancellation within 14 days **Discounts** None **Credit Cards** AE, MC, V **Check-In/Out** Customized **Smoking** Outside only **Pets** No (owners have outdoor cats) **Kids** Yes (if well behaved & supervised) **No-Nos** N/A **Minimum Stay** 2 night minimum in Casita **Open** All year **Hosts** David & Rosemary Brown, 11770 E. Rambling Trail, Tucson 85747 **Phone** (520) 298-1764 or toll-free (800) 982-1795 **Fax** (520) 722-4558 **E-mail** oasis@tucson-bed-breakfast.com **Web** www.tucson-bed-breakfast.com

HACIENDA DEL REY BED & BREAKFAST, Tucson

OVERALL ★★★★½ | QUALITY ★★★★½ | VALUE ★★★★ | PRICE RANGE $85–$95

From the road it is almost impossible to see the front of Hacienda del Rey through the thick forest of cactus and ironwood trees, but the entrance is through the side courtyard, where a small bridge, bougainvillea, and mesquite surround a dry, rocky creek bed. Security lights come on automatically for night arrivals, a legacy of the host's former business as a licensed security guard. Baby, the great Dane, and Killer are actually quite gentle dogs, but they provide a bit of extra security for the gem show regulars and business people (who like the easy access to I-10) filling this bed-and-breakfast each winter.

SETTING & FACILITIES

Location Marana; from I-10, just north of intersection of W. Ina & N. Cortaro Rds. **Near** Picture Rocks, Saguaro National Park West, Desert Museum, Tucson Mall **Building** 1996 Territorial-style hacienda w/ courtyard **Grounds** 4 acres of desert w/ cactus garden **Public Space** LR, DR, office, laundry **Food & Drink** Choice of full or cont'l breakfast in DR; self-service snack bar **Recreation** Golf, horse riding **Amenities & Services** Laundry, automatic outside security lighting, free Tucson International Airport transfers (advance notice)

ACCOMMODATIONS

Units 3 **All** TV/VCR, phone, data port, clock, ceiling fan, private courtyard entrance **Some** Handicap-accessible (1), 2 entrances (2), saltillo tile floors (2) **Bed & Bath** Queens; all private baths, 2 tubs. **Favorites** Pueblo Room has arrowhead collection on wall, Indian baskets, bow & arrow, dream catcher **Comfort & Decor** Each room is different; themes run from Mexican serapes and Pueblo Indian to cowboy and Western art.

RATES, RESERVATIONS, & RESTRICTIONS

Deposit 1 night or 50% of stay; refund minus $20 if cancellation within 2–3 weeks or re-rented **Discounts** Weekly **Credit Cards** AE, MC, V, D **Check-In/Out** 3–6 p.m./11 a.m. **Smoking** No **Pets** No (owners have 2 dogs) **Kids** Yes (ask first) **No-Nos** N/A **Minimum Stay** 2 nights during peak season **Open** All year **Hosts** Bill & Polly Ritchie, 7320 N. Cortaro Rd., Tucson 85743 **Phone** (520) 579-0425 **Fax** (520) 579-3830 **E-mail** N/A **Web** N/A

JEREMIAH INN BED & BREAKFAST, Tucson

OVERALL ★★★★ | QUALITY ★★★★½ | VALUE ★★★★ | PRICE RANGE $80–$120

A tranquil retreat named for the biblical verse "Oh that I had in the desert a lodging place for travelers" (Jeremiah 9:2) was built specifically as a bed-and-breakfast by the host, a Seattle building contractor, who crafted a hallway niche for a guest refrigerator and designed two laundry rooms. Guests have additional privacy on their side of the house, thanks to a side entrance near the parking area that bypasses a living room shared with the host family and their two boys. Overall, rooms are very spacious and clean, with lots of light and no frills.

SETTING & FACILITIES

Location Tucson's East Side, near intersection of Houghton Rd. & E. Catalina Hwy. **Near** Sabino Canyon, Mt. Lemmon, E. Tanque Verde restaurant row, Saguaro National Park East, Coronado National Forest **Building** 1995 Santa Fe stucco ranch house designed as B&B **Grounds** 3.3 acres w/ back yard patio and pool w/ deck in the Catalina Mountain foothills **Public Space** LR DR w/ pool view **Food & Drink** Full breakfast in DR, on patio, poolside, or in room; freshly baked cookies every morning; 24-hour complimentary beverages

Recreation Golf, horse riding, bird-watching **Amenities & Services** Pool, Jacuzzi, hall-way fridge w/ food bins for each room, 2 laundry rooms w/ irons

ACCOMMODATIONS

Units 5 **All** Phone, TV, robes, hair dryer, digital clock radio, ceiling fan **Some** Armoires **Bed & Bath** Queens plus sleeper sofas and single beds; all private baths, tubs **Favorites** Coronado, the smallest, entered via the bath, has the most dramatic views of surrounding mountains; Rincon has second most dramatic mountain views, desert prints on walls; Patagonia views prickly pear, birds, rabbits, deer, mountains **Comfort & Decor** Light Southwest, no frills, with whitewash pine, touches of Navajo. and cacti.

RATES, RESERVATIONS, & RESTRICTIONS

Deposit Reservations required; 7-day cancellation for refund minus fee **Discounts** Families, 4 nights or more, some packages **Credit Cards** AE, MC, V **Check-In/Out** 3–6 p.m./11 a.m. **Smoking** No **Pets** No **Kids** Yes **No-Nos** N/A **Minimum Stay** None **Open** All year **Hosts** Bob & Beth Miner, 10921 East Snyder Rd., Tucson 85749 **Phone** (520) 749-3072 or toll-free (888) 750-3072 **Fax** N/A **E-mail** info@jeremiahinn.com **Web** www.jeremiahinn.com

THE ROYAL ELIZABETH BED & BREAKFAST INN, *Tucson*

OVERALL ★★★★★ | QUALITY ★★★★½ | VALUE ★★★★ | PRICE RANGE $95–$180

An 1878 army officer's home converted into apartments in the 1940s, with a carriage house and servants' quarters incorporated into the building, the Royal Elizabeth reopened as a bed-and-breakfast in 1999 after a decade of vacancy. Now on the National Register of Historic Places with its original ceiling heights restored, the mansion is entered through a leaded- and beveled-glass front door leading past the front desk and lounge to a dining room under a skylight. Most rooms have private patios and private entrances onto a common patio and pool area bordering a relatively quiet downtown street. Thanks to its central location, this is one of the few Tucson bed-and-breakfasts to stay busy during the summer months.

SETTING & FACILITIES

Location Downtown **Near** Convention Center, museums, galleries, university, historic districts, government offices **Building** 1878 adobe mansion w/ wood interior **Grounds** 0.5 acre city lot w/ fenced front lawn, patio, pool & gardens **Public Space** DR w/ leaded-glass skylight, lounge w/ fireplace **Food & Drink** Full breakfast in DR; late afternoon refreshments **Recreation** Golf, jogging **Amenities & Services** Pool, hot tub, VCR library, ice machine, informal meeting spaces

ACCOMMODATIONS

Units 6 guest rooms, including 2 2-room suites **All** Sitting area, AC, ceiling fan, safe, digital clock, phone, armoire w/ satellite TV/VCR and fridge **Some** Private entrance (4), private patio (5), fainting couch (2) **Bed & Bath** Queens (4), doubles (2), additional sofa beds (2);

all private baths, tubs (2), jetted tub (1). **Favorites** Nicole Elizabeth Suite has sitting room bar, silk love seat, jetted tub, bay window overlooking pool, private entrance; Rose room has original 1923 rose wallpaper, desk, private porch **Comfort & Decor** Victorian antiques, love seats, fainting couches, throw rugs on wood floors, fine linens.

RATES, RESERVATIONS, & RESTRICTIONS

Deposit On a per-night basis; cancellations within 14 days receive full refund minus $25 fee, otherwise refund only if room rebooked **Discounts** Corp. **Credit Cards** AE, MC, V, D **Check-In/Out** 3–6 p.m./11 a.m. **Smoking** No **Pets** No **Kids** Yes (under parental supervision) **No-Nos** N/A **Minimum Stay** None **Open** All year **Hosts** Jack Nance & Robert Ogburn, 204 S. Scott Ave., Tucson 85701 **Phone** (520) 670-9022 or toll-free (877) 670-9022 **Fax** (520) 629-9710 **E-mail** info@royalelizabeth.com **Web** www.royalelizabeth.com

Valley of the Sun

At the center of the Valley of the Sun, Phoenix is a big-time city complete with extensive traffic jams, high-priced resorts, top restaurants, major league sports teams, championship golf courses, and excellent museums. A few bed-and-breakfasts have survived into the present megalopolis era thanks to grandfather clauses in the current rules favoring hotels, motels, and resorts. Opening a new bed-and-breakfast in Phoenix is a Sisyphean task, as an objection from a neighbor within a few miles can shut down the operation and wipe out the investment.

Most of the cities and suburbs ringing Phoenix regulate area bed-and-breakfasts in such a way that they are marginalized as part-time businesses or sidelines for real estate agents. Typically the rules make it difficult for bed-and-breakfasts to rent more than two rooms per night. One of the exceptions is Cave Creek, a funky cowboy-style town bordering Tonto National Forest 20 miles north of Scottsdale. Cave Creek is adjacent to the Boulders Resort in Carefree and is a good place for combining relaxation, recreation, and proximity to Phoenix.

Goodyear, a suburb 14 miles west of Phoenix, is named after the Goodyear Tire Co., which established plantations taking advantage of the furnace-like summer heat to grow cotton for tire cords. Appropriately, NASCAR, motorcycle, and other racing are the big events in Goodyear. South of Goodyear is Gila Bend, a nineteenth-century verdant oasis transformed into a dry, dusty, desolate twentieth-century truck stop by water diversion projects.

The only reason to pass through Gila Bend is to head south to Organ Pipe Cactus National Monument, preferably during the cool winter weather. An hour north of Organ Pipe is Ajo, where a bed-and-breakfast survives in what was a Phelps-Dodge company town until the polluting copper smelter shut down in 1985. East of Gila Bend is Casa Grande Ruins

National Monument. Aside from a bed-and-breakfast in Florence and hot-season desert cotton growing, the Casa Grande area is notable for a cool-season influx of golf club–toting snowbirds and RVs.

THE GUEST HOUSE INN, Ajo

OVERALL ★★★★ | QUALITY ★★★★½ | VALUE ★★★★★ | PRICE RANGE $79–$89

Originally built by Phelps Dodge to house visiting mining executives, when copper mining ended in the 1980s the renovated Guest House became a bed-and-breakfast. Of interest primarily for its proximity to Organ Pipe Cactus National Monument, the inn has its coterie of annual repeat visitors who come for a week every spring to follow the changing desert wildflower displays in this land of the giant saguaro cactus. Heavy cactus-shaped copper candlestick holders on the mantel over the fireplace are among the reminders of the town's mining heritage. An enclosed porch "hallway" fronts the guest rooms, keeping them cool on the hottest days.

SETTING & FACILITIES
Location At Ajo's only traffic light, go south on La Mina Ave. **Near** Organ Pipe Cactus National Monument, Kitt Peak National Observatory **Building** 1925 ranch-style copper company guest house **Grounds** Yard w/ bird-filled desert landscape **Public Space** LR w/ faux turquoise walls, ceiling fans, white leather sofas fronting fireplace; DR w/ long walnut table, leather chairs; latticed patio **Food & Drink** Full breakfast in DR; private dinners **Recreation** Desert exploration **Amenities & Services** TV, meetings, receptions

ACCOMMODATIONS
Units 4 guest rooms, 2 on each side of house **All** Ceiling fan, individual heat/AC, hair dryer **Some** Ice buckets **Bed & Bath** Queens (3), singles (1); all private baths, tubs (2) in north rooms **Favorites** Prescott on cool north side of house has carved dark wood four-poster bed w/ matching dresser, white bedspread w/ floral borders **Comfort & Decor** Glass and wood doors, shuttered closets, Victorian with desert paintings or more South-western Spanish style furnishings with desert hues.

RATES, RESERVATIONS, & RESTRICTIONS
Deposit Credit card; 3 days cancellation notice **Discounts** None **Credit Cards** MC, V, DC **Check-In/Out** 2 p.m./11 a.m. **Smoking** No (outdoors only) **Pets** No **Kids** Yes **No-Nos** N/A **Minimum Stay** None **Open** All year (except 2 days Christmas Eve) **Host** Mike Walker, 700 Guest House Rd., Ajo 85321 **Phone** (520) 387-6133 **Fax** N/A **E-mail** N/A **Web** N/A

ANDORA CROSSING, Cave Creek

OVERALL ★★★½ | QUALITY ★★★★ | VALUE ★★★★ | PRICE RANGE $100–$150

Andora Crossing combines 1920s Italian masonry trailer park rock walls with a 1950s ranch house and a 1960s expansion. "It's the Arizona desert unplugged with no phone, TV, e-mail or computer," says the hostess, an Arizona native who bought this eclectic desert retreat in 1994. Besides painting walls, doors, and floors in her unique way, the hostess's paintings of horses, agave, prickly pears, and clouded skies adorn the walls. The homey shared rooms have brick arches. Desert isolation amid Andora wash, a creek, saguaro, ironwood, mesquite, and jojoba make this a popular retreat.

SETTING & FACILITIES
Location 35 mi. north of Phoenix's Sky Harbor International Airport **Near** Carefree, Scottsdale **Building** 1920s rock walls, 1950s ranch house, 1960s remodeling **Grounds** 2.5 acres w/ wash, rock well, desert vegetation **Public Space** LR, DR **Food & Drink** Full breakfast in DR; pistachio jars; barbecues **Recreation** Golf, horse riding, hot-air ballooning, jeep tours **Amenities & Services** TV, stereo

ACCOMMODATIONS
Units 4 **All** Down comforter, boom box (tape/CD), clock, heat/AC **Some** Ceiling fan (3), fridge (2), microwave (1), bath salts (1) **Bed & Bath** King (1), queen (3), extra twins (2); all private baths, tub (3) **Favorites** Owl's Nest, a stand-alone guest house across the wash from main house, has 2 BRs, stenciled walls w/ stuffed owl, painted linoleum floor, metal zinnia lamp, porch w/ terra cotta Mexican chimney; Griffins Three has pink concrete floor, stained-glass panels, Mexican floral bowls over bed, paneled bath w/ Mexican tiles, block glass **Comfort & Decor** 1940s/1950s dude ranch style, white walls with patches of 1920s rock work, nature paintings, eclectic furnishings, some wood beams and trim, saltillo tiles, tiled baths.

RATES, RESERVATIONS, & RESTRICTIONS
Deposit 1 night (10-day cancellation for full refund) **Discounts** None **Credit Cards** None (cash or check only) **Check-In/Out** 4–6 p.m./11 a.m. **Smoking** Outside only **Pets** No (owner has dogs) **Kids** Yes **No-Nos** N/A **Minimum Stay** 2 nights **Open** Sept. 15–June 1 **Host** Karen Douglass, P.O. Box 7050, Cave Creek 85327 **Phone** (480) 488-3747 or toll-free (888) 488-3747 **Fax** N/A **E-mail** N/A **Web** www.andoracrossing.com

FULL CIRCLE RANCH, Cave Creek

OVERALL ★★★★½ | QUALITY ★★★★ | VALUE ★★★★ | PRICE RANGE $160–$275

On a rural road dead ending just before the saguaro-studded desert gives way to foothills, horse-friendly Full Circle Ranch is fronted by a saltillo tile entrance with fountains. Run by a former southern California aerospace engineer who calls himself host, cook, maid, servant, and friend, the rambling ranch house has a wagon wheel fronting a flagstone fireplace surrounded by artificial boulders. Realistic life-size figures of an Indian with a rifle and a grizzled old cowboy with a whiskey glass cause double-takes. Just past a kitchen with an island and Mexican tiles, saloon-style doors lead to the three lowest-priced original guest rooms. Two new more expensive rooms called casitas have patios and whirlpool tubs.

SETTING & FACILITIES
Location 35 mi. north of Phoenix's Sky Harbor International Airport **Near** Lake Pleasant, Carefree, Scottsdale **Building** 1960s ranch house moved here from Scottsdale in 1990s **Grounds** Rock waterfall & rooftop observation deck overlooking BLM lands w/ hills & desert vegetation **Public Space** LR, DR, game room, bar room, outdoor sitting areas **Food & Drink** Full breakfast in DR; dinners & charcoal/mesquite barbecues available **Recreation** Horse riding, golf, boating, fishing **Amenities & Services** Jacuzzi, pool, outdoor fire pits, indoor fireplaces, pool table, card tables, stereo, darts, lighted horse arena

ACCOMMODATIONS
Units 5 **All** Ceiling fan, TV, stocked fridge, robes, clock radio **Some** Desk (1), porch (2) **Bed & Bath** King (2), queen (2), twins (1); all private baths, whirlpool tub (2) **Favorites** Two new casitas have king bed, saltillo tile floors, patios, whirlpool tub, Mexican tile sink, tiled shower, separate toilet room **Comfort & Decor** Relatively spare, with some Southwest and Mexican accents, wood-paneled walls, timber furnishings, flagstone or saltillo floors, shutters.

RATES, RESERVATIONS, & RESTRICTIONS
Deposit 50% (14-day cancellation policy; otherwise liable for full amount) **Discounts** Extended stays **Credit Cards** AE, MC, V, D **Check-In/Out** 2–8 p.m./11 a.m. **Smoking** No **Pets** No (owner has friendly big black dog; horses welcome) **Kids** Over age 15 only) **No-Nos** N/A **Minimum Stay** None **Open** All year **Host** Jim Langan, 40205 N. 26th St., Cave Creek 85027 **Phone** (623) 465-7570 **Fax** (623) 465-7579 **E-mail** jlangan@fullcircleranch.com **Web** www.fullcircleranch.com

THE INN AT RANCHO SONORA, Florence

OVERALL ★★★½ | QUALITY ★★★★ | VALUE ★★★★ | PRICE RANGE $59–$150

The adjacent RV park, the mainstay of the family business, offers a number of shared facilities, including an attractive pool and Jacuzzi, in this middle-of-the-desert location halfway between Tucson (65 miles) and Phoenix. Many come here on prison-related business, as a facility is nearby, but at least half are visiting nearby Casa Grande Ruins or checking out Florence's small main strip that seems frozen in time as a movie and TV backdrop. The hosts can provide helpful hints on what to do and where to eat (e.g., L&B Inn for Mexican food), and help make this remote desert stop more rewarding.

SETTING & FACILITIES
Location 60 mi. SE of Phoenix; 5 mi. south of Florence on AZ 79 **Near** Casa Grande Ruins, Boyce Thompson Arboretum **Building** Renovated 1930s adobe motel **Grounds** Walled courtyard adjacent to RV park **Public Space** DR **Food & Drink** Cont'l breakfast buffet in DR **Recreation** Golf **Amenities & Services** Pool, Jacuzzi, picnic area, putting green, laundry, vending machines & kitchen shared w/ RV park

ACCOMMODATIONS
Units 5 guest rooms, 3 casitas **All** Private entrance, TV, individual heat/AC **Some** Phones **Bed & Bath** Kings, queens, twins; all private baths **Favorites** Fernando & Evangeline combine into suite w/ French doors, full kitchen, private patio; Casitas have 1 or 2 BRs, LRs, and complete kitchens **Comfort & Decor** Eclectic country and Western with Mexican tiled bath.

RATES, RESERVATIONS, & RESTRICTIONS
Deposit 7 day cancellation, 1 night charge on short stays; 1 month cancellation required on stays over a week, or charged for entire period **Discounts** Extended stays **Credit Cards** AE, MC, V, D, CB **Check-In/Out** Flexible **Smoking** Designated outside areas **Pets** Yes (if small; requires prior permission; $10) **Kids** Yes **No-Nos** N/A **Minimum Stay** None **Open** All year **Hosts** Brent & Linda Freeman, 9198 N. AZ 79, Florence 85232 **Phone** (520) 868-8000 or toll-free (800) 205-6817 **Fax** (520) 868-8000 **E-mail** rancho@c2i2.com **Web** www.c2i2.com/~rancho

INDIAN SPRINGS RANCH BED & BREAKFAST, Goodyear

OVERALL ★★★★½ | QUALITY ★★★★★ | VALUE ★★★★★ | PRICE RANGE $85–$100

Designed and built from scratch for a growing family by the retired air force pilot owners, Indian Springs incorporates Spanish stained-glass windows from a tour of duty in Spain. A helmeted conquistador window is set into a high-ceiling living room next to a marble-top pecan dining room set resting on oak floors beneath a chandelier. The Ponderosa Room, under a white arch-covered walkway, was once the living room, and the fireplace was used for cooking. The ranch books up a year in advance with a long waiting list for NASCAR, Winston, motorcycle, and stock car racing events at Phoenix International Raceway, and local corporations sometimes take rooms for a month or two at a time.

SETTING & FACILITIES
Location East of Phoenix; from I-10 Exit 131 go south 5.5 mi. on 115th Ave. past raceway **Near** Phoenix International Raceway, Estrella County Park **Building** 1974 Spanish hacienda w/ guest room wing **Grounds** Courtyard w/ saguaro, mesquite, birdhouse in trees, gated pool **Public Space** LR, DR, basement exercise room **Food & Drink** Full breakfast in DR; ice bucket & split for special occasions; lunch catering **Recreation** Golf, mountain biking, bird-watching, horse riding, vehicle racing **Amenities & Services** Weddings, receptions, horse corral

ACCOMMODATIONS

Units 4 guest rooms separate from main house **All** Private entrances, TV/VCR, iron & ironing board, lighted makeup mirror, hair dryer, plush colored robes, heating, microwave or fridge on request **Some** Kitchens (2), cooling (3), fireplace (1) **Bed & Bath** Queens (3), twins (1), roll-aways on request; all private baths, tubs, amenity-laden medicine cabinets **Favorites** Casita opens onto pool, has white walls, black beam divider, queen & twin trundle beds, double sink, cloud & sky shower curtains, complete kitchen, outside wrought-iron spiral staircase to deck; Ponderosa has fireplace, queen & extra-long double bed, kitchenette, white adobe & wood-paneled walls, Spanish stained glass **Comfort & Decor** Spanish and Western with mostly saltillo tile or flagstone floors, walls ranging from split pine log to rock and adobe with candlestick holders, beam wood ceilings.

RATES, RESERVATIONS, & RESTRICTIONS

Deposit 48-hour cancellation for full refund, except race weekends **Discounts** Corp., longer-term (no breakfast) **Credit Cards** None (cash or check only) **Check-In/Out** 1 p.m./11 a.m. **Smoking** No **Pets** No (owners have dog) **Kids** Yes (crib, booster chair available) **No-Nos** N/A **Minimum Stay** 2 nights on race weekends **Open** Oct. 1–April 30 (other times by special arrangement) **Hosts** Frank & Elaine Billingsley, 13132 W. Beverly Rd., Goodyear 85338 **Phone** (623) 932-2076 or toll-free (888) 426-1707 **Fax** (623) 932-9330 **E-mail** ebill_2000@yahoo.com **Web** www.indianspringsranch.com

HACIENDA ALTA BED & BREAKFAST, Phoenix

OVERALL ★★★★ | QUALITY ★★★★½ | VALUE ★★★★ | PRICE RANGE $90–$200

From busy Camelback Road a thick jungle of saguaro and desert plants is circled by a dirt road leading to Hacienda Alta, whose meditative back yard desert sculpture garden teems with quail, roadrunners, and cottontail rabbits. The back yard gate opens onto the Phoenician Resort golf course for early morning walks. The high-ceiling Western-style living room and dining room with vintage hand-carved and painted Mexican furniture is filled with photos and maps of relatives dating to the 1840s Mexican-American War. The multilevel property has its share of steps, the most impressive leading to the loft suite.

SETTING & FACILITIES

Location South slope of Camelback Mountain, near corner of 56th St. & E. Camelback Rd. **Near** Phoenician Resort, Scottsdale Fashion Square, Biltmore Fashion Park, Paradise Valley, parks, zoo, botanical garden, airport **Building** 1928 Territorial-style 3,300 sq. ft. 2-story adobe **Grounds** 3 acres w/ citrus trees, cactus & desert sculpture garden **Public Space** LR, DR **Food & Drink** Full breakfast in DR **Recreation** Golf, horse riding **Amenities & Services** Gate to walking/jogging path along Phoenician golf course (early a.m.)

ACCOMMODATIONS

Units 3 **All** TV/VCR, phone, ceiling fan **Some** Loft (1), patio **Bed & Bath** Queens, singles; all private baths, tubs (2) **Favorites** Loft suite has LR w/ fireplace, staircase, private upper patio, walls near ceiling tinted sunset hues, grapevine wrought-iron window **Comfort & Decor** White adobe walls, throw rugs on tile floors, beam ceilings, wrought iron, leaded glass, painted leather chairs, Mexican ceramic sinks.

RATES, RESERVATIONS, & RESTRICTIONS
Deposit 1 night; full refund with 10-day notice, half if shorter notice **Discounts** None **Credit Cards** None (cash or checks only; Canadian currency OK) **Check-In/Out** 3–6 p.m./11 a.m. **Smoking** No **Pets** Need to ask (individual basis; owners have dogs) **Kids** Yes **No-Nos** N/A **Minimum Stay** None **Open** All year **Hosts** Ed & Margaret Newhall, 5750 E. Camelback Rd., Phoenix 85018 **Phone** (480) 945-8525 **Fax** N/A **E-mail** N/A **Web** N/A

THE HARMONY HOUSE BED & BREAKFAST INN, Phoenix

OVERALL ★★★★ | QUALITY ★★★½ | VALUE ★★★★ | PRICE RANGE $100–$130

In a neighborhood of 1950s ranch houses and surrounded by a huge shady pine tree and a virtual orchard of flood-irrigated pecan, grapefruit, peach, date palm, and lemon trees, Harmony House was the original Tudor home ruling over this Phoenix neighborhood when it was a citrus orchard. Set back from 7th Avenue, the tick-tock of an antique German wall clock is the only sound heard over a dining room table dominated by a brass peacock crystal chandelier. The living room (which is rented out with the Banta Suite) has a TV, fireplace, and antique love seats, and it radiates a relaxed and informal, almost casual ambience.

SETTING & FACILITIES
Location North of corner of N. 7th & E. Glendale Aves. **Near** Airport, museums, parks, Glendale shops and restaurants, Phoenix Mountains Preserve **Building** 1934 English Tudor-style plantation home **Grounds** An acre w/ 22 fruit & nut trees **Public Space** Kitchen entrance, LR **Food & Drink** Cont'l breakfast in DR **Recreation** Golf, horse riding **Amenities & Services** Chemical-free (ozone) hot tub, 400-movie VCR library

ACCOMMODATIONS
Units 5 **All** TV **Some** Crystal chandeliers (2), ceiling fan (1), walk-in closets (2) **Bed & Bath** King, queen, twin & sofa beds; all private baths, tubs (3) **Favorites** The Banta Suite is closest to the hot tub, has the only ceiling fan, & comes with a queen sleeper sofa in the LR **Comfort & Decor** Victorian, with varying combinations of pedestal sinks, crystal chandeliers, dormer windows, wallpaper, carved wood furniture, and angled ceilings.

RATES, RESERVATIONS, & RESTRICTIONS
Deposit Refund minus $25 fee if cancellation over 14 days in advance; within 14 days refund only if room rebooked; no refund within 7 days. Policy also applies to early checkout **Discounts** None **Credit Cards** AE, MC, V, D **Check-In/Out** 4–6 p.m./10 a.m. **Smoking** Outside only **Pets** No (owners' 2 dogs stay outside) **Kids** Yes (over age 12 wel-

comed) **No-Nos** N/A **Minimum Stay** None **Open** All year **Hosts** Don Johnson & Fito
Licea, 7202 N. 7th Ave., Phoenix 85021 **Phone** (602) 331-9554 or toll-free (877) 331-9554
Fax (602) 395-0528 **E-mail** harmonybb2@aol.com **Web** www.bbonline.com/az/harmony

MARICOPA MANOR BED & BREAKFAST INN, Phoenix

OVERALL ★★★★½ | QUALITY ★★★★½ | VALUE ★★★★ | PRICE RANGE $89–$229

Within a block of a shopping plaza in a neighborhood of tall palm trees
fronting white 1920s Spanish-style haciendas, the 7,200-square-foot Maricopa Manor is moving to bolder colors and upgraded furnishings under its
new owners. For example, in addition to a kitchen, dining area, double
whirlpool tub, stained glass, and a fireplace between the bedroom and living room, the Manor Suite is now done up in gold lamé and royal blue. The
clientele is 80% business, the rest mostly romantic escapes seeking the luxury that abounds in the one- and two-bedroom suites here.

SETTING & FACILITIES
Location Near Uptown Plaza, corner of Central Ave. & Camelback Rd. **Near** Airport,
Biltmore Fashion Park, museums, parks, convention center, shops **Building** 1928 Spanish
mission style **Grounds** 1 acre w/ gazebo & pool **Public Space** LR, DR **Food & Drink**
Cont'l breakfast in DR or in picnic basket in guest room sitting area; bottled water, tea,
coffee in room **Recreation** Golf **Amenities & Services** Pool, hot tub

ACCOMMODATIONS
Units 7 suites **All** AC, robes, pool towels, fridge, cable TV/VCR, alarm clock, stereo/CD,
phone **Some** Fireplaces **Bed & Bath** Mostly kings; all private baths, tubs & Jacuzzi tubs
Favorites Siesta Suite has an LR fireplace, saltillo tile floor kitchen, carved wood dining
table, desk, sitting area; Reflection Path has deep lavender walls, fireplace, Jacuzzi, chrome
faucets, dining set **Comfort & Decor** Rooms are being upgraded with brighter colors
and more elegant furnishings.

RATES, RESERVATIONS, & RESTRICTIONS
Deposit Credit card; voucher for 1 night minus $50 fee if cancel within 14 days, otherwise $50 fee **Discounts** None **Credit Cards** AE, MC, V, D, DC **Check-In/Out** 4–6 p.m./11 a.m. **Smoking** No **Pets** No **Kids** Prefer age 16 and older **No-Nos** N/A **Minimum Stay** None **Open** All year **Hosts** Mark Tucker & Jeff Vadheim, 15 W. Pasadena Ave., Phoenix 85013 **Phone** (602) 274-6302 **Fax** (602) 266-3904 **E-mail** maricopamanor@aol.com **Web** www.maricopamanor.com

Grand Canyon Country

Grand Canyon Country stretches from the red rocks of Sedona north to Page and Lake Powell along the Utah border. The Grand Canyon has a more isolated, forested North Rim that closes with the winter snows and an immensely popular South Rim. There are no North Rim bed-and-breakfast options. The nearest bed-and-breakfasts to the South Rim are in Williams and Flagstaff.

Surrounded by ponderosa pine forests and mountain ski areas, Williams has the closest (58 miles) bed-and-breakfasts to the Grand Canyon's South Rim. Downtown Williams looks much like it did in the heyday of Route 66, with the old motels and endless curio shops paralleling the railroad tracks. Steam trains still chug from the historic Grand Canyon Railway depot in Williams to Grand Canyon Village in the South Rim. With only 2,500 people, Williams is a manageably small town.

Flagstaff is almost as close to the South Rim as Williams and is similarly surrounded by pine forests and ski areas. But Flagstaff has 46,000 people, two microbreweries, and many more motels sprawled around a railroad freight hub clanging with train traffic all hours of the day and night. Downtown is showing signs of becoming trendy, but the old buildings are still intact. The Lowell Observatory is famed for its discovery of the planet Pluto, and the Museum of Northern Arizona is among the state's best. Flagstaff is also near Native American ruins like Wupatki and Walnut Canyon National Monuments.

Scenic AZ 89A winds through mountainous oak forests from Flagstaff to Sedona, passing Slide Rock State Park and the colorful cliffs of Oak Creek Canyon. The second most popular international destination in Arizona after the Grand Canyon, Sedona is a New Age outpost replete with expensive art galleries and energy vortexes among the red rock formations.

During the hot summer months, the beaches around Lake Powell near Page are almost as jammed as Sedona in the fall. It's all about water play in Page, though the John Wesley Powell Museum and the Carl Hayden Visitor Center at Glen Canyon Dam are educational.

THE ALBERS HOUSE, *Flagstaff*

OVERALL ★★★★ | QUALITY ★★★★½ | VALUE ★★★★★ | PRICE RANGE $125

Bermed on three sides for quiet, the private suite behind the Albers House was formerly a two-car garage and coal chute for the original owners of the Flagstaff Steam Laundry. Fresh flowers are an indoor staple. Outside cosmos grow abundantly in summer, and tall sunflowers attract birds. The patio offers views of the San Francisco peaks, though the small pond fed by a Saint Francis statuary fountain is devoid of water lilies thanks to raccoons. In winter, the patio can be decorated with luminaries. Interior orange poured-concrete floor tiles provide winter warmth, as they are underlain by hot water tubing. Honeymooners like the total privacy, and families can add a bed.

SETTING & FACILITIES
Location Historic downtown district **Near** Grand Canyon, archaeological sites, Indian reservations, museums, galleries **Building** 1932 Santa Fe Revival **Grounds** Garden w/ hammock, greenhouse, fountain **Public Space** Patio **Food & Drink** Full breakfast in DR or on patio; afternoon snack; chocolates & fresh fruit 24 hours; dinners by special arrangement **Recreation** Biking, horse riding, fishing, winter sports **Amenities & Services** Weddings, birthday parties, reservations

ACCOMMODATIONS
Units 1 suite w/ private garden entry **All** Robes, hair dryers, phone, clock, iron & ironing board, fan, remote control stereo, bath amenities **Some** Rollaway bed (on request) **Bed & Bath** Queen; private bath w/ tub **Favorites** Suite has private entrance from garden, bricked alley parking spot, dining nook, separate bedroom w/ garden window behind antique Shaker bed w/ snowflake quilt **Comfort & Decor** Mission-style carved Spanish oak, Art Deco light fixtures, pewter candlestick lamp and framed mirrors, brown wicker chairs, French provincial dining set, American classic rocker, British armoire, fresh flowers, Louis XIV phone stand, Hoosier cabinet, bath with marble and claw-foot tub.

RATES, RESERVATIONS, & RESTRICTIONS
Deposit Credit card holds (7-day cancellation for refund minus $10) **Discounts** Cash payment, extended stays **Credit Cards** AE, MC, V **Check-In/Out** 3–6 p.m./11 a.m. **Smoking** Outside only **Pets** No (kennel referral; owners have cat) **Kids** Yes **No-Nos** N/A **Minimum Stay** 2 nights Sept. & Oct. weekends, holidays **Open** All year **Host** Mary Rabe, 705 N. San Francisco St., Flagstaff 86001 **Phone** (928) 779-0869 or toll-free (800) 285-7664 **Fax** (928) 779-9747 **E-mail** albershous@aol.com **Web** N/A

ASPEN INN BED & BREAKFAST, Flagstaff

OVERALL ★★★★ | QUALITY ★★★★ | VALUE ★★★★★ | PRICE RANGE $79–$99

Originally built by a local judge in what is still a quiet, residential, downtown neighborhood, in 1997 the Aspen Inn was turned into a bed-and-breakfast by its hosts, whose command of Spanish, German, and Italian makes them popular with Europeans. The white-walled living room has burgundy wood trim, fluted glass lights, floral touches, very light Southwestern accents, and a peace symbol by the fireplace. The formal dining room serves up quiches and crêpes on blue and white china from northern Spain. The rooms have either queen sofa futons or an alcove with extra bed.

SETTING & FACILITIES
Location 3 blocks from downtown **Near** Grand Canyon, archaeological sites, museums **Building** 1912 bungalow w/ Craftsman influences, burgundy wood trim **Grounds** Double residential lot w/ redwood deck behind high fence **Public Space** LR, DR **Food & Drink** Full breakfast in DR; fridge stocked w/ snacks, beverages **Recreation** Biking, horse riding, fishing, winter sports **Amenities & Services** Receptions, parties, multiple languages spoken, fax, computer

ACCOMMODATIONS
Units 3 **All** Robes, cable TV, phone (data port), hair dryer, smoke detectors, forced air radiators **Some** Gas stove (1), washer & dryer (1), futon (2) **Bed & Bath** Queen beds, 1 twin; all private baths, tub (1) **Favorites** Wilson room is blue & white w/ private back entrance, lace curtains, floral futon, gas stove, washer & dryer; peach-colored Peach Room has antique brass, century-old East Lake furnishings, candle lights, makeup mirror, dresser, overstuffed chairs, futon sofa; dark green Wyatt's Room has deep brown wood, contemporary sleigh bed, hallway bath w/ tub, alcove w/ twin bed popular w/ families **Comfort & Decor** Varied, includes textured white walls, wood trim, hardwood floors, rugs, antiques or contemporary furnishings, local art, upholstered chairs, armoire, pedestal sink.

RATES, RESERVATIONS, & RESTRICTIONS
Deposit 25% (no refund unless room re-rented) **Discounts** Whole house rental **Credit Cards** AE, MC, V, D, **Check-In/Out** 4–6 p.m./11 a.m. **Smoking** Back deck only **Pets** No **Kids** Yes **No-Nos** N/A **Minimum Stay** None **Open** All year **Hosts** Joe & Raquel Sanchez, 218 N. Elden, Flagstaff 86001 **Phone** (928) 773-0295 or toll-free (888) 999-4110 **Fax** (928) 226-7312 **E-mail** info@flagstaffbedbreakfast.com **Web** www.flagstaffbedbreakfast.com

BIRCH TREE INN BED & BREAKFAST, Flagstaff

OVERALL ★★★½ | QUALITY ★★★★ | VALUE ★★★★ | PRICE RANGE $69–$109

Across the street from Thorpe Park and city tennis courts in a neighborhood with aspen lined streets near Lowell Observatory, Birch Tree Inn is one of the region's oldest continuously operating bed-and-breakfasts, dating to 1989.

The rooms, including the yellow-and-blue tulip-themed Pella Room, which shares a bathroom with the navy blue–and-white Wicker Room, have a simple country feel complementing the rural feel of the neighborhood. The blue-and-white game room has horseshoes, a rifle, a washboard, and a cowboy hat on the wall behind the pool table and piano. Old Coke bottles and china service come together in the dining room.

SETTING & FACILITIES

Location 0.5 mi. from historic downtown, corner of N. Thorpe & Birch **Near** Grand Canyon, archaeological sites, Indian reservations, museums, galleries, parks **Building** 1917 2-story Craftsman bungalow w/ wrap-around porch **Grounds** 0.67 acres w/ aspen, elm, & birch trees; rocks, gazebo w/ hot tub **Public Space** LR w/ fireplace, game room, DR, front porch, deck **Food & Drink** Full breakfast in DR; early a.m. beverages in hallway outside rooms; afternoon refreshments; special dietary needs require advance notice **Recreation** Biking, horse riding, fishing, winter sports, tennis **Amenities & Services** Hot tub, TV, pool table, piano, fax, computer

ACCOMMODATIONS

Units 5 upstairs rooms **All** Robes, double-pane windows, AC **Some** Rocking chairs **Bed & Bath** King (1), queen (3), queen & twin (1); 3 private baths, 1 shared, tub (1) **Favorites** Southwest has lodgepole pine king bed, kachina dolls, dream catcher, sand paintings, muted sandstone, pastel colors, shower/tub; Carol's room has Shaker pine furniture, hunter green & beige colors **Comfort & Decor** Comfortable country feel with varied themes, quilts, hardwood floors, wallpaper, some wood paneling, antique armoires, or dressers.

RATES, RESERVATIONS, & RESTRICTIONS

Deposit Credit card holds (72-hour cancellation for refund minus $25 fee) **Discounts** None **Credit Cards** AE, MC, V, D **Check-In/Out** 4–6 p.m./11 a.m. **Smoking** No **Pets** No **Kids** Yes (over age 12) **No-Nos** N/A **Minimum Stay** None **Open** All year **Hosts** Sandy & Ed Znetko, Rodger & Donna Pettinger, 824 W. Birch Ave., Flagstaff 86001 **Phone** (928) 774-1042 or toll-free (888) 774-1042 **Fax** : (928) 774-8462 **E-mail** info@ birchtreeinn.com **Web** www.birchtreeinn.com

FALL INN TO NATURE, Flagstaff

OVERALL ★★★★ | QUALITY ★★★★ | VALUE ★★★★ | PRICE RANGE $69–$95

After a short drive along a dirt subdivision road lined with pine trees and white-fenced ranch houses, a chirping bird doorbell greets visitors to Fall Inn to Nature. The entryway features the hostess's antique cup and saucer and pillbox collections, as well as completed jigsaw puzzles of eagles, the Grand Canyon, Zion, and Sedona. The dining room has cuckoo clocks, a floral crochet and a gift corner selling small crafts, jams, and barbecue sauce. The host runs a tour company, and guests get discounts when combining personalized minivan tours with bed-and-breakfast stays. Only two rooms are rented at a time.

SETTING & FACILITIES
Location 6.5 mi. north of downtown on AZ 89 **Near** Grand Canyon, archaeological sites, museums **Building** 1996 ranch house w/ cedar exterior, white plaster interior **Grounds** 2.5 acres w/ trees, scrub **Public Space** LR, DR, patio **Food & Drink** Cont'l breakfast in DR or patio; cider & cookie (stays over 2 nights) **Recreation** Biking, horse riding, fishing, winter sports **Amenities & Services** Hot tub, TV, newspapers, minivan tours, food storage fridge

ACCOMMODATIONS
Units 3 **All** Robes, TV/VCR, phone, coffeemaker, ceiling fan, clock radio, first-aid kit **Some** Desk (1) **Bed & Bath** King/twins (1), queen (2); 1 private bath w/ tub, 1 shared **Favorites** Butterfly Room has queen bed, roll-away (on request), butterfly stenciling, mountain views, private bath w/ tub; kids like blue & pink floral rabbit room, which has king/twin beds, desk, rabbit dolls, china, porcelain & stencils, shared bath w/ double vanities **Comfort & Decor** Butterfly, bird, and rabbit themes, some timber furnishings, shared bath with block-glass window.

RATES, RESERVATIONS, & RESTRICTIONS
Deposit Credit card holds (7-day cancellation policy) **Discounts** Tour packages, multiple rooms, Jan.–April (1/2 price night on 3 night stay) **Credit Cards** AE, MC, V **Check-In/Out** 4–6 p.m./11 a.m. **Smoking** Outside **Pets** No (cats, dogs, farm animals on premises) **Kids** Age 6 and older **No-Nos** N/A **Minimum Stay** None **Open** 10 months (closed 2 months in winter; dates vary) **Hosts** Annette & Ron Fallaha, 8080 N. Colt Dr., Flagstaff 86004 **Phone** (928) 714-0237 or toll-free (888) 920-0237 **Fax** (928) 714-0237 **E-mail** fallinn@infomagic.com **Web** www.bbonline.com/az/fallinn

THE INN AT 410, Flagstaff

OVERALL ★★★½ | QUALITY ★★★★½ | VALUE ★★★ | PRICE RANGE $135–$190

As overpriced as it gets in this railroad town punctuated by rumbling freight trains, especially considering the property's paucity of amenities, the Inn at 410 is living off its past laurels under professional management that efficiently processes guest credit cards. In the name of relaxation there are no phones or TVs, and only the highest-priced Jacuzzi rooms have robes. Though a bit of a thoroughfare, the living room offers a fireplace and sitting spaces. If more than just a nice room matters, take scenic AZ 89A south to Sedona, where at these prices bed-and-breakfasts provide spectacular red rock views without train noise and compete with each other to offer service and amenities.

SETTING & FACILITIES
Location Downtown residential neighborhood, 4 blocks from Route 66 **Near** Grand Canyon, archaeological sites, museums **Building** 1907 gray 2-story Craftsman w/ white wood trim, shingle roof, stone foundation **Grounds** Stone front gates, patio, gazebo, flower garden w/ boulders **Public Space** LR, DR, porch **Food & Drink** Full breakfast in

DR; afternoon snacks **Recreation** Biking, horse riding, fishing, winter sports **Amenities & Services** N/A

ACCOMMODATIONS

Units 9, 6 upstairs **All** Coffeemaker, fridge, AC, ceiling fan, clock radio, hair dryer **Some** Robes (3), gas fireplace (8), handicap access (1) **Bed & Bath** King (1), queen (8); all private baths, tub (6), whirlpool tub (3) **Favorites** Southwest is dominated by bath w/ jetted tub & kiva-style gas fireplace surrounded by stainless steel w/ stylized petroglyphs, timber furnishings, O'Keeffe and Grand Canyon pictures, pottery **Comfort & Decor** Very varied, tastefully furnished; carpeted rooms may have wood trim, wallpaper, brick, sitting area with love seat or sofa.

RATES, RESERVATIONS, & RESTRICTIONS

Deposit 1 night or 50% for longer stays (7-day cancellation; 14 days w/ multiple rooms) **Discounts** None **Credit Cards** MC, V **Check-In/Out** 4–6 p.m./11 a.m. **Smoking** No **Pets** No **Kids** Yes (if well behaved; in Dakota and Suite Nature rooms) **No-Nos** N/A **Minimum Stay** 2 nights weekends April 1–Oct. 31; 3 nights some holidays **Open** All year **Hosts** Howard & Sally Krueger, 410 N. Leroux St., Flagstaff 86001 **Phone** (928) 774-2008 or toll-free (800) 774-2008 **Fax** (928) 774-6354 **E-mail** info@inn410.com **Web** www.inn410.com

JEANETTE'S BED & BREAKFAST, Flagstaff

OVERALL ★★★½ | QUALITY ★★★★ | VALUE ★★★★ | PRICE RANGE $115–$145

Geared to couples wanting to time-warp back to Arizona statehood in 1912, Jeanette's has pale 1920s and 1930s colors and artifacts like a walnut chevaroux from spinster aunts and risqué grandmothers. Even the creamy lime kitchen keeps to the theme with a porcelain sink, 1930s stove, 1938 refrigerator, and a maple counter crafted from an early 1900s carpenter's bench. Hallway decor includes a wood and Naugahyde bus seat, mannequins wearing old clothing, 1930s Redwing shoes, RC Cola memorabilia, photos of grandparents, and old typewriters and irons. Modern breakfast delicacies include smoothies and poached pears with tart cherry sauce.

SETTING & FACILITIES

Location 2 mi. east of downtown, below Mt. Elden **Near** Grand Canyon, archaeological sites, museums **Building** 1996 2-story gray & white late Victorian style w/ wide curved porch **Grounds** Pines, native plants, green school field in back **Public Space** LR, DR, hallways **Food & Drink** Full breakfast in DR; lemonade, cookies; fridge w/ beverages, snacks **Recreation** Biking, horse riding, fishing, winter sports **Amenities & Services** Fresh flowers, culinary weekend, 1960s New Year's Eve

ACCOMMODATIONS

Units 4, 3 upstairs **All** Hair dryer, iron & ironing board, homemade lye soap, bubble bath, large bath amenity basket **Some** Fireplace (1), porch (3) **Bed & Bath** King (1), queen (2), 2 doubles (1); all private baths, claw-foot tub (3), tub (1) **Favorites** Icie Vean's Room has sharecropper grandmother's metal beds, eye doctor's chair, dental cabinet, orange & black bath w/ tub & separate shower, shared porch; Grandma Amelia's Room has sitting area w/ fainting couch, fireplace, rug over hardwood floor, celluloid vanity set, leather bench, white wicker, porch **Comfort & Decor** Varies with room theme (female relatives), includes 1900–30 furnishings and antiques, modern paintings for sale.

RATES, RESERVATIONS, & RESTRICTIONS
Deposit 1 night (7-day cancellation policy) **Discounts** AAA **Credit Cards** MC, V, D **Check-In/Out** 4–6 p.m./11 a.m. **Smoking** No **Pets** No **Kids** No (age 16 or older allowed on occasion) **No-Nos** N/A **Minimum Stay** 2 nights May 1–Oct. 31, holidays **Open** All year **Hosts** Jeanette & Ray West, 3380 E. Lockett Rd., Flagstaff 86004 **Phone** (928) 527-1912 or toll-free (800) 752-1912 **Fax** N/A **E-mail** romance@jeanettesbb.com **Web** www.jeanettesbb.com

LAKE MARY BED & BREAKFAST, Flagstaff

OVERALL ★★★★ | QUALITY ★★★★ | VALUE ★★★★ | PRICE RANGE $80–$110

A quiet country property far from the trains on the road leading to Mormon Lake and Happy Jack, Lake Mary is a long, narrow ranch house with two living rooms separated by a kitchen. One guest room, Teddy Wicker, is upstairs directly above a comfortably furnished living room within earshot of the TV. The other living room on the side of the house with the two downstairs guest rooms has a magenta and gold cut velvet sofa, a fireplace, and stained glass. The Valentine Room has an angel theme, glass box doll display, old nightgowns, and a lace and Valentine wall collage.

SETTING & FACILITIES
Location 2.5 mi. south of downtown Flagstaff **Near** Sedona, lakes, Grand Canyon, archaeological sites, museums **Building** 75-ft.-long early 1930s ranch house w/ 1980s additions, enclosed wrap-around porch **Grounds** 1 acre w/ pine trees **Public Space** 2 LRs, DR, porch **Food & Drink** Full breakfast in DR; afternoon refreshments **Recreation** Biking, horse riding, fishing, winter sports **Amenities & Services** Data port, fax, TV

ACCOMMODATIONS
Units 3 **All** Robes, ceiling fan, hair dryer, clock radio, coffeemaker **Some** TV/VCR (1) **Bed & Bath** King (1), queen (2); all private baths w/ tub **Favorites** Teddy Wicker above LR, popular w/ families, has black wrought-iron king bed, nook w/ daybed, angled ceilings, skylights, wicker furnishings, TV, teddy bears, old school lunchboxes; Victorian has wood paneling, beige floral wallpaper, vanity bench for luggage, shuttered closets, bath w/ skylight & lace shower curtains **Comfort & Decor** Varied rooms include Victorian and Valentine themes, some wood paneling, wallpaper, skylights, lace, vanity bench, shuttered closets, dresser with mirror, collages, old nightgowns, dolls.

RATES, RESERVATIONS, & RESTRICTIONS
Deposit 1 night (3-day cancellation for refund minus $15) **Discounts** Weekdays **Credit Cards** MC, V **Check-In/Out** 4 p.m./11 a.m. **Smoking** Outside porch **Pets** No **Kids** Age 6 and older **No-Nos** N/A **Minimum Stay** None **Open** All year **Hosts** Frank & Christine

McCollum, 574 Lake Mary Rd., Flagstaff 86001 **Phone** (928) 779-7054 or toll-free (888) 241-9550 **Fax** (928) 779-7054 **E-mail** N/A **Web** www.lakemarybb-flagstaff.com

THE SLED DOG INN, *Flagstaff*

OVERALL ★★★½ | QUALITY ★★★★ | VALUE ★★★★ | PRICE RANGE $110–$185

On the grounds of an old dairy farm bordering Coconino National Forest, the Sled Dog uses old dairy barn wood for armoires and has old railroad trestles posts. Sled dog lessons are offered at a site seven miles northwest of Flagstaff. The attractive sunken living room has a stone fireplace, timber furnishings, deep green fabrics, ceiling fans, and double doors opening onto a pine needle–covered deck. The upstairs meeting room opens onto a hallway overlooking the lounge, and snowshoes and old ski poles are nearby. The owners live next door, and a manager cooks and runs the operation.

SETTING & FACILITIES
Location From Flagstaff go 6 mi. south on US 17 to Exit 333 (Mountainaire Rd.) **Near** Grand Canyon, Sedona, archaeological sites, museums, lakes **Building** 1997 2-story North Woods–style brown building w/ green roof **Grounds** 4 acres of meadow bordered by pine forest **Public Space** LR, DR, meeting room, deck **Food & Drink** Full breakfast in DR; coffee/tea available all day; group lunches, dinners **Recreation** Mountain biking, horse riding, fishing, hunting, para-gliding, winter sports **Amenities & Services** Sled dog lessons (winter), hot tub, sauna, rock-climbing wall, mountain bikes, groups (24 maximum)

ACCOMMODATIONS
Units 10, including 2 2-room suites **All** Phone jacks, heaters **Some** Ceiling fan (5), AC (5), handicap-accessible (1) **Bed & Bath** King (2) converting to twins, queen (5), queen & double (2), 2 doubles (1); all private baths with tub **Favorites** Northern Lights suite, a family favorite, has queen & 2 double beds, sled dog paraphernalia, lanterns, metal animal lamp bases **Comfort & Decor** Simple clean country feel, with white walls, wood trim, carpeting, rustic log and timber furnishings, armoires, animal themes, down comforters, screened windows, mostly small baths.

RATES, RESERVATIONS, & RESTRICTIONS
Deposit Full amount (15-day cancellation policy) **Discounts** Corp. groups, singles, weekdays **Credit Cards** AE, MC, V, D **Check-In/Out** After 4 p.m./11 a.m. (no late arrival restrictions) **Smoking** No **Pets** Yes (not allowed in public areas; must be attended & in portable kennel) **Kids** Yes **No-Nos** N/A **Minimum Stay** 2 nights on weekends **Open** All year **Hosts** Wendy White & Jaime Ballesteros, 10155 Mountainaire Rd., Flagstaff 86001 **Phone** (928) 525-6212 or toll-free (800) 754-0664 **Fax** (928) 525-1855 **E-mail** info@sleddoginn.com **Web** www.sleddoginn.com

CANYON COLORS BED & BREAKFAST, Page

OVERALL ★★★ | QUALITY ★★★★ | VALUE ★★★★★ | PRICE RANGE $50–$90

A rambling suburban ranch-style house whose living room walls are lined with oil and watercolor nature paintings—including the hostess's moody full moon canyon country night scene and stormy seashore—Canyon Colors seems almost like a small art museum, though it calls itself a Christian bed-and-breakfast. In actual practice this translates into genuine friendliness, a desire to be helpful, a Bible in every room, and a PG-rated family-oriented video library rather than active proselytizing, although they are more than happy to "talk Jesus." Families wanting to combine a wholesome home-style stay with Lake Powell fun will be happy here.

SETTING & FACILITIES

Location 6 mi. from lake; from Lake Powell Blvd., turn at South Navajo Dr. (corner w/ school) & go 0.7 mi. to 225 **Near** Lake Powell, Glen Canyon Dam, Antelope Canyon, Lee's Ferry, Marble Canyon, Paria Wilderness **Building** 1980 wood & plaster suburban ranch house **Grounds** 0.3 acre w/ cement backyard patio, trees, shrubs, jimson weed (Datura), & small above-ground pool **Public Space** LR, DR, back yard patio **Food & Drink** Full breakfast in DR or back yard patio; complimentary chips, salsa, iced tea for warm-weather arrivals, hot beverage & cookies for winter arrivals; gas grill for patio cooking; special dietary needs met **Recreation** Boating, golf **Amenities & Services** PG-rated video library, coolers & beach towels, laundry

ACCOMMODATIONS

Units 3 **All** Cable TV/VCR, fridge, Bible **Some** Fireplace (2) **Bed & Bath** Queens (3) plus additional futon queens (2); all private baths, Jacuzzi tub (1) **Favorites** Sunflower Room has yellow sunflower theme, Jacuzzi tub, wood-burning fireplace, queen, queen futon, & daybed **Comfort & Decor** Functional rooms with plenty of bed space for families; oil and watercolor canyon and nature scenes.

RATES, RESERVATIONS, & RESTRICTIONS

Deposit Credit card; cancellations 7 days prior to check-in date avoid charges **Discounts** None **Credit Cards** AE, MC, V, D, DC **Check-In/Out** Flexible **Smoking** Patio area only **Pets** No (owners have dog & cat w/ public space access) **Kids** Yes **No-Nos** N/A **Minimum Stay** None **Open** All year **Hosts** Rich & Bev Jones, P.O. Box 3657, Page 86040 **Phone** (520) 645-5979 or toll-free (800) 536-2530 **Fax** N/A **E-mail** canyoncolors@canyon-country.com **Web** canyon-country.com/colors.htm

ADOBE HACIENDA, Sedona

OVERALL ★★★ | QUALITY ★★★★ | VALUE ★★★★ | PRICE RANGE $159–$209

Overlooking a golf course several miles from the uptown Sedona action, Adobe Hacienda has a tan living room with a tile floor, ceiling fan, timber furniture, and a back door opening onto a relaxing patio with a fountain and Mexican firepot that transitions from flagstone to grass. Only the handicap-accessible Anasazi Room at the front of the property does not open onto the back patio. Most of the wall art by local artists is for sale, as are the Pendelton blankets on the beds. The owner's quarters, a two-room suite sleeping four, is being converted into a fifth guest room.

SETTING & FACILITIES

Location Village of Oak Creek **Near** Galleries, shops, state parks, national forest **Building** Modern ranch-style house **Grounds** 1 acre w/ pine trees in front, narrow flagstone strip w/ fountain looking across golf course in back **Public Space** LR, DR, patio **Food & Drink** Full breakfast in DR; drinks in fridge **Recreation** Golf, horse riding, biking, jeep touring **Amenities & Services** Patio receptions (40), wedding coordination

ACCOMMODATIONS

Units 4 **All** TV/VCR, gas fireplace, phone, CD/clock, ceiling fan, fridge, hair dryer, Pendelton blankets **Some** Double French doors opening to patio (3), handicap-accessible (1) **Bed & Bath** King (3), queen (1); all private baths, whirlpool tub (3) **Favorites** Vaquero Room has cowboy theme, metal four-poster bed, washboard above tub; Sedona Room is largest, has rustic Mexican wood furnishings, armoire, double wood doors leading to bath, saltillo tile floor, tiles around fireplace, Southwestern rugs, carved wood king bed, sleeper sofa **Comfort & Decor** Varied room themes include Old West, Mexican, Native American pueblo style, some with old barn wood, timber furnishings, brightly colored fabrics, stenciling, tiled bath, painted Mexican sink, separate glass shower.

RATES, RESERVATIONS, & RESTRICTIONS

Deposit 1 night or 50% on longer stays (balance due 10 days prior to arrival; 10-day cancellation for refund minus $25) **Discounts** Seasonal specials, singles **Credit Cards** AE, MC, V, D **Check-In/Out** 4–6 p.m./11 a.m. **Smoking** No **Pets** No **Kids** Yes **No-Nos** N/A **Minimum Stay** Holidays (e.g., 3 days Thanksgiving) **Open** All year **Hosts** Tatia & Jim Rauch, 10 Rojo Dr., Sedona 86351 **Phone** (928) 284-2020 or toll-free (800) 454-7191 **Fax** (928) 284-2047 **E-mail** info@adobe-hacienda.com **Web** www.adobe-hacienda.com

ADOBE VILLAGE GRAHAM INN, Sedona

OVERALL ★★★★★ | QUALITY ★★★★★ | VALUE ★★★★ | PRICE RANGE $169–$599

Apples, pears, and plums growing here are cooked into syrups and jams; bats swoop by at dusk; and an Our Lady of Forgiveness sculpted out of recycled 1950s automobiles graces the Purple Lizard casita. But Adobe Village Graham Inn stakes its reputation on providing luxury and being attentive to guest needs. Rooms in the main building hold their own, but the clay-walled casita compound with its own mesquite courtyard and pond are the top prize. Casita bread makers are timed to complete their loaves and drive guests wild with aromas on arrival, and the bathrooms are larger than most hotel rooms.

SETTING & FACILITIES
Location Village of Oak Creek **Near** Galleries, shops, state parks, national forest **Building** Contemporary Southwestern style, adjacent casita "village" added in 1998 **Grounds** Flagstone walkways, fruit trees, fountains w/ waterfalls **Public Space** LR, DR **Food & Drink** Full breakfast in DR or casita; afternoon appetizers; stocked fridges **Recreation** Golf, tennis, horse riding, biking, jeep touring **Amenities & Services** Pool, Jacuzzi, concierge service, turn-down service, laundry machines, mountain bikes

ACCOMMODATIONS
Units 7 rooms & 4 adobe casitas **All** Robes, fireplace, cable TV, AC, clock radio, CD player, phone (modem), hair dryer, iron & ironing board **Some** Balcony/patio (10), kitchenettes (casitas) **Bed & Bath** King, queen, twins; all private baths, whirlpool tub (10), steam shower (1) **Favorites** Sunset casita has Don Quixote sculpture on Amish sugar bin, twig chairs, tree-shaped wrought-iron bed, pyramidal bath fireplace fronting tiled tub & large picture window **Comfort & Decor** Varies widely, ranging from green carpets, yellow florals, and

white wicker in Garden Room to purple wallpaper and Southwestern style; 850-square-foot casitas have variegated tile or wood floors with throw rugs, tinted walls, some rocks, rattan, barn wood, stained glass, leather, waterfall shower.

RATES, RESERVATIONS, & RESTRICTIONS

Deposit 50% (balance due 15 days before arrival; 15-day cancellation notice for refund minus $25) **Discounts** Singles **Credit Cards** AE, MC, V, D **Check-In/Out** 3–6 p.m./11 a.m. **Smoking** Outside **Pets** No **Kids** Yes **No-Nos** N/A **Minimum Stay** None **Open** All year **Hosts** Stuart & Ilene Berman, 150 Canyon Circle Dr., Sedona 86351 **Phone** (928) 284-1425 **Fax** (928) 284-0767 **E-mail** adobe@sedonasfinest.com **Web** www. sedonasfinest.com

ALMA DE SEDONA INN, Sedona

OVERALL ★★★★½ | QUALITY ★★★★½ | VALUE ★★★★ | PRICE RANGE $99–$265

Across the street from Casa Sedona and around the corner from Boots & Saddles, Alma de Sedona Inn offers ample luxuries in a clean, understated manner. All the guest rooms have private entrances and private patios situated so that the views do not include other patios. Second-floor rooms, especially the Far Pavilions, which has a plush green upholstered headboard and footboard at the base of the bed, are most sought after for their views of the surrounding mountains. The handicap-accessible room has a double shower; the rest have jetted tubs and king beds.

SETTING & FACILITIES

Location West Sedona **Near** Galleries, shops, state parks, national forest **Building** 4 Southwestern-style sandstone-colored buildings built in late 1990s surround central courtyard **Grounds** 2 acres w/ junipers, red rock retaining walls, & native plantscaping

Public Space LR w/ fireplace, parlor w/ game table, DR **Food & Drink** Full breakfast in DR, poolside, or in room; afternoon appetizers; drinks, cookies all day **Recreation** Golf, horse riding, biking, jeep touring **Amenities & Services** Cooking classes, heated pool w/ twinkling lights (10-month season), fax

ACCOMMODATIONS

Units 12 **All** Fireplace, ceiling fan, cable TV, CD player, clock radio, robes, hair dryer, candles, wineglasses, coffeemaker, data port, private balcony/patio & entrance **Some** Handicap-accessible (1) **Bed & Bath** King beds; all private baths, jetted tub (11), double shower (1) **Favorites** World Traveler has 2d-floor sunset views, four-poster carved pine bed, armoire w/ TV, wicker furnishings, old tiger map & luggage; Zora's Legacy has dark cherry furnishings, desk, burgundy floral duvet, sleeper sofa, desk, header beams **Comfort & Decor** Each room is different, some with cherry wood furniture or Western motif; all are comfortably furnished with carpeting, valences, upholstered chairs, solid color walls, tile and wood baths, no clutter or frills.

RATES, RESERVATIONS, & RESTRICTIONS

Deposit 1 night or 50% of longer stays (15-day cancellation policy for full refund minus $20 handling fee) **Discounts** Low season **Credit Cards** AE, MC, V **Check-In/Out** 3–6 p.m./11 a.m. **Smoking** No **Pets** No **Kids** Over age 10 ($25/night fee) **No-Nos** N/A **Minimum Stay** 2 nights on weekends **Open** All year **Host** Lynn McCarroll, 50 Hozoni Dr., Sedona 86336 **Phone** (928) 282-2737 or toll-free (800) 923-2282 **Fax** N/A **E-mail** innkeeper@almadesedona.com **Web** www.almadesedona.com

APPLE ORCHARD INN BED & BREAKFAST, Sedona

OVERALL ★★★★½ | QUALITY ★★★★½ | VALUE ★★★★ | PRICE RANGE $135–$230

A former home of the Jordan family, who farmed apples here before selling off the land for development of the modern tourist town of Sedona, Apple Orchard Inn is the best uptown Sedona offering. Though only a six-block walk from the center of tourist activities, the inn feels secluded. Stone steps in the back yard lead down to a red rock waterfall flowing into a cooling pool next to the hot tub. Local art decorates the walls. An archaeologist, Steven Benedict, gives breakfast talks and offers guests customized tours to sites not on the jeep tour circuit.

SETTING & FACILITIES

Location Residential neighborhood 6 blocks north of uptown Sedona **Near** Galleries, shops, state parks, national forest **Building** 1950s 3-level ranch-style house remodeled into B&B in 1998 **Grounds** 2 wooded & landscaped acres w/ copper fountain & red rock waterfall **Public Space** LR, DR, patio **Food & Drink** Full breakfast in DR or patio; afternoon appetizers; stocked fridge in room **Recreation** Golf, tennis, horse riding, jeep tours, bird-watching **Amenities & Services** Hot tub, cooling pool, dinner & tour reservations, morning archaeological talks

ACCOMMODATIONS

Units 6 **All** Robes, fridge, TV/VCR, phone, hair dryer, clock radio **Some** Handicap-accessible (1), fireplace (2), patio (5) **Bed & Bath** King (6); all private baths with whirlpool tub **Favorites** Hideaway, honeymooner favorite, has rock art theme, fireplace, patio, 2-person whirlpool tub, and fridge; Steamboat Rock has red rock wall, floral motifs, large wood-framed mirror, glass-topped table w/ lace, stained-glass lamps **Comfort & Decor** Themes vary from rock art and Victorian to Old West, with some faux-textured walls, art by local artists, stained-glass lamps, headboards, armoires.

RATES, RESERVATIONS, & RESTRICTIONS

Deposit 1 night or 50% of longer stays (14-day cancellation for refund minus $25) **Discounts** Weekdays during low season (July, Aug., Nov.–Jan.) **Credit Cards** AE, MC, V **Check-In/Out** 3–6 p.m./11 a.m. **Smoking** No **Pets** No (owner has shitzu dog) **Kids** Over age 12 **No-Nos** N/A **Minimum Stay** 2 nights for Sat. stays **Open** All year **Hosts** Stephanie & Philip Sherwin, 656 Jordan Rd., Sedona 86336 **Phone** (928) 282-5328 or toll-free (800) 663-6968 **Fax** (928) 204-0044 **E-mail** appleorc@sedona.net **Web** www.appleorchardbb.com

BOOTS & SADDLES, Sedona

OVERALL ★★★½ | QUALITY ★★★★ | VALUE ★★★★ | PRICE RANGE $95–$245

Around the corner from Casa Sedona and Alma de Sedona, but much smaller than either, Boots & Saddles is run by the original proprietors of Territorial House, which was sold in late 2001. The total focus is now on the Boots & Saddles guests, who are given pampering options like dinner, in-room massage, and special romantic packages. Some patios look out on the backside of Alma Sedona and West Sedona's red rock formations. The idea here is to provide a relaxing retreat in close proximity to the outdoor and indoor attractions of Sedona.

SETTING & FACILITIES

Location West Sedona, 3 mi. from uptown **Near** : Galleries, shops, state parks, national forest **Building** A-frame cedar home remodeled in 1998 **Grounds** Small yard w/ wood swing, barbecue **Public Space** LR, DR **Food & Drink** Full breakfast in DR; afternoon snacks; optional dinners **Recreation** Golf, horse riding, biking, jeep touring **Amenities & Services** Hot tub, lodgepole pine swing

ACCOMMODATIONS

Units 4 **All** Robes, gas fireplace, CD/clock, hair dryer, iron & ironing board, fridge, phone, cable TV, ceiling fan, patio/balcony **Some** Individual AC/heat, central AC/heat, telescope (1) **Bed & Bath** Queen beds; all private baths, jetted tub (3) **Favorites** Gentleman Cowboy occupies whole upper floor, has barn wood wall accents, stone fireplace, ironwood headboard, love seat, table, 2 chairs, telescope, private balcony; Wrangler, smallest room, has private staircase from LR, sloping ceiling, pine wood, pedestal sink, timber bed, Western prints, blues & reds **Comfort & Decor** Country and Southwestern themes with carpeting, tiled floors, headboards, some sinks and tubs in main rooms, ample bath amenity baskets.

RATES, RESERVATIONS, & RESTRICTIONS

Deposit 50% to confirm and balance 30 days prior to arrival (8-day cancellation policy; 15 days for 2 rooms or 4 nights or more; refund minus $25 fee) **Discounts** Low season, multiple nights **Credit Cards** AE, MC, V, D **Check-In/Out** 4–6 p.m./11 a.m. **Smoking** Decks & garden only **Pets** No **Kids** Yes **No-Nos** N/A **Minimum Stay** 2 nights on weekends, 3 nights on holidays **Open** All year **Hosts** John & Linda Steele, 2900 Hopi Dr., Sedona 86336 **Phone** (928) 282-1944 or toll-free (800) 201-1944 **Fax** (928) 282-7977 **E-mail** info@oldwestbb.com **Web** bootsandsaddlesbb.com

BRIAR PATCH INN, Sedona

OVERALL ★★★★ | QUALITY ★★★★ | VALUE ★★★★ | PRICE RANGE $159–$295

Briar Patch, a popular group and family retreat operated by the same family for two decades, is also a nature escape for individuals. The creek is stocked with trout, swimming holes are nearby, and there are forested sitting areas and a massage gazebo alongside the creek. The main building has flagstone floors, Mexican carved wood and leather, kachinas, Native American artifacts, and a dark, woodsy feel. The cabins all stand alone, the best boasting creek views. Although a nature getaway, the *Wall Street Journal, New York Times,* and local newspapers are set out in the lounge.

SETTING & FACILITIES

Location Lower Oak Creek Canyon, 3.5 mi. north of uptown Sedona **Near** Flagstaff, galleries, shops, state parks, national forest **Building** Cabins clustered around main building **Grounds** 9 acres w/ trees, shrubs, sheep pasture bordering Oak Creek **Public Space** Lobby & lounge spaces w/ 2 fireplaces **Food & Drink** Full breakfast buffet (no meat) in living room, along creek, or picnic basket in room; snacks; afternoon soup (w/ meat, Tues.–Sun.; extra cost); outdoor gas grills **Recreation** Fishing, swimming **Amenities & Services** Phone, groups, summer classical violin & guitar (breakfast), newspapers, massage therapist

ACCOMMODATIONS

Units 18 stand-alone cabins, 3 w/ 2 BRs **All** AC, heating, fan, CD player, coffemaker, patio/deck **Some** Kitchen (14), wood-burning fireplace (16), rocking chairs **Bed & Bath** King (12), queen (6), twin (6), multiple beds (8); tub (4), jetted tub (1) **Favorites** Bunkhouse has jetted tub, flagstone floor, wood walls & ceiling, sunken sitting area, deck overlooking creek; Case de Piedra is all stone, w/ creek view from king bed **Comfort & Decor** Log cabin style with lodgepole pine furnishings, bright Southwest fabrics, wood or flagstone floors and area rugs, some rock and wood walls, sitting areas.

RATES, RESERVATIONS, & RESTRICTIONS

Deposit 1 night (10-day cancellation for refund minus $25; 30 days some holidays) **Discounts** Group **Credit Cards** AE, MC, V **Check-In/Out** 3–6 p.m./11 a.m. **Smoking** No **Pets** No (2 sheep) **Kids** Yes **No-Nos** N/A **Minimum Stay** 2 nights weekends, 3 nights holidays **Open** All year **Host** Rob Olson, 3190 N. AZ 89A, Sedona 86336 **Phone** (928) 282-2342 or toll-free (888) 809-3030 **Fax** (928) 282-2399 **E-mail** briarpatch@sedona.net **Web** www.briarpatchinn.com

CANYON VILLA INN, Sedona

OVERALL ★★★★★ | QUALITY ★★★★★ | VALUE ★★★★ | PRICE RANGE $189–$279

On the opposite end of the semicircular block housing Adobe Village Graham Inn and the more family-oriented Cozy Cactus, Canyon Villa has firmly established itself as one of Sedona's best, for the service as well as the Bell Rock and Courthouse Butte views. Indeed, the inn design staggers the rooms for best views. Canyon Villa is in the Village of Oak Creek, a separate city without the Sedona room tax, half a dozen miles from the uptown Sedona frenzy. A double-faced marble fireplace separates the high, slanting, beamed-ceiling living and dining rooms, both of which are popular gathering places with ceiling fans, skylights, and tall arched windows framing the red rocks beyond the pool. Trailheads are nearby.

SETTING & FACILITIES
Location Village of Oak Creek, 6 mi. south of uptown Sedona **Near** Galleries, shops, state parks, national forest **Building** 1992 Mediterranean villa style **Grounds** Patio w/ outdoor fireplace & rose garden w/ twig bench border Coconino National Forest **Public Space** LR, DR, library **Food & Drink** Full breakfast in DR; afternoon appetizers; evening deserts **Recreation** Golf, tennis, horse riding, biking, jeep touring **Amenities & Services** Year-round heated pool, turn-down service, chess set, piano, stereo, telescope

ACCOMMODATIONS
Units 11, 5 upstairs **All** Patio/balcony, robes, ceiling fan, CD/clock radio, cable TV **Some** Fireplace (4) **Bed & Bath** King (8), king/twins (2), queen (1), extra pullout beds (4); all private baths, 1 handicap-accessible, whirlpool tub **Favorites** Ocotillo has Southwest decor, fireplace, varied wallpapers, double vanity; Mariposa has fireplace, tub in room, separate shower **Comfort & Decor** Elegant furnishings, bordered ceilings, valences, floral and print comforters, triple sound-proofed walls, carpeting, armoires with TVs, some stained glass, French doors opening onto patios or balconies, ceramic baths, different colored towels in each room.

RATES, RESERVATIONS, & RESTRICTIONS
Deposit 1 night or 50% of longer stays (14-day cancellation for refund minus $25) **Discounts** Travel agents **Credit Cards** AE, MC, V, D **Check-In/Out** 3–6 p.m./11 a.m. **Smoking** No **Pets** No **Kids** Over age 10 **No-Nos** N/A **Minimum Stay** 2 nights weekends, holidays **Open** All year **Hosts** Les & Peg Belch, 125 Canyon Circle Dr., Sedona 86351 **Phone** (928) 284-1226 **Fax** (928) 284-2114 **E-mail** canvilla@sedona.net **Web** www.canyonvilla.com

CASA SEDONA, Sedona

OVERALL ★★★★ | QUALITY ★★★★½ | VALUE ★★★★ | PRICE RANGE $175–$255

Casa Sedona is just north of AZ 89A, across the street from Alma de Sedona and around the corner from Boots & Saddles. The proprietors, a former Dow Chemical company employee and his wife who have run bed-and-breakfasts in North Carolina and St. Augustine, Florida, live on the premises and direct a professional staff. Coyotes howl at night, but the rooms are safely removed pockets of luxury with single or double whirlpool tubs. A separate building has a lounge merging into an upper and lower dining room, and there is plenty of outdoor eating space.

SETTING & FACILITIES

Location West Sedona, 3 mi. from uptown **Near** Galleries, shops, state parks, national forest **Building** 1990s Southwest design by Frank Lloyd Wright protégé Mani Subra **Grounds** 1 acre w/ fountain, rocks, wood swing, roses, 40 flower species, junipers, pines **Public Space** Lounge w/ fireplace, upstairs & downstairs DRs, patio **Food & Drink** Full breakfast in DRs or garden; afternoon appetizers; 24-hour snacks & beverages **Recreation** Golf, horse riding, biking, jeep touring **Amenities & Services** 2 sun decks, hot tub

ACCOMMODATIONS

Units 16 **All** Robes, TV/VCR, fireplace, fridge, individual heat/AC, clock radio, phone, data port, ceiling fan, fireplace, balcony or patio, hair dryer, bath salts, magnifying makeup mirror **Some** Handicap-accessible (1) **Bed & Bath** King (8), queen (8); all private baths, jetted tub (15) **Favorites** Panache has rose carpet, large California wine poster, bath w/ burgundy stripe wallpaper, floral border, glass shower, separate tub **Comfort & Decor** Varied themes include lace, cowboys, Southwestern, and country French, with wood sleigh and metal four-poster beds, TV in armoire, timber or wood furnishings, ceiling borders.

RATES, RESERVATIONS, & RESTRICTIONS

Deposit 1 night or 50% of longer stays when reservation made, balance 14 days prior to arrival (14-day cancellation for refund minus $25) **Discounts** Singles **Credit Cards** AE, MC, V, D **Check-In/Out** 3–6 p.m./11 a.m. **Smoking** No **Pets** No **Kids** Over age 12 **No-Nos** N/A **Minimum Stay** Holidays, special event weekends **Open** All year **Hosts** Bob & Donna Marriott, 55 Hozoni Dr., Sedona 86336 **Phone** (928) 282-2938 or toll-free (800) 525-3756 **Fax** N/A **E-mail** casa@sedona.net **Web** www.casasedona.com

COUNTRY GARDENS BED & BREAKFAST, Sedona

OVERALL ★★★★½ | QUALITY ★★★★ | VALUE ★★★★ | PRICE RANGE $165–$225

Away from the uptown hubbub along a rural country road with horse ranches, Country Gardens is fronted by an old Civil War wagon, a wagon wheel gate, prickly pear, and a partially protected vegetable garden. A fountain with aquatic plants and fish fronts the entrance to a living room with timber furnishings, artwork nooks, and recessed lighting. The backyard has a large strip of grass with seating and stone tables for viewing the sunset. A private gate offers access to Coconino National Forest hiking and biking trails—Oak Creek and Dry Creek are within half a mile. All in all, a very relaxing way to explore Sedona.

SETTING & FACILITIES
Location 2 mi. north of Red Rock State Park, 6 mi. west of Uptown Sedona **Near** Red Rock Crossing, Coconino National Forest **Building** 1994 ranch-style house **Grounds** 2 acres w/ fountains, hammocks, wood swings on flagstone, night lights, stone tables **Public Space** LR w/ flagstone fireplace, DR **Food & Drink** Full breakfast in DR; guest gas barbecue **Recreation** Horse riding, fishing, golfing, hot-air ballooning, jeep tours **Amenities & Services** Full concierge services, weddings, fax, rolltop desk

ACCOMMODATIONS
Units 4, including stand-alone cottage **All** Robe, private entrance, TV/VCR, stereo, phone, clock, iron & ironing board, fridge, ceiling fan, fireplace/stove **Some** Kitchenette (2), coffeemaker (2) **Bed & Bath** Queen (3), full (1); all private baths, jetted tub (2) **Favorites** Grand Canyon Suite is stand-alone cottage w/ private fenced yard for massage, black wood-burning stove, metal Mexican mirrors; Suite Jerome is private A-frame w/ outside staircase, deck, 5 skylights, wood-burning fireplace, loft, 3 queen beds, saltillo tile, cranberry rugs, kitchenette **Comfort & Decor** Relatively spare white walls, lodgepole pine accents and furnishings, some wicker, love seat, mirrored armoire, hidden TV.

RATES, RESERVATIONS, & RESTRICTIONS
Deposit 1 night or 50% of stay (14-day cancellation for refund minus $25) **Discounts** None **Credit Cards** AE, MC, V **Check-In/Out** 2–4 p.m./11 a.m. **Smoking** No **Pets** No **Kids** No **No-Nos** N/A **Minimum Stay** 2 nights weekends, 3 nights holidays **Open** All year **Hosts** Dave & Sue Neimy, 170 Country Lane, P.O. Box 2603, Sedona 86339 **Phone** (928) 282-1343 or toll-free (800) 570-0102 **Fax** (928) 204-2246 **E-mail** reservations@sedonacountryinn.com or info@sedonacountryinn.com **Web** sedonacountryinn.com

COZY CACTUS BED & BREAKFAST, Sedona

OVERALL ★★★½ | QUALITY ★★★½ | VALUE ★★★★ | PRICE RANGE $100–$135

On the same circular street as Graham Inn/Adobe Village and Canyon Villa Inn, Cozy Cactus shares some of the same spectacular views but eschews the luxury of its bed-and-breakfast neighbors. The rooms at Cozy Cactus are as simple and basic as they come, but that is just fine with its clientele of outdoor hiking enthusiasts and families. Before hitting the trails, hikers carbo-load on banana praline muffins and buttermilk pear pancakes with vanilla maple syrup. Families like renting a back view room (Georgia O'Keeffe, Cowboy's Hideaway) and an adjacent front room to form a suite sharing a living room with a fireplace, TV, and kitchen.

SETTING & FACILITIES
Location Village of Oak Creek, near intersection of AZ 179 & Bell Rock Blvd. **Near** National monuments, state parks, archaeological sites, galleries, outlet shopping **Building** 1983 ranch house **Grounds** Backyard borders Coconino National Forest **Public Space** LRs (2), DR **Food & Drink** Full breakfast in DR; popcorn, coffee, tea in kitchen **Recreation** Golf, horse riding, biking, off-road & jeep tours, hot-air ballooning **Amenities & Services** TV/VCR, stereo, Internet connection, wood-burning fireplaces, kitchens

ACCOMMODATIONS

Units 5; some (4) combining into 2-BR suites (2) **All** Hair dryer, clock radio **Some** Red rock views (2), sliding glass doors to patio (3), ceiling fan (1) **Bed & Bath** King/twins (1), queen (4); all private baths w/ tub **Favorites** Georgia O'Keeffe has wood sleigh bed w/ black metal flower panels, leaf & flower pattern fabrics, banker's lamp **Comfort & Decor** Very basic and simple, one Victorian and four with light Southwestern touches, creamy Navajo white walls, black metal lamp, dresser and end table of oak, lodgepole pine, or red cedar.

RATES, RESERVATIONS, & RESTRICTIONS

Deposit 50% if over 1 night (14-day cancellation for refund minus $20 fee) **Discounts** Midweek during off-season (summer, winter), over 4 nights **Credit Cards** AE, MC, V, D **Check-In/Out** 4–6 p.m./11 a.m. **Smoking** Outside **Pets** No **Kids** Yes (crib, high-chair, & roll-away bed available) **No-Nos** N/A **Minimum Stay** 2–3 nights some high-season holidays, special events **Open** All year **Hosts** Bruce Baillie & Linda Caldwell, 80 Canyon Circle Dr., Sedona 86351 **Phone** (928) 284-0082 or toll-free (800) 788-2082 **Fax** N/A **E-mail** info@cozycactus.com **Web** www.cozycactus.com

CREEKSIDE INN AT SEDONA, Sedona

OVERALL ★★★★½ | QUALITY ★★★★½ | VALUE ★★★★ | PRICE RANGE $145–$300

Portraits of Victorian ladies decorate the hallways at Creekside Inn, which blends a traditional ranch-style house with Victorian decor and spacious grounds. Secluded and quiet yet close to galleries and shopping, this romantic honeymoon and anniversary hideaway has a period parlor with a fireplace and 1893 piano under the wood ranch house peaked-roof entry. Run by an English corporate world escapee, breakfast specialties include brandied grapes and fruit-filled oven pancakes. Brown and rainbow trout can be caught after a short hike across lawns with swings and picnic tables down to the dirt trail running alongside Oak Creek. Wildlife ranges from dragonflies, javelina, elk, and deer to blue herons, golden eagles, and ducks.

SETTING & FACILITIES

Location In valley off AZ 179, 0.8 mi. from uptown Sedona **Near** Galleries, shops, state parks, national forest **Building** 1986 ranch-style house remodeled into B&B in 1998 **Grounds** 3 acres w/ swings, picnic tables, creek **Public Space** LR, DR **Food & Drink** Full breakfast in DR; chocolates on bed; snacks, drinks; group lunches **Recreation** Golf, tennis, horse riding, biking, fishing **Amenities & Services** Weddings (100 people), reunions, corporate groups, meeting lounge (10 people)

ACCOMMODATIONS

Units 6 **All** Robes, hair dryer, desk, phone, TV/VCR, clock radio, fridge, coffeemaker, ceiling fan, AC, heat, patio **Some** Wood-burning fireplace (1), microwave (3) **Bed & Bath** Queen beds; all private baths w/ whirlpool tub **Favorites** Creek View Suite has organ lamp, bedside chandeliers, wood bed w/ ornate headboard, double vanity w/ makeup lights, bone china w/ English hunting scene on wall near toilet **Comfort & Decor** Spare white walls, wood trim, American Victorian antiques, French doors opening to patio, sitting area, oil-burning lamps, china plates.

RATES, RESERVATIONS, & RESTRICTIONS

Deposit Credit card holds (10-day cancellation policy) **Discounts** Groups, whole inn rentals **Credit Cards** AE, MC, V, D **Check-In/Out** 3–6 p.m./11 a.m. **Smoking** No **Pets** No **Kids** Over age 10 **No-Nos** N/A **Minimum Stay** 2 nights if Saturday included during high season **Open** All year **Hosts** Mark & Tammy Charlesworth, 99 Copper Cliffs Dr., Sedona 86336 **Phone** (928) 282-4992 or toll-free (800) 390-8621 **Fax** (928) 282-0091 **E-mail** info@creeksideinn.net **Web** www.creeksideinn.net

THE INN ON OAK CREEK, Sedona

OVERALL ★★★½ | QUALITY ★★★★ | VALUE ★★★ | PRICE RANGE $180–$275

A busy highway is just a few feet from the front door, but the Inn on Oak Creek is well sound-proofed. A private park under a heavily trafficked bridge offers seating along the grassy, tree-lined banks of Oak Creek overlooking tennis courts (another property) on the opposite side, albeit with highway sounds in the background. A newly enlarged common deck literally hangs over the creek, and water aficionados can choose from among seven rooms with private decks overlooking the creek. Proximity to galleries and shopping is a selling point here, but don't expect too much hospitality at this pricey property.

SETTING & FACILITIES

Location On AZ 179, 1 block from Tlaquepaque, across the street from Hillside shops & galleries **Near** Galleries, shops, state parks, national forest **Building** 1972 2-story shingle art gallery remodeled into B&B in 1995 **Grounds** Private park alongside creek below highway bridge has hammock, seating **Public Space** LR, DR, deck above creek **Food & Drink** Full breakfast in DR or outside deck; afternoon snacks; all day beverages, pastries; special dietary needs require advance notice **Recreation** Horse riding, fishing, golf, biking, tennis, jeep tours **Amenities & Services** N/A

ACCOMMODATIONS

Units 11 **All** Robe, hair dryer, TV/VCR, phone, gas fireplace **Some** Handicap-accessible (1), vaulted ceiling (3) **Bed & Bath** King (3), queen (8); all private baths with jetted tub **Favorites** Angler's Retreat is corner room w/ king bed, fly-fishing decor, & deck that can be used for creek fishing; Duck Pond has waterfowl theme, queen bed, deck w/ jetted tub overlooking creek **Comfort & Decor** Each room has different theme; in general the decor is simple but upscale country, with the best seven rooms having decks overlooking Oak Creek.

RATES, RESERVATIONS, & RESTRICTIONS

Deposit Within 7 days of booking (7-day cancellation policy) **Discounts** Stay 8 days, pay for 7 **Credit Cards** AE, MC, V, D **Check-In/Out** 3–6 p.m./11 a.m. **Smoking** Designated outdoor areas **Pets** No (local boarding available) **Kids** Yes (over age 10) **No-Nos** N/A **Minimum Stay** 2 nights on weekends **Open** All year **Hosts** Rick & Pam Morris, 556 AZ 179, Sedona 86336 **Phone** (928) 282-7896 or toll-free (800) 499-7896 **Fax** (928) 282-0696 **E-mail** info@sedona-inn.com **Web** www.sedona-inn.com

THE LANTERN LIGHT INN, Sedona

OVERALL ★★★★ | QUALITY ★★★★ | VALUE ★★★★ | PRICE RANGE $115–$295

Pine trees, junipers, and an oval blue sign mark the highway entrance to the Lantern Light Inn, which has an intimate dining and living room interior of dark woods, candles, angled beige walls, ceiling fans, Oriental accents, and fabrics in gold, blue, and burgundy. The only staircase, lined with the proprietor's photographs, is off-limits to guests because it leads to the hosts' private quarters. The inn is popular with international groups, which often divide up, with half the group going to the Grand Canyon and half touring Sedona. Fresh flowers and woodwind music are common at the inn, which faces Thunder Mountain, a popular movie backdrop in the heyday of Western cowboy movies.

SETTING & FACILITIES

Location West Sedona, on AZ 89A near intersection of Dry Creek Rd. **Near** City hall, galleries, shops, state parks, national forest **Building** 1970 & 1985 Spanish colonial & country-style buildings **Grounds** 0.5 acre w/ lanterns, shrubs & almond trees, & lily pond in back **Public Space** LR, DR, patios **Food & Drink** Full breakfast in DR; fridge stocked w/ drinks **Recreation** Golf, horse riding, biking, jeep touring **Amenities & Services** Conference room w/ fireplace, music studio, TV

ACCOMMODATIONS

Units 4 **All** Patio, AC, fridge, TV/VCR **Some** Kitchen (2), fireplace (2), private entrance (2) **Bed & Bath** King/twins (3), queen (1); all private baths w/ tubs **Favorites** 700-sq.-ft. Ryan Suite has yellow & blue floral BR w/ double doors opening to patio, 2d pink floral bedroom w/ shower, 2 baths, kitchen, DR, laundry room, huge white & rose floral LR, brick & wood fireplace, private flagstone & orange cement tile courtyard w/ fountain **Comfort & Decor** Varied with standard furnishings.

RATES, RESERVATIONS, & RESTRICTIONS
Deposit 1 night for short stays (10-day cancellation policy) **Discounts** Travel agents, extended stays **Credit Cards** None (cash, checks, or money orders only) **Check-In/Out** After 2 p.m./11 a.m. **Smoking** Outside only **Pets** No **Kids** Yes (east wing rooms only) **No-Nos** N/A **Minimum Stay** None **Open** All year **Hosts** Edward & Chris Varjean, 3085 W. AZ 89A, Sedona 86336 **Phone** (928) 282-3419 or toll-free (877) 275-4973 **Fax** (928) 203-9380 **E-mail** lanternlightinn@earthlink.net **Web** www.lanternlightinn.com

THE LODGE AT SEDONA, Sedona

OVERALL ★★★★ | QUALITY ★★★★ | VALUE ★★★★ | PRICE RANGE $125–$245

In the late 1950s, a doctor added a wing to a Mission-style building to house his family of 12 children. More recently, the Lodge at Sedona was a rehabilitation center and then a bed-and-breakfast. Under new ownership in late 2001, the old casual country style is being returned to a more traditional Mission style in keeping with Frank Lloyd Wright's concepts of harmonizing interiors with nature. This will mean a return to wood floors and natural materials like leather, as well as retaining the rock, brick fireplaces, and period stained glass. A new upstairs suite will be double the size of current suites and will have a waterfall shower. The expansive grounds are also being improved, with a pool and spa center being installed in a natural dip in the land.

SETTING & FACILITIES
Location Within 1 mi. of uptown Sedona **Near** Galleries, shops, state parks, national forest **Building** Arts & Crafts style, w/ added 1950s wing **Grounds** 2.5 wooded acres w/ ponds, rock gardens **Public Space** Lounge, DR, library, gift shop **Food & Drink** Full breakfast in DR or porch; afternoon snacks; early evening deserts; 24-hour fruit, beverages **Recreation** Golf, horse riding, biking, jeep touring **Amenities & Services** Labyrinth, pool, whirlpool, gazebo

ACCOMMODATIONS
Units 14 **All** TV/VCR, phone, 24-hour concierge, CD, radio, Internet connection, iron & ironing board, hair dryer **Some** Handicap-accessible (1), fireplace (12), private deck (3), ceiling fan, outdoor shower **Bed & Bath** King (4), king/extra long twins (4), queen (6); all private baths, jetted tub (8) **Favorites** Tea Room Suite has private deck, sitting area, fireplace, double whirlpool tub **Comfort & Decor** Country casual decor being restored to Mission style; each room will be different, with Japanese, Art Nouveau, Native American, cowboy themes.

RATES, RESERVATIONS, & RESTRICTIONS
Deposit 1 night or 50% of longer stays (14-day cancellation for refund minus $30) **Discounts** Inquire **Credit Cards** AE, MC, V, D **Check-In/Out** 3–8 p.m./11 a.m. **Smoking** No **Pets** No **Kids** Over age 11; $30 per person charge **No-Nos** N/A **Minimum Stay**

None **Open** All year **Host** Shelley L. Wachal, 125 Kallof Place, Sedona 86336 **Phone** (928) 204-1942 or toll-free (800) 619-4467 **Fax** (928) 204-2128 **E-mail** info@ lodgeatsedona.com **Web** www.lodgeatsedona.com

THE PENROSE BED & BREAKFAST, Sedona

OVERALL ★★★★ | QUALITY ★★★★ | VALUE ★★★★ | PRICE RANGE $140–$190

Nestled into a hillside fronting aptly named Castle Rock in a residential neighborhood with commanding views of Bell Rock and Courthouse Butte, the Penrose is one of Sedona's newest bed-and-breakfasts. Arches, windows, and balconies abound to maximize the commanding hillside views. The proprietors spent three years searching the Sedona area for the location and getting the necessary building permits. Several architects labored to turn the hostess's design inspiration into blueprints allowing the builder to accurately capture the bed-and-breakfast dream. There is ample luxury, but it is kept understated, almost austere, as the underlying ideology here is a spare Mediterranean feel that emphasizes the outside environment.

SETTING & FACILITIES
Location Village of Oak Creek **Near** National monuments, state parks, archaeological sites, galleries, outlet shopping **Building** 2000 2-story terra cotta Mediterranean w/ black wrought-iron balconies **Grounds** 3 acres on hillside below Castle Rock & bordering Coconino National Forest **Public Space** Entry room w/ piano & telescope, LR, 2 DRs, view deck **Food & Drink** Full breakfast in DR or on deck; afternoon snacks; fruit plate tops fridge w/ 24-hour beverages **Recreation** Golf, horse riding, biking, jeep tours, ballooning **Amenities & Services** T-shirt, guest book rating restaurants & activities

ACCOMMODATIONS
Units 5; 4 upstairs **All** Robes, TV/DVD, CD/clock radio, phone (1 hour free U.S. long distance), individual climate control **Some** Sitting area (1), patio & private entrance (1), balcony (4) **Bed & Bath** Queen (5); all private baths, tub (3), 2-person jetted tub (2), double shower (3) **Favorites** Downstairs Yavapai has private patio & entrance, metal lamps, brown leather chair, carved Indonesian wood furnishings, pedestal sink, double jetted tub w/ block glass window, Castle Rock view from toilet **Comfort & Decor** Clean white walls, ample windows with blinds opening up for views and privacy, saltillo tile floors downstairs, cherry laminate floors upstairs.

RATES, RESERVATIONS, & RESTRICTIONS
Deposit Credit card holds (10-day cancellation policy; money forfeited applied to future stay) **Discounts** Multiple-room rental, off-season weekdays, singles **Credit Cards** MC, V, D **Check-In/Out** 3–7 p.m./11:30 a.m. **Smoking** No **Pets** No **Kids** Yes **No-Nos** N/A **Minimum Stay** None **Open** All year **Hosts** Whitney & Christie Pope, 250 Red Butte Dr., Sedona 86351 **Phone** (928) 284-3000 or toll-free (888) 678-3030 **Fax** N/A **E-mail** info@thepenrose.com **Web** www.thepenrose.com

SADDLEROCK RANCH, Sedona

OVERALL ★★★★★ | QUALITY ★★★★½ | VALUE ★★★★★ | PRICE RANGE
$154–$189

A two-level deck with a 180° panorama of Sedona's red rock formations and a Jacuzzi cascading into a swimming pool front the Saddlerock Ranch house. The huge living room has a wood fireplace, massive beams, flagstone floor, piano, pool table, and 14-foot picture windows. The hostess, a potter with hotel industry experience, serves breakfast on a table fronting large picture windows with mesmerizing views. Pottery, kachinas, and paintings add to the ambience of the house, a.k.a city of Sedona Historic Landmark number 4. Formerly part of a 6,000-acre dude ranch used as a movie set in the 1940s and 1950s, the house became a bed-and-breakfast in 1990.

SETTING & FACILITIES
Location Hillside w/ panoramic views, 1 mi. from uptown Sedona and gallery district **Near** Galleries, shops, state parks, national forest **Building** 1940s classic ranch-style house w/ adobe, rock, wood beams **Grounds** 3 hillside acres w/ bonfire ring **Public Space** LR, DR, deck **Food & Drink** Full breakfast in DR; afternoon snacks; mints on pillow; large oatmeal raisin pecan cookies **Recreation** Golf, tennis, horse riding, biking, jeep tours **Amenities & Services** Jacuzzi, pool, wood-burning fireplace, piano, pool table, telescope, ice, microwave, laundry service, fax, Internet access

ACCOMMODATIONS
Units 3 rooms, including stand-alone casita **All** Cordless phone, TV/VCR, CD/clock, hair dryer, fridge, fireplace **Some** Stove inserted into fireplace **Bed & Bath** King (1), queen (2); all private baths w/ tub **Favorites** Saddlerock Room in main house where John Wayne once stayed has autographed portrait, long mirror behind bed, rock fireplace, carved maple leaf door **Comfort & Decor** Some rock and adobe walls, stained glass, pottery, oil paintings, armoires with fridge, carpeted baths, thick towels.

RATES, RESERVATIONS, & RESTRICTIONS
Deposit N/A (14-day cancellation policy) **Discounts** Low season, extended stays **Credit Cards** None (cash or check only) **Check-In/Out** 4–6 p.m./11 a.m. **Smoking** No **Pets** No (kennel referral; owner has schnauzer dogs) **Kids** Precrawling infants or over age 13 **No-Nos** N/A **Minimum Stay** None (prefer 2–3 nights) **Open** All year **Host** Fran Jackson Bruno, 255 Rock Ridge Dr., Sedona 86336 **Phone** (928) 282-7640 or toll-free (866) 282-7640 **Fax** (928) 282-6829 **E-mail** saddlerock@esedona.net **Web** www.saddlerockranch.com

STONE FLOWER BED & BREAKFAST, Sedona

OVERALL ★★★★ | QUALITY ★★★★ | VALUE ★★★★★ | PRICE RANGE $95–$110

In a rural area on the western edge of Sedona near pinyon pine and juniper forests, Stone Flower is an intimate and simple rural retreat. Travelers on a tight budget without the need of luxuries will find the price hard to beat. Views toward Cathedral Rock are offered from the hot tub and wood deck, and hammocks are available for relaxing. The book-lined living room has three sofas and is a favorite place for people to get acquainted and chat. The dining room has a wall lined with family pictures, including a news correspondent daughter with Mikhail Gorbachev in Moscow. The Last Chance gift shop offers wood flutes, quilts, and decorative petroglyph candles. The hosts, who speak several languages, value privacy and keep their exact address a secret until after booking.

SETTING & FACILITIES

Location Western Sedona **Near** Uptown Sedona, Red Rock Crossing, Coconino National Forest trails **Building** Compact rural house **Grounds** Native plantscaping w/ pond, patio **Public Space** LR, DR **Food & Drink** Full breakfast in DR; snack table; outdoor guest barbecue; special dietary needs **Recreation** Horse riding, swimming, fishing, golfing, skiing, tennis **Amenities & Services** Backcountry tours/reservations, multiple languages (Russian, Polish, German, Spanish), hot tub, 2 hammocks, fire pit, phone, stereo, gift shop

ACCOMMODATIONS

Units 3 **All** Clock **Some** Bay window w/ love seat (1) **Bed & Bath** Queen (3); all private baths with tub **Favorites** Green Room has double-glass doors opening onto deck, brass queen & single bed, wicker dresser & end tables **Comfort & Decor** White walls, angled stucco ceilings, skylights, timber furnishings, bench at foot of bed, simple wall decor such as Oriental rug and feathers, mirrored armoire.

RATES, RESERVATIONS, & RESTRICTIONS

Deposit 1 night (7-day cancellation policy) **Discounts** Singles, extended stays **Credit Cards** MC, V, DC, CB **Check-In/Out** 4–6 p.m./11 a.m. **Smoking** No **Pets** No **Kids** No **No-Nos** Incoming phone calls after 10 p.m. **Minimum Stay** 2 nights high season & holidays **Open** All year **Hosts** Helena & Dennis Sigman, N/A, Sedona 86336 **Phone** (928) 282-2977 or toll-free (800) 338-2334 **Fax** N/A **E-mail** sigman@stoneflower.com **Web** www.stoneflower.com

TERRITORIAL HOUSE, *Sedona*

OVERALL ★★★½ | QUALITY ★★★★ | VALUE ★★★★ | PRICE RANGE $100–$185

Started as a bed-and-breakfast by the owners of Boots & Saddles but under new ownership since late 2001, Territorial House retains its country feel. Old Arizona Territory maps line the staircase walls. The living room has a beam ceiling, a wagon wheel, leather furnishings, and an antique rifle on the wall above the stone fireplace. The dining room is most notable for its saltillo tiles. Stairways lead to the rooms, two of which combine into a two-room suite with queen and twin beds. Some tubs are in the main rooms, many of which have Western touches like saddles and stirrups.

SETTING & FACILITIES
Location Off intersection of AZ 89A & Dry Creek Rd., 4 mi. from uptown Sedona **Near** Cottonwood, galleries, shops, state parks, national forest **Building** Compact, 2-story, ranch-style house **Grounds** 3/4 acre; small back yard w/ flagstone, rocks, rose garden, native plants **Public Space** LR, DR, covered veranda **Food & Drink** Full breakfast in DR or veranda; afternoon snacks; fridge w/ drinks; candy in rooms **Recreation** Golf, horse riding, biking, jeep touring **Amenities & Services** Hot tub, microwave, TV/VCR, stereo

ACCOMMODATIONS
Units 4 **All** Robes, ceiling fan, fireplace, CD/clock radio **Some** Cable TV/VCR (3), phone (3), balcony (1), telescope (1) **Bed & Bath** King (2), queen (1), queen & twin (1); all private baths, whirlpool tub (2) **Favorites** Indian Garden is Pueblo style w/ private staircase, sloping wood roof, wicker & wood furnishings, balcony & telescope; Red Rock Crossing has canopied four-poster king bed, shuttered closets, glass cabinet w/ porcelain dolls, butacca chairs & table, whirlpool in room **Comfort & Decor** Country style with carpeted, wood & saltillo tile floors, some knotty pine, old wood headboards, florals, glass showers.

RATES, RESERVATIONS, & RESTRICTIONS
Deposit 50% to confirm and balance 30 days prior to arrival (8-day cancellation policy; 15 days for 2 rooms or 4 nights or more; refund minus $25 fee) **Discounts** Low season, multiple nights **Credit Cards** AE, MC, V, D **Check-In/Out** 4–6 p.m./11 a.m. **Smoking** Deck & garden only **Pets** No **Kids** Yes **No-Nos** N/A **Minimum Stay** None **Open** All year **Hosts** Larry & Suzanne Galisky, 64 Piki Dr., Sedona 86336 **Phone** (928) 204-2737 or toll-free (800) 801-2737 **Fax** (928) 204-2230 **E-mail** info@territorialhousebb.com **Web** www.territorialhousebb.com

A TOUCH OF SEDONA, Sedona

OVERALL ★★★½ | QUALITY ★★★★ | VALUE ★★★★ | PRICE RANGE $109–$159

Only a short walk from the uptown tourist action, A Touch of Sedona attracts a value-oriented clientele who like the relative quiet of this residential street so close to the galleries and shops. (More ambience and spacious grounds are available a block to the north at the Apple Orchard Inn, albeit at a higher price.) Nearby is the historic park commemorating the Jordan family apple orchard, which grew on this street before it was subdivided in the 1970s. Just south on Jordan Road is Sedona Memories Bakery and Cafe, whose sandwiches on homemade bread bring in tour buses and sell out early in the day.

SETTING & FACILITIES
Location Residential neighborhood 5 blocks north of uptown Sedona **Near** Galleries, shops, state parks, national forest **Building** 1990 California ranch-style **Grounds** Sage & mesquite desert landscaping **Public Space** LR, DR **Food & Drink** Full breakfast in DR; afternoon snacks; 24-hour fridge beverages **Recreation** Golf, tennis, horse riding, jeep tours **Amenities & Services** Guest fridge (unstocked), TV, stereo, fax

ACCOMMODATIONS

Units 5 **All** Patio, clock radio, ceiling fan, central AC/heat, hair dryer, iron & ironing board, phone jacks, TV **Some** Tile floor (1), carpeting (4), coffeemaker (1), desk (1) **Bed & Bath** King (3), queen (1), 2 queens (1); all private baths, tub (2) **Favorites** Roadrunner Studio has optional cont'l breakfast in room (added fee), 2 doors, four-poster white timber bed, coffeemaker, sofa, picture window, ample cabinet & shelf space, Southwest turquoise & pink accents; Hummingbird has slanting ceiling, 2 beds, desk, double vanity, stained-glass hummingbirds, etched-glass bird of paradise **Comfort & Decor** Themes vary from kachinas and hummingbirds to roadrunners, eagles, and wolves, with plain white walls, local pottery, armoires, lodgepole pine timber furnishings, some stained glass, wicker.

RATES, RESERVATIONS, & RESTRICTIONS

Deposit 1 night or 50% of longer stays (10-day cancellation for refund minus $15) **Discounts** None **Credit Cards** AE, MC, V, D **Check-In/Out** 4–6 p.m./11 a.m. **Smoking** No **Pets** No (kennel referrals) **Kids** Yes (if well behaved) **No-Nos** N/A **Minimum Stay** None **Open** All year **Hosts** Bill & Sharon Larsen, 595 Jordan Rd., Sedona 86336 **Phone** (928) 282-6462 or toll-free (800) 600-6462 **Fax** (928) 282-1534 **E-mail** touch@touchsedona.com **Web** www.touchsedona.com

WISHING WELL BED & BREAKFAST, Sedona

OVERALL ★★★★ | QUALITY ★★★★½ | VALUE ★★★★ | PRICE RANGE $195–$210

Though a hillside retreat with no phones or TVs in the rooms, Wishing Well has a living-room TV and English-style hallway phone booth. The living room is elegantly appointed with stained glass, brown ceiling beams, and green plants. As part of the transition to new owners, the previous proprietor's autographed wall of show business photos is disappearing and a new suite is being built. All rooms have decks with breathtaking views toward Sedona. However, power poles mar some views, and highway noise drifts up to the least favorite private decks. The innkeepers are always available, but with breakfast served in the room most guests come and go without seeing much of the hosts after check-in.

SETTING & FACILITIES

Location On a hillside above AZ 89A, 0.5 mi. north of uptown Sedona **Near** Galleries, shops, state parks, national forest **Building** Contemporary brown wood design spread across hillside **Grounds** Hillside w/ wishing well, rosemary hedges, fountains, statues, rock waterfall flowing into pool **Public Space** LR **Food & Drink** Cont'l breakfast on tray/cart in room **Recreation** Golf, tennis, horse riding, hot-air ballooning, jeep tours, bird-watching **Amenities & Services** English-style phone booth, TV, elevator

ACCOMMODATIONS

Units 6 **All** Robes, fireplace, fridge, binoculars, private deck & entrance **Some** Radio (on request) **Bed & Bath** King (3), queen (2); all private baths, outdoor jetted tub (4) **Favorites** Sunrise, Sunset has Spanish colonial furniture, carved four-poster king bed w/

canopy, wood-framed sliding glass door to lattice-shaded jetted tub, black & gold accents, unobstructed views; Morning Glory has double deck w/ jetted tub, white canopy queen bed, rose walls **Comfort & Decor** Spanish or Mexican furnishings, mostly white walls, vanity with makeup mirror, glass shower, separate toilet room.

RATES, RESERVATIONS, & RESTRICTIONS

Deposit None (credit card holds) **Discounts** Singles **Credit Cards** AE, MC, V, D **Check-In/Out** 3–6 p.m./11 a.m. **Smoking** No **Pets** No **Kids** Not encouraged **No-Nos** N/A **Minimum Stay** None **Open** All year **Hosts** Valda & Esper Esau, 995 N. AZ 89A, Sedona 86336 **Phone** (928) 282-4914 or toll-free (800) 728-9474 **Fax** (928) 204-9766 **E-mail** wishwell@sedona.net **Web** www.sedonawishingwell.com

THE JOHNSTONIAN BED & BREAKFAST, Williams

OVERALL ★★★½ | QUALITY ★★★½ | VALUE ★★★★ | PRICE RANGE $55–$75

The first bed-and-breakfast in Williams when it opened in 1987, but closed in recent years, this small Victorian ranch house in an old neighborhood with sycamore trees near Route 66 reopened under new owners on Memorial Day 2001 and began taking overflow from nearby Terry Ranch. A wide, carpeted spiral staircase lined with pictures leads to small rooms with stuffed animals; all the rooms share one downstairs bath. But the friendly hosts make it feel like home. Motorcyclists use the garage when it rains. Businesspeople log on to the satellite Internet connection. Groups make themselves at home in the downstairs living room, watch TV in the rocking chair, or play the piano or accordion.

SETTING & FACILITIES

Location Downtown, 3 blocks south of Route 66 **Near** Grand Canyon, Flagstaff, Route 66 **Building** 1900 blue & white Victorian w/ gingerbread behind white picket fence **Grounds** Small back yard being landscaped **Public Space** Downstairs LR, DR, upstairs lounge w/ TV, desk **Food & Drink** Full breakfast in DR; candy & fruit in room; snacks, beverages **Recreation** Golf, fishing, horse riding, winter sports **Amenities & Services** Phone, laundry, computer w/ satellite Internet hookup, TV, piano, accordion

ACCOMMODATIONS

Units 3 upstairs rooms **All** Clock, oil lamps **Some** Radio (1) **Bed & Bath** Queen (2), full-size (1); 1 shared bath downstairs, tub (1) **Favorites** Country Room has blue stuffed cat w/ red ball, wedding ring quilt, purple & white stuffed rabbit on old potty chair, stuffed bull, wardrobe mirror, hats hanging on wall, old chest, wood closet; Sweetheart Room has white teddy bear w/ red "be mine" heart, carved wood headboard, clock radio, rose dresser w/ silver vanity set, & white figurines w/ aftershave lotion & perfume **Comfort & Decor** Floral and maroon wallpapers, stuffed animals, original doors with big knobs and skeleton key locks, angled ceilings, quilts, rocking chairs, stuffed animals.

RATES, RESERVATIONS, & RESTRICTIONS

Deposit First night (7-day cancellation policy) **Discounts** Whole house rental **Credit Cards** MC, V **Check-In/Out** 3 p.m./10 a.m. **Smoking** No **Pets** No **Kids** Yes (by prior arrangement; need separate room) **No-Nos** N/A **Minimum Stay** None **Open** All year **Hosts** Bob & Cindy Lafollette, 321 W. Sheridan Ave., Williams 86046 **Phone** (928) 635-2178 or toll-free (866) 545-0467 **Fax** N/A **E-mail** johnstonianbnb@cindyse-biz.com **Web** www.johnstonian.com

THE RED GARTER BED AND BAKERY, Williams

OVERALL ★★★½ | QUALITY ★★★½ | VALUE ★★★★ | PRICE RANGE $85–$125

Built by a German tailor bent on making his fortune in America, the Red Garter was part of the 1890s saloon row across the street from the railway station. Female employees leaned out the upstairs windows of the Best Gal's Room (#1) and enticed cowboys into the bordello. Women lower on the pecking order lived in back near the two-story outhouse. The Madam's Room (#2) at the top of the staircase was positioned for monitoring the comings and goings. The proprietor, who has spent decades helping restore Williams, brings out old photos and gives history lessons next to the red-and-blue-striped barber pole in the downstairs gift shop. The downstairs bakery counter offers croissants, bagels, scones, and strudel.

SETTING & FACILITIES

Location Center, almost kitty-corner from regional Visitors Center & Grand Canyon Railroad depot **Near** Grand Canyon, Flagstaff, museums, archaeological sites **Building** 1897 brick Richardsonian Romanesque style **Grounds** Street in front, Route 66 in back **Public Space** Gift shop, bakery, DR **Food & Drink** Cont'l breakfast in DR **Recreation** Golf, fishing, horse riding, winter sports **Amenities & Services** Laundry room, midday meeting space

ACCOMMODATIONS

Units 4 upstairs rooms **All** Ceiling fan, clock radio, cable TV **Some** Hair dryer & iron (on request), private deck (1), skylights **Bed & Bath** Queen (3), queen & double (1); all private baths, tub (1) **Favorites** Best Gal's Room, near top of staircase called "the cowboy endurance test," has sitting area w/ red sofa & gas stove under street-facing windows, lace curtains, mirrored dresser, small illustrations of alluringly posed women, and white, green, & burgundy colors; Big Bertha has 2 beds, skylight, private deck **Comfort & Decor** High ceilings, dark pine trim, floral wallpaper, transom windows, antique mirrored armoires, risqué women and Western scenes on walls, black and white baths.

RATES, RESERVATIONS, & RESTRICTIONS

Deposit Credit card holds (7-day cancellation for refund minus 10%) **Discounts** Whole place rental, packages, Web specials, off-season specials (Nov., Feb.) **Credit Cards** AE,

MC, V, D **Check-In/Out** 4–8 p.m./11 a.m. **Smoking** No **Pets** No **Kids** Yes (over age 8)
No-Nos N/A **Minimum Stay** None **Open** Mid-Feb.–Nov. 30 **Host** John W. Holst, 137
W. Railroad Ave., Williams 86046 **Phone** (928) 635-1484 or toll-free (800) 328-1484 **Fax**
N/A **E-mail** info@redgarter.com **Web** www.redgarter.com

SHERIDAN HOUSE INN, Williams

OVERALL ★★★★★ | QUALITY ★★★★★ | VALUE ★★★★★ | PRICE RANGE
$135–$225

Nestled on a hillside surrounded by a ponderosa pine forest 59 miles south
of the Grand Canyon and 32 miles west of Flagstaff, Sheridan House has
upstairs and downstairs porches and patios in the main house with forest
views for eating and sipping wine. Besides breakfast, the former hotel chef
host keeps guests well fed with post–happy hour dinner specialties ranging
from Italian and Mexican to Jamaican jerk chicken, Caribbean seafood, and
Cuban yellow rice and black beans. One main house room is off the
kitchen; others are up and down a carpeted staircase. A building adjacent to
the main house has upstairs and downstairs two-bedroom suites.

SETTING & FACILITIES
Location 5 blocks south of Route 66 **Near** Grand Canyon, museums, archaeological
sites **Building** 1988 multilevel ranch-style house & adjacent 2-story 4-unit building
Grounds Flagstone patio merges into gov't-owned forests w/ hiking trail **Public Space**
LR, DR, entertainment room, fitness room, patio, porch **Food & Drink** Full breakfast &
buffet dinner in DR or outdoor deck; happy hour w/ snacks & beverages; stocked guest
fridge **Recreation** Golf, fishing, hunting, winter sports **Amenities & Services** Jacuzzi,
pool table, piano, fitness equipment, laundry

ACCOMMODATIONS
Units 8 units, including 2 2-BR suites **All** Ceiling fan, TV/VCR, stereo, hair dryer, clock
radio, iron & ironing board **Some** Fridge, coffeemaker, desk (2), fireplace (1), private patio
(1) **Bed & Bath** King (6), queen (2); all private baths, tub (7) **Favorites** Sycamore has bay
window sitting area, view of pines & squirrels, glass-top tables, green floral spreads, &
flower wall art **Comfort & Decor** Fine wood furnishings range from rosewood in Rosewood Room to oak in Oakwood room; some marble baths.

RATES, RESERVATIONS, & RESTRICTIONS
Deposit 1 night (7-day cancellation, full refund; up to 24 hours, forfeit 25% total reservation; 14-day holiday cancellation policy) **Discounts** None **Credit Cards** AE, MC, V, D
Check-In/Out 4–6 p.m./11 a.m. **Smoking** No **Pets** 1 room only (Oakwood, which has
patio) **Kids** Yes (well behaved only) **No-Nos** N/A **Minimum Stay** None **Open** Mid-
Feb.–Dec. 31 **Hosts** Steve & Evelyn Gardner, 460 E. Sheridan Ave., Williams 86046 **Phone**
(520) 635-9441 or toll-free (888) 635-9345 **Fax** (520) 635-1005 **E-mail** sheridan
house@thegrandcanyon.com **Web** www.thegrandcanyon.com/sheridan

TERRY RANCH BED & BREAKFAST, Williams

OVERALL ★★★★★ | QUALITY ★★★★½ | VALUE ★★★★ | PRICE RANGE $110–$155

Log walls, a wrap-around veranda with rocking chairs, and warm hospitality contribute to the comfortable country feel at Terry Ranch. Except during holidays, the living room sports a red, white, and blue theme with vintage flags, an old trunk doubling as a table, a wood fireplace, and plenty of comfortable sofas and chairs. The dining area, down the hall from the living room, serves up specialties like pumpkin chocolate muffins and caters to diabetic, vegan, and other special diets (guests are asked about dietary needs when booking over the phone). Room names like Eliza Jane and Mary Ann reflect back on family history.

SETTING & FACILITIES

Location East edge of town, corner of Quarterhorse & Rodeo Rds. **Near** Grand Canyon, Flagstaff, Indian ruins **Building** 1992 2-story log cabin w/ green sheet metal roof **Grounds** Cottonwood & numerous small conifer trees, flagstone, gazebo, arbor w/ seating, wood swing **Public Space** LR, DR, veranda **Food & Drink** Full breakfast in DR; packaged breakfasts for early tours; room basket w/ cider & snacks; special dietary needs **Recreation** Horse riding, rafting, fishing, birding, biking, golf, winter sports **Amenities & Services** Tour reservations, guest fridge, CD player

ACCOMMODATIONS

Units 4 downstairs rooms **All** Robes, ceiling fan, sitting area, gas-burning fireplace, cable TV/VCR, 2d door to veranda, quilt, clock, big bath amenity basket **Some** Rocking chairs **Bed & Bath** King (1), queen (3); all private baths w/ tub **Favorites** Honeymooners like blue & white Charlotte Malinda's carved wood fireplace ringed w/ blue tiles near bed, bath w/ blue bead board paneling & rose stencils; Hannah Louise has green cast iron bed, floral china display, 2 rocking chairs, trombone on wall **Comfort & Decor** Log and wallpaper walls, mirrored armoires, hardwood floors with rugs, black wrought-iron doors opening onto veranda, baths with claw-foot tubs and heat lamps.

RATES, RESERVATIONS, & RESTRICTIONS

Deposit $25 (7-day cancellation policy) **Discounts** Whole house rentals, packages (Nov. 1–Mar. 1), travel agents, week stays (1 night free) **Credit Cards** AE, MC, V, D **Check-In/Out** After 4 p.m./10 a.m. **Smoking** No **Pets** No (nearby boarding kennel; owners have friendly cats) **Kids** Yes (with advanced arrangement) **No-Nos** No alcohol served (may bring own) **Minimum Stay** None **Open** All year **Hosts** Del & Sheryl Terry, Glenn & Leisa Watkins, 701 Quarterhorse Rd., Williams 86046 **Phone** (928) 635-4171 or toll-free (800) 210-5908 **Fax** N/A **E-mail** info@terryranchbnb.com **Web** www.terryranchbnb.com

Indian Country

Indian Country stretches from the Four Corners region in the northeast corner of the state toward Tuba City just east of the Grand Canyon and includes the lands of the Navajo and Hopi Nations. Bed-and-breakfasts are few in number and hard to find. For Hopi Nation centers like Second Mesa, the only options may be a motel or a commute.

A Navajo hogan bed-and-breakfast stay is likely to be relatively primitive, much the way the ancestors lived, or maybe a little better than the ancestors had it, with perhaps a sleeping bag over a soft sheepskin on a hard dirt floor. Leave home any notions of fine mattresses and being pampered. Think cultural experience, camping out, and maybe a juniper sweat lodge with sage incense.

Window Rock, the Navajo Nation capital and tourism department headquarters, has two reliable hogan bed-and-breakfasts nearby. There are also bed-and-breakfasts in Monument Valley near the Utah border, but only one is easily located. To access other Indian Country areas, the only alternative may be directly contacting the Navajo Nation (phone (520) 871-6436) and hiring a tour guide (e.g., John Largo or Will Tsosie) to create a custom package including a hogan stay with a local family.

Even if it comes down to roughing it and commuting from a cheap motel along I-40 in Holbrook or Winslow, Indian Country is worth exploring. Homolovi Ruins State Park, a sacred gathering place of the Hopi clans three miles east of Winslow, has a thousand-room pueblo and river wildlife viewing areas. The 28-mile drive through the Petrified Forest National Park and Painted Desert, 25 miles east of Holbrook, are easily worth half a day. Deeper into Indian Country near Chinle is Canyon de Chelly National Monument, whose sandstone walls still enclose seasonal Navajo corn, livestock, and peach farms. Navajo National Monument near Kayenta has the Betatakin and Keet Seel Ruins.

GOAT SPRINGS HOSPITALITY, Fort Defiance

OVERALL ★★★ | QUALITY ★½ | VALUE ★★★★ | PRICE RANGE $180 ($100 FOR FIRST PERSON; $80/ADDITIONAL PERSON)

Navajo cultural is experienced while living primitively, like the grandparents did before moving into more modern log cabins. Several close-knit family generations living nearby still use the hogan for ceremonies, including weddings and graduations. Guests can accompany the host, who carries his golf driver with him when herding sheep and tending the yellow, white, and blue corn; take rug weaving lessons; or buy a rug from the hostess, a reading specialist elected to the Window Rock School Board. Farm activities and corn pollen ceremonies follow the seasons. Forget luxury, because sleeping on sheepskins on a dirt floor and using an outhouse is more akin to camping.

SETTING & FACILITIES
Location 3.5 mi. north of Window Rock on Indian Route (IR) 12 **Near** Navajo cultural center, Gallup, Petrified Forest, Canyon de Chelly **Building** 1990s east-facing "male" cement & wood Navajo hogan **Grounds** Farm pens w/ sheep, playground, pasture, & corn field w/ red sandstone mountain backdrop **Public Space** Farm, playground **Food & Drink** Traditional Navajo breakfast; traditional dinner option **Recreation** Hiking, herding sheep, rug weaving **Amenities & Services** Sweat lodge ($35/person; available without overnight stay), small rugs for sale

ACCOMMODATIONS
Units 1 hogan holding up to 10 people **All** No running water **Some** N/A **Bed & Bath** Sheepskin mattresses on floor; no bath (but water, soap, towels), outhouse behind tree **Favorites** Mud, plaster, & wood sweat lodge to side of hogan has rock bonfire & burning sage; men go first, then women **Comfort & Decor** Dirt floor, sofas, windows (not traditional), metal stove in center.

RATES, RESERVATIONS, & RESTRICTIONS
Deposit Depends on services desired (ask) **Discounts** None **Credit Cards** None (cash or money order only) **Check-In/Out** Customized **Smoking** Outside **Pets** Yes (family has dogs, sheep) **Kids** Yes **No-Nos** N/A **Minimum Stay** No **Open** Feb.–Nov. (snow closes) **Hosts** Lorraine & Jason Nelson, P.O. Box 183, Fort Defiance 86504 **Phone** (520) 729-2786 **Fax** N/A **E-mail** N/A **Web** N/A

TSE LI GAH SINIL' HOSPITALITY, Ganado

OVERALL ★★★½ | QUALITY ★★ | VALUE ★★★★ | PRICE RANGE $165 ($145/FIRST
PERSON; $20/ADDITIONAL PERSON)

Named after a white rock outcropping, Tse Li Gah Sinil' was established "to really experience what we have here, who we are as Navajo Dine people," says the hostess, who works for the Navajo Tourism Department and stays in a log cabin near the primitive hogan to provide food for guests by cooking in the fireplace or outdoors if warm. The grandparents tend sheep and livestock in nearby canyons and still use the hogan for the blessing way, Navajo weddings, and corn pollen ceremonies. The mostly adult clientele comes from as far away as Japan for strenuous hikes deep into Bear Canyon and to arroyos near corn fields to see petroglyphs and Anasazi ruins.

SETTING & FACILITIES
Location 11 mi. down a dirt road between Ganado & Window Rock **Near** Kinlichee Ruins Tribal Park, Cross Canyon, Navajo cultural center, Petrified Forest, Canyon de Chelly **Building** Late 1950s female (octagon) hogan **Grounds** Granite boulders, pinyons, & junipers **Public Space** Everything outside the hogan **Food & Drink** Traditional Navajo breakfast of blue corn meal, bacon, eggs, fruit, Navajo tea or coffee; lunch or dinner can be arranged there or can bring in own **Recreation** Hiking **Amenities & Services** Navajo storytelling, crafts demos (pottery, basketry, silver), ceremonies (requires advance arrangement)

ACCOMMODATIONS
Units 1 hogan, sleeps up to 10 comfortably **All** No electricity, no running water **Some** N/A **Bed & Bath** Twin beds (2) or sheepskin mattress on floor; portable tub in hogan, sweat lodge, outhouse **Favorites** Pinyon wood hogan with stone foundation & green roofing paper roof **Comfort & Decor** Beehive-style wood-burning pot-bellied stove and box of firewood in middle of wood-paneled octagonal room.

RATES, RESERVATIONS, & RESTRICTIONS
Deposit Negotiable; 14 days advance notice for cancellations **Discounts** None **Credit Cards** None (cash or check only) **Check-In/Out** By 6 p.m./11 a.m. **Smoking** No **Pets** Yes, must stay outside hogan; animals not allowed in ceremonial house **Kids** Yes **No-Nos** N/A **Minimum Stay** None **Open** April–Nov. (depending on snow) **Host** Christine Wallace, P.O. Box 1187, St. Michaels 86511 **Phone** (520) 871-4360 **Fax** N/A **E-mail** wallace@cia-g.com **Web** N/A

NAVAJO TRIBAL PARK VISIT THE HOGAN, Monument Valley

OVERALL ★★★ | QUALITY ★½ | VALUE ★★★★ | PRICE RANGE $20/PERSON

The Blacks' trips deep into Monument Valley have been written up in *Arizona Highways* magazine. Visit the Hogan is a new business for this Navajo family and is the only easily located bed-and-breakfast in this area that director John Ford made famous in films like *Stagecoach, My Darling Clementine, The Wagon Master,* and *Cheyenne Autumn.* Basically, the Blacks supply the sheepskin and dirt floor, and guests camp out like Old West traders inside the hogan, enjoying spectacular Monument Valley views (bring your own folding chair). The famous Goulding's Trading Post & Lodge is less than a mile away for those needing a real bed and some luxury.

SETTING & FACILITIES
Location Monument Valley, on US 163, 0.5 mi. south of Gouldings turnoff **Near** Kayenta, Mexican Hat **Building** 1 hogan, sleeps up to 15 **Grounds** Hosts live in trailers in back & to side are tour jeeps & horses **Public Space** Everything outside the hogan **Food & Drink** Regular American breakfast served in hogan **Recreation** Horse riding, jeep tours **Amenities & Services** Black's Hiking & Jeep Tours arranges tours

ACCOMMODATIONS
Units 1 hogan, has held 15 people **All** Lantern-shaped flashlight **Some** N/A **Bed & Bath** Sheepskin on floor, bring own sleeping bag or use theirs; no bath, outhouse only **Favorites** Hogan has spectacular views of Monument Valley **Comfort & Decor** Cedar log interior

RATES, RESERVATIONS, & RESTRICTIONS
Deposit None **Discounts** Groups **Credit Cards** None (cash or travelers checks) **Check-In/Out** No set times **Smoking** Outside **Pets** Yes (must stay outside hogan) **Kids** Yes **No-Nos** N/A **Minimum Stay** None **Open** All year **Hosts** Agnes & Roy Black, P.O. Box 310393, Mexican Hat 85431 **Phone** (520) 674-4111 or (435) 739-4226 or toll-free (800) 749-4226 **Fax** (435) 739-4226 **E-mail** N/A **Web** N/A

Western Border

The "coastline" of the dammed but still mighty Colorado River is Arizona's Western Border, a desert landscape intersected by mountain ranges. This area borders Nevada along the Colorado River from the blue waters of Lake Mead and Hoover Dam south through Lake Mohave. South of Davis Dam and Bullhead City, near Laughlin, Nevada, the muddy brown Colorado River flowing south into Mexico becomes the border between California and Arizona.

Beaches, campgrounds, marinas, and cantinas turn stretches of the Colorado River into watery desert playgrounds. But western Arizona's only bed-and-breakfasts are away from the water in Chloride and Kingman. An old silver mining town founded in 1862, Chloride has shrunk from 3,000 people and 75 operating mines to an artists' town of 300. Most folks driving US 93 linking Las Vegas and Phoenix cruise right by the Chloride turnoff, 17 miles north of Kingman, without even blinking.

At high noon the first and third Saturdays of most months, Chloride gunfighters stage a shootout, and a vaudeville show follows. A dirt road into the mountains outside town rewards the adventurous with Roy Purcell's soul-searching rock art murals. The big events in Chloride are the May and October "all-town yard sales" and June's Black Powder Days. Kingman boasts of being on Route 66, but it is mainly a pit stop 170 miles west of the Grand Canyon.

Southwest of Kingman on Old Route 66 is Oatman, an old gold-mining town that has declined from 20 saloons and a stock exchange into a touristy Old West spectacle with burros roaming the streets. Heading south along the Colorado River is Havasu City, a retirement town boasting the original London Bridge and three microbreweries serving periodic invasions of partying college students. Parker and Quartzite fill with RVs and over a million visitors for the winter gem shows and flea markets. But the desert empties when early spring temperatures climb into triple digits. Yuma, on the Mexican border, has an old territorial prison, a new microbrewery, a Japanese baseball team for spring training, and plenty of golf.

SHEPS OF CHLORIDE, Chloride

OVERALL ★★★ | QUALITY ★★★ | VALUE ★★★★ | PRICE RANGE $35–$65

Chloride, nestled in scrub-covered high desert mountains with silver chloride, is an old mining town turned funky by artists like Roy Purcell, whose colorful "inward search for self" murals decorate a rock outcrop east of town. Old Man Shep owned most of the town, and the boardwalk block with the bed-and-breakfast and several businesses named Sheps has been passed on intact over the years. The thick-walled adobe rooms here are as basic as they come, with a cozy mine shaft architecture crafted by the miners. Sheps Cafe has a pot-bellied stove, stools surrounding a counter lined with early 1900s tiles, and two strong women hand-shredding potatoes to go with enormous omelets that can sustain hungry miners for days. Across the street is an Old West town park named Cyanide Springs, where on the first and third Saturdays of the month gunfighters reenact a shootout in front of the Dead Ass Saloon.

SETTING & FACILITIES
Location About 17 mi. north of Kingman on AZ 93, near Grasshopper Junction, take Chloride turnoff heading east. After 4 mi. road turns into Tennessee in center of town. Turn right on Second, go 1 block **Near** Rock art murals, museums, collectibles shops, galleries, Old West park with vaudeville **Building** 8 units in 1860s miners' adobe; 4 units in early 1900s frame house built of railroad boxcar lumber **Grounds** Adobe has small courtyard, w/ Shep's RV Park in back & Old Western–style boardwalk w/ funky stores in front **Public Space** Frame house has porch & sitting room with TV **Food & Drink** Full breakfast menu in Sheps Cafe; lunch available **Recreation** Exploring small funky town with artists & Western history **Amenities & Services** Meetings (24), fax, laundromat

ACCOMMODATIONS
Units 12 guest rooms, 10 1-BR and 2 2-BR **All** Sitting room **Some** Phones, ceiling fans, thick adobe walls (8), paintings (2) **Bed & Bath** Twins (4), full-size doubles (4), queens (4); all private baths, shower (9) or tub (3) **Favorites** 2-BR suites, w/ spacious LRs **Comfort & Decor** Motel-like; very simple, clean, and austere.

RATES, RESERVATIONS, & RESTRICTIONS
Deposit 1 night deposit w/ reservation; 7-day cancellation for full refund **Discounts** Midweek specials **Credit Cards** AE, MC, V, D, DC **Check-In/Out** 2 p.m./11 a.m. **Smoking** In cafe **Pets** Special arrangement (usually not allowed) **Kids** Yes **No-Nos** N/A **Minimum Stay** None **Open** All year **Hosts** John and Bonnie McNeely , 9827 2nd St. , Chloride 86431 **Phone** Toll-free (877) 565-4251 **Fax** N/A **E-mail** jmcn1122@aol.com **Web** N/A

HOTEL BRUNSWICK, Kingman

OVERALL ★★★ | QUALITY ★★★ | VALUE ★★★★ | PRICE RANGE $25–$115

Kingman is mostly a stopping place between California/Nevada and the Grand Canyon. In 1909 the hotel opened as the region's first three-story building and was a paragon of luxury frequented by Hollywood stars. Cowboy star Andy "Jingles" Devine grew up next door. With the demise of Route 66, in 1977 the Brunswick was boarded up, along with much of downtown Kingman. In 1997 a renovated Brunswick reopened as a bed-and-breakfast. Under new French ownership in 1999 the Brunswick metamorphosed into a boutique hotel with a bar selling cigars. Europeans enjoy the period decor, watching the trains go by, and the bargain Cowboy/Cowgirl rooms, which have separate floors for men and women and shared bathrooms. But rooms with private bathrooms, particularly the suites, offer more comfort.

SETTING & FACILITIES

Location Downtown, on historic Route 66 (Andy Devine Ave.), between 3rd & 4th Sts. **Near** Locomotive & sports parks, museums, Route 66, train station, airfield **Building** Local tufa stone w/ veranda built in 1909, renovated 1997 **Grounds** Opens onto street & old Santa Fe Railroad depot **Public Space** Restaurant, bar, lobby **Food & Drink** Cont'l-plus breakfast; all meals available, well-stocked cash bar **Recreation** Golf, tennis, fitness center, horseback riding, herding cattle **Amenities & Services** Internet access, business center, car rental, massage, laundry

ACCOMMODATIONS

Units 24 guest rooms, including 9 sharing bath, 8 suites **All** AC, cable TV, phone **Some** Private baths (15), kitchen & DR (2) **Bed & Bath** Varies widely; 9 share 3 baths, 15 w/ showers or tubs **Favorites** Presidential suite **Comfort & Decor** Early 1900s feel, eclectic mix of furnishings.

RATES, RESERVATIONS, & RESTRICTIONS

Deposit None (24-hour cancellation) **Discounts** Corp., wedding, military, gov't, June–Oct. **Credit Cards** AE, MC, D, DC **Check-In/Out** Early/late available **Smoking** Designated areas only **Pets** No **Kids** Yes **No-Nos** N/A **Minimum Stay** None **Open** All year **Hosts** Gerard Guedon and Jessie Sayas-Guedon, 315 E. Andy Devine Ave., Kingman 86401 **Phone** (520) 718-1800 **Fax** (520) 718-1801 **E-mail** rsvp@hotel-brunswick.com **Web** www.hotel-brunswick.com

Central Territory

Arizona's Central Territory climbs into mountainous Prescott National Forest, providing relief from the scorching desert heat in the valleys below. Not surprisingly, the Central Territory is a cool summertime escape destination for Phoenix and the Valley of the Sun. On I-17 between Phoenix and Flagstaff is Montezuma Castle National Monument, which houses five- and six-story cliff apartments built by the Sinagua Indians in the twelfth century.

Near Cottonwood and Clarkdale is Tuzigoot National Monument, a climbable Sinaguan hilltop stone pueblo overlooking scenic flatlands that became a twentieth-century copper-mining waste dump. Clarkdale, a sleepy town of 2,000, was created because it was flat enough to house a copper smelter for ore mined in mountainous Jerome. Phelps Dodge closed the copper mines and smelter in the 1950s. Today Clarkdale is home to the Verde Canyon Railroad, which runs scenic four-hour round trips along the upper Verde River to the Perkinsville ghost town.

AZ 89A twists and turns through the mountains from Clarkdale to the terraced hillside town of Jerome. Named after New York financier Eugene Jerome, who bankrolled the copper production, shops selling art have replaced the Jerome mines. A Liars' Festival and chili cookoff are held in April, and Jerome's Victorian and other historic homes open for touring the third full weekend in May.

AZ 89A meanders southwest another 25 miles through pine-forested mountains from Jerome toward Prescott. An early Arizona Territory capital, Prescott came into existence as a gold-mining town. Almost every weekend there is a festival or event of some kind in the downtown Courthouse Plaza across from Whiskey Row. Horse racing runs from Memorial Day to Labor Day. The Phippen Museum of Western Art is situated across from giant granite boulders near Thumb Butte.

FLYING EAGLE COUNTRY BED & BREAKFAST, Clarkdale

OVERALL ★★★★★ | QUALITY ★★★★ | VALUE ★★★★★ | PRICE RANGE $85–$95

Two overstuffed white sofas, a piano, an inlaid Moroccan chess set, and a flagstone nook with a wood-burning stove mark the Flying Eagle Country entrance. A telescope aimed out the window across the Verde Valley magnifies the distant peaks above Flagstaff and Sedona. The views are equally inspiring from the white wrought-iron seating under the trees in the front yard. Javelina, birds, deer, and coyote frequent the gardens to munch on fallen apples, peaches, pears, persimmons, plumcots, pomegranates, figs, and other fruits, which guests are free to harvest between games of bocce ball on the lawn. The dining room has an open island for conversing while the Swedish hostess and her Hollywood studio prop-maker husband prepare breakfast.

SETTING & FACILITIES
Location Near Yavapai College, between Jerome & Cottonwood **Near** Prescott, Sedona, museums, national monuments, Verde Canyon Railroad **Building** 1981 2-story ranch house w/ wine cellar **Grounds** 1.8 acres w/ fruit trees, gardens w/ mints & sage, sitting area w/ Verde Valley view **Public Space** LR, DR, porch **Food & Drink** Full breakfast in DR **Recreation** Boating, rafting, rail excursions, hang gliding **Amenities & Services** Hot tub, telescope, Moroccan chess set, piano

ACCOMMODATIONS
Units 3 **All** Ceiling fan, clock radio, TV **Some** Individual AC (1), central AC (2) **Bed & Bath** Queen (3); all private baths, tub (1) **Favorites** Loft has private deck entrance, French doors, shuttered closet, antique wood furnishings, pine wood post & beam by bed; stand-alone guest house has kitchenette w/ microwave & full-size fridge, angled ceiling, wood-burning stove on flagstone island, beige carpet, light colors **Comfort & Decor** Varies from early American in guest house to Italian Provincial with polished parquet floors, small red rugs, whitish paisley floral bed covers.

RATES, RESERVATIONS, & RESTRICTIONS
Deposit Credit card holds (6-day cancellation notice for refund minus $15) **Discounts** Verde Canyon rail packages **Credit Cards** MC, V, D **Check-In/Out** 4–6 p.m./11 a.m. **Smoking** No **Pets** No (owners have cat) **Kids** Yes **No-Nos** N/A **Minimum Stay** None **Open** All year **Hosts** Kristus & Inger Bellamy, 2700 Windmill Lane, Clarkdale 86324 **Phone** (928) 634-0211 **Fax** N/A **E-mail** jandibellamy@msn.com **Web** www.flyingeagle country.com

GHOST CITY INN B&B, Jerome

OVERALL ★★★★ | QUALITY ★★★★ | VALUE ★★★★ | PRICE RANGE $85–$125

Built by Phelps Dodge to house mining executives, steeply terraced Ghost City is a short walk from the Main Street action. The hostess, a former nurse, successfully transferred her helping skills to pleasing guests. The host, Jerome's police chief, mounts a Harley to lead motorcycle tours of Southwest bed-and-breakfasts. A shared second-story veranda is popular for snacking, socializing, and watching the street below. The blue-and-white Cleopatra room is decorated with angels to ward off a ghost. Once notorious for bordellos, murders, and mayhem, this town of 500 people and steep narrow streets is currently Arizona's fourth most popular tourist destination with 1.5 million visitors annually.

SETTING & FACILITIES

Location 3.5 blocks from Jerome Historic District **Near** Museum, galleries, state parks, national monuments **Building** 1885/95 2-story double-veranda executive boarding house **Grounds** Steep multilevel hillside w/ koi pond, seating under grapevine-covered arbor **Public Space** TV/game room, DR **Food & Drink** Full breakfast in DR; afternoon snacks; 24-hour beverages; special event dinners **Recreation** Boating, rafting, rail excursions, motorcycles **Amenities & Services** Harley motorcycle rental, hot tub w/ sound system, murder mystery dinners

ACCOMMODATIONS

Units 6 **All** Robes, TV/VCR, fridge, clock radio, ceiling fan, fire alarm **Some** Private deck (1), shared front veranda (5), individual air coolers (2), central AC (4) **Bed & Bath** Queen (5), double (1); 2 private baths, 2 shared **Favorites** Miner's Suite has hardwood floor, Victorian antiques, sofa, carved-face chair, desk, Egyptian tapestry comforter, "Phelps Dodge" green color; Western room has timber bed, lassos, old cowboy chaps on wall; Northern Exposure has rolled pine cabin feel, wood fish on wall above bed, hunting & fishing theme **Comfort & Decor** Varies with room theme, may include lace, quilted fabrics, old brick chimney remnants, wood dresser, stained glass.

RATES, RESERVATIONS, & RESTRICTIONS

Deposit 1 night (7-day cancellation for refund minus $20) **Discounts** Multiple rooms, Harley motorcycle rental packages **Credit Cards** AE, MC, V, D **Check-In/Out** 4–7 p.m./11 a.m. ($20 late check-in fee) **Smoking** No **Pets** No **Kids** Yes (over age 11) **No-Nos** Loud late-night partying **Minimum Stay** None **Open** All year **Hosts** Alan & Jackie Muma, 541 Main St., P.O. Box T, Jerome 86331 **Phone** (928) 634-4678 or toll-free (888) 634-4678 **Fax** N/A **E-mail** reservations@ghostcityinn.com **Web** www.ghostcityinn.com

INN AT JEROME, Jerome

OVERALL ★★★½ | QUALITY ★★★½ | VALUE ★★★★ | PRICE RANGE $55–$85

Built to last after three fires at the end of the nineteenth century burned down the town, the Inn at Jerome makes up for its paucity of private bathrooms with a choice central location for shopping and Old West history buffs. Breakfast is at the Jerome Grille, where the blue jean–wearing hostess does double duty as bartender and waitress. Though the bed-and-breakfast breakfast menu looks limited, in actual practice even eggs Jerome (shredded beef, green chile sauce, melted cheeses, and carmelized onions on a flour tortilla) and the Copper Cliffs omelet (avocado, sour cream, enchilada sauce) can be ordered. Verde Valley views are available from the Victorian Rose, Little Daisy, and Memories of the Heart rooms.

SETTING & FACILITIES

Location Center of historic district, on Cleopatra Hill, next to police station **Near** Museums, state parks, national monuments, Prescott, Sedona **Building** 1899 2-story reinforced concrete storefront **Grounds** Front opens onto street, back is against hillside **Public Space** Lounge w/ fireplace, bar, restaurant, back porch **Food & Drink** Full breakfast at Jerome Grille; hot beverages in lounge; bar; lunch served at Grille **Recreation** Jeep & gold panning tours, mountain biking, fishing, horse riding, hot-air ballooning **Amenities & Services** Phone

ACCOMMODATIONS

Units 8 **All** Robes, down pillows, TV, clock radio, ceiling fan, pedestal sink, armoire **Some** Step-up four-poster bed (2) **Bed & Bath** Queen (6), full (2); 2 private baths, 3 shared **Favorites** Lariat and Lace has step-up four-poster timber bed (good for kids w/ sleeping bags underneath), barn wood armoire, blue & purple cowgirl print, distressed hardwood floor, horse lamp w/ woven wood shade, lace valences, shared bath **Comfort & Decor** Varied room themes include French Provincial, daisies and sunflowers, and Victorian, with stained glass, wrought iron, antique dark wood, and antiqued furnishings.

RATES, RESERVATIONS, & RESTRICTIONS

Deposit 1 night or 50% of stay (7-day cancellation for full refund) **Discounts** None **Credit Cards** AE, MC, V, D **Check-In/Out** 3–6 p.m./11 a.m. **Smoking** Back porch only **Pets** No **Kids** Yes **No-Nos** N/A **Minimum Stay** None **Open** All year **Host** Juanita Schuyler, 309 Main St., P.O. Box 91, Jerome 86331 **Phone** (520) 634-5094 **Fax** N/A **E-mail** innatjerome@sedona.net **Web** innatjerome.com

SURGEON'S HOUSE, Jerome

OVERALL ★★★★½ | QUALITY ★★★★ | VALUE ★★★★ | PRICE RANGE $100–$150

A rambling hillside residence designed by Arthur Kelly, one of the first black architects in Los Angeles, Surgeon's House was built so that Phelps Dodge could lure a doctor to this remote mountain mining town. The bed-and-breakfast encompasses two adjacent properties whose crumbled foundations enclose small pools and a waterfall. Views are unimpeded across the Verde Valley toward Sedona. The hostess, a charming conversationalist, bought the property from the mining company about a decade ago and lives on the lower level. Guests enter via the second level and climb a staircase lined with photos, paintings, quilts, garments, suitcases, and teddy bear to similarly decorated guest rooms.

SETTING & FACILITIES

Location Center, 2 blocks uphill from Main St. **Near** Museum, galleries, shops, state parks, national monuments **Building** 1916 Mediterranean reverse split-level hillside house **Grounds** Multiple level gardens w/ flagstone waterfall, pools, mural, sound system **Public Space** LR, sitting area w/ green plants, DR, porch **Food & Drink** Full breakfast in DR; 24-hour access to kitchen snacks & fridge beverages **Recreation** Boating, rafting, railroad excursions **Amenities & Services** Phone, in-house massage, personal walking tours, expeditions

ACCOMMODATIONS

Units 4 **All** Ceiling fan, radio, clock **Some** Kitchenette (1), private patio (1) **Bed & Bath** Kings (3), queen (1); all private baths, tub (2) **Favorites** Chauffeur's Quarters behind garage has kitchenette, private patio w/ garden; Master Suite is very large, w/ four-poster king bed, sitting room w/ daybed, walk-in closet, Verde Valley views **Comfort & Decor** Eclectic mix of furnishings, a clutter of items like teddy bears and Raggedy Ann dolls, and walls almost completely covered with paintings, posters, and framed articles; bathrooms range from black-and-white linoleum and tile to purple with stencils.

RATES, RESERVATIONS, & RESTRICTIONS

Deposit Full amount (under 4 days cancellation charged full amount & issued transferable gift certification w/ no expiration date) **Discounts** None **Credit Cards** MC, V **Check-In/Out** 4–6 p.m./11 a.m. **Smoking** No **Pets** Yes (prior arrangement required; owner has 2 cats; addition $25/night fee) **Kids** Yes (prior arrangement required) **No-Nos** N/A **Minimum Stay** None **Open** All year **Host** Andrea Prince, 101 Hill St., P.O. Box 998, Jerome 86331 **Phone** (928) 639-1452 or toll-free (800) 639-1452 **Fax** N/A **E-mail** andrea@surgeonshouse.com **Web** www.surgeonshouse.com

BRIAR WREATH INN BED & BREAKFAST, Prescott

OVERALL ★★★★½ | QUALITY ★★★★★ | VALUE ★★★★★ | PRICE RANGE
$100–$150

Entered via a sun porch with green carpeting and white wicker furniture, Briar Wreath has an elegant large living room with an antique slot machine and piano nook. Originally a ten-acre lumber mill owner's estate, Briar Wreath retains the original oak floors, walls, and stained ceilings. The remodeled green and white kitchen with its skylights and floral tile wallpaper is also noteworthy, as is the parquet dining table with its Waverly patterned window seating. The Suite and Provence room have private patios that double as private entrances. Proximity to the Historic Downtown District is another plus.

SETTING & FACILITIES
Location Downtown residential area, 6 blocks SE of town square **Near** Jerome, state parks, museums **Building** 1904 Craftsman-style house **Grounds** 1 acre w/ gazebo, flagstone pond, 500-year-old juniper trees **Public Space** LR, DR, sun porch **Food & Drink** Full breakfast in DR; afternoon wine; group lunches; private dinners; barbecues; 24-hour cookies, beverages **Recreation** Biking, horse riding, fishing **Amenities & Services** Jacuzzi, stationary bike, piano, weddings, receptions (100 outside), massage, aromatherapy

ACCOMMODATIONS
Units 4 **All** Robes, TV/VCR, ceiling fan, cassette/radio clock, hair dryers, bath amenities **Some** Private patio (2), sitting area (3) **Bed & Bath** Queen beds; all private baths, tub (3) **Favorites** Suite has sliding glass door to private deck, huge green & rose LR, separate bedroom w/ four-poster bed; Provence has wood paneling, green wallpaper, burgundy chairs, green plants growing in pot-bellied stove **Comfort & Decor** Luxurious French and English country feel with Waverly patterned soft furnishings, florals, hardwood floors, some carpeting, armoires, wicker, lace, wallpaper, wood paneling, green and dusty rose colors.

RATES, RESERVATIONS, & RESTRICTIONS
Deposit Credit card or 50% cash (5-day cancellation policy) **Discounts** Whole house rental, weekdays, winter (Nov. 1–May 1) **Credit Cards** AE, D **Check-In/Out** 3–6 p.m./11 a.m. **Smoking** No (ashtrays outside) **Pets** No (owners' 2 dogs stay in their living quarters) **Kids** Not encouraged **No-Nos** N/A **Minimum Stay** Only on holiday weekends **Open** All year **Hosts** Terry Fowler & Fred Munch, 232 S. Arizona St., Prescott 86303 **Phone** (928) 778-6048 **Fax** N/A **E-mail** office@briarwreath.com **Web** www.briarwreath.com

THE COTTAGES AT PRESCOTT COUNTRY INN BED & BREAKFAST, Prescott

OVERALL ★★★½ | QUALITY ★★★½ | VALUE ★★★★ | PRICE RANGE $69–$119

A throwback to the heyday of motor court motels, the Cottages at Prescott Country Inn would have even more appeal to nostalgia buffs if only there were a nearby diner with a flickering neon sign serving up sinkers to dunk in the hot joe. Jaguars, U-Haul vans, and cars with dogs, kids, and newly-weds jockey into the parking spaces ringing the interior of the horseshoe-shaped motor court. Don't look for too much luxury. But most cottages have two rooms and a kitchen, making them a good deal for self-sufficient travelers who want to spread out.

SETTING & FACILITIES

Location 3 blocks from downtown & town square **Near** Jerome, state parks, museums **Building** 1940s restored motor court motel **Grounds** Covered patio w/ barbecue, mostly central blacktop area lined w/ parking **Public Space** Front office **Food & Drink** Cont'l breakfast in room or 2 free passes to Waffles & More; coffee packs in room **Recreation** Biking, horse riding, fishing **Amenities & Services** Jacuzzi, weddings, parties

ACCOMMODATIONS

Units 12 **All** Cable TV, clock radio, coffeemaker, porch **Some** Kitchen (9), gas fireplace (10), AC, ceiling fan **Bed & Bath** King (6), queen (6), multiple beds (3); all private baths, tub (1) **Favorites** Honeymoon Mood Cottage (#16) has queen canopy bed in combination living/sleeping room, private deck; pink & blue Primrose Cottage has large room opening into kitchen, king canopy bed, armoire, rock fireplace, deck w/ swing; Hideaway Suite offers most privacy, has pantry, king canopy bed, tub, private deck **Comfort & Decor** Country style with eclectic mix of wood and bamboo furnishings, some dating back to 1940s and looking suitably worn, plain carpets, faded florals, plates, dolls, teddy bears, assorted bric-a-brac, small kitchens.

RATES, RESERVATIONS, & RESTRICTIONS

Deposit Credit card holds (72-hour cancellation) **Discounts** AAA, AARP **Credit Cards** AE, MC, V, DC **Check-In/Out** 3 p.m./11 a.m. **Smoking** Outside **Pets** Yes **Kids** Yes **No-Nos** N/A **Minimum Stay** None **Open** All year **Hosts** Rick & Janina Fenning, 503 S. Montezuma St., Prescott 86303 **Phone** (928) 445-7991 or toll-free (888) 757-0015 **Fax** (928) 717-1215 **E-mail** cottages@cableone.com **Web** www.virtualcities.com/ons/az/r/azr4801.htm

HASSAYAMPA INN, Prescott

OVERALL ★★★★ | QUALITY ★★★★ | VALUE ★★★★ | PRICE RANGE $109–$299

Half a block from the town square weekend action and across the street from the old Carnegie library and late-1800s Ellis Theater, the red brick

Hassayampa boasts bellmen opening doors and an operator for the 1920s gated elevator. Under the same ownership as Santa Fe's La Fonda since January 2001, the Hassayampa is "renewing" its original Mission look while keeping the best changes over the years. The Peacock Restaurant, whose breakfast specialties include lemon soufflé pancakes and crab cakes Benedict, is keeping its etched-glass peacock lady door and the booths that replaced the original diner counter.

SETTING & FACILITIES

Location Historic downtown **Near** Jerome, state parks, museums **Building** 1927 4-story Mission & Italian Renaissance hybrid designed by Henry Trost, a student of Chicago's famed Sullivan **Grounds** Brick-tiled gazebo area **Public Space** Spacious lobby w/ painted ceiling, lounges **Food & Drink** Full breakfast in restaurant; bar; lunch, dinner in restaurant **Recreation** Biking, horse riding, fishing **Amenities & Services** Banquet room, weddings, dance floor, 5 meeting rooms (45/room), broadband connections, elevator, limited room service hours, lobby piano

ACCOMMODATIONS

Units 68 rooms, including 11 suites **All** Cable TV, iron & ironing board, hair dryer, digital clock, phone w/ voice mail & data port **Some** Handicap-accessible **Bed & Bath** King (24), queen (27), 2 queens (17); all private baths, tub (many), jetted tub (1) **Favorites** Corner suites have best views; #304 has old glass w/ room number above door; #311, Norman Rockwell Suite, has Rockwell decor **Comfort & Decor** Eclectic mix under restoration to simulate Mission style with 1920s oak reproductions, peacock greens and blues, silk draperies, Victorian accents, wood bath ceilings; about ten rooms have original Castilian walnut furnishings with inlaid tiles, some leather desks, small hexagonal tiled baths.

RATES, RESERVATIONS, & RESTRICTIONS

Deposit Credit card holds (72-hour cancellation policy; 30 days for special events) **Discounts** Groups, romance getaway packages, golf packages **Credit Cards** AE, MC, V, D, DC **Check-In/Out** 3 p.m./noon **Smoking** In designated guest rooms **Pets** No **Kids** Yes **No-Nos** N/A **Minimum Stay** None **Open** All year **Host** Bradbury Corp., 122 E. Gurley St., Prescott 86301 **Phone** (928) 778-9434 or toll-free (800) 322-1927 **Fax** (928) 445-8590 **E-mail** inn1@mindspring.com **Web** www.hassayampainn.com

LYNX CREEK FARM, Prescott

OVERALL ★★★★½ | QUALITY ★★★★★ | VALUE ★★★★ | PRICE RANGE $85–$150

Among the earliest bed-and-breakfasts in the region, Lynx Creek Farm started in 1984 with a 500-square-foot guest house and added a luxurious log cabin building to meet demand in 1990. More recently, Lynx Creek added four stand-alone vacation units (no breakfast, but plenty of other luxuries; $160), two on the farm and two in town. For an extra $20, guests in the four log cabin rooms can add a second room and kitchenette to make a suite. This is also a working farm with pigs, milk goats, chickens, and

Nubian dogs. This is a popular family vacation spot for Phoenicians in summer, who come to escape the desert heat. Winter weekends, the decks with hot tubs and wood-burning stoves are popular.

SETTING & FACILITIES
Location Off AZ 69 Exit 291 (Onyx Rd.), 5 mi. east of Prescott **Near** Jerome, state parks, museums **Building** 1992 2-story log cabin & 1980 shingled guest house **Grounds** 32-acre organic farm w/ 200 adjoining acres of open gov't land w/ hiking trail **Public Space** Store, DR, patio **Food & Drink** Full breakfast in DR or on outside shaded deck; evening refreshments **Recreation** Biking, horse riding, fishing **Amenities & Services** Farm animal experiences

ACCOMMODATIONS
Units 6 B&B units, 4 stand-alone vacation units **All** Ceiling fan, AC, coffeemaker **Some** Private deck w/ hot tub (2), shared deck w/ hot tub & cool water pool (2), daybeds (2), loft w/ extra beds (1), kitchenette (optional) **Bed & Bath** King (6); all private baths, tub (6) **Favorites** White Wicker room has netting over bed, white wicker furniture, mirrored armoire, daybed, shared deck w/ hot tub & pool **Comfort & Decor** Themes range widely from cowboy to country garden; antique armoires, lanterns, quilts, wood paneling, wallpaper, view windows abound.

RATES, RESERVATIONS, & RESTRICTIONS
Deposit Credit card holds (14-day cancellation for refund minus 15% of total obligation) **Discounts** Multiple nights **Credit Cards** AE, MC, V, D **Check-In/Out** 4–6 p.m./11 a.m. **Smoking** No **Pets** Yes (if well behaved & supervised; owner has dogs, farm animals) **Kids** Yes (if well behaved & supervised) **No-Nos** N/A **Minimum Stay** 2 nights weekends, 4 units **Open** All year **Hosts** Greg & Wendy Temple, P.O. Box 4031, Prescott 86302 **Phone** (928) 778-9573 or toll-free (888) 778-9573 **Fax** N/A **E-mail** lcf@vacation-lodging.com **Web** vacation-lodging.com/lcf

PRESCOTT PINES INN BED & BREAKFAST, Prescott

OVERALL ★★★½ | QUALITY ★★★★ | VALUE ★★★★ | PRICE RANGE $65–$109 ($269 FOR CHALET)

Looking a bit like a roadside motel with wings on either side of the main building, Prescott Pines' creamy white and pink main house fronted by a rose arbor originally housed a family with 14 children on the old Haymore dairy farm. The main house has a reception desk and dining room. All the guest rooms are in guest houses with porches on either side of the main house. Though lacking in luxuries, Prescott Pines is popular with families because the price is reasonable, kitchens are available, and there is nothing breakable.

SETTING & FACILITIES
Location 1.3 mi. south of town square **Near** Jerome, state parks, museums **Building** 4 guest houses either side of 1934 former farm house **Grounds** Acre w/ pine, cedar, walnut,

& apple trees; garden, flagstone patio, swinging bench **Public Space** DR, reception area, patio **Food & Drink** Full breakfast in DR ($5); beverages, bottomless cookie jar, mints **Recreation** Biking, horse riding, fishing **Amenities & Services** Fax

ACCOMMODATIONS

Units 12 rooms, 1 3-BR chalet **All** Private outside entry, porch, ceiling fan, individual heat/AC, phone, cable TV **Some** Gas fireplace (3), kitchenette (5), full kitchen (3), track lighting, TV, clock radio **Bed & Bath** King (3), queen (9); all private baths, tub (10) **Favorites** 1,300-sq.-ft. 2-story chalet sleeping 8–10 has 3 BRs (king, 3 queens, queen futon), kitchen, wood-burning stove, DR, LR, deck w/ barbecue; Heather has king canopy bed, fireplace, glass-topped bamboo table, stained-glass nightlight; 2-room Foxglove has wood paneling, stencils, futon sofa, linoleum floor **Comfort & Decor** Simple country feel with partial wood paneling or floral wallpaper, tables, chairs, dresser, occasional Victorian accents, no fragile antiques.

RATES, RESERVATIONS, & RESTRICTIONS

Deposit 1 night or 50% for longer stays (7-day cancellation for 85% refund; 14–21 days for holidays, multiple rooms) **Discounts** Senior, midweek, corp., AAA, Internet, extended stays **Credit Cards** MC, V **Check-In/Out** 3–7 p.m./noon **Smoking** No **Pets** No **Kids** Yes **No-Nos** N/A **Minimum Stay** None **Open** All year **Hosts** Harry & Debbie Allen, 901 White Spar Rd., Prescott 86303 **Phone** (928) 445-7270 or toll-free (800) 541-5374 **Fax** (928) 778-3665 **E-mail** info@prescottpinesinn.com **Web** www.prescottpinesinn.com

CHEZ RINA, *Wickenburg*

OVERALL ★★★★½ | QUALITY ★★★★½ | VALUE ★★★★ | PRICE RANGE $85–$200

It is hard to picture a better place to relax in the high desert just an hour north of Phoenix. The front yard is landscaped with cacti, and the spacious back yard is equipped for comfort, with a barbecue, hot tub, fountain, artistic knickknacks, orange Mexican pottery, and plenty of chairs for viewing the gorgeous surroundings. Restaurant row runs along nearby AZ 60, and the nearby Desert Caballeros Museum is renowned. The hostess is a busy woman renovating a nearby motel, but she has enough friends around to make sure guests are taken care of. The detached casitas offer the most privacy and the best views and are best for long stays and kids.

SETTING & FACILITIES

Location In high desert, 60 mi. NW of Phoenix on AZ 93; from junction of AZ 93 & 60, go west on AZ 60 and then south on Saguaro Dr. to 4th house **Near** Museum, restaurants, mine tour, cattle ranches **Building** Recent vintage ranch house w/ 2 attached guest rooms & 2 detached casitas **Grounds** 3.5 acres w/ saguaro, palo verde, cacti, Mexican pottery, fountain overlooking spacious neighborhood back yards & mountains **Public Space** Mainly outdoor grounds, though guests are welcome to visit main house **Food & Drink** Breakfast served by customized arrangement **Recreation** Horses, golf **Amenities & Services** French & English spoken, hot tub, barbecue, free washer/dryer

ACCOMMODATIONS

Units 4 guest rooms, includes 1 detached 2-BR casita, 1 detached 1-BR, & 2 rooms w/ private entrances attached to main house **All** Wood ceiling, ceiling fan, coffeemaker, fridge, microwave oven **Some** Full fridge (1), full kitchen (2), mountain views from porch (2) **Bed & Bath** Queens (3), double (1); all private baths **Favorites** Dominic, a 2-BR detached casita w/ 2 full baths, beam ceiling, Southwest LR **Comfort & Decor** Simple, clean, uncluttered artsy Southwest flavor with plenty of wood, seating, big beds.

RATES, RESERVATIONS, & RESTRICTIONS

Deposit None **Discounts** None **Credit Cards** None (cash or checks only) **Check-In/Out** Customizable **Smoking** Outside only **Pets** Requires permission, 3 cats roam outside **Kids** Yes **No-Nos** N/A **Minimum Stay** None **Open** All year **Host** Rina Theriault, 701 S. Saguaro Dr., Wickenburg 85390 **Phone** (520) 684-0776 **Fax** (520) 684-1255 **E-mail** N/A **Web** N/A

Nevada

Las Vegas's 130,000 hotel rooms and 43 Strip casinos attract over 35 million visitors a year. But the closest thing in Vegas to a bed-and-breakfast is a wedding chapel–theme hotel dishing up a continental breakfast in the vicinity of tattoo parlors and bail bond offices. For a while a ritzy bed-and-breakfast was operating among the tall ponderosa pines and shady oaks of Mt. Charleston, 45 miles north of Las Vegas. But the southern Nevada bed-and-breakfast scene has mostly been coming up double zeros.

Nevada's meager bed-and-breakfast action is centered in the Reno-Tahoe territory around Carson City, Virginia City, and Genoa. Nestled in the Sierra Nevada foothills 20 miles east of Lake Tahoe and 450 miles north of Las Vegas, Genoa was known as Mormon Station when it became modern Nevada's first permanent settlement in 1851. The Mormon Station State Historic Park and Genoa Courthouse Museum are open from May to October.

Carson City and the silver-domed state Capitol are 12 miles north of Genoa. The Carson City mint, which struck Virginia City silver into dollars in the late nineteenth century, now houses the State Museum. The Virginia & Truckee Railroad's 21-mile route hauling precious metals from Virginia City's Comstock Lode to Carson City is celebrated at the Nevada State Railroad Museum. Virginia City, a touristy, Old West saloon town with annoying admission charges, is midway between Carson City and Reno.

About two hours west of Virginia City is Lake Tahoe, the world's second largest alpine lake. Lake Tahoe's bed-and-breakfasts are on the California side of the border, except for one in Nevada's Incline Village ski resort. An hour east of Virginia City on US 50 in Pony Express territory is Fallon, best known for the U.S. Navy Top Gun training center, the excellent Churchill County Museum, and heart o' gold cantaloupes.

Reaching Nevada's northernmost bed-and-breakfasts in cowboy country requires about a half-day drive from Reno or Virginia City toward Winnemucca and the Idaho border. The old ghost town of Unionville, about 30 miles south of Winnemucca, is where Samuel Clemens gave gold mining a fling before a career change to newspaper writing under the name Mark Twain for Virginia City's Territorial Enterprise. Paradise Valley, a scenic cattle ranching area, is 35 miles north of Winnemucca. Between Memorial Day and Labor Day, Winnemucca events include a mule show, a Basque festival, an Indian powwow, and the state's oldest rodeo.

Interstate 80 runs east from Winnemucca through the gold mining town of Battle Mountain en route to Elko. Elko's winter Cowboy Poetry Gathering attracts luminaries like Baxter Black. The National Basque Festival is in July, and September is Elko's classic car festival.

FOR MORE INFORMATION

Northern Nevada Bed & Breakfast Guild
c/o Wild Rose Inn
P.O. Box 605
Genoa, NV 89411
This group publishes a brochure with member information.

Nevada Commission on Tourism
401 N. Carson St.
Carson City, NV 89701
(775) 687-4322 or toll-free (877) 2000-nev. www.travelnevada.com or www.2000nevada.com
This group publishers accommodation and travel guides.

The Nevada Travel Network
www.nevadatravel.net

Nevada

DEER RUN RANCH BED & BREAKFAST, Carson City

OVERALL ★★★★ | QUALITY ★★★★ | VALUE ★★★★ | PRICE RANGE $85–$115

Across the road from Washoe Lake and fronted by alfalfa fields and Hay for Sale signs, Deer Run Ranch provides seating near a private pond alive with dragonflies and bullfrogs in summer. A very informal, art-filled place for nature lovers to relax and unwind. Deer are commonly spotted, owls screech and coyotes howl at night, and eagles and hawks circle overhead. Wood doors and a map-lined hallway separate the proprietors, an architect and a potter with a studio here, from the guest quarters, which include a private living room and patio. Families rent the place in summer, business-people stop by in winter, and couples come for weekend escapes.

SETTING & FACILITIES

Location From NV 395 Exit 42 north of Carson City, go 3.8 mi. east on East Lake Blvd. **Near** State & county parks, museums, Virginia City, Genoa, Reno, Lake Tahoe, Pyramid Lake **Building** 1983–4 passive-solar, timber-framed contemporary ranch-style house **Grounds** Pond, organic vegetable & wildflower garden, fruit trees, large alfalfa field **Public Space** Patio, living room w/ fireplace, DR **Food & Drink** Full breakfast in DR or on patio; beverage & snack starter pack; guest fridge **Recreation** Fishing, boating, biking, hang gliding, bird-watching, winter sports **Amenities & Services** Wood pool, horseshoes, phone (modem), TV/VCR

ACCOMMODATIONS

Units 2 rooms, each w/ private bath off hallway outside room **All** Robes, ceiling fan, clock radio, individual furnace heat **Some** Chief Winnemucca photo **Bed & Bath** Queen bed (2); each has private bath w/ tub **Favorites** Navajo Room has Navajo rugs, sand painting, window seat; Old Ranch Room has photos of area's early days **Comfort & Decor** Comfortable and informal, with window seats, reading lights, and lots of art work, including hostess's father's photographs

RATES, RESERVATIONS, & RESTRICTIONS

Deposit Credit card holds (10 days cancellation for full refund minus $10) **Discounts** Regular corp. customers **Credit Cards** AE, MC, V, D **Check-In/Out** 4–6 p.m./11 a.m. **Smoking** Outdoors & patios only; no cigars **Pets** No (owners have dogs, cats) **Kids** Yes (over age 6; need own room) **No-Nos** N/A **Minimum Stay** 2 nights on holidays, special-event weekends **Open** All year **Hosts** Muffy & David Vhay, 5440 Eastlake Blvd., Carson City 89704 **Phone** (775) 882-3643 **Fax** N/A **E-mail** N/A **Web** www.virtualcities.com/nv/deerrun.htm

ONCE UPON A TIME BED AND BREAKFAST, Elko

OVERALL ★★★½ | QUALITY ★★★½ | VALUE ★★★★ | PRICE RANGE $65–$75

A cowboy mural on the front of a garage with a 1932 Packard Roadster marks arrival at Once Upon a Time. A room with a Western cityscape wall mural is devoted to an elaborate model train setup with buildings and drawbridges. The Treasure of Sierra Madre bedroom has family heirlooms, like an old gold scale from a prospector grandfather, lanterns, mining lamps, and Civil War and logging photos. A kitchen counter makes it possible to sit in the dining room and chat with the hostess while breakfast is cooking. Many walls are covered with the host's drawings of old movie stars like Mary Pickford, W. C. Fields, and the Little Rascals.

SETTING & FACILITIES

Location Near downtown Elko **Near** Mountains, forests, lakes, casinos **Building** 1958 ranch style **Grounds** Wood deck, trees w/ hammock **Public Space** Living room w/ large-screen TV & stereo, DR, model train room, back porch **Food & Drink** Full breakfast in DR; outdoor guest barbecue, microwave use **Recreation** Skiing, golf **Amenities & Services** Model train room

ACCOMMODATIONS

Units 3 rooms, 2 w/ shared bath **All** AC, electric blanket, quilt, TV trays & chairs in closet, clock cassette radio **Some** Lighted closet **Bed & Bath** Queen beds; 1 private bath, 1 shared bath **Favorites** Pink Casablanca Bedroom has lace canopy bed w/ star quilt, optional feather mattress, sitting area, private bath w/ walk-in shower **Comfort & Decor** Mirrored closets, wood shutters, valences, movie star drawings, and themes varying from cowboys and Indians to mining

RATES, RESERVATIONS, & RESTRICTIONS

Deposit Credit card (7 days for full refund; otherwise forfeit 1 night) **Discounts** 3-night minimum package deals, extended stays **Credit Cards** AE, MC, V, D, DC **Check-In/Out** 3 p.m./11a.m. **Smoking** Outside on back porch **Pets** Yes (by prior arrangement only; owners have dog) **Kids** Yes (age 10 and older) **No-Nos** N/A **Minimum Stay** None **Open** All year **Hosts** Madeline & Michael Johnson, 537 14th St., Elko 89801 **Phone** (775) 738-1200 **Fax** N/A **E-mail** mjohnson@elko-nv.com **Web** N/A

THE 1906 HOUSE, Fallon

OVERALL ★★★½ | QUALITY ★★★½ | VALUE ★★★★ | PRICE RANGE $65

A turreted two-story pink building with a green roof along what Life magazine called "the loneliest road in America" (US 50), the 1906 House is a Fallon landmark faithfully restored by a former U.S. Navy officer and his wife. Beyond the wood and beveled-glass front door are the original uranium Vaseline glass lamp fixtures and hand-carved Tahoe pine woodwork. The parlor has a hardwood fireplace, and dining room cabinets display the crystal and china service. Around the corner is a thriving, almost old-fashioned small-town Main Street where Mexican food and hints of trendiness complement casinos. The clientele ranges from businesspeople during the week to families on weekends.

SETTING & FACILITIES

Location Center of town, on US 50 (S. Carson St.) 1 block south of Main St. **Near** U.S. Navy "Top Gun" training center, state parks, ghost towns, wildlife refuge **Building** 1904 classic Queen Anne Victorian **Grounds** Small grass & brick patio **Public Space** Parlor, DR, 2nd floor sitting area, back porch w/ half bath **Food & Drink** Full breakfast in DR; afternoon tea (iced in summer, hot in winter) **Recreation** Boating, fishing, golf, bird-watching **Amenities & Services** Phone, meetings (up to 45), tea parties

ACCOMMODATIONS

Units 2 guest rooms w/ shared bath, 1 w/ private bath (under renovation), 1 overflow room (doubles as office) **All** TV/VCR, digital clock radio **Some** Internet access (1) **Bed & Bath** Queen beds (all rooms); 1 private bath, 1 shared bath **Favorites** Rose Room in witch's hat turret has mansion bed, triple lace draperies, stenciling, red velvet fainting couch, Carolina mirror dresser; Violet Room has purple-and-green theme, iron sleigh bed, wicker chaise longue **Comfort & Decor** White walls and angled ceilings, a mix of antique and reproduction period furnishings; bath has large tiled shower w/ seat, floor and ceiling wallpaper, and twisting emergency stairway exit w/ "yellow brick road" stencils; hallway sitting area has family picture nook, floral chairs and carpets

RATES, RESERVATIONS, & RESTRICTIONS

Deposit 1 night (optional, if confirmation needed) **Discounts** None **Credit Cards** None (cash or check only) **Check-In/Out** 3 p.m./ 11 a.m. **Smoking** No **Pets** No (rare exceptions for older dogs; owners have 2 terriers) **Kids** Yes (over age 12) **No-Nos** Not having a good time **Minimum Stay** None **Open** All year **Hosts** Jerry & Suzanne Noonkester, 10 S. Carson St., Fallon 89406 **Phone** (775) 428-1906 **Fax** N/A **E-mail** the1906house@oasisol.com **Web** www.geocities.com/eureka/1219

WILD ROSE INN, *Genoa*

OVERALL ★★★★½ | QUALITY ★★★★½ | VALUE ★★★★ | PRICE RANGE $115–$180

Fronted by an elm tree with a swing and occasional grazing deer, the Wild Rose's beveled-glass doors open onto hardwood floors with Oriental-style rugs, antique Queen Anne chairs, red leather sofas, an antique oak roll-top desk, an Illinois butter churn, a Steinway grand piano, and watercolor art for sale. Contemporary beveled-glass dining room cabinets hold china and crystal. Though near summer and winter resorts like Lake Tahoe and Kirkwood, many guests walk to the 1865 Genoa Courthouse Museum. Others head down the block to the Genoa Bar, an 1800s gentleman's saloon with an 1840s diamond dust mirror, red oil lamps, and a red pool table over a trap door.

SETTING & FACILITIES

Location From Carson City go 8 mi. south on NV 395 and 4 mi. west on Genoa Lane (NV 206) **Near** Mormon Station State Park, Lake Tahoe, Carson City, Virginia City, Kirkwood ski resort **Building** 1989 replica Queen Anne Victorian **Grounds** 1.5 acres of gardens and natural landscape merging into native sage, locust, & cottonwoods **Public Space** Living room, DR, veranda **Food & Drink** Full breakfast in DR; afternoon full English tea; 24-hour snacks, beverages, & liquors in DR **Recreation** Gliding, mountain biking, boating, fishing, tennis, golf, winter sports, hot springs **Amenities & Services** Weddings, receptions, groups (up to 30), Douglas County Airport pick-up service (Minden; small planes)

ACCOMMODATIONS

Units 5 guest rooms, including 3d-floor penthouse suite **All** Ceiling fans, air-conditioning, digital clock radio **Some** Fridge (1), wet bar (1), optional TV (1) **Bed & Bath** King (1), queen beds (4); all private baths, tubs (4) **Favorites** Gables is 3d-floor penthouse w/ fridge, wet bar, 2 queen beds, day bed, sitting area, pink curtained skylight, 2 pedestal sinks **Comfort & Decor** Contemporary Victorian style w/ carpeting, wicker and wood furnishings, brass bed frames, sitting areas

RATES, RESERVATIONS, & RESTRICTIONS

Deposit Credit card (1-week cancellation for full refund minus $10 fee) **Discounts** Group, midweek corp. **Credit Cards** AE, MC, V **Check-In/Out** 4 p.m./11 a.m. **Smoking** Outside only **Pets** No (owner has cat) **Kids** Yes (over age 12) **No-Nos** N/A **Minimum Stay** None **Open** All year **Host** Sue Haugnes, 2332 Main St., P.O. Box 605, Genoa 89411 **Phone** (775) 783-9763 or toll-free (877) 819-4225 **Fax** (775) 783-9763 **E-mail** wildrose@pyramid.net **Web** wildrose-inn.com

HAUS BAVARIA BED AND BREAKFAST INN, Incline Village

OVERALL ★★★★ | QUALITY ★★★★ | VALUE ★★★★ | PRICE RANGE $99–$245

Nestled in the Sierra Nevada Mountains, the only bed-and-breakfast on the Nevada side of Lake Tahoe, Haus Bavaria is an alpine-style ski lodge. The upstairs living room has beam ceilings, knotty pine wood paneling, a flagstone fireplace, leather chairs and sofa, Bavarian bric-a-brac, and a balcony fronted by tall pine trees. The balconied rooms are all up a carpeted staircase with large angled windows. Late risers choose rooms with a west-facing exposure, and those wanting the early morning sun go for the east side. Though there are nearby beaches and casinos for summer play, the bed-and-breakfast gets most of its business for the winter ski slopes.

SETTING & FACILITIES

Location North shore of Lake Tahoe, between Crystal Bay & Sand Harbor **Near** Heavenly Valley ski area, lake, beaches, forest, casinos **Building** 1980 2-story European style guest house **Grounds** Flagstone pathways w/ aspens, conifers, manzanita, & summer flowers **Public Space** Upstairs lounge, living room, DR, patio **Food & Drink** Full breakfast in

DR **Recreation** Boating, fishing, mountain biking, tennis, golf, winter sports **Amenities & Services** Private beach access, ski rack, weddings, receptions (20 people)

ACCOMMODATIONS
Units 5 upstairs rooms **All** Balcony, double-pane windows, clock radio, modem jack, fan **Some** TV (2), desk (4), down comforter **Bed & Bath** King (4), queen bed (1); all private baths, tub (1) **Favorites** Room #2 in the back has yard views & faces west for late sleepers **Comfort & Decor** White walls and carpet, dark Douglas fir doors and trim, teak bureau and bed tables, sliding glass balcony door

RATES, RESERVATIONS, & RESTRICTIONS
Deposit 1 night (30 days for full refund minus $15 fee) **Discounts** Groups, extended stays **Credit Cards** AE, MC, V, D **Check-In/Out** 3 p.m./11 a.m. **Smoking** No **Pets** No (owner has 2 cats) **Kids** Yes (over age 12) **No-Nos** N/A **Minimum Stay** None **Open** All year **Host** Bick Hewitt, 593 N. Dyer Circle, P.O. Box 9079, Incline Village 89452 **Phone** (775) 831-6122; (800) 731-6222 **Fax** (775) 831-1238 **E-mail** N/A **Web** www.hausbavaria.com

STONEHOUSE COUNTRY INN, *Paradise Valley*

OVERALL ★★★★ | QUALITY ★★★★ | VALUE ★★★★ | PRICE RANGE $40–$95

A working cattle ranch with a private quail- and pheasant-hunting preserve, the living room at Stonehouse Country Inn has four soft sofas, ceiling fans, a burl table, old grain rakes, hay forks and a washboard around the fireplace, and a huge steelhead trophy above a big-screen TV and stereo. The proprietor's rack of working cowboy hats decorates the entrance near a table with brochures like "Wow That Cow! How Cattle Enrich Our Lives . . . and Enhance the Planet." Guest rooms are upstairs and have flexible bed arrangements, even bunks. Nearby Paradise Valley is worth exploring—it's part ghost town surrounded by cattle ranches.

SETTING & FACILITIES
Location From Winnemucca go 22 mi. north on US 95 and 13 mi. east on NV 290 **Near** Winnemucca, Unionville **Building** 1991 3-story, 7,000-sq.-ft. country house **Grounds** 1,100 acres of cattle pasture, meadows, lawns, large cottonwood trees, creek **Public Space** Enclosed front porch, DR, living room **Food & Drink** Cont'l breakfast in DR; self-service bar; barbecue & other meals by arrangement **Recreation** Hunting, fishing, biking, horse riding **Amenities & Services** Weddings, reunions, groups (400), hot tub, 5 RV hookups (30-ft. limit)

ACCOMMODATIONS
Units 7 **All** Portable fan, clock, guest journal **Some** Window sitting area **Bed & Bath** Kings (5), singles/twins/doubles (5); 5 private baths w/ tub, 1 shared bath **Favorites** Garvey Suite is largest, overlooks meadows & valley; has gold, purple, green & floral decor; leather & velvet chairs; large dresser; and king & single bed **Comfort & Decor** Clean modern country decor with Western touches; nothing fancy

RATES, RESERVATIONS, & RESTRICTIONS
Deposit None (but reservations required) **Discounts** Group **Credit Cards** None (cash or check only) **Check-In/Out** 4–6 p.m./11 a.m. (flexible) **Smoking** No **Pets** Dogs allowed outside (in kennels) during hunting season; horses welcome **Kids** Yes **No-Nos** N/A **Minimum Stay** None **Open** March–December **Host** Steve Lucas, P.O. Box 77, Paradise Valley 89426 **Phone** (775) 578-3530 **Fax** (775) 578-3716 **E-mail** stonehouse@m-hip.com **Web** stonehouse.freeservers.com

OLD PIONEER GARDEN COUNTRY INN, *Unionville*

OVERALL ★★★★½ | QUALITY ★★★★ | VALUE ★★★★★ | PRICE RANGE $75–$95

Unionville (population 20), a high-desert ghost town where Mark Twain failed as a gold miner before launching a brilliant writing career, is where a World War II navy fighter pilot from the U.S.S. Enterprise and his family fashion twig furniture and operate Old Pioneer Garden. It is also a farm, and at night bells tinkle and sheep bleat. Mrs. B's, the nearest restaurant, is inside Mr. B's Casino at the I-80 Mill City truck stop, where waitresses call patrons "sweetie." The local tungsten mine has been closed for 30 years, but the hosts have been steadily renovating 1860s houses, each better than the last and furnished like a time warp to the 1930s and 1940s.

SETTING & FACILITIES
Location From I-80 Mill City/Unionville Exit 32 mi. south of Winnemucca, go 17 mi. south on NV 400 to pavement's end and then 3 mi. on dirt road at Unionville historic marker **Near** Ghost towns, old mines, hot springs, Mark Twain cabin, Black Rock Desert **Building** 1860s pioneer stone, adobe & wood ranch houses & barn (Tack House) **Grounds** Fenced pastures w/ sheep, geese, horses **Public Space** Each house has kitchen, DR, living room, porch; play room (1) **Food & Drink** Full breakfast in Talcott House (owner's home) kitchen or outdoor gazebo; dinners by advance arrangement **Recreation** Fishing, boating,

hunting, horse riding, fossil hunting, bird-watching **Amenities & Services** Phone, pool table, play room, baby grand piano, antiques shop, goat milking-and goose egg–hunting lessons, weddings, groups, special events

ACCOMMODATIONS

Units 11 rooms, 6 w/ private baths **All** Framed original art **Some** Ceiling fan (4), fireplace (2), porch (4) **Bed & Bath** Queen beds (2), doubles (9); tubs (3), 6 private baths, 5 rooms w/ shared baths **Favorites** In Field House, Ocean View Hotel Apartment sign is above double doors separating sitting room w/ pasture & mountain views from queen bedroom w/ bird lamps, old travel trunks, rocking chair, sofas, mid–twentieth-century lampshades **Comfort & Decor** Relaxed country style with upholstered 1930s stuffed sofas and chairs, twig furniture, vintage lampshades, wood floors with throw rugs, old framed mirrors, varied art, and Western memorabilia

RATES, RESERVATIONS, & RESTRICTIONS

Deposit Credit card or $20 (refundable) **Discounts** Groups, travel agents **Credit Cards** None (cash or checks only) **Check-In/Out** 4–6 p.m./11 a.m. **Smoking** Outside only **Pets** Yes (1 room has pet door; owners have several cats, dogs; horses welcome) **Kids** Yes **No-Nos** N/A **Minimum Stay** None **Open** All year **Hosts** Lew & Mitzi Jones, 2805 Unionville Rd., Unionville 89418 **Phone** (775) 538-7585 **Fax** N/A **E-mail** catwomaninlove@yahoo.com **Web** www.virtualcities.com/nv/oldpioneer.htm

CHOLLAR MANSION, *Virginia City*

OVERALL ★★★½ | QUALITY ★★★★ | VALUE ★★★★ | PRICE RANGE $75–$125

An elegantly furnished former mine office and mining superintendent's residence with 12-foot-high ceilings and foot-thick wood floors, the Chollar Mansion has an old mine paymaster's booth and basement vault for storing Comstock Lode gold and silver. The location is convenient, overlooking the Chollar Mine and the Virginia and Truckee Railroad tracks, a short uphill walk from all the touristy Virginia City action on C Street. Compared to the Gold Hill Hotel, the Chollar Mansion makes a quiet retreat. But the long-term future of the bed-and-breakfast is in some doubt, as the owner was trying to sell the house for a bundle of bullion and the real estate agent was touting alternate uses for the property.

SETTING & FACILITIES

Location On the outskirts of Virginia City's historic downtown **Near** Museums, restaurants, saloons, Carson City, Reno, Lake Tahoe **Building** 1862 3-story red brick w/ white wood trim former mine office & adjacent 1870 cottage **Grounds** Small courtyard and side gardens **Public Space** Men's parlor, library, DR **Food & Drink** Cont'l breakfast in downstairs DR **Recreation** Biking, horse riding **Amenities & Services** Weddings, bookstore, house tours

ACCOMMODATIONS

Units 3 rooms in main house, 1 cottage across courtyard; 2 units share bath **All** TV, digital clock radio, ceiling fan **Some** N/A **Bed & Bath** King (2), queen (2); 1 shared bath, 2 private baths, tub (1) **Favorites** Suite #1 occupies half of house downstairs, has sitting room, florals, wood floor w/ room-size carpet **Comfort & Decor** Plaster walls, period antique furnishings

RATES, RESERVATIONS, & RESTRICTIONS

Deposit 1 night or 50% (14-day cancellation for refund minus $10; otherwise refund only if re-rented) **Discounts** None **Credit Cards** None (cash or traveler's checks only) **Check-In/Out** 2–6 p.m./11 a.m. **Smoking** No (outside only) **Pets** No (owners have 2 cats) **Kids** Yes (in cottage room only; $15/child; 2-child maximum) **No-Nos** N/A **Minimum Stay** None (except for special events) **Open** All year **Hosts** Ken & Kay Benton, P.O. Box 889, 565 S. D St., Virginia City 89440 **Phone** (702) 847-9777 **Fax** N/A **E-mail** N/A **Web** N/A

THE CROOKED HOUSE, Virginia City

OVERALL ★★★ | QUALITY ★★★★ | VALUE ★★★★ | PRICE RANGE $65–$125

A few blocks downhill from C Street's touristy action, Crooked House alternated between boarding house and private residence until restored to a late-1800s Comstock Lode ambience as a bed-and-breakfast in 1995. The front porch and funky rear upstairs balcony offer panoramas of the surrounding town and hillsides, which are rich in gold- and silver-mining history. The Suite and Gold Room, which share a bath, are connecting rooms with wood sleigh beds and hide-a-beds that combine into a two-bedroom family room sleeping six. Lovers of early morning light should choose the Suite or Rose Rooms to awaken at sunrise; late sleepers will be happier in the east-facing Gold and Peacock Rooms. When the proprietor leaves on airline business, the woman next door ministers to guests.

SETTING & FACILITIES

Location 3 blocks downhill from historic C St. **Near** Museums, restaurants, saloons, Carson City, Reno, Lake Tahoe **Building** 1876 faded lavender & white multistory wood Victorian **Grounds** Side yard & back garden w/ flagstone and gnarled trees **Public Space** Parlor, DR, front & back verandas **Food & Drink** Extended breakfast in DR **Recreation** Biking, horse riding **Amenities & Services** Emergency house phone

ACCOMMODATIONS

Units 4 **All** TV, drinking water **Some** N/A **Bed & Bath** Queen (4); 2 private baths, 1 shared bath **Favorites** Peacock room has private bath w/ claw-foot tub & shower; the suite is more spacious, but shares a shower w/ Gold Room; Rose room has four-poster bed and private bath w/ claw-foot tub **Comfort & Decor** White-and-black carpeted wood staircase leads to rooms w/ replica late-1800s wallpaper, hanging chandeliers, and comfortable antique period furnishings

RATES, RESERVATIONS, & RESTRICTIONS

Deposit Credit card or full cash deposit (14-day cancellation for full refund; otherwise refunds only for nights room is re-rented) **Discounts** Multiple room & whole house group & family rentals **Credit Cards** MC, V, D **Check-In/Out** 3 p.m./11 a.m. **Smoking** No (veranda or porch only) **Pets** Yes **Kids** Yes **No-Nos** N/A **Minimum Stay** 2 nights on special event weekends **Open** All year **Host** Patrick Gilmore, 8 S. "F" St., Virginia City 89440 **Phone** (775) 847-4447 or toll-free (800) 340-6333 **Fax** N/A **E-mail** crooked-house@gbis.com **Web** www.bbonline.com/nv/crookedhouse

GOLD HILL HOTEL, Virginia City

OVERALL ★★★½ | QUALITY ★★★★ | VALUE ★★★★ | PRICE RANGE $45–$145
(MORE FOR HOUSES)

On a steep hillside overlooking the highway and surrounded by Comstock Lode mines and old miner's shacks, the Gold Hill Hotel calls itself Nevada's oldest hotel and claims a pair of benign ghosts, William and Rosie. The four original historic hotel rooms above the bar in front are small enough that the canopy bed in the honeymoon favorite (#4) leaves no room for a ceiling fan, though the bath holds a claw-foot tub. The newer rooms, though less historic, are quieter and can be impressively spacious, the best having windowed sitting areas and wood-burning fireplaces. Motorcyclists favor the bar; summer weekends are packed with wedding receptions.

SETTING & FACILITIES

Location In Gold Hill, 1 mi. south of Virginia City on NV 342 **Near** Museums, restaurants, saloons, Carson City, Reno, Lake Tahoe **Building** 1859 multistory rubble, stone, & piled mortar hillside construction w/ newer additions **Grounds** Across street is brick and flagstone area w/ gazebo **Public Space** Lobby, bar, DR **Food & Drink** Cont'l breakfast in DR; French restaurant serves lunch & dinner Mon.–Sat., Sunday champagne brunch; bar is open evenings, all day Fri.–Sun. **Recreation** Boating, fishing, winter sports **Amenities & Services** Weddings, groups (150), bookstore, steam train stop (summer runs to Virginia City), lectures, special events

ACCOMMODATIONS

Units 18 rooms, including 4 houses and duplex **All** Clock radio, phone **Some** Comforter, ceiling fan, AC, balcony, TV, kitchen, claw-foot tub, fireplace, fridge **Bed & Bath** Kings, queens, doubles; all private baths, tubs (15) **Favorites** #6, 7, 9, & 10 have wood-burning fireplace, king bed, spacious sitting area by window, balcony **Comfort & Decor** Each room is a variation on period decor, with antiques, vintage wallpaper, and color schemes

RATES, RESERVATIONS, & RESTRICTIONS

Deposit Credit card holds (24-hour cancellation; 2-week notice for block booking) **Discounts** Groups, theater packages **Credit Cards** MC, V **Check-In/Out** 3 p.m./11 a.m. **Smoking** Yes (not in dining room) **Pets** Yes (3 units only) **Kids** Yes **No-Nos** N/A **Minimum Stay** None **Open** All year **Hosts** Carol & Bill Fain, P.O. Box 70, Virginia City 89440 **Phone** (775) 847-0111 **Fax** (775) 847-0604 **E-mail** N/A **Web** www.goldhillhotel.net

New Mexico

New Mexico borders Arizona in the west, Mexico in the southwest, Texas in the east and southeast, Colorado in the north, Oklahoma's Panhandle in the northeast, and Utah in the Four Corners (northwest). Spanish colonial, Mexican, and Native American influences are particularly pronounced here. When the glaciers of the last major Ice Age swept across much of North America 11,000 years ago, New Mexico was a Native American refuge.

Ancient petroglyphs, archaeological ruins, and functioning Native American pueblos and communities are found throughout New Mexico. Each of New Mexico's 22 Native American pueblos and tribes is a sovereign government with its own laws, off-limits areas, restrictions, and fees (e.g., for entry and photography). Native American arts-and-crafts fairs, turquoise and silver jewelry, pottery, dance ceremonies, rug auctions, and festivals are powerful attractions. New Mexico bed-and-breakfasts often book months in advance when Native American events are scheduled nearby.

New Mexico has approximately 270 bed-and-breakfasts, many of which are seasonal or part-time businesses that are difficult to locate or contact. Most of the 70 or so members of the New Mexico Bed & Breakfast Association strive to distinguish themselves as professional innkeepers and tend to be relatively safe bets. The vast majority of New Mexico's bed-and-breakfasts are concentrated in the Central region around Albuquerque and in the North Central region around Santa Fe and Taos.

The Albuquerque airport in central New Mexico is a common entry point for the state. Albuquerque's museums, cultural centers, and nearby Native American pueblos are often bypassed in the rush to traverse the 63 miles to Santa Fe. Santa Fe is the state capital, and it is hard to top for history, culture, shopping, restaurants, museums, and Southwestern ambience. Villages like Corrales, Bernalillo, and Algodones are on the old El Camino Real paralleling Interstate 25 between Albuquerque and Santa Fe.

Northeast New Mexico extends into the prairies and has few bed-and-breakfasts, being more of a scenic stopping place en route to Taos or Santa Fe from the Midwest. Bed-and-breakfasts are also scarce outside Farmington in the Northwest. Southeast bed-and-breakfasts are clustered around Cloudcroft, Ruidoso, and Lincoln. Southwest New Mexico has well over a dozen bed-and-breakfasts scattered among cities like San Antonio, Socorro, Hillsboro, Kingston, Silver City, Gila, Mesilla, and Las Cruces.

FOR MORE INFORMATION

New Mexico Bed & Breakfast Assoc. (inspects its members), P.O. Box 2925, Santa Fe, NM 87504. Toll-free (800) 661-6649, www.nmbba.org.

New Mexico Dept. of Tourism (state tourism info), phone (505) 827-7400 or toll-free (800) 733-6396, e-mail enchantment@newmexico.org, www.newmexico.org.

New Mexico Indian Tourism Assoc., P.O. Box 340, Church Rock, NM 87311, phone (505) 726-0878.

New Mexico Vacation Guide (issued annually). Published by New Mexico Magazine (for complimentary distribution by New Mexico Department of Tourism), www.nmmagazine.com.

Santa Fe Visitor Information Center, 491 Old Santa Fe Trail, P.O. Box 20002, Santa Fe, NM 87503, phone (505) 827-7336, e-mail vcenter@state.nm.us, www.santafe.org.

Taos County Chamber of Commerce, P.O. Drawer I, Taos, NM 87571, phone (505) 758-3873 or toll-free (800) 732-8267, e-mail info@taoschamber.com, www.taoschamber.com.

Southeast

From the San Andreas Mountains north of Alamogordo and Carrizozo, southeast New Mexico extends east to Clovis, Hobbs, and west Texas's sparsely populated Panhandle Plains. Southeast New Mexico stretches south through Roswell and Carlsbad to the vast open Big Bend country desert of west Texas. Towns are few and far between in the vast desert expanses, and the few bed-and-breakfasts are mostly clustered in the cooler mountainous elevations northeast of Alamogordo.

Alamogordo, a long strip mall–like stretch of fast foods and motels, primarily services Holloman Air Force Base and the White Sands Missile Range, where the world's first atomic bomb was exploded at the Trinity Site (not open to the public). Easily accessed from bed-and-breakfasts in Las Cruces, Mesilla, High Rolls, Cloudcroft, and Ruidoso, Alamogordo also has the yucca-studded gypsum sand dunes of White Sands National Monument, a toy-train museum, the International Space Hall of Fame, and a Space Center Complex with an IMAX theater and planetarium.

Cloudcroft, a small mountain-resort town 18 miles northeast of Alamogordo and 20 miles north of the Sacramento Peak National Solar Observatory, is popular for bird-watching, horseback riding, and skiing in Lincoln National Forest. Ruidoso, the major mountain-resort town and a cool summer escape for west Texans, has a microbrewery, quarterhorse racing from May to Labor Day, golf, and plentiful shopping. Thanks to 10 chairlifts, 54 runs, and a ski school with snowboarding lessons at the Mescalero Tribe's Ski Apache resort, Ruidoso is a bustling winter playground.

An hour northeast of Ruidoso is Lincoln, which has restored frontier buildings and Billy the Kid history. Roswell, a city of 45,000 an hour east of Lincoln, has the International UFO Museum and Research Center. West of Lincoln on US 380 are Capitan's Smoky Bear Historical State Park and

Carrizozo. A crossroads, Carrizozo is near the gold-mining ghost town of White Oaks, the volcanic Valley of Fires Recreation Area, and Three Rivers Petroglyphs National Recreation Site. Every year brings fresh rumors (hopes) of a bed-and-breakfast opening in Artesia or Carlsbad, near Carlsbad Caverns National Park.

THE LODGE, Cloudcroft

OVERALL ★★★★ | QUALITY ★★★★ | VALUE ★★★★ | PRICE RANGE $99

In a 9,200-foot-elevation mountain village encircled by Lincoln National Forest, the ten rustic Pavilion Bed-and-Breakfast rooms built by the Alamogordo and Sacramento Railway predate the elegant main lodge a quarter of a mile up the hill. The Pavilion has its own cavernous 200-person ballroom, the Sacramento, complete with peaked ceiling, stone fireplace, windowpane mirrors, lace curtains, movie theater, and bowling alley. Originally mainly a summer escape from the desert heat, the nearby family-style ski slopes are now also a major draw. Guests share the Lodge facilities with hotel guests and eat breakfast in the Lodge restaurant, Rebecca's.

SETTING & FACILITIES
Location Center **Near** Ruidoso, Alamagordo, White Sands **Building** Early 1900s brown wood w/ red trim & wraparound porch **Grounds** Gazebo **Public Space** Lounge, bar, restaurant, patio (in main lodge) **Food & Drink** Full breakfast in Rebecca's; lunch, dinner, Sunday brunch; group catering **Recreation** Biking, horse riding, hunting, tennis, golf, fishing, rappelling, volleyball, croquet, horseshoes, winter sports **Amenities & Services** 9-hole golf course, golf & gift shops, fitness room, massage, seasonal pool, hot tub, sauna, soda machine, microwave, weddings, groups (200)

ACCOMMODATIONS
Units 10 Pavilion guest rooms **All** Cable TV, phone (modem), ceiling fan, coffeemaker, comforter **Some** Fireplace (4), gas furnace (2), baseboard heat (8), iron and ironing board, robes & hair dryer (on request) **Bed & Bath** King (1), queen (9); all private baths, jetted tub (4) **Favorites** 505B, largest of 4 luxury suites w/ gas fireplaces & jetted tubs, has king & queen trundle bed, sleeps 8; 505A has 2 BRs, gray floral wallpaper in tiled bath **Comfort & Decor** Carpeted rooms have cabin feel with floor-to-ceiling wood paneling, dressers or armoires, vanities with pedestal sinks, wood and wallpapered bathrooms

RATES, RESERVATIONS, & RESTRICTIONS
Deposit 1 night (14-day cancellation policy) **Discounts** Varied packages, AARP, AAA **Credit Cards** AE, MC, V, D, DC **Check-In/Out** After 4 p.m./noon **Smoking** No **Pets** Yes (small pet; $100 deposit, $25 nonrefundable for cleaning) **Kids** Yes **No-Nos** N/A **Minimum Stay** Some holidays & weekends **Open** All year **Host** Lisa Thomassie, 1 Corona Pl., P.O. Box 497, Cloudcroft 88317 **Phone** (505) 682-2566 or toll-free (800) 395-6343 **Fax** (505) 582-2715 **E-mail** thelodge-nm@zianet.com **Web** www.thelodgeresort.com

GOOD LIFE INN, High Rolls

OVERALL ★★★★★ | QUALITY ★★★★½ | VALUE ★★★★ | PRICE RANGE $120–$170

Bordered by a forest, cattle and horse pasture, and 114 Red Delicious apple trees, the Good Life Inn specializes in romantic retreats and weddings. Indeed, after opening in July 2000 the proprietors did a dozen weddings the first year, often supplying the photography, catering, and marriage services. The Secret Garden Suite, occupying a whole floor, has an 850-square-foot porch used for weddings. The concrete dining room floor is painted as faux green and brown wood. The adjacent brick living room has beam ceilings, rag-painted walls, a wood stove, plump leather sofa, big-screen TV, stained-glass lamps, and antiques.

SETTING & FACILITIES

Location 10 mi. east of Alamogordo, 8 mi. west of Cloudcroft **Near** White Sands, forests **Building** 1978 trilevel 4,000-sq.-ft. brick ranch house **Grounds** 4 acres w/ peach & pear trees, creek, small waterfall **Public Space** LR, DR, game room, porch **Food & Drink** Full breakfast in DR, patio, or room; sunset beverages; bottled water in rooms; dinners; group catering **Recreation** Biking, horse riding, fishing, winter sports **Amenities & Services** Indoor hot tub, exercise equipment, dance floor, bar, pool table, darts, piano, big-screen TV, massage, receptions, weddings (200)

ACCOMMODATIONS

Units 3 **All** TV/VCR, satellite music, CD player/clock, fridge, microwave, coffeemaker, ceiling fan **Some** Makeup mirror (1), iron & hair dryer (on request) **Bed & Bath** Queen (2), full-size (1); all private baths **Favorites** Victorian-style Tea Rose Suite has full-size partial-canopy bed, angel and small-girl pictures, antique cherub end table, separate vanity w/ double sinks, water closet; Kokopelli Suite has iron four-poster bed, Native American decor **Comfort & Decor** Carpeted rooms with varied themes, tables for two, fluted glass, multicolor rag-painted walls

RATES, RESERVATIONS, & RESTRICTIONS

Deposit 50% or 1 night (2-week cancellation policy; 1 month for multiple rooms) **Discounts** Multiple nights **Credit Cards** AE, MC, V, D **Check-In/Out** 3 p.m./noon **Smoking** No **Pets** No (owners have cat, dog) **Kids** Yes (over age 14) **No-Nos** N/A **Minimum Stay** 3 nights on holidays **Open** All year **Hosts** Guillian & Melise Zoe, 164 Karr Canyon Rd., High Rolls 88325 **Phone** (505) 682-5433 or toll-free (866) 543-3466 **Fax** N/A **E-mail** goodlifeinn@aol.com **Web** www.goodlifeinn.com

CASA DE PATRÓN B&B INN, Lincoln

OVERALL ★★★★ | QUALITY ★★★★ | VALUE ★★★★ | PRICE RANGE $77–$107

Territorial legislator Juan Patrón's residence and an outlaw hangout in the late 1800s, Casa de Patrón books full a year in advance for August's Billy the Kid pageant. Just down the road from Capitan's Smokey Bear Museum, the Casa's main house contains Juan's Old Store with an old telephone pole bed surrounded by punched-tin reading lights, a collection of 100 historic washboards, and Bob Boze Bell's Billy the Kid art for sale on the walls. All in all, a relaxing base steeped in Old West history for exploring southeast New Mexico from Ruidoso to Roswell.

SETTING & FACILITIES

Location 30 min. NE of Ruidoso **Near** State monuments, forests, museums, Roswell **Building** 1860s New Mexico Territorial adobe, additional buildings added in 1980s & 1990s **Grounds** 5 acres w/ courtyards; Chinese elm, apple, peach, & almond trees; mowed gamma grass pastures extending to mesa slopes **Public Space** 2 LRs, 2 DRs **Food & Drink** Full breakfast in DRs, cont'l breakfast in casitas; dinner by arrangement; group catering **Recreation** Golf, fishing, biking, horse riding **Amenities & Services** Piano, pipe organ, small meetings

ACCOMMODATIONS

Units 7 guest rooms in 4 buildings **All** Clocks, individual heat, ceiling fan **Some** Robes (1), radio/tape deck (4), fridge (4), coffeemaker (4), fireplace (2), kitchen (2) **Bed & Bath** King (1), queen (3), queen & twins (1), twins (1); all private baths, tub (2), jetted tub (1) **Favorites** Casita de Paz, popular w/ families, has 2 BRs, LR, full kitchen, redwood deck; Casita Bonita, popular w/ honeymooners, has black wrought-iron spiral staircase to loft, futon sofa bed, adobe brick walls, saltillo tile floor, bamboo chairs, kitchen **Comfort & Decor** Viga ceilings, punched Mexican tin, Billy the Kid art, tiled baths; some porches, recessed lighting, rocking chairs, wood paneling, wicker

RATES, RESERVATIONS, & RESTRICTIONS

Deposit Credit card holds (7-day cancellation policy) **Discounts** Extended stays (6 or more nights) **Credit Cards** MC,V **Check-In/Out** 3–8 p.m./ noon **Smoking** Outdoors **Pets** No **Kids** Yes **No-Nos** N/A **Minimum Stay** None (except holidays) **Open** March–Oct. (by special arrangement during winter months) **Hosts** Jeremy & Cleis Jordan, P.O. Box 27, Lincoln 88338 **Phone** (505) 653-4676; (800) 524-5202 **Fax** (505) 653-4671 **E-mail** patron@pvtnetworks.net **Web** www.casapatron.com

APPLE TREE BED & BREAKFAST INN, Ruidoso

OVERALL ★★★½ | QUALITY ★★★★½ | VALUE ★★★★ | PRICE RANGE $79–$129

Though near a microbrewery, many restaurants, galleries, and shops, the Apple Tree may be too motel-like for many bed-and-breakfast aficionados. But for the west Texans flooding this town to escape the summer heat, this is as fine a place as any for a summer weekend of horse racing, as the 7,000-foot elevation provides a cooling respite from the desert heat. In winter, skiing is the passion here. The chief complaint is the outdoor walk between guest rooms and the fine indoor spa pavilion.

SETTING & FACILITIES

Location Central **Near** Museums, galleries, Indian reservations **Building** Conglomeration of former apartments, restaurant, healing center, shop space **Grounds** Patio **Public Space** Spa pavilion w/ robes, TV/VCR, stereo, DR **Food & Drink** Full breakfast in DR; special dietary needs require advance notice **Recreation** Horse racing & riding, boating, swimming, fishing, golf, winter sports **Amenities & Services** 2 hot tubs, steam & exercise rooms, massage, weddings, reunions

ACCOMMODATIONS

Units 11 **All** Cable TV, phone, clock radio, carpet, private entrance **Some** Fireplace (6), full kitchen (6), coffeemaker (9), ceiling fan (8), box fan (3), hair dryer (on request), iron (on request) **Bed & Bath** King (5), queen (7); all private baths, jetted tub (6), tub (5) **Favorites** 1,100-sq.-ft. Rock House has stone exterior, interior archways, wood paneling, 2 BRs; San Antonio, honeymoon favorite, has four-poster bed w/ gauze veil, fireplace, carpeted bath, jetted tub **Comfort & Decor** White walls, plantation shutters, upholstered chairs; upper rooms have ceiling fan and tiled bath; most lower rooms have fireplace and carpeted bath with jetted tub

RATES, RESERVATIONS, & RESTRICTIONS
Deposit 1 night or 50% (refund minus $25 for 14-day cancellation; 30 days for group, holiday, special event dates) **Discounts** Extended stay, ski packages, Tues. free (with restrictions) **Credit Cards** AE, MC, V, D **Check-In/Out** 3–8 p.m./11 a.m. **Smoking** No **Pets** Rock House only **Kids** Rock House only **No-Nos** N/A **Minimum Stay** None **Open** All year (may close first week April, Nov.) **Hosts** Bill Querin & Sandra Davis, 100 Lower Terrace, Ruidoso 88345 **Phone** (505) 257-1717 or toll-free (877) 277-5322 **Fax** (505) 257-1718 **E-mail** appletreebb@zianet.com **Web** www.appletreebb-spa.com

Southwest

From US 60 north of Socorro, New Mexico's southwest stretches south to the Texas and Mexico borders. New Mexico's southwest also extends west from the Arizona border to the San Andreas Mountains east of I-25. Evidence of a Native American presence here dates back several thousand years. Don Juan de Onate trekked in with colonists from Mexico City and claimed the area for Spain in 1598.

Mexican festivals like Cinco de Mayo and the Day of the Dead are big events. Las Cruces, New Mexico's second largest city with 78,000 people, is on the Rio Grande River 40 miles north of El Paso, Texas. Bordering Las Cruces is Mesilla, where fields of cotton, chiles, and alfalfa are interspersed with pecan orchards. The Gadsden Purchase, transferring this strip of southern New Mexico from Mexico to the United States, was ratified in Old Mesilla in 1854. White Sands National Monument, an hour to the northeast of Old Mesilla's shop-lined plaza, is a major area attraction. Rock Hound State Park, 60 miles west of Las Cruces, near Deming, allows each visitor to haul off 15 pounds of agates and quartz crystals. Two hours west of Las Cruces near Lordsburg are the ghost towns of Shakespeare and Steins.

Two hours north of Las Cruces on I-25 is Socorro and one of two New Mexico cities named San Antonio. This San Antonio is where legendary hotelier Conrad Hilton started out. Bosque del Apache National Wildlife Refuge's November Festival of the Cranes celebrates the greater sandhill crane migration. Socorro has an excellent microbrewery and the New Mexico Institute of Mining and Technology museum. The National Radio Astronomy Observatory's VLA (Very Large Array) and visitor center are an hour west of Socorro.

Mountainous NM 152 wends slowly through the old mining towns of Hillsboro and Kingston to Silver City, a drive best undertaken during the day to avoid hitting livestock. Silver City's Western New Mexico University Museum has a renowned Mimbres pottery collection. Tortuously slow roads head north to Gila Cliff Dwellings National Monument.

CASITAS DE GILA GUESTHOUSES, Gila

OVERALL ★★★★ | QUALITY ★★★★ | VALUE ★★★★ | PRICE RANGE $90–$175

After seven years operating a bed-and-breakfast in Ireland, a former geology professor and his wife built these high-desert dwellings on cliffs above a floodplain for self-sufficient types who enjoy doing their own cooking. Dinner meats or full meals can be ordered from the 30,000-acre cattle ranch next door, the Double E, which also offers trail rides through former Apache lands. A self-guided nature trail explains the geology and ecology shaped by the creek running through the property. A wilderness retreat three miles from the nearest paved road and far from restaurants, the bed-and-breakfast is hard to find at night.

SETTING & FACILITIES
Location 30 mi. west of Silver City **Near** Mines, ghost towns, national forest, Indian ruins **Building** 1998–9 Southwestern adobe-style design **Grounds** 70 acres w/ vegetable & herb garden, pinyon pine, juniper, yucca, grasslands, creek **Public Space** Covered table, hiking trail **Food & Drink** Cont'l breakfast in room; stocked fridge & kitchen shelves; dinner delivery available **Recreation** Horse riding, biking, fishing, rock hunting **Amenities & Services** Hot tub, binoculars, telescope, hammock, family reunions

ACCOMMODATIONS
Units 5 guest houses (casitas), 4 in duplexes **All** Robes, quilt, ceiling fan, thermostat, fireplace, hair dryer, clock radio, iron, fireplace, phone, full kitchen, LR, sleeper sofa, board games, outdoor barbecue, porch **Some** Handicap accessible (1) **Bed & Bath** Queen (3), double & twin (2); all private baths, tub (4) **Favorites** Animalito has sombreros on walls, Southwest rugs on brown cement floor, carved animals & petroglyphs on kiva fireplace, horseshoe lamp, metal lizard towel rack, Mexican chairs; Sun & Moon has 2 BRs, carved theme headboards **Comfort & Decor** Carved animals on front door, beam and plank ceiling, white walls with local art, black wrought iron, colored cement floors with radiant heat, recessed lighting, dresser, coat rack, and tile sink

RATES, RESERVATIONS, & RESTRICTIONS
Deposit 50% (21-day cancellation for refund minus $25 fee) **Discounts** Extended stays **Credit Cards** AE, MC, V, DC, D **Check-In/Out** 3–6 p.m./10 a.m. **Smoking** No **Pets** No (owners have dogs, horses) **Kids** Yes **No-Nos** N/A **Minimum Stay** None **Open** All year **Hosts** Becky & Michael O'Connor, P.O. Box 325, Gila 88038 **Phone** (505) 535-4455 or toll-free (877) 923-4827 **Fax** (505) 535-4456 **E-mail** info@casitasdegila.com **Web** www.casitasdegila.com

THE ENCHANTED VILLA BED & BREAKFAST, Hillsboro

OVERALL ★★★½ | QUALITY ★★★★½ | VALUE ★★★★ | PRICE RANGE $40–$70

On NM 152, fronted by mulberry, cottonwood, and apple trees, the Enchanted Villa doubles as a tour bus feeding stop. Indeed, the hostess's full catering license comes in handy when families rent the whole property for holidays or Boy Scout groups turn the living room into a sleeping-bag city. The living room has Southwestern accents, a family photo wall, a fireplace, and bifold windows that effectively air out the place after smokers. Hunters, bikers, and travelers seeking off-the-beaten path alternatives to Santa Fe frequent this apple-growing old mining town. Beware of the slow mountainous highway after dark, as deer and cattle populate the roadway.

SETTING & FACILITIES
Location Historic district, 30 mi. SW of Truth or Consequences & 9 mi. east of Kingston **Near** Silver City, forest **Building** 1941 Territorial-style adobe **Grounds** 2.5 acres w/ lava terraces, 2 patios, birch, pine & juniper trees, hammock, chair swing **Public Space** LR, DR, patio **Food & Drink** Full breakfast in DR; candy; picnic lunches; dinner by arrangement; full group catering **Recreation** Biking, birding, boating, swimming, fishing, hunting **Amenities & Services** TV/VCR, weddings (150), workshops (40)

ACCOMMODATIONS
Units 5 **All** Ceiling fan, wind-up clock, board games **Some** Desk (1) **Bed & Bath** King & 2 twins (1), queen & twin (2), queen (1), twin (1); all private baths, tub (3) **Favorites** Sir Victor room has white walls w/ turquoise accents, queen bed, shuttered walk-in closet, Native American artifacts, local watercolors, bath w/ pedestal sink & green plant rack; Santa Fe, largest, has king, 2 twins, gray & orange alcove, linoleum bath w/ large mirror **Comfort & Decor** Carpeted rooms have tables, chairs, large windows, shutters; some have sitting areas

RATES, RESERVATIONS, & RESTRICTIONS
Deposit Full amount (1-week cancellation policy) **Discounts** Extended stays, special promos **Credit Cards** None (cash or check only) **Check-In/Out** After 1 p.m./11:30 a.m. **Smoking** Allowed in 1 guest room & LR **Pets** No (owners have outdoor cats, dogs) **Kids** Yes **No-Nos** N/A **Minimum Stay** None **Open** All year **Host** Maree Westland, P.O. Box 456, Hillsboro 88042 **Phone** (505) 895-5686 **Fax** NA **E-mail** maree@riolink.com **Web** N/A

THE BLACK RANGE LODGE, Kingston

OVERALL ★★★★ | QUALITY ★★★★ | VALUE ★★★★ | PRICE RANGE $49–$139

New Mexico's largest town during the mining boom a century ago and a ghost town by World War I, Kingston's largest building is now the Black Range Lodge. On rural residential Main Street, the lodge combines a cavalry and miner boarding house with old saloon and casino foundations. The proprietors, a former film directorial assistant and musician/Frisbee star, sponsor straw bale workshops and publish *The Last Straw,* a natural construction quarterly, from a computer-lined room off the kitchen. Three overflow bedrooms up sleeping capacity to 27 for family reunions and business group retreats.

SETTING & FACILITIES
Location 0.5 mi. west of NM 152 **Near** Silver City, forest **Building** 1884 brick boarding housing, expanded into 3-story 9,000-sq.-ft. stone & log edifice in 1934 **Grounds** 2.5 acres w/ 16 bamboo species in Permaculture landscape, bananas & ginger in straw bale greenhouse **Public Space** LR, game room, TV/conference room, DR, kitchen, porches **Food & Drink** Full breakfast in DR or patio; vegetarian bias; guest fridge & microwave **Recreation** Biking, birding, boating, swimming, fishing **Amenities & Services** Pool table, pianos, arcade games, hot tub, RV hookups, massage, groups (70)

ACCOMMODATIONS
Units 7 **All** Dresser **Some** Multiple beds (4), radiant floor heat (2 floors) **Bed & Bath** King (2), queen (5); all private baths, cast-iron tub (2) **Favorites** Old adobe room #3 has entry w/ desk & single bed, step down to queen BR w/ floral bedspreads & bookshelves, bath w/ greenhouse banana view, deck; brick room #4 has queen, single, & alcove w/ bunk beds, animals painted on green walls, white tin ceiling **Comfort & Decor** A melange of stone, brick, adobe and super-insulated straw bale walls, beam ceilings, creaking wood floors, dressers, desks, tiled baths and showers fitted into odd spaces

RATES, RESERVATIONS, & RESTRICTIONS
Deposit Credit card holds (no cancellation penalties) **Discounts** Inquire **Credit Cards** MC, V, D **Check-In/Out** 3–6 p.m./noon **Smoking** No **Pets** Yes (if well-behaved, $5/night; chickens, turkeys, cats share grounds) **Kids** Yes **No-Nos** N/A **Minimum Stay** None **Open** All year **Hosts** Catherine Wanek & Pete Fust, 119 Main St., Kingston 88042 **Phone** (505) 895-5652 **Fax** (505) 895-3326 **E-mail** blackrange@zianet.com **Web** www.zianet.com/blackrange/lodge

INN OF THE ARTS BED & BREAKFAST, Las Cruces

OVERALL ★★★½ | QUALITY ★★★★ | VALUE ★★★★ | PRICE RANGE $75–$105

Centrally located on a busy street near all the downtown action, Inn of the Arts is a walled compound with much of the front downstairs area devoted to an art gallery with everything from the hostess's photography to paintings of all shapes, sizes, and media by mostly regional artists. The inn recently slimmed down from 22 to 9 rooms (all named after artists) in the main white-walled adobe building. Rooms in the surrounding structures are being converted into condo and time-share units by the host, an architect. Not all guests have been happy with the changes, but given the Las

Cruces location (rather than Santa Fe), the rates here remain very reasonable. In the past, groups have rented out all rooms and had meals catered.

SETTING & FACILITIES

Location Center, historic district **Near** Museums, university, White Sands **Building** Restored century-old 2-story Territorial adobe **Grounds** Gazebo **Public Space** Lobby, art gallery, DR **Food & Drink** Full breakfast in DR; snacks, beverages on request **Recreation** Golf, fishing, water sports **Amenities & Services** Piano, TV, fax, e-mail, exercise room, massage, hair styling, marriage services, receptions, weddings (50)

ACCOMMODATIONS

Units 9 guest rooms **All** Ceiling fan, clock radio **Some** Bidet (2), fireplace (3), kitchenette (3), fridge (on request) **Bed & Bath** Queen (5), 2 queens (2), queen & twin (2); all private baths, tub (2) **Favorites** Maria Martinez has timber bed, kiva fireplace, red skull serape, small saltillo tile bath w/ shower/tub **Comfort & Decor** White walls, dark wood floors and accents, relatively sparsely furnished, some carved wood, twig, and Mexican furnishings, smallish baths with saltillo tile floors, some pedestal sinks

RATES, RESERVATIONS, & RESTRICTIONS

Deposit Credit card holds (negotiable cancellation policy; inquire) **Discounts** AAA, AARP, travel agents, corp., gov't., extended stay **Credit Cards** AE, MC, V, D, DC **Check-In/Out** 3–6 p.m./11 a.m. **Smoking** No **Pets** Yes (owners must provide kennels; $15 surcharge) **Kids** Yes (requires prior approval) **No-Nos** N/A **Minimum Stay** None **Open** All year **Hosts** Linda & Jerry Lundeen, 618 S. Alameda, Las Cruces 88005 **Phone** (505) 526-3326 or toll-free (888) 526-3326 **Fax** (505) 647-1334 **E-mail** lundeen@innofthearts.com **Web** www.innofthearts.com

T. R. H. SMITH MANSION BED & BREAKFAST, Las Cruces

OVERALL ★★★★ | QUALITY ★★★★ | VALUE ★★★★ | PRICE RANGE $70–$130

Named after a local bank president who built the house and was kept from living here by a 1914 bankruptcy scandal, T. R. H. Smith Mansion changed

hands several times before becoming a bed-and-breakfast in 1995. Located on a busy corner close to all the downtown action, the mansion's pecan trees and lawns with black wrought-iron furniture lend a hint of more rural origins. The living room walls are sponge-painted mustard and blue. The dark beam-ceiling dining room features stained-glass windows and a large glass cabinet displaying the hostess's porcelain and china collections. Also notable is the plant-laden sun room, which has glasshouse-style and green sponge-painted walls.

SETTING & FACILITIES

Location Historic Alameda Depot District **Near** Museums, university, White Sands **Building** 1914 Prairie style w/ high beamed ceilings **Grounds** 0.5 acre corner lot w/ 4 pecan trees **Public Space** LR, DR, garden room, porch **Food & Drink** Full breakfast in DR or garden room **Recreation** Golf, fishing, water sports **Services** Piano, fax, e-mail, receptions, meetings (60)

ACCOMMODATIONS

Units 4 **All** AC, phone (data port), radio cassette clock **Some** Fireplace (1), feather comforter (1) **Bed & Bath** King (2), queen (2); all private baths, tub (3) **Favorites** Americas, largest, has white walls, loveseat facing wood-burning fireplace, feather comforter, gray sloping cabinet, dark carved wood furnishings, walk-in closets, Mexican folk art, punched tin, lace, mountain & garden views; European has upholstered king bed headboard, upholstered & wood furnishings, tapestry patterns, turquoise & pink rose floral fabrics, pink tiled tub/shower **Comfort & Decor** Hardwood floors, desks, dressers, roomy closets, varied world travel themes including Old World, Americas, Southwest, and Polynesian items, like seashell display, Caribbean paintings, drum tables, and kachinas

RATES, RESERVATIONS, & RESTRICTIONS

Deposit 1 night (7-day cancellation or gift certificate as refund) **Discounts** Weekdays, packages **Credit Cards** AE, MC, V, D **Check-In/Out** 3–6 p.m./11 a.m. **Smoking** No (outside or sun porch) **Pets** Yes (small pets, $20; owners have dog) **Kids** Yes **No-Nos** N/A **Minimum Stay** None **Open** All year **Hosts** Marlene & Jay Tebo, 900 N. Alameda Blvd., Las Cruces 88005 **Phone** (505) 525-2525 or toll-free (800) 526-1914 **Fax** (505) 524-8227 **E-mail** smithmansion@zianet.com **Web** www.smithmansion.com

HAPPY TRAILS, Mesilla

OVERALL ★★★★½ | QUALITY ★★★★ | VALUE ★★★★ | PRICE RANGE $85–$150

In the middle of farm country, surrounded by alfalfa fields and pecan orchards, yet only three miles southwest of downtown Las Cruces, Happy Trails is a wood-beamed horse and family folk art haven. A mile-long canal trail for horses and people meanders through pecan orchards to Old Mesilla. Honeymooners favor the carpeted La Casita guest house, which has a blue-and-red kerchief quilt on its king bed, a kitchenette, cowboy and cactus tiles, and kiva and twig towel racks in a sunset-yellow bath streaked with red. Rooms share a courtyard with a pecan tree, pool, and red chile mural. Breakfast is served in a new sun room.

SETTING & FACILITIES
Location 1 mi. from Old Mesilla **Near** Las Cruces, museums, university **Building** 1952 adobe brick Territorial hacienda w/ 1990s tin roof **Grounds** 10 acres w/ brick courtyard, gazebo, sycamores, 3-acre vineyard, 6-acre pecan orchard **Public Space** LR, DR **Food & Drink** Full breakfast in DR; fridge w/ 24-hour beverages, snacks **Recreation** Golf, fishing, bird-watching, boating **Amenities & Services** Pool, hot tub, laundry, computer, TV/VCR, stereo, microwave, chuck wagon, parties, weddings (100)

ACCOMMODATIONS
Units 2 guest rooms & 1 guest house **All** Hair dryer, radio, clock, ceiling fan **Some** TV/VCR (on request), phone (1), kitchenette (1), handicap accessible (1) **Bed & Bath** King & double futon (1), queen (1), queen & double (1); all private baths, tub (1) **Favorites** Aspen & Willow connect as suite w/ sliding door to courtyard, cattle, Indian maiden, saguaro & Pueblo murals, stylized diamondbacks, carved Indian heads, vintage radio, old carom table, & Victorian touches like old hats on wall & lace curtains **Comfort & Decor** Extensive folk painting includes botanical, Native American, and Western murals; painted window frames and light switches; longhorn skulls; timber beds; quilts; shutters; French doors; and saltillo tiles

RATES, RESERVATIONS, & RESTRICTIONS
Deposit Credit card holds (7-day cancellation notice or gift certificate refund) **Discounts** Gov't., extended stays **Credit Cards** AE, MC, V **Check-In/Out** 2 p.m./noon **Smoking** No **Pets** Yes (corral for horses) **Kids** Yes **No-Nos** N/A **Minimum Stay** None **Open** All year **Hosts** Sylvia & Barry Byrnes, 1857 Paisano Rd., Mesilla 88005 **Phone** (505) 527-8471 **Fax** N/A **E-mail** N/A **Web** www.las-cruces-new-mexico.com

MESON DE MESILLA, Mesilla

OVERALL ★★★★ | QUALITY ★★★★ | VALUE ★★★★ | PRICE RANGE $45–$140

Just blocks from historic Old Mesilla's quaint plaza and shops, Meson de Mesilla is best known locally for its restaurant open to the public for breakfast and dinner. The dining room has Southwestern stained-glass windows, changing displays of local art, and an atrium with a tiled wall. The full-service bar opens onto a patio area with a pool. Tents go up around the pool for group functions, which the restaurant caters. Though Mesilla has been considered a separate city since its days as a Butterfield Stagecoach stop, for all practical purposes it is a rural Las Cruces suburb.

SETTING & FACILITIES
Location 0.75 mi. south of I-10 Exit 140 in Las Cruces **Near** Museums, galleries, Las Cruces, White Sands **Building** Late 1980s 2-story w/ wraparound porch **Grounds** 1 acre

w/ brick patio, small poolside rose garden, memorial stone **Public Space** Lobby, restaurant, bar, patio **Food & Drink** Full breakfast in DR; bar; dinner; catering **Recreation** Golf, fishing, bird-watching, boating **Amenities & Services** Pool, free laundry, soda machine, banquet room (78), weddings, groups (300)

ACCOMMODATIONS

Units 15 guest rooms **All** Phone (data port), ceiling fan, TV **Some** Second sliding glass door (14), kiva fireplace (3), iron & hair dryer (on request) **Bed & Bath** King (3), queen (7), double (2), twin (1), 2 twins (2); all private baths, jetted tub (1), tub (14), **Favorites** Kachina & Kiva are sunny corners w/ Organ Mountain views from balcony; Kokopelli suite connects w/ double-bedded Mimbres, has carved wood four-poster king bed, Southwestern/Mexican decor, kiva fireplace, block glass window above jetted tub **Comfort & Decor** Varied decor ranges from 1960s with marbles in Kiva room to White Sands mural in Kachina, plain pastels in San Albino and Yucca, parquet or carpet floors, some armoires with TVs, glass-topped tables, and love seats.

RATES, RESERVATIONS, & RESTRICTIONS

Deposit Credit card holds (no cancellation penalty imposed) **Discounts** Weekly rates **Credit Cards** AE, MC, V, D, DC, CB **Check-In/Out** 3–6 p.m./11 a.m. **Smoking** No **Pets** No **Kids** Yes **No-Nos** N/A **Minimum Stay** None **Open** All year **Host** Robert Morris 1803 Avenida de Mesilla, P.O. Box 1212, Mesilla 88046 **Phone** (505) 525-9212 or toll-free (800) 732-6025 **Fax** (505) 527-4196 **E-mail** N/A **Web** www.travelguides.com/inns/full/NM/6096.html

---

CASA BLANCA BED & BREAKFAST, *San Antonio/Socorro*

OVERALL ★★★½ | QUALITY ★★★★ | VALUE ★★★★ | PRICE RANGE $70–$90

From October's Bosque del Apache National Wildlife Refuge sandhill crane migration through spring songbird season, birders flock to Casa Blanca. Many grab a hot morning drink from the stove and disappear for a chilly day of winter bird-watching, returning to warm themselves in the barn sauna beneath a Casablanca movie poster. A bird feeder replica of the house is visible from the kitchen window. Near the front entrance is a framed receipt from Conrad Hilton's father, whose adobe near the local train station started his son on a service tradition that became the Hilton hotel chain.

SETTING & FACILITIES

Location 10 mi. south of Socorro, 8 mi. north of Bosque del Apache National Wildlife Refuge **Near** Wetlands, reservoirs, museums, ghost towns, Indian ruins, radio observatory **Building** 1880 Victorian farmhouse w/ double adobe walls, barn **Grounds** 1 acre w/ fields, barn, pump house; apricot, apple, cherry, peach & pecan trees; white Concord grapevines **Public Space** 2 LRs, DR, porch w/ swings **Food & Drink** Cont'l breakfast in DR **Recreation** Bird-watching, golf, fishing, hunting, biking, rock climbing **Amenities & Services** Sauna, exercise bike, mountain bikes, piano, TV/VCR, bird feeder

ACCOMMODATIONS

Units 3 guest rooms **All** Robes, electric blanket, clock, electric baseboard heat **Some** Roll-away bed (1), wood-burning stove (1), private outdoor entrance (2), handicap accessible bath (1) **Bed & Bath** Queen (2), double & twin (1); all private baths, jetted tub (1), tub (1) **Favorites** Heron has carpet, private outdoor entrance, some wood paneling, wheelchair-accessible bath w/ tiled jetted tub, steps into main house; Crane has brick floor, wood-burning stove, mirrored armoire, back yard view, wood-paneled bath w/ shower **Comfort & Decor** Varied—nothing too fancy. Brick or carpet floors, Mexican chairs, some wood paneling

RATES, RESERVATIONS, & RESTRICTIONS

Deposit Credit card holds (1-week cancellation policy) **Discounts** Extended off-season stays (Sept., Oct., Apr., May) **Credit Cards** MC, V **Check-In/Out** 5–7 p.m./11 a.m. **Smoking** No **Pets** Yes (requires prior approval; owner has dog) **Kids** Yes **No-Nos** N/A **Minimum Stay** None **Open** Labor Day to Memorial Day **Host** Phoebe Wood, P.O. Box 31, San Antonio 87832 **Phone** (505) 835-3027 **Fax** N/A **E-mail** casablancabandb@hotmail.com **Web** N/A

BEAR MOUNTAIN LODGE, Silver City

OVERALL ★★★½ | QUALITY ★★★★ | VALUE ★★★★ | PRICE RANGE $100–$180

Nestled among the hills and mesas of the Pinos Altos Mountains, Bear Mountain Lodge evolved from housing boys with mental problems to being a bed-and-breakfast under the guidance of an avid birder, Myra McCormick, who left the property to the Nature Conservancy of New Mexico upon her death. This splendid 6,250-foot-elevation lodge, which devotes a dining room wall to photos of the original owners, makes its own organic berry jams. The lounge is truly a great room with wood beams and stone fireplaces. Though lacking the front desk hospitality expected by discerning travelers, the Nature Conservancy members packing the place and banding birds find more than enough luxury in this fine institutional offering.

SETTING & FACILITIES

Location 3 mi. north of Silver City **Near** Museums, galleries, ghost towns, forest **Building** 1920s 2-story adobe-style lodge, remodeled in 2000 **Grounds** 178 acres w/ trails, bird-feeding station, small pond, rock-lined stream **Public Space** Lounge, DR, library, porches **Food & Drink** Full breakfast in DR; vegan, vegetarian, & special diets if requested when reserving; 24-hour beverages, snacks; sack lunch or dinner by arrangement **Recreation** Biking, horse riding, fishing, bird-watching **Amenities & Services** Computer, barbecue, resident naturalist, conferences, weddings

ACCOMMODATIONS

Units 11 guest rooms, 4 sharing private LR w/ gas fireplace **All** Ceiling fan, evaporative cooling, radiant floor heat, clock **Some** Robes (6), double sleeper sofa (4), balcony (4), kitchen (1), handicap accessible (1) **Bed & Bath** King (7), queen (3), 2 doubles (1); all private baths, jetted tub (4), tub (6) **Favorites** Wren's Nest is private guest house w/ kitchen **Comfort & Decor** Mission style with beam ceilings, hardwood floors, Southwestern rugs, painted wardrobes, bear paw coasters, and wood ceiling baths and tile floors

RATES, RESERVATIONS, & RESTRICTIONS

Deposit Credit card holds (2-week cancellation for refund minus $15) **Discounts** None **Credit Cards** AE, MC, V **Check-In/Out** 2–9 p.m./11 a.m. **Smoking** No **Pets** No (dogs roam grounds; horse boarding $15/night) **Kids** Yes (over age 10) **No-Nos** N/A **Minimum Stay** 2 nights **Open** All year **Host** The Nature Conservancy , P.O. Box 1163, Silver City 88062 **Phone** (505) 538-2538 or toll-free (877) 620-bear **Fax** (505) 534-1827 **E-mail** innkeeper@bearmountainlodge.com **Web** www.bearmountainlodge.com

THE COTTAGES, Silver City

OVERALL ★★★★½ | QUALITY ★★★★½ | VALUE ★★★★ | PRICE RANGE $89–$199

Half a mile down a dirt road with black wrought-iron gates and a herd of deer feeding on alfalfa, the Cottages include a white-washed red-brick home built by a wealthy heiress. Three adjacent luxury cottages originally housed the caretaker, chauffeur, and guests; javelina, fox, wolf, bobcat, and other wildlife roam the area. The Cottages, which are down paths with little village signs, are stocked with ample food and extras like disposable cameras. Bathroom and medicine cabinet amenities cover almost every contingency and include yellow rubber duckies. If anything more is needed, just attach a note to the door.

SETTING & FACILITIES

Location 7 blocks north of US 180 **Near** Museums, galleries, ghost towns, forest **Building** 1939 country French w/ copper downspouts, adjacent 1939 cottages **Grounds** 200 acres w/ alfalfa field, trails, old silver mine, forest, brick courtyard w/ fountain **Public Space** LR, DR, porch **Food & Drink** Fridge and picnic basket stocked with cont'l breakfast items, snacks; dessert in cottages or DR **Recreation** Biking, horse riding, fishing, bowling **Amenities & Services** Local newspaper

ACCOMMODATIONS

Units 2 suites in main house, 3 cottages **All** Private entrance, TV/VCR, phone (modem), microwave, hair dryer, ceiling fan, fireplace, nonallergenic feather bed **Some** Private patio (3), full kitchen (3), slippers (3) **Bed & Bath** King, queen; all private baths, tub (3) **Favorites** Fountain Suite has queen bed, antiques, signed Apollo astronaut photos, walk-in closets; Mountain View has brass queen bed, knotty pine beam ceiling, pecan paneling, hall wall stencils, basket-weave bath tile **Comfort & Decor** Sitting area with rugs on plank floor, French antiques, wallpaper ceiling border, French doors opening to flagstone patio, wallpapered bath, vanity area, and mirrored closets

RATES, RESERVATIONS, & RESTRICTIONS

Deposit Credit card holds (72-hour cancellation policy) **Discounts** Extended stays (8th night free) **Credit Cards** AE, MC, V, D **Check-In/Out** 5 p.m./11 a.m. **Smoking** Outside **Pets** No (pet boarding nearby) **Kids** No **No-Nos** N/A **Minimum Stay** 2 nights (3 on holidays) **Open** All year **Hosts** Mike & Colleen Michaels, P.O. Box 2562, 2037 Cottage San Rd., Silver City 88062 **Phone** (505) 388-3000 or toll-free (800) 938-3001 **Fax** N/A **E-mail** N/A **Web** www.silvercitycottages.com

Central

Founded by the Spanish in 1706 near Native American pueblos along the Rio Grande River facing the western slopes of the Sandia Mountains, Albuquerque is the central crossroads for all New Mexico. Central Avenue, alternately seedy and hip enough for jazz and kicks, encompasses old Route 66. I-25 runs north from Las Cruces in southwest New Mexico through Albuquerque before turning northeast to Santa Fe and the Colorado border. I-40 runs west from Amarillo, Texas, through Albuquerque en route to Gallup and Arizona's Petrified Forest and Grand Canyon National Parks.

With about 400,000 of New Mexico's 1.7 million residents, Albuquerque is definitely the state's population center. Bed-and-breakfasts book full the week of the International Balloon Fiesta in October and are a popular alternative lodging when conferences and conventions come to town. Old Town, a happening mix of adobe and Victorian buildings with galleries, restaurants, and museums, celebrates the founding of this city named for the duke of Albuquerque in April. Though the weather in this 5,000-foot elevation city is relatively moderate, the Sandia Mountains have snow for winter skiing.

Central New Mexico's Native American heritage can be experienced in the many pueblos outside the metropolitan area. In Albuquerque's West Mesa just south of Corrales, Petroglyph National Monument has hiking trails among lava flows and several thousand petroglyphs. The relaxing rural village of Corrales is 15 miles north of Albuquerque airport and even closer to Old Town. A mile or so north of Corrales, Bernalillo has Coronado State Monument and a Spanish mission with a Zuni sun symbol. Jemez Springs, 50 miles north of Albuquerque on NM 4, is tucked away among forested red rocks near the Jemez Pueblo.

BÖTTGER-KOCH MANSION BED & BREAKFAST, *Albuquerque*

OVERALL ★★★★★ | QUALITY ★★★★½ | VALUE ★★★★ | PRICE RANGE $109–$250

Fronting Old Route 66 (Central Ave.), a few blocks walk from the Old Town restaurants and museums, the elegant and refined Böttger-Koch Mansion was a popular urban stopping place for Machine Gun Kelly and his gang during the Prohibition era. Today it is bordered by a school and a large city parking lot, which guests use. Family black-and-white photos decorate the upstairs hallway. The hostess does the cooking and decorating, included some detailed floral artworks. The decor and room arrangements change from time to time, as inspiration strikes, so it is not your imagination if favorite rooms seem different each visit.

SETTING & FACILITIES
Location Old Town, 1 block from Plaza **Near** Downtown, museums, galleries, shops, convention center, airport **Building** 1912 American Foursquare w/ pressed-tin roof **Grounds** Courtyard w/ Chinese elm trees **Public Space** LR, DR, upstairs sitting area **Food & Drink** Full breakfast in DR; 24-hour beverages, snacks; special dietary needs; Thurs. high teas mid-Oct.–Apr.; special occasion teas **Recreation** Biking, horse riding, hot-air ballooning, golf **Amenities & Services** TV, massage, facials, spa services, upstairs guest kitchen

ACCOMMODATIONS
Units 8 **All** Robes, comforters, hair dryers, cable TV/VCR, clock radio **Some** Kitchen (1), remote-controlled heat/cooling (6), ceiling fan (7), original tin ceiling (3), pedestal sink (7) **Bed & Bath** King (4), queen (3), twin (1), tub (2); all private baths, claw-foot tub (2), jetted tub (1) **Favorites** Skye Elizabeth has queen four-poster bed w/ fishnet canopy, mahogany vanity, floral & striped burgundy tapestry chairs, blue-tiled bath w/ chandelier & claw-foot tub **Comfort & Decor** Victorian elegance with frilly lace lampshades; floral art and patterns; wood, marble, and carpet floors; step-up beds with plenty of tasseled pillows and lace; some fluted glass; mirrored armoires; and daybeds

RATES, RESERVATIONS, & RESTRICTIONS
Deposit 1 night or 50% (14-day cancellation for refund minus $25) **Discounts** Corp., AAA, AARP, whole house rental, historic inns promos **Credit Cards** AE, MC, V, D, DC **Check-In/Out** 3–6 p.m./11 a.m. **Smoking** Outside **Pets** No **Kids** Yes **No-Nos** N/A **Minimum Stay** None **Open** All year **Host** Yvonne Koch, 110 San Felipe NW, Albuquerque 87104 **Phone** (505) 243-3639 or toll-free (800) 758-3639 **Fax** (505) 243-4378 **E-mail** BottgerK@aol.com **Web** www.bottger.com

CASA DEL GRANJERO, Albuquerque

OVERALL ★★★★½ | QUALITY ★★★★ | VALUE ★★★★ | PRICE RANGE $79–$179

A walled compound on a narrow residential street a mile from October's balloon fiesta site, Casa del Granjero has three guest rooms in the main 6,000-square-foot adobe. A seven-foot-tall sharpened wood coyote fence surrounds four rooms with a guest kitchen in the 3,800-square-foot guest house across the street. The skylighted living room has a brown kiva fireplace, clerestory windows, and oryx, buffalo, and antelope heads. A sauna and hot tub are safely ensconced in a stand-alone wood-paneled public room that can be privately reserved, complete with a stereo, skylights that open, and snack and beverage service.

SETTING & FACILITIES
Location 15 mi. NW of Albuquerque International Airport **Near** Museums, International Balloon Fiesta **Building** 1825 Territorial hacienda, 1958 adobe ranch house **Grounds** 3 acres w/ courtyard, gazebo, small waterfall, lily/goldfish pond, raspberries, roses, fruit trees, swings **Public Space** LR (2), DR (2), TV room, business office, porches **Food & Drink** Full breakfast in DR or patio; snacks, beverages; special dinners; open kitchen; catering **Recreation** Golf, horse riding, biking, ballooning, tennis **Amenities & Services** Hot tub, sauna, barbecue, laundry, kitchen, Internet access, fax, photocopier, scanner, big-screen TVs, stereo, phones, meeting room (35), parties, weddings (100 outside)

ACCOMMODATIONS
Units 7 **All** Robes, kiva fireplace, ceiling fan, hair dryer, clock **Some** TV (3) **Bed & Bath** King & twin(s) (3), queen & twin(s) (4); all private baths, tub (3), double shower (1), water closet (5) **Favorites** Cuarto Grande has LR, floral painted archway, twig furnishings, saltillo floor, tiled double shower **Comfort & Decor** Varied themes, brick, tile or carpet floors, some futons, quilts, lace, murals, large closets, carved wardrobes, French doors, and stained glass

RATES, RESERVATIONS, & RESTRICTIONS
Deposit Credit card holds (14-day cancellation) **Discounts** Gov't., groups, AAA, extended stays, repeat guests, romance packages **Credit Cards** AE, MC, V, D, but check or cash requested **Check-In/Out** 11 a.m.–2 p.m./11 a.m. **Smoking** No **Pets** Yes (1 small pet room; horse stable; owners have horses, goat, cats) **Kids** Yes **No-Nos** N/A **Minimum Stay** None **Open** All year **Hosts** Victoria & Butch Farmer, 414 C de Baca Lane, Albuquerque 87114 **Phone** (505) 897-4144 or toll-free (800) 701-4144 **Fax** (505) 897-9788 **E-mail** granjero@prodigy.net **Web** www.innewmexico.com

CINNAMON MORNING BED & BREAKFAST, Albuquerque

OVERALL ★★★★½ | QUALITY ★★★★½ | VALUE ★★★★ | PRICE RANGE $79–$185

Heavily Mexican-influenced with bright yellows and oranges alternating with cream walls, Cinnamon Morning has large outdoor and candlelit indoor kitchens. When the weather is warm, the outdoor kitchen serves up breakfasts and caters meals for meetings. In cooler weather, dining and meetings shift indoors. The hostess faux paints and stencils the walls and adds color to the furniture, and the host handles the remodeling chores. The folk art is mostly Mexican, though there are Peruvian painted pigskins, ceramic asparagus stalk tables, sunflowers, and fabric lizards. The atmosphere is very informal, and guests can help themselves to a beer from the fridge.

SETTING & FACILITIES

Location I mi. north of Old Town **Near** Downtown, museums **Building** 1930s remodeled Mexican-influenced adobe, adjacent building **Grounds** 3 acres w/ flagstone courtyard, covered patio, ceramic fireplaces, small waterfall, fountain, koi, globe willow & cherry trees **Public Space** LR, DR, patio **Food & Drink** Full breakfast in DR or courtyard; 24-hour snacks, beverages; vegetarian w/ advance notice; candy in rooms; meeting meals catered **Recreation** Biking, horse riding, hot-air ballooning, golf **Amenities & Services** Barbecue, guest fridge, business services, meetings (40)

ACCOMMODATIONS

Units 6 **All** Robes, hair dryer, ceiling fan, clock **Some** Kitchen (1), phone (3), TV/VCR (2), stereo (1), private entrance (2), fireplace (3) **Bed & Bath** King (2), queen (3), double (1); all private baths **Favorites** 2-BR guest house suite has kitchen, DR, LR w/ fireplace, phone, TV, stereo, daybed **Comfort & Decor** Textured cream and brightly colored walls, wood ceilings, saltillo tile floors, some shutters, archways, armoires, stenciled wood trim, upholstered and carved wood furnishings, large closets, Western and Mexican art, and tiled baths

RATES, RESERVATIONS, & RESTRICTIONS

Deposit Credit card holds (14-day cancellation for full refund; 30 days for holidays) **Discounts** Corp., extended stays **Credit Cards** AE, MC, V, D, DC **Check-In/Out** After 3 p.m./noon **Smoking** Outdoors **Pets** Encouraged (in Guest House rooms; dogs have full run of fenced yard; owners have cats, dogs) **Kids** Yes **No-Nos** N/A **Minimum Stay** None **Open** All year **Hosts** Sue & Dick Percilick, 2700 Rio Grande Blvd. NW, Albuquerque 87104 **Phone** (505) 345-3541 or toll-free (800) 214-9481 **Fax** (505) 342-2283 **E-mail** dpercilick@aol.com **Web** www.cinnamonmorning.com

DEVONSHIRE ADOBE INN LTD BED & BREAKFAST, *Albuquerque*

OVERALL ★★★★ | QUALITY ★★★★ | VALUE ★★★★ | PRICE RANGE $80–$130

Building regulations prohibited a Victorian exterior, but the local government could not stop Devonshire Adobe's Texas host and English hostess from bringing Tuesday through Friday afternoon high teas to Albuquerque. The dark walnut dining room has old oak English pub tables, lace tablecloths, ferns, floral wreaths, and lace-curtained French doors opening onto a garden courtyard. Catering and cakes are big business here, and musicians play for events from the mezzanine overlooking the atrium. A hallway is lined with photos of the hostess's cakes created to resemble patterned Southwestern pottery, gold Mayan face masks, Mexican leopards, and boar's heads. The entry room has pink chairs, a green sofa, a grandfather clock, and a spinning wheel.

SETTING & FACILITIES
Location 16 mi. NW of Albuquerque International Airport **Near** Museums, Petroglyph National Monument **Building** 1996 nondescript steel-frame northern New Mexico exterior w/ Victorian interior **Grounds** Courtyard, small garden **Public Space** LR, DR, parlor, atrium w/ fountain & lace-curtained skylight, porch **Food & Drink** Full breakfast in DR or atrium; tea on arrival; afternoon English high tea in DR, atrium, or courtyard; event catering; special dietary needs w/ advance notice **Recreation** Golf, horse riding, biking, ballooning **Amenities & Services** Guest bath, fax, e-mail, large-screen TV, meetings, birthday teas, weddings, special events (75 outside; 50 for sit-down dinners)

ACCOMMODATIONS
Units 7 **All** Phone (modem), clock, ceiling fan, coffeemaker **Some** Fridge (4), balcony (3), fireplace (1), handicap accessible (1), iron, hair dryer, cable TV (on request) **Bed & Bath** Queen (6), twin (1); all private baths, tub (6) **Favorites** Alexander, the largest, has four-poster carved mahogany bed, sitting area, gas fireplace, fridge, balcony **Comfort & Decor** Victorian style with varied themes, antiques, mirrored dressers or armoires, family heirlooms like old maps, musical instruments, war medals, and tapestries

RATES, RESERVATIONS, & RESTRICTIONS
Deposit 50% (14-day cancellation for refund minus $10 if re-rented) **Discounts** Group **Credit Cards** AE, MC, V, D **Check-In/Out** 4 p.m./noon **Smoking** No (porch, garden) **Pets** No **Kids** Yes **No-Nos** N/A **Minimum Stay** None (except balloon festival) **Open** All year **Hosts** Pat & Jay Power, 4801 All Saints Rd., Albuquerque 87120 **Phone** (505) 898-3366 **Fax** (505) 898-8793 **E-mail** devon@nmia.com **Web** www.devonshireadobeinn.com

HACIENDA ANTIGUA, Albuquerque

OVERALL ★★★★ | QUALITY ★★★★ | VALUE ★★★★ | PRICE RANGE $99–$229

In a residential area between Casa del Granjero and the railway tracks, Hacienda Antigua is a quiet relaxing retreat near Albuquerque's Old Town. Catering to individual travelers rather than groups and wedding parties, Hacienda Antigua strives to maintain a relaxing ambience around its pool and gardens. The main adobe at one time had 28 rooms housing a local family and was a watering stop for horses with a mercantile store, cantina, and chapel. The living room still has some of that yesteryear feel with its slanting beam ceilings and fireplace. Rooms here are standards with queen beds and more spacious haciendas with king beds, sitting areas, and added amenities.

SETTING & FACILITIES
Location 10 mi. NW of Albuquerque International Airport **Near** Museums, Old Town **Building** 1790s adobe hacienda **Grounds** 3 acres w/ courtyard, large cottonwood tree,

fountain, hammock, ramada, raised bed garden, wildflowers, grasses, & apple, peach, plum, & pear trees **Public Space** LR, DR, porch **Food & Drink** Full breakfast buffet in DR; 24-hour snacks, beverages; water & snacks in rooms **Recreation** Golf, horse riding, biking, ballooning, tennis **Amenities & Services** Pool, hot tub, fax, ironing board, small functions (15)

ACCOMMODATIONS

Units 8 **All** Robes, wood-burning kiva fireplace, fridge, coffeepot, clock radio, bath salts, hair dryer, down comforter **Some** Fireplace (7), cable TV (4), phone (4), iron **Bed & Bath** King & daybed (4), queen & twin (2), queen (2); all private baths, jetted tub (2), double shower (2) **Favorites** La Sala is a hacienda room w/ wood paneling, sitting area, wicker furnishings **Comfort & Decor** Low doorways, beam ceilings, 2-foot-thick adobe walls, brick floors, throw rugs, armoires, quilts, folk art, Guatemalan textiles. Four hacienda suites have sitting/eating areas with sofa, table and chairs, separate doors to bath with whirlpool tub or double shower

RATES, RESERVATIONS, & RESTRICTIONS

Deposit 1 night (10-day cancellation policy) **Discounts** AAA, senior, Internet specials **Credit Cards** MC, V **Check-In/Out** 4–7 p.m./11 a.m. **Smoking** No **Pets** Yes **Kids** Yes **No-Nos** N/A **Minimum Stay** None **Open** All year **Hosts** Mark Brown & Keith Lewis, 6708 Tierra Dr. NW, Albuquerque 87107 **Phone** (505) 345-5399 or toll-free (800) 201-2986 **Fax** (505) 345-3855 **E-mail** info@haciendantigua.com **Web** www.haciendantigua.com

JAZZ INN BED & BREAKFAST, Albuquerque

OVERALL ★★★★ | QUALITY ★★★★ | VALUE ★★★★ | PRICE RANGE $69–$109

A haven for jazz musicians playing local gigs, the JazZ Inn sunken living room has been the scene of house party sessions with Herb Ellis, Mose Allison, Archie Shepp, and other jazz artists whose autographed portraits line the hallway walls. Self-proclaimed artists, community activists, and jazz fanatics, the proprietors arrange for jazz artists to visit Albuquerque and produce CD titles, such as George V. Johnson Jr.'s LiVe!@JazZInn. Central Avenue (Route 66) and the downtown trolley line are around the corner from the brown stucco bed-and-breakfast with turquoise trim. The atmosphere is informal, and the house fridge policy is "ask and you shall eat."

SETTING & FACILITIES

Location Downtown, 4 blocks from Convention Center **Near** University, museums, galleries, zoo, aquarium, parks **Building** Century-old eclectic Southwestern Victorian **Grounds** Wood fence surrounds dirt patio w/ Siberian elms, sculpture, cacti **Public Space** Sunken LR, DR **Food & Drink** Full breakfast in DR; "home-style" food access **Recreation** Biking **Amenities & Services** Wheelchair ramp, grand piano, 5,000 LP/CD/tape library, parties, weddings (75 guests)

ACCOMMODATIONS

Units 5 **All** Tape/CD player, clock radio, ceiling fan **Some** Armoire, phone (modem), fax **Bed & Bath** Queen (3), double (1), double & twin (1); all private baths, tub (3) **Favorites** Duke Ellington Suite, largest room, has trunk fronting queen bed, Route 66 memorabilia and horns on walls, bay window w/ green plants, morning glory stained-glass above claw-foot tub; Herb Ellis Suite entry has twin daybed & half bath, second room w/ double bed & full bath, cowboy & kachina art **Comfort & Decor** Mix of antique and contemporary furnishings with jazz, cowboy, Native American, and African motifs, rugs on wood plank floors

RATES, RESERVATIONS, & RESTRICTIONS
Deposit 50% (15-day cancellation for refund minus $15 fee; 30-day cancellation and full advance payment for conventions, balloon fiesta; fully transferable vouchers issued) **Discounts** Jazz concert packages **Credit Cards** AE, MC, V, D **Check-In/Out** 3–6 p.m./11 a.m. **Smoking** No **Pets** Yes (requires prior approval) **Kids** Yes **No-Nos** N/A **Minimum Stay** None **Open** All year **Hosts** Sophia & Nicholas Peron, 111 Walter St. NE, Albuquerque 87102 **Phone** (505) 242-1530 or toll-free (888) jazzinn **Fax** (505) 242-1530 **E-mail** 111bnb@swcp.com **Web** www.jazzinn.com

LOS POBLANOS INN, Albuquerque

OVERALL ★★★★★ | QUALITY ★★★★½ | VALUE ★★★★ | PRICE RANGE $135–$250

Set back from the road along a tree-lined entry and fronted by a lotus pond, farm fields, grazing churro sheep, strutting peacocks, and a St. Isidro sculpture, Los Poblanos and the adjacent 15,000-square-foot La Quinta Cultural Center were designed by architect John Gaw Meem. Architects researching Santa Fe style settle into the leather chairs of the hardwood library here to study New Mexico history and architecture. The spacious, angled living room features hardwood floors, two fireplaces, and several sitting nooks. The McCormick and twin-bedded Sor Juana rooms connect into a family suite. The Simms Suite has his-and-hers dressing rooms, a private greenhouse patio, and a hot tub.

SETTING & FACILITIES
Location Village of Los Ranchos, 4 mi. north of Old Town **Near** Museums **Building** 1800s ranch house expanded as New Mexico Territorial in 1934, Cultural Center, barn, silos **Grounds** 25 acres w/ pond, orchards, extensive formal gardens, fountains, courtyard, farm fields **Public Space** LR, DR, kitchen/cantina, conservatory, library, porches **Food & Drink** Full breakfast in DR or cantina; afternoon tea, snacks; fridge w/ beverages **Recreation** Biking, horse riding, hot-air ballooning, golf, bird-watching **Amenities & Services** Cable TV, national newspapers, business retreats, social functions (100)

ACCOMMODATIONS
Units 6 **All** Phone (data port), fireplace **Some** Patio w/ hot tub (1), TV (1), fridge (2), swamp coolers, ceiling fans, desks **Bed & Bath** King (3), queen (2), twins (1); all private baths, tub (5) **Favorites** Girard Guest House has LR, pottery folk art, stenciled BR floor, wicker, upholstery, carved wood, carpeted bath **Comfort & Decor** Open adobe feel, carved wood furnishings, New Mexico antiques, colorful folk art, paintings, punched-tin frames, tile, and ironwork

RATES, RESERVATIONS, & RESTRICTIONS
Deposit 50% (10-day cancellation for refund minus 10%; 100% deposit & 30 days cancel-
lation for Dec. 21–Jan. 2 & Balloon Fiesta) **Discounts** Corp., extended stays **Credit
Cards** AE, MC, V **Check-In/Out** 3–6 p.m./noon **Smoking** Outside portals **Pets** No
(boarding arrangements at nearby kennels) **Kids** Yes **No-Nos** N/A **Minimum Stay**
None **Open** All year **Hosts** Odette Schuler, Armin & Penny Rembe, 4803 Rio Grande
Blvd. NW, Albuquerque 87107 **Phone** (505) 344-9297 or toll-free (866) 344-9297 **Fax**
(505) 342-1302 **E-mail** info@lospoblanos.com **Web** www.lospoblanos.com

THE POTTERIES BED & BREAKFAST, Albuquerque

OVERALL ★★★★ | QUALITY ★★★½ | VALUE ★★★★ | PRICE RANGE $85–$100

Located in a quiet residential neighborhood, the Potteries is run by a potter who can be a source of advice for buyers of contemporary and traditional art. The hostess's tastes run toward her own pottery, carved wood
chests, and Japanese scrolls, which are displayed in one of the two living
rooms. A mile away are Rio Grande Nature Conservancy paths and trails
that run alongside irrigation ditches (acequias) and bosques (wetlands).
Though the location has a quiet rural feel, I-40 is only three miles to the
south and downtown Albuquerque and the convention center are an easy
commute.

SETTING & FACILITIES
Location 4 mi. north of Old Town **Near** Old Town, museums **Building** 1971 rambling
adobe ranch house w/ attached greenhouse, private pottery studio **Grounds** 1 acre w/
trees, patio **Public Space** LR w/ fireplace, second LR w/ artwork, DR, porch **Food &
Drink** Full breakfast in DR **Recreation** Biking, horse riding, hot-air ballooning, golf, bird-
watching **Amenities & Services** Piano, TV

ACCOMMODATIONS
Units 2 **All** TV, clock radio, portable heater **Some** Private entrance (1), porch (1), coffeemaker (1), phone (1), private AC (1), makeup lights (1) **Bed & Bath** King & twin
trundle (1), double (1); all private baths, tub (1) **Favorites** Southwestern has porch, private entrance, shuttered doors to king bed, sitting area w/ twin trundle bed, large walk-
in closet, coffeemaker, private phone line, makeup lights; Quilt Room has a star quilt
behind antique maple spool double bed, hope chest, bath across hall w/ pottery, old barn
wood art & paintings **Comfort & Decor** Wood beam ceilings, old family furnishings,
Italian tile floors, throw rugs, large closet with dresser inside, baths with brick tile floors
and tiled sinks

RATES, RESERVATIONS, & RESTRICTIONS
Deposit 1 night (10-day cancellation) **Discounts** Extended stay (7 days or longer gets
10% off) **Credit Cards** None (cash, check only) **Check-In/Out** 2–5 p.m./noon **Smoking** Patio, greenhouse **Pets** Need to ask (young dogs discouraged; owner has dog) **Kids**

Yes **No-Nos** N/A **Minimum Stay** None **Open** All year **Host** Liz Anderson, 4100 Dietz Farm Circle, Albuquerque 87107 **Phone** (505) 344-3144 or toll-free (800) 795-3144 **Fax** N/A **E-mail** lizpotteries@earthlink.net **Web** www.collectorsguide.com/thepotteries

HACIENDA VARGAS BED & BREAKFAST INN, *Algodones*

OVERALL ★★★★½ | QUALITY ★★★★ | VALUE ★★★★ | PRICE RANGE $79–$149

On a bend in the old El Camino Real (Route 66), horse-friendly Hacienda Vargas combines an old stagecoach stop, chapel, general store, and casita into a romantic rural getaway. The triangular yard with a turquoise bell tower tolling for weddings is sandwiched between Amtrak rails and highway. A long entry has French doors opening to the patio, a wood stove, knight, and skylight. The stand-alone casita's two suites have a private courtyard. The sponge-painted pink and turquoise San Felipe has garden stencils and a double whirlpool tub. The Western-patterned Santa Ana's bath has weathered barn wood and a pressed-tin ceiling.

SETTING & FACILITIES
Location 24 mi. north of Albuquerque, 25 mi. south of Santa Fe **Near** Museums, pueblos **Building** 150–200-year-old adobe hacienda combines 2 buildings, century-old adobe casita **Grounds** 2 acres w/ courtyard, gazebo, bell tower, pond, cottonwood & elm trees **Public Space** Entry, DR, library **Food & Drink** Full breakfast in DR; evening beverages, snacks **Recreation** Golf, horse riding, biking **Amenities & Services** Phone, fax, computer, strolling guitars, wedding chapel, meetings, parties (250)

ACCOMMODATIONS
Units 7 **All** Ceiling fan, clock **Some** Fireplace (6), tape/radio (6), irons, hair dryers, phones (on request) **Bed & Bath** Queen (6), double (1); all private baths, claw-foot tub

(3), jetted tub (4) **Favorites** Santa Fe bridal suite has low entry w/ steps, sitting area, fireplace, brick floor, block glass, 2-person jetted tub **Comfort & Decor** You'll find a blend of old and more modern, wood frame and adobe walls, wood-burning and gas fireplaces, some inlaid tiles, beam ceilings, brick and saltillo tile floors, mirrored armoires, varied antiques and reproductions, and old radios

RATES, RESERVATIONS, & RESTRICTIONS

Deposit Credit card holds (10-day cancellation for refund minus $35 fee; different rules for peak periods) **Discounts** Extended stays, romance packages, whole hacienda rentals, groups **Credit Cards** AE, MC, V **Check-In/Out** 4–6 p.m./11 a.m. **Smoking** No **Pets** Yes (w/ advance notice; horses welcome: owners have dogs, cats, horses) **Kids** Yes **No-Nos** N/A **Minimum Stay** None **Open** All year **Hosts** Richard & Cynthia Spence, 1431 NM 313, P.O. Box 307, Algodones 87001 **Phone** (505) 867-9115 or toll-free (800) 261-0006 **Fax** (505) 867-0640 **E-mail** stay@haciendavargas.com **Web** www.haciendavargas.com

LA HACIENDA GRANDE, Bernalillo

OVERALL ★★★★★ | QUALITY ★★★★ | VALUE ★★★★ | PRICE RANGE $99–$139

At the end of a narrow gravel lane between the villages of Corrales and Algodones, La Hacienda Grande is a former stagecoach stop on the old El Camino Real running between Santa Fe and Mexico City. In the same family from 1711 to 1995, La Hacienda is still surrounded by the Santa Ana Indian reservation, horse pastures, and cottonwood trees. All the guest rooms, five of which open onto the courtyard, are different, because they were added one room at a time over the years. The step-down dining room, formerly a winery, stable, and chapel, has barrel chairs and a glass-topped Santa Fe latilla table.

SETTING & FACILITIES

Location 19 mi. north of Albuquerque International Airport **Near** Museums, parks, historic sites, pueblos **Building** 1700s Spanish hacienda **Grounds** Courtyard, patio, grape arbor, roses **Public Space** LR, DR **Food & Drink** Full breakfast in DR or courtyard; pre-breakfast room beverage tray; candlelight dinners, picnic baskets **Recreation** Horse riding, biking, golf **Amenities & Services** TV/VCR, fax, copier, secretarial services, flower arrangements, massage, meetings, weddings (150)

ACCOMMODATIONS

Units 6 **All** Phone jack, hair dryer, iron, ironing board **Some** Private entrance (5), fireplace (5), TV/VCR (2), phone (on request) **Bed & Bath** Mix of kings, queens, doubles, rollaways; all private baths, jetted tub (1), tub (1) **Favorites** Cochiti has alcove entry w/ latilla screens, ladder, kiva fireplace, 2-century-old brick floor, purple & maroon wardrobe; San Felipe, the largest, has white wicker furnishings, wrought-iron bed, wood stove, double jetted tub **Comfort & Decor** High beam ceilings, 2.5-feet-thick adobe walls, saltillo tile or brick floors, mats and Southwestern rugs, black wrought-iron chandeliers, sitting areas with Mexican and twig chairs, plus wood wardrobes

RATES, RESERVATIONS, & RESTRICTIONS
Deposit 1 night or 50% (11-day cancellation for refund minus $15; 30 days for holidays, markets; 60 days for balloon festival; transferable gift certificate issued) **Discounts** Packages **Credit Cards** AE, MC, V, D, DC **Check-In/Out** 4–6 p.m./11 a.m. **Smoking** No (courtyard) **Pets** Yes (advance permission needed) **Kids** Yes **No-Nos** N/A **Minimum Stay** None **Open** All year **Hosts** Gayle & Ray Richmond, 21 Barros Lane, Bernalillo 87004 **Phone** (505) 867-1887 or toll-free (800) 353-1887 **Fax** (505) 771-1436 **E-mail** lhg@swcp.com **Web** www.lahaciendagrande.com

CASA DE ALEGRIA BED & BREAKFAST, Corrales

OVERALL ★★★★ | QUALITY ★★★★ | VALUE ★★★★ | PRICE RANGE $79–$129

Looking out across horse and cattle pastures to the Sandia Mountains in the distance, Casa de Alegria is one of over a dozen bed-and-breakfasts in this quiet village adjoining Albuquerque. Down a dirt road off a narrow, paved country lane, Casa de Alegria has three rooms in an L-shaped wing surrounding the courtyard. A fourth room inside the house is used mostly for overflow. The main house is technically the domain of the hosts, but guests are often made welcome under the skylight in the gathering room with smoothies whipped up from fruit growing on the grounds. Many prefer relaxing outside in the hammock or hot tub and enjoying the Sandia Mountain and rural views, or just gazing at goldfish in the small rock pond.

SETTING & FACILITIES
Location 16 mi. north of Albuquerque International Airport **Near** Museums, galleries, historic sites, pueblos **Building** Late 1990s hacienda **Grounds** 4 acres w/ courtyard, patio, hammock, small waterfall flowing into rock pond **Public Space** TV/stereo room **Food & Drink** Full breakfast in DR or courtyard; chocolates; special dietary needs **Recreation** Horse riding, biking, hot-air ballooning, golf, fishing, bird-watching **Amenities & Services** Hot tub, organ, microwave, Spanish spoken, parties, weddings (30)

ACCOMMODATIONS
Units 4 **All** Fireplace, ceiling fan, AC, TV, clock radio, fresh flowers, radiant floor heat **Some** Handicap accessible (1), VCR (1) **Bed & Bath** Queen; all private baths, tub (1) **Favorites** Coyote, the largest room, has VCR for TV, basic wood furniture, tub & shower; Jack Rabbit Room differs from others in having a wide shower w/ a seat for handicap accessibility **Comfort & Decor** High ceilings, saltillo tile floors, white walls with black-and-white photos, down comforters, simple wood furnishings, candelabra light fixtures, closets, and pedestal sinks

RATES, RESERVATIONS, & RESTRICTIONS
Deposit Credit card holds (72-hour cancellation for 90% refund) **Discounts** Seniors, whole house rental **Credit Cards** AE, MC, V **Check-In/Out** 4–7 p.m./11 a.m. **Smoking** No (courtyard) **Pets** No **Kids** Yes **No-Nos** N/A **Minimum Stay** None **Open** All year

Host Sonia Bettez, P.O. Box 90, Corrales 87048 **Phone** (505) 890-0176 or toll-free (888) 320-3456 **Fax** (505) 890-6998 **E-mail** alegriainn@cs.com **Web** www.new-mexico-inn.com

HACIENDA MANZANAL, Corrales

OVERALL ★★★★★ | QUALITY ★★★★½ | VALUE ★★★★ | PRICE RANGE $85–$125

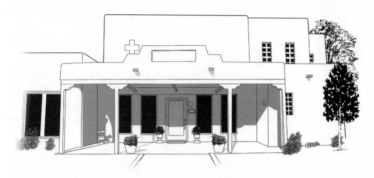

Along a shady rural lane with speed bumps and a strictly enforced 30 mph speed limit, Hacienda Manzanal is in an area with dark nights (no street lights) whose quiet is punctuated by the local dogs, roosters, and coyotes. Manzanal is Spanish for apple orchard, like the one next door. A horse ranch borders another side, and a back gate leads to an acequia (irrigation canal) trail into town frequented by horses, bikes, and pedestrians. The living room has a saltillo tile floor, an old dry goods store posting machine, a "one cent honest weight" scale, plus family antiques from Nebraska and rocking chairs.

SETTING & FACILITIES

Location 15 mi. north of Albuquerque International Airport **Near** Museums, galleries, historic sites **Building** 2001 2-story Pueblo/Territorial style **Grounds** 1 acre w/ courtyard, fountain, elm, cottonwood, & 16 apple trees **Public Space** LR, DR **Food & Drink** Full breakfast in DR or courtyard; afternoon refreshments; 24-hour beverages; special diets **Recreation** Horse riding, biking, hot-air ballooning, golf **Amenities & Services** TV/VCR, stereo, portable phone, meetings, parties, weddings (40)

ACCOMMODATIONS

Units 4 **All** Modem jack, gas fireplace, ceiling fan, radiant floor heat, clock radio, hair dryer **Some** Handicap accessible (1), sofa bed (2) **Bed & Bath** King (2), queen (2); all private baths, jetted tub (1), tub (2) **Favorites** San Juan has outdoorsy feel, fishing gear, antique rifles, duck decoys, carved bear holding fish, loveseat/bed; French Provincial Orchard Room has beam ceilings, Tudor countryside mural, 2 armoires, writing table, lace curtains, frilly lampshades, double sinks, apple tree mural above jetted tub **Comfort & Decor** Varied themes, dressers or armoires, closets, trunks, teddy bears and dolls, upstairs block-glass windows.

RATES, RESERVATIONS, & RESTRICTIONS
Deposit I night (7-day cancellation policy) **Discounts** Extended stays, corp., whole house rental, Internet packages **Credit Cards** AE, MC, V, D **Check-In/Out** 5–6:30 p.m./10 a.m. **Smoking** No (outside) **Pets** No (owner's pets stay on their side of house) **Kids** Yes (over age 6 preferred) **No-Nos** Lock outside doors if returning after 10 p.m. **Minimum Stay** None **Open** All year **Hosts** Sue & Norm Gregory, 300 W. Meadowlark Lane, Corrales 87048 **Phone** (505) 922-1662 or toll-free (877) 922-1662 **Fax** (505) 922-1909 **E-mail** hmf@haciendamanzanal.com **Web** www.haciendamanzanal.com

YOURS TRULY BED & BREAKFAST, Corrales

OVERALL ★★★★★ | QUALITY ★★★★½ | VALUE ★★★★ | PRICE RANGE $98–$135

On a hill just above a speed trap in this go-slow community where the signs say Drive Slow and See Our Village, Drive Fast and See Our Judge, Yours Truly soothes visitors with classical music in a living room with a brick floor, beam ceilings, and a balloon festival pin display. The Spirit Room bathroom is entered via swinging saloon doors. Woodrow, a wooden man, is alternately bent into service as a table with outstretched drink-holder arms or straightened into a coat rack. The kitchen clock reads "Who cares?" Indeed, cares can melt away while gazing at the Sandia Mountains.

SETTING & FACILITIES
Location 16 mi. north of Albuquerque International Airport **Near** Museums, parks, historic sites, pueblos **Building** 1990s contemporary hillside adobe **Grounds** Patios, metal kachina & roadrunner sculptures, rock fishpond, hammock, whiskey barrel fountain, sage, cactus, wildflowers **Public Space** LR, DR **Food & Drink** Full breakfast buffet in DR; pre-breakfast tray outside room w/ flowers, fruit, bread, coffee; candy jar in room; happy hour snacks & drinks **Recreation** Horse riding, biking, hot-air ballooning, golf **Amenities & Services** Stereo, fax/copier, hot tub, barbecue, guest fridge, meetings

ACCOMMODATIONS
Units 4 **All** Robes, gas fireplace, AC, cable TV, lip balm, iron & ironing board, hair dryer, radio, clock, flashlight **Some** Phone (2), VCR (2), ceiling fan (2), candles **Bed & Bath** King (3), king & single (1); all private baths, tub (1), dbl. shower (2) **Favorites** Kachina has blue & yellow accents, tiered sitting areas, wired stand for orange sink, Kokopelli candles, private back entrance **Comfort & Decor** Brick floors, some high slanting wood ceilings, window seats, wavy walls, block glass, full-length mirrors, reading lights, barbed-wire cacti, and humorous Southwestern art set the tone here

RATES, RESERVATIONS, & RESTRICTIONS
Deposit I night (3-day cancellation for refund minus $25 fee) **Discounts** Off-season (Nov.–March), various specials **Credit Cards** AE, MC, V, D, DC **Check-In/Out** "When you can"/"when you have to" **Smoking** No **Pets** Yes (requires prior approval) **Kids** Yes

(requires prior approval) **No-Nos** N/A **Minimum Stay** None **Open** All year **Hosts** Pat & James Montgomery, 160 Paseo de Corrales, Corrales 87048 **Phone** (505) 898-7027 or toll-free (800) 942-7890 **Fax** (505) 898-9022 **E-mail** yourstrulybb@aol.com **Web** www.bbyourstruly.com

THE DANCING BEAR BED & BREAKFAST, Jemez Springs

OVERALL ★★★★½ | QUALITY ★★★★ | VALUE ★★★★ | PRICE RANGE $80–$130

Reached via a slow (30 mph) but scenic mountain road passing pueblos and red rocks, Dancing Bear is a retreat in a small village with a mineral springs bathhouse and pottery workshops. The living room has cathedral ceilings and floor-to-ceiling windows that come to a point like the bow of a boat, providing views across the patio to the red rock mesa bordering the Jemez River. The cozy rounded living room also has a large central fireplace warming the dining area. A mini-gallery sells sage smudge sticks, sculpted bears, dream catchers, and pottery from Jemez Pueblo.

SETTING & FACILITIES
Location 50 mi. north of Albuquerque **Near** Bandelier, Los Alamos, Indian pueblos, hot springs, forests **Building** 1985 contemporary wood & glass, 2 stories **Grounds** Patio backed by sandstone mesa, Jemez River, cottonwood trees **Public Space** LR, DR **Food & Drink** Full breakfast in DR or patio; afternoon snacks; special dietary needs; small group lunches, dinners **Recreation** Biking, fishing, rafting, winter sports **Amenities & Services** Mini-gallery, barbecue, weddings, meetings, reunions (25 people)

ACCOMMODATIONS
Units 4 guest rooms, 1 upstairs **All** Robes, TV/VCR, clock radio, hair dryer, water pitcher, ceiling fan **Some** Fridge (2), coffeemaker (2), patio (1) **Bed & Bath** King (2), king/2 singles (1), queen waterbed (1); all private baths, tub (2) **Favorites** Santa Fe, the largest, has pale pink color, fireplace, king bed, shuttered closet w/ fridge & double roll-away, leather loveseat, carpeted marble bath, water closet, green plants, pottery, and sliding glass door to patio. Bear's Den has peaked ceiling, mint green color, skylight, king bed, sleeper sofa, makeup lights, shower w/ seats **Comfort & Decor** Bear motif, teddy bears, stone sculptures, paintings, rocking chairs, punched-tin light fixtures, and reading areas

RATES, RESERVATIONS, & RESTRICTIONS
Deposit 50% of first night (7-day cancellation policy) **Discounts** Seniors, extended stays **Credit Cards** MC, V, D **Check-In/Out** 3–6 p.m./11 a.m. **Smoking** No **Pets** No **Kids** Yes **No-Nos** N/A **Minimum Stay** None (2 nights preferred on weekends) **Open** All year **Host** Carol Breen, 314 San Diego Dr., P.O. Box 128, Jemez Springs 87025 **Phone** (505) 829-3336 or toll-free (800) 422-3271 **Fax** (505) 825-3395 **E-mail** Dancingbear@sulphur canyon.com **Web** www.dancingbearbandb.com

DESERT WILLOW BED & BREAKFAST, Jemez Springs

OVERALL ★★★★½ | QUALITY ★★★★ | VALUE ★★★★ | PRICE RANGE $90–$135

Like Dancing Bear, Desert Willow is a rural retreat along the Jemez River bordered by red mesas and public forest lands. Modern art dominates, from the abstract canvases at the entrance to the blue crackle front door and sculpture garden with heads from around the world. The Dragonfly Cottage, a self-contained, stand-alone two-bedroom retreat with a living room and full kitchen, is not served breakfast. The main house has two upstairs rooms sharing a common lounge. The dining room has a brick floor; homemade chocolate truffles compete with a healthier fruit bowl at snack time. The host's chocolate truffles have attracted enough raves that he is opening a candy shop.

SETTING & FACILITIES
Location Mile marker 16 on NM 4, 50 mi. north of Albuquerque **Near** Bandelier, Los Alamos, Indian pueblos, hot springs, forests **Building** 1998 northern New Mexico–style w/ moss-colored stucco exterior, tin roof **Grounds** 1 acre bisected by Jemez River, 2 flagstone patios, boulders, drought-tolerant landscape, sculptured head collection, pine & cottonwood trees **Public Space** Upstairs LR, DR, library **Food & Drink** Full breakfast in DR (no breakfast in cottage); evening chocolate truffles, fruit bowl **Recreation** Biking, fishing, rafting, winter sports **Amenities & Services** Satellite TV/VCR, phone

ACCOMMODATIONS
Units 2 guest rooms, 1 standalone cottage **All** Fresh flowers, down comforter, ceiling fan, hair dryer, clock **Some** Full kitchen (1), TV/VCR (1), phone (1), fireplace (1), porches (1) **Bed & Bath** Queen (3); tub (3); all private baths **Favorites** Self-contained Dragonfly Cottage has many windows, 2 BRs w/ platform queen beds, full kitchen, LR w/ fireplace, brick floors, TV/VCR, phone, wicker furnishings, large deck **Comfort & Decor** Sponge-painted walls, four-poster canopied beds, sitting area, contemporary paintings, woodcuts, pottery, gold carpet, radiant floor heat, and tiled baths

RATES, RESERVATIONS, & RESTRICTIONS
Deposit None **Discounts** Extended stays **Credit Cards** AE, MC, V **Check-In/Out** 2–6 p.m./11 a.m. **Smoking** No **Pets** No (owners have cat, dog) **Kids** Yes (in cottage) **No-Nos** N/A **Minimum Stay** 2 nights for cottage **Open** All year **Host** Leone Wilson, 15975 NM 4, P.O. Box 255, Jemez Springs 87025 **Phone** (505) 829-3410 **Fax** (505) 829-3410 **E-mail** wilsons@desertwillowbandb.com **Web** www.desertwillowbandb.com

RIVERDANCER INN, Jemez Springs

OVERALL ★★★★ | QUALITY ★★★★ | VALUE ★★★★ | PRICE RANGE $109–$160

Along foothills fronting the Jemez River, Riverdancer features a "healing house" offering "à la carte therapeutic or spa body treatments," involving movement, bodywork, seaweed wraps, spirituality, and nature walks. More like a motel complex in feel than the smaller and more intimate Dancing Bear or Desert Willow, Riverdancer is nonetheless a relaxing retreat for those seeking a healing experience. The huge main lounge area has a reception desk, skylights, green plants, a high pine beam ceiling with tongue-and-groove planks, ceiling shelves displaying Native American baskets and pottery, kachinas, saltillo tile floors, and soft upholstered sofas and chairs surrounding a big-screen TV and a cattle skull above the kiva fireplace. The saltillo tile hallways are punctuated with wooden steps and art display niches.

SETTING & FACILITIES
Location 60 mi. NW of Albuquerque **Near** Bandelier, Los Alamos, Indian pueblos, hot mineral springs, forests **Building** Mid-1990s hacienda built as B&B **Grounds** 5 acres w/ tiered brick patio, Buddha fountain, peach trees, hammock, labyrinth **Public Space** Lounge, DR, casita for wraps & energy healing **Food & Drink** Full breakfast in DR; 24-hour beverages; organic vegetarian dinners **Recreation** Biking, fishing, bird-watching, winter sports **Amenities & Services** TV, massage, laundry

ACCOMMODATIONS
Units 7 **All** TV, phone, clock radio, first-aid kit **Some** Kitchen (1), hair dryers **Bed & Bath** King (3), queen (3), twin (1); jetted tub (1), tub (6); all private baths. **Favorites** Zuni has queen bed, tiled sink w/ makeup lights, sliding glass door to patio; suite has LR, queen bed, kitchen, saltillo tile floor w/ radiant heat **Comfort & Decor** Each room is named after Native American tribe and offers solid basic furnishings, baskets, pottery, Southwestern-style rugs, tiled sinks, and makeup mirrors

RATES, RESERVATIONS, & RESTRICTIONS
Deposit 1 night or 50% (10 days for refund minus 15% on 1-night reservations) **Discounts** Bodywork & retreat packages, whole property rental **Credit Cards** MC, V, D **Check-In/Out** 2–7 p.m./11 a.m. **Smoking** No **Pets** No (resident dog) **Kids** Yes (over age 10) **No-Nos** N/A **Minimum Stay** None (except holidays) **Open** All year **Host** Linsay Locke , 16445 NM 4, Jemez Springs 87205 **Phone** (505) 829-3262 or toll-free (800) 809-3262 **Fax** (505) 829-3262 **E-mail** reservations@riverdancer.com **Web** www.riverdancer.com

Northwest

Northwest New Mexico borders Utah, Colorado, and Arizona in the Navajo Nation at the Four Corners, the only point in the United States where four state corners converge. From the Four Corners, northwest New Mexico extends east along the Colorado border beyond Farmington and Bloomfield toward Navajo Lake State Park. Northwest New Mexico also stretches along the Arizona border south of Gallup to the Zuni Reservation, then east toward El Morro and El Malpais National Monuments, Grants, and the Acoma and Laguna Indian Reservations along I-40 west of Albuquerque.

Bed-and-breakfast businesses are few and hard to find outside Farmington. The northwest population center and one of New Mexico's largest cities with 34,000 people, Farmington is best known for its coal mining and oil and gas production. At the confluence of the San Juan, Animas, and La Plata Rivers, the Navajo name for Farmington is To-Tah, which means three waters. Farmington has an excellent new museum, old trading posts, golf courses, shopping malls, and a microbrewery.

Aztec Ruins National Monument, 15 miles northeast of Farmington, has a restored ceremonial kiva and remnants of a sandstone pueblo apartment complex with hundreds of rooms. The desolate Bisti/De-Na-Zin Wilderness south of Farmington is a geologic spectacle of badlands and hoodoos. Half an hour west of Farmington is the Navajo Nation city of Shiprock, named after the basaltic remnants of a 3-million-year-old extinct volcano that seemingly shimmers and floats like a ship when the light is right. Often photographed for geology textbooks as a classic example of a volcanic neck with radiating dikes, Shiprock is a sacred Navajo site (climbing is prohibited). Mesa Verde National Park in Colorado is 1.5 hours to the north. Chaco Culture National Historic Park is accessible via dirt roads 1.5 hours south of Farmington.

CASA BLANCA INN, Farmington

OVERALL ★★★★½ | QUALITY ★★★★½ | VALUE ★★★★ | PRICE RANGE $78–$160

In a quiet residential hillside neighborhood above the main drag, Casa Blanca is a relaxed and friendly base for exploring the area and its many trading posts. Originally designed by trader Miriam Taylor, whose portrait appears in the dining room opposite jungle-like green wallpaper and wrought-iron windows, Casa Blanca's longtime staff of Charlotte, Rosie, and Nate makes guests feel at home. Australian doves sing in the green-carpeted living room, and French doors open to the patio. A sunken library has brick and wood walls, a saltillo tile floor, Southwestern rugs, and a flagstone fireplace.

SETTING & FACILITIES

Location 2 blocks north of Main St. **Near** Trading posts, Anasazi ruins, forest, lakes **Building** 1940s Mission style **Grounds** 2 acre wooded hillside w/ patio, gazebo, hammock, flowering hyacinth **Public Space** LR, DR, library **Food & Drink** Full breakfast in DR, patio, or bed; afternoon tea; take-out lunches, dinner **Recreation** Golf, fishing, boating **Amenities & Services** Concierge, valet, turn-down, laundry, free airport shuttle, hot tub, stereo, piano

ACCOMMODATIONS

Units 6 guest rooms, 1 guest house **All** Robes, TV/VCR, phone, clock radio **Some** Ceiling fan (4), hair dryer & butler basket (on request), laundry room (1), patio (2), sun porch (1) **Bed & Bath** King (3), queen (3), king & queen (1); all private baths, jetted tub (1), tub (3) **Favorites** Caballero, original master BR, has king bed, carved headboard, dark wood furnishings, private patio, malachite makeup table, double sinks, green & white tile bath; Sequito, up green carpet staircase, has French doors, king bed, iron headboard, armoire, love seat, green plants, wicker furnishings, sun porch, double sinks **Comfort & Decor** Wood or wicker furnishings; some upholstery and antiques; varied headboards or canopies, desks, or tables; dressers or armoires; varied art on walls

RATES, RESERVATIONS, & RESTRICTIONS

Deposit Credit card holds (7-day cancellation for full refund) **Discounts** AAA, corp., extended stays **Credit Cards** AE, MC, V, D **Check-In/Out** 4–7 p.m./11 a.m. **Smoking** Patio **Pets** No **Kids** Yes **No-Nos** N/A **Minimum Stay** None **Open** All year **Hosts** Tammy & Floyd Jensen, 505 E. La Plata St., Farmington 87401 **Phone** (505) 327-6503 or toll-free (800) 550-6503 **Fax** (505) 326-5680 **E-mail** casablancanm@hotmail.com **Web** www.farmington-nm-lodging.com

SILVER RIVER ADOBE INN, Farmington

OVERALL ★★★½ | QUALITY ★★★★ | VALUE ★★★★ | PRICE RANGE $75–$175

Perched on a sandstone bluff overlooking the San Juan River and a bird fly-way, the Silver River Adobe mixes San Juan Pueblo adobe brick with post-and-beam construction. Rough-sawn green beams from local forests, an aged wood patina, organic oat grain waffles, maple syrup, and organic apple juice, are part of the environmentally sound approach. Along with the many trading posts, being midway between Mesa Verde and Chaco and down the road from the Aztec and Salmon Ruins draws tourists here. During the winter, Farmington bed-and-breakfasts tide themselves over with the business trade that services the local medical and mining industries.

SETTING & FACILITIES

Location 2.5 mi. west of downtown **Near** Trading posts, Anasazi ruins, forest, lakes **Building** 1980s adobe & ponderosa pine Roy Davin design w/ recent additions **Grounds** 4 acres w/ cottonwoods on sandstone cliffs above river **Public Space** DR **Food & Drink** Cont'l breakfast in DR **Recreation** Golf, fishing, bird-watching **Amenities & Services** Piano, small weddings, workshops

ACCOMMODATIONS

Units 3 **All** Private entrance, ceiling fan, phone, clock **Some** Full kitchen (1) **Bed & Bath** King (1), queen (2); all private baths **Favorites** Cliffrose Suite has wood paneling & adobe brick, 14-inch-thick exposed ceiling beams, San Juan River view windows, carved wood furnishings, black wrought-iron bed, LR, pottery, baskets, kachinas, full kitchen, Mexican tile shower **Comfort & Decor** Passive solar heat, radiant heat cement floors, Southwestern rugs, wood walls and ceilings, reading lamps, local oil paintings, punched-tin mirror frames, marble or Mexican tile showers.

RATES, RESERVATIONS, & RESTRICTIONS

Deposit 1 night or 50%; 14-day notice for refund **Discounts** Extended stays, golf & fishing packages **Credit Cards** AE, MC, V **Check-In/Out** 4–7 p.m./11 a.m. **Smoking** No **Pets** Yes **Kids** Yes (over age 12) **No-Nos** N/A **Minimum Stay** None **Open** All year **Hosts** Diana Ohlson & David Beers, 3151 W. Main St., P.O. Box 3411, Farmington 87499 **Phone** (505) 325-8219 or toll-free (800) 382-9251 **Fax** (505) 325-5074 **E-mail** sribb@cyberport.com **Web** www.cyberport.com/silveradobe

North Central

North Central New Mexico, the bed-and-breakfast center of the state, stretches into the mountainous Carson and Santa Fe National Forests north of Albuquerque. Santa Fe and Taos are the major destinations. Bed-and-breakfasts are also scattered among smaller high-elevation towns like Truchas, Chimayo, Abiquiu, Espanola, and Chama. Skiers flock to the Sangre de Cristo Mountains and Taos Ski Valley after Thanksgiving. Rafters take to the rivers after the snow melts in spring. Thanks to the 7,000-foot elevation, Taos and Santa Fe summers are mild.

A log and adobe building built over Native American ruins by the Spanish in 1610, Santa Fe's Palace of the Governors was the territorial capitol into the twentieth century. Now a museum on a street lined with Native American arts and crafts vendors, the palace is near the 400-year-old Plaza. Nearby are the Fine Arts and Georgia O'Keeffe Museums, the Institute of American Indian Arts, and New Mexico's top shopping streets.

Though Santa Fe is arguably the cultural center and has deeper historic roots, Taos has a much more varied array of bed-and-breakfasts spread over a wider geographic area. Santa Fe bed-and-breakfasts are restricted to commercial zones by local ordinance, and owners can hire professional innkeepers and live elsewhere. Taos ordinances are geared toward having owners living on the property and being hosts, though larger properties often get some front desk help.

Taos has 7,000 residents and eight museums, including the Kit Carson Home and the 21-room Spanish Colonial Martinez Hacienda. Taos Society of Artists paintings are displayed at the Harwood Foundation and Ernest Blumenschein Home. The Millicent Rogers Museum delves into history and culture. Most of Taos's annual 2 million visitors come from neighboring Texas and Colorado, though the city is a popular driving destination from around the Midwest.

The High Road to Taos meanders scenically north from the crossroads town of Espanola. Chimayo is noted for its weavers and the healing miracles at El Santuario. Georgia O'Keeffe's badlands landscape scenes can be seen heading north from Abiquiu to Chama on US 84.

CASA DEL RIO, Abiquiu/Espanola

OVERALL ★★★★ | QUALITY ★★★½ | VALUE ★★★★ | PRICE RANGE $100–$125

A small sign and closed livestock gate half a mile past mile marker 199 on US 84 mark the short dirt road leading to Casa del Rio, which is bordered by open Bureau of Land Management land. Now in its fourteenth year as a bed-and-breakfast in the Ghost Ranch country made famous by Georgia O'Keeffe's paintings, Casa del Rio features a partially rounded kiva-style meditation room with a traditional Southwestern viga and latilla ceiling. The Rio Chama flows across the property; it is muddy in summer but fishable in winter. Hummingbirds seasonally buzz the patio, and migratory birds fly overhead.

SETTING & FACILITIES
Location 10 mi. south of Abiquiu, 10 mi. north of Espanola **Near** Santa Fe, Taos, Ghost Ranch, Bandelier, forests **Building** 1980 Pueblo-style adobe **Grounds** 12 acres of native landscape, river, brick patio w/ small waterfall, goldfish pond **Public Space** LR, DR, meditation room **Food & Drink** Full breakfast in DR **Recreation** Fishing, hunting, horse riding, biking, bird-watching **Amenities & Services** Meditation space

ACCOMMODATIONS
Units 4 guest rooms **All** Fridge, clock **Some** Fireplace (2), radiant floor heat (2), daybed (1) **Bed & Bath** King (1), queen (3) **Favorites** La Casita has tile entrance, wood floor, old mine lintels, king bed, kiva fireplace, pottery lamps, stump ottoman, baling twine & braided leather closet, junipers overhanging private walled patio w/ white wrought-iron furniture & swinging chair **Comfort & Decor** Handcrafted wood and Mexican furnishings, viga and latilla ceilings, saltillo tile floors, Southwestern rugs, punched-tin frames and fixtures, paintings for sale on walls, decorative Talavera-tiled bath sinks, outdoor sitting areas

RATES, RESERVATIONS, & RESTRICTIONS

Deposit 50% or 1 night (21-day cancellation for full refund; $20 rebooking fee; full payment & no refund for major holiday weekends) **Discounts** None **Credit Cards** AE, MC, V, D **Check-In/Out** 4–6 p.m./10–11 a.m. **Smoking** No **Pets** No (owners have dogs, horses, sheep) **Kids** Yes (over age 12) **No-Nos** N/A **Minimum Stay** 2 nights for major holidays, local festivals **Open** All year **Hosts** Eileen Sopanen & Mel Vigil, #19946 US 84, P.O. Box 702, Abiquiu 87510 **Phone** (505) 753-2035 or toll-free (800) 920-1495 **Fax** (505) 753-2035 **E-mail** casadelrio@newmexico.com **Web** www.bbonline.com/nm/casadelrio

THE PARLOR CAR BED & BREAKFAST, Chama

OVERALL ★★★★ | QUALITY ★★★★ | VALUE ★★★★ | PRICE RANGE $50–$90

Built by Chama's first banker during the Roaring Twenties, the Parlor Car is conveniently across the from the Cumbres and Toltec Scenic Railroad station. Each room is named after a railroad man, including the lowest-priced Fredrick Henry Harvey, whose private bathroom is across the hall. The living room has bay windows, a white pressed-tin ceiling, rock fireplace, black leather sofa and chairs, stained-glass lamps, horse sculptures, and cowboy and sheep paintings. The veterinarian host tries to keep the premises allergen-free. Breakfast is served on beveled-glass place mats with gold-trimmed white china, crystal, and silver. The library features trout pictures and fluted glass lights.

SETTING & FACILITIES

Location Across street from train station **Near** Colorado border, Taos, Santa Fe **Building** Mid-1920s 2-story rock & adobe Tudor w/ metal roof **Grounds** Hammock, umbrella, 6 apple trees, lilies, lilacs, roses, hollyhocks, columbines, cosmos **Public Space** LR, DR, library **Food & Drink** Full breakfast in DR; cookies on arrival; bottled water in rooms; bedtime pillow treats; picnic lunches **Recreation** Hunting, fishing, boating, winter sports **Amenities & Services** Piano, ironing facilities, basketball court

ACCOMMODATIONS

Units 3 guest rooms **All** TV/VCR, clock **Some** Hair dryer (on request) **Bed & Bath** Queen; all private baths, jetted tub (1) **Favorites** George Mortimer Pullman, original lady's sun & sewing room, has floral theme, high-tech brass bed w/ adjustable softness, feather pillows, down comforter, 2-person jetted tub; William Jackson Palmer has mahogany decor, century old rugs, 2 armoires, iron coat stand, gentleman's valet, stained-glass reading lamps **Comfort & Decor** Wood floors, rugs, chandeliers, dark wood furnishings, family antiques, period reproductions, armoires, full-length mirror, quilts or embroidered bedspreads, lace curtains

RATES, RESERVATIONS, & RESTRICTIONS

Deposit Credit card holds (7-day cancellation for full refund; 4 days for 50% refund) **Discounts** Extended stays, repeat visits, railroad volunteers **Credit Cards** AE, MC, V, D, CB

Check-In/Out 3–6 p.m./11 a.m. **Smoking** No **Pets** No (kennel space arranged, $15/day) **Kids** Yes (if well-behaved) **No-Nos** N/A **Minimum Stay** None **Open** All year **Hosts** Wendy & Bonsall Johnson, 311 Terrace Ave., P.O. Box 967, Chama 87520 **Phone** (505) 756-1946 or toll-free (888) 849-7800 **Fax** N/A **E-mail** N/A **Web** www.parlorcar.com

CASA ESCONDIDA BED & BREAKFAST, Chimayo

OVERALL ★★★ | QUALITY ★★★★ | VALUE ★★★½ | PRICE RANGE $80–$140

In a rural area known for its weaving families and the healing Santuario de Chimayo church, Casa Escondida is under new ownership. The living room retains its beam ceilings, brick floor, and kiva fireplace. The four rooms in the main house seem destined to retain their Spanish Colonial character. However, the smaller, more basic outside garden rooms, which carry the lowest price tags, may undergo some cosmetic improvements. The new owner, a refuge from the Ohio business world, is very adept at handling the phones. Hopefully, on-site hospitality will follow when her new home nearby is completed.

SETTING & FACILITIES
Location Rio Arriba County Road 100, west of intersection of NM 76 & Santa Fe CR 98 **Near** Espanola, Santa Fe, Taos, Bandelier, Indian pueblos **Building** Spanish Colonial **Grounds** 6 acres w/ pastures, foothills **Public Space** LR, DR **Food & Drink** Full breakfast in DR; 24-hour beverage, snacks; box lunch; prior arrangement for special dietary needs **Recreation** Fishing, hunting, horse riding, boating, biking, bird-watching, winter sports **Amenities & Services** Hot tub, stereo

ACCOMMODATIONS
Units 8 **All** Robes **Some** Fireplace (3), wood stove (1), kitchenette (1), private patio/deck (3) **Bed & Bath** Queen (1), queen & twin (2), full-size (3), full & 2 twins (1), full & twin (1); all private baths, tub (6) **Favorites** Casita Escondida guest house has kiva fireplace, wrought-iron queen bed, trundle daybed, sitting room, French doors to dining area, kitchenette, private deck; upstairs Kiva Room has pine floor, small sitting area, kiva fireplace, angled A-frame timber ceiling, queen & twin beds, window for tiled tub **Comfort & Decor** Saltillo tile, brick, wood and carpet floors, beam or tongue-and-groove ceilings, some French doors, and sitting areas

RATES, RESERVATIONS, & RESTRICTIONS
Deposit Credit card holds (14-day cancellation policy; gift certificate issued when money kept) **Discounts** Extended stays, groups **Credit Cards** MC, V **Check-In/Out** 4–6 p.m./11 a.m. **Smoking** No **Pets** Yes (restrictions; ask first; $10/night) **Kids** Yes **No-Nos** N/A **Minimum Stay** None **Open** All year **Host** Belinda Bowling, P.O. Box 142, Chimayo 87522 **Phone** (505) 351-4805 or toll-free (800) 643-7201 **Fax** (505) 351-2575 **E-mail** casaes@newmexico.com **Web** www.casaescondida.com

HACIENDA RANCHO DE CHIMAYO, Chimayo

OVERALL ★★★½ | QUALITY ★★★★½ | VALUE ★★★★ | PRICE RANGE $59–$105

Across the street from the terraced gardens of Restaurante Rancho de Chimayo, the Hacienda is run by a family tracing its roots to late 1600s Spanish colonial migrations from Mexico. Once the family home, all the rooms in this restored adobe open onto a courtyard. The Hacienda is almost midway between Taos and Santa Fe and makes an acceptable base for exploring the surrounding areas. However, compared to the offerings in Taos and Santa Fe, the Hacienda seems relatively spartan and isolated. For some, this is precisely the reason to come here, along with the famous Santuario Chimayo and the family weaving shops in the area.

SETTING & FACILITIES
Location On Santa Fe CR 98 **Near** Espanola, Santa Fe, Taos, Bandelier, Indian pueblos **Building** 1800s Territorial-style adobe home, restored in 1984 **Grounds** Courtyard, willows **Public Space** Lobby **Food & Drink** Cont'l breakfast in lobby, room, or courtyard, or 50% off at Restaurante Rancho de Chimayo; lunch, dinner at restaurant **Recreation** Fishing, hunting, horse riding, boating, biking, bird-watching, winter sports **Amenities & Services** Gallery, TV

ACCOMMODATIONS
Units 7 **All** Fireplace, coffeemaker **Some** Hide-a-bed (3), daybed (1), private balcony (3), fridge (1), robes & hair dryer (on request) **Bed & Bath** King (2), king/twin (2), queen (2), double (1); all private baths, tub **Favorites** Siete has cherry wood furnishings, king or twin beds, sitting area w/ double hide-a-bed, floral bedspread, fireplace, private balcony, connecting door to Seis; Cuatro has queen bed, wicker & wood furnishings, fridge, desk, fireplace, sitting area, connecting door to Tres, which has brass king bed & wicker furnishings **Comfort & Decor** Uncluttered, w/ white-washed adobe walls, beam and plank ceilings, carved wood, wicker and upholstered furnishings, some antiques, desks, iron or wood beds, and floral wallpaper and fabrics

RATES, RESERVATIONS, & RESTRICTIONS
Deposit Credit card holds (10-day cancellation policy) **Discounts** Off-season (Nov.–March, except holidays) **Credit Cards** AE, MC, V **Check-In/Out** 2–8 p.m./ noon **Smoking** No **Pets** No (resident cat) **Kids** Yes (over age 9) **No-Nos** N/A **Minimum Stay** None **Open** All year **Hosts** Jaramillo family, P.O. Box 11, Chimayo 87522 **Phone** (505) 351-2222 **Fax** N/A **E-mail** N/A **Web** N/A

ADOBE ABODE, Santa Fe

OVERALL ★★★★ | QUALITY ★★★★ | VALUE ★★★★ | PRICE RANGE $145–$185

Originally a military officer canteen, Adobe Abode maintains some of the original hardwood floors and kitchen cabinets despite redecorating every five years. Red, green, yellow, and blue chairs punctuate the gray and white in a living room with white beam ceilings, a fireplace, and sofas. French doors lead to a dining room with a walnut-stained oak floor, metal chandelier, timber table, painted wood Aunt Jemima and Java puppets. The three back rooms with private patio entrances are best for families. The largest, the red-accented yellow and blue Provence Suite, has a living room with a fireplace and sofa.

SETTING & FACILITIES
Location 4 blocks from Plaza **Near** Downtown, museums, galleries **Building** 1907 Southwest style **Grounds** Patio, tree **Public Space** LR, DR **Food & Drink** Full breakfast in DR; sherry & cookies **Recreation** Horse riding, fishing, biking, golf, tennis, winter sports **Amenities & Services** Self-check-in service

ACCOMMODATIONS
Units 6 **All** Robes, hair dryer, duvet, coffeemaker, cable TV, ceiling fan, phone, answering machine, iron & ironing board **Some** Private entrance (3), fireplace (2), desk (5), handicap accessible (1) **Bed & Bath** Queen (5), twin (1); all private baths, tub (4) **Favorites** Bronco has 12-ft. beam ceilings, kiva fireplace, four-poster pine bed w/ saddle & lariat, snowshoes & cowboy boots, French door patio entrance, bath skylights; Cabin in Woods has red walls w/ black trim, fishnets & bags on timber bed, old English chair, marble desk, red armoire, bath w/ yellow walls, blue & white tiles, skylight, twig mirror, duck decoy, shower **Comfort & Decor** Carpet, brick, or hardwood floors, color schemes like pink and gray or yellow and blue with red accents, rustic and antique furnishings, punched-tin mirrors, some bath skylights

RATES, RESERVATIONS, & RESTRICTIONS
Deposit 1 night w/ credit card (14-day cancellation for refund minus 10% of entire reservation; 30 days for holidays) **Discounts** None **Credit Cards** MC, V, D **Check-In/Out** After 2 p.m./11 a.m. **Smoking** No **Pets** No (owners have dog) **Kids** Yes (in back rooms) **No-Nos** N/A **Minimum Stay** None **Open** All year **Host** Pat Harbour, 202 Chapelle, Santa Fe 87501 **Phone** (505) 983-3133 **Fax** (505) 424-3027 **E-mail** pat@adobeabode.com **Web** www.adobeabode.com

ALEXANDER'S INN, Santa Fe

OVERALL ★★★★ | QUALITY ★★★★ | VALUE ★★★★ | PRICE RANGE $80–$175

On a narrow, older residential street, Alexander's, Carolyn Lee's first Santa Fe bed-and-breakfast, is named after her son. The front porch overlooking the street and an especially flowery garden is a popular hangout for soaking up the warmth of the noonday sun. The living room has stenciled white walls, floral-cushioned wicker chairs, plenty of potted green plants, and a foyer with a tall grandfather clock and window seats. The low kitchen counter is a very popular spot, and it is typically crowded with a variety of baked treats. Even the shared bathroom is a cavernous, double-vanity, skylighted delight loaded with green plants, a rough wood ceiling, lavender-tinged walls, green and morning glory tiles, and stenciled floral borders.

SETTING & FACILITIES

Location 0.5 mi. east of Plaza **Near** Museums, galleries **Building** 1903 Craftsman style **Grounds** Front flower garden, back yard deck, apricot & locust trees **Public Space** LR, DR **Food & Drink** Cont'l breakfast in DR or deck; all-day snacks, beverages **Recreation** Horse riding, fishing, biking, golf, tennis, winter sports **Amenities & Services** Hot tub, health club privileges

ACCOMMODATIONS

Units 7 **All** Robes, hair dryer, phone, clock radio or clock & boom box, bath amenities **Some** Fireplace (3), cable TV (5), kitchen (1) **Bed & Bath** King (2), queen (4), twins (1); 5 private baths, 1 shared, tub (2), claw-foot tub (1), jetted tub (1) **Favorites** Lilac downstairs has brick fireplace, orange stained-glass windows, wood floor, sitting area, step-up bath, pedestal sink, claw-foot shower/tub; Cottage, a family favorite, has saltillo tile floor, kiva fireplace, sofa futon, kitchen, spiral staircase to low-ceilinged loft, jetted tub **Comfort & Decor** Mix of antique and wicker furnishings, angled ceilings and alcoves, green plants, floral decor, and reading lamps

RATES, RESERVATIONS, & RESTRICTIONS

Deposit 1 night (14-day cancellation for refund) **Discounts** Low season, repeat customers **Credit Cards** MC, V, D **Check-In/Out** After 2 p.m./11 a.m. **Smoking** No **Pets** Yes (if well behaved; $20) **Kids** Yes (over age 12) **No-Nos** N/A **Minimum Stay** 2 nights on weekends **Open** All year **Hosts** Keith Gore & Carolyn Lee, 529 E. Palace Ave., Santa Fe 87501 **Phone** (505) 986-1431 or toll-free (888) 321-5123 **Fax** (505) 982-8572 **E-mail** alexanderinn@aol.com **Web** www.alexanders-inn.com

CASA DE LA CUMA BED & BREAKFAST, Santa Fe

OVERALL ★★★★ | QUALITY ★★★★ | VALUE ★★★★ | PRICE RANGE $75–$145

On a hillside just north of the Plaza action, Casa de la Cuma is far enough from the hubbub and traffic to be relaxing. At the same time, the bed-and-breakfast is only a brisk half-mile walk from the major museums, galleries, shops, churches, and restaurants ringing the Plaza. On the downside, only Room #1 and the suite have private bathrooms. But for families and people who know each other, sharing the combination hallway bath offers economies. Indeed, despite the shared bath, Room #3 has its charms if you like the blend of dream catchers, serapes, and John Wayne illustrations.

SETTING & FACILITIES

Location 5 blocks north of Plaza **Near** Downtown, museums, galleries, pueblos **Building** 1945 adobe style **Grounds** Pine tree, fire pit, flagstone pond **Public Space** LR, DR **Food & Drink** Cont'l breakfast in DR; afternoon snacks; 24-hour beverages **Recreation**

Horse riding, fishing, biking, golf, tennis, winter sports **Amenities & Services** Modem jack, fridge, microwave

ACCOMMODATIONS
Units 4 All Robes, hair dryer, clock radio, cable TV, iron & ironing board **Some** Desk (2), ceiling fan (2), wood-burning stove (1), kitchenette (1), stereo (1), VCR (1) **Bed & Bath** King (1), king/twins (1), queen (2); 2 private baths, 2 shared, tub (2) **Favorites** Room #1 has king bed, wood-burning stove, private patio entrance, mirror above desk, ceiling fan, Huichol embroidery, blue & white tiled sink, shower/tub; Suite has LR w/ queen sleeper sofa, queen in BR, wall niches w/ pottery, kitchenette, stereo, VCR, stall shower **Comfort & Decor** White walls, lace curtains, hardwood floors, Mexican carved-wood furniture, TVs in armoires, light Western themes like O'Keeffe and cowboys

RATES, RESERVATIONS, & RESTRICTIONS
Deposit 1 night or 50% (10-day cancellation policy) **Discounts** Extended stays (over 1 week), Internet specials **Credit Cards** AE, MC, V, D **Check-In/Out** 3 p.m./11a.m. **Smoking** No **Pets** No (cat on premises) **Kids** Yes (under age 7 in suite) **No-Nos** N/A **Minimum Stay** 2 nights on weekends **Open** All year **Hosts** Dona & John Fisher, 105 Paseo de la Cuma, Santa Fe 87501 **Phone** (505) 983-1717 or toll-free (888) 366-1717 **Fax** (505) 983-2241 **E-mail** info@casacuma.com **Web** www.casacuma.com

THE DON GASPAR COMPOUND INN, *Santa Fe*

OVERALL ★★★★★ | QUALITY ★★★★½ | VALUE ★★★★ | PRICE RANGE $95–$295

On a narrow, one-way, tree-lined street of old adobe residences and professional offices a block and a half southwest of the kiva-shaped state capitol, the walled Don Gaspar Compound is quiet and spacious. Families and groups like the 1,500-square-foot two-bedroom/two-bath, antique oak–furnished Mission-style house with its ample outdoor partying area. A small double futon room boosts the sleeping capacity to six, and there are two wood-burning fireplaces, warm red upholstery, sponged yellow walls, dark woods, a kitchen, hand-painted china, bath murals, and washer and dryer. Individual business travelers gravitate toward the two spacious Mission-style casitas.

SETTING & FACILITIES
Location 6 blocks south of Plaza **Near** Capitol **Building** 4 historic homes in Arts & Crafts, Territorial, Adobe pueblo styles **Grounds** Brick courtyard, tulip gardens, fountains, apple, peach, apricot trees **Public Space** DR, patio **Food & Drink** Cont'l plus breakfast buffet (1 entree) in DR, courtyard, or room; coffee beans in room **Recreation** Horse riding, fishing, biking, golf, tennis, winter sports **Amenities & Services** Groups

ACCOMMODATIONS
Units 10 **All** Fridge, microwave, coffeemaker, coffee grinder, clock radio, phone, swamp cooler, humidifier **Some** Full kitchen (3), washer & dryer (1), ceiling fans, VCRs, fireplaces, handicap accessible (1) **Bed & Bath** King (9), queen (1); all private baths, tub (4), jetted tub (5) **Favorites** Courtyard Casita has full kitchen, DR, LR, walled courtyard w/ roses, bath w/ tiled mural, pedestal sink, jetted tub **Comfort & Decor** Mission and Adobe styles, indoor and outdoor sitting areas, sponge-painted walls, oak and tile floors, shuttered windows, carved timber and upholstered furnishings, wardrobes, metalwork frames, Mexican tiles, and some bath murals

RATES, RESERVATIONS, & RESTRICTIONS
Deposit Credit card holds (14-day cancellation for full refund; gift certificate for forfeited nights) **Discounts** Internet specials, singles, extended stays, seasonal (fall, spring) **Credit Cards** AE, MC, V **Check-In/Out** 3 p.m./11 a.m. **Smoking** No **Pets** No **Kids** Yes **No-Nos** N/A **Minimum Stay** 2 nights high season, 3 nights holidays, special events, groups **Open** All year **Hosts** Trudy O'Connor & Shirley Isgar, 623 Don Gaspar Ave., Santa Fe 87501 **Phone** (505) 986-8664 or toll-free (888) 986-8664 **Fax** (505) 986-0696 **E-mail** info@dongaspar.com **Web** www.dongaspar.com

GRANT CORNER INN, Santa Fe

OVERALL ★★★★½ | QUALITY ★★★★ | VALUE ★★★★ | PRICE RANGE $130–$240

Next door to the Georgia O'Keeffe Museum and kitty-corner from Santa Fe County's administrative offices, the white picket–fenced Grant Corner Inn and its iron lattice porch occupy a bustling corner near all the Plaza shops, churches, and museums. The public is invited to breakfast and the popular Sunday brunch served up in the blue-and-white rabbit motif dining room. The gift shop sells house-made jams along with rabbit jewelry. The halls are lined with a black-and-white photo history of the inn and its inhabitants, including the hostess, who still receives original guests from when the inn first opened 20 years ago. This inn has been voted the best bed-and-breakfast in Santa Fe by several local magazines.

SETTING & FACILITIES
Location 2 blocks NW of Plaza **Near** Museums, galleries **Building** Early 1900s 3-story brick Colonial, 2-room stand-alone adobe guest house **Grounds** 0.8 acres w/ wisteria-covered gazebo, weeping willow trees **Public Space** Reception/gift shop, DR/parlor, upstairs lounge, porch **Food & Drink** Full breakfast in DR; Sun. brunch; 24-hour beverages, snacks; afternoon tea; picnic lunches; special dinners; catering **Recreation** Horse riding, fishing, biking, golf, tennis, winter sports **Amenities & Services** Parties, weddings (50–75)

ACCOMMODATIONS
Units 10 **All** Robes, hair dryer, TV, clock radio, ceiling fan, phone **Some** Fireplace (1), fridge (8), coffeemaker (3), AC (8), VCR (4), balcony (3) **Bed & Bath** King (3), queen (6), twins (1); all private baths, jetted tub (3) **Favorites** Elena's Boudoir has French furnishings, sage & mauve fabrics, recessed lights, sitting area, daybed, his & hers closets, canopied king feather bed, marble desk, fridge, coffeemaker, antique vanity, jetted tub **Comfort & Decor** The first two floors are hardwood, the third, carpeted. You'll also find traditional fabrics and patterns, armoires, hidden TVs, quilts, comforters, four-poster and brass beds, some French doors, baths with brass fixtures, and antique or Mexican tiled sinks

RATES, RESERVATIONS, & RESTRICTIONS
Deposit 1 night or 50% (10-day cancellation policy; 30 days for longer stays) **Discounts** Extended stays, Internet specials **Credit Cards** AE, MC, V **Check-In/Out** 3–6 p.m./noon **Smoking** No **Pets** No **Kids** Yes (over age 6) **No-Nos** N/A **Minimum Stay** None (except holidays) **Open** All year **Host** Louise Stewart, 122 Grant Ave., Santa Fe 87501 **Phone** (505) 983-6678 or toll-free (800) 964-9003 **Fax** (505) 983-1526 **E-mail** info@grantcornerinn.com **Web** www.grantcornerinn.com

HACIENDA NICHOLAS, Santa Fe

OVERALL ★★★★ | QUALITY ★★★★ | VALUE ★★★★ | PRICE RANGE $95–$160

Friendly, casual, and under the same ownership as Alexander's but with its own staff, Hacienda Nicholas mixes Provence and Southwestern styles with colorful Mexican tiles and carved woods. The handicap-accessible Sunflower Room has French doors, a wood floor, beam ceilings, clerestory windows, and a red, white, and blue tiled bath. The three rooms surrounding the courtyard have outside entrances, saltillo tile entryways, and kiva fireplaces. The four other rooms are accessible only via the main house, which has a living room with a horned elk skull over the fireplace, cowboy and horse art, old timber tables, and orange and blue Southwestern sofas.

SETTING & FACILITIES
Location 3 blocks east of Plaza **Near** Museums, galleries **Building** Early 1900s adobe style **Grounds** Enclosed patio, flagstone courtyard, fireplace, terra cotta pots, roses **Public Space** LR, DR **Food & Drink** Full breakfast in DR or patio; all-day snacks, beverages **Recreation** Horse riding, fishing, biking, golf, tennis, winter sports **Amenities & Services** Guest fridge

ACCOMMODATIONS

Units 7 **All** Robes, cable TV, phone, AC **Some** Fireplace (3), pedestal sink (4), handicap accessible (1) **Bed & Bath** King (3), queen (4); all private baths, tub (6) **Favorites** Nicholas has brick entry, sitting room, fireplace w/ inlaid tile scenes, blue & yellow colors, cowboy & landscape paintings, B&W Indian chief photo, carpet area w/ wrought-iron king bed, colorfully tiled bath w/ carved wood & tin mirror **Comfort & Decor** Southwestern and Provence, hand-troweled plaster over adobe walls, carved wood lintels, carpet, wood or saltillo tile floors, wrought-iron and four-poster timber beds, Gustave Baumann prints, colorful Mexican tin mirrors, sitting areas with carved Mexican pine, some inlaid tile scenes, dark wood trims and lace curtains, bathrooms with botanical and brightly colored tiles, some with stenciling and murals

RATES, RESERVATIONS, & RESTRICTIONS

Deposit 1 night (14-day cancellation for refund) **Discounts** Low season **Credit Cards** MC, V, D **Check-In/Out** After 2 p.m./11 a.m. **Smoking** No **Pets** Yes **Kids** Yes **No-Nos** N/A **Minimum Stay** 2 nights on weekends **Open** All year **Host** Glennon Grush, 320 E. Marcy St., Santa Fe 87501 **Phone** (505) 992-8385 or toll-free (888) 284-3170 **Fax** (505) 982-8572 **E-mail** haciendanicholas@aol.com **Web** www.haciendanicholas.com

LA TIENDA INN & DURAN HOUSE, Santa Fe

OVERALL ★★★½ | QUALITY ★★★★ | VALUE ★★★★ | PRICE RANGE $100–$195

Two blocks from the Georgia O'Keeffe Museum, La Tienda Inn and Duran House serves up continental breakfast in the room or in a relaxing courtyard patio. Rooms are in three remodeled historic buildings a few blocks from the main downtown hustle and bustle. The only second-story room is Aurora's in Duran House. Rosa's, Maria's, and Victoriana's Rooms in the Duran House have porches. Afternoon tea is served in the common room of the old adobe store, which also houses a motel-like reception desk. Most rooms have Gustave Baumann prints, though two have black-and-white photos of Native Americans.

SETTING & FACILITIES

Location 0.5 mi. west of Plaza **Near** Downtown, museums, galleries **Building** Extensively renovated late-1800s adobe farmhouse, 1900 Territorial house, 1920s adobe store **Grounds** Courtyard, fountain, crabapple trees **Public Space** Reception, common room w/ fireplace, patio **Food & Drink** Cont'l breakfast in room or garden; afternoon tea; beverages, snacks; bottled water in room **Recreation** Horse riding, fishing, biking, golf, tennis, winter sports **Amenities & Services** Guest comment book

ACCOMMODATIONS

Units 11 **All** Cable TV, phone, clock radio, heat, flowers, private entrance **Some** Fireplace (5), fridge (10), AC (10), ceiling fan (most), hair dryer (on request), handicap accessible (1) **Bed & Bath** King (3), king/twins (2), queen (6); all private baths, tub (10) **Favorites** Romero has creamy adobe walls, tile & hardwood floor, wood ceiling, sun porch, picket-fenced terrace; Maria's has sloping turquoise wood floor, weathered wood table, kiva fire-place, stuffed floral chairs, shuttered windows, green end tables, candlestick lamps, porch **Comfort & Decor** Varied, with carpet, wood and tile floors, wood or stucco ceilings, some weathered wood tables, antiques, and Southwest-style rugs and furnishings.

RATES, RESERVATIONS, & RESTRICTIONS

Deposit 1–2 nights (14-day cancellation for refund minus $15) **Discounts** Groups, win-ter midweek **Credit Cards** MC, V **Check-In/Out** 3–7 p.m./11 a.m. **Smoking** No **Pets** No (resident cat) **Kids** Yes **No-Nos** N/A **Minimum Stay** 2 nights weekends, 3 nights holidays, 4 nights Indian market **Open** All year **Hosts** Barbara Watson and James Meyer, 445 W. San Francisco St., Santa Fe 87501 **Phone** (505) 989-8259 or toll-free (800) 889-7611 **Fax** (505) 820-6931 **E-mail** info@latiendabb.com **Web** www.latiendabb.com

THE MADELEINE INN, *Santa Fe*

OVERALL ★★★½ | QUALITY ★★★★ | VALUE ★★★★ | PRICE RANGE $70–$160

Formerly Preston House, the hypoallergenic Madeleine is now under the same ownership as Alexander's Inn. On a quiet dead-end street a short walk from all the Plaza attractions, the Madeleine was built by Chinese migrant workers. Hence, a black-and-gold Chinese bamboo-style staircase graces a yellow-and-white living room adorned with carved dark woods, stained glass, bay windows, and a comfortable floral sofa. The small Sweet Pea Room and slightly larger Geranium Room offer bargain rates for those who can live with a shared bath. The top-floor Ivy Room has a spiral staircase to the garden. Two rooms in a detached garden guest house are pricier alterna-tives for those desiring more privacy.

SETTING & FACILITIES

Location 0.25 mi. east of Plaza **Near** Museums, galleries, shops **Building** 1886 multi-story Queen Anne Victorian **Grounds** Flagstone patio, English garden, apricot tree **Pub-lic Space** LR, DR **Food & Drink** Full breakfast in DR **Recreation** Horse riding, fishing, biking, golf, tennis, winter sports **Amenities & Services** Hot tub, health club privileges

ACCOMMODATIONS

Units 8 **All** Robes, hair dryer, clock radio, ceiling & floor fans **Some** Fireplace (2), pedestal sink (4) **Bed & Bath** King (4), queen (3), twin (1); 6 private baths, 1 shared, tub (3) **Favorites** Morning Glory has stained glass above metal king bed, white floral tiles fronting carved fireplace, large mirrored wardrobe, pedestal sink in room, step-down bath w/ angled ceiling & floral wallpaper; Columbine has small chandelier, dark wood trim, wall-paper, stained glass above bay window, fireplace, metal king bed, large mirrored wardrobe **Comfort & Decor** A semi-random mix of original house antiques and recent furnish-ings, lace curtains, some open closets, some large wardrobes, angled ceilings, window seats, and sinks in room

RATES, RESERVATIONS, & RESTRICTIONS
Deposit I night (14-day cancellation for refund) **Discounts** Low season (Nov. 16–March 16, except holidays), repeat customers **Credit Cards** MC, V, D **Check-In/Out** After 2 p.m./11 a.m. **Smoking** No **Pets** No **Kids** No **No-Nos** N/A **Minimum Stay** 2 nights on weekends **Open** All year **Hosts** George Padilla & Carolyn Lee, 106 Faithway St., Santa Fe 87501 **Phone** (505) 982-3465 or toll-free (888) 877-7622 **Fax** (505) 982-8572 **E-mail** madeleineinn@aol.com **Web** www.madeleineinn.com

SPENCER HOUSE BED & BREAKFAST INN, Santa Fe

OVERALL ★★★★ | QUALITY ★★★★ | VALUE ★★★★ | PRICE RANGE $99–$176

In a semi-residential neighborhood around the corner from the Georgia O'Keeffe Museum and the downtown Plaza action, Spencer House is fronted by trumpet vines frequented by hummingbirds. A white picket fence and tan stucco wall surround a small relaxing front patio with green wrought-iron furniture. The sunny dining room faces the patio and has a wood ceiling, candlestick chandeliers, and green wicker chairs. The living room has a red sofa, aged wood chairs, and kiva fireplace. The back two rooms are used for small kids, because with only bathroom walls in common there is little noise.

SETTING & FACILITIES
Location 4 blocks from Plaza **Near** Museums, galleries **Building** 1923 tin-roofed Mediterranean adobe, restored in 1993 **Grounds** Patio, roses, lavender, mint, trumpet vine, honeysuckle, poppies **Public Space** LR, DR, porch **Food & Drink** Full breakfast in DR; 24-hour beverages; fresh baked goods; bottled water at check-in **Recreation** Horse riding, fishing, biking, golf, tennis, winter sports **Amenities & Services** Laundry pickup & delivery, e-mail access, computer use

ACCOMMODATIONS
Units 6 **All** Hair dryer, bath amenities, down comforter, quilt, heater, AC **Some** Ceiling fan (5), clock radio (3), clock (3), daybed (1), fireplace (2), cable TV (1), patio (2), kitchen (1) **Bed & Bath** Queen (5), twins (1); all private baths tub (4), jetted tub (2) **Favorites** Welsh has private entrance, beam ceiling, kiva fireplace, wicker chairs & tables, TV in armoire, step-up four-poster beds, individual AC/heat, private patio; Cottage Room has lintels, posts, lots of windows, full kitchen, track lighting, lace curtains, blinds, wood sleigh queen bed, daybed, wood-burning fireplace, jetted tub **Comfort & Decor** Wood floors, Oriental carpets, wood and wicker furnishings, wardrobes, dressers, reading lamps, pedestal sinks, punched-tin lampshades, several baths with skylights, fans, and heaters

RATES, RESERVATIONS, & RESTRICTIONS
Deposit 50% (14-day cancellation policy) **Discounts** None **Credit Cards** AE, MC, V **Check-In/Out** 3–5 p.m./10:30 a.m. **Smoking** No **Pets** No (2 resident dogs) **Kids** Yes

(over age 12) **No-Nos** N/A **Minimum Stay** None **Open** All year **Hosts** Jan McConnell
& John Pitlak, 222 McKenzie St., Santa Fe 87501 **Phone** (505) 988-3024 **Fax** (505) 984-
9862 **E-mail** jan@spencerhse-santafe.com **Web** www.spencerhse-santafe.com

WATER STREET INN BED & BREAKFAST, Santa Fe

OVERALL ★★★★ | QUALITY ★★★★ | VALUE ★★★★ | PRICE RANGE $100–$248

A rambling two-story adobe complex across the street from the Santa Fe
Stages theater and next door to a piano bar–dinner restaurant, Water Street
Inn is very modern in its amenities and a short walk to all the Plaza action.
The four suites in the back of the building are closest to the latilla-shaded
hot tub and have sitting rooms, extra beds, and a shared courtyard with a
wisteria and fountain. The lounge, which offers early morning coffee, is a
comfortable mix of leather furnishings, a kiva fireplace, Southwest pottery,
patterned fabrics, and shuttered windows.

SETTING & FACILITIES
Location 2.5 blocks west of Plaza **Near** Downtown, museums, galleries **Building** Early
1900s adobe, 2d story added, renovated mid-1990s **Grounds** Landscaped patio, courtyards **Public Space** Lounge, DR, sun deck, patio **Food & Drink** Cont'l breakfast in DR
or sun deck; happy hour w/ wine in lounge or patio; turn-down bread & cookies **Recreation** Horse riding, fishing, biking, golf, tennis, winter sports **Amenities & Services** Sheltered hot tub, ice machine, guest fridge, turn-down, groups, weddings

ACCOMMODATIONS
Units 12 **All** Cable TV/VCR, phone, voice mail, clock radio/CD player, hair dryer, fresh
flowers **Some** Handicap accessible (1), private patio (3), fireplace (10), ceiling fan (8) **Bed
& Bath** King (4), queen (8); all private baths, tub (11), jetted tub (1) **Favorites** Room #4
has curtained four-poster king bed, banco twin bed, down chaise longue in sitting area, kiva
fireplace, brick floor, pink morning glory archway to blue-tiled bath; Village Suite has viga &
cove ceiling, turquoise fireplace w/ yellow petroglyphs **Comfort & Decor** Southwest
colors, track lighting, carved wood and leather furnishings, pine armoires, antique and four-
poster beds, carpet, wood or brick floors, some beam ceilings, and shutters

RATES, RESERVATIONS, & RESTRICTIONS
Deposit 50% (14-day cancellation for refund minus 10%; 1 year raincheck for forfeited
nights) **Discounts** Internet specials **Credit Cards** AE, MC, V, D **Check-In/Out** 2–6
p.m./11 a.m. **Smoking** No **Pets** Yes **Kids** Yes **No-Nos** N/A **Minimum Stay** Holidays,
special events only **Open** All year **Host** Mindy Mills, 427 W. Water St., Santa Fe 87501
Phone (505) 984-1193 or toll-free (800) 646-6752 **Fax** (505) 984-6235 **E-mail**
info@waterstreetinn.com **Web** www.waterstreetinn.com

ADOBE & PINES INN, Taos

OVERALL ★★★★ | QUALITY ★★★★½ | VALUE ★★★★ | PRICE RANGE $95–$185

Down a short dirt road just north of Mile Marker 41 on NM 68, Adobe and Pines still retains original sound-smothering 1830s adobe walls in four rooms. The large living room in the main hacienda has a beam ceiling, brick floor, yellow walls, blue tiles, large paintings, tan kiva fireplace, sofas, and rocking chairs. A sunny dining room is stocked with twig furniture. The 900-square-foot Puerta Amarillo, the largest room, has a private court-yard with hammocks, suede sofas, picture windows, a large-screen TV, double vanities, and a double jetted tub. Puerta Turquese—a stand-alone cottage with a full kitchen for cooking, two kiva fireplaces, bedroom, and a sitting area—is an extended-stay favorite; visitors like the combo of space, amenities, and ambiance there.

SETTING & FACILITIES

Location 4 mi. south of downtown Plaza **Near** Museums, Visitor Center **Building** 1832 adobe hacienda, 1990s casitas **Grounds** 2.5 acres, flagstone courtyard, spring tulips, fountain, stone bridge over irrigation canal; apple, cherry, cottonwood, willow, conifer, & elm trees **Public Space** LR, DR **Food & Drink** Full breakfast in DR; wine, beer on check-in; special dietary needs w/ advance notice **Recreation** Biking, rafting, fishing, hunting, horse riding, golf, winter sports **Amenities & Services** Massage, phone, weddings, groups

ACCOMMODATIONS

Units 9 **All** Clock, radio/CD player **Some** Fireplace (8), kitchenette (3), full kitchen (1), fridge (7), satellite TV (3), AC (1), hair dryer (optional) **Bed & Bath** King (1), queen (7); all private baths, jetted tub (5), tub (2), dry sauna (1) **Favorites** Puerta Rosa has private blue door courtyard entrance, rose walls, vaulted ceiling, black wrought iron, leather sofa, Mexican chairs, sunken bath w/ wood floor, tiled 2-person tub, fireplace, copper chairs, sauna **Comfort & Decor** Beam ceilings, brick and tile floors, sitting areas or second rooms, shutters or wood blinds, picture windows, some bath fireplaces, and private patios

RATES, RESERVATIONS, & RESTRICTIONS

Deposit 50% (15-day cancellation for refund minus $15 fee; otherwise 50% deposit forfeiture) **Discounts** Extended stays, recreation packages **Credit Cards** MC, V **Check-In/Out** 3–6 p.m./11 a.m. **Smoking** No **Pets** Yes ($10/night; horse boarding nearby) **Kids** Yes **No-Nos** N/A **Minimum Stay** None **Open** All year **Host** Cathy Ann Connelly, 4107 NM 68, P.O. Box 837, Rancho de Taos 87557 **Phone** (505) 751-0947 or toll-free (800) 723-8267 **Fax** (505) 751-8423 **E-mail** adobepines@newmex.com **Web** www.adobepines.com

ALMA DEL MONTE SPIRIT OF THE MOUNTAIN BED & BREAKFAST, Taos

OVERALL ★★★★½ | QUALITY ★★★★½ | VALUE ★★★★ | PRICE RANGE $136–$245

On the same rural Hondo Seco Road as Little Tree Bed and Breakfast, Alma del Monte is a relaxed adult retreat. Picture windows and mountain views abound. Pumice and concrete walls muffle sound. The hostess, formerly of Chicago, stays to her upstairs quarters at the front of the house unless summoned. The south-facing, passive solar guest rooms are downstairs at the back of the house. Chips, salsa, and other goodies are available 24 hours in the kitchen. The kitchen counter opens onto spacious dining and living room areas with corbels, beam ceilings, saltillo tile floors, Oriental rugs, a grand piano, a chess table, and outdoor views.

SETTING & FACILITIES

Location Between Arroyo Hondo & Arroyo Seco, 10 mi. NW of Plaza **Near** Museums, Taos Ski Valley **Building** 1996 Southwestern Pueblo/hacienda style **Grounds** 11.5 acres, courtyard, fountain, arbor, rose garden, hammocks **Public Space** LR, DR **Food & Drink** Full breakfast in DR; afternoon refreshments; 24-hour beverages, snacks, stocked fridge; organic, vegetarian available **Recreation** Biking, rafting, fishing, hunting, horse riding, golf, winter sports **Amenities & Services** Hot tub, VCR, massage, open kitchen, chess table, grand piano, ski rack

ACCOMMODATIONS

Units 5 **All** Gas fireplace, thermostat, radiant floor heat, down comforter, ceiling fan, phone, clock radio, hair dryer, iron, ironing board **Some** Private garden (3) **Bed & Bath** King (some convert into twins); all private baths, jetted tub **Favorites** Hank's has sunrise mountain views, canopied wood & wrought-iron bed, love seat & chair around kiva fireplace, private garden **Comfort & Decor** Beam ceilings, saltillo tile floors, sitting area with gas kiva fireplace, eclectic antiques, desks, dressers, some wicker, rocking chairs, skylights, and Southwestern touches like kiva towel racks

RATES, RESERVATIONS, & RESTRICTIONS

Deposit 1 night or 50% (14-day cancellation for refund minus 10% fee; 30 days, groups, ski season) **Discounts** Low season **Credit Cards** AE, MC, V **Check-In/Out** 4–6 p.m./11 a.m. **Smoking** Outside **Pets** No (owner's dog, cat not allowed in guest rooms) **Kids** Yes (over age 16) **No-Nos** N/A **Minimum Stay** None (except Christmas) **Open** All year **Host** Suzanne Head, 372 Hondo Seco Rd., P.O. Box 1434, Taos 87571 **Phone** (505) 776-2721 or toll-free (800) 273-7203 **Fax** (505) 776-8888 **E-mail** info@almaspirit.com **Web** www.almaspirit.com

AMERICAN ARTISTS GALLERY HOUSE
BED & BREAKFAST, Taos

OVERALL ★★★★½ | QUALITY ★★★★½ | VALUE ★★★★ | PRICE RANGE $80–$195

On a short dead-end road off NM 68, just south of the Ramada Inn de Taos, the American Artists Gallery House has three great Jacuzzi rooms and is well situated for exploring Taos. Though not serious competition to local art dealers, the Gallery Pinon cottage does boast an R. C. Gorman print and a stained-glass Star of David. Most rooms have metal sculptures. But breakfasts overshadow the artwork for sale on the walls of the main building. House favorites include the red onion tart with sweet potato fries, French toast Grand Marnier, and Tuscany breakfast burrito.

SETTING & FACILITIES
Location I mi. south of Plaza **Near** Museums, Visitor Center **Building** 5 adobe, frame, & Pueblo-style buildings **Grounds** 2 acres, flagstone paths, xeriscape **Public Space** Lounge, DR **Food & Drink** Full breakfast in DR; late afternoon deserts; guest fridge w/ beverages **Recreation** Biking, rafting, fishing, hunting, horse riding, golf, winter sports **Amenities & Services** Hot tub, USA Today newspaper

ACCOMMODATIONS
Units 10 **All** Wood-burning kiva fireplace, CD player, clock radio, coffeemaker, hair dryer, nightlight **Some** Robes (3), cable TV (5), radiant floor heat (3), fridge (9), wet bar (3), phone/data port (4), kitchen (1), private outdoor entrance (9) **Bed & Bath** King/twins (3), queen (7); all private baths, jetted tub (3), tub (2) **Favorites** Best Jacuzzi room has 12-ft. ceiling, skylights, Carmen Velarde fireplace, aspen desk, French doors, water closet **Comfort & Decor** Southwestern, saltillo tile or wood floor, wood and wrought-iron furnishings, metal sculptures, some wood ceilings, wardrobes, hammered-metal doors, Mexican tile baths

RATES, RESERVATIONS, & RESTRICTIONS
Deposit I night or 50% (14-day cancellation for refund minus $15; 30 days, holidays) **Discounts** Internet specials, extended stays, low season (Nov.–mid-Dec., Apr.) **Credit Cards** AE, MC, V, D **Check-In/Out** 3–6 p.m./11 a.m. **Smoking** No **Pets** Yes (in 3 guest rooms; prior approval needed; hosts have dog) **Kids** Yes (by prior arrangement; cribs available) **No-Nos** N/A **Minimum Stay** 2 nights weekends, 3 nights holidays **Open** All year **Hosts** Charles & LeAn Clamurro, 132 Frontier Lane, P.O. Box 584, Taos 87571 **Phone** (505) 758-4446 or toll-free (800) 532-2041 **Fax** (505) 758-0497 **E-mail** aagh@america-nartistbandb.com **Web** www.taosbedandbreakfast.com

CASA BENAVIDES BED & BREAKFAST INN, *Taos*

OVERALL ★★★½ | QUALITY ★★★★½ | VALUE ★★★★ | PRICE RANGE $89–$240

On the same block as the Kit Carson Museum and across the street from La Doña Luz, Casa Benavides started expanding when neighbors wed and began buying neighboring buildings. Though good from an historic preservation standpoint, bigness makes the bed-and-breakfast harder to distinguish from the large commercial inns lining the main highway and offering free breakfasts. Although the rooms and buildings have variety and are not totally lacking in character, the first stop in the motel-like reception is as satisfying a cultural experience as a mini-mart. Indeed, despite quality furnishings and the promise of a good meal on pretty plates, first contact is enough of a turnoff to send curious drive-by guests scurrying elsewhere for a better deal.

SETTING & FACILITIES
Location 0.5 block east of Plaza **Near** Museums, galleries **Building** 6 buildings, Pueblo adobes, trading posts, artists' studios, Victorian **Grounds** Flagstone patio, flowers, trees **Public Space** Lobby, DR **Food & Drink** Full breakfast in DR; afternoon tea **Recreation** Biking, rafting, fishing, hunting, horse riding, golf, winter sports **Amenities & Services** 2 outdoor hot tubs, massage room, spa treatments, family store discounts, fax, phone room, meeting rooms, groups (30)

ACCOMMODATIONS
Units 32 **All** Cable TV/VCR, clock, down comforter, AC or ceiling fan **Some** Kitchenette, stereo, fridge, patio, balcony **Bed & Bath** King (14), king & twin (1), queen (10), 2 queens (5), 2 singles (2); all private baths, tubs **Favorites** Rio Grande has timber furnishings, wood floor, beam ceilings, skylight, kiva fireplace, canopied king bed, daybed, drum end table, easy chair, quilt & rawhide bench, fridge, Native American art **Comfort & Decor** Very varied. Antique and carved-wood furnishings; Southwestern fabrics; tile, oak, and flagstone floors; some family heirlooms; paintings by noted Taos artists; Mexican tile baths

RATES, RESERVATIONS, & RESTRICTIONS
Deposit 1 night or 50% (10-day cancellation policy) **Discounts** None **Credit Cards** AE, MC, V, D **Check-In/Out** 3–7 p.m./11 a.m. **Smoking** Outdoors **Pets** No **Kids** Yes **No-Nos** N/A **Minimum Stay** None **Open** All year **Hosts** Tom & Barbara McCarthy, 137 Kit Carson Rd., Taos 87571 **Phone** (505) 758-1772 or toll-free (800) 552-1772 **Fax** (505) 758-5738 **E-mail** casabena@newmex.com **Web** www.taos-casabenavides.com

CASA DE LAS CHIMENEAS BED & BREAKFAST INN, *Taos*

OVERALL ★★★★★ | QUALITY ★★★★½ | VALUE ★★★★ | PRICE RANGE $150–$325

A Territorial-style mansion hidden behind seven-foot walls and 17 tall cottonwood trees on a quiet street, Casa de las Chimeneas (House of Chimneys) lives up to its reputation as New Mexico's top bed-and-breakfast. An executive chef and staff prepare two meals a day. A concierge is available to arrange avocado facial masks, herbal steam tents, his-and-hers packages (golf, spa), and even trip planning from Albuquerque if need be. La Sala de Patron and Sombraje combine into a two-room suite with a private walled patio. Territorial has a six-foot jetted tub and motorized skylight, though many prefer the rustic Rio Grande.

SETTING & FACILITIES
Location 2.5 blocks SE of Plaza **Near** Museums, galleries **Building** 1925 Spanish hacienda **Grounds** 0.9 acres, courtyard, fountains, herbs, vegetables, 8,000 bulbs, roses, cottonwood trees **Public Space** LR, DR **Food & Drink** Full breakfast in DR; light supper buffet; room fridge w/ beverages; dinners in room; dietary restrictions **Recreation** Biking, rafting, fishing, hunting, horse riding, golf, winter sports **Amenities & Services** Full concierge, spa services, massage, hot tub, workout room, sauna, laundry, family reunions, elopements

ACCOMMODATIONS
Units 8 **All** Robes, cable TV/VCR, fireplace, hair dryer, clock radio, CD player, phone, modem jack, fridge, teapot, iron, ironing board, humidifier, shoe dryer, private entrance **Some** Handicap-accessible (1), wet bar (4), ceiling fan (4), ski rack (7), motorized skylight (2), private patio (1) **Bed & Bath** King (5), king/twins (1), queen (1), 2 queens (2); all private baths, tub (4), jetted tub (3), double shower/sauna (1), 3-jet steam shower (1) **Favorites** 500-sq.-ft. Library Suite has motorized skylight, private patio, game table, king bed, sofa queen, wardrobe, double vanity, 3-jet steam shower, water closet **Comfort & Decor** Plush down pillows, some wardrobes/armoires, skylights, beam ceilings, French doors

RATES, RESERVATIONS, & RESTRICTIONS
Deposit 50% (14-day cancellation; gift certificate if room not re-rented) **Discounts** Internet specials, low season, packages **Credit Cards** AE, MC, V, D, DC **Check-In/Out** 3 p.m./11 a.m. **Smoking** No **Pets** No **Kids** Yes **No-Nos** N/A **Minimum Stay** None **Open** All year **Hosts** Susan Vernon, 405 Cordoba Rd., Box 5303 NDCBU, Taos 87571 **Phone** (505) 758-4777 or toll-free (877) 758-4777 **Fax** (505) 758-3976 **E-mail** info@visittaos.com **Web** www.visittaos.com

CASA ENCANTADA BED & BREAKFAST INN, Taos

OVERALL ★★★★ | QUALITY ★★★★ | VALUE ★★★★ | PRICE RANGE $95–$155

On a bend in a narrow road just off US 64, Casa Encantada nonetheless maintains its serenity. The Casa, which calls itself "the little property that grew," is actually an eclectic collection of edifices built over the past two centuries. The modern main house, which has a reception area and courtyard popular for summer music and group functions, is protectively isolated behind tall adobe-style walls penetrated via a turquoise wood door. The 1,000-square-foot Casita, which sleeps six, has a private courtyard, kitchen, laundry, folk design–covered walls, and a master bedroom with a kiva fireplace.

SETTING & FACILITIES
Location 1 mi. east of Plaza **Near** Museums, galleries **Building** Late 1800s adobe hacienda, early 1900s main house, 1970s additions **Grounds** 1 acre w/ courtyard, hidden patios, gardens, fountain, hammocks **Public Space** LR, atrium DR **Food & Drink** Full breakfast in DR; cookies at check-in **Recreation** Biking, rafting, fishing, hunting, horse riding, golf, winter sports **Amenities & Services** Piano, live weekend music, groups, weddings (30)

ACCOMMODATIONS
Units 9 **All** TV/VCR, hair dryer, fridge, clock radio, coffeemaker, teddy bear, private entrance, patio **Some** Kitchenette (3), fireplace (6), ceiling fan (2), sofa sleeper (2), futon (2), laundry (1), radiant floor heat (1) **Bed & Bath** King (3), queen (6); all private baths, tub (7) **Favorites** Santa Fe, honeymoon favorite, has framed wood doorway, LR fireplace opening onto king BR, twig cross, wingback chair, overstuffed love seat **Comfort & Decor** Eclectic mix of primitive and formal, mostly traditional Southwest style with plaster over adobe walls; turquoise accents; beam ceilings; wood, tile, and flagstone floors; wood, wicker, and Mexican furnishings; tile and kiva fireplaces; folk and contemporary art; antiqued frames, mirrors, and dressers

RATES, RESERVATIONS, & RESTRICTIONS
Deposit 1 night or 50% (10-day cancellation for refund minus $10) **Discounts** Internet specials, AAA, AARP, gov't. **Credit Cards** AE, MC, V, D **Check-In/Out** 4–6 p.m./11 a.m. **Smoking** No **Pets** Yes (dogs, cats on premises) **Kids** Yes **No-Nos** N/A **Minimum Stay** None (except Christmas) **Open** All year **Hosts** Sharon & Linda Nicholson, 416 Liebert St., 6460 NDCBU, Taos 87571 **Phone** (505) 758-7477 or toll-free (800) 223-8267 **Fax** (505) 737-5085 **E-mail** encantada@newmex.com **Web** www.casaencantada.com

CASA EUROPA, Taos

OVERALL ★★★★★ | QUALITY ★★★★½ | VALUE ★★★★★ | PRICE RANGE $85–$165

A luxurious, horse-friendly walled compound on a narrow country lane close to several museums and all the town action, Casa Europa is best known as a romantic retreat. Many rooms have themes, and all are full of small surprises, like the Austrian crystal chandelier and tiled scene above the bed in the Taos Mountain Room. The French Room has an 1860 French brass bed and a dressing area with French door windows overlooking Taos. Willow has a sitting area with a daybed, a Hopi theme painted under the glass-topped desk and tapestry fabric on carved wood chairs.

SETTING & FACILITIES
Location 1.3 mi. SW of Plaza **Near** Museums, galleries **Building** 200-year-old Territorial adobe, 1940s 2d story, 1980s modernization **Grounds** 0.5 acre, flagstone courtyards, willows, aspens, 5.5 acres of horse pasture across street **Public Space** LR, upstairs sitting area, DR, gallery **Food & Drink** Full breakfast in DR; late afternoon pastries or hors d'oeuvres, beverages **Recreation** Biking, rafting, fishing, hunting, horse riding, golf, winter sports **Amenities & Services** Hot tub, Swedish sauna, fireplace, concierge services, laundry

ACCOMMODATIONS

Units 7 **All** Robes, hair dryer, fireplace, desk, phone, clock radio, bath scale **Some** Cable TV (5), CD player (1), kitchen (1), daybed **Bed & Bath** King/twins (2), queen (5); all private baths, jetted tub (1), hot tub (2) **Favorites** 5-room Apartment Suite has kitchen, DR, hot tub; 3-room Southwest Suite has wood stove, jetted tub, bidet **Comfort & Decor** Eclectic mix of antique European and Southwestern furnishings, white-washed walls, dark beam ceilings, carpet, saltillo tile and brick floors, Mexican tin and brass mirrors, some lantern-style lights, skylights, crystal chandeliers, sitting areas with daybeds, dressing areas, marble or tiled baths

RATES, RESERVATIONS, & RESTRICTIONS

Deposit 1 night or 50% (14-day cancellation for refund minus $15) **Discounts** None **Credit Cards** MC, V **Check-In/Out** 3–6 p.m./11 a.m. **Smoking** No **Pets** Yes (selected rooms w/ approval; horse boarding) **Kids** Yes (cribs available) **No-Nos** N/A **Minimum Stay** None (except holidays) **Open** All year **Hosts** Rudi & Marcia Zwicker, 840 Upper Ranchitos Rd. (HC 68, Box 3F), Taos 87571 **Phone** (505) 758-9798 or toll-free (888) 758-9798 **Fax** (505) 758-9798 **E-mail** casa-europa@travelbase.com **Web** www.casaeuropanm.com

---

COTTONWOOD INN, Taos

OVERALL ★★★★ | QUALITY ★★★★½ | VALUE ★★★★ | PRICE RANGE $95–$175

At the intersection of NM 150 (Taos Ski Valley Road) and 230, bordered in back by sheep pasture with guinea hens running outside, Cottonwood Inn is a luxury retreat for skiing and fly-fishing. The hosts are all-around outdoor and fly fishing enthusiasts, and a fly fishing worktable sits atop the upstairs hallway. The second-floor Territorial room has a butterfly wall tapestry, balcony, sunken tub, and sitting area with kiva fireplace. The Buckaroo combines cowhide upholstery, lasso-waving metal cowboys, timber and bark beetle–galleried furniture with lace curtains and a drum table.

SETTING & FACILITIES

Location 6 mi. NW of Plaza **Near** Museums, Taos Ski Valley **Building** 1950s 2-story tan stucco Territorial adobe **Grounds** Aspen, apple, apricot, & plum trees; herbs; cutting flowers; rock fountain **Public Space** LR, 2 DR **Food & Drink** Full breakfast in DR; afternoon snacks; 24-hour cold beverages **Recreation** Biking, rafting, fishing, hunting, horse riding, golf, winter sports **Amenities & Services** Hot tub, TV/VCR, ice machine, CD player, meetings, weddings

ACCOMMODATIONS

Units 8 **All** Hair dryer, clock **Some** Fireplace (6), private entrance (5), patio/balcony (5), coffeemaker (3), fridge (3), wet bar (2), ceiling fan (1), kitchenette (1) **Bed & Bath** King & 2 twins (1), queen & twin (2), queen (5); all private baths, tub (4), jetted tub (3), hot tub (1), steam shower (2) **Favorites** Mesa Vista has 2d-floor private exterior entrance, antique carved-oak bed, fireplace, skylighted rotunda w/ hot tub, skylighted steam shower **Com-**

fort & Decor Traditional Southwest with varied themes. Beam ceilings; carved wood, leather; wicker and wrought-iron furnishings; saltillo tile, cement; and carpet floors; some shutters; skylights; kiva fireplaces; Mexican tile baths

RATES, RESERVATIONS, & RESTRICTIONS

Deposit I night or 50% (14-day cancellation for full refund) **Discounts** Internet specials, romance, massage, spa & ski packages **Credit Cards** AE, MC, V, D **Check-In/Out** 4–7 p.m./11 a.m. **Smoking** No **Pets** No (chickens, dogs, cats on premises) **Kids** No **No-Nos** N/A **Minimum Stay** None **Open** All year **Hosts** Bill & Kit Owen, HCR 74 Box 24609, Taos 87529 **Phone** (505) 776-5826 or toll-free (800) 324-7120 **Fax** (505) 776-1141 (call first) **E-mail** cottonbb@newmex.com **Web** www.taos-cottonwood.com

---

DOBSON HOUSE SOLAR EARTH SHIP, *Taos*

OVERALL ★★★★½ | QUALITY ★★★★ | VALUE ★★★★ | PRICE RANGE $110–$130

A Discovery Channel alternative energy tourism site, Dobson House is a Michael Reynolds "earthship" design insulated with 2,000 soil-packed discarded tires and powered by 22 solar panels. The 1,600-square-foot circular glass living room weaves European antiques and Southwestern style around ponderosa pine columns, red sandstone flooring, and a frame of 20,000 recycled aluminum cans. An art-lined 100-foot-long tile-inlaid stairway that glitters in the dark leads to two guest suites with old tires and bottles cemented into a drip-irrigated patio. The adjacent mesa and valley landscape, mostly Bureau of Land Management land, has hot springs, catch-and-release trout fly-fishing, hiking, and mountain biking trails.

SETTING & FACILITIES

Location 13 mi. NW of Plaza **Near** Museums, Rio Grande Gorge Bridge, Earthship Tour Office (www.earthship.org) **Building** 6,000-sq.-ft. contemporary (1996) solar adobe "earthship" **Grounds** 25 acres, bird feeder, drip irrigated herbs, native plants **Public Space** LR, DR, library **Food & Drink** Full breakfast in DR; afternoon snacks; dinner, vegan, vegetarian w/ advance notice **Recreation** Biking, rafting, fishing, horse riding, hot-air ballooning, bird-watching, winter sports **Amenities & Services** Piano, 16-in. telescope, weddings, retreats

ACCOMMODATIONS

Units 2 guest rooms, stand-alone 1,200-sq.-ft. casita under construction **All** Hair dryer, down comforter, clock, makeup mirror, bath amenities, flashlight, Chilean rain sticks **Some** Wood stove (1), gas log stove (1) **Bed & Bath** Queen & queen sleeper sofa; all private baths **Favorites**. Gorge View has Great Barrier Reef bedspread, gas log stove, green & yellow tiled bath **Comfort & Decor** Southwestern style, 500 square feet, adobe walls, beam ceilings, 8-foot windows, stone floors, throw rugs, sunken sitting areas, bright fabrics, free-standing stoves, private tiered patios, Mexican tile showers, towel racks

RATES, RESERVATIONS, & RESTRICTIONS

Deposit 1 night or 50% (2-week cancellation for refund minus $25; 4 weeks, holidays) **Discounts** Internet specials **Credit Cards** None (cash or check only) **Check-In/Out** After 4 p.m./11 a.m. **Smoking** No **Pets** No (resident dog, cat) **Kids** Yes (over age 14) **No-Nos** N/A **Minimum Stay** None (3 nights on holidays) **Open** All year **Hosts** Joan & John Dobson, P.O. Box 1584, El Prado 87529 **Phone** (505) 776-5738 **Fax** N/A **E-mail** dobhouse@newmex.com **Web** www.newmex.com/dobsonhouse

DRAGONFLY JOURNEYS, Taos

OVERALL ★★★★ | QUALITY ★★★★ | VALUE ★★★★ | PRICE RANGE $110

On the High Road to Taos (NM 518), bordering a trout creek called Rio Grande del Rancho, Dragonfly Journeys combines a bed-and-breakfast with a black-and-white photography darkroom and a clay pottery studio. Ideal for raku, the studio includes a wood stove and CD player, plus an extruder, slab roller, pottery wheel, two electric kilns, a portable raku kiln, and sandpit. Musicians and painters are welcome to use the space like a studio. An outdoor space inside a thicket of pine and cedar trees is used by art classes for guided meditation. The skylighted solarium has a pine ceiling, saltillo tile floors, green plants, sliding glass doors, picture windows, and upholstered rocking chairs.

SETTING & FACILITIES

Location 10 mi. SE of Taos Plaza in Carson National Forest **Near** Visitor Center, museums **Building** 1989 adobe-style cottage, adjacent adobe studios **Grounds** 1.3 acres surrounded by pinyon pine, cedar, & juniper forest, hiking trails, creek, hummingbird garden **Public Space** Solarium **Food & Drink** Full breakfast in solarium; cookies at check-in; 24-hour hot beverages **Recreation** Biking, rafting, fishing, hunting, horse riding, golf, winter sports **Amenities & Services** Art workshops, flagstone basketball court, B&W photography darkroom, clay & raku pottery studio

ACCOMMODATIONS

Units 1 2-room suite **All** Robes, satellite TV, stereo, hair dryer, clock radio, phone, microwave, toaster oven, coffeemaker, fridge, dishes, silverware, TV trays, ironing board, toiletries, private entrance **Some** N/A **Bed & Bath** Double bed (2); shared bath w/ tub **Favorites** Robin & Hummingbird Rooms differ only in wall art **Comfort & Decor** Basic and simple. Dresser, wood bench, B&W photography, raku masks, sculptures, pottery, handmade coffee cups

RATES, RESERVATIONS, & RESTRICTIONS

Deposit 50% (10-day cancellation for full refund minus $10 fee) **Discounts** None (artists may barter) **Credit Cards** AE, MC, V, D **Check-In/Out** 3–6 p.m./11 a.m. **Smoking** Outside, except when high fire danger **Pets** No (2 dogs on property) **Kids** Yes (over age 5)

No-Nos N/A **Minimum Stay** 2 nights **Open** Mid-Apr.–Dec. 30 **Hosts** Pamala Dean & Karen Fielding, 6690 NM 518, P.O. Box 2539, Taos 87571 **Phone** (505) 751-3220 **Fax** (505) 751-0131 **E-mail** dragonfly@taosarttetreat.com **Web** www.taosarttretreat.com

HACIENDA DEL SOL, *Taos*

OVERALL ★★★★½ | QUALITY ★★★★½ | VALUE ★★★★ | PRICE RANGE $95–$250

Formerly home to art patron Mabel Dodge and her Pueblo Indian husband, Tony Luhan, the sprawling Hacienda del Sol has dining and living rooms on opposite sides of the house. The living room has a dark beam ceiling, a light hardwood floor, ample leather seating around a kiva fireplace, a large portrait of Luhan against a purple background, a Jonathan Warm Day Pueblo painting, and niches filled with retablos, saints, and figurines. The back yard has flagstone walkways with petroglyph-style carvings, carved and sculpted santos, tall shade trees, and views across Pueblo Indian lands toward Taos Mountain. The host, a former caterer, creates specialties like huevos benedictos.

SETTING & FACILITIES
Location 1.5 mi. NW of Plaza **Near** Museums, galleries **Building** Restored 1804 adobe, newer guest house wing **Grounds** 1.2 acres w/ courtyards; redwood deck; cottonwood, elm, willow, & blue spruce trees; lilacs, tulips, daffodils **Public Space** LR, DR, gift shop, patio **Food & Drink** Full breakfast in DR or patio; afternoon refreshments **Recreation** Biking, rafting, fishing, hunting, horse riding, winter sports **Amenities & Services** Hot tub, TV, concierge tour planning, newspapers

ACCOMMODATIONS
Units 11 **All** Robes, hair dryer, sewing kit, clock, CD player, phone (data port), fan **Some** Fridge (8), fireplace (10) **Bed & Bath** Kings, queens, doubles, twins, daybeds; all private baths, tub (8), jetted tub (3), steam room (2) **Favorites** La Sala del Don has beam ceiling, skylights, sitting area around kiva fireplace, wood floor, red & turquoise rug, wood-paneled bath w/ blue & white tiles, makeup lights **Comfort & Decor** Pueblo style with low arched doorways, white adobe walls, dark beam ceilings, wood and brick floors, rugs, punched-tin frames, baskets, quilts, retablos, old trunks, Jonathan Warm Day prints

RATES, RESERVATIONS, & RESTRICTIONS
Deposit 1 night or 50% (14-day cancellation for refund minus $15; 30 days for holidays) **Discounts** Internet specials; ski, spa, & llama trek packages **Credit Cards** AE, MC, V, D, DC **Check-In/Out** 3–6 p.m./11 a.m. **Smoking** No **Pets** No **Kids** Yes **No-Nos** N/A **Minimum Stay** None **Open** All year **Hosts** Dennis Sheehan & Elton Moy, 109 Mabel Dodge Lane, P.O. Box 177, Taos 87571 **Phone** (505) 758-0287 **Fax** (505) 758-5895 **E-mail** sunhouse@sunhaciendadelsol.com **Web** www.taoshaciendadelsol.com

INN ON THE RIO, Taos

OVERALL ★★★★ | QUALITY ★★★★ | VALUE ★★★★ | PRICE RANGE $89–$139

On a rural road but conveniently close to galleries and restaurants, Inn on the Rio is whimsically painted inside and out by local folk artists. Holly-hocks, wildflowers, a niche with a St. Francis sculpture, and an old neon sign front the inn's folksy main adobe. Inside the skylighted yellow-and-brown gathering room are sofas, antlers, cattle skulls, horseshoes, a huge Carmen Velarde kiva fireplace, and a gallery wall of local paintings and metalwork. Guest rooms are under loggias in the motor court of the reno-vated 1950s Fiesta Motel, best known locally for pioneering neon signage and swimming pools.

SETTING & FACILITIES

Location 1.5 mi. east of Plaza **Near** Museums, galleries **Building** 250-year-old adobe main building, 1950s Pueblo-style motor court wings restored mid-1990s **Grounds** 2 acres, 200 spring-blooming lilac bushes, 150-year-old silver cottonwoods, box elder trees, path w/ 8 bird feeders **Public Space** Lounge, reception, DR **Food & Drink** Cont'l plus breakfast in DR or patio; all-day beverages, snacks **Recreation** Biking, rafting, fishing, hunt-ing, horse riding, golf, winter sports **Amenities & Services** Seasonal heated pool, hot tub, barbecue, games, bicycles

ACCOMMODATIONS

Units 12 **All** Phone, TV, thermostat **Some** Connecting rooms **Bed & Bath** King (4), queen & double (7), queen (1); all private baths, tub (2) **Favorites** Room #9 has old gar-den tools affixed to side of building, outside painting of scarecrow holding pitchfork; Room #5 has barbed wire coils, cowboy hats, red bandana fabrics, cattle skull, leather chair, bath w/ Southwestern & horse stencils **Comfort & Decor** Motel style w/ colorful hand-painted furniture, wrought iron, folk art walls and baths, varied theme decor ranging from gardening hats and rake heads to metal horses and Mexican spurs

RATES, RESERVATIONS, & RESTRICTIONS

Deposit Credit card holds (14-day cancellation policy) **Discounts** Internet specials, ski packages, adjoining rooms **Credit Cards** AE, MC, V, D **Check-In/Out** After 2 p.m./11 a.m. **Smoking** No (designated smoking area) **Pets** Yes (dogs only) **Kids** Yes **No-Nos** N/A **Minimum Stay** None (2–3 days on holidays) **Open** All year **Hosts** Robert & Julie Cahalane, 910 Kit Carson Rd., Taos 87571 **Phone** (505) 758-7199 or toll-free (800) 859-6752 **Fax** (505) 751-1816 **E-mail** info@innontherio.com **Web** www.innontherio.com

LA DOÑA LUZ INN, *Taos*

OVERALL ★★★★ | QUALITY ★★★★ | VALUE ★★★★ | PRICE RANGE $59–$199

Across the street from Casa Benavides and the Kit Carson Museum, La Doña Luz is fronted by a colorful mural emblazoned with its former name, El Rincon, and a 1909 trading post/museum started by Ralph Meyer, the host's grandfather. The idea here is to capture the original primitive Taos artist feel and mix in modern amenities. The room and staircase maze at La Doña Luz is like wandering through a cacophonous museum. There are Spanish Colonial antiques and early 1800s icons, twentieth-century Taos paintings, Native American buckskins, Kit Carson memorabilia, and a 1610 oak-burl cup to go with a 1600s hand-dug water well near the communal kitchen.

SETTING & FACILITIES
Location 0.5 block east of Plaza **Near** Museums, galleries **Building** 200-year-old adobe combines old fort, living quarters **Grounds** 3 patios **Public Space** Reception, LR, kitchen **Food & Drink** Cont'l breakfast in DR or patio **Recreation** Biking, rafting, fishing, hunting, horse riding, golf, winter sports **Amenities & Services** Museum/shop

ACCOMMODATIONS
Units 15 **All** TV/VCR, stereo, radio, clock, hair dryer, iron, ironing board **Some** Wood-burning fireplace (13), full kitchen (2), washer/dryer (2), balcony (3), private patio (1), robes (1), sofa bed (4), daybed (4), laundry (2) **Bed & Bath** King (4), queen (6), 2 queens (1), queen & 2 singles (1), full (1), 2 fulls (1); all private baths, tub (2), jetted tub (10), hot tub (4) **Favorites** Rainbow has loft, full kitchen, 2 kiva fireplaces, balcony, steep narrow staircase, rooftop deck w/ hot tub, laundry room **Comfort & Decor** Very varied and eclectic, New Mexico/Taos style, beam ceilings, bright colors, carved wood, oil paintings, tile and plank floors, some murals and painted headboards, skylights, colorful Spanish tiled baths

RATES, RESERVATIONS, & RESTRICTIONS

Deposit Credit card holds (7-day cancellation for refund; 14 days, holidays) **Discounts** None **Credit Cards** MC, V **Check-In/Out** 3–9 p.m./11 a.m. **Smoking** No **Pets** Yes (if well behaved; $10/night, full damage responsibility) **Kids** Yes **No-Nos** N/A **Minimum Stay** 3 nights major holidays **Open** All year **Hosts** Nina Meyers & Paco Castillo, 114 Kit Carson Rd., Taos 87571 **Phone** (505) 758-4874 or toll-free (800) 758-9187 **Fax** (505) 758-4541 **E-mail** info@ladonaluz.com **Web** www.ladonaluz.com

LA POSADA DE TAOS, Taos

OVERALL ★★★★ | QUALITY ★★★★ | VALUE ★★★★ | PRICE RANGE $95–$165

Bert Phillips's wagon axle broke in 1898, stranding him in Taos, where he stayed and founded the Taos arts colony and built La Posada as a home. A bed-and-breakfast since 1982, La Posada is nicely situated near the Harwood Museum and Plaza shops and galleries. From the front portal an arched larch entry opens onto an eclectically furnished living room with a white beam ceiling, brown tile fireplace, green leather chairs, valor sofa, carved-wood coffee table, and kachinas. The Beutler and El Solecito jetted tub rooms book up three to four months in advance for weekends, but the stand-alone honeymoon house is also a good choice.

SETTING & FACILITIES

Location Historic district, 2.5 blocks from Plaza **Near** Museums, galleries, Taos Pueblo **Building** 1905 adobe **Grounds** 0.5 acres w/ courtyard, rock waterfall, small pond, perimeter flowers **Public Space** LR, DR, patio **Food & Drink** Full breakfast in DR; afternoon snacks; 24-hour beverages in fridge, ice, hot water; water pitcher in room **Recreation** Biking, rafting, fishing, hunting, horse riding, golf, winter sports **Amenities & Services** CD player, TV/VCR, board games

ACCOMMODATIONS

Units 6 **All** Clock radio, hair dryer **Some** TV (2), phone (2), ceiling fan (3), wood-burning kiva fireplace (5), patio (5) **Bed & Bath** King/twins (1), queen (5); all private baths, jetted tub (2), tub (1) **Favorites** El Solecito has LR entry, old Mexican doors opening to private flagstone patio w/ pine tree, baskets hanging on blue & white walls, twig headboard, TV, phone, skylight over blue-tiled jetted tub **Comfort & Decor** Beam ceilings, brick and saltillo tile floors, carved wood, Mexican and antique furnishings, wardrobes, punched-tin and copper frames and fixtures, quilts

RATES, RESERVATIONS, & RESTRICTIONS

Deposit 1 night or 50% (10-day cancellation for refund minus $15; 30 days for holidays) **Discounts** Internet specials, romantic weekend; golf, river, & ski packages **Credit Cards** AE, MC, V, D **Check-In/Out** 4–6 p.m./11 a.m. **Smoking** No **Pets** No (owners have poodle, outdoor cat) **Kids** Yes **No-Nos** N/A **Minimum Stay** None **Open** All year **Hosts** Sandy & Alan Thiese, 390 Juanita Lane, P.O. Box 1118, Taos 87571 **Phone** (505) 758-8164 or toll-free (800) 645-4803 **Fax** (505) 751-4196 **E-mail** laposada@newmex.com **Web** www.laposadadetaos.com

LAUGHING HORSE INN, *Taos*

OVERALL ★★★★ | QUALITY ★★★½ | VALUE ★★★★ | PRICE RANGE $58–$130

Formerly Laughing Horse magazine publisher Spud Johnson's home and a gathering place for literary legends like D. H. Lawrence and Alice B. Toklas, the Laughing Horse became a hippie commune crash pad in 1968. Despite the kiva fireplace and Southwestern paintings, the music-lined living room still has the ambience of a hippie era. Eight rooms share three hallway baths, and backpackers climb kiva ladders in stereo-equipped lofts. The dining area hangout is an old wood table and bench under a punched metal lamp in the kitchen, across from the red London phone booth and candlelit Jerry Garcia shrine.

SETTING & FACILITIES
Location 1.5 mi. NW of Plaza **Near** Museums, galleries, Taos Pueblo **Building** 1887 brown adobe hacienda w/ lavender trim, 1970s added greenhouse-style east wing & second-story Earthship **Grounds** Trees **Public Space** LR w/ kiva fireplace, DR, kitchen, gift shop **Food & Drink** Cont'l breakfast in kitchen/DR **Recreation** Biking, rafting, fishing, hunting, horse riding, winter sports **Amenities & Services** Hot tub, mountain bikes, stove, hair dryer, phone, extensive music collection

ACCOMMODATIONS
Units 11 **All** Electric blanket, fan, cable TV/VCR, clock radio, stereo, incense & burners **Some** Lofts (5) **Bed & Bath** Queens, doubles, singles; 3 private baths, 3 shared **Favorites** Earthship Penthouse (sleeping 6) tops ramshackle staircase, is sunny A[GOTHIC]-frame w/ greenhouse-style windows, large sitting area/BR w/ 2 sofas & large-screen TV, additional BR & loft, wardrobe, wood stove, sun deck, tile shower, water closet **Comfort & Decor** Rustic, hippie commune feel with barky log & unfinished pine panel walls, wood and flagstone floors, Southwestern and brown cow fabrics, Huichol and folk art, east wing with kiva ladders for loft sleeping, largest west wing rooms with high beam ceilings and four-poster beds

RATES, RESERVATIONS, & RESTRICTIONS
Deposit Credit card holds (72-hour cancellation policy; 14 days for holidays) **Discounts** Group, seasonal, weekday **Credit Cards** MC, V, D **Check-In/Out** 3–6 p.m./11 a.m. **Smoking** No (outside) **Pets** Yes (well-behaved & socialized; $5/night) **Kids** Yes **No-Nos** N/A **Minimum Stay** None **Open** All year **Host** Bob Bodenhamer, 729 Paseo del Pueblo Norte, P.O. Box 4889, Taos 87571 **Phone** (505) 758-8350 or toll-free (800) 776-0161 **Fax** (505) 751-1123 **E-mail** laughinghorse@laughinghorseinn.com **Web** www.laughinghorse inn.com

LITTLE TREE BED & BREAKFAST, Taos

OVERALL ★★★★½ | QUALITY ★★★★½ | VALUE ★★★★ | PRICE RANGE $105–$155

On a rural road midway between the Plaza in downtown Taos and Taos Ski Valley to the north, Little Tree is built with Taos Pueblo-style exposed adobe rather than completely covered with more durable adobe-colored plasters and stucco. The hosts, Ritz-Carlton refugees hoping to raise search-and-rescue dogs, claim calmer sleep comes with exposed adobe. Many interior walls have an old-fashioned "alise" finish, a mixture of wheat paste, straw, and mica, adding glitter and sparkle. Exterior walls need yearly maintenance to keep from washing away. The main house has a blue leather sofa, kiva fireplace, poured concrete floor tiles, and friendly pets ensconced under beam ceilings.

SETTING & FACILITIES
Location Arroyo Hondo, 10.6 mi. NW of Plaza **Near** Museums, Taos Ski Valley **Building** Late 1980s adobe **Grounds** Coyote fence, courtyard, flagstone path, wind chimes, 1,700 bulbs blooming Apr.–Nov. **Public Space** LR, DR, library **Food & Drink** Full breakfast in DR; afternoon refreshments; Belgian chocolates in rooms **Recreation** Biking, rafting, fishing, hunting, horse riding, golf, winter sports **Amenities & Services** Guest bath, stereo, phone, telescope, concierge service

ACCOMMODATIONS
Units 4 **All** Robes, hair dryer, TV/VCR, quilt, comforter, private entrance **Some** Private courtyard (2) **Bed & Bath** Queen; all private baths, tub (3) **Favorites** Juniper, honeymoon suite, has whimsical cowboy art, hats, lasso, spurs, blue & white kiva fireplace, greens & plaids, private courtyard w/ leafy willow branch shelter, 2-person air bubble tub **Comfort & Decor** Themes include cowboy, Spanish Colonial, Native American, and Victorian; saltillo tile or poured-mud floors, rugs, beam ceilings, glittery adobe wall finish, tile baseboards, tin mirror frames, some antiques, retablos, armoires, rocking chairs, lace, and sponge-painted bathrooms

RATES, RESERVATIONS, & RESTRICTIONS
Deposit 1 night or 50% (14-day cancellation for refund minus 10% processing fee) **Discounts** Internet specials, repeat guests **Credit Cards** MC,V **Check-In/Out** 4–6 p.m./11 a.m. **Smoking** No (outdoors) **Pets** Yes (depends on pet; owners have black Belgian dogs, black cat) **Kids** Yes (inquire first) **No-Nos** N/A **Minimum Stay** 2 nights (some exceptions) **Open** All year **Hosts** Maggie & Gordon Johnston, P.O. Drawer II, Taos 87571 **Phone** (505) 776-8467 or toll-free (800) 334-8467 **Fax** (505) 776-3870 **E-mail** little@littletreebandb.com **Web** www.littletreebandb.com

OLD TAOS GUESTHOUSE BED & BREAKFAST, TAOS

OVERALL ★★★★ | QUALITY ★★★★ | VALUE ★★★★ | PRICE RANGE $75–$145

Across the street from San Geronimo Lodge, the rustic and relaxed Old Taos Guesthouse has gone through several incarnations over the years, including farmhouse, artist's studio, and dude ranch. Three rooms still have the almost-two-century-old original thick adobe walls. Families have connecting room options. Turquoise-colored Room 5 has a carved green door and connects to Room 4, with queen and twin beds. The ski slope–loving hosts carved the doors and many of the furnishings, including the turquoise wardrobe with punched tin from rolled-out cans in Room 7. The host, a former U.S. Navy Seal, bakes wild cherry muffins and strawberry bread for continental breakfasts.

SETTING & FACILITIES

Location 1.8 mi. east of Plaza **Near** Museums, galleries **Building** Rambling 1800s adobe hacienda w/ veranda, added onto during past 180 years **Grounds** 7.5 acres, deck, fire pit, fruit trees, alfalfa, horses, cottonwoods, spruce trees **Public Spac** LR, DR **Food & Drink** Full or cont'l breakfast in DR; 24-hour beverages **Recreation** Biking, rafting, fishing, hunting, horse riding, golf, winter sports **Amenities & Services** Hot tub, phone, guest fridge, piano, stereo, board games

ACCOMMODATIONS

Units 9 **All** Outdoor entrance **Some** Gas log kiva fireplace (4), wood-burning fireplace (1), full kitchen (1), phone (1), TV (1) **Bed & Bath** King (2), queen (6), twin (1); tub (3) **Favorites** Room #1 has window quilts for privacy, king bed on large 2-step wood platform, fold-out couch, crib space, full kitchen, wood-burning fireplace, ceiling fan, 2d bath w/ wall/ceiling mural, tub **Comfort & Decor** Hand-carved doors, handcrafted wood and twig furnishings, wardrobes, punched-tin light fixtures, Mexican tile sinks, some oak floors, skylighted baths, daybeds, beam ceilings, recessed wall niches with Southwestern artifacts, skylights

RATES, RESERVATIONS, & RESTRICTIONS

Deposit 1 night or 50% (10-day cancellation for refund minus $10) **Discounts** Internet specials **Credit Cards** MC, V **Check-In/Out** 3–6 p.m./11 a.m. **Smoking** No **Pets** Yes **Kids** Yes **No-Nos** "Leave neckties at home" **Minimum Stay** 2 nights on high-season weekends **Open** All year **Hosts** Tim & Leslie Reeves, 1028 Witt Rd., Taos 87571 **Phone** (505) 758-5448 or toll-free (800) 758-5448 **Fax** (505) 758-8885 **E-mail** oldtaos@ newmex.com **Web** www.oldtaos.com

SALSA DEL SALTO BED & BREAKFAST INN, Taos

OVERALL ★★★★½ | QUALITY ★★★★½ | VALUE ★★★★ | PRICE RANGE $85–$285

On the road north from the downtown Plaza to Taos Ski Valley, Salsa del Salto is noted for mountain views, French ski team connections, and large gatherings. Tents erected on lawns near the tennis court and pool have hosted 150 people for weddings. The living room in the contemporary two-story main building, designed by Antoine Predock, has large mountain view picture windows, two sitting areas, and a stone fireplace. The 1,000-square-foot, peaked-ceiling "apartment" has horse pasture views from the master bedroom, a skylighted kitchen with bird's-eye maple cabinets and a six-burner professional stove, several sofas, and an R. C. Gorman tile creation.

SETTING & FACILITIES
Location Arroyo Seco, 10 mi. NW of Plaza **Near** Taos Ski Valley **Building** 1970 2-story Southwest contemporary, 1992 2d building **Grounds** 4 acres, courtyard **Public Space** LR, DR **Food & Drink** Full breakfast in DR; afternoon snacks; 24-hour beverages **Recreation** Biking, rafting, fishing, hunting, horse riding, golf, winter sports **Amenities & Services** Pool, hot tub, sun deck, tennis court, fridge, microwave, meetings, family reunions, weddings (150)

ACCOMMODATIONS
Units 11 **All** Hair dryer, clock radio, radiant floor heat, down comforter **Some** TV (6), VCR (3), fireplace (4), ceiling fan (5), fridge (3), daybed, sofa bed **Bed & Bath** King (7), 2 queens (2), queen (1), twins (1); all private baths, tub (9), jetted tub (2) **Favorites** Master Room has copper-accented fireplace, corner window seat, fridge, TV/VCR, leather chairs, sofa bed, partially carpeted blue tile bath, window behind tub, double vanity, water closet, bidet **Comfort & Decor** Light Southwest feel. Carved timber furnishings with touches of color paint, dressers or wardrobes, nightstands, metal fixtures, some leather chairs, white-washed pine, Southwestern watercolors, drum tables, love seats, double vanities, balconies

RATES, RESERVATIONS, & RESTRICTIONS
Deposit 50% (14-day cancellation for full refund) **Discounts** Low season **Credit Cards** AE, MC,V **Check-In/Out** 3–7 p.m./11 a.m. **Smoking** No **Pets** No **Kids** Yes (over age 6) **No-Nos** N/A **Minimum Stay** Weekends & holidays only **Open** All year **Hosts** Mary Hockett & Dadou Mayer, #543 Taos Ski Valley Rd., P.O. Box 1468, El Prado 87529 **Phone** (505) 776-2422 or toll-free (800) 530-3097 **Fax** (505) 776-5734 **E-mail** salsa@taosnm.com **Web** www.bandbtaos.com

SAN GERONIMO LODGE, *Taos*

OVERALL ★★★★ | QUALITY ★★★½ | VALUE ★★★★ | PRICE RANGE $95–$150

Across the street from the more intimate Old Taos Guesthouse, San Geronimo seems more motel-like and specializes in hosting groups. Indeed, family reunions, wedding parties, and other groups often book rooms at both bed-and-breakfasts to minimize transportation and best satisfy everyone's needs. The Lodge provides hand puppets to entertain kids, a fun chile-pepper shaped pool, an on-site massage therapist, massage rooms, a meeting room with a piano and kiva fireplace, handicap-accessible facilities, and activities like free concerts, archaeology, and native plant club meetings. Best rooms include the six uppers with decks and Taos Mountain views, two of which have wood-burning fireplaces.

SETTING & FACILITIES
Location 1.8 mi. east of Plaza **Near** Museums, galleries **Building** 1925 Pueblo-style adobe w/ Territorial flourishes, renovated in 1994 **Grounds** Tall trees, historic irrigation ditch, gardens w/ walking log, hay bale, twig arbor **Public Space** Lounge, DR, second floor sitting area w/ green plants **Food & Drink** Full breakfast in DR; afternoon snacks **Recreation** Biking, rafting, fishing, hunting, horse riding, golf, winter sports **Amenities & Services** Hot tub, pool, piano, chess set, concierge service, free concerts, massage, meeting room, conferences, workshops (60)

ACCOMMODATIONS
Units 18 **All** TV, phone (data port), hair dryer **Some** Handicap accessible (2), gas fireplace (5), wood-burning fireplace (3) **Bed & Bath** King (2), queen (12), 2 queens (1), queen & double futon (1), 2 twins (1); all private baths, tub (16) **Favorites** Room #12 has Murphy queen bed, massage table **Comfort & Decor** Motel-like with white and terra cotta colors, wood and twig furnishings, shared patios and decks, some beam ceilings, pottery niches, kiva fireplaces with inlaid tiles, metalwork mirrors, pull-up window shades, lace curtains, bathrooms with Mexican tile and pedestal sinks

RATES, RESERVATIONS, & RESTRICTIONS
Deposit 1 night or 50% (10-day cancellation for full refund; 30 days, Dec. 21–Jan. 2; forfeiture of amount of entire stay) **Discounts** Groups **Credit Cards** AE, MC, V, D **Check-In/Out** 3–7 p.m./11 a.m. **Smoking** No **Pets** Yes (special rooms; resident dogs, cats) **Kids** Yes **No-Nos** N/A **Minimum Stay** None (except Christmas) **Open** All year **Host** Pat Hoffman, 1101 Witt Rd., Taos 87571 **Phone** (505) 751-3776 or toll-free (800) 894-4119 **Fax** (505) 751-1493 **E-mail** sgl@newmex.com **Web** www.sangeronimolodge.com

STEWART HOUSE BED & BREAKFAST, Taos

OVERALL ★★★★ | QUALITY ★★★★ | VALUE ★★★★ | PRICE RANGE $65–$200

The handcrafted folk art concoction of Taos artist Charles Stewart, Stewart House appears at first glance haphazardly assembled from pieces of weathered wood, stone, and whatever else topped the trash heap or the cat left on the doorstep that particular day. After a long stint as the eccentric artist's studio and home, Stewart House has been remodeled into a surprisingly comfortable bed-and-breakfast. Two rooms in the main house have easy access to a living room shared family-style with the hosts. Two comfortable rooms, Fiesta and Ranch, are in an adjacent stand-alone casita. The cavernous barn with its sleeping loft is at the back of the property.

SETTING & FACILITIES
Location 5 mi. NW of Plaza **Near** Museums, Ski Valley, Gorge Bridge, Old Blinking Light **Building** 1950s eclectic, eccentric barn wood & stone folk architecture **Grounds** 2 acres, small trees, flagstone paths, sculpted wood, hammock **Public Space** LR, DR **Food & Drink** Full breakfast in DR (no breakfast in barn) **Recreation** Biking, rafting, fishing, hunting, horseback riding, golf, winter sports **Amenities & Services** Hot tub, TV/VCR, phone, modem hookup, fridge, microwave, drum, board games, children's library, airport transportation, weddings, groups (20)

ACCOMMODATIONS
Units 6 **All** Robes, hair dryer, clock, coffeemaker, private entrance **Some** Patio (5), TV (5), VCR (1), fireplace (2), ceiling fan (2), kitchen (1), laundry (1) **Bed & Bath** King (2), queen (4); all private baths, tub (3) **Favorites** Barn, popular w/ groups, sleeps 6–11, has skylighted loft, kitchen, DR, laundry, but no breakfast; Fiesta has desk, best patio **Comfort & Decor** Beam ceilings, carved wood doors, folk art, bright colors, some log walls & futons

RATES, RESERVATIONS, & RESTRICTIONS
Deposit 50% (10-day cancellation for refund minus $10 fee, plus 5% if credit card deposit) **Discounts** Extended stays, seniors, return visitors **Credit Cards** AE, MC, V **Check-In/Out** 4–6 p.m./11 a.m. **Smoking** No **Pets** No (owners have dogs; dogs sometimes allowed in selected rooms; no cats) **Kids** Yes **No-Nos** N/A **Minimum Stay** None **Open** All year **Hosts** John & Sandy Snyder, #46 NM 150, P.O. Box 3020, Taos 87571 **Phone** (505) 776-2557 or toll-free (888) 505-2557 **Fax** (505) 776-2557 **E-mail** stewart-house@laplaza.org **Web** laplaza.org/~stwrths

TOUCHSTONE INN & SPA, *Taos*

OVERALL ★★★★½ | QUALITY ★★★★½ | VALUE ★★★★ | PRICE RANGE $105–$350

Fronted by the main highway and separated from Taos Pueblo lands in back by barbed wire, Touchstone is an adult-oriented retreat. The clothing-optional hot tub, CD-playing sauna, facials, wraps, and body polishing in the massage room vie for attention with outdoor massages facing Taos Mountain. The multicolored tile baths are particularly attractive, the best with tiled R. C. Gorman women. However, some care is warranted, as every adobe doorway is a small step up or down. Dining is in a greenhouse-like solarium among the watercolors of proprietor Bren Price, whose studio shares the property.

SETTING & FACILITIES
Location 1.5 mi. NW of Plaza **Near** Museums, galleries, Taos Pueblo **Building** Traditional adobe, 1990 renovations & 2d-story additions **Grounds** 2 acres w/ 2 double hammocks, cottonwood trees, wildflowers, playing fountains **Public Space** LR, DR, massage room **Food & Drink** Full breakfast in DR; 24-hour beverages, snacks **Recreation** Biking, rafting, fishing, hunting, horse riding, golf, winter sports **Amenities & Services** Hot tub, sauna, massage, wraps, facials, ice maker, fridge, baby grand piano, weddings, group retreats

ACCOMMODATIONS
Units 7 **All** Robes, hair dryer, cable TV/VCR, CD or tape player, phone, coffeemaker, wine glasses, ceiling fan, private patio, outside entrance **Some** Fireplace (4), kiva candle stove (3) **Bed & Bath** King (2), king/twins & queen sofa bed (1), queen (3), queen & full (1); all private baths, jetted tub (3), tub (3) **Favorites** Royale has king or 2 twins, queen sleeper, private deck, kiva stove, wet bar, skylight over jetted tub **Comfort & Decor** Classic Southwestern, with beam ceilings, Oriental or cowhide rugs, wall textiles, watercolors, skulls, lizards, leather, down comforters, afghans, some antiques and glass-topped desks, and tiled baths

RATES, RESERVATIONS, & RESTRICTIONS
Deposit 1 night or 50% (2-week cancellation for refund minus $30 fee; 30 days, Dec. 15–Jan. 8) **Discounts** Spa packages, off-season, AAA, extended stay **Credit Cards** MC, V **Check-In/Out** 4 p.m./11 a.m. **Smoking** No **Pets** No **Kids** Yes (over age 12) **No-Nos** N/A **Minimum Stay** 2 nights (3 nights Christmas, some holidays) **Open** All year **Host** Bren Price, 110 Mabel Dodge Lane, P.O. Box 1885, Taos 87571 **Phone** (505) 758-0192 or toll-free (800) 758-0192 **Fax** (505) 758-3498 **E-mail** touchstone@taosnet.com **Web** www.touchstoneinn.com

THE WILLOWS INN BED & BREAKFAST, Taos

OVERALL ★★★★ | QUALITY ★★★★ | VALUE ★★★★ | PRICE RANGE $100–$165

A thick-walled adobe estate on US 64, the Willows is best known as artist E. Martin Hennings's former home and studio. The main ranch house (where the hosts live) has kiva fireplaces, leather sofas, dark beam ceilings, light wood floors, and Southwestern rugs, as well as Hopi and Zuni kachinas for sale. Flagstone courtyards open onto guest rooms surrounding the main house. Room themes mirror regional history, including Anasazi (pottery, drums, kachinas), cowboy (cowhide, lantern, spurs), and conquistador. A host career change involving trombone study in Tucson means hired hands will likely be on duty until new owners arrive.

SETTING & FACILITIES
Location 0.5 mi. east of Plaza **Near** Museums, galleries **Building** 1926 Pueblo Revival, 1989 hacienda guest wing **Grounds** 1 acre, courtyards, fountains, pond, hammock, roses, willows, cottonwoods **Public Space** LR, DR, library/game room **Food & Drink** Full breakfast, optional early cont'l, in DR or patio; late afternoon snacks & beverages; special dietary needs w/ advance notice **Recreation** Biking, rafting, fishing, hunting, horse riding, golf, winter sports **Amenities & Services** Pool, TV/VCR, piano, stereo, phone, modem access, board games, darts, fly tying table

ACCOMMODATIONS
Units 5 **All** Private entrance, wood-burning fireplace, humidifier, hairdryer, bath amenity basket **Some** Fridge (1), microwave (1), CD player (1), clock radio (1), clock (4), electric kettle (2), fan (5) **Bed & Bath** Queens; all private baths, tub (4), jetted tub (1) **Favorites** 500-sq.-ft. Hennings' Studio sleeping 5 has Country French decor, sofa sleeper, daybed, desk, game table, fridge, microwave, CD player, private patio, block glass, jetted tub **Comfort & Decor** Beam ceilings, plank floors, rugs, dressers or armoires, oil lamps, candles, punched tin, Mexican tile baths, and porches

RATES, RESERVATIONS, & RESTRICTIONS
Deposit 50% or 1 night (14-day cancellation for full refund) **Discounts** Extended stays, singles **Credit Cards** AE, MC, V, D **Check-In/Out** 4–7 p.m./11 a.m. **Smoking** Outdoors **Pets** No (dogs, cats on premises) **Kids** Yes **No-Nos** N/A **Minimum Stay** 2 nights on holiday weekends (3–5 nights Christmas season) **Open** All year **Hosts** Janet & Doug

Camp, 412 Kit Carson Rd., Box 6560 NDCBU, Taos 87571 **Phone** (505) 758-2558 or toll-free (800) 525-taos **Fax** (505) 758-5445 **E-mail** willows@willows-taos.com **Web** www.willows-taos.com

RANCHO ARRIBA BED & BREAKFAST, Truchas

OVERALL ★★★½ | QUALITY ★★★½ | VALUE ★★★★ | PRICE RANGE $50–$70

At 8,400 feet elevation along the High Road to Taos with the Jemez and Sangre de Cristo Mountains in the distance, Rancho Arriba is a ranch with character run by a character who rode the Santa Fe Trail on horseback. The host built the hacienda in the early 1960s using 150-year-old windows and bricks. A 1980s water well, solar hot water heater, electrical wiring, and TV are among the few creeping concessions to modernity. An old wood stove cooks eggs from the ranch chickens. A favorite summer pastime is sitting on the front porch watching lightning storms. Livestock roam the curvy mountain roads after dark, and the town's small cafe/gallery closes after lunch. So plan to eat dinner early and arrive in daylight.

SETTING & FACILITIES
Location 8 mountainous mi. NE of Chimayo **Near** Santa Fe, Taos, Pecos Wilderness, forests **Building** 1965 hacienda-style adobe, electricity & water added in 1980 **Grounds** 25 acres w/ courtyard, pasture, hay barns, 2 greenhouses w/ nasturtiums, tomatoes, parsley **Public Space** LR, DR, porch **Food & Drink** Full breakfast in DR; dinner w/ advance arrangement **Recreation** Fishing, hunting, horse riding, biking **Amenities & Services** Microwave, fridge, fax, FM radio, TV

ACCOMMODATIONS
Units 3 **All** Electric blankets **Some** Robes (2) **Bed & Bath** Double bed (3); 1 private bath, 1 shared bath, claw-foot tub (1), tub (1) **Favorites** New room under construction has high wood ceiling, lace curtains, space for roll-away bed, private greenhouse-style bath **Comfort & Decor** White plaster over adobe walls, log beam (viga) & latilla ceilings, pine plank floor, Southwestern-style throw rugs, owner-carved beds, handmade barn wood furniture, old window pottery shelf, mirror, reading lights, local landscape paintings, greenhouse style baths w/ large windows

RATES, RESERVATIONS, & RESTRICTIONS
Deposit 1 night (1-week cancellation for refund) **Discounts** Extended stays **Credit Cards** MC, V **Check-In/Out** 5–7 p.m./11 a.m. **Smoking** No (outside) **Pets** No (owner has horses, chickens) **Kids** Yes **No-Nos** N/A **Minimum Stay** None **Open** All year **Host** Curtiss Frank, P.O. Box 338, Truchas 87578 **Phone** (505) 689-2374 **Fax** (505) 689-2665 **E-mail** rancho@ranchoarriba.com **Web** www.ranchoarriba.com

Texas

Most of Texas's 800 to 1,000 bed-and-breakfasts are in the Hill Country, an hour drive north from San Antonio or west from Austin, the state capital famous for its bat colony and music clubs. San Antonio, a major convention town and site of the Alamo, anchors the South Texas Plains region. San Antonio has done a good job maintaining its Spanish and Mexican heritage, and its low-rise downtown and Riverwalk have an excellent selection of bed-and-breakfasts. But heading west from San Antonio toward El Paso and New Mexico, the vast Big Bend country and panhandle plains of west Texas, the bed-and-breakfasts become scarcer than the water sources in the bleak desert landscape.

Most Texans stick to the Hill Country for vacations and weekend escapes, because these areas are also within three or four hours driving distance of major population centers like Dallas, Fort Worth, and Houston. The tiny Hill Country city of Fredericksburg accounts for about a third (320 and counting) of the bed-and-breakfasts and guest houses in Texas. Bluebonnets and other wildflowers carpeting the spring landscape are a major attraction, as are a new crop of wineries and roadside stands selling umpteen varieties of pecans and peaches.

Second to the Hill Country in bed-and-breakfast numbers is the Prairies and Lakes region. Stretching from Texas's northern border with Oklahoma toward Brenham, an hour north of Houston and the Gulf Coast and west almost to San Antonio, Prairies and Lakes includes the Dallas/Fort Worth metroplex. Dallas, a major convention center loaded with hotel and motel rooms, treats bed-and-breakfasts like varmints. Bed-and-breakfasts have found it easier to establish in Fort Worth, an aerospace/cowboy city about 45 minutes west of Dallas, and in quaint outlying towns like Granbury.

In the Gulf Coast region, Houston and Galveston are still big oil industry towns, though they are becoming better known for their medical centers and museums. Texans in general don't rush to the beaches like Californians do, with a few exceptions, like for bird-watching and spring breaks in places like South Padre Island. Galveston, a cruise ship port, is mainly a draw for nearby inland cities like Beaumont and Houston. Gulf Coast cities like Corpus Christi are better noted for refineries and industry than beach play. Bed-and-breakfasts, though they do exist outside of Houston and Galveston around the Gulf Coast region, tend not to be in the same league as the Hill Country best.

The Piney Woods region in east Texas borders Texas's allies from the old Confederacy, Louisiana and Arkansas. As the name implies, this is a region full of pine forests, unlike the rest of Texas. Jefferson, where the modern bed-and-breakfast movement started in Texas, is a former steamboat port seemingly frozen in time with its old Greek Revival homes. Tyler, a former Confederate stronghold, has more recently metamorphosed from an oil center to famous rosebush industry, whose blooms are a major attraction May through October.

FOR MORE INFORMATION

Historic & Hospitality Accommodations of Texas (HAT). A non-profit bed-and-breakfast association that inspects its member properties. (800) HAT-0368; info@hat.org; www.hat.org

Texas Accommodation Guide (issued annually). P.O. Box 149249, Austin, TX 78714-9249; (800) 452-9292; www.txlodging.com

Texas State Travel Guide (published annually). Texas Dept. of Transportation, 150 E. Riverside Dr., Austin, TX 78714-9249; www.dot.state.tx.us, www.traveltex.com or www.texashighways.com

Hill Country

The Hill Country is Texas's vacation hot spot. Wildflowers usually begin blooming in March and April, and the art galleries can never stock enough paintings of oak trees and fields of bluebonnets. Many of the back roads are still open range; night drivers need to be particularly careful not to hit wandering deer or longhorns. Lake recreation abounds between Austin and Burnet, but the countryside around Burnet and Llano is hunting territory.

Many of Austin's bed-and-breakfasts are clustered around the west campus of the University of Texas. Yet all are still close to the state capitol's impressive dome of pink Hill Country stone and the Sixth Street music clubs. Austin's Congress Avenue Bridge is famous as a March-through-October migratory roosting haven for colonies of insectivorous Mexican free-tailed bats. Mason, just north of Fredericksburg, has the Eckert James River Bat Preserve, which hosts May–October evening tours of bat maternity caves.

Fredericksburg has more bed-and-breakfasts and guest houses than any other city in the Southwest, with over 320. The area was settled by hardworking but dirt-poor German immigrants who used the local limestone to construct their subsistence farmhouses in the nineteenth century. Many of these old farmhouses have been renovated into bed-and-breakfast buildings.

An old ship-shaped hotel once owned by the parents of Admiral Chester Nimitz now houses the National Museum of the Pacific War on Fredericksburg's Main Street. Nearby Luckenbach is famous for its country music gatherings. Stonewall offers LBJ Ranch tours. Kerrville, best known in Texas for its summer camps, also has the Cowboy Artists of America Museum. Communities like Gruene, New Braunfels, Comfort, and Vanderpool also have attractions, such as antiques shops, dance halls, and state parks.

AUSTIN FOLK HOUSE BED AND BREAKFAST, Austin

OVERALL ★★★★ | QUALITY ★★★★ | VALUE ★★★★ | PRICE RANGE $69–$119

A creamy white building with blue trim a block from the Governors' Inn, the hostess's former employer, the Austin Folk House opened its door for business October 2001. A large student apartment complex sits between the Folk House and the bustling University of Texas west campus. The brunt of the student noise is borne by Room #9, a corner room only rented out when there is a full house. Southern folk art, mostly "primitive" black artists collected by the hostess's parents, lines the upstairs "gallery" hallway. Rooms #5 and #6 have the highest concentrations of art. A fireplace and sofa are downstairs.

SETTING & FACILITIES

Location 2 blocks west of Univ. of Texas **Near** Museums, parks, downtown **Building** 1880 High Victorian Italianate villa mixed w/ Prairie style, recently renovated **Grounds** Opens onto street corner **Public Space** LR, DR, kitchen, upstairs sitting area **Food & Drink** Full breakfast buffet in DR; evening wine; 24-hour snacks, beverages; special dietary requests **Recreation** Golf, biking, jogging, boating, fishing, swimming, water sports **Amenities & Services** Fax, phone, photocopies, office supplies, laundry

ACCOMMODATIONS

Units 9 **All** Robes, cable TV/VCR, hair dryer, phone, voice mail, clock radio/sound machine, coffeemaker, iron, ironing board, shaving mirror, bath pillow, air purifier, central AC/heat, ceiling fan **Some** High-speed Internet access (by request; fee), private entrance (1), handicap-accessible (1) **Bed & Bath** King (4), queen (5); all private baths, tub (7) **Favorites** Room #7 has canopied ironwork king bed, red & gold fabrics, Oriental rug, Chagall lithograph, beaded folk art, fluted glass lamps, closet; Room #1, which is handicap-accessible, has carpet, queen bed, mirrored armoire **Comfort & Decor** Antiques, dark wood furnishings, parquet floors or carpets, wrought-iron or wood sleigh beds, closets or armoires, drapes, blinds, stained glass, desks, Southern folk art.

RATES, RESERVATIONS, & RESTRICTIONS

Deposit None (72-hour cancellation policy) **Discounts** Univ., state gov't., extended stays **Credit Cards** AE, MC, V, D **Check-In/Out** 3 p.m./noon **Smoking** No **Pets** Yes **Kids** Yes **No-Nos** N/A **Minimum Stay** None **Open** All year **Hosts** Sylvia & Chris Mackey, 506 W. 22nd St., Austin 78705 **Phone** (512) 472-6700 or toll-free (866) 472-6700 **Fax** N/A **E-mail** sylvia@austinfolkhouse.com **Web** www.austinfolkhouse.com

THE BROOK HOUSE BED & BREAKFAST, Austin

OVERALL ★★★★½ | QUALITY ★★★★½ | VALUE ★★★★★ | PRICE RANGE $89–$119

In a quiet neighborhood around the corner from a facial spa, restaurants, and a large used bookstore, the Brook House is under the same ownership as the Governors' Inn and Carrington's Bluff. Though urban, the lodgings have a relaxed, almost country feel. Evenings present the constant temptation of ducking into the kitchen for cookies and ice cream. Guest rooms are in the main house and in a backyard carriage house and cottage. The Blue and Green main house rooms have private screened-in porches. Carriage House rooms have either a lower deck or an upstairs kitchen and are often rented together by families.

SETTING & FACILITIES

Location 7 blocks north of Univ. of Texas **Near** Downtown, museums, parks **Building** 1922 2-story Colonial Revival Country style, carriage house, cottage **Grounds** Covered patio, arbor, post oaks, cedar elms **Public Space** LR, DR, foyer, kitchen, guest bath, porches **Food & Drink** Full breakfast in DR or porch; breakfast in bed package available; 24-hour beverages, snacks, ice cream **Recreation** Golf, biking, jogging, boating, fishing, swimming, water sports **Amenities & Services** Cable TV/VCR, phone, fridge, newspaper, groups (100)

ACCOMMODATIONS

Units 6 **All** Cable TV, phone, voice mail, data port, hair dryer, clock radio, coffeemaker, iron, AC, ceiling fan **Some** Kitchen (2), screened porch (2), private entrance (2) **Bed & Bath** King (1), queen (5); all private baths, tub **Favorites** Sally's Room has king bed, original fainting couch, burgundy color scheme, floral fabrics, claw-foot tub; Delia's Cottage has antique oak furnishings, floral decor, sitting area w/ trundle sofa, kitchen w/ fridge &

microwave, private porch **Comfort & Decor** High ceilings, stained glass, antiques, iron, brass, pine and oak beds, armoires, dressers, some floral wallpapers and fabrics, fainting couches, desks, rocking chairs.

RATES, RESERVATIONS, & RESTRICTIONS

Deposit Credit card holds (72-hour cancellation policy) **Discounts** Gov't., univ., week-days, AARP **Credit Cards** AE, MC, V, D, **Check-In/Out** 3 p.m. or later/noon **Smoking** Porches, grounds **Pets** Yes (some limits) **Kids** Yes **No-Nos** N/A **Minimum Stay** Graduation, football weekends) **Open** All year **Hosts** Lisa & Matt Wiedeman, 609 W. 33rd St., Austin 78705 **Phone** (512) 477-0711 toll-free (800) 871-8908 **Fax** (512) 476-4769 **E-mail** brookhouse@earthlink.net **Web** www.governorsinnaustin.com

CARRIAGE HOUSE INN/RANCH HOUSE INN, Austin

OVERALL ★★★★★ | QUALITY ★★★★½ | VALUE ★★★★ | PRICE RANGE $100–$150

Before the host and hostess married, they were operating the neighboring Ranch House and Carriage House Inns as two separate bed-and-breakfasts in this rural-feeling residential neighborhood. The Carriage House's Cahaba Room has an antique Victrola and large upper deck. An antique cedar fence surrounds the gray, two-bedroom Ranch House. The attractive living and dining rooms have a leather sofa, cedar tables, granny's 80-year-old pickle jar, and an antique postage stamp quilt and washboard on the wall. The hostess, whose son has a food allergy, is very sensitive to special dietary needs and grows organic herbs, vegetables, and flowers.

SETTING & FACILITIES

Location 6 blocks west of Univ. of Texas **Near** Museums, parks, downtown **Building** 1930s Colonial 2-story wood carriage house, 1900 lava-wall bungalow **Grounds** 0.5 acre, gazebo, lily/fish pond, small rock waterfall, bird feeders, crape myrtles, pecan, mulberry, & Spanish oak trees **Public Space** LR, DR, upper deck in carriage house; LR, DR, kitchen in bungalow **Food & Drink** Full breakfast in DR or room; 24-hour beverages; kosher, vegan, allergies, special diets **Recreation** Golf, biking, jogging, boating, fishing, swimming, water sports **Amenities & Services** Fresh flowers, massage

ACCOMMODATIONS

Units 5 **All** Cable TV, phone, hair dryer, microwave or stove, coffeemaker, fridge, iron, ironing board, clock, central AC/heat, porch/deck **Some** Full kitchen (1), shared kitchens (2), robes (3), air filters (on request) **Bed & Bath** King (2), queen (3); all private baths, tub (1), jetted tub (1) **Favorites** Nolen Room has a king bed, secret bedpost cabinet, sofa, dragonfly stained-glass lamp, glass shower opening into room, water closet, shared kitchen **Comfort & Decor** Antiques and reproduction dark carved-wood furnishings, original longleaf pine and oak floors, lace curtains, large mirrors, wooden beds, pedestal sinks, tiled baths.

RATES, RESERVATIONS, & RESTRICTIONS

Deposit Credit card holds (72-hour cancellation policy) **Discounts** Gov't., extended stays, packages **Credit Cards** AE, MC, V, D **Check-In/Out** 3–6 p.m./11:30 a.m. **Smoking** No **Pets** No **Kids** Yes (weekdays) **No-Nos** N/A **Minimum Stay** 2 nights holidays, football weekends **Open** All year **Hosts** Tressie & Jim Damron, 1110 W. 22 1/2 St., Austin 78705 **Phone** (512) 472-2333 or toll-free (866) 472-2333 **Fax** (512) 476-0218 **E-mail** dcarriagehouse@aol.com **Web** www.carriagehouseinn.org

CARRINGTON'S BLUFF, Austin

OVERALL ★★★★ | QUALITY ★★★★ | VALUE ★★★★ | PRICE RANGE $79–$129

Recently purchased by a former Governors' Inn/Brook House employee, Carrington's Bluff is literally perched on a bluff. The grassy front yard has a 500-year-old oak tree and looks down on busy Lamar Boulevard, Pease District Park, and the Shoal Creek Trail. The main building has three downstairs guest rooms opening onto the dining and living areas. A green carpeted staircase with a seascape painting leads to two upstairs guest rooms. The two-level suite has its own entrance on the far end of a long front porch lined with wicker rocking chairs. Across the street is the three-bedroom Writers' Cottage, a bungalow with a shared full kitchen.

SETTING & FACILITIES

Location 10 blocks west of downtown **Near** Museums, parks **Building** 1877 English Country farmhouse, 1920s bungalow **Grounds** 1 acre, gazebo, oak trees **Public Space** LR, DR, porch; separate LR, DR, kitchen in bungalow **Food & Drink** Full breakfast buffet in main house DR; 24-hour snacks, beverages **Recreation** Golf, tennis, biking, jogging, boating, fishing, swimming, water sports **Amenities & Services** Piano, business services, groups, weddings (200)

ACCOMMODATIONS

Units 9 **All** Cable TV, coffeemaker, hair dryer, phone, data port, clock radio, newspaper, iron, ironing board, AC, ceiling fan **Some** Full kitchen (1), balcony (1) **Bed & Bath** King (2), queen (7); all private baths, tub (7) **Favorites** Evelyn Carrington has lace-curtained

French doors opening to DR, corner park-view bay windows, white floral sleeper sofa, dressing area, mirrored bureau & armoire; Suite has full kitchen, downstairs parquet floor & rugs, 2 carpeted upstairs bedrooms, wicker furnishings & baby carriage, sleeper sofa, stained-glass clock, desk, balcony, full & half baths **Comfort & Decor** English and American antiques, floral fabrics, wallpaper ceiling borders, hardwood floors and Oriental rugs, carpets in bungalow, four-poster beds, bureaus, armoires, some pedestal sinks.

RATES, RESERVATIONS, & RESTRICTIONS

Deposit Credit card holds (72-hour cancellation policy) **Discounts** Gov't., univ., weekdays, AARP **Credit Cards** AE, MC, V, D **Check-In/Out** 3 p.m. or later/noon **Smoking** No **Pets** Yes (house cat) **Kids** Yes **No-Nos** N/A **Minimum Stay** None **Open** All year **Hosts** Phoebe & Jeff Williams, 1900 David St., Austin 78705 **Phone** (512) 477-0711 or toll-free (888) 290-6090 **Fax** (512) 478-2009 **E-mail** N/A **Web** carringtonsbluff.citysearch.com

THE GOVERNORS' INN, Austin

OVERALL ★★★★½ | QUALITY ★★★★½ | VALUE ★★★★★ | PRICE RANGE $89–$119

Fronted by a "Red 'Dillo" (free campus and downtown transport) stop on a west campus street bustling with college students, the Governors' Inn is particularly popular with visiting professors. The yellow building with blue wrap-around porches and white trim hosts larger weddings and group functions than its sister property, the Brook House. Breakfast is served buffet-style in a serving room with a fireplace. French doors lead to a dining room with red-and-white magnolia wallpaper and a constant background of classical music. The urban beat is experienced from the balcony and a downstairs porch furnished with swings, white wicker, and wrought iron.

SETTING & FACILITIES

Location 4 blocks west of Univ. of Texas campus **Near** Downtown, museums, parks **Building** 1897 Neoclassical Victorian **Grounds** Stone wall surrounds yard **Public Space** LR, DR, serving room, kitchen, foyer, guest bath, wrap-around porch, upper balcony **Food & Drink** Full breakfast buffet in DR; breakfast in bed package available; 24-hour beverages, snacks, ice cream; candlelight dinners; special dietary needs **Recreation** Golf, biking, jogging, boating, fishing, water sports **Amenities & Services** Piano, secretarial services, newspaper, fax, Internet access, office supplies, massage, manicure, pedicure, groups, weddings (200)

ACCOMMODATIONS

Units 10 **All** Robes, hair dryer, cable TV, phone, answering machine, data port, clock radio, iron, ironing board, coffeemaker, ceiling fan **Some** Private entrance (1) **Bed & Bath** King (3), queen (7); all private baths, claw-foot tub (8) **Favorites** Room #10, the John Connelly, opens onto LR downstairs, has floral king canopy bed, green plants, lavender, white & maroon tile bath, pedestal sink **Comfort & Decor** Rooms named after Texas governors have Victorian antiques, floral fabrics, canopied beds, mirrored armoires, cushioned chairs, tables, molding, wood floors, rugs, tiled bath floors.

RATES, RESERVATIONS, & RESTRICTIONS

Deposit Credit card holds (72-hour cancellation policy) **Discounts** Single, gov't., univ., AARP, whole house **Credit Cards** AE, MC, V, D **Check-In/Out** 3 p.m. or later/noon **Smoking** Porches, grounds **Pets** Yes (some limits) **Kids** Yes **No-Nos** N/A **Minimum Stay** Graduation, football weekends **Open** All year **Hosts** Lisa & Matt Wiedeman, 611 W. 22nd St., Austin 78705 **Phone** (512) 479-0638 or toll-free (800) 871-8908 **Fax** (512) 476-4769 **E-mail** governorsinn@earthlink.net **Web** www.governorsinnaustin.com

LAZY OAK BED AND BREAKFAST, Austin

OVERALL ★★★★ | QUALITY ★★★★ | VALUE ★★★★ | PRICE RANGE $85–$125

In a south Austin residential neighborhood two blocks from Congress Avenue's antiques and vintage clothing shops, Lazy Oak is a laid-back retreat. The living room has turquoise wood floors, walls lined with paintings for sale, and whirring ceiling fans hanging from a 1960s Styrofoam tile ceiling. Every third Sunday evening, Lazy Oak hosts up to 30 people for a small living room concert in which all the proceeds ($10/person) go to the musicians. Business travelers, many part of performing arts road shows, are weekday regulars. Many nonprofit groups hold fund-raisers here. A big, grassy back yard with running water and a fishpond becomes a wildflower field every spring.

SETTING & FACILITIES

Location 1.5 mi. south of downtown's Congress Avenue Bridge **Near** Museums, parks **Building** 1911 2-story Plantation farmhouse **Grounds** 1 acre, spring wildflowers, fish pond **Public Space** LR, DR/kitchen, porch **Food & Drink** Full breakfast buffet-style in DR or room; 24-hour beverages, fruit, snacks **Recreation** Golf, biking, boating, fishing, water sports **Amenities & Services** Hot tub, fridge, stereo, exercise machines, in-room massage, concerts, *NY Times,* groups (50)

ACCOMMODATIONS
Units 5 **All** Robes, hair dryer, TV, phone, data port, clock, iron, ceiling fan **Some** VCR (on request) **Bed & Bath** King (1), king & queen (1), queen (2), 2 doubles (1); all private baths, 2 tubs (1), jetted tub (1) **Favorites** Downstairs suite has 2 BRs, separate sitting room, king & queen beds, desk, wrought-iron birdcage, 2 baths w/ 2 tubs **Comfort & Decor** Eclectic mix of 1920s and 1930s antiques, 1960s Styrofoam tile ceilings, shiplap and plaster walls, carpets, beveled-glass mirrors, bed lamps, wardrobes, dressers, desks, local artwork, painted bath floors, original block glass showers

RATES, RESERVATIONS, & RESTRICTIONS
Deposit None (7-day cancellation policy) **Discounts** Extended stays, state gov't., non-profit groups, whole house, low-season (Jan., Aug.), Internet specials **Credit Cards** AE, MC, V, D **Check-In/Out** After 3 p.m./noon **Smoking** No **Pets** No (outdoor dog on premises) **Kids** Over age 15 **No-Nos** N/A **Minimum Stay** None **Open** All year **Hosts** Renee & Kevin Buck, 211 W. Live Oak, Austin 78704 **Phone** (512) 447-8873 or toll-free (877) 947-8873 **Fax** N/A **E-mail** lazyoakinn@aol.com **Web** www.lazyoakbandb.com.

ROCKIN RIVER INN, Center Point

OVERALL ★★★★½ | QUALITY ★★★★ | VALUE ★★★★★ | PRICE RANGE $80–$150

On the Guadalupe River bike route between Kerrville and Bandera's dude ranches, Rockin River offers bicyclists and motorcyclists a large secure parking barn. The swimming pool is fed with 73° F spring water. Parties along the banks of the limestone-bottom river are the real treat here, particularly during the warm summer and late fall months. Large partying groups are often allowed to pitch tents and sleep out along the river. Guest rooms are away from the river. But 1,000 square feet of upstairs and downstairs wrap-around porches with saltillo tile floors, punched-tin fixtures, and swings are a breezy alternative.

SETTING & FACILITIES
Location On Guadalupe River **Near** Comfort, Kerrville, Fredericksburg, San Antonio **Building** 1882 red metal–roofed Spanish Mission style, 1900 arched additions **Grounds** 2.5 acres, river frontage, fish pond, spring, cypress trees **Public Space** LR, DR, kitchen, upstairs lounge, porches **Food & Drink** Full breakfast in DR; afternoon snacks **Recreation** Biking, water sports, fishing, bird-watching, hunting **Amenities & Services** Pool, satellite TV, stereo, fridge, AC, business meetings (10), parties (40 seated; over 100 outdoors)

ACCOMMODATIONS
Units 5 **All** Hair dryer, ceiling fan **Some** Private entrance (1), coffeemaker (1), TV (1) **Bed & Bath** King (1), king/twins (1), queen (1), full (1), full & twin (1); 3 private baths, 1 shared bath, tub (4) **Favorites** Rio Grande Suite has Texas flag fabrics, sleeping alcove, artful iron stars framing king bed, daybed, cowboy art, private porch entrance, coffeemaker, TV, large vanity, water closet **Comfort & Decor** Themes include Texas, wildflowers, New Orleans, and English; varied antiques, longleaf pine floors, white 20-inch-thick plaster-covered stone walls, oak and dark wood furnishings, iron and four-poster wood beds, sitting areas or shared sun porch, tiled baths.

RATES, RESERVATIONS, & RESTRICTIONS
Deposit 1 night (7-day cancellation for full refund) **Discounts** Group, whole house **Credit Cards** Not accepted (cash or check only) **Check-In/Out** 3–6 p.m./11 a.m. **Smoking** No **Pets** Yes (requires approval; dog on premises) **Kids** Over age 3 **No-Nos** N/A **Minimum Stay** 2 nights April–Aug. **Open** All year **Hosts** Ken & Betty Wardlaw, c/o P.O. Box 631, Fredericksburg 78624 **Phone** (830) 997-0443 or toll-free (866) 424-0576 **Fax** (830) 997-0040 **E-mail** relax@rockinriverinn.com **Web** www.rockin riverinn.com

THE MEYER BED & BREAKFAST ON CYPRESS CREEK, Comfort

OVERALL ★★★★ | QUALITY ★★★★ | VALUE ★★★★★ | PRICE RANGE $79–$99

Bordering the 1854 National Historic District built by German Free-thinkers, the Meyer's1857 stagecoach stop is now a decorator's studio. The main building, the Gast Haus, was built as a hotel in the 1880s when the railroad supplanted the stagecoach. The front porch has twig furniture with floral tapestry cushions. Outside is an old hoist once used to lift trunks into second-floor guest rooms. A grandfather clock stands guard in the foyer. A nearby staircase leads to a hallway lined with Meyer family photos and two upstairs guest rooms. The dining room has a gas stove, wooden rocking horse, and ranch view across Cypress Creek.

SETTING & FACILITIES

Location 1 block from Historic District **Near** Kerrville, Fredericksburg, San Antonio **Building** 1887 2-story Gast Haus, 1872 cottages, 1920 Julia Ellenburger House/Meyer Hotel **Grounds** Fountain, small pond **Public Space** LR, DR **Food & Drink** Full breakfast in DR **Recreation** Biking, water sports, fishing, bird-watching, hunting **Amenities & Services** Pool, hot tub, groups, weddings

ACCOMMODATIONS

Units 9 **All** Cable TV, hair dryer, makeup mirror, coffeemaker, iron, ironing board, clock, AC **Some** Gas stove (5), 2d bed **Bed & Bath** King (2), queen (7); all private baths, tub (8) **Favorites** Room #411, 2-room suite upstairs in Gast Haus, has white paneled walls & ceilings, ceiling fan, desk, trundle daybed, rocking chair, gas stove, large vanity, enclosed porch w/ wicker furnishings & river view; Room 301 in Ellenburger House has wood floor downstairs, upstairs carpets, sitting area w/ 2d bed, antique dresser, vanity **Comfort & Decor** Mix of wicker and wood furnishings, antiques, carpets, quilts, stained-glass lamps, rocking chairs, sitting areas and/or second full or twin beds, mostly wood blinds, some separate vanities and medicine cabinets, tiled baths.

RATES, RESERVATIONS, & RESTRICTIONS

Deposit Credit card holds (5-day cancellation policy) **Discounts** None **Credit Cards** AE, MC, V, D **Check-In/Out** 2–6 p.m./11 a.m. **Smoking** No **Pets** No **Kids** Yes (must be well behaved) **No-Nos** N/A **Minimum Stay** 2 nights holidays, special events **Open** All year **Hosts** Vicki & Shane Schleyer, 845 High St., Comfort 78013 **Phone** (830) 995-2304 or toll-free (888) 995-6100 **Fax** (830) 249-2138 **E-mail** stay@meyerbnb.com **Web** www.meyerbedandbreakfast.com

TIN STAR RANCH, *Enchanted Rock State Natural Area*

OVERALL ★★★★ | QUALITY ★★★½ | VALUE ★★★★ | PRICE RANGE $69–$150

Thirteen miles north of Fredericksburg via open range roads with roaming cattle, Tin Star Ranch slopes gently uphill. Registered longhorns, white-tailed deer, bikers, and shooters mingle with Euro-cowboys behind branch and barbed wire fences. Tin Star's limestone Alamo replica, wooden Old West facades, corral of sculptural horses, and shooting range are across from the Longhorn Palace, a new Old West–style saloon topped with spartan bed-and-breakfast bunk rooms. The cabins near the front of the property exude old Texas ambience and add far more luxury, albeit with no breakfast. Another half dozen bed-and-breakfast rooms are planned.

SETTING & FACILITIES

Location 5 mi. south of Enchanted Rock **Near** Fredericksburg **Building** 4 log & limestone cabins, old saloon replica **Grounds** 370 acres, oaks, junipers, pond, windmill, replica Old West town facades **Public Space** Saloon, shooting center **Food & Drink** Guest room breakfast in saloon; no breakfast in cabins; saloon meals, pizza oven **Recreation** Biking, rock climbing, horse riding, shooting **Amenities & Services** Shooting range, rifle rentals, barbecues, laundry, RV/tent camping, groups (saloon seats 160), weddings (parking for over 1,000 cars)

ACCOMMODATIONS

Units 4 cabins, 14 guest rooms above saloon **All** Chairs **Some** TV/VCR (4), fridge (4), microwave (4), coffeemaker (4), clock radio/cassette (4) **Bed & Bath** King (2), 2 queens (1), queen & 2 twins (1), single/double bunks (14); all private baths, jetted tub (4) **Favorites** Settler's Cabin and Homestead have upstairs & downstairs rooms **Comfort & Decor** Saloon rooms are small, simple and sparsely furnished with one or two sets of single and/or double bunks, a closet, and carved wood chair. Cabins combine Old West, Mexican, and German decor with antiques, stone and timber walls, polished wood floors, Southwestern rugs, wood-burning stoves/fireplaces, leather chairs, kitchenettes, wet bars, porches, rocking chairs, jetted tubs.

RATES, RESERVATIONS, & RESTRICTIONS

Deposit Credit card holds (10-day cancellation for refund minus $25) **Discounts** Weekdays **Credit Cards** AE, MC, V, D **Check-In/Out** 3–6 p.m./11 a.m. **Smoking** Porch **Pets** Yes **Kids** Infants; over age 10 **No-Nos** N/A **Minimum Stay** 2 nights weekends **Open** All year **Host** "Shooki", P.O. Box 111, Fredericksburg 78624 **Phone** (830) 685-3464 or toll-free (800) 722-8564 **Fax** (830) 685-3524 **E-mail** N/A **Web** www.tinstarranch.com

AB BUTLER'S DOGTROT AT TRIPLE CREEK, Fredericksburg

OVERALL ★★★★ | QUALITY ★★★★ | VALUE ★★★★ | PRICE RANGE $135

Transported to Fredericksburg from Cloyd's Landing on the shared Kentucky and Tennessee Cumberland River border, Ab Butler's is a classic early American dogtrot cabin. Once a Civil War hospital, Ab Butler's is actually two cabins sharing a covered open-air passageway called a dogtrot. Livestock was often sheltered in the covered passageway, prompting the alternative name "double-pen cabin." Now plunked down in front of the hosts' stone and plaster home, Ab Butler's is a primitive countryside retreat. Though nearby back roads are popular with bikers, sports enthusiasts need to beware: Because these digs lack TV, the Fredericksburg Brewing Company downtown on Main Street is the only place to watch the big game, and it closes by 9 p.m. most nights.

SETTING & FACILITIES
Location 4 mi. north of downtown, along Marshall Creek **Near** Museums, parks **Building** 1800s 2-story Kentucky dogtrot cabin, 1998 reconstructed in TX **Grounds** 5 acres, live oak, post oak, & pecan trees; seasonal creek; hammocks; fire pit **Public Space** Porch **Food & Drink** Full breakfast left in fridge in room **Recreation** Golf, tennis, swimming, fishing, boating, biking, horse riding **Amenities & Services** Horseshoes, bicycles

ACCOMMODATIONS
Units 2 **All** Phone, CD player/radio, board games, coffee grinder, coffeemaker, microwave, wood-burning fireplace, central heat/AC, ceiling fan **Some** N/A **Bed & Bath** King beds; private baths, jetted tub **Favorites** Marshall Creek Suite & Cumberland River Suite are mirror images, each w/ former parental downstairs sleeping quarters now a sitting room w/ board games & upstairs where children traditionally slept now an adult BR with jetted tub **Comfort & Decor** Primitive wood interior with downstairs living room and stone fireplace, upstairs bedroom, handmade soaps, front porch with swings and twig furnishings.

RATES, RESERVATIONS, & RESTRICTIONS
Deposit Credit card holds (7-day cancellation for full refund) **Discounts** Internet specials **Credit Cards** MC, V, D **Check-In/Out** 3 p.m./11 a.m. **Smoking** No **Pets** No (hosts have golden retriever) **Kids** No **No-Nos** N/A **Minimum Stay** 2 nights weekends **Open** All year **Hosts** Nan & Robert Mosely, 801 Triple Creek Rd., Fredericksburg 78624 **Phone** (830) 997-8279 or toll-free (877) 262-4366 **Fax** (830) 990-8580 **E-mail** reservations@abbutler.net **Web** www.abbutler.net

ALTE WELT GÄSTHOF/115 AUSTIN PLACE, Fredericksburg

OVERALL ★★★★½ | QUALITY ★★★★½ | VALUE ★★★★ | PRICE RANGE $150

A deliberate attempt to break from the Country and Victorian styles so prevalent among bed-and-breakfasts, the two multiroom suites at Alte Welt Gästhof and 115 Austin Place opt for the distressed and 1930s Manhattan period looks. Homestead decorator Charyl Coleman, who did the much more noir and distressed look of San Antonio's Havana Riverwalk Inn, successfully pulled off the time-warp feel here. Alte Welt Gästhof occupies the upper floors (above retail stores) of a Main Street commercial building. Austin Place is a single-story house behind Main Street. These spacious, unhosted guesthouses provide coupons for excellent pastries and even cappuccinos.

SETTING & FACILITIES
Location Downtown shopping district **Near** Museums, parks **Building** 1915 Basse block, 1930s Manhattan style **Grounds** Patio **Public Space** Sun room **Food & Drink** Coupon for cont'l breakfast at 3 nearby bakeries; beverages; wine, chocolates, appetizers at check-in

Recreation Golf, tennis, swimming, fishing, boating, biking, horse riding **Amenities & Services** Day spa services, carriage rides, romance packages, small meetings

ACCOMMODATIONS

Units 4 **All** Robes, cable TV, phone, fridge, microwave, coffeemaker, central heat/AC, ceiling fan **Some** Deck w/ private Jacuzzi (2), private garden (1), roll-away bed (on request) **Bed & Bath** Queen beds; all private baths, jetted tub (1), hot tub (2) **Favorites** 3-room Gasthof suite has comfortable LR facing Main Street, spoons & weathered baby shoes on DR wall, 1920s-style vanity, original pressed-tin ceiling **Comfort & Decor** Distressed, seemingly-abandoned-for-decades look, old trunks over armoires, faded and cracked photos, weathered silver mirrors, European antiques, and 1920s fabrics predominate at Alte Welt Gasthof. 115 Austin has more color, 1930s Manhattan fabrics. Both have multiple-room suites, period furnishings, hardwood floors, sisal rugs, canopied beds, tiled baths.

RATES, RESERVATIONS, & RESTRICTIONS

Deposit Credit card holds (7-day cancellation for refund minus $35) **Discounts** Internet/e-mail specials, weekend standbys, "same day" weekday reservations **Credit Cards** AE, MC, V, D **Check-In/Out** 3 p.m./11 a.m. **Smoking** No **Pets** No **Kids** No **No-Nos** N/A **Minimum Stay** None **Open** All year **Hosts** Ron & Donna Maddux, 909 E. Main St., P.O. Box 631, Fredericksburg 78624 **Phone** (830) 997-0443 or toll-free (888) 991-6749 **Fax** (830) 997-0040 **E-mail** stay@texas-bed-n-breakfast.com **Web** www.texas-bed-n-breakfast.com

---

CAMP DAVID, Fredericksburg

OVERALL ★★★★ | QUALITY ★★★★ | VALUE ★★★★ | PRICE RANGE $95–$125

Groups wanting to be close to the Main Street shopping district like Camp David's clustering of relatively self-sufficient cabins around a main house. Each cabin's kitchen includes a stove with an oven, a refrigerator, a microwave, and a coffeemaker. Front porches are equipped with white wood rocking chairs for enjoying the night air or listening to the Main Street traffic whiz by. Two blocks to the north, where Main Street forks and the main highway continues north into Mason, is an impressive castle edifice housing Friedhelm's Bavarian Inn. Friedhelm's budget menu items tend to disappoint, but the most expensive marbled, marinated rib-eye steaks are a favorite of locals in the know.

SETTING & FACILITIES

Location Downtown **Near** Museums, parks **Building** 1920s New England–style house, 5 cottages **Grounds** Courtyard, arbor, pecans **Public Space** Deck **Food & Drink** Full breakfast delivered to room **Recreation** Golf, tennis, swimming, fishing, boating, biking, horse riding **Amenities & Services** Barbecue, groups

ACCOMMODATIONS

Units 6 **All** Cable TV/VCR, phone, clock, central heat/AC, ceiling fan **Some** Full kitchen (5), kitchenette (1), gas fireplace (5) **Bed & Bath** King (4), 2 kings (1), king & single (1); all private baths, tub (2), jetted tub (4) **Favorites** Cypress has blue & cream country look, angled ceilings, saltillo tile floors, navy blue sofa & chairs, decorative (not functional) fireplace, king & single beds, tub; Pecan Cottage shares main house w/ hosts, has blue LR w/ blue tea service, kitchenette w/ fridge, microwave, coffeemaker, 2 BRs w/ king beds, queen sleeper sofa, tub **Comfort & Decor** Country flavor with floral wallpaper, sitting areas around fireplaces, carpets or saltillo tile floors, wood furnishings, wardrobes, some canopied beds, comforters, lace curtains, blinds, pedestal sinks, front porches w/ rocking chairs.

RATES, RESERVATIONS, & RESTRICTIONS

Deposit Credit card holds (10-day cancellation for refund minus $25) **Discounts** Weekdays **Credit Cards** AE, MC, V, D **Check-In/Out** After 2 p.m./11 a.m. **Smoking** Outside **Pets** No **Kids** Yes (over 12 years) **No-Nos** N/A **Minimum Stay** 2 nights event weekends **Open** All year **Hosts** Molly & Bob Sagebiel, 708 W. Main St., Fredericksburg 78624 **Phone** (830) 997-7797 or toll-free (866) 427-8374 (reservations) **Fax** (830) 997-8282 **E-mail** gasthaus@ktc.com **Web** www.fbglodging.com/tradtown/campdavid.htm

CHUCK WAGON INN, Fredericksburg

OVERALL ★★★★½ | QUALITY ★★★★ | VALUE ★★★★ | PRICE RANGE $115–$150

Adjacent to the Gillespie County Airport and grazing cattle, the Chuck Wagon is named after the chuck wagons that the host hauls around Texas for parades and to advertise his food business. The host and hostess, who have been long involved in catering and cooking, put on a good show, particularly when pulling in the chuck wagon. A covered patio area referred to as the cantina is a rustic common gathering area from which to survey the surroundings. Many of the cabins have downstairs sitting and eating areas and an upstairs sleeping loft.

SETTING & FACILITIES

Location 3 mi. SW of downtown **Near** Museums, parks **Building** 1854 German dairy farmhouse, 1850 log cabin, cottages **Grounds** 10 acres **Public Space** DR, covered patio **Food & Drink** Full breakfast in DR **Recreation** Golf, tennis, swimming, fishing, boating, biking, horse riding **Amenities & Services** Chuck wagon rides

ACCOMMODATIONS

Units 5 **All** TV, microwave, fridge **Some** VCR (2), fireplace (2) **Bed & Bath** King beds; all private baths, claw-foot tub (1), jetted tub (4) **Favorites** Bolinger Cabin has stone fireplace, timber & limestone chink walls, wood floors, rugs, porch w/ swings & rocking chairs, water closet fashioned from old outhouse, jetted tub; Larry Bill's Chuck Wagon has downstairs sitting area & chuck wagon–style breakfast nook, upstairs king bed & jetted tub, balcony; Miss Becky features Hill Country decor, downstairs sitting area & tiled breakfast nook, upstairs white picket fence headboard, jetted tub, balcony **Comfort & Decor** Mostly rustic old-fashioned cabin look. Eclectic mix of wood, timber, and modern upholstered furnishings, plus hardwood floors, rugs, stone, old wood and plaster walls, curtains, shelves, cabinets, modern carved-wood beds, some separate sitting and dining areas, dishes, wet bars, porches, patios or balconies.

RATES, RESERVATIONS, & RESTRICTIONS
Deposit Credit card holds (7-day cancellation for refund minus $35) **Discounts** Extended stays **Credit Cards** AE, MC, V, D **Check-In/Out** 3–6 p.m./11 a.m. **Smoking** No **Pets** No **Kids** No **No-Nos** N/A **Minimum Stay** None **Open** All year **Hosts** Sam & Becky Higgins, c/o P.O. Box 631, Fredericksburg 78624 **Phone** (830) 997-0443 or toll-free (888) 991-6749 (reservations) **Fax** (830) 997-0040 **E-mail** stay@fredericksburg-lodging.com **Web** www.fredericksburg-lodging.com/chuck/default.htm

CORNER COTTAGE, Fredericksburg

OVERALL ★★★★ | QUALITY ★★★★ | VALUE ★★★★ | PRICE RANGE $89–$109

The Corner Cottage honors Hill Country "Sunday house" construction tradition with an outside staircase. Hill Country farmers traditionally made the slow journey from the countryside to Fredericksburg for Saturday markets. They stayed overnight in their Sunday houses, going to church Sunday morning before heading home. Sunday house staircases allowed young men to come in late from Saturday night dances without waking the rest of the family. Each suite here is like its own little Sunday house with a downstairs living area and upstairs sleeping quarters. Neighborhood children like to fish from the bridge across the street for a big bass named Billy supposedly living in Barons Creek.

SETTING & FACILITIES
Location Downtown, 3 blocks from Main St. **Near** Museums, parks **Building** 1990 Fredericksburg style **Grounds** Corner lot w/ pecans, tree swing, hammock, bird & squirrel feeders **Public Space** DR, porch **Food & Drink** Full breakfast in DR or front porch; bottled water in rooms; special dietary needs w/ advance arrangement **Recreation** Golf, tennis, swimming, fishing, boating, biking, horse riding **Amenities & Services** Bikes

ACCOMMODATIONS
Units 3 **All** Cable TV/VCR, boom box, phone, coffeemaker, fridge, microwave, iron, ironing board, central heat/AC, gas fireplace **Some** Sleeper sofa (2), ceiling fan (2) **Bed & Bath** King (1), queen (2); all private baths, jetted tub (3), no shower (1) **Favorites** Twigley's Treehouse has 3 entrances, spiral staircase, burgundy throw rugs, large stuffed bear family, Chinese chess set in windowed sitting area, queen bed w/ floral duvet, bath w/ jetted tub, handheld shower, & bluebird tree house theme **Comfort & Decor** Country flavor, blues and yellows, polished wood floors, stone fireplaces, downstairs sitting areas and kitchenettes, upstairs bedrooms, quilted wall hangings, mirrored wardrobes, sofas/love seats, upstairs baths with floral wallpaper and recessed lighting.

RATES, RESERVATIONS, & RESTRICTIONS
Deposit Credit card holds (10-day cancellation for refund minus $25) **Discounts** Extended stays, weekdays **Credit Cards** AE, MC, V, D **Check-In/Out** After 2 p.m./11 a.m. **Smoking** No **Pets** No (owner has dog) **Kids** Over age 12 **No-Nos** N/A **Minimum Stay** None **Open** All year **Hosts** Marsha Traweek, 305 S. Orange, Fredericksburg

78624 **Phone** (830) 990-8265 or toll-free (866) 427-8374 (reservations) **Fax** (830) 997-8282 **E-mail** gasthaus@ktc.com **Web** www.fbglodging.com

FREDERICKSBURG BED & BREW, *Fredericksburg*

OVERALL ★★★★ | QUALITY ★★★½ | VALUE ★★★★ | PRICE RANGE $89

Opened in October 1994, the Bed & Brew is typical of Fredericksburg eateries, closing down its ale and lager taps at 9 p.m. most weekday nights and by 10 p.m. on weekends. But what is bad for partying and oompah music is good for those sleeping upstairs. The pine entry staircase and hall-way floors have an old boarding house feel. But the guest rooms are distinctively decorated, each by a different design, antique, or furnishings store. The largest rooms, named after the Country Lodge, Rustic Style, and Red Stallion stores, all face Main Street. The Country Lodge's timber decor includes antlers, old skis, paddles, and a fish tapestry. Rustic Style has wagon-wheel chandeliers and a cowboy-and-Indian wardrobe.

SETTING & FACILITIES
Location Downtown shopping district **Near** Museums, parks **Building** 1890s renovated former farm equipment/machine repair shop **Grounds** Opens onto city street **Public Space** Restaurant, beer garden w/ old well & stage **Food & Drink** Coupon for beer samplers in restaurant; microbrewery lunches, dinners **Recreation** Golf, tennis, swimming, horse riding, biking **Amenities & Services** TV, phone, beer garden musical shows

ACCOMMODATIONS
Units 12 **All** Individually controlled central heat/AC, clock, ceiling fan **Some** Handicap-accessible (1) **Bed & Bath** Queen beds; all private baths, tub (5) **Favorites** Bordello Room has shutters, old wardrobe, black wrought-iron header, love seat–like footer, tub; Garden Room, largest & quietest, is the only downstairs room, handicap-accessible former storage space, has corrugated aluminum sides, wood ceiling, garden implements on walls, upholstered seating; Settlers Room has wallpaper, original pressed-tin ceiling, canopied wrought-iron bed, shutters, lace curtains **Comfort & Decor** Each custom designed with a different theme (e.g., Hunter, Settler, Cowboy) and theme artifacts, mostly wood floors and rugs, some carpets, wood or wrought-iron beds, wicker or wood furnishings, wardrobes, some wallpaper, shutters and/or curtains.

RATES, RESERVATIONS, & RESTRICTIONS
Deposit Credit card holds (14-day cancellation policy) **Discounts** Usually none **Credit Cards** MC, V **Check-In/Out** 4 p.m./11 a.m. **Smoking** No **Pets** No **Kids** No **No-Nos** N/A **Minimum Stay** None **Open** All year **Hosts** Restaurant host/hostess (Jasper, Wendy, et al.), 245 E. Main St., Fredericksburg 78624 **Phone** (830) 997-1646 **Fax** N/A **E-mail** dasbier@ktc.com **Web** www.yourbrewery.com

HAUSSEGEN, *Fredericksburg*

OVERALL ★★★★½ | QUALITY ★★★★½ | VALUE ★★★★ | PRICE RANGE $115–$300

One block south of the Main Street downtown shopping district is Haussegen's crown jewel, the Log House, an eighteenth-century Amish cottage transported here from southern Pennsylvania. Behind the Log House is the smaller Fachwerk Cottage, built by Christian Durst, one of Fredericksburg's early German stone masons. These are in essence no-host accommodations. The hosts now live on ten rural acres five miles outside of town. There they are expanding their bed-and-breakfast offerings by renovating and installing a jetted tub in the first of five old cabins. These cut-stone cabins and their twig porch furnishings have already attracted easel-toting painting classes.

SETTING & FACILITIES
Location Downtown shopping district (2), 3 mi. NE of town (1) **Near** Museums, parks **Building** 1770s Pennsylvania Amish 2.5-story log house, 1800s Fachwerk Cottage, & 1852 stone farmhouse **Grounds** Patio (downtown); 10 acres NE of town w/ creek, springs, prickly pears, junipers, oaks **Public Space** Patio **Food & Drink** Cont'l breakfast left in room **Recreation** Golf, tennis, swimming, fishing, boating, biking, horse riding **Amenities & Services** Board games

ACCOMMODATIONS
Units 3 guest rooms in 2 locations **All** Kitchen/kitchenette, cable TV/VCR, stereo, fireplace, heat/AC **Some** Stove (1), dishwasher (1) **Bed & Bath** Queen (2), 3 queens, double, & single (1); jetted tub (1) **Favorites** 3-BR, 3.5-bath Log House, fronted by picket fence, has stenciled wood floors, Oriental rugs, harvest DR table seating 8, kitchen w/

stove, microwave, dishwasher, and fridge, 2 fireplaces, 2 showers, jetted tub; Fachwerk Cottage has LR w/ cathedral ceiling, rock fireplace, queen sleeper sofa, kitchenette w/ coffeemaker, china, cutlery, microwave & fridge, rocking chairs on porch **Comfort & Decor** Separate living rooms and bedrooms, period furnishings, fireplaces, timber and limestone walls, rough-hewn beams, tall ceilings, rock porches, no daily housekeeping.

RATES, RESERVATIONS, & RESTRICTIONS

Deposit Credit card holds (7-day cancellation for refund minus $35) **Discounts** Not usually **Credit Cards** AE, MC, V, D **Check-In/Out** 3–6 p.m./11 a.m. **Smoking** No **Pets** No **Kids** Over age 5 **No-Nos** N/A **Minimum Stay** 2 nights weekends **Open** All year **Hosts** Jan & Bill Borron, 104 E. Austin St., Fredericksburg 78624 **Phone** (830) 997-9907 or toll-free (877) 997-6923 **Fax** (830) 997-1021 **E-mail** reservations@haussegen.com **Web** www.haussegen.com

HOFFMAN HAUS, *Fredericksburg*

OVERALL ★★★★ | QUALITY ★★★★½ | VALUE ★★★★ | PRICE RANGE $120–$190

Though across the street from a livestock auction site and grazing longhorns, Hoffman Haus is just a short walk from the National Museum of the Pacific War (Admiral Nimitz Museum) and all the Main Street action. Meetings are a big business here. The Great Hall expands to 1,700 square feet with a stage, and the adjacent conservatory, library, dining/bar rooms, and courtyard further expand the reception space. The resident innkeeper lives in a stone house near the gardens. A 5,000-gallon rain water collection tank, which fills with rooftop runoff after two good rains, irrigates the gardens.

SETTING & FACILITIES

Location Downtown, 1 block south of Main St. **Near** Museums, parks **Building** 1835 log cabin, 6 cottages **Grounds** 2 acres, waterfall, fishpond **Public Space** DR, wine room, library **Food & Drink** Breakfast basket delivered to room; afternoon wine, snacks; beverages in room **Recreation** Golf, tennis, swimming, fishing, boating, biking, horse riding **Amenities & Services** Piano, VCR, meeting hall, weddings, groups (50)

ACCOMMODATIONS

Units 11 **All** Cable TV/VCR, coffeemaker, fridge, ceiling fan **Some** Wood-burning stove/fireplace (7), wet bar (2), hair dryer (on request) **Bed & Bath** King (5), queen (3), queen & 2 twins (2), queen & double (1); all private baths, tub/jetted tub **Favorites** Texas Star Suite has private outdoor staircase entrance, BR w/ longhorn over carved-wood bed, LR w/ queen sofa & daybed, pine plank floors, lots of funky mirrors, balcony, water closet, 1.5 baths; Morning Star Suite has antique wrought-iron queen bed, 2 twins in loft, fireplace, cowboy, cattle & Indian pictures, pedestal sink, jetted tub **Comfort & Decor** Mostly Texas frontier themes; rock, log, and chink walls; wood paneling; some open beam ceilings; carved wood and wrought-iron beds; antiques; reading lights; quilts; lace curtains; stained glass; some pedestal sinks.

RATES, RESERVATIONS, & RESTRICTIONS

Deposit Credit card holds (7-day cancellation for full refund) **Discounts** None **Credit Cards** AE, MC, V **Check-In/Out** 3–6 p.m./11 a.m. **Smoking** No **Pets** Yes **Kids** Yes **No-Nos** N/A **Minimum Stay** 2 nights weekends **Open** All year **Hosts** Joy & Ted Cureton, 608 E. Creek Street, Fredericksburg 78624 **Phone** (830) 997-6739 or toll-free (800) 899-1672 **Fax** (830) 997-3755 **E-mail** watkins@ctesc.net **Web** www.hoffmanhaus.com

MAGNOLIA HOUSE, Fredericksburg

OVERALL ★★★★ | QUALITY ★★★★ | VALUE ★★★★ | PRICE RANGE $95–$115

Designed by local architect and banker Edward Stein, whose work includes downtown Fredericksburg's Gillespie County Courthouse, the red brick Magnolia House preserves a slice of Roaring Twenties Texas life. The toughness of Hill Country life and the banker's instinct for frugality can be seen in the old pantry water pump and the system of capturing rain water from the roof and running it over limestone into cisterns. Other interesting features include double-sided cabinets and a built-in dining room buffet and cupboards. The living room has a candle fireplace, chandelier, and beachscapes from Knysa and Port Elizabeth in the host's native South Africa.

SETTING & FACILITIES

Location Downtown **Near** Museums, parks **Building** 1923 Craftsman **Grounds** 0.75 acre narrow lot w/ stone patio, fountain, fishpond **Public Space** LR, DR, breakfast room **Food & Drink** Full breakfast in breakfast room; afternoon snacks, beverages; 24-hour cold drinks **Recreation** Golf, tennis, swimming, fishing, boating, biking, horse riding **Amenities & Services** Flowers, stereo

ACCOMMODATIONS

Units 5 **All** Robes, cable TV, clock radio, flashlight, ceiling fan **Some** Private entrance (2), fireplace (2), kitchen (1) **Bed & Bath** King (2), queen (3); all private baths, tub (3), claw-foot tub (2) **Favorites** American Beauty has floral wallpaper, blue & pink accents, step-up bath w/ low slanting ceiling, pedestal sink; Bluebonnet Suite has floral stencils, blue & white tiled kitchen w/ fridge, microwave, double sink, & utensils, wood-burning stone fireplace, floral watercolors, landscape oils & photos, private entrance, claw-foot tub **Comfort & Decor** Varied decor, wood floors and floral rugs downstairs, carpets upstairs, lace curtains, Venetian blinds, mirrored dressers, murals, stencils, wall art, tiled baths (some off hallway), some pedestal sinks and water closets.

RATES, RESERVATIONS, & RESTRICTIONS

Deposit None, except when full house, which is 99% of weekends (7-day cancellation policy) **Discounts** AAA, AARP, occasional weekday specials, packages **Credit Cards** AE, MC, V, D **Check-In/Out** After 2 p.m./11 a.m. **Smoking** No **Pets** No **Kids** Yes (over age 6 weekdays; over age 12 weekends) **No-Nos** N/A **Minimum Stay** 2 nights weekends **Open** All year **Hosts** David & Dee Lawford, 101 E. Hackberry, Fredericksburg 78624 **Phone** (830)

997-0306 or toll-free (800) 880-4374 **Fax** (830) 997-0766 **E-mail** magnolia@hctc.net
Web www.magnolia-house.com

OLD HOME PLACE GUEST RANCH, *Fredericksburg*

OVERALL ★★★★½ | QUALITY ★★★★½ | VALUE ★★★★ | PRICE RANGE $149–$169

Across the street from the Pedernales River, the horse-friendly Old Home
Place is far enough off the beaten track to afford plenty of privacy. The
relaxing, rock-lined pool is within earshot of distant TX 16 and surveys
pastures with grazing goats and horses. Petri's Barn and the Lungkwitz
Cabin are completely detached from the main house, which is the private
domain of the hostess sisters. Only the yellow, gold, and black Pedernales
Suite, the only room with carpets, eschews the Western look for a French
Country theme. The tin tub and outdoor shower beneath the windmill
belong to the stone-walled Windmill Suite.

SETTING & FACILITIES
Location 6 mi. SW of Fredericksburg **Near** Museums, parks **Building** 1860s limestone
farm **Grounds** 19 acres, windmill, pastures, hammock, roses, herb garden, arbor, oaks,
junipers, cedars **Public Space** Office/reception **Food & Drink** Cont'l-plus breakfast in
room **Recreation** Golf, tennis, swimming, fishing, boating, biking, horse riding **Amenities
& Services** Pool, massage, spa treatment room

ACCOMMODATIONS
Units 4 **All** Robes, TV/VCR, stereo, phone, central heat/AC, kitchenette w/ coffeemaker,
fridge, microwave **Some** Outdoor hot tub (1) **Bed & Bath** King (2), queen (2); all private
baths, claw-foot tub (1), jetted tub (2) outdoor shower (1) **Favorites** Lungkwitz Cabin
has red oak logs from western Kentucky, Texas cowboy look, loft w/ king bed, stone fireplace, pressed-tin kitchen ceiling, stained glass around jetted tub, stone shower; Petri Barn
has narrow "rifle-shot windows," kiva fireplace, ladder towel rack, stone & glass shower,
private walled patio w/ cedar hot tub **Comfort & Decor** Limestone walls, high wood
ceilings, rugs on wood and stone floors, wrought-iron or French beds, antiques, armoires,
sofas, Western touches like wagon-wheel chandeliers, patio or porch.

RATES, RESERVATIONS, & RESTRICTIONS
Deposit Credit card holds (10-day cancellation for refund minus $25) **Discounts**
Extended stays **Credit Cards** AE, MC, V, D **Check-In/Out** 3–6 p.m./11 a.m. **Smoking** No
Pets Yes (outdoor cats, dogs; horses boarded) **Kids** Yes **No-Nos** N/A **Minimum Stay** 2
nights **Open** All year **Hosts** Toni Williams & Cheryl Griebenow, 979 Old Kerrville Rd., Fredericksburg 78624 **Phone** (830) 990-1183 or toll-free (866) 427-8374 (reservations) **Fax**
(830) 990-1323 **E-mail** info@oldhomeplacefbg.com **Web** www.oldhomeplacefbg.com

THE ORCHARD INN, *Fredericksburg*

OVERALL ★★★★★ | QUALITY ★★★★½ | VALUE ★★★★ | PRICE RANGE $125–$160

A duck pond, hay field, and pine trees impart a distinct rural feel to the Orchard Inn. To discourage walk-in traffic and maintain privacy, the inn lacks signage, though it is next door to Das Peach Haus, the hosts' country store. The incognito inn's skylighted living and dining rooms have a varied array of paintings. Some guest rooms have an upstairs bedroom with a downstairs living-room bath.

SETTING & FACILITIES

Location 2 mi. from downtown **Near** Museums, parks **Building** 1892 German Victorian, 1870 log cabin w/ renovations & additions, 1892 Pullman car **Grounds** 60 acres, hay field, catfish & perch pond, fountain **Public Space** LR, DR, library **Food & Drink** Full breakfast in DR; picnic baskets **Recreation** Golf, tennis, swimming, fishing, boating, biking, horse riding **Amenities & Services** Concierge services, newspaper, phone, paddleboats, fishing poles, telescope, binoculars, stereo, board games, massage, wedding receptions (75)

ACCOMMODATIONS

Units 5 guest rooms, 1 railroad car **All** Private entrance, individual heat/AC, clock radio, hair dryer, fresh flowers **Some** TV/VCR (5), phone & kitchenette (railcar) **Bed & Bath** King (5), queen (railcar); all private baths, tub (2), jetted tub (4) **Favorites** German Suite has green concrete floor, prewar carved Black Forest lamp and Venetian light fixtures, original German landscape paintings, Prince Frederick photo, a tapestry, beer steins, extra-long & extra-wide window seat doubling as twin bed, jetted tub **Comfort & Decor** Varied room themes, angular architecture, some log and limestone chink walls, moldings, acidetched concrete floors, wicker and wood furnishings, makeup lights.

RATES, RESERVATIONS, & RESTRICTIONS

Deposit Credit card holds (10-day cancellation for refund minus $35; 3 weeks, holidays, special events) **Discounts** Weekday Internet specials **Credit Cards** AE, MC, V, D **Check-In/Out** 3–6 p.m./11 a.m. **Smoking** No **Pets** No (owners have dog) **Kids** Over age 12 **No-Nos** Drinks on furniture (use coasters) **Minimum Stay** 2 nights weekends **Open** All year **Hosts** Annette & Mark Wieser, 1364 S. US 87, Fredericksburg 78624 **Phone** (830) 990-0257 or toll-free (800) 439-4320 **Fax** (830) 990-0257 **E-mail** orchard@ beecreek.net **Web** www.orchard-inn.com

PALO ALTO CREEK FARM, Fredericksburg

OVERALL ★★★★½ | QUALITY ★★★★½ | VALUE ★★★★ | PRICE RANGE $135–$250

Surrounded by oaks and a cattle fence across from a creek frequented by deer, Palo Alto Creek is an isolated retreat for honeymooners and others wanting to be left alone. A representative of the host drops off a continental breakfast, and there is no daily housekeeping to interrupt private moments. (These types of unhosted guest houses with no set breakfast times are fairly common in Fredericksburg and are usually booked through reservation services.) The Itz House has a steep staircase, some low ceilings, several beds, an old-time sleeping porch, two bathrooms, a full kitchen with stove and dishwasher, and a wood-burning fireplace.

SETTING & FACILITIES

Location 5 mi. NE of Fredericksburg **Near** Parks, museums **Building** 2-story farmhouse (Itz House), 1855 log cabin, 1880s barn **Grounds** Windmill, swinging chairs, oak trees **Public Space** Barn massage therapy room **Food & Drink** Cont'l breakfast left by room in morning **Recreation** Golf, tennis, swimming, fishing, boating, biking, horse riding **Amenities & Services** Massage

ACCOMMODATIONS

Units 3 **All** Robes, phone, TV (limited reception), VCR, ceiling fan, porch **Some** Full kitchen (1), kitchenette (2), gas log fireplace (2), wood-burning fireplace (1), stereo (2) **Bed & Bath** King (2), 2 queens, 2 twins, bunks (1); all private baths, tub (1), jetted tub (2) **Favorites** Log cabin, where original family raised 8 kids, now has French doors, beamed ceilings, fieldstone LR fireplace, antique jelly cabinet w/ TV & stereo, king bed, upstairs massage room; kitchenette w/ fridge, microwave, & coffeemaker; back porch w/ swinging chairs; bath w/ candles around jetted tub & kiva fireplace **Comfort & Decor** Antiques, folk art, antlers/longhorns, comfortable leather, twig and upholstered furnishings, track lighting, skylights, plenty of windows, old wardrobes, wood, limestone and plaster walls, limestone floors, porches with rocking chairs.

RATES, RESERVATIONS, & RESTRICTIONS

Deposit Credit card holds (10-day cancellation for refund minus $25) **Discounts** Extended stays, weekdays **Credit Cards** MC, V, D **Check-In/Out** 3–6 p.m./11 a.m. **Smoking** No **Pets** No **Kids** No **No-Nos** N/A **Minimum Stay** 2 nights weekends

Open All year **Host** Brooke Schweers, c/o 231 W. Main St., Fredericksburg 78624 **Phone** (830) 997-0022 (day) or toll-free (866) 427-8374 (reservations) **Fax** (830) 997-8282 **E-mail** pacf@ktc.com **Web** www.paloaltocreekfarm.com

RUNNYMEDE COUNTRY INN, Fredericksburg

OVERALL ★★★★★ | QUALITY ★★★★½ | VALUE ★★★★ | PRICE RANGE $85–$150

Opened in October 2000, Runnymede was built from scratch as a bed-and-breakfast in an oak and pasture area adjacent to TX 16. The hosts, who live in a nearby house, originally opened Austin's Governors' Inn and its sister properties as bed-and-breakfasts, then developed Fredericksburg's Camp David. Runnymede has four main house guest rooms upstairs, the stand-alone Thatcher and two-bedroom Hathaway Cottages, and an unfenced swimming pool. Hathaway's white picket fence encloses a yard with a windmill, bird bath, and weathervane. Hathaway also has a wood-burning fireplace in the living room, two queen beds upstairs, a king bed downstairs, and two bathrooms.

SETTING & FACILITIES

Location 4 mi. SW of downtown **Near** Museums, parks, Kerrville **Building** 2000 English Country 2-story, 2 stand-alone cottages **Grounds** Gazebo, post & live oaks, cattle & sheep pasture **Public Space** LR w/ fireplace, 2 DRs, patio **Food & Drink** Full breakfast in DR **Recreation** Golf, tennis, swimming, horse riding, biking **Amenities & Services** Pool, fridge, meeting area, groups (40), weddings (100)

ACCOMMODATIONS

Units 6 **All** Satellite TV/VCR, phone, CD player, ceiling fan **Some** Full kitchen (1), kitchenette (1), fireplace (2) **Bed & Bath** King (2), king & queen (2), king & 2 queens (1), king & twin (1); all private baths, jetted tub **Favorites** Kensington Suite in main house has pitched yellow ceilings, floral borders, overstuffed floral chairs, king & queen beds; Thatcher Cottage has gray frame exterior, blue & white interior, large room w/ canopied king bed, twin bed, queen sleeper sofa, love seat, fireplace, microwave, fridge, coffeemaker, pedestal sink, separate shower, rocking chairs on porch **Comfort & Decor** English country flavor, some antiques, oak and dark wood furnishings, floral wallpaper, quilts, carpets.

RATES, RESERVATIONS, & RESTRICTIONS
Deposit Credit card holds (10-day cancellation for refund minus $25) **Discounts** Weekdays, extended stays, Fredericksburg Artists' School, other packages **Credit Cards** AE, MC, V, D **Check-In/Out** After 2 p.m./11 a.m. **Smoking** No **Pets** No (outdoor cats) **Kids** Yes (infants & over age 12 in cottages) **No-Nos** N/A **Minimum Stay** 2 nights event weekends **Open** All year **Hosts** Gwen & David Fullbrook, 184 Fullbrook Lane, Fredericksburg 78624 **Phone** (830) 990-3613 or toll-free (866) 427-8374 (reservations) **Fax** (830) 997-8282 **E-mail** gasthaus@ktc.com **Web** www.fbglodging.com/traditional country/runnymedecountryinn.htm

THE GRUENE MANSION INN, *Gruene*

OVERALL ★★★★ | QUALITY ★★★★ | VALUE ★★★★ | PRICE RANGE $115–$215

Surrounded by cash crops of cotton until the boll weevil and the Great Depression almost removed the town from the map, the Gruene Mansion Inn is now part of a small, revived downtown. Neighboring buildings include a dance hall with live country-and-western music, the riverside Gristmill restaurant, and another bed-and-breakfast, the Gruene Homestead Inn. Two restaurants on the rear sides of the property provide plenty of space for wedding receptions. Steep bluffs crashing down into the Guadalupe River preclude letting young children run loose. Some guest rooms are on the bluffs and have wooden porches overlooking the river.

SETTING & FACILITIES
Location Downtown **Near** Dance hall, restaurants, New Braunfels **Building** 1872 mansion, carriage house, barn, corn crib **Grounds** Paths to restaurants, river bluffs **Public Space** Lobby, DR, serving room, gift shop, wraparound porch **Food & Drink** Cont'l breakfast buffet in DR or patio **Recreation** Golf, horse riding, fishing, water sports **Amenities & Services** Front desk, weddings

ACCOMMODATIONS
Units 30 guest rooms, 8 w/ upstairs and downstairs **All** Cable TV, coffeemaker, fridge, clock, porch or balcony **Some** Ceiling fan, trundle bed, fireplace, hair dryer (on request) **Bed & Bath** King, queen, double; all private baths, tub (most; some w/ tub only, no shower; some shower only) **Favorites** Room 10 has upstairs and downstairs, pressed white tin ceiling, white wood walls, black molding, green shutters, green cushions on white wicker furniture, lace canopy bed, gas log fireplace, private porch, bath w/ claw-foot tub on stone floor **Comfort & Decor** Rooms vary greatly (former owner was interior decorator), many with white wood walls, wood floors with area rugs, floral fabric strips, antiques, quilts, some canopy beds, fabric ceilings, white wicker and wood furnishings, mirrored dressing tables.

RATES, RESERVATIONS, & RESTRICTIONS

Deposit 50% or 1 night (7-day cancellation for refund minus $15; forfeited monies applicable to future stays) **Discounts** Inquire **Credit Cards** MC, V **Check-In/Out** 2:30 p.m./noon **Smoking** No **Pets** No **Kids** Not encouraged, but older children OK **No-Nos** Candles in rooms **Minimum Stay** 2 nights most weekends **Open** All year **Host** Jackie Walcott, 1275 Gruene Rd., Gruene 78130 **Phone** (830) 629-2641 **Fax** (830) 629-7375 **E-mail** frontdesk@gruenemansioninn.com **Web** www.gruenemansioninn.com

RIVER OAKS LODGE, Ingram

OVERALL ★★★★½ | QUALITY ★★★★ | VALUE ★★★★ | PRICE RANGE $95–$150

Across the highway from a river yielding 60-pound catfish, River Oaks is popular for reunions. Families like the two-bedroom River House, which has a kitchen, dining room, additional living room sleeping, and a large screened porch. Rooms 3–7 open onto an upper deck looking across the highway toward the river. Room 4 at the top of the staircase has a solid door behind the sliding glass door, muffling highway noises. The main house has many windows, comfortable napping chairs, textured yellow limestone walls outlining the state of Texas, a white ceiling with molding, and black-and-white cruiser and speedboat photographs.

SETTING & FACILITIES

Location 15 mi. west of Kerrville **Near** Fredericksburg, San Antonio **Building** 1930s heavily windowed 2-story Texas Hill Country limestone, late-1990s restoration **Grounds** 3 acres slope down to highway fronting Guadalupe River, old well **Public Space** LR, DR, porch, upper deck **Food & Drink** Full breakfast buffet in DR; special dietary needs by advance arrangement **Recreation** Golf, biking, boating, fishing, swimming, horse riding, bird-watching **Amenities & Services** TV/VCR, barbecue, answering machine, board games, 24-hour concierge, groups (20–30)

ACCOMMODATIONS

Units 10 **All** Data port, clock, heat/AC, ceiling fan **Some** TV (3), phone (1), screened porch (1), kitchen (1) **Bed & Bath** Queen (4), queen & extra bed(s) (4), full (2); all private baths, tub (3) **Favorites** Suite #3, upstairs corner, has side windows looking out on lighted oaks for a tree house feel, low angled ceiling, white wicker furnishings, red accents, individual thermostat, opens onto deck w/ river view **Comfort & Decor** Simple clean lines, 1950s colors, sliding glass doors (most), sitting areas, variously colored wicker furnishings, oak floors, sisal rugs, platform beds, floral comforters, aqua blue baths with black-and-white tiled floors and vanities.

RATES, RESERVATIONS, & RESTRICTIONS

Deposit 1 night (10-day cancellation for refund minus $25) **Discounts** Extended stays **Credit Cards** AE, MC, V **Check-In/Out** 4 p.m./11 a.m. **Smoking** No **Pets** No **Kids** Yes **No-Nos** N/A **Minimum Stay** 2 nights **Open** All year **Host** Linda Day, HCR 78, Box

231-B, Ingram 78025 **Phone** (830) 367-4214, toll-free (800) 608-2596, or toll-free (866) 895-5515 (reservations) **Fax** (830) 367-7507 **E-mail** linday@riveroakslodge.com **Web** www.riveroakslodge.com

RIVER RUN BED & BREAKFAST INN, Kerrville

OVERALL ★★★★½ | QUALITY ★★★★½ | VALUE ★★★★ | PRICE RANGE $100–$139

At the rural edge of town bordering a creek flowing into the Guadalupe River, River Run sits on part of an 1847 land grant reward to Colonel Jack Hays of the Texas Rangers. Next door is the Riverside Nature Center. Tall windows, 30-foot ceilings, the host's old pharmacist's counter, and leather and green floral tapestry seating surround the living room fireplace. The host, a Texas Hill Country guidebook author, named the downstairs rooms after Texas Rangers and the upper rooms after Texas authors. The wrap-around front porch has rocking chairs for watching this energy-efficient bed-and-breakfast recycle their tree leaves into mulch.

SETTING & FACILITIES
Location 4 blocks from downtown **Near** Fredericksburg, San Antonio, Comfort, museums **Building** 1996 2-story German Hill Country style w/ sloping tin roof, limestone walls **Grounds** 2 acres bordering Town Creek w/ hammock, chinaberry trees **Public Space** LR, DR, library **Food & Drink** Full breakfast in DR; afternoon snacks; 24-hour beverages **Recreation** Golf, biking, boating, horse riding, fishing, bird-watching **Amenities & Services** Piano, TV, chess, board games, newspaper, fax, e-mail access, AC, Texas history library, groups, weddings

ACCOMMODATIONS
Units 6 **All** Cable TV, phone, data port, clock, ceiling fan **Some** Private entrance (2), VCR (2), handicap-accessible (1), hair dryer, iron, ironing board (on request) **Bed & Bath** Queen beds; all private baths w/ whirlpool tub **Favorites** Kelton Suite downstairs has most privacy, metal bed, Texas Ranger gunfighter belt, long wicker mirror, wisteria stencils, alcove w/ daybed & rocking chair **Comfort & Decor** Wicker and wood furnishings, antiques, quilts, pine floors, white walls, nine-foot ceilings, floral ceiling borders, dressing tables, Texas history books and memorabilia, reading lights, vanities, some stenciling, shutters upstairs, curtains downstairs, separate showers.

RATES, RESERVATIONS, & RESTRICTIONS
Deposit Credit card holds (6-day cancellation for refund minus $10) **Discounts** Gov't., corp., whole inn group rental **Credit Cards** AE, MC, V, D **Check-In/Out** 3–6 p.m./11 a.m. **Smoking** No **Pets** No **Kids** Over age 15 **No-Nos** N/A **Minimum Stay** 2 nights holidays, special event weekends **Open** All year **Hosts** Jean & Ron "Honest Doc" Williamson, 120 Francisco Lemos St., Kerrville 78028 **Phone** (830) 896-8353 or toll-free (800) 460-7170 **Fax** (830) 896-5402 **E-mail** riverrun@ktc.com **Web** www.riverrunbb.com

THE INN ABOVE ONION CREEK, Kyle

OVERALL ★★★★★ | QUALITY ★★★★★ | VALUE ★★★★ | PRICE RANGE $175–$275
(INCLUDES DINNER)

Five miles down a roller coaster–like two-lane paved country road, the Inn above Onion Creek is a limestone and wood country hideaway mixing pioneer style with luxuries. Porches with twig furniture offer nighttime views of Austin's lights. A terraced swimming pool beckons on hot days. Surrounding government-owned land is being left undeveloped to protect aquifers, making the inn a haven for owls, deer, coyote, and wild turkeys. Indeed, a deer-proof fence protects the garden tomatoes, okra, herbs, and flowers. Both dinner and breakfast are included in the tariff, though this is a dry county (i.e., BYOB).

SETTING & FACILITIES

Location 25 mi. SW of Austin **Near** Wimberley **Building** 1990s 2-story early Texas style **Grounds** 322 acres, gazebo, fenced garden, oaks, cedar elms, hollies, mountain laurels, redbuds, walking trails **Public Space** LR w/ fireplace, DR, porch, sun deck, guest bath **Food & Drink** Full breakfast & dinner in DR; 24-hour snacks **Recreation** Golf, tennis, horse riding, water sports **Amenities & Services** Pool, piano, stereo, massage, board games, fridge, business meetings (12), wedding receptions (100)

ACCOMMODATIONS

Units 9 **All** Robes, hair dryer, fireplace, TV/VCR, stereo, radio, clock, coffeemaker, data port, shared or private porch, ceiling fan **Some** Handicap-accessible (1), kitchenette (1), wet bar, fridge **Bed & Bath** King, queen; all private baths, jetted tub (6), double shower (3) **Favorites** 2-story Kuykendall Suite in main building has 2 fireplaces, wet bar, fridge, sofa bed, double vanity, 1.5 baths **Comfort & Decor** Early Texas pioneer look, weathered old Mexican farm house doors w/ grillwork, varied raised bed styles, sitting areas around limestone fireplaces, old pioneer family photos, beveled-glass mirrors, desks, armoires, carpets, porch ceiling fans, separate block glass showers with seats, water closets.

RATES, RESERVATIONS, & RESTRICTIONS

Deposit 1 night (7-day cancellation for refund minus $15) **Discounts** Weekdays **Credit Cards** AE, MC, V **Check-In/Out** 3–6 p.m./11 a.m. **Smoking** No **Pets** No (dog on premises) **Kids** Over age 12 **No-Nos** N/A **Minimum Stay** 2 nights on weekends **Open** All year **Hosts** Jannie & John Orr, 4444 TX 150 W, Kyle 78640 **Phone** (512) 268-1617 or toll-free (800) 579-7686 **Fax** (512) 268-1090 **E-mail** innkeepers@innaboveonion creek.com **Web** www.innaboveonioncreek.com

THE FULL MOON INN, *Luckenbach*

OVERALL ★★★★ | QUALITY ★★★★ | VALUE ★★★★ | PRICE RANGE $125–$200

Surrounded by wheat fields and grazing cattle, the Full Moon Inn's main log cabin was built by Luckenbach's founder, Edmund Kuntz, when this was still a stagecoach stop and people rode in for Dance Hall Saturday nights. South Grape Creek on the other side of the road has tall trees, small bass, and swimming. In 2002 the ship captain host, still active with Gulf of Mexico shrimp boats, opened a new seafood restaurant, the Full Moon Saloon and Grill. The atmosphere is very casual, with a pickup counter and umbrellas for outdoor eating.

SETTING & FACILITIES
Location 8 mi. SE of Fredericksburg **Near** LBJ Ranch, wineries, museums, parks **Building** 1860 refurbished log cabin, smokehouse, cottages **Grounds** 12 acres, creek, apple, peach, plum apricot, cypress, & pecan trees **Public Space** DR, lobby, restaurant **Food & Drink** Full breakfast in DR; Tues.–Fri. dinner; catering; wedding cakes **Recreation** Biking, swimming, fishing, horse riding, golf **Amenities & Services** Fax, e-mail, concierge, culinary weekends, weddings, meetings (300)

ACCOMMODATIONS
Units 6 **All** Porch, ample bath amenities, fresh flowers, ceiling fan **Some** Full kitchen (1), fireplace (2), CD player (1), handicap-accessible (1) **Bed & Bath** King & queen (1), queen (5); all private baths, jetted tub (2), tub (5) **Favorites** Grape Suite, used for weddings, has full kitchen, separate bedroom, blue & purple carpet, old sewing machine/ table, oil painting of grapes, 2 roll-away beds in closet; 1800s Log Cabin has low front door, red carpet, king bed in downstairs BR, sofa, upstairs sleeping loft w/ angled ceiling, mirrors shaped like window frames, old photos, paintings & certificates in hallway, private entrance **Comfort & Decor** Limestone, timber, and old barn wood cabins have antiques, white plaster walls, dressers, tables, chairs, mirrors, armoires.

RATES, RESERVATIONS, & RESTRICTIONS

Deposit Credit card holds (10-day cancellation for refund minus $25) **Discounts** Week-days, AAA **Credit Cards** MC, V, D **Check-In/Out** 3–6 p.m./11:30 a.m. **Smoking** No **Pets** Yes (pig, guinea fowl on premises) **Kids** Yes **No-Nos** N/A **Minimum Stay** 2 nights weekends **Open** All year **Host** Capt. Matthew Carinhas, 3234 Luckenbach Rd., Freder]icksburg 78624 **Phone** (830) 997-2205 or toll-free (800) 997-1124 **Fax** (830) 997-1115 **E-mail** info@fullmooninn.com **Web** www.fullmooninn.com

MASON SQUARE/RED DOOR B&B, Mason

OVERALL ★★★½ | QUALITY ★★★★ | VALUE ★★★★ | PRICE RANGE $55–$80

A large plaza with tall pecan trees and an old courthouse is across the street from the Red Door and Mason Square bed-and-breakfasts. Red Door has four guest rooms above Hinckley's Country Store, an old-fashioned five-and-dime. Mason Square's three smaller and narrower guest rooms are above commercial offices closer to where US 87 and TX 29 intersect. Undemanding groups like Mason Square's privacy and make do with fewer amenities. Both bed-and-breakfasts have their own kitchenette/dining areas. Mason Square has a tiny sitting area with a few chairs. The Red Door's larger living room has a wood-burning fireplace and TV.

SETTING & FACILITIES

Location Downtown, Courthouse Square **Near** Fredericksburg, Bat Cave **Building** 1890s 2-story balconied commercial rock structures w/ downstairs stores & offices **Grounds** Open onto main street, plaza **Public Space** LR, DR/kitchenette, balcony **Food & Drink** Cont'l breakfast in DR **Recreation** Biking, boating, fishing, hunting **Amenities & Services** TV/VCR, portable phone, microwave, toaster oven, fridge, dishwasher, sink, kitchen utensils

ACCOMMODATIONS

Units 7 **All** Clock radio, ceiling fan **Some** Data port, coffeemaker (4), individual heat/AC (4), roll-away bed, hair dryer, iron, ironing board (on request) **Bed & Bath** King (5), queen (2); all private baths, jetted tub (2) **Favorites** Room #3 in Red Door has sage green color, burgundy accents, dark brown wood furnishings, small corner sitting area, lavender bench, deep windows, data port, jetted tub, separate shower; Room #4, honey-moon favorite in quiet back of Red Door, has blue color, pink carpet, woven canopy bed, small sitting area, jetted tub, separate shower **Comfort & Decor** Victorian woodwork, original ten-foot pressed-tin ceilings, opalescent stained-glass transoms, oak floors, car-pets, antiques, four-poster beds, dressers, armoires, reading lamps, open closet space, and floral wallpaper in baths.

RATES, RESERVATIONS, & RESTRICTIONS

Deposit Credit card holds (72-hour cancellation for refund minus $15) **Discounts** Week-days, gov't., churches, groups **Credit Cards** MC, V **Check-In/Out** 2 p.m./noon **Smoking** No **Pets** No **Kids** Yes (well-behaved; at Mason Square) **No-Nos** N/A **Minimum Stay** 2

nights holiday weekends **Open** All year **Hosts** Monica & Brent Hinckley, P.O. Box 298, Mason 76856 **Phone** (915) 347-6398 or toll-free (800) 369-0405 **Fax** N/A **E-mail** hinck5415@hctc.net **Web** N/A

WILLOW CREEK RANCH, Mason

OVERALL ★★★★½ | QUALITY ★★★★ | VALUE ★★★★★ | PRICE RANGE $50–$65 ($75–$100, NO BREAKFAST UNITS)

A working ranch four miles down a dirt road, Willow Creek has two bed-and-breakfast rooms and three stand-alone no-breakfast lodgings with full kitchens and barbecues. The Ranch has over 35 bird species, and borders a fly-fishing river (19 species, including bass, catfish, perch, sunfish). The picnic area along the Llano River is especially popular with groups. The main house has leather sofas, kachinas, and a dining area with sculptures next to a granite kitchen counter. A double door leads to a screened porch with carved Mexican furniture for poolside eating. The parlor has a fireplace under the original weathered green ceiling.

SETTING & FACILITIES
Location 14 mi. SE of Mason **Near** Fredericksburg, Bat Cave **Building** 1876 German stone farmhouse, east wing added, restored 2000 **Grounds** 100 acres, pastures, riverbank picnic area **Public Space** LR, DR, parlor w/ fireplace, screened porch, pool dressing room **Food & Drink** Full breakfast in DR or porch **Recreation** Biking, boating, fishing, swimming, bird-watching **Amenities & Services** Pool & whirlpool (adults only), TV/DVD, stereo, grand piano, e-mail access, groups, weddings (150)

ACCOMMODATIONS
Units 5 **All** Clock, ceiling fan, central heat/AC **Some** Microwave (1), fridge (1), coffeemaker (1), breakfast (2) **Bed & Bath** Queen (1), full (1); all private baths, claw-foot tub (1), tub (1) **Favorites** Ranch House Guest Room inside main house has queen bed, granite-topped longleaf pine dresser, mixed media Indian paintings, bath w/ eggs, bird nests; Guest House, original stand-alone stone smokehouse above wine/root cellar, has vaulted ceiling, pine beams, antique mirror, wicker table, lace curtains, granite steps to outside bath **Comfort & Decor** Southwestern and German styles, beaded board walls and ceilings, stone walls with German style plastering, quilt or comforter, dresser or armoire, wood and saltillo tile floors, rugs, R. C. Gorman prints.

RATES, RESERVATIONS, & RESTRICTIONS
Deposit $25/unit (72-hour cancellation for full refund) **Discounts** Whole property rentals, no breakfast **Credit Cards** Not accepted (cash or check only) **Check-In/Out** 3 p.m./noon **Smoking** No **Pets** No **Kids** Yes **No-Nos** N/A **Minimum Stay** None **Open** All year **Hosts** Dennis & Kay Evans, P.O. Box 1599, Mason 76856 **Phone** (915) 347-6781 or toll-free (888) 281-7242 **Fax** N/A **E-mail** willowcr@hctc.net **Web** www.willowcreekranchtexas.com

LAMB'S REST INN, New Braunfels

OVERALL ★★★★½ | QUALITY ★★★★ | VALUE ★★★★ | PRICE RANGE $95–$225

A tranquil river retreat 25 miles north of San Antonio and 40 miles south of Austin, the Lamb's Rest adds fresh flowers to its china and crystal breakfast settings. Riverbank relaxation is a popular pastime, as are countryside excursions and strolls through the nearby town of Gruene. Candles add romantic ambience to guest rooms like the periwinkle-blue Peggotty's Seaside Cottage. Quilly's Antiques strives for a French Country feel with a balcony, floral wallpaper, red and yellow walls, a sleigh bed, and an alcove with a fireplace and daybed. Grapes Inn offers up a pewter canopy bed and window seating.

SETTING & FACILITIES

Location On Guadalupe River, 1 mi. from Gruene **Near** San Antonio **Building** 1969 contemporary ranch house **Grounds** 1 acre, fountain, trees **Public Space** LR w/ fireplace, DR, decks **Food & Drink** Full breakfast in DR or porch; afternoon snacks; 24-hour beverages **Recreation** Golf, tennis, horse riding, fishing, water sports **Amenities & Services** Pool, hot tub, large-screen TV/VCR, piano, groups (16), weddings (30)

ACCOMMODATIONS

Units 4 guest rooms, 1 2-BR suite, 1 cottage **All** Robes, TV/VCR, hair dryer, CD/clock radio, coffeemaker, iron, ironing board, down comforter, ceiling fan **Some** Full kitchen (1), fireplace (2), desk (2) **Bed & Bath** King (1), queen (5); all private baths, jetted tub (3) **Favorites** Buttertub Farm, 2-BR suite, has yellow walls; red, white & blue plaid fabrics; alcove w/ white picket fence behind full-size wicker bed; birdhouses; two entrance doors. River Cottage has shabby chic decor, king bed, balcony, double jetted tub **Comfort & Decor** Country style, lamb themes; brightly colored walls or wallpaper; florals and plaids; family antiques; wicker, wood, and metal furnishings; sitting areas; reading lamps; rocking chairs; armoires; dressing tables; carpets; makeup mirrors.

RATES, RESERVATIONS, & RESTRICTIONS

Deposit 1 night (1-week cancellation for refund minus $10) **Discounts** Weekday corp. **Credit Cards** MC, V, D **Check-In/Out** 4 p.m./11 a.m. **Smoking** No **Pets** No **Kids** Over age 12 **No-Nos** N/A **Minimum Stay** 2 nights weekends, 3 nights holidays **Open** All year **Hosts** George & Judy Rothell, 1385 Edwards Blvd., New Braunfels 78132 **Phone** (830) 609-3932 or toll-free (888) 609-3932 **Fax** (830) 620-0864 **E-mail** lambsbb@aol.com **Web** www.bbhost.com/lambsrestbb

CRYSTAL RIVER INN, San Marcos

OVERALL ★★★★ | QUALITY ★★★★ | VALUE ★★★★ | PRICE RANGE $85–$150

A conglomeration of buildings spread across a city block, the Crystal River Inn specializes in getaway packages ranging from writing workshops and romantic interludes to murder mystery weekends. The three Young House guest rooms open onto a private lobby with a microwave, coffeemaker, and refrigerator. Rock House rooms open onto a common sitting area adding a phone and TV. Smokers opt for the Tex-Mex Neuces, which has a private back door opening onto the patio. Business travelers favor the Llano, which has a desk, love seat, wingback reading chair, and two bright walls of windows.

SETTING & FACILITIES
Location Historic district **Near** University **Building** 1883 Victorian, 1930s rock house **Grounds** Rose garden, pecan trees, fountain, fish pond, gazebo, covered patio **Public Space** LR, DR, gift shop **Food & Drink** Full breakfast in DR or bed (special arrangement); 24-hour snacks, beverages; picnics; catering; special dietary needs w/ advance notice **Recreation** Golf, tennis, horse riding, fishing, water sports **Amenities & Services** Phone, data port, microwave, fridge, TV/VCR, stereo, tour arrangements, weddings (300)

ACCOMMODATIONS
Units 8 guest rooms & 3 2-BR suites **All** TV **Some** Robes (4), VCR (4), fireplace (2), phone (5), ceiling fan (9) **Bed & Bath** King (4), queen (6), 2 doubles (1); all private baths, tub (7), claw-foot tub (3) **Favorites** Medina, popular w/ honeymooners, has green & rose walls, fireplace, elevated four-poster bed; San Marcos Suite has double-sided fireplace, canopied king & twin beds, bath skylight; 2-BR Rio Grande, most private, has Tex-Mex decor, kitchenette **Comfort & Decor** Varied styles include English Country, Victorian, and Southwestern, with antiques, sitting areas, armoires, some wallpaper/fabric walls and desks, carpets or hardwood floors with area rugs.

RATES, RESERVATIONS, & RESTRICTIONS
Deposit 50% (48-hour cancellation weekdays; 1 week for weekends; 3 weeks for groups, package events) **Discounts** Corp., weekday singles, extended stays, Internet specials, packages **Credit Cards** AE, MC, V, D, DC **Check-In/Out** After 3 p.m./noon **Smoking** No **Pets** Discouraged **Kids** Yes (requires advance arrangement) **No-Nos** N/A **Minimum Stay** 2 nights weekends **Open** All year **Hosts** Cathy, Mike, & Sarah Dillon, 328 W. Hopkins, San Marcos 78666 **Phone** (512) 396-3739 or toll-free (888) 396-3739 **Fax** (512) 396-6311 **E-mail** info@crystalriverinn.com **Web** www.crystalriverinn.com

ROSE HILL MANOR, Stonewall

OVERALL ★★★★½ | QUALITY ★★★★ | VALUE ★★★★ | PRICE RANGE $115–$150

A Texas Hill Country Wine Trail tasting stop for Alamosa Cellars (oddly situated in dry San Saba County), Rose Hill Manor sits atop a gently sloping hillside fronted by a hay field. The LBJ Ranch is about three miles north, off US 290. Four guest rooms are in the main house and have enclosed porches. Two cottages, Oak Grove and Hilltop, are away from the main house and have satellite TV, coffeemakers, and open decks. Two new buildings with four additional suites will have carpets, fireplaces, floral wall-paper, and glass-enclosed porches. The dining room has upholstered tapestry seating, burgundy floral carpets, and evening views of deer.

SETTING & FACILITIES

Location 17 mi. SE of Fredericksburg **Near** LBJ Ranch, Fredericksburg, Luckenbach, parks, museums **Building** 1990s 2-story Charleston Plantation, cottages **Grounds** 38 acres, hay field, cedar trees, herb garden **Public Space** LR, DR, DR/parlor, bar, hallway gift/bookshop, porches **Food & Drink** Full breakfast in DR or bar; afternoon snacks; 24-hour beverages; Texas wine tasting at check-in Sun.–Thurs.; Fri. & Sat. dinners **Recreation** Biking, boating, fishing, horse riding, bird-watching **Amenities & Services** Piano, bicycles, concierge services, wine tours, hayrides,

ACCOMMODATIONS

Units 10 **All** Private porch, heat/AC **Some** TV, coffeemaker and clock radio (cottages), hair dryer, iron (on request) **Bed & Bath** King (6), queen (4); all private baths, tub **Favorites** Sunrise Room has wood floor, rugs, rattan & dark wood furnishings, queen four-poster bed, white & wallpapered walls **Comfort & Decor** Dark wood period antiques, frilly bedside lamps, rattan, wood floors or carpets, four-poster beds, armoires, mirrored dressers, sitting areas, French doors opening onto verandas (main house), some floral wallpaper, tapestry upholstery, double vanities, and pedestal sinks.

RATES, RESERVATIONS, & RESTRICTIONS

Deposit Credit card holds (10-day cancellation for refund minus $10) **Discounts** Weekdays, military **Credit Cards** AE, MC, V, D **Check-In/Out** 3–6 p.m./11 a.m. **Smoking** No **Pets** No **Kids** Yes (age 12 weekend nights; any age Sun.–Thurs.; 3 people per room maximum) **No-Nos** N/A **Minimum Stay** 2 nights weekends, some holidays **Open** All year **Hosts** Patricia & Robert VanderLyn, 2614 Upper Albert Rd., Stonewall 78671 **Phone** (830) 644-5541 or toll-free (877) rosehil **Fax** (830) 644-2248 **E-mail** stay@rose-hill.com **Web** www.rose-hill.com

BLUEBIRD HILL BED & BREAKFAST, Utopia

OVERALL ★★★★½ | QUALITY ★★★★ | VALUE ★★★★ | PRICE RANGE $95–$125

Arrowheads and fossil seashells mark the entrance to Bluebird Hill. The anthropologist hostess does storytelling based on two decades of compiling local oral histories. The Texas Star Suite has cowboy decor, open beam ceilings, punched-copper fixtures, sliding glass doors to a private deck and outdoor staircase, a kitchenette, and a single bed and queen sleeper sofa in the living room. Further down the road, behind a locked cattle gate at Indian Blanket Ranch, is the Hideaway Cabin. The Cabin has an 1840 Betsy Ross bed, early Texas cowhide chairs, a fireplace, a sunken room with more beds and a loft.

SETTING & FACILITIES

Location 10 mi. west of Utopia **Near** Vanderpool **Building** Early Texas German farmhouse, 1840s-style cabin w/ 1986 additions **Grounds** 250 acres, creek, live oaks, hammock, fire pit, cattle grazing land w/ drift fences **Public Space** LR, DR, library, garden room, patio **Food & Drink** Full breakfast in DR or cabin **Recreation** Biking, boating, fishing, horse riding, bird-watching **Amenities & Services** Indoor hot tub, barbecue, 2 fireplaces, 2 satellite TVs, stereo, phone, Texas history books, bird & bat tours, storytelling, cowboy songs

ACCOMMODATIONS

Units 2 guest rooms, 1 cabin **All** Robes, hair dryer, clock radio, first-aid kit **Some** TV (1), private deck (1), full kitchen (1), kitchenette (1), phone (1), board games (1) **Bed & Bath** King (1), queen (2); all private baths, claw-foot tub (1), tub (1) **Favorites** Bird Nest gets morning sun, has warbler nests on wall, floral & bird prints, bird lamp shade, double vanity **Comfort & Decor** Varies greatly, includes wicker and wood furnishings, Texas antiques, rocking chairs.

RATES, RESERVATIONS, & RESTRICTIONS

Deposit 50% (7-day cancellation for refund of 50% of deposit) **Discounts** None **Credit Cards** None **Check-In/Out** 3–6 p.m./11 a.m. **Smoking** No **Pets** No **Kids** Over age 10 in main house; younger in cabin **No-Nos** Gun use or fireworks; motorized vehicles on trails **Minimum Stay** 2 nights Sept.–May; 3 nights holidays, spring break; 4 nights Memorial Day–Labor Day **Open** All year **Hosts** Lora Garrison & LeAnn Sharp, Box 697, Utopia 78884 **Phone** (830) 966-3525 **Fax** (830) 966-3519 **E-mail** leann@friolodging.com **Web** www.friolodging.com/bluebird

TEXAS STAGECOACH INN, *Vanderpool*

OVERALL ★★★★½ | QUALITY ★★★★ | VALUE ★★★★ | PRICE RANGE $115–$145

In western Bandera County, 75 miles southwest of Fredericksburg, the Texas Stagecoach Inn aptly calls itself "miles from nowhere." The inn borders a stretch of river suitable for bird-watching, canoeing, and catch-and-release bass and catfish fishing (bring your own equipment), but not swimming. Two upstairs rooms share a private common area with a desk. The white, wood-paneled living room is entered via a river-facing backdoor. It has an arrowhead collection, original 1950s woven steer hide and rope furnishings, and arrowhead-shaped tables. The 1950s west Texas theme extends to plates with green and white cowboys on bucking broncos.

SETTING & FACILITIES

Location 85 mi. NW of San Antonio **Near** Kerrville, Comfort, Bandera **Building** 1885 Hill Country Ranch, rebuilt & expanded **Grounds** 3 acres fronting river, pecan trees, old well **Public Space** LR, DR, pantry, gift shop/gallery **Food & Drink** Full breakfast buffet in butler's pantry; 24-hour snacks, beverages **Recreation** Biking, boating, fishing, horse riding, bird-watching **Amenities & Services** Piano, fridge, canoes

ACCOMMODATIONS

Units 5 **All** Robes, clock **Some** Private balcony (1) **Bed & Bath** King (4), 2 queens (1); all private baths, tub (4) **Favorites** Button Willow Canyon Suite has antique carved dresser, wood vanity table, bird house built of old barn wood & antique ceiling tin, birding books, French doors to private balcony, green plants in large tiled bath; Cottonwood Canyon Suite has large dressing room w/ hat boxes, Texas art, art books, horse head–embossed green leather chair, cedar bench at foot of bed, lots of sunlight **Comfort & Decor** Texas touches like horseshoe-shaped headboard and horseshoe fixtures, wood paneling, carpets, some stained glass, mirrored armoires, dressers.

RATES, RESERVATIONS, & RESTRICTIONS

Deposit 1 night or 50% (w/ 14 days' notice, 1 rescheduling change allowed; otherwise forfeit deposit) **Discounts** Extended stays, singles, honeymoon/anniversary specials **Credit Cards** Not accepted **Check-In/Out** 4–6 p.m./10 a.m. **Smoking** No **Pets** No **Kids** Yes (2-queen BR only; no roll-aways) **No-Nos** N/A **Minimum Stay** 2 nights weekends, 3 nights holidays **Open** All year **Hosts** David, Karen, Lindsay, & Trevor Camp, Ranch Road 187, HC 02 Box 166, Vanderpool 78885 **Phone** (830) 966-6272 or toll-free (888) 965-6272 **Fax** (830) 966-6273 **E-mail** stageinn@swtexas.net **Web** www.bbonline.com/tx/stagecoach

Prairies and Lakes

Prairies and Lakes encompasses a wide slice of Texas life from the Oklahoma border and the Dallas/Fort Worth metroplex south to the wheat fields and hilly ranch country just east of San Antonio and Austin. Dallas metamorphosed from being a dusty nineteenth-century flyspeck of a small town on the vast prairies into a metropolis when it became a major railroad hub. Famed for its oil wealth, Dallas is now a national business and trade center, central to the East and West Coasts in the airline age. Although business and conventions are usually the initial lure, Dallas offers a rich array of museums and an assortment of diversions ranging from the arts to professional sports.

Nicknamed Cow Town, nearby Fort Worth has successfully grafted the aerospace industry and museums onto its Old West heritage of the stockyards and partying cowboys driving cattle on the Chisholm Trail. The metroplex bed-and-breakfast offerings are relatively few in number, but most are good values when compared with local hotel prices.

An hour's drive north, east, or south of the metroplex are numerous relatively unknown small towns, like Granbury and Glen Rose, offering the adventurous a mushrooming number of bed-and-breakfast choices. Moving on down into central Texas, towns like Salado (population 1,381) offer a mix of shopping, Texas design, and countryside. Waco, a big city of 100,000 by central Texas standards, is the home for Baylor University, the Texas Ranger Hall of Fame, and the Dr. Pepper Museum.

An hour north of Houston, the southernmost extent of Prairies and Lakes, is a little-known group of Washington County towns with names like Brenham, Round Top, Gay Hill, Independence, and Bellville. Antiques, spring wildflowers, longhorns, and ranch life are among the attractions in what was prime cotton country in the heyday of the Confederacy. Washington on the Brazos State Park is the place to go for the history of the Texas Republic. Nearby Bryan/College Station houses Texas A&M University and the George H. Bush Presidential Library.

TEXAS RANCH LIFE, Bellville

OVERALL ★★★★★ | QUALITY ★★★★ | VALUE ★★★★ | PRICE RANGE $135–$290 (INCLUDES CATCH-AND-RELEASE BASS FISHING)

Spring weekends are roundup time at Texas Ranch Life, a working cattle ranch where groups can barbecue, ride, and learn cattle roping. The Lodge House has two upstairs and two downstairs guest rooms. Four other houses are rented on a whole-house basis, with an option for delivery of a breakfast basket loaded with homemade Czech kolaches. Kitchens are also stocked with juices, cereals, milk, and a coffeemaker. The Barn, which has a large game room with a VCR and pool table, can accommodate group overflow. The hosts, lawyers by training, live on another ranch seven miles away.

SETTING & FACILITIES
Location 15 mi. SE of Brenham **Near** Parks **Building** 1900 lodge house, 1940s cabin, 1869 Methodist youth house, 1880s dogtrot lake house, 1850s Confederate house **Grounds** 1,800 acres, lake **Public Space** Barn, cattle arena, game room **Food & Drink** Full breakfast in barn or cont'l breakfast basket delivered to house; barbecues **Recreation** Golf, fishing, biking **Amenities & Services** Trail rides, VCR, pool table, bird hunting, groups, weddings (200–300)

ACCOMMODATIONS
Units 4 guest rooms, 4 houses **All** TV/VCR, clock, ceiling fan **Some** Full kitchen (4), stereo (2), daybeds **Bed & Bath** Kings, queens, twins; all private baths, jetted tub (1), tubs **Favorites** Lake House, secluded in center of ranch, has private bird-hunting preserve, turquoise & white walls, stencils, maroon accents, green & yellow doors, roll-top desk, leather seating, double & single beds, sleeper sofa, shutters, Western art; Room #4, upstairs in Lodge House, has fine carved-wood furniture, duck illustrations, double vanity **Comfort & Decor** Individual houses have living room, dining room, kitchen, varied decor, antiques, Oriental rugs on wood floors, wood paneling, German stenciling, fine carved-wood furnishings, Texas artifacts, leather, armoires, rocking chairs, sofas, desks, porches, vanities.

RATES, RESERVATIONS, & RESTRICTIONS
Deposit 1 night (7-day cancellation policy) **Discounts** Group, whole ranch, packages **Credit Cards** AE, MC, V **Check-In/Out** 3–6 p.m./11 a.m. **Smoking** No **Pets** No (horse stalls available) **Kids** Yes **No-Nos** N/A **Minimum Stay** 2 nights **Open** All year **Hosts** Taunia & John Elick, P.O. Box 803, Bellville 77418 **Phone** (979) 865-3649 or toll-free (866) TEX-ASRL **Fax** (979) 865-9461 **E-mail** info@texasranchlife.com **Web** www.texasranchlife.com

ANT STREET INN, Brenham

OVERALL ★★★★★ | QUALITY ★★★★½ | VALUE ★★★★ | PRICE RANGE $95–$135

Occupying a full city block, the Ant Street Inn can host several hundred people for events under tents. The 4,000-square-foot ballroom seats 250 for wedding receptions and hosts antique auctions every other month. The library converts into an eight-person meeting room with a DSL Internet connection. The dining room resembles a saloon with a bar, huge stained-glass dome light, and individual tables. Guest rooms are named after Southern cities. The Charlotte Room has board game decor. Voodoo dancers, alligators, an 1883 Mississippi map, and an Odd Fellows poster compete for attention in the New Orleans Room.

SETTING & FACILITIES

Location Downtown, Ant Street Historic District **Near** Parks, museums, shops **Building** 1890s 2-story brick Renaissance Revival **Grounds** Arbor, fountain, roses, cottonwood tree **Public Space** Lobby, DR, guest bath, upstairs lounge, library, ballroom, gift shop, porches **Food & Drink** Full breakfast buffet in DR; early morning coffee; 24-hour ice cream, cold beverages; Fri., Sat. wine/apple cider hour **Recreation** Golf, fishing, water sports, biking **Amenities & Services** Internet access, fridge, coffeemaker, retreats, wedding receptions (250)

ACCOMMODATIONS

Units 14 **All** Robes, hair dryer, cable TV, phone, data port, clock radio, iron, ironing board, ceiling fan **Some** Handicap-accessible (1), VCR (2; also on request), fireplace (1), fridge (2), rollaway bed (on request), desk **Bed & Bath** Queen (12), 2 queens (1), double (1); all private baths, tub (8), jetted tub (1) **Favorites** Handicap-accessible San Antonio Room has porch door, fireplace, tall windows w/ cast-iron bars, fridge, wet bar, bath phone, double vanity, jetted tub, & tiled shower **Comfort & Decor** American antiques or distressed look, stained glass, crown molding, exposed brick, original pine floors and rugs, high upstairs ceilings, full- and half-tester beds, fainting couches, oil paintings.

RATES, RESERVATIONS, & RESTRICTIONS

Deposit Credit card holds (10-day cancellation policy) **Discounts** Corp. **Credit Cards** AE, MC, V, D **Check-In/Out** 3 p.m./11 a.m. **Smoking** Back porch **Pets** No **Kids** Over age 12 **No-Nos** N/A **Minimum Stay** Some holidays **Open** All year **Hosts** Pam & Tommy Traylor, 107 W. Commerce, Brenham 77833 **Phone** (979) 836-7393 or toll-free (800) 481-1951 **Fax** (979) 836-7595 **E-mail** stay@antstreetinn.com **Web** www.ant streetinn.com

FAR VIEW—A BED & BREAKFAST ESTATE, Brenham

OVERALL ★★★★½ | QUALITY ★★★★ | VALUE ★★★★ | PRICE RANGE $85–$195

A suburban estate where bats drink from the swimming pool on summer nights and the Texas state flag flies, Far View was built on a hill away from a swampy nearby bayou. The two-story brick building with white and green trim, designed by San Jacinto Monument architect A. C. Finn, has lots of French doors to promote airflow. The dining room has a 1930s floral tapestry and original stained glass. A stairway lined with photos documenting the history of the house leads to five upstairs rooms, many with desks for business travelers. A hallway amenity closet contains a corkscrew and wine glasses.

SETTING & FACILITIES

Location 15 blocks south of downtown **Near** Museums, parks **Building** 1925 Prairie style, 1994 renovation **Grounds** 2 acres, flagpole, ponderosa pines, oaks, pyrancantha, wisteria **Public Space** LR, DR, sun room, breakfast nook **Food & Drink** Full breakfast in DR; 24-hour ice cream, beverages; dinner parties **Recreation** Golf, fishing, water sports, biking **Amenities & Services** Pool, TV, putting green, phone, Internet access, horseshoes, croquet, iron, groups (70)

ACCOMMODATIONS

Units 8 **All** Robes, hair dryer, clock radio **Some** Full kitchen (1), fridge (1), phone (5), TV (5), private balcony (2) **Bed & Bath** King (5), queen (2), double (1); all private baths **Favorites** Star Room has big white star on ceiling, wrought-iron king bed, love seat, mistletoe wallpaper, plaid accents, mirrored armoire, Southwestern rugs, shuttered doors to private balcony; Carriage House Suite has 2 BRs, queen & king beds, sleeper sofa, dining area, lavender bricks, floral wallpaper, some wicker, dishwasher, microwave, coffeemaker, fridge **Comfort & Decor** Wood paneling, beaded wood ceilings with wallpaper borders, wood floors with area rugs, chrome and brass fixtures, armoires, some desks, shutters or shades.

RATES, RESERVATIONS, & RESTRICTIONS

Deposit 1 night (7-day cancellation for refund minus $10) **Discounts** Midweek corp., extended stays, Internet specials **Credit Cards** AE, MC, V, D **Check-In/Out** 3–6 p.m./11 a.m. **Smoking** No **Pets** No **Kids** Over age 12 **No-Nos** N/A **Minimum Stay** 2 nights weekends **Open** All year **Hosts** David & Tonya Meyer, 1804 S. Park St., Brenham 77833

Phone (979) 836-1672 or toll-free (888) farview **Fax** (979) 836-5893 **E-mail** stay@farviewbedandbreakfast.com **Web** www.farviewbedandbreakfast.com

INGLESIDE BED & BREAKFAST, Brenham

OVERALL ★★★★ | QUALITY ★★★★ | VALUE ★★★★ | PRICE RANGE $85–$120

A red brick home with black shutters, white trim, and a green porch floor, Ingleside is a short walk from downtown restaurants, the Funky Art Cafe, and the Brenham Fine Arts League. The hostess also owns a downtown tea room, A Place in Thyme. There are no phones or TVs in the guest rooms, but the den in the back of house has a TV and VCR. The upstairs hall lounge has a glass cabinet with *National Geographic* magazines dating back to 1913, a phone, fax, and data port. Classical music typically plays in the living room, which has a fireplace and piano.

SETTING & FACILITIES
Location 1.5 blocks east of downtown historic district **Near** Museums, parks **Building** 1923 2-story brick merchant's home **Grounds** Patio, fountain w/ frogs, oaks, pecans, swings **Public Space** LR, DR, den, upstairs lounge, butler's pantry, porch **Food & Drink** Full breakfast in DR; afternoon wine & cheese; water, mints in room; hot beverages, ice in butler's pantry **Recreation** Golf, fishing, water sports, biking **Amenities & Services** TV/VCR, phone, data port, fax, piano, microwave, fridge

ACCOMMODATIONS
Units 5 **All** Sound machine, clock, ceiling fan **Some** Robes (2), roll-away bed & hair dryer (on request) **Bed & Bath** King/twins (1), queen (1), full (3); 3 private baths, 1 shared bath, tub (2) **Favorites** Canopy Room has a canopied queen bed, yellow & blue colors, faux fireplace topped w/ ceramic cats, cobalt glass & blue beer steins, two dressers, an old water filter, tub; Victorian Room has 5-piece chocolate marble set w/ German silver pulls, robes, shared shower & half baths w/ Princess Room **Comfort & Decor** Eclectic mix of antiques, wood furnishings, quilts, carpets, wallpaper, blinds, lace, dressers, some armoires, etched glass, sitting areas with rocking chairs, loveseats.

RATES, RESERVATIONS, & RESTRICTIONS
Deposit 1 night (7-day cancellation for refund minus $10) **Discounts** N/A **Credit Cards** MC, V **Check-In/Out** 3–6 p.m./noon **Smoking** Porch, garden **Pets** No **Kids** Over age 12 years **No-Nos** N/A **Minimum Stay** H holiday, event weekends) **Open** All year **Host** Connie Hall, 409 E. Main, Brenham 77833 **Phone** (979) 251-7707 **Fax** (979) 251-7717 **E-mail** N/A **Web** N/A

MURSKI HOMESTEAD BED & BREAKFAST, Brenham

OVERALL ★★★★ | QUALITY ★★★★ | VALUE ★★★★ | PRICE RANGE $110–$135

A former cotton farm whose roots go back to the host family's Polish grandfather, Murski Homestead retains an 80-foot-deep, hand-dug 1919 well used to store butter. The enclosed dining room, originally the back porch, faces the old smokehouse. The front porch, which catches the north–south breezes, has white wood paneling, a ceiling fan, and several cats sharing the wicker rocking chairs and swing. The hostess makes and sells old-fashioned herbal soaps (see her other website at www.soapsbyhand.com) and uses the communal kitchen for gourmet cooking classes emphasizing organic herbs. Herbal cooking and wine and desert weekend party packages are available, and the hostess cooks for private parties.

SETTING & FACILITIES
Location 1.5 mi. from downtown **Near** Museums, parks, Ant Street Historic District **Building** 1896 dogtrot cabin, modernized & enclosed **Grounds** 100 acres, pond, old pecan orchard **Public Space** DR, kitchen, porches **Food & Drink** Cont'l-plus breakfast (left in fridge) in DR or porch; mints, water in room; late afternoon wine & cheese; snack basket; lunch, in-room dinners; catering **Recreation** Golf, fishing, water sports, biking **Amenities & Services** Microwave, fridge, board games, weekend parties & cooking classes, groups, wedding receptions (65)

ACCOMMODATIONS
Units 3 **All** Private entrance, coffeemaker, clock radio **Some** Satellite TV (1), roll-away bed (on request) **Bed & Bath** King (1), queen (1), 2 twins (1); all private baths, claw-foot tub (1) **Favorites** Sage room has king bed, sage green walls, antler lamp, satellite TV, pedestal sink, claw-foot tub **Comfort & Decor** Original dogtrot cabin walls, ceilings, wood floors, shuttered storm windows, armoires, old family quilts, antique lamps and chairs, corn shuck or wicker baskets at foot of bed, broomstick walk-in closet, sitting areas with rocking chairs, table.

RATES, RESERVATIONS, & RESTRICTIONS
Deposit 1 night (7-day cancellation for refund minus $25; 30-day cancellation for holidays, special events) **Discounts** Sun.–Wed., groups, whole house, Internet packages **Credit Cards** MC,V **Check-In/Out** 4–6 p.m./11 a.m. **Smoking** No **Pets** No (cat, donkeys, ducks, cows on premises) **Kids** Over age 12 **No-Nos** N/A **Minimum Stay** None **Open** All year **Host** Pamela Murski, 1662 Old Independence Rd., Brenham 77833 **Phone** (979) 830-9143 or toll-free (877) 690-0676 **Fax** (979) 836-0764 **E-mail** soap@alpha1.net **Web** www.murskihomesteadbb.com

THE BROWNING PLANTATION, *Chappell Hill*

OVERALL ★★★★ | QUALITY ★★★★ | VALUE ★★★★ | PRICE RANGE $125–$150

An hour northwest of Houston, the Browning Plantation originally housed Colonel W. W. Browning, a cattle-raising civic leader and staunch Confederate whose 67 slaves helped farm the surrounding acreage. During the manor house restoration some closets became bathrooms. Thus, two second-story rooms have half baths and a shared third-story full bath flanked by men's and women's dressing rooms. One more flight of stairs leads to panoramic area views from the rooftop widow's walk. The first- and second-story verandas provide their own views and rocking chairs. The ample acreage and grand hallway staircase for bridal descents make this a popular wedding venue.

SETTING & FACILITIES
Location 5 mi. east of Brenham **Near** Museums, parks **Building** 1857 Greek Revival plantation manor **Grounds** 10 acres, fish pond **Public Space** LR, DR, den, porches **Food & Drink** Full breakfast buffet in DR; 24-hour snacks, beverages; group catering; cake design **Recreation** Golf, horse riding, fishing, biking **Amenities & Services** Pool, hot tub, board games, satellite TV, stereo, fax, phone, groups, weddings (250)

ACCOMMODATIONS
Units 5 **All** Robes, hair dryer, iron, ironing board, coffeemaker, ceiling fan **Some** Decorative fireplace (2), porch entry (2) **Bed & Bath** Queen (3), queen & twin (2); 3 private baths, 1 shared bath, tub (2) **Favorites** Moonlight & Magnolias, downstairs honeymoon favorite, has full-tester queen bed, fireplace, dressing area, private veranda entrance, stained glass in bath; Touched by an Angel has fireplace, sofa, angel collection, 2d-floor veranda door, shower **Comfort & Decor** Varied themes, pastel colors, antiques, armoires, plantation or tester beds, 12-foot ceilings, wood floors, area rugs, some vanities.

RATES, RESERVATIONS, & RESTRICTIONS
Deposit 1 night or 50% (7-day cancellation for refund minus $20) **Discounts** Midweek, off-season, corp., group, Internet specials **Credit Cards** MC, V **Check-In/Out** 3 p.m./11 a.m. **Smoking** Verandas, pool deck **Pets** No (exceptions by advance arrangement) **Kids** Over age 12 **No-Nos** N/A **Minimum Stay** None (except certain holiday, special event weekends) **Open** All year **Hosts** Marilyn & Waddy Watkins, 9050 Browning St., Chappell Hill 77426 **Phone** (979) 836-6144 or toll-free (888) 912-6144 **Fax** N/A **E-mail** plantation1@msn.com **Web** www.browningplantation.com

AMELIA'S PLACE, Dallas

OVERALL ★★★★ | QUALITY ★★★★ | VALUE ★★★★★ | PRICE RANGE $95–$145

Deep in the heart of downtown Dallas, two blocks from the Convention Center on a trolley-bus stop corner, Amelia's Place has a Scrabble board tile facade. The hostess, a catfish-cooking Louisiana great-grandmother, served up six months of breakfasts and lunches to the local homeless who helped renovate the building. A guest bathroom sign says "Sexism is a social disease." Whistling is obligatory (house rules) climbing the stairs to the huge third-floor living room, which has whirring ceiling fans, original penthouse windows, weathered white paint on brown wood ceiling beams, brick walls, creamy raspberry archways, and black cabinets.

SETTING & FACILITIES
Location Downtown, corner of Young & St. Paul Sts. **Near** City Hall, Arts District, museums, parks **Building** 1920s 3-story factory, renovated in 1997 **Grounds** Fronts city

streets **Public Space** LR, lounge, DR, guest bath **Food & Drink** Full breakfast in DR; 24-hour beverages **Recreation** Golf, biking **Amenities & Services** Piano, TV, fridge, laundry, iron & ironing board, Union Station pickup, bicycles, Scrabble tables, board games

ACCOMMODATIONS

Units 7 **All** Heat/AC, clock radio **Some** Full kitchen (1) **Bed & Bath** King (1), king/twins (1), 2 queens (1), queen (1), double (2), twin (1); 5 private baths, 1 shared, jetted tub (1) **Favorites** First floor corporate apartment has full kitchen, love seat, double Murphy bed, red, white & blue colors, private outside entrance, jetted tub; Njoki has Afro-American art, 2 queen beds, makeup lights, curtain room divider **Comfort & Decor** Notable Dallas women themes, original steel ceiling beams and brick walls (or plaster), sound-proofing, rocking chairs, dressers, old tea chests, candles, closets, large mirrors, creamy raspberry baths with black-and-white tiles.

RATES, RESERVATIONS, & RESTRICTIONS

Deposit Credit card holds (7-day cancellation for 1-night stays, 30 days for multiple nights; no cancellation of multiple rooms for multiple nights) **Discounts** None **Credit Cards** AE, MC, V, D, DC, CB **Check-In/Out** Noon–9 p.m./3 p.m. **Smoking** Public areas only **Pets** No **Kids** Not recommended **No-Nos** Using 3d floor after 10 p.m. **Minimum Stay** None **Open** All year **Host** Amelia Jenkins, 1775 Young St., Dallas 75201 **Phone** (214) 651-1775 or toll-free (888) 651-1775 **Fax** (214) 761-9475 **E-mail** ameliaj@flash.net **Web** www.ameliasplace.com

HÔTEL ST. GERMAIN, *Dallas*

OVERALL ★★★★½ | QUALITY ★★★★½ | VALUE ★★★ | PRICE RANGE $290–$650

Less than a mile from downtown and the business district, Hôtel St. Germain caters to a corporate clientele and families with children on weekdays.

Come weekends, families are more tightly screened to weed out noisy children who might disturb honeymooning couples. For many the Philip Johnson–designed Crescent Court office complex across the street with its upscale hotel and neo-French shopping mall symbolize the Dallas decadence of oil boom days. The St. Germain's elegant French restaurant is a popular local splurge for special occasions. Indeed, when the restaurant is booming the guest rooms seem to be almost an afterthought.

SETTING & FACILITIES

Location Uptown, across street from Crescent Court **Near** Downtown, museums **Building** 1906 dormered 3-story European style mansion **Grounds** Courtyard **Public Space** Lobby, parlor, library, DR/restaurant **Food & Drink** Cont'l breakfast in DR or served by butler in room; dinner in French restaurant (Tues.–Sat.; $85); catering **Recreation** Golf, biking **Amenities & Services** Handicap-accessible, valet/butler service, 24-hour concierge desk, turn-down service, weddings/groups (175)

ACCOMMODATIONS

Units 7 suites **All** Robes, hair dryer, fireplace, TV/VCR, radio/CD player/clock, mini-bar **Some** Balcony (2), wood-burning fireplace (5) **Bed & Bath** King (2), queen (5); all private baths, tub (3), jetted tub (3) **Favorites** Suite 6, the priciest offering, has a Mallard bed & dresser, ball & claw table, twin pedestal sinks, jetted tub; Suite 5 has blue damask, French doors opening to large wrap-around balcony, B&W tiled bath w/ shower; Suite 4, intermediate in price and size, has lace, silks, vanity, jetted tub; Suite 7 has a draped Napoleonic sleigh bed, jetted tub **Comfort & Decor** Predominately Victorian decor with a variety of opulent French and Creole antiques, canopied beds, armoires, some baths with fireplaces or deep soaking tubs.

RATES, RESERVATIONS, & RESTRICTIONS

Deposit Full amount of stay (7-day cancellation for full refund; otherwise no refund) **Discounts** Corp., travel agent **Credit Cards** AE, MC, V **Check-In/Out** 4 p.m./noon **Smoking** No **Pets** Yes ($50 deposit) **Kids** On individual basis **No-Nos** N/A **Minimum Stay** None **Open** All year (closed Christmas and 10 days in Aug.) **Host** Claire Heymann, 2516 Maple Ave., Dallas 75201 **Phone** (214) 871-2516 or toll-free (800) 683-2516 **Fax** (214) 871-0740 **E-mail** N/A **Web** www.hotelstgermain.com

THE SOUTHERN HOUSE, *Dallas*

OVERALL ★★★★ | QUALITY ★★★★ | VALUE ★★★★★ | PRICE RANGE $90–$125

In a residential neighborhood with a trolley stop a mile from downtown and three blocks from the Crescent Court complex, the Southern House is a suburban-style haven. Both corporate travelers and conventiongoers find this an intimate escape from the downtown hustle and bustle. Weekends bring a more romantic mix of couples. The hostess pens one-act plays and hangs her abstract cityscapes and portraits on the walls. Besides a lower-level side deck, an outdoor spiral staircase opens onto a second-story deck. The spacious living room has a wood floor and rugs, shuttered windows, leather and upholstered furnishings, and a black fireplace with a built-in marble bench.

SETTING & FACILITIES

Location Uptown, State-Thomas Historic District **Near** Downtown, the Crescent, Arts District, museums **Building** 1997 3-story modified Prairie style **Grounds** Patio, front courtyard **Public Space** LR, DR, decks, guest bath **Food & Drink** Full breakfast in DR or patio; afternoon beverages; stocked guest fridge; private lunches, dinners **Recreation** Golf, biking, jogging **Amenities & Services** Laundry, iron, ironing board, Convention Center drop-offs, weddings (50 buffet, 24 sit-down)

ACCOMMODATIONS

Units 3 **All** TV, clock, hair dryer **Some** Stereo (1), individual AC/heat (2), roll-away (on request) **Bed & Bath** Queen (2), full-size (1); all private baths, tub (2) **Favorites** Rear Window has downtown view, Bali/Indonesian decor, painted faces on cabinets, sitting alcove w/ sofa, track lighting; Room with a View in 3d-story former attic has lodge-feel w/ greens & maroons, angled ceilings, downtown view, ceiling fan, stereo, large sitting area w/ plaid sofa, turned wood table, Texas flag, glass & tile shower **Comfort & Decor** Eclectic mix of room themes ranging from Asian to Deco, pleated fabric bottom-up window shades, dressers, wardrobes, old trunks, vanity tables, carpet, and parquet floors.

RATES, RESERVATIONS, & RESTRICTIONS

Deposit Credit card holds (24-hour cancellation policy) **Discounts** Weekdays, gov't, singles, extended stays **Credit Cards** AE, MC, V **Check-In/Out** After 3 p.m./11 a.m. **Smoking** No **Pets** No (poodle on premises) **Kids** No **No-Nos** N/A **Minimum Stay** None **Open** All year **Host** Pam Southern, 2625 Thomas Ave., Dallas 75204 **Phone** (214) 720-0845 **Fax** N/A **E-mail** pam@southernhouse.com **Web** www.southernhouse.com

AZALEA PLANTATION, Fort Worth

OVERALL ★★★★½ | QUALITY ★★★★ | VALUE ★★★★ | PRICE RANGE $125–$159

A relaxing outpost in the Fort Worth suburbs, Azalea Plantation has a sunken lounge area with chintz-patterned curtains, a broken pottery table topped with glass candy, and display cabinets with a sherry decanter hidden among the floral Depression-era chintz. An 1860 carved-wood Texas desk is among the artifacts collected by the host, a Fort Worth and Old West history buff. The dining room features a 12-foot china hutch, black floral carpet, and the hostess's spoon collection. The guest rooms all have floral names and floral decor, except the Bluebonnet, which has the floral name but Texas cowboy decor.

SETTING & FACILITIES

Location Oakhurst, 10 min. east of downtown **Near** Stockyards **Building** 1949 Plantation-style parsonage **Grounds** 2 acres w/ large oaks, gazebo, bird bath **Public Space** LR w/ fireplace, sunken lounge, DR **Food & Drink** Full breakfast buffet in DR; snacks, beverages; special dietary needs w/ advance notice; group dinners **Recreation** Golf, fishing, boating, water sports, horse riding **Amenities & Services** Stereo, TV/VCR, massage, flowers, volleyball, horseshoes, croquet, groups (20)

ACCOMMODATIONS

Units 4 **All** Robes, TV, CD player/radio/clock **Some** Kitchenette (2), stocked fridge (2), VCR (2), ceiling fan (2), balcony (2) **Bed & Bath** King (3), queen (1); all private baths, tub (1), jetted tub (3) **Favorites** Bluebonnet Bungalow, a cowboy-style cottage, has Civil War queen bed w/ marbleized balls, second BR w/ wrought-iron wagon-wheel double bed, maroon cowboy curtains, saddle, horse bookends, cowboy portraits, cowhide rug, rocking chair, kitchenette w/ full-size fridge & microwave **Comfort & Decor** Varied room themes range from Southwestern to very floral, mix of wood and upholstered furnishings, some antiques, wrought-iron and four-poster beds, imaginative lamps, sitting areas, curtains, blinds, mirrors, dressers, desks, lace shower curtains.

RATES, RESERVATIONS, & RESTRICTIONS

Deposit 1 night (72-hour cancellation policy) **Discounts** Whole property, corp., extended stay **Credit Cards** MC, V **Check-In/Out** 3–6 p.m./11 a.m. **Smoking** No **Pets** No **Kids** Not encouraged (case-by-case acceptance) **No-Nos** N/A **Minimum Stay** For major events only **Open** All year **Hosts** Martha & Richard Linnartz, 1400 Robinwood Dr., Fort Worth 76111 **Phone** (817) 838-5882 or toll-free (800) 68-RELAX **Fax** (817) 838-5882 (call first) **E-mail** info@azaleaplantation.com **Web** www.azaleaplantation.com

ETTA'S PLACE, Fort Worth

OVERALL ★★★★½ | QUALITY ★★★★½ | VALUE ★★★★★ | PRICE RANGE $125–$150

From the outside, Etta's Place looks like a brick office building. Inside is another world sheltered from the downtown hustle and bustle. The Music Room has elegant red leather and tan wood furnishings, plus a baby grand piano. The adjacent library features a giant globe and sliding glass doors to a patio shared with the dining room. A floral tapestry and dining room plate collection add formal notes. A bottle-cap U.S. flag and antique soda machine hint at casualness and fun. For those with a penchant for spreading out, three 700-square-foot suites have sitting areas plus kitchens with four-burner stoves and dishwashers.

SETTING & FACILITIES

Location Downtown, Sundance Square **Near** Stockyards **Building** 1990s 4-story brick commercial-office style **Grounds** Interior brick patios **Public Space** Music room, library, DR, mezzanine coffee nook, enclosed patio, garden terrace, guest bath **Food & Drink** Full breakfast in DR or patio; beverages in coffee nook; bottled water in rooms; private dinners **Recreation** Golf, boating, fishing, horse riding **Amenities & Services** Concierge, massage, piano, board games, fax, photocopies, weddings (40 seated), receptions (80–120)

ACCOMMODATIONS

Units 9 **All** Robes, hair dryer, cable TV, clock radio, phone, voice mail **Some** Handicap-accessible (1), full kitchen (3), VCR (3), sitting area (5), coffeemaker (5), ceiling fan (8) **Bed & Bath** King (4), queen (4), full-size (1); all private baths, tub **Favorites** Annie's Suite, honeymoon favorite isolated on 3d floor, has iron & wood sleigh bed, punched-metal lamps, blue wicker chairs w/ floral maroon cushions, blue armoire, full kitchen; Laura's Lounge, a spacious corner king, has sitting area, coffeemaker **Comfort & Decor** Varied color schemes, a mix of furnishings ranging from antiques to contemporary and wicker, blinds, carpets, a table, some rocking chairs and armoires, tiled baths.

RATES, RESERVATIONS, & RESTRICTIONS

Deposit Credit card holds (72-hour cancellation policy) **Discounts** Weekday corp., extended stay **Credit Cards** AE, MC, V, D, DC **Check-In/Out** 3–6 p.m./11 a.m. **Smoking** Outside **Pets** Yes (small; $10/night) **Kids** Over age 10 **No-Nos** N/A **Minimum Stay** None **Open** All year **Host** Leslie Benson, 200 W. Third St., Fort Worth 76102 **Phone** (817) 654-0267 **Fax** (817) 878-2560 **E-mail** N/A **Web** N/A

THE TEXAS WHITE HOUSE BED & BREAKFAST, Fort Worth

OVERALL ★★★★ | QUALITY ★★★★½ | VALUE ★★★★ | PRICE RANGE $125–$185

Adjacent to the Fairmount National Historic District, the Texas White House is becoming a couples' getaway from the stresses of Dallas. The wrap-around porch fronts a busy street, but bubble bath and candles turn the claw-foot tubs in the main house into fonts of relaxation. It gets even more sybaritic in the cavernous, barn-like carriage house at the back of the property, where jetted tubs and a sauna await. Families like the denim-and-leather Longhorn suite in the carriage house, because the living room has a Murphy bed as well as a leather love seat, recliner, built-in desk, chestnut floors, pine furnishings, and recessed lighting.

SETTING & FACILITIES

Location 5 min. from downtown/Sundance Square **Near** Stockyards **Building** 1910 Country style w/ 1994 additions, 2002 carriage house **Grounds** Gazebo **Public Space** LR w/ fireplace, DR, porch **Food & Drink** Full breakfast in DR; 24-hour snacks, beverages **Recreation** Golf, biking, fishing, boating, water sports, horse riding **Amenities & Services** Fridge, fax, surge suppressor, turn-down service, groups, receptions

ACCOMMODATIONS

Units 3 guest rooms, 2 carriage house suites **All** Robes, cable TV, clock radio, phone, data port, iron, ironing board, heat/AC, ceiling fan **Some** Stocked fridge (2), VCR (2), CD/tape player, desk (3), sauna (1) **Bed & Bath** King/twins (1), queen (4); all private baths, claw-foot tub (3), jetted tub (2) **Favorites** Lone Star, business favorite, has deep dark wood antiques, stained-glass Texas flag, old church pew in sitting area, small hallway to closet-size bath; Mustang, upstairs in carriage house, has cream walls, barn red accents, lots of windows, Deco furnishings, sauna, jetted tub **Comfort & Decor** Some antique wood furnishings, wicker, floral wallpaper, lace curtains, blinds, old trunks, beveled glass, armoires, wood floors, area rugs, sitting areas with rocking chairs.

RATES, RESERVATIONS, & RESTRICTIONS
Deposit 1 night (5-day cancellation policy) **Discounts** Multiple nights, packages **Credit Cards** AE, MC, V, D, DC, CB **Check-In/Out** Customized to guest schedule **Smoking** Front porch **Pets** No **Kids** Yes **No-Nos** N/A **Minimum Stay** None **Open** All year **Hosts** Grover & Jamie McMains, 1417 Eighth Ave., Fort Worth 76104 **Phone** (817) 923-3597 or toll-free (800) 279-6491 **Fax** (817) 923-0410 **E-mail** stay@texaswhitehouse.com **Web** www.texaswhitehouse.com

MARIPOSA RANCH, *Gay Hill/Independence*

OVERALL ★★★★★ | QUALITY ★★★★½ | VALUE ★★★★ | PRICE RANGE $85–$205

A 100-acre working cattle ranch with seven renovated buildings, the Mariposa Ranch is about Texas history. The Davy Crockett Quarters have carved Mexican furnishings, a saddle, and saloon-style swinging doors leading to the toilet stall. The Sam Houston Suite has a Victorian mirrored armoire, bidet, claw-foot tub, and lace. The Ranch Hand's Bunkhouse has red, white, and blue sponge-painted walls. The 1825 Texas Ranger Cabin has punched-metal star lamps and an upstairs loft crib with teddy bears. The Settlers' Cottage and Homestead House satisfy those who need three bedroom. The grounds can accommodate tents for two weddings with optional butterfly releases.

SETTING & FACILITIES
Location 10 mi. north of Brenham **Near** Parks, lake, museum **Building** 1836 2-story Greek Revival, early-1800s log cabin, 1920s farmhouse, 4 other buildings **Grounds** 100 acres, 2 ponds, ferns, oaks, arbor, hammock, greenhouse **Public Space** LR, DR, chapel **Food & Drink** Full breakfast buffet in DR; private dinners **Recreation** Golf, fishing, water sports, biking **Amenities & Services** Piano, horseshoes, massage, wagon rides, cookouts, meetings, weddings (150)

ACCOMMODATIONS
Units 11 **All** Robes, TV/VCR, fridge, microwave, coffeemaker, clock radio, individual AC/heat, ceiling fan, porch **Some** Fireplace (7), full kitchen (2), CD player, hair dryer (on request) **Bed & Bath** King (1), queen (10); all private baths, tub (2), claw-foot tub (5), jetted tub (4) **Favorites** Fern Oaks Cottage, smallest room, liked by honeymooners for privacy, has floral wallpaper, fireplace, loveseat, porch, jetted tub **Comfort & Decor** Varied mix of cowboy and Victorian farm house designs includes antiques, cowboy, and Texas Ranger theme items, loveseats, rocking chairs.

RATES, RESERVATIONS, & RESTRICTIONS
Deposit 1 night or 50% (10-day cancellation for refund minus $25 or full amount credited to future visit within 6 months; 30-day cancellation for holidays, special events, groups;

full amount nonrefundable for antiques weekends) **Discounts** Corp., group, weekday, Internet specials **Credit Cards** AE, MC, V **Check-In/Out** 3–6 p.m./11 a.m. **Smoking** No **Pets** No (animals on premises) **Kids** Yes (well-behaved; selected rooms) **No-Nos** N/A **Minimum Stay** None **Open** All year **Hosts** Johnna & Charles Chamberlain, 8904 Mariposa Lane, Brenham 77833 **Phone** (979) 836-4737 or toll-free (877) 647-4774 **Fax** (979) 836-4712 **E-mail** info@mariposaranch.com **Web** www.mariposaranch.com

NUTT HOUSE HOTEL, Granbury

OVERALL ★★★★ | QUALITY ★★★★ | VALUE ★★★★ | PRICE RANGE $150–$175

Erected on the site of the blind Nutt brothers' original log mercantile store to house both the store (ground level) and hotel (above the store), the Nutt House Hotel was designated a state historic landmark in 1968. The original hotel included a restaurant with Southern cooking, and the new Grady Spears' Nutt House Restaurant plans to serve country-style haute cuisine. The grand plan of renovating the hotel into a bed-and-breakfast includes revitalizing the historic downtown plaza area. The hosts are best known for operating a Fredericksburg bed-and-breakfast, Ab Butler's Dogtrot at Triple Creek, and are teamed with another Fredericksburg couple, Ron and Donna Maddux, who operate Alte Welt Gästhof and 1st Class Bed & Breakfast Reservation Service. Another Fredericksburg operator, Jan Borron of Haussegen Bed & Breakfast, is the interior designer.

SETTING & FACILITIES
Location Downtown plaza, 35 mi. SE of Fort Worth **Near** Opera house, state parks, Glen Rose **Building** 1893 limestone hotel/mercantile store **Grounds** Opens onto city street/town square **Public Space** Lobby/lounge, restaurant, day spa **Food & Drink** Cont'l breakfast in DR; beverages in bar; Texas country cooking in restaurant **Recreation** Golf, fishing, boating, water sports, horse riding, biking **Amenities & Services** Phone, data port, massage

ACCOMMODATIONS
Units 7 **All** Robes, cable TV, clock radio, hair dryer, individual heat/AC, duvet, iron, ironing board, ceiling fan **Some** Double vanities **Bed & Bath** King (2), queen (5); all private baths, jetted tub **Favorites** Donna's Suite, among the largest, has king bed w/ handcrafted headboard, double dresser, double jetted tub **Comfort & Decor** Combines period look and modern amenities, beaded-board ceilings, moldings, hardwood floors, sisal rugs, antique armoires, dressers, Ralph Lauren fabrics, upholstered wood furnishings, towel warmers, 100 square feet or larger baths.

RATES, RESERVATIONS, & RESTRICTIONS
Deposit Credit card holds (7-day cancellation for refund minus $35; otherwise lose cost of entire stay) **Discounts** Internet specials **Credit Cards** AE, MC, V, D **Check-In/Out** After 3 p.m./11 a.m. **Smoking** No **Pets** No **Kids** No **No-Nos** N/A **Minimum Stay** 2

nights weekends **Open** All year **Hosts** Nan & Robert Mosely, 121 E. Bridge St., Granbury 76048 **Phone** (830) 997-0443 or toll-free (888) 678-0813 **Fax** N/A **E-mail** stay@nutt-house-hotel.com **Web** www.nutt-house-hotel.com

HEART OF MY HEART RANCH, Round Top

OVERALL ★★★★½ | QUALITY ★★★★½ | VALUE ★★★★ | PRICE RANGE $135–$225

Since its 1970s opening, Heart of My Heart Ranch has attracted 23,000 guests to this town of 77 people an hour northwest of Houston. The main building's wrap-around porch with rocking chairs overlooks a large pond stocked with bass, catfish, and perch. Cattle graze in the distance. The hallway has a grandfather clock, duck stamp illustrations, and a pistol said to have belonged to Wyatt Earp. Guest rooms are scattered among several buildings, adding privacy. Heart of My Heart is also the title of the host's book telling the story of an early frustrated love requited later in life.

SETTING & FACILITIES

Location 20 mi. west of Brenham **Near** Museums, parks **Building** 1985 Victorian farmhouse, 1836 log cabin, adults-only Frontier House, stand-alone cottage, carriage house **Grounds** 110 acres, pond **Public Space** LR, DR, porch **Food & Drink** Full breakfast buffet in DR; 24-hour snacks, beverages; breakfast in bed, picnic lunches, group catering available **Recreation** Golf, tennis, horse riding, fishing, biking, bird-watching **Amenities & Services** Heated pool, hot tub, piano playground equipment, boats, bikes, barbecue, storytelling, conference room w/ full kitchen, AV equipment, groups (25)

ACCOMMODATIONS

Units 12 **All** Robes, color TV/VCR, phone, clock, ceiling fan **Some** Stereo (1), fireplace (4) **Bed & Bath** King (2), queen (9), doubles (1), sleeper sofa/daybed/second beds (8); all private baths, tub (8), jetted tub (1), no shower (1) **Favorites** Almeida's Room has oak queen bed, alcove w/ twin bed, chocolate marble dresser; Honeymoon Suite has four-poster queen bed, sitting area w/ fireplace & sleeper sofa, porch **Comfort & Decor** Varies from rustic log cabin to more traditional farm style with antiques and quilts.

RATES, RESERVATIONS, & RESTRICTIONS

Deposit $50 per night (no refunds; rescheduling Sun.–Thur. only) **Discounts** Group, state gov't., corp. **Credit Cards** AE, MC, V, D **Check-In/Out** 3–8 p.m./11 a.m. **Smoking** No **Pets** No (kennel nearby; cats, dogs, farm animals on premises) **Kids** Yes **No-Nos** N/A **Minimum Stay** 2 nights regular weekends, 3 nights holidays **Open** All year **Hosts** Frances & Bill Harris, P.O. Box 106, 403 Florida Chapel Rd., Round Top 78954 **Phone** (979) 249-3171 or toll-free (800) 327-1242 **Fax** (979) 249-3171 **E-mail** heart17@cvtv.net **Web** www.heartofmyheartranch.com

OUTPOST @ CEDAR CREEK, Round Top

OVERALL ★★★★½ | QUALITY ★★★★ | VALUE ★★★★ | PRICE RANGE $100–$200

On a rural farm road five miles west of Round Top, the Outpost is a collection of six restored farm buildings, many formerly abandoned for decades. Children do best in the oak dogtrot cabins with bunk beds, particularly the twig-and-timber Colorado Cabin with its porch swing, fish and duck decor, antler hangers, zebra-painted cowhide rugs, and tree stump tables. The Barn Cottage Suite and two-bedroom Victorian Cottage House offer cable TV and private porches with English cottage gardens. Trailer life hankerings are answered in a vintage 32-foot Airstream land cruiser with a galley kitchen, stereo, and TV.

SETTING & FACILITIES
Location 15 mi. south of Brenham **Near** Museums **Building** 1920s restored hay barn, 1880s farmhouses, early-1800s dogtrot cabins, Airstream trailer **Grounds** 51 acres, old farm equipment, antique roses, native gardens, ponds, pergola, bird feeders **Public Space** LR, DR, cookhouse **Food & Drink** Full breakfast in DR; afternoon snacks, beverages **Recreation** Golf, horse riding, bird-watching, biking **Amenities & Services** Kitchen, ice machine, laundry, TV, phone, e-mail access, fax, binoculars, groups (60 inside, 150 outside)

ACCOMMODATIONS
Units 9 **All** Outdoor porch, CD/clock radio **Some** Fireplace (2), full kitchen (3), DR (2), cable TV (3), stereo (1) **Bed & Bath** Queen & bunks (2), queen & doubles/twins (4), 2 doubles/twins (2); 7 private baths, 1 shared bath, claw-foot tub **Favorites** Tejas dogtrot cabin has vintage Texas look, barn wood doors, queen & bunk beds **Comfort & Decor** Either rustic pioneer or English country garden look, mostly weathered wood or log walls, log and plank or corrugated metal ceilings, rugs and animal hides on longleaf pine floors, some brick floors, armoires, twig and carved Mexican furnishings, lace.

RATES, RESERVATIONS, & RESTRICTIONS
Deposit 50% (8-day cancellation for refund; otherwise no refund) **Discounts** Weekdays, corp., groups, packages **Credit Cards** AE, MC, V **Check-In/Out** 3 p.m./11 a.m. **Smoking** No **Pets** No (dogs, cats on premises) **Kids** Not encouraged (log cabin bunks by prior arrangement) **No-Nos** N/A **Minimum Stay** None (2 nights certain event weekends) **Open** All year **Host** Leonore Prudhomme, 5808 Wagner Rd., Round Top 78954 **Phone** (979) 836-4975 or toll-free (888) 433-5791 **Fax** (979) 836-7577 **E-mail** stay@ outpostatcedarcreek.com **Web** www.outpostatcedarcreek.com

THE INN AT SALADO BED & BREAKFAST, *Salado*

OVERALL ★★★★ | QUALITY ★★★★ | VALUE ★★★★ | PRICE RANGE $70–$160

Surrounded by antiques shops, boutiques, galleries, and restaurants on Main Street, the Inn at Salado has no need for TVs. Business travelers flock here individually and for small weekday group retreats. Weekends bring in the shop-til-you-drop crowd, couples, and wedding parties. Weddings take place in a blue-and-white wood country chapel with the original 1901 wood floor and modern heating and air conditioning. A large catering kitchen and staff chef service groups in the adjacent 2,000-square-foot covered pavilion. Inn guests can use the microwave and refrigerator in the main house kitchen and dip into the pretzel and cookie jars.

SETTING & FACILITIES
Location Historic District, North Main at Pace Park Dr. **Near** Shops, creek, bridges **Building** 1872 I-plan Vernacular w/ Classical & Victorian detailing, side house, cottage, 1901 chapel **Grounds** 2 acres w/ oak trees, old stone well, brick paths, patios **Public Space** Lobby, LR, DR, kitchen **Food & Drink** Full breakfast in DR; all-day beverages, snacks; lunch, dinner, snack catering **Recreation** Golf, horse riding, creek wading **Amenities & Services** VCR, projection equipment, speaker system, fax & copy services, business groups (2 rooms, 1,200 sq. ft.), weddings (200)

ACCOMMODATIONS
Units 8 **All** Phone, clock radio, ceiling fan **Some** Fireplace (3), wood-burning stove (1), private porch (3), roll-away beds (selected rooms on request) **Bed & Bath** King (2), queen (5), 2 singles (1); all private baths, jetted tub (1), claw-foot tub (8) **Favorites** Baylor House, stand-alone cottage, has canopied queen bed, separate sitting room w/ sofa bed, private porch, 2 full baths, jetted tub **Comfort & Decor** Slight Victorian or country feel, antiques, floral fabrics, wallpaper, light blue wood floors, sitting areas, rocking chairs, armoires.

RATES, RESERVATIONS, & RESTRICTIONS
Deposit Credit card holds (72-hour cancellation policy; longer for multiple rooms; 50% charge for short-notice cancellations)) **Discounts** Corp., weekdays **Credit Cards** AE, MC, V, D **Check-In/Out** After 3 p.m./noon **Smoking** No **Pets** No **Kids** Yes (if "very well

behaved") **No-Nos** N/A **Minimum Stay** None (2 nights certain holidays, special events) **Open** All year **Hosts** Rob & Suzanne Petro, P.O. Box 320, Salado 76571 **Phone** (254) 947-0027 or toll-free (800) 724-0027 **Fax** (254) 947-3144 **E-mail** rooms@inn-at-salado.com **Web** www.inn-at-salado.com

THE KATY HOUSE BED & BREAKFAST, Smithville

OVERALL ★★★★ | QUALITY ★★★★ | VALUE ★★★★ | PRICE RANGE $95–$115

From the old engine house punch clock next to the front door to the dining room lanterns and old steam gauges, the Katy House is like a museum celebrating Jay Gould's former railroad, the Missouri, Kansas & Texas (MK&T). Katy is the name given to the Kansas and Texas portion of the railroad. Old stock and gold bond certificates line the stairway to the three upstairs rooms in the main house. Two rooms in an adjacent duplex are available for children and pets. The host, who has a penchant for restoring old railroad artifacts, worked his way up from brakeman and conductor to become a Union Pacific engineer.

SETTING & FACILITIES
Location Downtown **Near** Parks **Building** 1909 Classic Revival Mediterranean brick villa, 1923 wood buildings **Grounds** Fish pond, birdhouses, old railroad crossing signs **Public Space** LR w/ fireplace, DR, library, porch **Food & Drink** Full breakfast in DR; 24-hour hot beverages, lemonade **Recreation** Horse riding, fishing, hunting, golf **Amenities & Services** Katy railroad history library

ACCOMMODATIONS
Units 5 guest rooms, 2 in separate back building **All** Cable TV/VCR, phone, coffeemaker, clock radio, individual AC/heat **Some** Full kitchen (1), microwave (3), fridge (3), ceiling fan (4) **Bed & Bath** Queen beds; all private baths, claw-foot tub **Favorites** Katy Tower in outside wood building has stained glass, boot & cowhide motif lamp, Texas flag rocking chair & shower curtain, private porch; Conductors Quarters has sofa bed for families, full kitchen w/ shanty stove, metal train signs & gauges **Comfort & Decor** Wood paneling, wood floors, blinds, armoires, railroad artifacts like porcelain drumheads and freight car grab iron towel racks, dresser, desk, baths with marble, wainscoting, horse bridle toilet paper holders.

RATES, RESERVATIONS, & RESTRICTIONS
Deposit 1 night (72-hour cancellation policy) **Discounts** Corp., gov't., extended stays **Credit Cards** AE, MC, V, D **Check-In/Out** 2 p.m./noon **Smoking** No **Pets** Yes (1 room for dogs w/ prior arrangement; house dog) **Kids** Yes (1 room in separate building) **No-Nos** N/A **Minimum Stay** None **Open** All year **Hosts** Bruce & Sallie Blalock, 201 Ramona, P.O. Box 803, Smithville 78957 **Phone** (512) 237-4262 or toll-free (800) 843-5289 **Fax** N/A **E-mail** innkeeper@katyhouse.com **Web** www.katyhouse.com

THE COTTON PALACE, Waco

OVERALL ★★★★½ | QUALITY ★★★★½ | VALUE ★★★★ | PRICE RANGE $99–$129

On a residential street adjacent to downtown and near Baylor University, the Cotton Palace serves as a reminder of Waco's nineteenth-century status as one of the world's largest cotton producers. Roy Elspeth Lane, the original architect of Waco's Cotton Palace exhibition center, designed this mansion. The hostess, a Waco native who teaches broadcast and public speech, renovated the building and turned it into the kind of bed-and-breakfast she would want to stay at. One public room contains the memorabilia of her father, Baylor's longtime baseball coach, Dutch Schroeder. The four second-floor guest rooms have jetted tubs and robes.

SETTING & FACILITIES
Location Center **Near** Museums, university, Crawford **Building** 1916 Arts & Crafts, additions & 1999 renovation **Grounds** Organic gardens **Public Space** LR w/ fireplace, DR, sun porch, upper sitting area, guest bath **Food & Drink** Full breakfast buffet in DR; 24-hour snacks, beverages **Recreation** Biking, horse riding, fishing, boating **Amenities & Services** TV, phone, board games, checkers table, newspaper, meetings (30)

ACCOMMODATIONS
Units 6 **All** Cable TV/VCR, clock radio, hair dryer, iron, ironing board, duvet, ceiling fan **Some** Robes (4), phone/data port (3) **Bed & Bath** King (2), queen (3), 2 singles & trundle (1); all private baths, tub (1), jetted tub (4) **Favorites** Eren's Suite has blue, yellow, & rose color scheme, separate sitting area, sofa bed, oak-paneled king bed, pedestal sink, marble shower, jetted tub; Amanda's Room, a monochromatic study in gray & white, has a mahogany queen mansion bed, separate shower, jetted tub w/ seat; Jennifer's Room downstairs has purple carpets, textured yellow walls, floral fabrics, four-poster queen bed, down

comforter **Comfort & Decor** Varied antiques, colorful textured walls, wallpaper, desks, dressers, mirrored dressing tables, wood floors, carpets, rocking chairs, ottomans, marble vanities, recessed bath lighting.

RATES, RESERVATIONS, & RESTRICTIONS

Deposit Credit card holds (72-hour cancellation policy) **Discounts** Honeymoon packages, corp., gov't., extended stays **Credit Cards** AE, MC, V **Check-In/Out** 3–6 p.m./11 a.m. **Smoking** No **Pets** No **Kids** Over age 12 **No-Nos** N/A **Minimum Stay** None **Open** All year **Host** Becky Hodges, 1910 Austin Ave., Waco 76701 **Phone** (254) 753-7294 **Fax** N/A **E-mail** cottonpalace@aol.com **Web** www.thecottonpalace.com

Piney Woods

The Piney Woods is east Texas. From ragtime pianist Scott Joplin's home-town of Texarkana in the northeast where Texas borders Arkansas, the Piney Woods parallels the Louisiana border south almost to Beaumont in the Gulf Coast region. The Texas bed-and-breakfast movement began in the small east Texas town of Jefferson in the 1970s.

During the nineteenth century, Jefferson was a thriving steamboat port trading with New Orleans. With a population of 30,000 Jefferson was then the second-largest Texas port, surpassed only by the ocean port of Galveston. A town with beautiful Greek Revival homes for its many merchants, Jefferson told financier Jay Gould not to sully its streets with railroad tracks. Gould, whose private railcar is now ironically parked across the street from Jefferson's Excelsior Hotel, turned Dallas into the railroad center instead. Then, when an engineer with dynamite changed Caddo Lake's flow, steamboat traffic shifted en masse to Shreveport and Jefferson's merchant population moved on.

Now a quaint town of 2,615 people with most of the original Greek Revival buildings, Jefferson is like a piece of history, frozen in time, but with over a dozen bed-and-breakfasts. The old homes open for tours the first weekend in May and the first two weekends in December. One of the region's biggest attractions is the First Monday Trade Days in Canton, where antiques and crafts are traded "sunup til sundown" Thursday through Sunday prior to the first Monday of each month.

Tyler, the east Texas population center with 84,000 people, draws 100,000 visitors for the six-day, late-September, livestock-oriented East Texas Fair. The mid-October Texas Rose Festival and the 38,000 rosebushes blooming from May to October at the Municipal Rose Garden and Museum also draw many visitors to this former Confederate stronghold–

turned–rosebush production center. To the south of Tyler, Nacogdoches has some historical interest as the city where the Texas Revolution against Mexico started in 1832.

AIRY MOUNT INN, Burnet

OVERALL ★★★★ | QUALITY ★★★★ | VALUE ★★★★ | PRICE RANGE $95–$125

Longhorns graze the pastures and rambunctious dogs guard Airy Mount, which is in the heart of hunting country. Though friendly at heart, the canines love to put on displays of fierceness by baring their fangs, jumping at car windows, and gnawing at front tires of moving vehicles. Airy Mount was built on a breezy hill by a Confederate general and his former Kentucky slaves (later freed) to better thwart Indian attacks. The hosts occupy the stone house near the windmill. Guests share a separate two-story stone building. Guns, longhorn skulls, big game animals, and birds are mounted on the 18-inch-thick limestone walls.

SETTING & FACILITIES

Location 1 mi. east of downtown **Near** Lakes, parks **Building** 1878/84 stone house & stable, new roof & remodeling **Grounds** 38 acres, grazing pastures, windmill **Public Space** LR, DR, kitchen **Food & Drink** Full candlelight breakfast in DR **Recreation** Fishing, hunting, boating, water sports, horse riding **Amenities & Services** TV/VCR, phone, barbecue, Western dances, receptions

ACCOMMODATIONS

Units 1 3-room suite, 2 guest rooms **All** Clock radio, ceiling fan **Some** TV/VCR (2), fireplace (1) **Bed & Bath** King & single daybed (1), queen (1), 2 doubles (1); all private baths, tub **Favorites** Santa Fe Suite contains original safe room where women and children were boarded up and hidden from attacking Indians, red metal hospital king bed w/ Confederate emblem, antique daybed, Texas-shaped mirror, Confederate water pitcher & bowl, claw-foot tub, water closet; General's Room has carpets, floor heater, leather chairs, old Confederate flag, deer heads, mounted ducks, TV/VCR, large vanity **Comfort & Decor** Rustic mix of Texas and Confederacy antiques, mounted animals, hide rugs, old trunks, Native American paintings, carpets or plank floors, beam ceilings, rock walls, wallpaper, dressers, wardrobes, desks, rocking chairs.

RATES, RESERVATIONS, & RESTRICTIONS

Deposit Credit card holds (72-hour cancellation policy) **Discounts** Packages **Credit Cards** MC, V (4% extra charged to total for credit card payments) **Check-In/Out** 2–8 p.m./noon **Smoking** No **Pets** No (dogs roam yard) **Kids** Yes (over age 5) **No-Nos** N/A **Minimum Stay** None **Open** All year **Hosts** Rosanne & Charles Hayman, RR 3, Box 280, Burnet 78611 **Phone** (512) 756-4149 **Fax** (512) 756-5135 **E-mail** info@airymount.com **Web** www.airymount.com

1ST BED & BREAKFAST IN TEXAS—PRIDE HOUSE, Jefferson

OVERALL ★★★★ | QUALITY ★★★★ | VALUE ★★★★ | PRICE RANGE $75–$175

Opened in 1975 and still under the same ownership, Pride House was recognized by the state legislature as Texas's first bed-and-breakfast. The main house has six rooms with ceiling fans, including the small attic rooms. But all the TVs are in the four-room cottage and stand-alone two-bedroom house with king and queen beds. The main dining room has stained glass, purple walls, a black-and-white linoleum floor, a curved window mirror, and a fireplace. Most guests tend to drive in from the Dallas area, about three hours west. The courthouse and historic district are six blocks away.

SETTING & FACILITIES
Location Commercial district **Near** Museums, historic homes **Building** 1889 stick Victorian Italianate, cottage, 2-BR house **Grounds** Front yard **Public Space** LR, DR, porch **Food & Drink** Full breakfast buffet in DR or porch, or basket delivered to room; 24-hour snacks, beverages **Recreation** Fishing, hunting, boating, water sports, horse riding **Amenities & Services** Portable wheelchair ramp, USA Today newspaper, weddings, groups (25)

ACCOMMODATIONS
Units 11 **All** Hair dryer, lighted makeup mirror, clock radio **Some** Fireplace (3), cable TV (6), ceiling fan (6), shared kitchen (4) **Bed & Bath** King (3), king & queen (1), queen (5), queen & twins (2); all private baths, tubs (5), jetted tub (1) **Favorites** Royal George has bay window, sitting area, gold stars on blue ceiling, stained-glass windows, desk, pedestal sink; the Suite, largest room, in cottage, has sunken LR, blue & white plaid curtains, wood-burning stove, recessed lighting, half dozen chairs, desk, double sinks, water closet **Comfort & Decor** Main house rooms have Victorian decor, armoires, stained glass, carpets, colorful walls, black claw-foot tubs; four cottage rooms mix Creole and Victorian influences, wood floors, rugs, shared kitchen.

RATES, RESERVATIONS, & RESTRICTIONS
Deposit 1 night (7-day cancellation policy; no refunds major holidays) **Discounts** Midweek, Internet specials **Credit Cards** AE, MC, V, D **Check-In/Out** After 3 p.m./11 a.m. **Smoking** No **Pets** No **Kids** Yes **No-Nos** N/A **Minimum Stay** 2 nights weekends **Open** All year **Host** Sandy Spalding, 409 Broadway St., Jefferson 75657 **Phone** (903) 665-2675 or toll-free (800) 894-3526 **Fax** (903) 665-3901 **E-mail** jefftx@mind.net **Web** www.jeffersontexas.com

OLD MULBERRY INN BED & BREAKFAST, Jefferson

OVERALL ★★★★½ | QUALITY ★★★★½ | VALUE ★★★★ | PRICE RANGE $70–$169

A 5,500-square-foot house with a 55-foot-long foyer, the Old Mulberry Inn was designed to be a bed-and-breakfast and fit harmoniously into this historic Greek Revival neighborhood. Painted clouds top the library's 30-foot-high ceiling. Danish Christmas plates grace the dining room, where the host serves up mulberry treats. Guest rooms are downstairs in the main building. The hosts live in a removed upstairs wing, just a buzzer press away. The no frou-frou, cookbook-writer host, who edited the home and garden section of a central California newspaper, fashioned some of the fabrics and lamps, including a cotton mill spindle lamp in the Star Room.

SETTING & FACILITIES
Location 7 blocks from historic district **Near** Museums, historic homes **Building** 1996 raised Louisiana Plantation style w/ Greek Revival columns **Grounds** 0.67 acres, arbor, small sculptures, bird bath, 100-year-old mulberry & large pecan **Public Space** LR, DR, library/lounge, porches **Food & Drink** Full breakfast buffet in DR; early morning coffee, biscotti; 24-hour snacks **Recreation** Fishing, hunting, boating, water sports, horse riding **Amenities & Services** Massage, electronic air filtering

ACCOMMODATIONS
Units 5 **All** Cable TV/VCR, clock radio, candles, central heat/AC, ceiling fan **Some** Hair dryer (on request) **Bed & Bath** King (3), queen (2); all private baths, claw-foot tub (3), jetted tub (1) **Favorites** Sophie's Room has Provençal French country feel, yellow & blue Waverly fabrics, sunflowers, antiqued white armoire, old white door headboard, bird house lamp, window-shaped mirror, tiles, plates **Comfort & Decor** Eclectic, raised four-poster carved-wood rice beds, armoires, dressers, writing tables, upholstered and wood chairs, pine heartwood floors, recessed halogen lights, cabinets/shelves, mulberry pillows, ceramic tile baths with 100-year-old doors, and nightlights.

RATES, RESERVATIONS, & RESTRICTIONS
Deposit Credit card holds (7-day cancellation for refund minus fee) **Discounts** Weekday, corp., AAA, Jan. & Aug. specials **Credit Cards** AE, MC, V, D **Check-In/Out** 3–7 p.m./11 a.m. **Smoking** No **Pets** No **Kids** Older kids only **No-Nos** N/A **Minimum Stay** Special events, holiday weekends **Open** All year **Hosts** Donald & Gloria Degn, 209 Jefferson St., Jefferson 75657 **Phone** (903) 665-1945 or toll-free (800) 263-5319 **Fax** N/A **E-mail** mulberry@jeffersontx.com **Web** www.oldmulberryinn.com

STEAMBOAT INN, *Jefferson*

OVERALL ★★★★ | QUALITY ★★★★ | VALUE ★★★★ | PRICE RANGE $95–$110

A white one-story house with green trim in a tree-lined residential neighborhood, the Steamboat Inn is within a block of two museums and all the historic district action. Around the corner is Jefferson's Old Fashion Hamburger Store, where the friendly waitresses serve up incredibly large pecan pie slices. Also nearby is Auntie Skinners, a biker favorite, as it is just about the only place in this almost dry county serving alcohol and staying open late. A pleasant assemblage of salvageable buildings, the Steamboat Inn has a long plank hallway, a crystal chandelier and sponged brownish-orange walls lined with illustrations of the steamboats that docked in the old port of Jefferson.

SETTING & FACILITIES
Location Historic district **Near** Museums, historic homes **Building** Greek Revival, assembled in1993 from pieces of 3 100–150-year-old homes **Grounds** I acre, fountain **Public Space** LR, DR, long hallway, porch **Food & Drink** Full breakfast buffet in DR; 24-hour snacks, beverages in kitchen; fruit bowl in hall **Recreation** Fishing, hunting, boating, water sports, horse riding **Amenities & Services** Microwave, fridge, board games, fax, phone, data port, in-room massage/spa services

ACCOMMODATIONS
Units 4 **All** Fireplace, TV/VCR, coffeemaker, clock radio, ceiling fan **Some** Shared porch (2) **Bed & Bath** King (3), queen (1); all private baths, claw-foot tub **Favorites** Mittie Stephens, named after steamboat that caught fire & sank in nearby Caddo Lake, has 1840s armoire, reproduction of antique wood queen bed, oars on wall, shared porch w/ wicker seating **Comfort & Decor** Each room has picture of namesake steamboat, mix of antiques and reproductions, sitting area, color schemes varying from pink, green, and mauve to blue and white, wallpaper, plank floors and ceilings, fluted glass.

RATES, RESERVATIONS, & RESTRICTIONS
Deposit Credit card holds (7-day cancellation policy; 30 days for whole house rental) **Discounts** Corp., gov't., weekdays, whole house, celebration packages **Credit Cards** AE, MC, V, D **Check-In/Out** 3 p.m./11 a.m. **Smoking** Outside **Pets** No **Kids** Yes (over age 8) **No-Nos** N/A **Minimum Stay** 2 nights holiday/special event weekends **Open** All year **Hosts** Byron & Amy Haden, 114 N. Marshall St., Jefferson 75657 **Phone** (903) 665-8946 or toll-free (877) 665-8946 **Fax** (903) 665-7884 **E-mail** info@steamboatinnhefferson.com **Web** www.steamboatinnjefferson.com

PINE CREEK LODGE, Nacogdoches

OVERALL ★★★★ | QUALITY ★★★★ | VALUE ★★★★ | PRICE RANGE $95–$150

Since starting out with a cabin on the hilly family farm, Pine Creek Lodge has expanded into a cluster of seven buildings. The pond is stocked with bass and channel catfish, and wild turkeys are sometimes sighted in the woods. The main building has three dining rooms for functions, which are the big business here. The farm even has its own greenhouse to grow ferns for weddings. Though Nacogdoches occupies an important niche in the early history of modern Texas, the city itself has little to offer most sight-seers. Consequently, weekday room rates drop precipitously—to as low as $55.

SETTING & FACILITIES
Location 10 mi. west of Nacogdoches **Near** Forests, lakes **Building** 7 buildings, vary from contemporary to rustic cabins **Grounds** 140 acres, 700 rosebushes, large fish pond, creek **Public Space** Lobby, lounge, DRs, decks, guest baths, poolside cabana **Food & Drink** Cont'l breakfast in room weekdays (full breakfast if 4 or more rooms occupied); full breakfast weekends in DR; fruit, candy, beverages; picnics; candlelight steak dinners by reservation **Recreation** Golf, swimming, fishing, biking **Amenities & Services** Pool, golf driving range, function room, meetings (100), banquets (260)

ACCOMMODATIONS
Units 17 **All** Robes, TV/VCR, phone, clock, fridge, coffeemaker, microwave, individual heat/AC, private entrance, ceiling fan **Some** Outdoor hot tub (2), fireplace (2), private decks **Bed & Bath** King (15), queen (2); all private baths, jetted tub (2), tub (13) **Favorites** 2 upstairs rooms in main building have decks w/ private hot tubs; 2 1-BR cottages have fireplaces, jetted tubs; 2 garden building rooms have porches & flower gardens; 3 Creek House rooms have private decks w/ creek views **Comfort & Decor** Varies from rustic to contemporary, creamy Sheetrock walls and ceilings, carpets, handmade yellow pine furnishings, some wallpaper, recessed lighting, sleeper sofas, vanities.

RATES, RESERVATIONS, & RESTRICTIONS
Deposit 1 night (14-day cancellation policy) **Discounts** Weekdays **Credit Cards** AE, MC, V, D **Check-In/Out** 3 p.m./11 a.m. **Smoking** Outside **Pets** No **Kids** Yes **No-Nos** Alcohol **Minimum Stay** None **Open** All year **Hosts** Michael Pitts & Family, 341 Pine

Creek Rd., Nacogdoches75964 **Phone** (936) 560-6282 or toll-free (888) 714-1414 **Fax** (936) 560-1675 **E-mail** info@pinecreeklodge.com **Web** www.pinecreeklodge.com

KIEPERSOL ESTATES BED & BREAKFAST, Tyler

OVERALL ★★★★★ | QUALITY ★★★★½ | VALUE ★★★★ | PRICE RANGE $130–$200

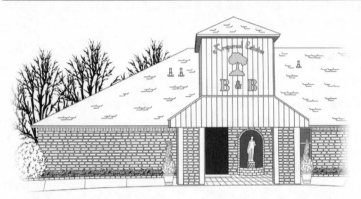

Opened in late 1999 by an East Texas farming entrepreneur who originally hailed from South Africa, Kiepersol Estates seems patterned after the elegant small wine estate hotels found outside of Cape Town. Ponds are stocked with catfish, bass, and perch. Weathered Western barn wood walls, a stone brick fireplace, and black-and-white landscape and family photographs enliven the bar and lounge areas. A leather lounge is set aside for nonsmokers. Cigar smokers can indulge in an adjacent lounge upholstered with tapestries. The restaurant has a window into the wine cellar and serves up steaks cut and aged from whole loins on site.

SETTING & FACILITIES

Location 11 mi. south of Tyler **Near** Museums **Building** 1999 country estate **Grounds** 386 acres, ponds, gazebo, pine trees, 14 acres of grapevines, winery **Public Space** Nonsmoking lounge, cigar lounge, bar, restaurant **Food & Drink** Full breakfast in DR; dinner in restaurant; private event meals **Recreation** Golf, fishing, biking, horse riding **Amenities & Services** Sat. group horse & carriage tours, cigars, chapel (40), private large group DR (130), small group DRs (14; 40)

ACCOMMODATIONS

Units 5 **All** Robes, hair dryer, satellite TV, phone, clock, ceiling fan **Some** Private patio (3), patio fan (3), hot tub (3), iron (on request) **Bed & Bath** King beds; all private baths, clawfoot tub **Favorites** Champagne Room, largest, popular for wedding nights & anniversaries, has champagne & green color scheme, faux-painted walls, wallpaper, private enclosed patio w/ jetted tub; Paarl Room, a corner room w/ pond view, & Coastal Room also have private enclosed patios w/ jetted tubs **Comfort & Decor** Opulent, mostly antique leather and dark wood furnishings, greens, burgundies, florals, four-poster wood or metal beds, Oriental carpets on wood floors, fluted glass, wainscoting, wallpaper, faux painting, brocade curtains, pleated shades, water closets.

RATES, RESERVATIONS, & RESTRICTIONS

Deposit Credit card holds (48-hour cancellation policy) **Discounts** Weekdays **Credit Cards** AE, MC, V, D **Check-In/Out** 3 p.m./11 a.m. **Smoking** No **Pets** No (peacocks on premises) **Kids** Yes **No-Nos** N/A **Minimum Stay** None **Open** All year **Host** Andra Wilman, 21508 Merlot Lane, Tyler 75703 **Phone** (903) 894-3300 **Fax** (903) 895-4140 **E-mail** bandb@kiepersol.com **Web** www.kiepersol.com or www.keepusall.com

Gulf Coast

The Gulf Coast region stretches west from the Texas–Louisiana border along the Gulf of Mexico to the Mexican border near Harlingen and Brownsville. White sand beaches and salt marshes compete with shipping ports, oil drilling rigs, refineries, and factories for this stretch of coastline. Alas, Gulf Coast bed-and-breakfasts are few and far between, relatively rare species compared to the far more numerous oil rigs and refineries.

Unless they live in a nearby city, most Texans do not head to the Gulf Coast when they want a good bed-and-breakfast experience. Which is not to say that this is not a rewarding place to visit. The bird-watching, beaches, museums, oil rigs, chess games, ship movements, seafood, shopping, and other amusements can certainly be fun along the Strand in Galveston when the weather is warm and sunny and the storm windows remain open.

After Houston and Galveston, the bed-and-breakfast scene really thins out near the coast, though the Stacia Leigh in Galveston has an arrangement to sail to another bed-and-breakfast near Rockport and Corpus Christi. Between this book's Appendix and the Internet, intrepid adventurers can certainly paste together a Gulf Coast bed-and-breakfast itinerary meandering southwest from Houston or Galveston down to South Padre Island and the Mexican border at Matamoros. The choices will be few, and Hill Country pampering will usually not be an option, but at least it's Texas and near the beach, right?

The maze of freeways and spread out nature of Houston make it a sister city to Los Angeles in geographic spirit. Be prepared for torn-up streets and lots of detours through the outstanding medical and impressive museum districts until Houston completes its rapid transit system. Hobby Airport commuters will particularly appreciate the location of Hidden Oaks Bed and Breakfast.

THE QUEEN ANNE BED & BREAKFAST, Galveston

OVERALL ★★★★ | QUALITY ★★★★ | VALUE ★★★★ | PRICE RANGE $90–$180

People come from Dallas, San Antonio, and Austin, but most Queen Anne guests coming to play on the Strand are from nearby Houston and Beaumont. Front, back, and side Cape Cod–style sun porches with rocking chairs and swings are popular for catching the sea breezes, and a coffeepot and refrigerator stocked with soft drinks are nearby. The stereo system floods the porches and dining areas with music (typically light jazz). The chandeliered dining room features crystal, candles, and china. The Cape Hatteras, Cape May, and Cape Cod rooms all have connecting doors and can be turned into multiroom suites.

SETTING & FACILITIES
Location 6 blocks from Strand **Near** Dock, museums **Building** 1905 Queen Anne Victorian **Grounds** Small front fish pond, sego palms **Public Space** LR, DR, porches, guest bath **Food & Drink** Full breakfast in DR; afternoon wine & cheese; 24-hour beverages **Recreation** Golf, fishing, biking **Amenities & Services** Bicycles, TV/VCR, phone, iron, hair dryer, fridge, stereo, groups, weddings (32 sit-down, 50 standing)

ACCOMMODATIONS
Units 6 **All** Robes, clock, heat/AC, ceiling fan **Some** Private entrance (1), fridge (1), coffeemaker (1), cable TV (1), CD player (1) **Bed & Bath** King (2), queen (4); all private baths, jetted tub (1) **Favorites** The Suite, the only ground-level room, has the best amenities, private entrance, lavender color, white trim, seashell collection, canopied queen bed, beveled-glass armoire, green plants, wood & wicker furnishings, double jetted tub; Cape May forms connecting suite, has king bed, sitting area w/ sleeper sofa, floral tapestry fabrics **Comfort & Decor** Lace curtains, shuttered windows, carpets, walnut, burl veneer, other wood furnishings, armoires, dressing tables, some sitting areas and sleeper sofas, floral fabrics, pedestal sinks.

RATES, RESERVATIONS, & RESTRICTIONS
Deposit Credit card holds (5-day cancellation policy) **Discounts** Weekdays, Internet specials, anniversary/honeymoon packages **Credit Cards** AE, MC, V, D **Check-In/Out** 3 p.m./11:30 a.m. **Smoking** Porches **Pets** No **Kids** Over age 12 **No-Nos** N/A **Minimum Stay** 2 nights May–late Aug., some holidays, special events **Open** All year **Hosts** Ron & Jackie Metzger, 1915 Sealy Ave., Galveston 77550 **Phone** (409) 763-7088 or toll-free (800) 472-0930 **Fax** (409) 765-6525 **E-mail** N/A **Web** www.welcome.to/queenanne

STACIA LEIGH BED & BREAKFAST ABOARD THE CHRYSEIS, Galveston

OVERALL ★★★★ | QUALITY ★★★★ | VALUE ★★★★ | PRICE RANGE $125–$200

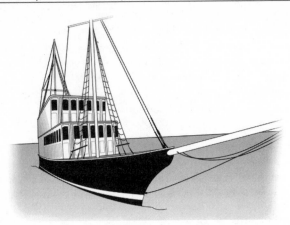

Originally built with Oregon pine masts in Le Havre, France, and dubbed the Chryseis, this 120-foot-long schooner did a tour of duty as Italian dictator Benito Mussolini's World War II yacht. Rescued from decay and transformed into the Stacia Leigh bed-and-breakfast in 1999, the Chryseis has a 46-foot-long upper lounge and a more private lower lounge with white wicker furnishings. The dock also has two levels, as well as a glass-enclosed dining area with ceiling fans and heating. An outdoor hot tub looks out on oil industry jack-ups, semi-submersibles, and ships. The Strand action is only a block away.

SETTING & FACILITIES

Location Texas Cruise Ship terminal, behind Fisherman's Wharf Restaurant **Near** The Strand, museums, ground transit systems **Building** 1906 floating luxury yacht **Grounds** 4,000 sq. ft. of wood plank dock **Public Space** Upper lounge, lower lounge, deck DR, guest bath **Food & Drink** Full breakfast in DR; afternoon snacks, beverages **Recreation** Golf, fishing, biking **Amenities & Services** Hot tub, yacht cruises, parties, weddings (195)

ACCOMMODATIONS

Units 11 **All** TV, clock radio **Some** Stereo (1) **Bed & Bath** King (8), queen (3); all private baths, jetted tub (8) **Favorites** Truman Suite, a V-berth where the bow narrows, has skylights above bed, privacy windows for honeymooners, plenty of portholes, jetted tub; Nimitz and Eisenhower Suites, lower stern (below deck) honeymoon favorites, have seating where hull juts up, 6 water-level portholes, jetted tub; Roosevelt Suite has long hallway, 25 curving lower deck windows, boat-shaped wall cabinet, wood paneling, jetted tub **Com-**

fort & Decor Sparse ship-like furnishings, nautical decor like shells and starfish, porthole windows, white wood paneling, cabinets, small table, colorful director's chairs.

RATES, RESERVATIONS, & RESTRICTIONS
Deposit Credit card holds (7-day cancellation policy) **Discounts** Corp., multiple rooms, extended stays, package deals, Internet specials **Credit Cards** AE, MC, V, D **Check-In/Out** 3 p.m./11 a.m. **Smoking** No **Pets** No **Kids** Over age 15 **No-Nos** N/A **Minimum Stay** 2 nights weekends from May 1–Oct. 1 **Open** All year **Hosts** Pat & Bonnie Hicks, Pier 22 at Harborside Dr., Galveston 77550 **Phone** (409) 750-8858 **Fax** N/A **E-mail** innkeeper@stacia-leigh.com **Web** www.stacia-leigh.com

ANGEL ARBOR BED & BREAKFAST INN, Houston

OVERALL ★★★★ | QUALITY ★★★★ | VALUE ★★★★ | PRICE RANGE $95–$125

Five blocks north of I-10 (the Katy Freeway) in an area known for its abundance of law offices, Angel Arbor does a brisk weekday business with corporate clients, many here to work on legal matters. The rooms are named after angels, an angel statue graces the stairway, and an outdoor angel fountain offers relief from worldly troubles. Three rooms are upstairs in the main house and share a solarium with wicker furnishings and a full-size refrigerator. Just in case, a mini-fridge is hidden away inside a closet. The basement has a twin-bedded room. An adjacent cottage has two rooms with jetted tubs that can be combined into a balconied suite.

SETTING & FACILITIES
Location Houston Heights, corner of 9th & Heights Blvd. **Near** Parks, museums, downtown **Building** 1923 red-brick Georgian, adjoining cottage **Grounds** Gazebo, angel statue **Public Space** LR w/ fireplace, DR, solarium **Food & Drink** Full breakfast in DR; 24-hour beverages; snack baskets; murder mystery group dinners, teas **Recreation** Golf, tennis **Amenities & Services** Upstairs & downstairs guest fridges, groups (20)

ACCOMMODATIONS
Units 6 guest rooms, 4 in main house **All** Robes, hair dryer, TV/VCR, phone, iron, ironing board, clock radio, zoned AC, ceiling fan **Some** Fridge (2), tape player **Bed & Bath** Queen (5), twins (1); all private baths, claw-foot tub (2), jetted tub (4) **Favorites** Angelique Room has cherry sleigh bed, love seat, view deck; Raphael has canopy bed, original hallway bath w/ added double sinks, jetted tub **Comfort & Decor** Burgundy carpets and dark woods (like mahogany and cherry) in main house, wicker and American oak furnishings in adjoining cottage, four-poster and canopy beds, wallpaper ceiling borders, mirrored dressers, armoires, love seats and desks or tables and chairs, shuttered windows, lace shower curtains.

RATES, RESERVATIONS, & RESTRICTIONS
Deposit Credit card holds (72-hour cancellation policy) **Discounts** Internet specials **Credit Cards** AE, MC, V, D **Check-In/Out** After 3 p.m./11:30 a.m. **Smoking** No **Pets** No

Kids Over age 12 **No-Nos** N/A **Minimum Stay** None **Open** All year **Hosts** Marguerite & Dean Swanson, 848 Heights Blvd., Houston 77007 **Phone** (713) 868-4654 or toll-free (888) 810-0092 **Fax** (713) 861-3189 **E-mail** b-bhoutx@wt.net **Web** www.angelarbor.com

HIDDEN OAKS BED & BREAKFAST, Houston

OVERALL ★★★★★ | QUALITY ★★★★½ | VALUE ★★★★★ | PRICE RANGE $95–$179

A walled oasis in a quiet residential neighborhood, hidden away from the endless strip mall bordering I-45 (the Gulf Freeway) near Hobby Airport, Hidden Oaks is a remnant of an 1820s 13,000-acre cattle ranch land grant from Stephen Austin. Built by a descendent of an original "Old Three Hundred" settler, Hidden Oaks gets its fair share of weekday business travelers. The Rosa Christie Suite dressing room and large grounds are popular for weddings. The small Samuel Room's Murphy bed folds up to provide additional function space adjoining the living room. A new pavilion with a dance floor is under construction.

SETTING & FACILITIES
Location Hobby Airport/Broadway exit **Near** Downtown, parks, Kemah Waterfront, NASA, Galveston **Building** 1927 Plantation style, adjacent carriage house **Grounds** 1.5 acres, cherub fountain, animal sculptures, herb garden, large oak trees, palms **Public Space** LR w/ fireplace, DR, porch **Food & Drink** Full breakfast in DR; snacks, beverages in room **Recreation** Golf, tennis, jogging **Amenities & Services** Grand piano, big-screen TV/VCR, computer, Internet access, hot tub, massage, newspaper, basketball court, weddings (75–100)

ACCOMMODATIONS
Units 4 All Robes, hair dryer, coffeemaker, TV/VCR, CD player, phone, data port, ceiling fan **Some** Fridge (3), microwave (3), coffeemaker (3), full kitchen (1), stereo (1) **Bed &**

Bath King (2), queen (2); all private baths, tub (2), jetted tub (1) **Favorites** 500-sq.-ft. Rosa Christie Suite has upholstered king headboard, sitting room w/ sofa & daybed, fireplace, dolphin clock, long narrow dressing area w/ lighted mirror; Carriage House has antique oak queen bed, stained-glass lamps, full kitchen, stereo, double jetted tub, stall shower **Comfort & Decor** Mostly large rooms have high-quality wood furnishings and fabrics, ample wardrobe space, sitting areas with sofa beds.

RATES, RESERVATIONS, & RESTRICTIONS

Deposit Credit card holds (72-hour cancellation policy) **Discounts** Corp., singles, weekdays **Credit Cards** AE, MC, V, D **Check-In/Out** 3–6 p.m./11 a.m. **Smoking** Outside **Pets** No (kennel arrangements available) **Kids** Over age 12 **No-Nos** N/A **Minimum Stay** None **Open** All year **Hosts** Phil & Maria Fillingame, 7808 Dixie Dr., Houston 77087 **Phone** (713) 640-2457 or toll-free (888) 305-0204 **Fax** (713) 640-2505 **E-mail** hiddenoaks@houston.rr.com **Web** www.hiddenoaksbnb.com

PATRICIAN BED & BREAKFAST INN, Houston

OVERALL ★★★★ | QUALITY ★★★★ | VALUE ★★★★ | PRICE RANGE $80–$150

A few blocks walk from the Fine Arts, Contemporary Arts, Health and Medical Science, and Natural Science Museums, the Patrician is popular with both business travelers and wedding parties. A new deck and 14-foot gazebo accommodates the wedding business. Business travelers have access to meeting and working spaces, as well as an early breakfast option. The dining room walls are sponge-painted red and lined with old family photographs. An upstairs refrigerator is stocked with beverages, and a microwave is in the hall. Two new attic guest rooms have roll-top desks, claw-foot tubs, and pedestal sinks.

SETTING & FACILITIES

Location Museum District **Near** Downtown, Texas Medical District, parks, Rice University **Building** 1919 Colonial Revival mansion **Grounds** Fountain, gazebo, deck, lights on trees **Public Space** Foyer, LR w/ fireplace, DR, solarium, guest bath **Food & Drink** Full breakfast in DR; 24-hour beverages; group murder mystery dinners; catering **Recreation** Golf, tennis, jogging **Amenities & Services** Fax, AV equipment, CD player, microwave, fridge, event planning, weddings (80)

ACCOMMODATIONS

Units 7 **All** Robes, hair dryer, cable TV, phone, data port, voice mail, clock radio, ceiling fan **Some** VCR (3), CD player (2), iron & ironing board (5), private patio (1) **Bed & Bath** Queen beds; all private baths, claw-foot tub (2), jetted tub (4) **Favorites** Lollie Dee has burl walnut bed, sofa bed, clouds & stars painted on ceiling, tile mural surrounding double jetted tub, separate shower, private patio; Annalyse has blue floral wallpaper, lots of windows, Victorian bed, sofa bed, walk-in shower, jetted tub **Comfort & Decor** Antiques, stained glass, original wavy glass, sitting areas, sponged-painted walls (blues, pinks, greens), botanical wallpapers, some painted sky ceilings.

RATES, RESERVATIONS, & RESTRICTIONS

Deposit Credit card holds (7-day cancellation policy; otherwise responsible for full amount of stay) **Discounts** Singles **Credit Cards** AE, MC, V, D **Check-In/Out** 4–7 p.m./11 a.m. **Smoking** No **Pets** On individual basis w/ prior approval; dog on premises **Kids** Yes **No-Nos** N/A **Minimum Stay** 2 nights on weekends **Open** All year **Host** Pat Thomas, 1200 Southmore Blvd., Houston 77004 **Phone** (713) 523-1114 or toll-free (800) 553-5797 **Fax** (713) 523-0790 **E-mail** information@texasbnb.com **Web** www.texasbnb.com

Zone 17

South Texas Plains

San Antonio anchors the northeast corner of the South Texas Plains, a region stretching south toward the cotton, citrus, and vegetable farming areas around Weslaco and McAllen and west toward the small city of Eagle Pass bordering Mexico along the Rio Grande River. With over a million people, San Antonio is by far the most populated city in this relatively sparsely inhabited region studded with hilly cattle ranches, oaks, and pecans.

As far as bed-and-breakfasts go, there is not much in this region outside of San Antonio. But that's okay—San Antonio is worth several days itself, and the city borders both the Hill Country and Prairies and Lakes zones, which have the largest concentrations of bed-and-breakfasts in Texas. Interesting Hill Country towns like Gruene, New Braunfels, Comfort, Kerrville, and Fredericksburg are within an hour's drive of San Antonio. Houston is only three hours of driving time, and Austin is about half that distance.

San Antonio's Riverwalk is the center of tourist and convention action. Excellent restaurants and museums abound. The botanical garden is topnotch. Four missions are part of the Spanish colonial and Mexican heritage. The Institute of Texas Cultures in Hemisphere Park is an eye-opening introduction to the 27 ethnic groups that built this diverse state. Late April is the ten-day Fiesta San Antonio. The rodeo and livestock show comes to town in February. The Texas Folklife Festival happens in June.

The Alamo remains a reminder of the struggle for independence in a downtown remarkable for the relative paucity of the skyscrapers that make most downtowns alienating experiences. A good public transportation system links together a vibrant art scene and neighborhoods of historic homes, like the King William and Monte Vista Historic Districts.

BECKMANN INN AND CARRIAGE HOUSE
BED & BREAKFAST, San Antonio

OVERALL ★★★★½ | QUALITY ★★★★ | VALUE ★★★★ | PRICE RANGE $110–$150

At the southernmost edge of the Riverwalk and King William Historic District, Beckmann Inn is within three blocks of the artist studios, theater, and microbrewery at the Blue Star Arts Complex. The living room, entered via a burled red pine door, has a Parisian wood mosaic floor, a Mexican tile fireplace, 14-foot ceilings, and tall windows. Arched opaque glass doors lead to a formal dining room decorated with over half a century of German anniversary plates from the nearby Pioneer Flour Mill. Indeed, the inn traces its lineage back to the Guenther Flour Mill family in the late 1800s.

SETTING & FACILITIES

Location King William Historic District **Near** Museums, parks, galleries **Building** 1886 Greek Victorian w/ adjacent carriage house, porches & rooms added **Grounds** 0.8-acre corner lot w/ pecan trees, flowers, & Victorian landscape behind cypress fence **Public Space** LR w/ fireplace, DR, solarium, porch **Food & Drink** Full breakfast in DR; 24-hour snacks, beverages **Recreation** Golf, biking, horse riding, tennis, jogging **Amenities & Services** Concierge services, piano, stereo, fax, computer, e-mail

ACCOMMODATIONS

Units 5 **All** Robes, cable TV, fridge, phone, data port, clock radio, iron, ironing board, heat/AC, ceiling fan **Some** Fireplace (1), private entrance (4), brick patio (Carriage House) **Bed & Bath** Queen beds; all private baths, tub (1) **Favorites** Upstairs Carriage House room, a honeymoon privacy favorite, has separate sitting area, shared brick patio, flower boxes; Library Room has fireplace, bird cage w/ greenery, Italian Anris wood carving collection, walk-in closet **Comfort & Decor** Floral fabric themes, white walls, wallpaper ceiling border, eight-foot-tall carved wood beds, desks, armchairs, antique trunks, armoires, shuttered windows, carpet or wood floor and area rug, pedestal sink.

RATES, RESERVATIONS, & RESTRICTIONS

Deposit 1 night (14-day cancellation for refund minus $20) **Discounts** Corp. **Credit Cards** AE, MC, V, D, DC **Check-In/Out** 4–5 p.m./11 a.m. **Smoking** Outside **Pets** No **Kids** Yes (but only 2 occupants allowed per room) **No-Nos** N/A **Minimum Stay** 2 nights on weekends **Open** All year **Hosts** Betty Jo & Don Schwartz, 222 E. Guenther St., San Antonio 78204 **Phone** (210) 229-1449 or toll-free (800) 945-1449 **Fax** (210) 229-1061 **E-mail** beckinn@swbell.net **Web** www.beckmanninn.com

BONNER GARDEN BED & BREAKFAST, San Antonio

OVERALL ★★★★ | QUALITY ★★★★ | VALUE ★★★★ | PRICE RANGE $85–$125

In the heart of San Antonio's Monte Vista Historic District and near the downtown bus line, Bonner Garden celebrates artist Mary Bonner in this concrete and steel mansion designed by architect Atlee B. Ayres. In a neighborhood of imposing mansions, this rose-colored building with green shutters boasts Bonner's original studio and several of her oils and watercolors. The formal dining room is as eclectic as the guest rooms, mixing an 1870 table from the British embassy in Denmark with Laredo, Texas, hotel chairs and an Italian crystal chandelier. Black leather furnishings and a stereo make the living room popular.

SETTING & FACILITIES
Location 2 mi. north of downtown/Riverwalk **Near** Museums, parks **Building** 1910 replica of early 1600s Italian villa **Grounds** 2.3-acre corner lot w/ fish pond, wedding arch **Public Space** LR w/ fireplace, DR, lounge, rooftop deck **Food & Drink** Full breakfast in DR; 24-hour snacks, beverages **Recreation** Golf, biking, horse riding **Amenities & Services** Pool, stereo, computer, Internet access, very small weddings (4 people)

ACCOMMODATIONS
Units 6 **All** TV/VCR, phone, clock radio **Some** Fireplace (5), fridge (1), coffeemaker (1), hair dryer & iron (on request) **Bed & Bath** King (2), queen (4); all private baths, tub (1), jetted tub (2) **Favorites** Portico Room, originally house tea room, has B&W tile floor, four-poster carved rice king bed, porcelain fireplace; Studio, Mary Bonner's original art studio, has saltillo tile floor, wood ceiling, white rock wall behind iron canopy queen bed, fridge, coffeemaker **Comfort & Decor** Eclectic mix of antiques and comfortable furnishings; decor themes ranging from garden to Chinese, huge armoires, mirrors, desks, wood and tile floors, area rugs, Mary Bonner prints, and local art.

RATES, RESERVATIONS, & RESTRICTIONS
Deposit Credit card holds (72-hour cancellation policy) **Discounts** Extended stay, weekday corp., singles **Credit Cards** AE, MC, V, D **Check-In/Out** 1 p.m./11 a.m. **Smoking** No **Pets** No **Kids** Over age 2; 1 family at a time) **No-Nos** N/A **Minimum Stay** 2 nights on weekends **Open** All year **Hosts** Jan & Noel Stenoien, 145 E. Agarita Ave., San Antonio 78212 **Phone** (210) 733-4222 or toll-free (800) 396-4222 **Fax** (210) 733-6129 **E-mail** noels@onr.com **Web** www.bonnergarden.com

NOBLE INNS: JACKSON HOUSE (JH) & AARON PANCOAST CARRIAGE HOUSE (PCH), San Antonio

OVERALL ★★★★★ | QUALITY ★★★★½ | VALUE ★★★★ | PRICE RANGE $120–$225

A predominately German settlement known as Sauerkraut Bend, San Antonio's King William Historic District was home to the property host's great-grandfather, who constructed Pancoast Carriage House across the street from the Ogé House. After successfully converting the Pancoast into a bed-and-breakfast in 1991, the Noble family opened the renovated Jackson House as a bed-and-breakfast with a stained-glass enclosed swim spa in 1995. The Pancoast is more about self-sufficiency, with an expanded continental breakfast dropped off the night before in a private downstairs suite and two upstairs suites sharing kitchen, living, and dining areas.

SETTING & FACILITIES

Location King William Historic District, 4 blocks from downtown **Near** Museums, parks, galleries **Building** 1894 & 1896 Victorians **Grounds** Landscaped gardens, patios **Public Space** LR, DR **Food & Drink** Full breakfast in DR (JH); cont'l breakfast in suite (PCH); afternoon beverages, snacks, evening sherry, stocked fridge (JH) **Recreation** Golf, biking, jogging **Amenities & Services** Concierge, Rolls Royce limo, turn-down service, bicycles, enclosed swim spa (JH), outdoor pool & whirlpool (PCH), groups & business retreats (18)

ACCOMMODATIONS

Units 6 guest rooms (JH), 3 suites (PCH) **All** Robes, fireplace, hair dryer, TV **Some** Full kitchen (PCH), iron, ironing board, makeup mirror (on request) **Bed & Bath** King (2), queen (7); all private baths, claw-foot tub (4), jetted tub (4) **Favorites** Room 5, upstairs in JH, has sitting alcove w/ fireplace & dormer windows, tiled shower w/ bench; Suite 1, downstairs in PCH, has private LR, DR, full kitchen, double jetted tub **Comfort & Decor** Fine carved-wood and marble furnishings, antiques, armoires, William Morris and

Waverly wallpapers, original longleaf pine floors or carpet (uppers), candelabra lights over oval bath mirrors.

RATES, RESERVATIONS, & RESTRICTIONS
Deposit 1 night (14-day cancellation for refund minus $20) **Discounts** Group, corp. **Credit Cards** AE, MC,V, D **Check-In/Out** 3 p.m./11 a.m. **Smoking** Outside **Pets** No **Kids** Over age 13 in JH; all ages in PCH **No-Nos** N/A **Minimum Stay** 2 nights on weekends **Open** All year **Hosts** Donald & Liesl Noble, 102 Turner St., San Antonio 78204 **Phone** (210) 225-4045 or toll-free (800) 221-4045 **Fax** (210) 227-0877 **E-mail** stay@nobleinns.com **Web** www.nobleinns.com

O'CASEY'S BED & BREAKFAST, San Antonio

OVERALL ★★★★ | QUALITY ★★★★ | VALUE ★★★★★ | PRICE RANGE $79–$99

In the early 1900s residential Monte Vista Historic District, O'Casey's is particularly popular with families visiting nearby Trinity University, where the hosts formerly taught music. Though lacking the room amenities and jetted tubs of the more elegant Inn at Craig Place (see Appendix) a block away, O'Casey's provides ample comfort, a friendly ambience, and good value. La Fonda Mexican restaurant (less than three blocks away on Main Street) has been a neighborhood institution since 1932. A theatrical group passing through left O'Casey's with five leprechaun murals. A leprechaun holding coffee and pancakes graces the family-style dining room, where the hosts hold court and guests chat each morning.

SETTING & FACILITIES
Location 2 mi. north of Alamo/downtown Riverwalk **Near** Museums, parks, Trinity University **Building** 1904 2-story merchant's house w/ columns & balcony added later, carriage house in rear **Grounds** Patio, pecan tree **Public Space** LR w/ fireplace, DR **Food & Drink** Full breakfast in DR, porch or garden **Recreation** Golf, biking, horse riding **Amenities & Services** Piano, computer, newspaper, board games

ACCOMMODATIONS
Units 7 **All** TV **Some** Shared balcony (2), deck (1), full kitchen (2) **Bed & Bath** King (3), queen (3), 2 full (1); all private baths, tub (6) **Favorites** Blarney Loft, former hayloft in stand-alone Carriage House, has low ceiling, brown wicker & wood furnishings, wallpaper ceiling border, carpet, king bed, alcove w/ single bed, full kitchen, large deck, tile shower; Londonderry Suite in back of main house has sleeping leprechaun mural, 2d room w/ twin day & trundle beds, old chest, claw-foot tub **Comfort & Decor** Antique wood and wicker furnishings, some desks, rocking chairs, wardrobes, mirrored dressers, wood floors, area rugs, lace curtains, blinds, teddy bears, mostly small baths.

RATES, RESERVATIONS, & RESTRICTIONS
Deposit Credit card holds (7-day cancellation policy) **Discounts** Weekday, singles **Credit Cards** AE, MC,V, D **Check-In/Out** Flexible, customized **Smoking** No **Pets** Yes (2 rooms only; $10) **Kids** Yes (Carriage House only) **No-Nos** N/A **Minimum Stay**

None **Open** All year **Hosts** John & Linda Casey, 225 W. Craig Place, San Antonio 78212 **Phone** (210) 738-1378 or toll-free (800) 738-1378 **Fax** (210) 733-9408 **E-mail** info@ocaseybnb.com **Web** www.ocaseybnb.com

THE OGÉ HOUSE INN ON THE RIVERWALK, San Antonio

OVERALL ★★★★½ | QUALITY ★★★★½ | VALUE ★★★★ | PRICE RANGE $155–$225

Elegant and formal, with a 90% occupancy rate year-round, the three-story Ogé House is so popular that the front door remains locked to prevent guests from being disturbed by the hordes of tourists on walking tours through this historic homes district. Nonetheless, the green wrought-iron and wicker furnishings of the front porch and veranda offer relaxation. Though not as close to the river as the Riverwalk Inn, which is about two blocks away, the Ogé House back lawn borders the river and offers easy access to this quiet (compared to downtown) southern portion of the Riverwalk.

SETTING & FACILITIES
Location King William Historic District, 5 blocks from downtown **Near** Museums, galleries, parks **Building** 1857 Antebellum mansion, upper floors added in 1870s **Grounds** 1.5 acres w/ roses, herb garden, wrought-iron gazebo **Public Space** Foyer, lobby, sunken library, DR, upstairs lounge **Food & Drink** Full breakfast in DR or veranda; 24-hour snacks, beverages; port wine in rooms **Recreation** Golf, biking, horse riding, jogging **Amenities & Services** Fax, copier, newspapers (national & local)

ACCOMMODATIONS
Units 10 (5 suites, 5 rooms) **All** Robes, cable TV, phone, voice mail, data port, clock radio, iron, ironing board, individual heat/AC, ceiling fan **Some** Fireplace (7), private porch (1), shared veranda (4), VCR **Bed & Bath** King (5), queen (5); all private baths, tub (9) **Favorites** River View Suite has private staircase & river-view porch, king bed, fireplace **Comfort & Decor** Elegant yet comfortable mix of European and American antiques reminiscent of Antebellum era, carpet or wood floors with area rugs, armoires, closets, desks, makeup mirrors, lace curtains, drapes.

RATES, RESERVATIONS, & RESTRICTIONS
Deposit 1 night or 50% (14-day cancellation for refund minus $20; 60 days for holidays, special events; otherwise liable for entire amount of stay) **Discounts** Weekday corp., singles **Credit Cards** AE, MC, V, D, DC **Check-In/Out** 1–6 p.m./11 a.m. **Smoking** No **Pets** No **Kids** No **No-Nos** N/A **Minimum Stay** 2 nights on weekends (up to 4 nights for special events) **Open** All year **Hosts** Patrick & Sharrie Magatagan, 209 Washington St., San Antonio 78204 **Phone** (210) 223-2353 or toll-free (800) 242-2770 **Fax** (210) 226-5812 **E-mail** ogeinn@swbell.net **Web** www.ogeinn.com

San Antonio, Texas 269

RIVERWALK INN, San Antonio

OVERALL ★★★★½ | QUALITY ★★★★½ | VALUE ★★★★★ | PRICE RANGE $99–$155

Under the same ownership as the urbane Riverwalk Vista, the rustic Riverwalk Inn is fronted by gas lamps and overlooks the quiet (no boats) south end of the river. The historic King William district is a block south, and all the downtown action is just ten minutes north along the Riverwalk. The Tennessee log cabin design and room names pay homage to Alamo defenders like Davy Crockett and James Bowie. Local storytellers occasionally drop by during breakfast to flesh out the history. An 80-foot front porch lined with rocking chairs invites relaxation and contemplation. Flickering lights above the fireplaces add a romantic touch to the rooms.

SETTING & FACILITIES

Location Riverwalk Parkway, 0.5 mi. south of Alamo **Near** Museums, galleries, parks **Building** Five 1840/1860s 2-story Tennessee log houses combined **Grounds** Fronted by city-maintained native plant/wildflower garden **Public Space** DR **Food & Drink** Expanded cont'l breakfast (1 entree) in DR; beverages all day; evening deserts **Recreation** Golf, biking, horse riding, jogging **Amenities & Services** Conference room (12), slide/overhead projectors

ACCOMMODATIONS

Units 11 **All** Fridge, coffeemaker, phone, cable TV, clock radio, individual heat/AC, shared porch/balcony **Some** Fireplace (9), river views (9), hair dryer & iron (on request) **Bed & Bath** King (2), queen (9); all private baths, showers only **Favorites** Gruene in main building has canopy bed, some weathered furnishings, punched-tin fixtures, upholstered chairs; Austin, the honeymoon favorite, at end of long porch, is most private; 2 uppers have higher ceilings, superior balcony views **Comfort & Decor** Rustic country feel with antiques, weathered doors, polished wood and flagstone floors, beam ceilings, track lighting, four-poster beds, patchwork quilts, rocking chairs, and slate-floor showers.

RATES, RESERVATIONS, & RESTRICTIONS
Deposit 1 night (10-day cancellation for refund minus $15 fee) **Discounts** Corp., gov't **Credit Cards** AE, MC, V, D **Check-In/Out** 3–6 p.m./11 a.m. **Smoking** Designated outdoor areas **Pets** No (cat on premises) **Kids** Yes (but fire regulations allow only 2 occupants per room) **No-Nos** N/A **Minimum Stay** 2–3 days weekends, holidays, special events **Open** All year **Hosts** Tracy & Jan Hammer, 329 Old Guilbeau, San Antonio 78204 **Phone** (210) 212-8300 or toll-free (800) 254-4440 **Fax** (210) 229-9422 **E-mail** innkeeper@riverwalkinn.com **Web** www.riverwalkinn.com

RIVERWALK VISTA, San Antonio

OVERALL ★★★★½ | QUALITY ★★★★★ | VALUE ★★★★ | PRICE RANGE $150–$250

Conveniently situated half a block from the Convention Center and across the street from River Center Mall, Riverwalk Vista opened September 18, 2001. Under the same ownership as the Riverwalk Inn, Riverwalk Vista is a boutique inn with amenities for businesspeople and funky street signs, quilts, and enlarged postcard images of old San Antonio lining the hallways. The boardroom boasts a cast-iron column, windows fronting the lounge, voice conferencing, a magnetic/writeable wall, and digital projection. Rooms reflect downtown history, and down the street is the site of an 1880s store opened by the host's grandfather.

SETTING & FACILITIES

Location Downtown Riverwalk, corner of Alamo, Commerce & Losoya Sts. **Near** Alamo, museums, galleries, parks **Building** 1883 3-story San Antonio–style commercial building, refurbished to 1920s/30s style **Grounds** Opens onto urban street **Public Space** 3 lounges, DR **Food & Drink** Cont'l breakfast in DR; 24-hour fruit, beverage; complimentary bottled water, cookies in room; mini-bar, snack basket; group catering **Recreation** Golf, biking, horse riding **Amenities & Services** Concierge, business center, board room (12), meeting room (25)

ACCOMMODATIONS

Units 17 **All** Robes, hair dryer, clock, sleep machine, 26-in. TV/DVD/VCR, cordless speaker phone, Internet access, safe, iron, ironing board, makeup mirror, fridge, coffeemaker, ceiling fan **Some** Handicap-accessible (1), sitting area (most), connecting rooms **Bed & Bath** King (2), queen (15); all private baths **Favorites** Riverwalk Vista Suite has sitting area overlooking Riverwalk, king bed; Dullnig Suite wraps around bustling street corner, has 3 BRs, queen sleeper sofa in LR, 3 baths **Comfort & Decor** High ceilings, original oversized double-paned windows, longleaf pine floors, some original brick walls, Dutch leather chairs, ottomans, armoires, Restoration Hardware fixtures, wrought iron, recessed lighting, fish bowl on desk, makeup mirrors, granite counters, slate showers with clear glass doors.

RATES, RESERVATIONS, & RESTRICTIONS

Deposit 1 night (10-day cancellation for refund minus $15) **Discounts** Corp., gov't **Credit Cards** AE, MC, V, D **Check-In/Out** Before 6 p.m./11 a.m. **Smoking** No **Pets** No **Kids** Yes **No-Nos** N/A **Minimum Stay** None **Open** All year **Hosts** Tracy & Jan Hammer, 262 Losoya St. , San Antonio 78205 **Phone** (210) 223-3200 or toll-free (866) 898-4782 **Fax** (210) 223-4278 **E-mail** info@riverwalkvista.com **Web** www.riverwalkvista.com

RUCKMAN HAUS BED & BREAKFAST, San Antonio

OVERALL ★★★★ | QUALITY ★★★★ | VALUE ★★★★ | PRICE RANGE $85–$125

On a sloping corner lot across the street from a Montessori school, Ruckman Haus opened in August 2001. Around the corner is the nation's second-oldest municipal park, 46,000-acre San Pedro Springs Park, which has added lighted tennis courts, a playhouse, and meditative pools since being declared public land by Spain's King Philip V in 1729. The hosts, who live in the basement, added a stained-glass door with a mail chute and five body shower jets to the English Room. The third-floor Highlands Room squeezes Scottish accents and an alcove with two extra beds for families under low, sloping ceilings.

SETTING & FACILITIES

Location 2 mi. NW of downtown/Riverwalk **Near** Museums, park **Building** Early 1900s Spanish-influenced 3-story stucco **Grounds** Statuary, oleander, ferns, patio, adding pond **Public Space** LR, DR, kitchen, porch **Food & Drink** Full breakfast in DR, porch, patio, or room; afternoon margarita hour; 24-hour snacks, beverages; kitchen use **Recreation** Golf, biking, horse riding, jogging, tennis **Amenities & Services** Dog run

ACCOMMODATIONS

Units 5, all upstairs **All** Cable TV, phone, data port, clock, coffeemaker, individual heat/AC, ceiling fan **Some** Stocked fridge (1), wet bar (1), private deck (1) **Bed & Bath** Queen; all private baths, claw-foot tub (1), body jet shower (2) **Favorites** Sun Room has Spanish Colonial bed w/ matching secretary, sun porch w/ wicker furnishings, textured yellow walls, gold accents, exposed brick, stocked fridge, wet bar, Texas star table, spiral staircase to private deck, dark blue & yellow tiled bath w/ body jet shower **Comfort & Decor** Varied European themes, stained glass, armoires, colorful textured walls, mostly wood floors and window blinds, sitting areas, tile and wallpaper baths, some glass block.

RATES, RESERVATIONS, & RESTRICTIONS

Deposit Credit card holds (7-day cancellation for refund minus $10; otherwise forfeit 1 night) **Discounts** Weekday corp. **Credit Cards** AE, MC, V, D **Check-In/Out** 3–9 p.m./noon **Smoking** Outside **Pets** Yes (2 dogs, 2 cats on premises) **Kids** Over age 6 **No-Nos** N/A **Minimum Stay** None **Open** All year **Hosts** Ron & Prudence Ruckman, 629 W. French, San Antonio 78212 **Phone** (210) 736-1468 or (210) 422-8681 or toll-free (866) 736-1468 **Fax** (210) 736-1468 **E-mail** theruckmans@earthlink.net **Web** www.ruckmanhaus.com

Utah

Utah is a geological treasure chest of layered sandstone cliffs, red rock canyons, buttes, mesas, pinnacles, arches, spires, and hoodoos. Since becoming Utah Territory under Brigham Young in 1850, the state has grown from a collection of predominately Mormon settlements and Native American tribes into an international destination that hosted the 2002 Winter Olympics. Salt Lake City, the capital, is centered between Provo and Ogden in northern Utah's 100-mile-long Metro-Wasatch Front. The 72-mile-long Great Salt Lake is second only to the Dead Sea in salinity. The Great Salt Lake Desert extends west to the Nevada border and includes the Bonneville Speedway, Dugway Proving Grounds, and vast military no-travel zones. Bear Lake, a 28,000-year-old earthquake-created freshwater lake, stretches across the Idaho border near Garden City. Numerous manmade reservoirs around the state have become water recreation havens, including Jordanelle and Deer Creek Reservoirs near the Midway and Park City Olympic ski venues. The Snow Basin Olympic Super G site, Powder Mountain, and Nordic Valley are accessible from Ogden, Huntsville, Mountain Green, and Eden.

Eastern Utah shares the Flaming Gorge National Recreation Area with Wyoming to the north and Dinosaur National Monument with Colorado to the east, but it is almost devoid of bed-and-breakfasts. Central Utah has descended into a bit of a funk. Once there were dozens of bed-and-breakfasts in small towns like Ephraim, Fillmore, Gunnison, Manti, Marysvale, Monroe, Mt. Pleasant, Nephi, Salina, and Spring City. Most have closed or been put up for sale. Only Manti remains a central Utah bed-and-breakfast stronghold, thanks to its Mormon Temple and summer festival.

Southwestern Utah is easily reached from both Salt Lake City and Las Vegas. St. George is notable for mild weather in a state that gets extremes of summer heat and winter cold. The roads east from St. George lead through

Hurricane, Virgin, Rockville, and Springdale to Zion National Park. About 50 miles north of St. George is Cedar City's summer Shakespeare Festival. The Brian Head ski area, Cedar Breaks National Monument, and Panguitch Lake are west of Panguitch and east of Cedar City. Panguitch, Glendale, and Mt. Carmel are intermediate to Zion and Bryce Canyon National Parks. Tropic and Escalante are near Bryce Canyon and Kodachrome Basin. Torrey, Teasdale, and Hanksville are close to Capitol Reef.

Southeastern Utah is notable for river rafting, jeep touring, Native American rock art, National Parks like Canyonlands and Arches, National Monuments like Hovenweep and Natural Bridges, and State Parks like Dead Horse, Goosenecks, Edge of the Cedars, and Goblin Valley. Green River, Moab, Monticello, Blanding, and Bluff are among the bed-and-breakfast possibilities.

FOR MORE INFORMATION

Bed & Breakfast Inns of Utah, phone (801) 374-8400, www.bbiu.org

Ski Utah, 150 W. 500 South, Salt Lake City, UT 84101; phone (801) 534-1779 or toll-free (800) ski-utah, www.skiutah.com.

Utah Accommodations Guide (published annually; includes dozens of other tourism sources). Utah Travel Council, Council Hall, Salt Lake City, UT 84114; phone (801) 538-1030 or toll-free (800) 200-1160, www.utah.com

Utah Hotel & Lodging Assoc. (co-publishes Utah Accommodations Guide), www.lodgingutah.com

North

Northern Utah is a vast expanse of desert, forest, and mountain stretching from Bear Lake bordering Idaho and the Wyoming border in the northeast to the Nevada state line in the west. The Great Salt Lake, a shallow feeding ground for seagulls (the state bird), and the Great Salt Lake Desert keep the west sparsely populated.

Salt Lake City is home to the state capitol and over 150,000 people; it is as cosmopolitan as it gets in this 2-million-person state. Upscale neighborhoods and old Victorian homes grace the blocks around the granite state capitol. Microbreweries and college hangouts are plentiful, and sports teams like the NBA's Utah Jazz play in the downtown arena. But Mormon culture frowns on caffeine, and the ubiquitous urban corner cappuccino shop is a no-go here. Temple Square, a 10-acre city block enclosed by 15-foot walls, houses the six spires of the Latter Day Saints Temple and the acoustic dome of the Mormon Tabernacle Choir.

South of Salt Lake City is Provo, home to Brigham Young University. North of Salt Lake City, sandwiched between the steep, granite Wasatch Mountains on the east and the Great Salt Lake on the west, is Ogden. A railroad hub with an air force base, Ogden and smaller cities (like Eden, Huntsville, and Mountain Green) are gateways to ski areas like Snow Basin, Powder Mountain, and Nordic Valley.

North of the Olympic ski areas, the bed-and-breakfast scene fades dramatically. Logan and adjacent Providence attract university travelers, local business and wedding trade, and occasional tourists heading from Salt Lake City to Yellowstone National Park. Garden City entices with summer water recreation, the September Mountain Man Rendezvous, and winter snowmobiling at Bear Lake.

Summer water recreation and winter skiing near the Midway and Park City Olympic venues make for year-round fun east of Salt Lake City. Park City is an old silver-mining town with housing terraced up a mountainside and a downtown shopping district below. The big January event is the independent filmmakers festival at Robert Redford's Sundance Institute.

SNOWBERRY INN & BREAKFAST, Eden

OVERALL ★★★ | QUALITY ★★★½ | VALUE ★★★★ | PRICE RANGE $65–$115

Party animals wanting to ski Nordic Valley, Powder Mountain, and Snow Basin will find themselves at home here, as will young families with bunk bed–loving kids. The Snowberry Inn hosts, a young family with children, live in a large loft across from the upstairs guest rooms. The inn exudes a mountain-man feel with high log beam ceilings, timber walls, saltillo tiles, antlers, chainsaws, skis, snowshoes, hanging plants, large ceiling fans, and a mantel lined with beer bottles and glasses. The downstairs game room, near an "undersea" guest room with bunk beds, has a pool table, TV, and darts.

SETTING & FACILITIES
Location Across from Pineview Reservoir, 10 mi. NE of Ogden **Near** Ski slopes, lakes **Building** Contemporary high-ceiling 2-story & basement log cabin style **Grounds** Mostly open space facing mountains, w/ a few trees, flower garden **Public Space** Lounge, gift shop, game room **Food & Drink** Full breakfast in DR **Recreation** Boating, fishing, biking, golf, horse riding, bird-watching, winter sports **Amenities & Services** Hot tub, piano, pool table, TV, darts, massage

ACCOMMODATIONS
Units 7 **All** CD/clock radio **Some** TV (1; first-come, first-served), rocking chair (1) **Bed & Bath** Queen (7), bunks (2); all private baths, tub (1) **Favorites** Alaskan has 1 log wall w/ Eskimo masks, antique table, canopy timber bed, claw-foot tub; Mountain Man has skis on log & wood paneled walls, log bed, stuffed bobcat & bear, makeup lights; carpeted Family Room has timber bunks, log fish sink, ample luggage rack space, underground sea theme **Comfort & Decor** Very basic, mostly white plaster walls, an occasional log cabin–style wall, log and antique sleigh beds, minimal furnishings.

RATES, RESERVATIONS, & RESTRICTIONS
Deposit 25% nonrefundable Dec. 20–April 1 (7-day cancellation policy; 25% fee if less than 7 days) **Discounts** Multiple nights **Credit Cards** AE, MC, V, D **Check-In/Out** After 4 p.m./noon **Smoking** No **Pets** Yes (owners have dogs, cats) **Kids** Yes **No-Nos** N/A **Minimum Stay** None **Open** All year **Hosts** Roger & Kim Arave, 1315 UT 158, Eden 84310 **Phone** (801) 745-2634 or toll-free (888) 334-3466 **Fax** (801) 745-0585 **E-mail** sberryinn@aol.com **Web** snowberryinn.com

EAGLE FEATHER INN, Garden City

OVERALL ★★★½ | QUALITY ★★★½ | VALUE ★★★★ | PRICE RANGE $48–$90

A stand-alone house on a corner lot on the main highway, Eagle Feather is the only Bear Lake bed-and-breakfast on the Utah side of the border (the Idaho side also has bed-and-breakfasts). The living room has eagle photos, a carved wood eagle, wood and upholstered chairs, a sleeper sofa, and a wood floor with throw rugs. Most of the time the whole bed-and-breakfast is rented out to families, some of whom make use of the over 120 miles of groomed snowmobile trails in winter (there is also ice fishing and skiing). Bear Lake, a 28,000-year-old earthquake-created freshwater lake with warm summer waters (60–70° F, June–July), is also the locale for the Mountain Man Rendezvous in September.

SETTING & FACILITIES

Location Across the road from Bear Lake, 3 blocks south of the junction of US 89 & UT 30 **Near** Bear Lake, Idaho border **Building** Single family house **Grounds** Large lawns **Public Space** LR, kitchen, DR **Food & Drink** Cont'l breakfast in DR **Recreation** Fishing, boating, swimming, biking, golf, bird-watching, winter sports **Amenities & Services** TV/VCR, laundry room, kitchen, gas barbecue, hot tub, volleyball net, lawn chairs, parking for boats, RVs, snowmobiles

ACCOMMODATIONS

Units 3 **All** Quilt, digital clock **Some** Private deck (1), desk (1) **Bed & Bath** Queen; all private baths, tub (1) **Favorites** Sun Room behind kitchen has 2 queen beds, desk, sliding glass door to private deck **Comfort & Decor** Pink or blue color scheme, carpeting or wood floors with throw rugs, basic wood and wicker furnishings, botanical and eagle decor.

RATES, RESERVATIONS, & RESTRICTIONS

Deposit 1 night (14-day cancellation for refund; tougher policy for whole house rental) **Discounts** Whole house rentals (no breakfast), 7 nights (pay for 6), off season (Oct. 1–Dec. 14, March 15–May 31) **Credit Cards** MC,V **Check-In/Out** 4 p.m./11 a.m. **Smoking** No **Pets** Yes (in front rooms w/ wood floors; extra charge; owners have dogs) **Kids** Yes **No-Nos** N/A **Minimum Stay** None **Open** All year **Hosts** Elizabeth & Peter Slonek, 135 S. Bear Lake Blvd., Garden City 84028 **Phone** (435) 946-2846 or toll-free (877) 977-2846 **Fax** N/A **E-mail** slonek@dcdi.net **Web** www.go-utah.com/eaglefeatherinn

VALLEY HOUSE INN, Huntsville

OVERALL ★★★★½ | QUALITY ★★★★ | VALUE ★★★★ | PRICE RANGE $99–$179

Winter is high season at Valley House, which is near the Snow Basin Olympic Super G site, Powder Mountain, and Nordic Valley. Summer water enthusiasts are only six blocks from a boat marina. The Shooting Star Saloon on the same block attracts the motorcycle crowd. A Trappist Monastery and Mormon historic sites are also nearby. Unlike Snowberry in nearby Eden, Valley House is decidedly upscale, attracting couples to breakfast on private patios. After passing through a front entrance with a cuckoo clock and chandelier, guests ascend a floral carpeted staircase leading to the rooms and a floral and wicker sitting area.

SETTING & FACILITIES
Location 3 blocks from Pineview Reservoir, 12 mi. east of Ogden on UT 39 **Near** Olympic ski slopes, lakes, Mormon historic sites **Building** 1872 red brick w/ white trim **Grounds** 1 acre of lawns, sitting areas **Public Space** Upstairs LR **Food & Drink** Breakfast in room or on lawn; cider & cookies in room on arrival **Recreation** Golf, biking, fishing, boating, swimming, winter sports **Amenities & Services** N/A

ACCOMMODATIONS
Units 3 suites, all upstairs **All** Large-screen TV/VCR, AC **Some** Gas fireplace (2), electric fireplace (1), balcony (2) **Bed & Bath** Queen beds; all private baths, whirlpool tub (2), claw-foot tub (1) **Favorites** Crystal Palace, a honeymoon favorite, has steam room, whirlpool tub, gilded mirror & roses over white marble fireplace, floral carpeting, breakfast patio; Log Haven has old stove, wood floor, bark walls, antler chandelier over log bed, lantern lights, faux rock fireplace; Enchanted Castle has sauna w/ tape deck, brick walls, beam ceiling, dark woods, gray marble floor, armoire, knights' coats of arms **Comfort & Decor** Very varied, includes contemporary, log cabin, and castle motifs, original wood, sinks in old dressers, antiques, green and burgundy accents.

RATES, RESERVATIONS, & RESTRICTIONS
Deposit Credit card holds (7-day cancellation policy) **Discounts** Weekdays, non–ski season **Credit Cards** AE, MC, V, D **Check-In/Out** 4 p.m./noon **Smoking** No **Pets** No **Kids** Yes (roll-away for 1 child; babies OK) **No-Nos** N/A **Minimum Stay** None **Open** All year **Hosts** Jim & Ruth May, 7318 East 200 South, Huntsville 84317 **Phone** (801) 745-8259 or toll-free (888) 791-8259 **Fax** (801) 745-1035 **E-mail** website@valleyhouseinn.com **Web** www.valleyhouseinn.com

LOGAN HOUSE INN AND CONFERENCE CENTER, Logan

OVERALL ★★★★ | QUALITY ★★★★½ | VALUE ★★★★ | PRICE RANGE $99–$175

Popular with university and high-tech local businesses, as well as the local wedding and anniversary trade, Logan House also gets it share of summer visitors, many staying several nights to catch the full cycle of Utah's summer opera festival. International travelers also stay overnight here, as Logan is a stopping place on the route between Los Angeles, Salt Lake City, and Yellowstone National Park. The entry to Logan House has a large figurine candlestick sculpture, a brass chest, and a floral watercolor beneath a coat rack.

A wood travel chest doubles as a table in the living room, where a green floral sofa faces a fireplace mantel topped with a stained-glass village.

SETTING & FACILITIES
Location Downtown **Near** University, national forest **Building** 1890s 3-story Georgian Manor **Grounds** Shade trees, blue swinging bench **Public Space** LR, DR, porch **Food & Drink** Full breakfast in DR or room **Recreation** Fishing, boating, biking, golf, horse riding, winter sports **Amenities & Services** Receptions (300 people), piano

ACCOMMODATIONS
Units 6 **All** TV/VCR, phone, data port, AC, ceiling fan **Some** Fireplace (4), balcony (1), handicap-accessible (1) **Bed & Bath** King (1), queen (4), 2 doubles (1); all private baths, whirlpool tub **Favorites** Veranda Suite has windowed sitting area, tan brick walls, wood floors, fireplace, bath w/ columns over black tub, B&W floor tiles, gilded mirror, fluted-glass fixtures; burgundy & white Library has 500 books in dark cherry bookcases, track lighting, fireplace, metal globe, four-poster queen bed; Master Suite has columned king bed, fireplace, balcony **Comfort & Decor** Combines English country style, modern art, high ceilings, molding, glass-topped tables, upholstered chairs, reading lamps, antique armoires, leaded glass, shutters, wrought iron, brick, plaid bedspreads, and brass fixtures.

RATES, RESERVATIONS, & RESTRICTIONS
Deposit Full amount at time of reservation ("firm cancellation policies") **Discounts** Group, corp. **Credit Cards** AE, MC, V, D, DC **Check-In/Out** 4–6 p.m./11 a.m. **Smoking** No **Pets** No **Kids** Yes **No-Nos** N/A **Minimum Stay** None **Open** All year **Hosts** Rod & Marion Vaughn, 168 North 100 East, Logan 84321 **Phone** (435) 752-7727 or toll-free (800) 478-7459 **Fax** (435) 752-0092 **E-mail** loganinn@loganhouseinn.com **Web** www.loganhouseinn.com

BLUE BOAR INN, Midway

OVERALL ★★★★★ | QUALITY ★★★★★ | VALUE ★★★★ | PRICE RANGE $150–$295

Near the Olympic cross-country ski venue and five golf courses, Blue Boar Inn boasts a fine dining restaurant lined with paintings. A dark wood and stone pub has a boar's head over the fireplace and 150-year-old French tavern tables. A big blue boar is painted on the front of the building and, lest anyone forget, a cuddly toy boar is in each room. Far from boorish, each guest room is named after a famous author and stocked with that author's books to fight boredom. The best rooms have private patios or sitting areas with bay windows.

SETTING & FACILITIES
Location 20 mi. south of Park City **Near** Olympic ski slopes **Building** Swiss country style w/ stones, turret **Grounds** Small patio, herb garden **Public Space** Restaurant, pub, upstairs sitting area w/ chess table, deck **Food & Drink** Full breakfast in restaurant; afternoon snacks; bottled water; lunch & dinner Tues.–Sat.; special event catering **Recreation**

Golf, biking, fishing, boating, horse riding, winter sports **Amenities & Services** Meeting room (16), receptions, elevator, turn-down, fresh flowers

ACCOMMODATIONS
Units 14 **All** Robes, satellite TV/VCR, gas fireplace, clock, data port, hair dryer, makeup mirror, individual AC/heat **Some** Handicap-accessible (1), patio **Bed & Bath** King, queen; all private baths, jetted tub (13) **Favorites** Shakespeare suite has tan florals, upholstered love seat, shuttered windows above jetted tub surrounded by pedestals; Rudyard Kipling has tiger pillows on striped chairs, silver elephants on black bedspread; Jane Austin has small patio, lots of wood, blue florals **Comfort & Decor** Varied author-related themes, feather beds, shuttered windows, light wood trim, dark wood furnishings, high ceilings in suites, some sitting areas, floral carpets and fabrics, stained glass.

RATES, RESERVATIONS, & RESTRICTIONS
Deposit 1 night on booking (full payment 14 days before arrival; 30-day cancellation for full refund; under 14 days cancellation forfeits full cost of stay) **Discounts** Inquire **Credit Cards** AE, MC, V, D **Check-In/Out** 3 p.m./noon **Smoking** No **Pets** No **Kids** Yes **No-Nos** N/A **Minimum Stay** None **Open** All year **Hosts** Jay & Sandy Niederhauser, 1235 Warm Springs Rd., P.O. Box 1299, Midway 84049 **Phone** (435) 654-1400 or toll-free (888) 650-1400 **Fax** (435) 654-6459 **E-mail** innkeeper@theblueboarinn.com **Web** www.theblueboarinn.com

INN ON THE CREEK, Midway

OVERALL ★★★★ | QUALITY ★★★★★ | VALUE ★★★★ | PRICE RANGE $145–$195 ($135–$765 CHALETS)

In a gated community with a golf course, guests enter the Inn on the Creek via a typical hotel-style marble reception near the restaurant. Besides the 8 bed-and-breakfast rooms in the main building, there are 32 chalet rooms ranging from studios to five-bedroom units with kitchens that can sleep 20. The Norwegian ski team rented most of the chalets for the 2002 Winter Olympics, as nearby Soldier Hollow ski park was the cross-country and biathlon venue. There is no knowledgeable innkeeper hanging around to help out, but the surrounding area has an abundance of water sports, golf, and ski opportunities.

SETTING & FACILITIES
Location Heber Valley, 20 mi. south of Park City **Near** Olympic ski slopes **Building** 1990s European chalet style **Grounds** Small pond w/ wooden foot bridge overlooks golf course **Public Space** Lobby, restaurant **Food & Drink** Cont'l breakfast in restaurant; lunch, dinner; event catering **Recreation** Golf, biking, fishing, boating, horse riding, winter sports **Amenities & Services** Pool & hot tub (summer only), video library (fee), massage, flowers, weddings (200)

ACCOMMODATIONS
Units 8 rooms in main building, plus 32 chalet rooms **All** TV, phone, hair dryer, digital alarm clock, coffeemaker, ceiling fan, fireplace, balcony **Some** Sofa sleepers **Bed & Bath**

King beds; all private baths, jetted tub **Favorites** French Legacy (#1) has patio w/ wood table & chairs overlooking golf course, wicker & wood four-poster bed, manor house & architectural detail drawings; English Traditional (#7) has tan tones w/ hints of lavender, white shutters over sliding door opening to patio w/ mountain views **Comfort & Decor** Very elegant, with carved-wood or painted armoire, two or three layers of pillows, some vaulted ceilings and skylights, furnishings of oak, cherry, other woods.

RATES, RESERVATIONS, & RESTRICTIONS

Deposit Required (48-hour cancellation policy enforced) **Discounts** Groups, midweek, extended stays **Credit Cards** AE, MC, V, D, DC **Check-In/Out** 3 p.m./11 a.m. **Smoking** No **Pets** No **Kids** Not allowed in main building rooms, but OK in chalet rooms **No-Nos** N/A **Minimum Stay** None **Open** All year **Hosts** Kent & Pauline Perry, 375 Rainbow Lane, P.O. Box 1000, Midway 84049 **Phone** (435) 654-0892 or toll-free (800) 654-0892 **Fax** (435) 654-5871 **E-mail** info@innoncreek.com **Web** www.innoncreek.com

HUBBARD HOUSE, Mountain Green

OVERALL ★★★ | QUALITY ★★★½ | VALUE ★★★★ | PRICE RANGE $55–$149

Nine miles from the Snow Basin Olympic downhill and slalom action, Hubbard House has expanded to ten rooms, which will hopefully fill with business traffic and Forest Service workers. Many guests here are visiting relatives in Ogden, but Hubbard House is expanding parking from 14 to 33 spaces to appeal to more groups. The proprietor, who has lived here since 1971 and operated the bed-and-breakfast for seven years, welcomes horses to use the corral space. The front porch, a good lemonade drinking venue on hot summer days, has the best Wasatch Mountain views.

SETTING & FACILITIES

Location 10 mi. SE of Ogden, I-84, Exit 92 **Near** Ski slopes, lakes **Building** 1928 brown brick Stickley w/ front porch, barn wing **Grounds** 1.5 acres w/ fields, trees, horse corral **Public Space** DR, porch **Food & Drink** Full breakfast in DR or room **Recreation** Fishing, boating, hunting, golf, winter sports **Amenities & Services** Hot tub, group room

ACCOMMODATIONS

Units 10 **All** TV, phone jack **Some** VCR, ceiling fan, phone (optional) **Bed & Bath** King (2), queen (8); 4 private baths, 3 shared, tubs (6), whirlpool tub (1) **Favorites** Tack Room has barn wood walls, tongue & groove cedar floor, green rug, leather chair, round wood table, covered wagon atop dresser, small boots, serape, bucking bronco picture, horse tiles above jetted tub **Comfort & Decor** Small rustic barn wing rooms have unfinished pine, old barn wood, dressers, end tables, chairs, Western accents; main house has pink or white walls, some stained glass, desks, sofa sleepers, wood floors with throw rugs, pedestal sinks, small shared baths.

RATES, RESERVATIONS, & RESTRICTIONS

Deposit Credit card holds (3-day cancellation for refund minus $15; 50% if cancel on arrival date) **Discounts** Groups, extended stays, frequent visitors **Credit Cards** AE, MC, V, D **Check-In/Out** 4 p.m./noon **Smoking** Front porch, outdoors **Pets** Yes (prior approval needed; owner has outdoor cats; horses welcome) **Kids** Yes **No-Nos** N/A **Minimum Stay** None **Open** All year **Hosts** Don & Gloria Hubbard, 5648 W. Old Hwy Rd., Mountain Green 84050 **Phone** (801) 876-2020 or toll-free (800) 815-2220 **Fax** N/A **E-mail** hubbhouse@aol.com **Web** www.hubbardhouse.com

1904 IMPERIAL HOTEL, Park City

OVERALL ★★★½ | QUALITY ★★★½ | VALUE ★★★★ | PRICE RANGE $80–$245

Before being restored as a 1900s-style B&B, the 1904 Imperial Hotel served stints as a boarding house for silver miners, bordello, and apartment building. Across the street from a microbrewery, stone steps lead to a small comfortably upholstered purple lounge with a ceiling fan, fireplace, dark woods, and blue-green carpeting. An adjacent shop sells coffee, juices, and snacks. Each room is named after an old silver mine in the area. Locals come here for one-night summer stays when rates are lowest. During winter skiers sign up for individual times to use the indoor hot tub.

SETTING & FACILITIES

Location Downtown **Near** Ski slopes, recreational reservoirs **Building** 1904 3-story miner's boarding house, restored in 1987; on National Register of Historic Landmarks **Grounds** Opens onto street **Public Space** Lounge, DR, patio **Food & Drink** Full breakfast in DR or patio (summer); afternoon refreshments **Recreation** Golf, biking, horse riding, fishing, boating, winter sports **Amenities & Services** Hot tub, groups (10–15 best)

ACCOMMODATIONS

Units 10 **All** Robes, down comforters, phone, cable TV **Some** VCR (on request), quilt (2) **Bed & Bath** King (2), queen (7), twins (1), tub (1); all private baths, Roman tub (7), clawfoot tub (1) **Favorites** Little Belle has balcony, Main St. access; Anchor Room has king bed, spiral staircase to loft w/ twin beds **Comfort & Decor** Casual mix of modern functional and early 1900s Victorian furnishings, period color schemes, replica wallpaper, wood molding, tailored lace curtains, gray tiled baths.

RATES, RESERVATIONS, & RESTRICTIONS

Deposit Complex policy toughest in winter (Nov. 20–April 15, or when ski lifts are open) when 50% is due within 90 days of arrival, balance within 30 days of arrival, and 30-day cancellation policy for refund minus 1 night nonrefundable deposit; 1 night deposit and 72-hour summer cancellation policy **Discounts** Groups (off-peak, non–ski times), whole hotel rental, off-season **Credit Cards** AE, MC, V, D **Check-In/Out** 4 p.m./11 a.m. **Smoking** No **Pets** No **Kids** Yes **No-Nos** Candles **Minimum Stay** None (except holiday weekends, special events) **Open** All year **Hosts** Nancy McLaughlin, Donna Ferguson, and Karen Hart, 221 Historic Main St., P.O. Box 1628, Park City 84060 **Phone** (435) 649-1904 or toll-free (800) 669-utah **Fax** (435) 645-7421 **E-mail** stay@1904imperial.com **Web** www.1904imperial.com

ANGEL HOUSE INN, Park City

OVERALL ★★★★½ | QUALITY ★★★★½ | VALUE ★★★★ | PRICE RANGE $125–$305

At Angel House the rooms have angel names and themes. But skiers seem more interested in skiing to lunch on Main Street, the adjacent Town Lift to Park City Mountain Resort, and the Quitting Time ski run terminus nearby. The purple-carpeted living room has stained glass, lavender chairs, a floral sofa, and an elaborately carved fireplace surrounded by crystals, brass Asian divinities, and angels. The dining room decor changes seasonally and may include china, crystal, depression glass, a lace tablecloth, and flowers. The hostess, a former intensive care nurse, also rents out an adjoining condo with two hot tubs.

SETTING & FACILITIES
Location Downtown **Near** Ski slopes, recreational reservoirs **Building** 1889 Queen Anne Victorian, 1989 redesigned as inn **Grounds** Hillside rock garden w/ wildflowers, hammock, cottonwood trees **Public Space** LR, DR **Food & Drink** Full breakfast in DR; afternoon snacks; fridge w/ 24-hour beverages, snacks; in-room catering; spring–summer picnic baskets **Recreation** Golf, biking, horse riding, fishing, boating, winter sports **Amenities & Services** Hot tub, ski storage, TV/VCR, stereo, ministerial services, weddings (20)

ACCOMMODATIONS
Units 9 **All** Phone (modem), down comforter, clock, hair dryer **Some** TV (5), roll-away bed **Bed & Bath** King (1), queen (8); all private baths, claw-foot tub (3), tub (6) **Favorites** Victoria has bay window w/ rose quartz & crystal stained-glass angel, antique French burl veneer bed, hand-painted melted glass lamp, French bed & porcelain Victorian dolls, TV atop old French bar **Comfort & Decor** Victorian look with antiques and reproduction furnishings, tapestry or brocade floral bedspreads, antique window molding, and angel artwork.

RATES, RESERVATIONS, & RESTRICTIONS
Deposit Ski season, 1 night w/ full payment 30 days before arrival (45-day cancellation for refund minus $25; 30–44 days forfeits 1 night; 29 days loses all) **Discounts** Summer, group, AAA, senior **Credit Cards** AE, MC, V, D, DC **Check-In/Out** 3 p.m./11 a.m. **Smoking** No **Pets** No (owners have cat) **Kids** Yes (over age 12, precrawling infants) **No-Nos** N/A **Minimum Stay** 4 nights ski season (Jan.–April), special events **Open** All year **Hosts** Joe & Jan Fisher-Rush, 713 Norfolk Ave., P.O. Box 159, Park City 84060 **Phone** (435) 647-0338 or toll-free (800) angel-01 **Fax** (435) 655-8524 **E-mail** info@angelhouse inn.com **Web** www.angelhouseinn.com

THE OLD MINERS' LODGE, Park City

OVERALL ★★★½ | QUALITY ★★★★ | VALUE ★★★★ | PRICE RANGE $70–$270

Twenty stone steps lead up the hillside to the Old Miners' Lodge, but in winter many prefer to ski in. Indeed, amenities like bike and ski storage and chairlift proximity are major attractions. The lodge, formerly a small hotel and married miner apartments, is now under the same ownership as the 1904 Imperial Hotel. All the rooms reflect Park City history. For example, the "Black Jack" Murphy room is named after a miner who typified the Old West ethic of shoot first and ask questions later. He was hanged for shooting a claim jumper in the back.

SETTING & FACILITIES
Location Downtown **Near** Ski slopes, recreational reservoirs **Building** 1890 2-story gray wood, newer back rooms **Grounds** Gazebo, deck **Public Space** LR, DR, porch **Food & Drink** Full breakfast in DR; afternoon refreshments; ice machine, guest fridge **Recreation** Golf, biking, horse riding, fishing, boating, winter sports, hot-air ballooning **Amenities & Services** Hot tub, bike & ski storage, meetings

ACCOMMODATIONS
Units 12 **All** Robes, down comforter, digital clock, iron & ironing board **Some** Fridge (3), phone (on request), ceiling fan (8) **Bed & Bath** King (4), queen (6), doubles (2); all full baths, tub (11) **Favorites** Jedidiah Grant Suite steps down to king bed, 2 twin beds, enclosed porch, panoramic town views, green & purple w/ pink & white stripes, claw-foot tub; "Black Jack" Murphy has log cabin–style entry, mining theme **Comfort & Decor** Very basic furnishings, varied room themes reflecting persons in Park City history.

RATES, RESERVATIONS, & RESTRICTIONS
Deposit Winter ski season (Nov. 20–April 15), 1 night nonrefundable deposit, 50% 90 days prior to arrival, balance 30 days before arrival (30-day cancellation for refund minus 1 night); summer, 1 night (72-hour cancellation for full refund) **Discounts** Group **Credit Cards** AE, MC, V, D, DC **Check-In/Out** 2–6 p.m./noon **Smoking** No **Pets** No (hosts have dog) **Kids** Yes **No-Nos** N/A **Minimum Stay** None (except holidays, special events) **Open** All year **Hosts** Hugh Daniels & Susan Wynne, 615 Woodside Ave., P.O. Box 2639, Park City 84060 **Phone** (435) 645-8068 or toll-free (800) 648-8068 **Fax** (435) 645-7420 **E-mail** stay@oldminerslodge.com **Web** www.oldminerslodge.com

WASHINGTON SCHOOL INN, Park City

OVERALL ★★★★½ | QUALITY ★★★★½ | VALUE ★★★★ | PRICE RANGE $95–$395

A public school from 1889 until closed by declining enrollments in 1931, and one of the few buildings surviving the great fire of 1898, Washington School is as luxurious as it gets in this former mining town turned touristy Olympic ski resort. Rooms book up a year in advance for ski season. After climbing cement steps to register in the burgundy-and-turquoise living room with its red leather seating and fireplace, guests get a coveted Park City parking pass. Rooms are reached via staircases and hallways with pink floral–patterned black carpets, seating, and green plants.

SETTING & FACILITIES
Location Downtown, 1 block from Main Street **Near** Ski slopes, recreational reservoirs **Building** 1889 limestone, 1985 renovation into inn **Grounds** Hillside w/ veranda, wood deck **Public Space** LR, mezzanine, DR, porch **Food & Drink** Full breakfast in DR; afternoon snacks; 24-hour beverages **Recreation** Fishing, boating, golf, horse riding, winter sports **Amenities & Services** Sauna, hot tub, ski lockers, TV/VCR, office, Internet access, meeting room

ACCOMMODATIONS
Units 11 rooms, 3 suites **All** Robes, phone, digital clock radio, bath amenities **Some** Internet access (suites), TV, fireplace **Bed & Bath** King, queen, doubles, twins; all private baths, tub **Favorites** Miss Thatcher (#310) has angled ceilings, black carpet w/ salmon & white florals, brown wallpaper w/ white florals, brown wicker w/ magenta cushions, gilded mirror above brick gas fireplace, Renaissance tapestry, 2 desks, cable TV, four-poster queen bed, town-view tub **Comfort & Decor** Varied plush decor includes quality antiques, dark woods, upholstered furnishings, wicker, wallpaper, and florals.

RATES, RESERVATIONS, & RESTRICTIONS
Deposit Ski season (Nov. 23–April 3) pay 1 night at booking, balance 45 days before arrival (60-day cancellation for refund minus $25; 30–59 days forfeit 1 night; 30 days or less forfeit full payment) **Discounts** Whole house rental (summer) **Credit Cards** AE, MC, V **Check-In/Out** Any time after 11 a.m./11 a.m. **Smoking** No **Pets** No **Kids** Yes (over age 8) **No-Nos** N/A **Minimum Stay** 4–5 nights winter ski weekends, holidays **Open** All year **Hosts** Nancy Beaufait & Delphine Covington, 543 Park Ave., Park City 84060 **Phone** (435) 649-3800 or toll-free (800) 824-1672 **Fax** (435) 649-3802 **E-mail** washinn@xmission.com **Web** www.washingtonschoolinn.com

PROVIDENCE INN, Providence

OVERALL ★★★ | QUALITY ★★★★ | VALUE ★★★★ | PRICE RANGE $69–$229

Originally known as the Rock Meeting House, the Rock Church portion of the Providence Inn is often rented out separately as a wedding chapel. A parlor separate from the powder blue and white living and dining rooms can be closed off for use by wedding parties. The Georgian wing third story, added in recent years when the inn was a senior citizen home, contains six smallish queen rooms. The first- and second-story king rooms and the king suites in the back of the property are by far the best and have the added option of breakfast in the room.

SETTING & FACILITIES
Location Just south of Logan **Near** University, Wasatch-Cache National Forest **Building** 1871 rock church w/ 1926 3-story brick Georgian wing **Grounds** Century-old trees **Public Space** LR, parlor, DR **Food & Drink** Full breakfast in DR or in king rooms **Recreation** Fishing, boating, biking, golf, horse riding, winter sports **Amenities & Services** Wedding chapel (seats 120)

ACCOMMODATIONS

Units 15 **All** TV/VCR **Some** Fireplace, hair dryer **Bed & Bath** King (9), queen (6); all private baths, each w/ jetted tub **Favorites** English Cottage, 1 of 3 king suites, has linoleum entry w/ sink & cuckoo clock, living room w/ red carnation sofa, fireplace, wood dining set, leather & upholstered chairs, rocking chair, armoire w/ TV, heart-shaped jetted tub, red-curtained shower, double sinks w/ large mirror, separate toilet stall, English countryside pictures **Comfort & Decor** Very varied, as each room has a different theme, like Monet, Van Gogh, Colonial, Old Mill Pond, Pioneer Home, Cape Cod, Rose Garden, Victorian, New Orleans; ranges from plastered walls with borders to wood paneling, wicker or wood furnishings, upholstered or wrought-iron chairs, four-poster metal canopy to timber beds.

RATES, RESERVATIONS, & RESTRICTIONS

Deposit N/A; 7-day cancellation policy **Discounts** Corp., groups **Credit Cards** AE, MC, V, D, DC **Check-In/Out** 4 p.m./11 a.m. **Smoking** No **Pets** No **Kids** Yes **No-Nos** N/A **Minimum Stay** None **Open** All year **Hosts** Various duty managers, 10 S. Main, P.O. Box 99, Providence 84332 **Phone** (435) 752-3432 or toll-free (800) 480-4943 **Fax** (435) 752-3482 **E-mail** provinn@providenceinn.com **Web** www.providenceinn.com

HINE'S MANSION, Provo

OVERALL ★★★★ | QUALITY ★★★★½ | VALUE ★★★★ | PRICE RANGE $99–$199

A good stopping place for those with business or a conference to attend in Provo, Hine's Mansion processes guests efficiently and provides ample luxury. Indeed, the reception desk is strategically located midway between the kitchen and front room for maximum efficiency. The front room has a white marble fireplace, white sofas, burgundy carpets, stained glass, and a crystal chandelier. About half the clientele is local, many here for anniversaries, honeymoons, and birthdays. The out-of-state half is typically here on Brigham Young University business or to visit friends and family. Though far from the Olympic slopes around Park City, the mansion also hosts a smattering of skiers in winter. Basically, this is a backwater outpost compared to more cosmopolitan Salt Lake City an hour to the north.

SETTING & FACILITIES

Location Downtown, off I-15, Exit 268 near corner of University Ave. & Center St. **Near** Lakes, rivers, museums, Park City, Salt Lake City **Building** 1895 3-story red-brick Victorian **Grounds** Corner lot w/ koi pond in front **Public Space** LR, DR **Food & Drink** Full breakfast in DR; cider in room; evening fruit, cookies **Recreation** Golf, fishing, boating, winter sports **Amenities & Services** Soda vending machine, piano

ACCOMMODATIONS

Units 9 **All** Robes, TV/VCR, clock radio, stereo **Some** Pedestal sink **Bed & Bath** King, queen; all private baths, 2-person whirlpool tub (9) **Favorites** Penthouse occupies entire top floor, has vaulted ceilings, 2 chandeliers, large-screen TV; Country Garden near front door has sunken bed area, wood furnishings, brick & ivy wallpaper **Comfort & Decor** An eclectic mix of varied Victoriana-like gilt-framed mirrors, stained glass, marble, crystal, carpeting, wallpaper, and eccentricities like Cabin Fever, a room with antlers on the brick wall and timber furnishings.

RATES, RESERVATIONS, & RESTRICTIONS
Deposit I night (7-day cancellation for refund minus fee) **Discounts** Corp., weekday, other (inquire) **Credit Cards** AE, MC, V, D **Check-In/Out** 4–6 p.m./I I a.m. **Smoking** No **Pets** No **Kids** Not encouraged (need separate rooms) **No-Nos** N/A **Minimum Stay** None **Open** All year **Hosts** Sandi & Gene Henderson, 383 West 100 South, Provo 84601 **Phone** (801) 374-8400 or toll-free (800) 428-5636 **Fax** (801) 374-0823 **E-mail** grhenderson@enol.com **Web** www.hinesmansion.com

THE ANNIVERSARY INN—SOUTH TEMPLE, Salt Lake City

OVERALL ★★★ | QUALITY ★★★★ | VALUE ★★★ | PRICE RANGE $119–$369

Those who shy away from bed-and-breakfasts because they seem too personal might find the Anniversary Inn the perfect compromise, as it gets about as personal as a convenience store. The inn combines a front desk almost on par with the downtown Motel 6 with some imaginative rooms that the locals genuinely love. The flights of fancy in this old mansion are wild and far-flung, ranging from the Hayloft (cheapest room), Neptune's Cave, Mysteries of Egypt, Jungle Safari, and Savannah Nights to Secret Garden, Sultan's Palace, and Phantom of the Opera. It sells out often enough that the same corporate enterprise has a second property in Salt Lake City, Anniversary Inn—Salt City Jail, with 36 more choices, including repeats of favorites like Phantom of the Opera.

SETTING & FACILITIES
Location Downtown, about 7 blocks from Temple Square **Near** State capitol, university, museums, state offices **Building** 1889 Queen Anne Victorian mansion **Grounds** Flower garden, century-old trees, Masonic Temple park next door **Public Space** Lobby **Food & Drink** Cont'l breakfast in guest room; cider in room on arrival; free cheesecake **Recreation** Boating, fishing, biking, golf, winter sports **Amenities & Services** N/A

ACCOMMODATIONS
Units 13 **All** Surround sound stereo, large-screen TV, triple sheeting, phone, clock **Some** Fireplace **Bed & Bath** King, queen; all private baths, jetted tub **Favorites** Mysteries of Egypt is decorated to look like the inside of a pharaoh's tomb; Kahn Mansion Suite has chessboard table, carved wood chairs & bed, deep burgundy color, rose floral carpet, bath w/ B&W marble, gray tiles, arches, & pillars **Comfort & Decor** Each room is very varied, ranging from enchanted forest trees and jungle murals to almost traditional in the President's Quarters and Anniversary Inn Suite.

RATES, RESERVATIONS, & RESTRICTIONS
Deposit Credit card holds (48-hour cancellation policy) **Discounts** AAA **Credit Cards** AE, MC, V, D **Check-In/Out** After 5 p.m./noon ($25 fee for early arrival or late checkout)

Smoking No **Pets** No **Kids** Small children not welcome **No-Nos** N/A **Minimum Stay** None **Open** All year **Host** Todd Crawford, 678 E. South Temple, Salt Lake City 84102 **Phone** (801) 363-4900 or toll-free (800) 324-4152 **Fax** N/A **E-mail** jkirkland@ anniversaryinn.com **Web** www.anniversaryinn.com

ANTON BOXRUD BED & BREAKFAST, Salt Lake City

OVERALL ★★★★ | QUALITY ★★★★ | VALUE ★★★★ | PRICE RANGE $69–$140

Around the corner from the Armstrong Mansion and the Anniversary Inn, Anton Boxrud attracts skiers in winter and single business travelers all year. The old gentleman's smoking room was converted into a guest business office to meet business demand. Romantics can use the concierge service for tickets, flowers, and other special requests. Only two rooms share a wall and no room is above another, relative quiet prevails. Coffee is poured from antique Bavarian china, and cinnamon buns and stuffed toast are served on linens with fresh flowers. The front porch, next to a large stained-glass window, and the TV room by the rose-wallpapered fireplace are favored snacking and socializing venues.

SETTING & FACILITIES

Location Downtown, 7 blocks from Temple Square **Near** State capitol, university, museums, government offices **Building** 1901 pink 2-story Victorian w/ gray & white trim **Grounds** Backyard grape arbor **Public Space** LR, DR, front porch, downstairs bath **Food & Drink** Full breakfast in DR or on porch; chocolates in room; 24-hour snacks, beverages; private dinners by arrangement **Recreation** Boating, fishing, biking, golf, winter sports **Amenities & Services** Hot tub, business office (phone, fax, copier, modem), meetings (10 or fewer), covered parking, concierge

ACCOMMODATIONS

Units 7 **All** Robes, down comforter, bath amenities, ceiling fan, clock radio **Some** Marble & wrought-iron baker's racks in bath (2) **Bed & Bath** King (1), queen (5), single (1); 5 private baths, 2 shared, tub (2), whirlpool tub (1) **Favorites** Queen Suite has large jetted tub w/ lace drapes, oval-mirrored armoire, oak sleigh bed, tapestries; Grandma's Hideaway (#7) has king & roll-away bed in angled attic alcove, wicker sitting area, fainting couch, artificial white roses **Comfort & Decor** Lace curtains, eclectic mix of old and new furniture, stained glass, modern baths with tile floors, gilded mirrors, pedestal sinks.

RATES, RESERVATIONS, & RESTRICTIONS

Deposit Credit card holds (14-day cancellation for refund minus $25) **Discounts** Whole house rental, meetings **Credit Cards** AE, MC, V, D, DC **Check-In/Out** After 2 p.m./11:30 a.m. **Smoking** No **Pets** No (owner has white terrier) **Kids** Yes (under age 10 requires special arrangement) **No-Nos** N/A **Minimum Stay** None **Open** All year **Host** Jane Johnson, 57 South 600 East, Salt Lake City 84102 **Phone** (801) 363-8035 or toll-free (800) 524-5511 **Fax** (801) 596-1316 **E-mail** antonboxrud@attbi.com **Web** www.antonboxrud.com

ARMSTRONG MANSION BED AND BREAKFAST, Salt Lake City

OVERALL ★★★★½ | QUALITY ★★★★½ | VALUE ★★★★ | PRICE RANGE $99–$229

Built at the close of the nineteenth century by a former mayor known for inducing harmony between the city's Mormons and non-Mormons, Armstrong Mansion was one of the first homes here to have piped-in running water. Though it bills itself locally as a romantic weekend getaway and floral decor abounds, the location and consistent service also make the mansion a weekday favorite with business travelers. Fluted-glass fixtures, an abundance of hand-carved wood, and a parlor with antiques and an ornate ceiling mark the entry. Room themes reflect the months of the year, and the passage of time is marked in Cherished Years, the attic room containing decorated storage trunks.

SETTING & FACILITIES

Location Downtown, 7 blocks from Temple Square **Near** State capitol, university, museums, government offices **Building** 1893 red-brick Queen Anne Victorian **Grounds** Fence encloses shrubbery, off-street parking **Public Space** LR, DR, sitting areas each floor **Food & Drink** Full breakfast in DR; basket w/ sparkling cider in rooms; beverages, snacks **Recreation** Boating, fishing, biking, golf, winter sports **Amenities & Services** Elevator, meetings/groups

ACCOMMODATIONS

Units 13 **All** Scented candle, feather duvet, TV/VCR, phone, digital clock, radiator, central AC/heat **Some** Robes (larger rooms), pedestal sink, fireplace (most not operational) **Bed & Bath** King (3), queen (10); all private baths, jetted tubs (11), tub (1) **Favorites** February Interlude has Victorian Valentine theme, maroon carpet, wrought-iron spiral staircase to turret w/ whirlpool & shower; December Dreams has lighted Christmas tree, patterned tile floor, painted ceiling, huge display cabinet, angel & dried poinsettias atop mirrored armoire, quilt on wall above jetted tub **Comfort & Decor** Varied room themes reflect months of year; most have Victorian elegance, molding, stencils, garlands, Armstrong family photos, armoires (some beveled glass), and stained glass.

RATES, RESERVATIONS, & RESTRICTIONS

Deposit 1 night (7-day cancellation for refund minus $25) **Discounts** Groups, meetings, whole house rental **Credit Cards** AE, MC, V, D, DC **Check-In/Out** 3 p.m./11 a.m. **Smoking** No **Pets** No (exceptions require special arrangement, deposit) **Kids** Yes **No-Nos** N/A **Minimum Stay** None **Open** All year **Hosts** Dave & Judy Savage, 667 East 100 South, Salt Lake City 84102 **Phone** (801) 531-1333 or toll-free (800) 708-1333 **Fax** (801) 531-0282 **E-mail** inkeeper@armstrong-bb.com **Web** www.armstrong-bb.com

BRIGHAM STREET INN, *Salt Lake City*

OVERALL ★★★★½ | QUALITY ★★★★½ | VALUE ★★★★ | PRICE RANGE $125–$185

A favorite among those in Salt Lake City for business downtown and at the nearby University of Utah, Brigham Street Inn is on a tree-lined residential street within 15 minutes walking distance of the urban action. The excellent beds are a major attraction here, as are the dual living rooms that allow for private meetings. When this mansion was restored into a bed-and-breakfast in 1982, different interior design teams took charge of each room and came up with distinctive solutions to the angled ceilings, bay windows, and sitting areas. Rooms 1–3 are sunniest. Only Room 4 has a balcony. Rooms 1 and 2 have connecting doors, though Room 1's huge bathroom is outside off the hallway. Rooms 6–8 are the highest and most visually interesting angled-ceiling uppers.

SETTING & FACILITIES

Location Residential neighborhood NE of downtown **Near** Temple Square, state capitol, downtown, Univ. of Utah, museums **Building** 1898 3-story red brick Victorian on National Register of Historic Places **Grounds** Off-street parking in back near carriage house **Public Space** 2 LRs, DR **Food & Drink** Cont'l breakfast in DR; snacks; 24-hour fridge access **Recreation** Boating, fishing, biking, golf, winter sports **Amenities & Services** 24-hour service

ACCOMMODATIONS

Units 9, all upstairs **All** Robes, cable TV, clock radio, phone, makeup mirror, trouser rack **Some** Fireplace (5), balcony (1), VCR **Bed & Bath** King (5), queen (3), twin (1); all private baths, tub (5), whirlpool tub (1) **Favorites** Room 7 has deep blue wallpaper, mirror above maple fireplace, whiskey barrel, king bed, angled ceiling; Room 9 is ground-level suite w/

private garden entrance, ceiling fan, kitchen, double whirlpool tub, sleeper sofa **Comfort & Decor** Each room is distinctively furnished, some with wood paneling, sponge-painted walls, bay windows with seating, ceiling molding, glass-topped tables and desks, high-quality dark wood and bamboo furnishings, and rich fabrics.

RATES, RESERVATIONS, & RESTRICTIONS

Deposit 1 night (48-hour cancellation for full refund) **Discounts** Locally advertised specials, frequent guests **Credit Cards** AE, MC, V **Check-In/Out** 3 p.m./11 a.m. **Smoking** No **Pets** No **Kids** Yes **No-Nos** N/A **Minimum Stay** None **Open** All year **Hosts** Spence Eccles family, 1135 E. South Temple, Salt Lake City 84102 **Phone** (801) 364-4461 or toll-free (800) 417-4461 **Fax** (801) 521-3201 **E-mail** N/A **Web** www.brigham streetinn.citysearch.com

HAXTON MANOR, Salt Lake City

OVERALL ★★★★ | QUALITY ★★★★½ | VALUE ★★★★ | PRICE RANGE $100–$170

From the outside it looks like just another large old house in this tree-lined residential neighborhood boasting over half a dozen bed-and-breakfasts, but inside Haxton Manor exudes the rich country manor ambience of Olde England. A ceiling fan whirs above the hardwood living room floors in the summer. In winter an overstuffed sofa and chairs surround the fireplace and stained-glass lamps and garden illustrations on the walls make for a comforting retreat. Book lovers will like the Bristol Room's book wallpaper, nightstand, old book tables, and book-upholstered chair and ottoman. Look your best here, as the innkeepers snap a Polaroid keepsake of each guest.

SETTING & FACILITIES

Location Downtown's Historic Avenues District, 10 blocks from Temple Square **Near** State capitol, Trolley Square, university, museums, government offices **Building** 1906 3-story country manor house, restored in 1997 **Grounds** Front lawn, parking in back **Public Space** LR, library, DR, front porch **Food & Drink** Full breakfast in DR; 24-hour complimentary candies, bottled water, soft drinks **Recreation** Boating, fishing, biking, golf, winter sports **Amenities & Services** Next-day laundry, fitness center, fax machine, English limousine (airport service)

ACCOMMODATIONS

Units 6 **All** Robes, ceiling fan, clock radio, individual thermostat, down comforter, TV/VCR, speaker phone, voice mail, data port, desk **Some** Fireplace (2) **Bed & Bath** Queens; all private baths, jetted tub (4) **Favorites** Brighton, a honeymoon favorite, has bay window, mirrored armoire, burgundy tones, separate vanity, jetted tub w/ shower; Sussex, a popular wedding night & anniversary alcove, has jetted tub behind bedroom curtain, blue carpet, crackled gold walls, wood & embossed metal headboard, stuffed chairs by fireplace sitting area **Comfort & Decor** English country manor style with sponge-painted walls, stenciling, some wallpaper, lace curtains, dark wood dressers, armoires, garlands, and fluted glass.

RATES, RESERVATIONS, & RESTRICTIONS
Deposit Credit card (10-day cancellation for full refund; otherwise forfeit 50%) **Discounts** Groups, corp., whole house rentals **Credit Cards** AE, MC, V, D **Check-In/Out** 3 p.m./11 a.m. **Smoking** No **Pets** No **Kids** No **No-Nos** N/A **Minimum Stay** None **Open** All year **Hosts** Buffi & Douglas King, 943 East South Temple, Salt Lake City 84102 **Phone** (801) 363-4646 or toll-free (877) 930-4646 **Fax** N/A **E-mail** innkeepers@ haxtonmanor.com **Web** www.haxtonmanor.com

THE INN ON CAPITOL HILL, *Salt Lake City*

OVERALL ★★★★ | QUALITY ★★★★★ | VALUE ★★★★ | PRICE RANGE $139–$229

On a hillside convenient to government offices and Temple Square, with plenty of stairs for exercise, the Inn on Capitol Hill is richly furnished from the stained-glass sextant window in the basement Explorer Room to the Tiffany lamps in the uppermost Great Salt Lake room. Each room reflects an aspect of Utah state history. There is something for every taste, whether it's the red brick walls and large train engine model in the small Railroad Room or the more romantic rose antiqued armoire and stone tiles of the Desert Rose Room. The original master bedroom of the mansion is now the Colonization Room, which has a huge cattle horn–shaped arch above the whirlpool tub.

SETTING & FACILITIES
Location 2 blocks north of Temple St., 6 blocks south of state capitol **Near** Temple Square, museums, university, government offices **Building** 1906 Second Renaissance Revival–style 4-story mansion **Grounds** Well-manicured lawns (no seating) **Public Space** LR, music room w/ fireplace & 2 pianos, DR **Food & Drink** Full breakfast in DR; snacks during day **Recreation** Boating, fishing, biking, golf, winter sports **Amenities & Services** Weddings, receptions (60–70 people)

ACCOMMODATIONS
Units 13 **All** TV/VCR, clock, AC, phone, armoire **Some** Fireplace (5), balcony (3), patio (2) **Bed & Bath** King (4), queen (9); all private baths, jetted tub (13) **Favorites** Great Salt

Lake in former top-floor ballroom has Tiffany lamps, sloping ceilings, sitting area, king bed, bath alcove w/ green plants. Legacy shares balcony w/ Statehood, has good downtown views, beveled glass, green & lavender Victorian chairs **Comfort & Decor** Each room is very different, with antiques, floral themes, and decor depicting different aspects of Utah history from the red, white, and blue of statehood to the drums, arrows, and petroglyphs of the Ute Indians; sinks are embedded in dresser-style vanities.

RATES, RESERVATIONS, & RESTRICTIONS
Deposit Credit card (21-day cancellation policy) **Discounts** Regionally (UT, ID) advertised specials (ask) **Credit Cards** AE, MC, V **Check-In/Out** 3:30 p.m./11 a.m. **Smoking** No **Pets** Not encouraged, but some exceptions are made **Kids** Yes (under age 8 requires prearrangement) **No-Nos** N/A **Minimum Stay** None **Open** All year **Host** Aleshia Marshall, 225 N. State St., Salt Lake City 84103 **Phone** (801) 575-1112 or toll-free (888) 8-THE-INN **Fax** (801) 933-4957 **E-mail** reservations@utahinn.com **Web** www.utahinn.com

PEERY HOTEL, Salt Lake City

OVERALL ★★★★ | QUALITY ★★★★½ | VALUE ★★★★ | PRICE RANGE $88–$165

Built in 1910 just after completion of the Union Pacific and Denver Rio Grande railroad depots to service the successful mining-related businesses in the mountains around Salt Lake City, the flat-roofed Peery Hotel has large light wells separating the wings that provide natural light. Renovated in 1999, the original wood-paneled lobby is still intact, complete with leather-topped writing desk, wainscoting, oak staircase, fireplace, marble-topped sideboards, carved angels, and egg-and-dart motif ceiling. The lobby comes alive with piano music two or three evenings per week. King and queen parlor rooms and double queen rooms are largest and have extra phones and TVs, as well as robes. Most rooms have desks (smaller rooms have tables) for business travelers, who also appreciate the high-speed Internet access.

SETTING & FACILITIES
Location Downtown, near Exchange Place Historic District **Near** Museums, microbreweries, state capitol, university, temple, railroad depot **Building** 1910 E-shaped, Prairie Style, 3-story post-&-beam construction gray brick w/ white trim & classical revival motifs **Grounds** Opens onto city street **Public Space** Lobby, restaurants, sitting areas each

floor **Food & Drink** Full breakfast buffet in restaurant; seafood/steakhouse & grill all meals **Recreation** Boating, fishing, biking, golf, winter sports **Amenities & Services** Complimentary airport shuttle, whirlpool, fitness center, valet, room service, 10 meeting rooms (largest seats 150)

ACCOMMODATIONS

Units 73 **All** 25-in. TV, voice mail, data port, high-speed Internet access, coffeemaker w/ Starbucks coffee, hair dryer, iron & ironing board, digital alarm clock **Some** Robes, fridge (on request), sleeper sofas **Bed & Bath** King (11), 2 queens (5), queen (57); all private baths, tubs (many) **Favorites** 340 is large corner king parlor; 323–332 & 225–232 are larger, some w/ kings & sitting areas in quieter interior of building's E-shape **Comfort & Decor** European boutique look, with antique reproductions, armoires, canopied beds, vase-shaped bath lights, and pedestal sinks.

RATES, RESERVATIONS, & RESTRICTIONS

Deposit Credit card (24-hour cancellation) **Discounts** Airline, corporate, AAA, various specials **Credit Cards** AE, MC, V, D **Check-In/Out** 3 p.m./11 a.m. **Smoking** No **Pets** No **Kids** Yes **No-Nos** N/A **Minimum Stay** None **Open** All year **Host** Lynda Tovar, 110 W. Broadway, Salt Lake City 84101 **Phone** (801) 521-4300 or toll-free (800) 331-0073 **Fax** (801) 364-3295 **E-mail** reservations@peeryhotel.com **Web** www.peeryhotel.com

SALTAIR BED AND BREAKFAST, Salt Lake City

OVERALL ★★★ | QUALITY ★★★½ | VALUE ★★★★ | PRICE RANGE $55–$149

Salt Lake City's oldest continuously operating bed-and-breakfast, Saltair is named after an old Great Salt Lake amusement park. Besides rooms and cottages, eight executive suites and a two-bedroom bungalow with kitchens and no breakfast are popular with families of patients in nearby hospitals (e.g., burn unit). Rooms are small compared to cottages, which sleep several people and have more amenities. The three bed-and-breakfast rooms, sharing a bath with a shower, are best rented by families. Sweet Sage's painted wooden cowboy with lariat and wall-mounted barbed wire collection are hits with kids and Western buffs.

SETTING & FACILITIES

Location Downtown, near Trolley Square **Near** Masonic Temple, Temple Square, university, museums **Building** 1903 Victorian, 1870s cottages **Grounds** Back patio w/ hammock, barbecue **Public Space** Parlor, TV room, DR, front porch **Food & Drink** Full breakfast in DR; cottages get cont'l breakfast; free saltwater taffy, beverages, evening snacks **Recreation** Boating, fishing, biking, golf, winter sports **Amenities & Services** Hot tub

ACCOMMODATIONS

Units 5 rooms & 3 cottages **All** Robes, comforters, fresh flowers (rooms) **Some** Cable TV (cottages), phone (cottages), fireplace (cottages), **Bed & Bath** Queen (7), single (1); 2 private baths, tub (1), jetted tub (1) **Favorites** Sego Lily has small green & cream sitting area w/ fireplace, dark floral wallpaper, mirrored closet, brass coat rack, antique rocker, beveled mirror over dresser, private bath. Cottages have bedroom, extra folding or Murphy beds in LR, full kitchen **Comfort & Decor** Rooms are eclectic and varied, with brass antique beds, comfortable mattresses, lace, tasseled lampshades, armoires, dressers.

RATES, RESERVATIONS, & RESTRICTIONS

Deposit Credit card (Dec. 1–April 30, 30-day cancellation for refund minus $25; May 1–Dec. 30, 10-day cancellation) **Discounts** Extended stays, hospital-related, summer & Internet specials **Credit Cards** AE, MC, V, D **Check-In/Out** 3:30 p.m./11 a.m. **Smoking** No **Pets** Cottages only **Kids** Cottages only **No-Nos** N/A **Minimum Stay** None **Open** All year **Hosts** Jan Bartlett & Nancy Saxton, 164 South 900 East, Salt Lake City 84102 **Phone** (801) 533-8184 or toll-free (800) 733-8184 **Fax** (801) 595-0332 **E-mail** saltair@saltlakebandb.com **Web** www.saltlakebandb.com

Central

The western boundaries of sparsely populated central Utah extend north along the Nevada border from Garrison near Great Basin National Park to the Goshute Indian Reservation. US 50 traverses the western two-thirds of central Utah, a desert with some sand dunes, lava flows, valleys, and north–south mountains like the Confusion Range. Delta, the high desert population center (3,000 people), has several gas stations and low-budget motels but no bed-and-breakfasts.

The more forested eastern part of central Utah runs from the northern tip of Capitol Reef National Park to the Manti–La Sal National Forest north of Fairview, a town of 1,000. Most towns are along Interstates 15 and 70, which run north–south and east–west, respectively. Much of the area is mountainous, and most is covered by the Manti–La Sal, Fishlake, and Dixie National Forests. Cabins, campgrounds, and motels are the main lodgings for the summer outdoor recreational activities. Bed-and-breakfasts have not gained a major foothold here, and winter snows bring a quick end to tourist season.

Along I-15 the big town is Fillmore, population 2,000, which has the Territorial Statehouse State Park. Surrounded by cattle ranching and alfalfa fields in Millard County, Fillmore was named after U.S. president Millard Fillmore, a friend to persecuted Mormons. Nephi has a decent Mexican restaurant and is a good place to get on the Mt. Nebo scenic drive. Tiny Salina on I-70 has good breakfasts at the Mad House Cafe on Main Street and good lunches and dinners at Mom's Cafe, but the only bed-and-breakfast is gone.

Only Manti, a friendly town of 2,300 on a scenic section of UT 89, has a solid lineup of bed-and-breakfasts. Main Street is lined with old-fashioned malt and shake shops. People ride their horses down the side streets, and the impressive Manti LDS Temple lures visitors here to be married. The annual Mormon Miracle Pageant in June draws over 100,000 visitors who partake of pancake breakfasts on the sloping temple lawns.

HISTORIC MANTI HOUSE INN, Manti

OVERALL ★★★★ | QUALITY ★★★★ | VALUE ★★★★ | PRICE RANGE $59–$129

Originally built in the late 1880s as a hotel for workers constructing the nearby Manti Temple, the Historic Manti House was renovated by its new owners in late 2000. The Manti House owes some of its success to the continuing popularity of the impressive hillside Manti Temple, which acts as a magnet attracting couples from around the region for marriage ceremonies. Indeed, two Manti House banquet rooms serving luncheons for up to 100 people are popular for wedding parties. The hardwood-floor dining room also serves up prime rib and chicken dinners amid old photos of historic mansions, a fireplace, mirrors, and fluted glass lamps. There is a small gift store on the premises.

SETTING & FACILITIES
Location Downtown, corner of Fourth North & UT 89 (Main St.) **Near** Lakes, forest, state parks, temple, historic sites **Building** 1880s stone hotel **Grounds** Big cottonwood tree, gazebo **Public Space** Gazebo **Food & Drink** Full breakfast in DR; candies; catered luncheons; dinner restaurant **Recreation** Fishing, boating, water sports, golf, 4-wheeling **Amenities & Services** Gift shop, wedding receptions (100 people), meetings, piano

ACCOMMODATIONS
Units 7, all upstairs **All** Cable TV/VCR, digital clock, quilt **Some** Balcony (1), gas fireplace (2), wood stove (2), ceiling fan **Bed & Bath** Queen (6), double (1); all private baths, tub (3), jetted tub (2) **Favorites** Honeymoon Suite has angled ceiling, garden murals, step-up canopied queen bed, fireplace, pine dresser, private entrance stairway to DR, balcony, jetted tub; Joseph Fielding Smith room has stone wallpaper design, BR sink w/ decoy duck & wood-framed hexagonal mirror, dried flowers, tree, claw-foot tub, stall shower **Comfort & Decor** Varied wallpapers, antique furnishings, marble- and glass-topped tables, wood dressers, some sponge-painted walls, wood and metal frame beds, pedestal sinks, some claw-foot tubs.

RATES, RESERVATIONS, & RESTRICTIONS
Deposit Credit card (3-day cancellation for refund minus $30 fee) **Discounts** Inquire **Credit Cards** MC, V **Check-In/Out** 3 p.m./11 a.m. **Smoking** No **Pets** No **Kids** Yes **No-Nos** N/A **Minimum Stay** None **Open** All year **Hosts** Jennifer & Jason Nicholes, 401 N. Main St., Manti 84642 **Phone** (435) 835-0161 or toll-free (800) 835-7512 **Fax** (435) 835-0161 **E-mail** mantihouseinn@mstar2.net **Web** www.mantihouse.com

THE LEGACY INN BED & BREAKFAST & GIFT SHOP, Manti

OVERALL ★★★½ | QUALITY ★★★★ | VALUE ★★★★ | PRICE RANGE $75–$95

Every June for the past three decades, Manti, a town of fewer than 3,000 residents with a Main Street lined with old-fashioned malt and shake shops, hosts over 100,000 visitors for the annual Mormon Miracle Pageant. The Legacy Inn is kitty-corner from the hillside temple, whose sloping lawns hold 13,000 chairs for pancake breakfasts. Indeed, the octagonal Tower Room, with its stained-glass temple views is one reason Legacy Inn books for the festival a year in advance. People statewide come to be married and visit the temple, which is why Manti bed-and-breakfasts are thriving when most other central Utah bed-and-breakfast have closed. The Legacy Inn gift shop sells marbles, homemade jellies, chocolate truffles, and the hostess's patchwork quilts.

SETTING & FACILITIES

Location Center, across from temple **Near** Lakes, forests, state parks, historic sites **Building** 1988 Victorian country style **Grounds** Rose garden **Public Space** LR, DR, family room, covered patio **Food & Drink** Full breakfast in DR; early evening refreshments; chocolate truffles in room; dinner on request **Recreation** Fishing, boating, water sports, golf, 4-wheeling **Amenities & Services** Gift shop, TV/VCR

ACCOMMODATIONS

Units 4 **All** CD/clock **Some** Gas fireplace (2) **Bed & Bath** Queen beds, twins; all private baths **Favorites** Family Suite has bedroom w/ queen bed, family room w/ 2 twin beds & futon, brick fireplace; Country Garden Room has mahogany bed draped in lace, upholstered rose chairs, fireplace, separate vanities, large bath w/ stained glass; Master Suite has four-poster plantation bed, fireplace, sitting area, stained-glass bath window **Comfort & Decor** Comfortable country style with patchwork quilts, some sitting areas, oak furnishings, canopied beds, antique church stained glass.

RATES, RESERVATIONS, & RESTRICTIONS

Deposit Credit card (cancellation within 7 days, otherwise responsible for all nights room not rebooked) **Discounts** Multiple nights, whole house rental **Credit Cards** MC, V **Check-In/Out** 1 p.m./11 a.m. **Smoking** No **Pets** No (occasional exceptions) **Kids** Yes **No-Nos** N/A **Minimum Stay** None **Open** All year **Hosts** Jan & Mike Crane, 337 North 100 East, Manti 84642 **Phone** (435) 835-8352 **Fax** N/A **E-mail** stay@legacyinn.com **Web** www.legacyinn.com

YARDLEY INN & SPA, Manti

OVERALL ★★★★ | QUALITY ★★★★½ | VALUE ★★★★ | PRICE RANGE $60–$160

In this town along UT 89 where people ride horses down the street, the Yardley Inn is extending its successful bed-and-breakfast business with spa services. Besides massage and exercise rooms, there are tubs for hydrotherapy, an infrared sauna, and an array of equipment for everything from rearranging the chi to colonic, color, sound, and other detoxification therapies. Backyard greenhouse organic food may find its way into the dark wood and stone wall dining room, which is overlooked by a book-lined mezzanine lounge. The living room has a grandfather clock, piano, fireplace, chandelier, and yellow interior with white trim. The best rooms are the three suites, particularly the two honeymoon suites, which have robes, jetted tubs, and fireplaces.

SETTING & FACILITIES

Location Downtown **Near** Lakes, forest, state parks, temple, historic sites **Building** Huge, rambling multistory home **Grounds** Greenhouse w/ organic food plants, patio **Public Space** LR, DR, upstairs lounge, massage room, infrared sauna, hydrotherapy tub, exercise room **Food & Drink** Full breakfast in DR; candlelight dinners **Recreation** Fishing, boating, water sports, golf, 4-wheeling **Amenities & Services** Piano, colonic therapy equipment, chi machine, bio-electronic detox, sound & light therapy, resonator, Kirilian photography,

ACCOMMODATIONS

Units 6 **All** Satellite TV/VCR, clock, individual AC/heat **Some** Robes (3), fireplace (2), skylight (1), balcony (1) **Bed & Bath** King (3), queen (3); all private baths, tub (3), jetted tub (2) **Favorites** Lavender & Lace has a huge carpeted BR w/ step down into a jetted tub, vanity, fireplace, mirrored closet, lavender floral mural, balcony. Wedgewood Room is done up in blue & white **Comfort & Decor** High-quality dark wood furnishings, varied color schemes, some florals, molding, carpet, some mirrored closets.

RATES, RESERVATIONS, & RESTRICTIONS

Deposit Credit card holds (7-day cancellation policy) **Discounts** Groups **Credit Cards** AE, MC, V, D **Check-In/Out** 3 p.m./11 a.m. **Smoking** No **Pets** No **Kids** Yes **No-Nos** N/A **Minimum Stay** None **Open** All year **Hosts** Gill & Marlene Yardley, 190 South 200 West, Manti 84642 **Phone** (435) 835-1861 or toll-free (800) 858-6634 **Fax** N/A **E-mail** N/A **Web** N/A

Southwest

Southwestern Utah covers an immense amount of ground, from the Arizona and Nevada borders in the southwest corner of the state to Glen Canyon National Recreation Area along the Colorado River in the east. Deserts, canyons, forested mountains, rivers, streams, and eroded sandstone formations in stunning red, orange, white, and gray are all part of the landscape. Besides Grand Staircase–Escalante and Cedar Breaks National Monuments and several worthwhile state parks, southwestern Utah has Capitol Reef, Bryce Canyon, and Zion National Parks.

Often accessed from Las Vegas, St. George is one of the gateways to Zion and Bryce Canyon National Parks. Winters are mild enough in St. George that Brigham Young established his winter home here in a neighborhood now teeming with bed-and-breakfasts. St. George has Utah's first Mormon temple, historic homes, an art museum, and free concerts the first Monday of the month (May–October) in Vernon Worthen Park. An hour to the east is Zion, and there are bed-and-breakfasts en route to the park's west entrance in towns like Rockville, Virgin, and Springdale.

North of St. George, Cedar City books up during the summer months for the Utah Shakespeare Festival. Brian Head Resort, a winter ski area, and Cedar Breaks National Monument are less than an hour from Cedar City. Panguitch, along the Sevier River seven miles north of the Bryce Junction (intersection of US 89 and UT 12), is under an hour from Panguitch Lake, Red Canyon, and Bryce Canyon National Park. Glendale and Mount Carmel Junction are closer to Zion's east entrance. Kanab, once popular for shooting cowboy movies, is 70 miles north of the Grand Canyon's North Rim.

Tropic is ideally located east of Bryce Canyon and northwest of Kodachrome Basin State Park's moody sandstone spires and hoodoos. About an hour east of Tropic is Escalante, a good jumping-off place for backcountry exploration of Grand Staircase–Escalante National Monument. Torrey and Teasdale are the preferred stopping places for exploring the petroglyphs, fruit orchards, old Mormon pioneer settlements, and towering sandstone reefs of Capitol Reef National Park.

BAKER HOUSE BED & BREAKFAST, Cedar City

OVERALL ★★★★★ | QUALITY ★★★★½ | VALUE ★★★★★ | PRICE RANGE $99–$159

A favorite of locals for anniversaries, honeymoons, and getaways, the opulent Baker House has Jacuzzi tubs in rooms named after famous poets, like Keats and Browning. Extreme privacy is provided by eight-inch-thick bathroom walls with soundproofing separating the rooms. A volume of poetry by each room's namesake poet adds a literary touch. The dining room is surrounded by bay windows, and breakfast is around a round table with a lazy Susan. The ornate parlor features Victorian floral sofas, hand-carved wingback Italian chairs, and a big-screen TV. By many measures the best bed-and-breakfast in town, Baker House combines the best modern amenities with classic Victorian architectural style. Rooms book up very quickly from mid-June to mid-October for the Utah Shakespeare Festival.

SETTING & FACILITIES
Location Southern edge of town **Near** Brian Head Ski Resort, Cedar Breaks, lakes, theaters **Building** 1998 3-story Queen Anne Victorian mansion **Grounds** Sloping lawn w/ rock garden, Victorian carriage **Public Space** Parlor, DR **Food & Drink** Full breakfast in DR; specialties include stuffed French toast, enchiladas; chocolate & bottled water in room; bottomless cookie jar & drinks in DR guest fridge any time **Recreation** Fishing, boating, winter sports, golf, theater **Amenities & Services** Homemade soaps, entertainment center w/ big screen TV, nature sound tapes

ACCOMMODATIONS
Units 5 **All** Ming robes, makeup mirror, hair dryer, gas fireplace, AM/FM cassette alarm clock, data port, ceiling fan, TV/VCR, poetry book **Some** Phones on request **Bed & Bath** Kings; all private baths, Jacuzzi tubs **Favorites** Emerson has sitting room, floral wallpaper, 2-way fireplace, deep maroons & lavender, floral wallpaper, mountain view; Shelley has wrought-iron bed, deep burgundy colors, mountain view; Byron on 3d floor has heart-shaped tub favored by newlyweds, gold carpet, blue & rose florals **Comfort & Decor** Exudes luxury with rich dark woods, top-to-bottom plushness, and an excellent merger of modernity with traditional New England Victorian style.

RATES, RESERVATIONS, & RESTRICTIONS
Deposit Credit card (1-week cancellation; $25 fee) **Discounts** Groups, off-season **Credit Cards** AE, MC, V, D, DC **Check-In/Out** 3–8 p.m./11 a.m. **Smoking** Outside only **Pets** No **Kids** Yes (over age 13) **No-Nos** N/A **Minimum Stay** None **Open** All year **Hosts** Lori & Tony Baker, 1800 Royal Hunte Dr., Cedar City 84720 **Phone** (435) 867-

5695 or toll-free (888) 611-8181 **Fax** (435) 867-5694 **E-mail** thebakers@netutah.com
Web www.bbhost.com/bakerhouse

BARD'S INN, Cedar City

OVERALL ★★★★ | QUALITY ★★★★ | VALUE ★★★★ | PRICE RANGE $75–$90

Like most of Cedar City, Bard's Inn reaches its seasonal business peak from
mid-June through mid-October during the Utah Summer Games and Tony
Award–winning (best regional theater) Shakespeare Festival, when early
reservations are strongly advised. Besides enjoying the convenience of walking to the theater, a highly regarded lunch and dinner restaurant, Adriana's,
is next door in this residential suburb near the town center and I-15. Bard's
Inn has memorabilia reflecting the host's lifelong interest in mining and
antique stained glass from old mining mansions, as well as costumes and
Shakespeare play memorabilia from the local festival. The Oberon and Fal-
staff rooms have connecting doors forming a kitchenette suite.

SETTING & FACILITIES
Location 2 blocks from town center and Shakespearean theaters **Near** Brian Head Ski
Resort, Cedar Breaks, lakes, theaters **Building** 1908 2-story bungalow **Grounds** 0.3 acre
yard **Public Space** LR, DR, glass porch, upstairs lounge **Food & Drink** Full breakfast in
DR or glass porch; upstairs lounge fridge; restaurant next door serves lunch, dinner
Recreation Fishing, boating, winter sports, golf, theater **Amenities & Services**
Enclosed front porch w/ heat/AC, TV

ACCOMMODATIONS
Units 7 **All** Hair dryer **Some** Private outside entrance (2), kitchenette (2) **Bed & Bath**
Queens, 2nd twins or doubles; all private baths, tubs **Favorites** Mistress Ford has private
outside entrance to downstairs sitting area, old mining baron mansion furnishings like a
mirrored dressing table; Beatrice has basement brick & wallpaper alcove w/ queen & twin,
Henry VIII costumes & sketches, kitchenette w/ full fridge, 4-burner stove; Oberon is
handicap-accessible w/ kitchenette, pineapple stenciling, Gibson Cambria icebox **Comfort & Decor** Varies with room theme; rich wood and brass furnishings, antique stained
glass, floral bedspreads, fruit stenciling, angled ceilings, mining memorabilia, Ming antiques.

RATES, RESERVATIONS, & RESTRICTIONS
Deposit 1 night (10-day cancellation) **Discounts** None **Credit Cards** AE, MC, V
Check-In/Out 1:30 p.m./11 a.m. **Smoking** No **Pets** No **Kids** Yes **No-Nos** N/A **Mini-
mum Stay** None **Open** All year (Nov.–May by prior arrangement) **Hosts** Audrey & Jack
Whipple, 150 South 100 West, Cedar City 84720 **Phone** (435) 586-6612 **Fax** N/A
E-mail N/A **Web** N/A

THE BIG YELLOW INN BED & BREAKFAST, Cedar City

OVERALL ★★★★★ | QUALITY ★★★★½ | VALUE ★★★★★ | PRICE RANGE $85–$120 ($180 SUITE)

The Big Yellow Inn is Cedar City's newest bed-and-breakfast and badly needed because of a chronic room shortage from mid-June through mid-October for the Utah Shakespeare Festival, which won a 2000 best regional theater Tony Award. Superbly designed rooms skillfully convey themes ranging from nautical and safari to Mediterranean and English. Ample public spaces with a Victorian period feel or a more modern look make it hard to go wrong here. At one time the Garden Cottage (see Appendix) and Bard's Inn were the unchallenged top bed-and-breakfasts in Cedar City, but first the Baker House and now the Big Yellow Inn have upped the ante.

SETTING & FACILITIES
Location From Interstate 15, Exit 59 go east on 200 North and south on 300 West **Near** Brian Head Ski Resort, Cedar Breaks, lakes, theaters **Building** Newly built Georgian Revival **Grounds** Backyard has fish pond, grape arbor, & fountain **Public Space** Living room, DR, library, sitting areas, porches **Food & Drink** Full breakfast in DR **Recreation** Fishing, boating, winter sports, golf, theater **Amenities & Services** Guest office w/ computer, DSL connection, fax, copier

ACCOMMODATIONS
Units 11 guest rooms; 5 on 1st floor, 5 on 2d floor, penthouse suite **All** AC, Internet access **Some** Fireplace (3), balcony (3), handicap-accessible (lower level) **Bed & Bath** Kings (3), queens (6), 1 king, queen, & single, 1 queen & single; all private baths **Favorites**

Gable suite is 900-sq.-ft. top-floor penthouse w/ king, queen, twins, sitting room, fireplace, double Jacuzzi, telescope; Bon Voyage has queen & single sofa beds, nautical theme w/ peach & navy blue color scheme; the Hunter, Stitch in Time, & Blue Haven rooms combine into a family suite w/ a separate hallway door **Comfort & Decor** Each room has an individual theme with matching antiques and curios, deep mahogany woods, quilts or chenille bedspreads; public rooms have stained-glass lamps, grandfather clocks, lace, crown moldings, and a Victorian feel or adopt modern themes like plaids

RATES, RESERVATIONS, & RESTRICTIONS

Deposit Credit card (2-week cancellation notice; otherwise no refund unless room rebooked) **Discounts** Corp. rate for single travelers, multiple rooms for families, entire floors **Credit Cards** MC, V **Check-In/Out** 4–8 p.m./11 a.m. **Smoking** No (not permitted within 25 feet of the inn) **Pets** No **Kids** Yes (under age 8 requires preapproval) **No-Nos** N/A **Minimum Stay** None **Open** All year **Hosts** Scott & Barbara Hunt, 234 South 300 West, Cedar City 84720 **Phone** (435) 586-0960 **Fax** (435) 586-0961 **E-mail** stay@bigyellowinn.com **Web** www.bigyellowinn.com

ESCALANTE'S GRAND STAIRCASE BED & BREAKFAST INN, Escalante

OVERALL ★★★½ | QUALITY ★★★★ | VALUE ★★★★ | PRICE RANGE $65–$105

Easy to find on West Main Street, a block from the popular Prospector Inn motel and walking distance to restaurants, the main building at Escalante's Grand Staircase encloses the office and dining room under a high wood ceiling and skylights with Indian drums and log furnishings. The main building has the only room with just one queen bed, the blue-colored Country Room. The other rooms are in the Carriage House wing further back from the main highway, and a short walk to the Great Room for breakfast and gift purchases. Guest rooms are notable for their use of barn wood and murals of petroglyphs, granaries, and points of local interest.

SETTING & FACILITIES

Location Center of town, on main highway **Near** State and national parks **Building** 1998–99 Western main building, stand-alone guest room wing **Grounds** Picnic table area **Public Space** Great room in main house **Food & Drink** Full breakfast in DR; special dietary needs w/ advance notice **Recreation** Biking, horse riding, fishing **Amenities & Services** Mountain bike rental, tour services

ACCOMMODATIONS

Units 5 guest rooms, 1 in main house **All** Phone, TV, AC/heat **Some** Handicap-accessible (1), coffeemaker (4) **Bed & Bath** King (1), queens (4), 2nd queen or double (3); all private baths, tubs **Favorites** Sage has canopied king, leather headboard, sage green colors; Clay has 2 queens, reddish clay color, handicap accessibility; Cadet is 380 sq. ft., blue w/ 2 queens **Comfort & Decor** Barn wood, frame mirrors, murals behind dressers, Zapotec rugs on wall, vanities, baths with tile floors.

RATES, RESERVATIONS, & RESTRICTIONS

Deposit Credit card (7-day cancellation policy) **Discounts** None **Credit Cards** MC, V **Check-In/Out** 3–6 p.m. (after 9 p.m. on request)/10:30 a.m. **Smoking** No (smoking area outside) **Pets** No **Kids** Yes (need advance permission if under age 10) **No-Nos** N/A **Minimum Stay** None **Open** All year **Hosts** Tom & Linda Mansell, 280 W. Main, P.O. Box 657, Escalante 84726 **Phone** (435) 826-4890 or toll-free (866) 826-4890 **Fax** N/A **E-mail** linda@escalantebnb.com **Web** www.escalantebnb.com

RAINBOW COUNTRY BED & BREAKFAST, Escalante

OVERALL ★★★½ | QUALITY ★★★½ | VALUE ★★★★★ | PRICE RANGE $40–$65

The signs along UT 12 say turn at the Chevron station for Rainbow Country, but the Chevron became an Amoco a few years back. The hostess is too busy raising kids and running a small rock shop plus the Broken Bow Arch campground (an old sign still calls it "sss") on Main Street to update the highway signs. Rainbow Country's entrance is attractive enough, once you find it. The circular driveway is lined with cottonwood trees and the sundeck faces a meadow-like lawn. The rooms all have two beds, and the below-ground "gathering room" has a wood-burning stove, microwave popcorn, pool table, and big-screen TV.

SETTING & FACILITIES

Location East side of town, near Escalante High School and Amoco station **Near** Escalante Petrified Forest & Anasazi Indian Village State Parks, Calf Creek, Bryce Canyon and Capitol Reef National Parks **Building** 1990 split-level ranch-style modular, prefabricated **Grounds** 3 desert acres **Public Space** Living room, DR, downstairs play room, sundeck **Food & Drink** Full breakfast in DR; microwave popcorn available **Recreation** Horse riding, biking, fishing **Amenities & Services** Hot tub, pool table, big-screen TV, phone

ACCOMMODATIONS

Units 4 guest rooms, 3 downstairs **All** Robes, radio alarm clock, central heat/AC **Some** Hair dryer (on request), desk (1) **Bed & Bath** Queens (2), doubles, twins; all private baths, tubs (2) **Favorites** Large queen & double room sleeps 4, has tub; upstairs has double & twin, tub & walls w/ old lumber saws, wheat sickles, horse harnesses, & washboards **Comfort & Decor** Half the rooms are ordinary but very comfortable in keeping with the modular prefab look; the two theme rooms are garden and old equipment (themes are promised for other rooms).

RATES, RESERVATIONS, & RESTRICTIONS

Deposit Credit card (24-hour cancellation policy) **Discounts** Longer stays **Credit Cards** MC, V **Check-In/Out** 4 p.m./11 a.m. **Smoking** No **Pets** Yes (if small; owner has pets) **Kids** Yes **No-Nos** N/A **Minimum Stay** None **Open** All year (closed Dec. 24 & 25) **Hosts** Clark & Catherine Barney, 586 East 300 South, Escalante 84726 **Phone** (435) 826-4567 or toll-free (800) 252-8824 **Fax** N/A **E-mail** rainbow@color-country.net **Web** www.color-country.net/~rainbow

EAGLE'S NEST BED & BREAKFAST, *Glendale*

OVERALL ★★★★ | QUALITY ★★★½ | VALUE ★★★★ | PRICE RANGE $79–$107

Well worth the short dirt-road detour into the mountains past cattle pastures and cowboys in pickup trucks, Eagle's Nest's elevation is 6,000 feet elevation with snow in winter (snow plows open the roads) and feeders attracting hummingbirds. The cathedral-ceilinged living room furnished by the well-traveled hosts, who migrated here from Mill Valley, California, is intentionally without electronic media. Instead there are overstuffed chairs, reading materials, games, a piano, and a fireplace. Sitting around in the shade of mountain oaks, maples, and pinion pines watching for deer and other wildlife on the front patio is a popular pastime. The property opens onto Bureau of Land Management land with hiking trails, and the hot tub is popular at night.

SETTING & FACILITIES

Location From US 89, go 1.6 mi. north at Mile Marker 92 (B&B sign) on dirt road **Near** Zion National Park, Bryce Canyon National Park, Cedar Breaks, Coral Pink Sand Dunes State Park, Navajo Lake, Grand Staircase-Escalante National Monument **Building** Remodeled 1950s summer home w/ fallout shelter **Grounds** 13 mountainous acres w/ 2 springs **Public Space** Living room, DR **Food & Drink** Full breakfast in DR; evening wine or beer; bedside brownies; guest kitchen w/ microwave & fridge; dietary requirements accommodated w/ advance notice **Recreation** Horse riding, fishing, boating, hiking **Amenities & Services** Hot tub

ACCOMMODATIONS

Units 4 **All** Varied antiques **Some** Loft (1), outside entrance (1), gas fireplace (2) **Bed & Bath** King (1), 2 queens (1), full size (1), twins (1); all private baths, tubs (3) **Favorites** Oriental Suite, a honeymoon favorite, has California king, futon couch, Tibetan lucky signs & prayer wheels, Japanese masks, fireplace, shower; Anasazi Suite has 2 queens, fireplace, private entrance; Loft has 2 floors w/ twin beds, crystals, burgundy & gold brocade, paisleys **Comfort & Decor** Very varied: for example, Oriental, Southwestern, country garden with French antiques.

RATES, RESERVATIONS, & RESTRICTIONS

Deposit 1 night (14-day cancellation for refund) **Discounts** None **Credit Cards** MC, V, D **Check-In/Out** 5–8 p.m./11 a.m. **Smoking** No (outside only) **Pets** No (owners have cat & dog) **Kids** Yes (if well behaved; breakables) **No-Nos** N/A **Minimum Stay** None (except holidays) **Open** All year **Hosts** Shanoan & Dearborn Clark, P.O. Box 160, 500 W. Lydia Canyon Rd., Glendale 84729 **Phone** (435) 648-2200 or toll-free (800) 293-6378 **Fax** (435) 648-2221 **E-mail** innkeeps@eaglesnestbb.com **Web** www.eaglesnestbb.com

HISTORIC SMITH HOTEL BED & BREAKFAST, Glendale

OVERALL ★★★ | QUALITY ★★★ | VALUE ★★★ | PRICE RANGE $44–$80

During daily business hours the living room, which has a fireplace, doubles as an antiques store with lots of little items, and the guest entrance to the Historic Smith Hotel is through the dining room. Oak, rattan, apple crisp, and a 1920s wood-burning stove set the tone, which is more like an old-fashioned country boarding house than a hotel. Guests can watch trucks rumble down the noisy highway from the front porch or move to the quieter upstairs back porch for more pastoral gazing at the tree swing, goldfish pond, organic food gardens, and small alfalfa field nestled below the mountains. This is a particularly good stop for bikers, being on the main highway, and groups renting the whole hotel get a 20% discount.

SETTING & FACILITIES
Location Center of town, on US 89 **Near** Zion National Park, Bryce National Park, Coral Pink Sand Dunes State Park, Grand Staircase–Escalante National Monument **Building** 1927 2-story pioneer-style boarding house **Grounds** 2 acres includes acre of alfalfa, goldfish pond, tree swing, organic herbs, vegetables, fruit trees **Public Space** Living room, DR, screened porch **Food & Drink** Full breakfast in DR **Recreation** Horse riding, hiking **Amenities & Services** Hot tub, laundry, barbecue, picnic table, tree swing, antiques store, hallway phone

ACCOMMODATIONS
Units 7 guest rooms, 6 upstairs **All** Ceiling fan, TV **Some** Alarm clock, wood floor (1), handicap-accessible (1) **Bed & Bath** King, queen, doubles (5), bunks (1); 5 private baths, 1 shared bath, tubs (4) **Favorites** Room #5 is largest, has king bed, French armoire, private front porch, tub; #7 has queen bed, shower, sponged blue walls, blue carpet, private staircase entrance; #8 downstairs is handicap-accessible w/ timber-framed double bed, colorful patchwork quilt, tub **Comfort & Decor** Rather ordinary with touches of inspiration like sponge-painted or floral walls, lilac crewel, colorful patchwork quilts.

RATES, RESERVATIONS, & RESTRICTIONS
Deposit Credit card holds (48-hour cancellation) **Discounts** AAA, AARP, over 3 nights, groups, whole house rental **Credit Cards** MC, V **Check-In/Out** 3–7 p.m./10 a.m. **Smoking** No **Pets** Depends on pet; need to ask first; owners have an Australian cattle dog, Bandit **Kids** Yes **No-Nos** N/A **Minimum Stay** None **Open** All year **Hosts** Rochelle & Bunny, 295 N. Main, P.O. Box 106, Glendale 84729 **Phone** (435) 648-2156 or toll-free (800) 528-3558 **Fax** (435) 648-2156 **E-mail** smith_hotel@email.com **Web** N/A

JOY'S BED & BREAKFAST, Hanksville

OVERALL ★★★ | QUALITY ★★★ | VALUE ★★★★ | PRICE RANGE $50

Dogs dart down the middle of the rural road where Joy's is located, 27 miles south of the buttes, badlands, and Paleozoic outcrops of Goblin Valley State Park and 30 miles east of the domes, spires, and sandstone escarpments of Capitol Reef. The hostess, a retired uranium miner, came to appreciate Mushroom Valley's (now Goblin Valley) landscape after she stopped mining there and opened Wayne County's first bed-and-breakfast. The living room is comfortably furnished with sofas and chairs, and the jewelry and pottery displays are for sale. Family photos line the hallway. It's "like going back home to Mom's," says Joy, who limits herself to one set of guests and one child at a time.

SETTING & FACILITIES
Location From junction of UT 95 & 24, go west on UT 24 (100 North) and south on Center St. (1 block west of post office) **Near** Capitol Reef & Canyonlands National Parks, Goblin Valley State Park, Bullfrog Marina (Lake Powell), Wild Horse Canyon **Building**1970s white ranch-style "rambler" w/ black trim **Grounds** 1 acre w/ summer flower gardens **Public Space** Living room, DR, front porch **Food & Drink** Full breakfast in DR **Recreation** Hiking, camping, boating **Amenities & Services** Special arrangements w/ Blondies, restaurant & gift shop owned by Joy's son

ACCOMMODATIONS
Units 3 **All** Basic furnishings **Some** TV (1) **Bed & Bath** Queens; 2 shared baths w/ tub (1) and stall shower (1) **Favorites** Not a big difference among the rooms **Comfort & Decor** Home-like, with basic comfortable furnishings, carpets, wallpaper, and turquoise, blue pastel, and pink color schemes.

RATES, RESERVATIONS, & RESTRICTIONS
Deposit Credit card (12-hour cancellation policy) **Discounts** None **Credit Cards** AE, MC, V **Check-In/Out** Customized **Smoking** No **Pets** No **Kids** Yes (1 only; must call first) **No-Nos** N/A **Minimum Stay** None **Open** March 31–Oct. 31 **Host** Joy Mecham, P.O. Box 151, 296 S. Center, Hanksville 84734 **Phone** (435) 542-3252 **Fax** (435) 542-3858 **E-mail** N/A **Web** ww1.bbgetaways.com/wc.dll?ddm~morelist~14566

VIOLA'S GARDEN BED AND BREAKFAST, Kanab

OVERALL ★★★½ | QUALITY ★★★½ | VALUE ★★★★ | PRICE RANGE $76–$125

The newest bed-and-breakfast in Kanab, a crossroads town with a bustling motel row tied to its past as a Hollywood Western movie location, Viola's fortuitously opened its doors just as all the other Kanab bed-and-breakfasts shut theirs. The hostess's grandparents bought this Victorian house from the 1912 Sears Roebuck catalog and finished the walls, electricity and plumbing piecemeal over the decades as finances permitted. Dark cherry and mahogany woods grace the dining room and parlor, which has a traditional wood mantel fireplace. The Lilac, Cherry Blossom, and Apple Blossom Rooms all share a deck facing the back yard hot tub, and the neighbors here are friendly and helpful.

SETTING & FACILITIES

Location Center of town **Near** Coral Pink Sand Dunes State Park, Bryce Canyon, Zion National Park, Lake Powell, Pipe Spring National Monument **Building** "Avoca" (no. 109) ordered from 1912 Sears and Roebuck's Modern Homes Catalogue **Grounds** Backyard w/ cherry tree, greenhouse, & hot tub **Public Space** Formal parlor, DR, sun room, front veranda **Food & Drink** Full breakfast in DR **Recreation** Golf, fishing, horse riding **Amenities & Services** Hot tub

ACCOMMODATIONS

Units 5 **All** AC, clocks **Some** Shared deck (3), private patio (1), pedestal sink in room (1) **Bed & Bath** Queens; all private baths, tubs, some w/ no showers **Favorites** The upstairs Rose Garden Room has painted fairies on the claw-foot tub, mountain views; English Garden Room has a private balcony **Comfort & Decor** Victorian, with swags and lace curtains, angled ceilings, antiques, dark woods, wood-framed beds, claw-foot tubs.

RATES, RESERVATIONS, & RESTRICTIONS

Deposit Credit card **Discounts** None **Credit Cards** MC, V **Check-In/Out** Arrange when booking **Smoking** No **Pets** No (2 house cats) **Kids** No **No-Nos** N/A **Minimum Stay** None **Open** All year **Hosts** Von & Nileen Whitlock, 250 North 100 West, Kanab 84741 **Phone** (435) 644-5683 **Fax** N/A **E-mail** info@violas-garden.com **Web** www.violas-garden.com

ARROWHEAD BED & BREAKFAST, Mt. Carmel

OVERALL ★★★★ | QUALITY ★★★★ | VALUE ★★★★ | PRICE RANGE $69–$125

Set back from US 89 and surrounded by a white fence, an old wagon wheel, and horse and cattle pastures, Arrowhead is a luxurious ranch house that makes a good base for exploring the areas between Bryce and Zion National Parks and south toward the Grand Canyon's forested North Rim. The luxurious living room has a stone fireplace and big-screen TV and opens onto a patio for outdoor breakfasts. The adjacent deck has a pool and hot tub for relaxation. The hosts can arrange horseback riding into the nearby mountains, where the wildlife ranges from deer and elk to golden and bald eagles.

SETTING & FACILITIES

Location Along US 89, 2 mi. north of Mt. Carmel Junction at Mile Marker 84 **Near** Zion National Park, Bryce Canyon National Park, Coral Pink Sand Dunes State Park, Grand Staircase–Escalante National Monument **Building** 1985 2-story ranch house w/ stone facade **Grounds** White fence surrounds 12 acres of pasture fronting US 89 **Public**

Space Living room, DR, deck **Food & Drink** Full breakfast in DR or patio; guest kitchen **Recreation** Horse riding, horseshoes, skiing, fishing, hunting, bird-watching, volleyball, basketball, hiking **Amenities & Services** Pool table, pool, hot tub, big screen TV, exercise equipment, barbecue

ACCOMMODATIONS
Units 5 **All** TV/VCR **Some** Fridge & microwave (1), futon sofa (1) **Bed & Bath** King (1), queens (4); all private baths, Jacuzzi (1), tubs (3) **Favorites** Yellow Rose Suite is yellow and blue w/ yellow roses, four-poster king, queen roll-out, double Jacuzzi, dressing room, fridge, microwave, private poolside entrance **Comfort & Decor** Antique furniture, wood-frame beds, lace curtains, handmade comforters.

RATES, RESERVATIONS, & RESTRICTIONS
Deposit 1 night (cancellation 10 days before arrival date for refund) **Discounts** Extended stays, multiple rooms, Nov. 30–March 1 **Credit Cards** MC, V **Check-In/Out** 3–9 p.m./11 a.m. **Smoking** Patio **Pets** No (ranch has 2 dogs, cats, chickens, other animals) **Kids** Yes **No-Nos** N/A **Minimum Stay** None **Open** All year **Hosts** Jim & Jane Jennings, P.O. Box 5561, 2155 S. State St., Mt. Carmel 84755 **Phone** (435) 648-2569 or toll-free (888) 821-1670 **Fax** (435) 648-2781 **E-mail** dueljl@color-country.net **Web** www.arrowheadbb.com

ROCKY TOP RANCH BED AND BREAKFAST,
Mt. Carmel Junction

OVERALL ★★★½ | QUALITY ★★★½ | VALUE ★★★★★ | PRICE RANGE $65–$75

From the highway, a quarter mile from the Buffalo Grill restaurant, a dirt road leads through a gate with two metal cattle skulls to secluded Rocky Top Ranch. The owners spent several years piecing together a complete house reached by wood stairs above a stand-alone garage. The hostess spent years working at the Thunderbird motel in nearby Mt. Carmel Junction and, not being a morning person, brings a continental breakfast up the night before. Thus, guests have complete freedom in their own private, secluded ranch house a short walk from the main house. The surrounding hills can be hiked or ridden in ATVs, or (better yet) bring your horse.

SETTING & FACILITIES
Location UT 9, Mile Marker 47, 3 mi. east of Zion National Park east entrance & 9.7 mi. west of Mt. Carmel Junction (US 89) **Near** Zion National Park, Bryce Canyon, Kanab **Building** Cabin built above garage **Grounds** 15 acres w/ horse pastures in mountain foothills **Public Space** Porch, outdoor areas **Food & Drink** Cont'l breakfast brought to room night before **Recreation** Horse riding, ATVs **Amenities & Services** barbecue, fire pit, horseshoes, 2 RV hookups, horse boarding

ACCOMMODATIONS
Units 1 house **All** Full kitchen w/ stove, microwave, & large fridge; ceiling fan; sliding glass door to redwood deck **Some** N/A **Bed & Bath** King and single; private bath **Favorites**

Rustic cabin built above garage **Comfort & Decor** Wood paneling, Southwestern art on walls, angled light maroon ceiling, carpeted dining room with octagonal wood table, and rustic wood bath.

RATES, RESERVATIONS, & RESTRICTIONS
Deposit None **Discounts** None **Credit Cards** None (cash or check only) **Check-In/Out** Flexible **Smoking** No **Pets** Yes (owner has cats & dogs; horses welcome) **Kids** Yes **No-Nos** N/A **Minimum Stay** None **Open** March–Nov. (depending on weather) **Hosts** Ralph & Colleen Carlson, P.O. Box 123, Orderville 84758 **Phone** Toll-free (877) 548-9800 **Fax** N/A **E-mail** rocky@color-country.net **Web** N/A

ZION WATERSIDE LODGE, Mt. Carmel Junction

OVERALL ★★★★ | QUALITY ★★★½ | VALUE ★★★★ | PRICE RANGE $89–$169

Carved out of a surrounding working cattle ranch to fill a niche for groups, Zion Waterside Lodge sells out well in advance for family reunions during the summer months. Rooms are spare and clean Western-style sleeping places. The real action is outdoors in this self-proclaimed "bed-and-breakfast-style lodge." Ponds stocked with catfish, trout, and bass; hiking and biking trails; and square dances in the barn are popular with groups. This family-run, group-oriented lodge provides ample escapes from business meetings and is one of the few places where kids can swim in a pond and run amok.

SETTING & FACILITIES
Location Clear Creek Ranch, 2 mi. east of Zion National Park's east entrance; from UT 9, Mile Marker 46, turn onto Northfork Rd **Near** Airstrip, Zion National Park, Bryce Canyon **Building** Modern, 2-story wood lodge w/ ample decks **Grounds** 600 acres w/ ponds, meadows, forested mountains **Public Space** DR, lounge w/ fireplace and satellite TV/VCR **Food & Drink** Full breakfast or breakfast basket; box or picnic lunches, family-style dinners, bedtime desserts available for groups **Recreation** Canoeing, fishing, biking, golf, horse riding, Ping Pong, volleyball, horseshoes, skeet shooting **Amenities & Services** Children's playground, seasonal swimming pond, guest office work area, meeting rooms, pavilion, outdoor fire pit, amphitheater, laundry

ACCOMMODATIONS
Units 9 guest rooms, 4 upstairs & 5 downstairs, includes 2 2-BR family suites **All** Ceiling fan **Some** Sinks **Bed & Bath** Queens, some w/ additional singles; all private baths, tubs (2) **Favorites** Family suites w/ adjoining rooms connected; loft has twin beds for kids **Comfort & Decor** Simplicity and spareness, with white walls, rustic light pine wood, and log furnishings, horseshoe hangers, Southwestern carpet patterns

RATES, RESERVATIONS, & RESTRICTIONS
Deposit Credit card; $25 cancellation fee, cancellations less than 24 hours in advance charged for 1 night **Discounts** Groups **Credit Cards** MC, V **Check-In/Out** 3 p.m./11 a.m. **Smoking** No **Pets** No **Kids** Yes **No-Nos** N/A **Minimum Stay** None **Open** All year

Host Dixie McCorvey, P.O. Box 167, Orderville 84758 **Phone** Toll-free (800) 486-6511 **Fax** (435) 648-2301 **E-mail** information@zionwatersidelodge.com **Web** www.zionwater sidelodge.com

PANGUITCH ANGLERS FLY SHOP AND INN, *Panguitch*

OVERALL ★★★ | QUALITY ★★★½ | VALUE ★★★★ | PRICE RANGE $55–$150 (HIGHER RATES INCLUDE FISHING)

Halfway between Las Vegas and Salt Lake City at the old Hillsdale ghost town site, the Anglers Fly Shop and Inn was born in 2001 amid roadside pastureland bisected by a river with brown trout and cottonwood trees. Panguitch translates as "big fish" in the Paiute Indian language, and the surrounding area is renowned for trout fishing. Weathered ghost-town lumber adds a rustic feel, though the bed-and-breakfast radically changed an old house, keeping only the facade and pine floor while adding modern amenities like plumbing and flush toilets. Picnic benches and a pond appeal to people preferring painting, writing, and relaxing. The shop is worth a stop for fly talk and admiring Brooklyn-born Vinnie's amazingly lifelike fish and duck carvings.

SETTING & FACILITIES
Location Hillsdale ghost town; from junction of UT 89 & 12, go 2 mi. south on UT 89 to Mile Marker 123 **Near** Lakes, Red Canyon, Bryce Canyon National Park, Cedar Breaks, wildlife museum **Building** 2001 restoration of 1915–17 "new fancy house" **Grounds** 155 acres, includes 2-acre pond, picnic table, and 2 mi. of fishing river **Public Space** LR w/ fireplace, kitchen **Food & Drink** Cont'l breakfast; snacks; kitchen use **Recreation** Fishing, boating **Amenities & Services** Fishing gear, guided trips

ACCOMMODATIONS
Units 4 guest rooms, 1 in fly shop **All** Heating **Some** Partially handicap-accessible (1), armoires (2) **Bed & Bath** Queens (3), doubles (1); all private baths, tubs (2) **Favorites** Paneled room adjacent to fly shop has private entrance, electric fireplace, angler theme quilts, Creole wicker, two doubles, shower; largest upper has 2 iron-framed queen beds, river view **Comfort & Decor** Rustic with pine wood, antiques, fly-fishing themes.

RATES, RESERVATIONS, & RESTRICTIONS
Deposit 1 night (72-hour cancellation for refund) **Discounts** Groups, weekly rates **Credit Cards** MC, V **Check-In/Out** 3 p.m./11 a.m. **Smoking** No **Pets** No (can be boarded at nearby kennel; owners have dogs) **Kids** Yes **No-Nos** N/A **Minimum Stay** None **Open** All year **Hosts** Vince Salvato & Bobbi Bryant, UT 89, MM 123, P.O. Box 41, Panguitch 84759 **Phone** (435) 676-8950 **Fax** (435) 676-8519 **E-mail** info@ panguitchanglers.com **Web** panguitchanglers.com

THE RED BRICK INN OF PANGUITCH, Panguitch

OVERALL ★★★★ | QUALITY ★★★★ | VALUE ★★★★ | PRICE RANGE $65–$150

Originally the area's first hospital, the Red Brick Inn of Panguitch is popular with local residents, many of whom were born in this building or who, during a later boarding house era, lived here as newlyweds. Locals now fight among themselves over who will stay here when their large families take over the town for reunions. The bed-and-breakfast conversion (changes are evident every visit) is the handiwork of a San Bernadino, California, couple with catering and construction backgrounds who began their bed-and-breakfast search before being married over 15 years ago. They fell in love with the town while visiting friends running the Flying M coffee shop on North Main Street. The inn is notable for its artistic architectural design solutions and Peggy's talk-of-the-town cookies and muffins.

SETTING & FACILITIES

Location 1.5 blocks from 4-way stop sign on corner of Main & Center Sts. **Near** Lakes, Red Canyon, Bryce Canyon National Park, Cedar Breaks, Brian Head Ski Resort, wildlife museum **Building** 1930s Dutch colonial **Grounds** Large rural back yard for playing bocce ball; greenhouse, chicken coop, fire pit, Jacuzzi, & gazebo in various stages of planning & construction **Public Space** Living room, DR **Food & Drink** Full breakfast in DR; afternoon snacks; home-baked cookies in rooms; picnic lunches available **Recreation** Horse riding, fishing, mountain biking, skiing **Amenities & Services** House phone, big-screen TV

ACCOMMODATIONS

Units 7 units, 4 upstairs, 2- & 3-BR suites **All** TV/VCR, clock radio **Some** Ceiling fans, sitting areas, full kitchen (1), separate entrance (2) **Bed & Bath** Kings, queens, doubles; 5 private baths, 1 shared bath, some tubs **Favorites** Weekend at the Seashore has New England theme, white picket-fence headboard, wall heater, seashore painting; Lazy B has cowboy state plates, huge lariat, and cast-iron horseshoes in sitting area; Hideout in basement is 3-BR red rock cave w/ fireplace, wagon wheel chandelier, bellows coffee table **Comfort & Decor** Each room unique with creative folk art design solutions—stacks of vintage suitcases as nightstands, sleeping bag comforter, and oar windows in North Woods Room; jailhouse theme with bars and brass key ring in two-room suite.

RATES, RESERVATIONS, & RESTRICTIONS

Deposit 25% (72-hour cancellation for refund) **Discounts** 3d night half price, 5th night free, winters, Brian Head ski packages, groups **Credit Cards** AE, MC, V, D **Check-In/Out** after 3 p.m./12 p.m. **Smoking** No **Pets** Yes (if small; owners have cat) **Kids** Yes **No-Nos** N/A **Minimum Stay** None **Open** All year **Hosts** Brett & Peggy Egan, 161 North 100 West, Panguitch 84759 **Phone** (435) 676-2141 or toll-free (866) red-brik **Fax** (435) 676-2141 **E-mail** peggy@redbrickinnutah.com **Web** www.redbrickinnutah.com

HUMMINGBIRD INN BED & BREAKFAST, Rockville

OVERALL ★★★★ | QUALITY ★★★½ | VALUE ★★★★★ | PRICE RANGE $45–$95

On tree-lined UT 9 (Main St.), five miles east of Grafton Ghost Town and seven miles west of Zion National Park, Hummingbird Inn lets the light in through two stories of windows. A large sunken living room lights up its fireplace in winter and displays Navajo hummingbird jewelry for sale. A spiral staircase leads to a loft/library, and a small solarium grows green plants. The dining room windows look out on a garden with hummingbird feeders and the long corolla flowering species favored by hummers. Although not as luxurious as the best bed-and-breakfasts in St. George, 40 miles to the west, Hummingbird offers the advantages of an intimate and attractive house that is only seven miles from Zion National Park headquarters and Springdale shops and restaurants.

SETTING & FACILITIES
Location Near Zion National Park, state parks, St. George, forests, ghost towns **Building** 1990s 2-story Southwest style w/ abundant windows **Grounds** 1 acre w/ horse pasture behind yard **Public Space** LR, DR, loft/library **Food & Drink** Full breakfast in DR **Recreation** Biking, horse riding, fishing, river tubing, bird-watching, tennis **Amenities & Services** Sundeck, fireplace, play area for badminton, croquet, horseshoes

ACCOMMODATIONS
Units 4 **All** Ceiling fan **Some** TV/VCR (2) **Bed & Bath** King (1), queen (3); all private baths, tub (3), jetted tub (1) **Favorites** Spanish-style Isabella has large conquistador picture, cutwork feather quilt, roses painted on drapes & ceiling border; Sara Elizabeth, early Pioneer style, is romantic favorite w/ angled ceiling, king bed w/ floral bedspread, love seat in sitting area, TV/VCR, double jetted tub **Comfort & Decor** Basic furnishings reflecting historical periods from Native American to Spanish colonial to pioneer, mostly carpeted w/ dark woods, some pinks, maroons

RATES, RESERVATIONS, & RESTRICTIONS
Deposit None (48-hour cancellation policy) **Discounts** Extended stays **Credit Cards** None **Check-In/Out** 3 p.m./11 a.m. **Smoking** No **Pets** No **Kids** Yes **No-Nos** N/A **Minimum Stay** None **Open** All year **Host** Connie Terry, 37 W. Main St., Rockville 84763 **Phone** (435) 772-3632 or toll-free (800) 964-bird **Fax** N/A **E-mail** N/A **Web** N/A

HARVEST HOUSE BED & BREAKFAST AT ZION, Springdale

OVERALL ★★★½ | QUALITY ★★★★ | VALUE ★★★★ | PRICE RANGE $90–$110

Harvest House is a very comfortable, home-style bed-and-breakfast near shops, restaurants, and the entrance to Zion National Park. Although motels near Zion regularly fill to capacity during the summer, bed-and-breakfasts have had a hard time surviving in Rockville and Springdale. Upstairs rooms, particularly the two with private decks, are popular for their mountain views. The living room, a comfortable gathering place with angled ceilings, white walls, and sofas, has satellite TV to keep in touch with the outside world after a day in the park. Aching muscles from a day of hiking can be soothed in a back yard hot tub near a koi pond.

SETTING & FACILITIES

Location 0.5 mi. from park entrance **Near** Zion National Park, state parks, forests **Building** 1989 Prairie style **Grounds** 0.5 acres w/ gardens, koi pond surrounded by rocks & lawn **Public Space** Front porch **Food & Drink** Full breakfast in DR; coffee bar, guest fridge **Recreation** Biking, horse riding, fishing, river tubing, bird-watching, tennis **Amenities & Services** Hot tub, satellite TV, bicycle storage

ACCOMMODATIONS

Units 4 guest rooms, 3 upstairs **All** Ceiling fan **Some** Decks (2), sofa bed (1) **Bed & Bath** Queen; all private baths, tub (3) **Favorites** Watchman, the largest room, has light wood furniture, queen bed, queen sofa bed, private deck overlooking mountains; Upper Sunset has wicker furnishings, sitting area w/ sofa & coffee table, private deck w/ mountain views; late risers like Lower Sunset, a downstairs room w/ Mission-style furniture and no morning sun **Comfort & Decor** White and wicker themes with green accents, Mission- and Vaughn-style wood furnishings, tables, chairs, some sitting areas and private decks.

RATES, RESERVATIONS, & RESTRICTIONS

Deposit Credit card holds **Discounts** Inquire **Credit Cards** AE, MC, V **Check-In/Out** 4–6 p.m./11 a.m. **Smoking** No **Pets** No **Kids** Yes (over age 6) **No-Nos** N/A **Minimum Stay** None **Open** All year **Hosts** David & Elaine Bennett, 29 Canyon View Dr., P.O. Box 125, Springdale 84767 **Phone** (435) 772-3880 **Fax** N/A **E-mail** harvesthous_Utah@yahoo.com **Web** www.harvesthouse.net

NOVEL HOUSE INN AT ZION, Springdale

OVERALL ★★★ | QUALITY ★★★★ | VALUE ★★★★ | PRICE RANGE $85–$115

Although the facade is rather ordinary and the property is easily mistaken for a modern motel, the interior furnishings are finer quality. Each room has a furniture theme related to a famous author, but the decor is not as rich as that found at the Blue Boar Inn, another Utah bed-and-breakfast with an author theme. But considering the reasonable price and close proximity to Zion National Park, couples without kids or pets will find this an acceptable stop, albeit slightly stiff and sometimes pretentious. Though Novel House advertises itself as romantic, couples seeking romantic quarters will find much better away from the park in St. George. The best room is the living room, which has a fireplace, chess table, and plenty of books.

SETTING & FACILITIES

Location Near park entrance, corner of Zion Park Blvd. & Paradise Rd. **Near** Zion National Park, state parks, forests **Building** 1995 contemporary tan 2-story stucco **Grounds** 2 acre lot w/ mountains in background **Public Space** LR, DR, porch **Food & Drink** Full breakfast in DR **Recreation** Biking, horse riding, fishing, river tubing, bird-watching, tennis **Amenities & Services** Groups

ACCOMMODATIONS

Units 10 **All** TV, phone, central AC/heat **Some** N/A **Bed & Bath** King (5), queen (5); all private baths, tub **Favorites** Bronte Room, popular w/ honeymooners, has king bed, love seat, dark woods; Count Leo Tolstoy is country Russian in feel **Comfort & Decor** Each room has different author theme, nothing too fancy, most with wood four-poster bed, armoires and wardrobes, dressers or vanity tables, upholstered or carved or wingback wood chairs, some antiques.

RATES, RESERVATIONS, & RESTRICTIONS

Deposit Credit card holds (7-day cancellation) **Discounts** Group, corp., AAA, seniors **Credit Cards** AE, MC, V, D **Check-In/Out** 4–7 p.m./11 a.m. **Smoking** No (outside) **Pets** No **Kids** No **No-Nos** N/A **Minimum Stay** None **Open** All year **Hosts** Ross & Norma Clay, 73 Paradise Rd., P.O. Box 188, Springdale 84767 **Phone** (435) 772-3650 or toll-free (800) 711-8400 **Fax** (435) 772-3651 **E-mail** novelhouse@novelhouse.com **Web** www.novelhouse.com

GREENE GATE VILLAGE, St. George

OVERALL ★★★★★ | QUALITY ★★★★★ | VALUE ★★★★★ | PRICE RANGE $79–$139

Greene Gate Village is a village of eight elegant courtyard houses with places in Mormon pioneer history. The sign out front speaks the plain truth when it says elegant and affordable. Each house is fronted by a plaque honoring a Mormon church personality. For instance, 11 children were raised

in the two-bedroom Tolley House, and early pioneers prepared for the arduous California trek in the Grainery. But it is hard to conceive of pioneer hardships among Greene Gate's five bridal suites and amenities like skylights, private porches, futon sofas, and tiled whirlpool tubs. The one concession to funk is the Depression-era Conoco and Gilmore Dixie gas pumps alongside the gravel parking area.

SETTING & FACILITIES

Location Historic District, between I-15 & Bluff St., just south of Brigham Young's winter house **Near** Historic Mormon buildings, parks, museums **Building** 8 houses, some dating back to late 1800s and National Historic Register **Grounds** Brick & grass courtyards w/ trees, flowers, benches **Public Space** Reception area, courtyard **Food & Drink** Full breakfast in Bentley House; Bentley House serves dinner Thurs.–Sat., caters receptions **Recreation** Golf, tennis, winter sports **Amenities & Services** Groups, receptions, pool

ACCOMMODATIONS

Units 16 rooms in 8 houses, 4 2-BR units **All** Microwave, fridge, phone, TV **Some** VCR, pool (2), tennis court (1), full kitchen (2), kitchenette (2), fireplace (8) **Bed & Bath** Kings, queens, twins (Greene House), often multiple beds; all private baths, whirlpool tubs (5) & tubs **Favorites** Christmas Cottage has Christmas tree in living room, fireplace, ceiling fan, whirlpool tub near king bed, kitchenette; Lysann has private balcony & skylight over tub; Green Hedge has 3 rooms sharing a common LR w/ fireplace & kitchen, including Kristyl w/ whirlpool tub room **Comfort & Decor** Each house is slightly different, though the tendency is toward Victorian and pioneer themes but tempered with mostly carpeted baths and luxuries like sitting rooms with futon sofas and malachite-tiled whirlpool tubs (Judd House).

RATES, RESERVATIONS, & RESTRICTIONS

Deposit Credit card (3-day cancellation for refund; 30 days for Greene House) **Discounts** Corp., groups (2 nights or longer; no breakfast w/ Greene and Miles End House rentals); golf packages **Credit Cards** AE, MC, V, D **Check-In/Out** 3 p.m./11 a.m. **Smoking** No **Pets** No **Kids** Yes **No-Nos** N/A **Minimum Stay** None **Open** All year **Hosts** Mark & Barbara Greene, 76 W. Tabernacle St., St. George 84770 **Phone** (435) 628-6999 or toll-free (800) 350-6999 **Fax** (435) 628-6989 **E-mail** stay@greenegate.com **Web** www.greenegatevillage.com

AN OLDE PENNY FARTHING INN BED & BREAKFAST, St. George

OVERALL ★★★★ | QUALITY ★★★★ | VALUE ★★★★ | PRICE RANGE $59–$115

Behind a white picket fence, tall shade trees make the patio, with its views of historic Native American red cliffs, the favored morning and late afternoon beverage sipping place at An Olde Penny Farthing. The host, a San Francisco Bay–area architectural worker with English roots, expresses his creativity in details like the handicap-accessible, Southwestern Morning Dove's saltillo tile bath floor, 4-foot-deep and 7.5-foot-long tub, and double shower. A small room without a bath has an extra double bed for families and also serves as a business workspace. The hostess, a licensed nurse, contributed the antique bed pan display above the blue wood staircase. The comfortable maroon living room has a green and white fireplace and doubles as a group meeting space.

SETTING & FACILITIES
Location Historic Downtown District **Near** Zion National Park, Snow Canyon State Park, Red Cliffs, museums, historic buildings **Building** 120-year-old Victorian-style pioneer adobe w/ rock foundation & 18-in.-thick walls, stucco added later **Grounds** Street corner patio w/ hillside views **Public Space** LR, DR, patio **Food & Drink** Full breakfast in DR or patio; banana carrot muffins and multiberry crêpes most notable; special diets w/ prior arrangement **Recreation** Golf, winter sports **Amenities & Services** Weddings, receptions, family reunions, business meetings

ACCOMMODATIONS
Units 5 guest rooms, 3 can combine into suite **All** AC, ceiling fan, TV/VCR, fridge, digital clock, data port **Some** Handicap-accessible (1), sitting room (1), fireplace (1), pull-chain water closet toilet (3 uppers) **Bed & Bath** King (1), queens (4); all private baths, extra deep & extra long tub (1), whirlpool tubs (2), claw-foot tubs (2) **Favorites** Betsy Ross has old 13-star flag; 13-ft.-high ceiling; red, white, & blue assorted Americana; four-poster queen. Winston Churchill is largest, has beam ceiling, dark pub green & burgundy colors, king bed, painted pine bath floors; Bridal Suite has skylight, double whirlpool tub, fireplace, large sitting room **Comfort & Decor** Varies with room themes; floors range from saltillo tile and flagstone to painted wood, some wood beam and planked ceilings, beds vary from oak to iron and peeler log.

RATES, RESERVATIONS, & RESTRICTIONS
Deposit Credit card (3-day cancellation policy; 1 week for holiday weekends, special events) **Discounts** Group whole house rental (up to 15 people) **Credit Cards** AE, MC, V, D **Check-In/Out** 4–8 p.m./11 a.m. **Smoking** No **Pets** Yes (small dog ok; owners have dog) **Kids** "Call; it depends . . ." **No-Nos** N/A **Minimum Stay** None **Open** All year **Hosts** Alan & Jacquie Capon, 278 North 100 West, St. George 84770 **Phone** (435) 673-7755 or toll-free (800) 943-2920 **Fax** N/A **E-mail** oldepenny@sginet.com **Web** www.oldepenny.citysearch.com

QUICKSAND AND CACTUS BED & BREAKFAST, St. George

OVERALL ★★★ | QUALITY ★★★ | VALUE ★★★★ | PRICE RANGE $60–$90

Mormon pioneer history buffs will enjoy sharing the wood-floor and beam-ceiling living room in the former home of Mormon historian Juanita Brooks, a college dean who resigned for marriage and children and then established her professional reputation tracking down pioneer diaries and writing at night. *Quicksand and Cactus,* the title of Brook's autobiography, is the name of the bed-and-breakfast run by a local graphics artist. A stone mason constructed the two-room rock house in 1877 using scrap from church buildings and in 1877 added an adobe kitchen (now a bedroom). A sleeping porch, now part of a room, was added during the World War II era. The National Register honey locust tree in front was planted in 1879.

SETTING & FACILITIES

Location 2 blocks from Historic District in residential neighborhood **Near** Opera house, museums, galleries, shops, Ancestor Square, national and state parks **Building** Conglomeration of an 1877 2-room rock house, 1887 adobe, and 1941 sleeping porch **Grounds** 0.3 acre w/ flagstone walkway, metal sculptures, roses, santolina, honey locust, & mulberry **Public Space** Living room, DR, front & back porches **Food & Drink** Full breakfast in DR **Recreation** Golf, winter sports, biking **Amenities & Services** Mormon history info

ACCOMMODATIONS

Units 3 **All** Private entrance, AC, ceiling fan, TV/VCR, digital clock radio **Some** Connect as suite (2) **Bed & Bath** Queens (2), double (1); all private baths, claw-foot tubs w/ hand showers **Favorites** Bedroom 1 has floral wallpaper, pedestal sink, extra room for kids **Comfort & Decor** Each room is different and may include floral wallpaper and comforters, wainscoting, wood furnishings, framed flower, and bird and cat etchings.

RATES, RESERVATIONS, & RESTRICTIONS

Deposit Credit card **Discounts** None **Credit Cards** MC, V, D **Check-In/Out** 3 p.m./11 a.m. **Smoking** No **Pets** No (owner has cat) **Kids** Yes **No-Nos** N/A **Minimum Stay** None **Open** All year **Host** Carla Fox, 346 N. Main St., St. George, 84770 **Phone** (435) 674-1739 or toll-free (800) 381-1654 **Fax** N/A **E-mail** quiksand@infowest.com **Web** www.infowest.com/quicksand

SEVEN WIVES INN, St. George

OVERALL ★★★★★ | QUALITY ★★★★½ | VALUE ★★★★★ | PRICE RANGE $75–$150

After Utah became a state and the U.S. government outlawed polygamy in 1882, Benjamin Johnson hid in the attic (Jane's room) and secretly visited his seven wives in the rooms below. Hence, the home is now known as the Seven Wives Inn. Each room is named after a wife (rooms in the neighboring President's House are named after Mormon church presidents' wives) and contains the history of that wife (one liberated lady even dumped Benjamin) and a blank journal for guests to express their thoughts (the inn does its best to remove X-rated pages, but parental discretion is advised). Breakfast specialties like blueberry oat pancakes and parfaits composed of homemade granola, nonfat yogurt, and fruit can be eaten on the polygamist's patio overlooking a quiet, tree-lined residential street and Brigham Young's winter house.

SETTING & FACILITIES

Location Historic District, kitty-corner from Brigham Young's winter house **Near** Museums, galleries, shops, historic buildings, national & state parks **Building** 1873 & 1883 neighboring 2-story pioneer houses & cottage **Grounds** Tree-shaded yard w/ pool **Public Space** LRs, DR, patio **Food & Drink** Full breakfast in DR or patio; English afternoon tea (Wed.–Fri.); 5-course dinners by Chef Leo; jazz & murder mystery dinners **Recreation** Golf, tennis, biking, winter sports **Amenities & Services** Pool (Apr.–Oct.), Seven Wives label bayberry soap, massage, body wraps, botanical skin care, aromatherapy, bicycles, free access to gym

ACCOMMODATIONS

Units 13 **All** TV, phone **Some** VCRs, claw-foot tubs **Bed & Bath** Kings (2), queens (11), 2nd twin beds (2); all private baths, tubs (7), whirlpool tubs (4) **Favorites** Melissa suite has canopied four-poster, Victorian furnishings, fireplace, double whirlpool; Ada Cottage has pioneer-style furniture, Gothic Temple windows, kitchenette, double shower, whirlpool tub; Sarah room has Roaring Twenties decor, sun room, fireplace, private porch, 1927 Model T Ford whirlpool tub **Comfort & Decor** Varies among relatively spacious rooms with very comfortable beds, floral pillows, understated country elegance, and simplicity generally prevailing from attic alcoves with angled ceilings and stenciling to rooms with French doors, lace, and period wallpapers.

RATES, RESERVATIONS, & RESTRICTIONS

Deposit Credit card (3-day cancellation for full refund minus $10 fee) **Discounts** Corp. singles (Sun.–Thur.) **Credit Cards** AE, MC, V, D **Check-In/Out** 3–9 p.m./11 a.m. **Smoking** No **Pets** No **Kids** By prior arrangement **No-Nos** N/A **Minimum Stay** None **Open** All year **Hosts** Shellee Taylor & Rosie Chero, 217 North 100 West, St. George 84770 **Phone** (435) 628-3737 or toll-free (800) 600-3737 **Fax** N/A **E-mail** info@sevenwivesinn.com **Web** www.sevenwivesinn.com

MULEY TWIST INN, Teasdale

OVERALL ★★★★ | QUALITY ★★★★ | VALUE ★★★★★ | PRICE RANGE $70–$90

Around the corner from a white Mormon church and almost flush against a sandstone mountain, Muley Twist is the creation of a desert-loving couple who spend winters ski-patrolling Aspen and summers exploring Hell's Hole and other local mountain bike trails. Surrounded by a pinion pine and Utah juniper forest, the green-roofed, cedar-sided inn is fronted by a large wraparound porch with views of the Mummy Cliffs and Gorilla Rocks. A ripple-rock sandstone perimeter wall is planted with drought-tolerant flowers and herbs like penstemon, Russian sage, and hyssop. The six-foot-diameter pine dining room table has a carved leaf motif perimeter; provides chairs stained green, blue, and mahogany to match the carpet; and is tucked in a bay window alcove with mountain views.

SETTING & FACILITIES

Location 3.5 mi. SW of Torrey **Near** Capitol Reef National Park, town of Escalante **Building** 1996 modern 2-story cedar farmhouse w/ wraparound porch **Grounds** 30 acres of natural forest **Public Space** Living room, DR, wraparound porch **Food & Drink** Full breakfast in DR; lunch, dinner, & special event catering by Cafe Diablo **Recreation** Fishing, biking, horse riding **Amenities & Services** Weddings, special events

ACCOMMODATIONS

Units 5 guest rooms, 4 upstairs **All** Phone, clock radio **Some** Handicap-accessible (1) **Bed & Bath** Queens, trundle bed (1), rollaway available; all private baths, tubs **Favorites** Mountain Room has small Norfolk pine, Nepal & Peru mountain photos, Aspen mining claims map, green-stained furnishings w/ leaf carvings, classic quilts; Prairie Room is larger, has bay window, pencil-post bed, pine-stained armoire topped w/ quilt display **Comfort & Decor** Simple and comfortable rooms with varied nature themes, like canyon and desert, antelope and prickly pear metal sculptures, nature photos and watercolors, carved- and stained-wood furnishings, homemade duvets, classic quilts, wood-framed beveled mirrors; baths have pedestal sink, tile floor.

RATES, RESERVATIONS, & RESTRICTIONS

Deposit Credit card (10-day cancellation policy) **Discounts** Groups **Credit Cards** AE, MC, V **Check-In/Out** 4–9 p.m./11 a.m. **Smoking** No **Pets** No (pets must remain outside) **Kids** Yes (if well behaved) **No-Nos** N/A **Minimum Stay** None **Open** April 1–Oct. 28 **Hosts** Eric & Penny Kinsman, Box 117, 125 South, Teasdale 84773 **Phone** (435) 425-3640 or toll-free (800) 530-1038 **Fax** N/A **E-mail** muley@rof.net **Web** www.go-utah.com/muleytwist

SKYRIDGE, Torrey

OVERALL ★★★★ | QUALITY ★★★★ | VALUE ★★★★ | PRICE RANGE $107–$158

Reached via a short gravel road across from the Wonderland Inn motel, SkyRidge lives up to its name with magnificent views encompassing Capitol Reef and the surrounding mountains. The owners, who moved here from Mendocino on the California coast and designed the house, created custom art furnishings, like the living room's sponge-painted, slate-colored sheetrock fireplace hammered with 30 pounds of roofing nails. Edgy checks and stripes complement dyed and scored slate-like concrete floors; caged finches chirp in the dining room. Painted and glazed sand- and mud-textured walls are lined with watercolors for sale. Shelves of painted wood hens, Navajo mud sheep, and other gift items for sale compete with large mountain view windows for attention.

SETTING & FACILITIES

Location Just east of the intersection of UT 12 & 24 **Near** Capitol Reef National Park, Escalante **Building** Early 1990s 3-story territorial style **Grounds** 75 ridge-top acres

Public Space Living room, DR **Food & Drink** Full breakfast in DR; 24-hour beverages; evening hors d'oeuvres **Recreation** Horse riding, biking, fishing **Amenities & Services** Hot tub, massage (fee)

ACCOMMODATIONS

Units 6 **All** TV/VCR, phone, clock, hair dryer **Some** Private deck w/ hot tub (2), private patio **Bed & Bath** King (1), queens (5); all private baths, double whirlpool (1), tubs (4) **Favorites** Sagebrush on 2d floor has king, private deck w/ hot tub; Pinon on 2d floor also has deck w/ hot tub **Comfort & Decor** Eclectic mix of antiques, wicker, owner-created art furnishings, and numerous mountain view windows.

RATES, RESERVATIONS, & RESTRICTIONS

Deposit Credit card (14-day cancellation policy; fee imposed) **Discounts** Winter **Credit Cards** MC,V **Check-In/Out** 4–6 p.m./ 11 a.m. **Smoking** No (outside only) **Pets** No **Kids** Yes **No-Nos** N/A **Minimum Stay** 2 nights weekends May–June, Sept.–Oct. **Open** All year **Hosts** Sally Elliot & Karen Kesler, P.O. Box 750220, Torrey 84775 **Phone** (435) 425-3222 **Fax** (435) 425-3222 **E-mail** skyridge@color-country.net **Web** www.bbiu.org/skyridge

BRYCE POINT BED & BREAKFAST, Tropic

OVERALL ★★★★ | QUALITY ★★★★ | VALUE ★★★★ | PRICE RANGE $55–$120

The hallway is decorated with family pictures, and most guest rooms at Bryce Point are named after the hosts' four children and their spouses. The host couple, who married out of high school just after World War II, even had their grown children decorate some guest rooms, mostly with adult occupation themes, like aviation. The three upstairs guest rooms, reached via a staircase topped with antlers, are nearest a huge redwood deck with good views of Powell Peak at sunset and a Bryce Canyon view at sunrise. Europeans particularly like the intimate family experience here, feeling it broadens their cultural understanding between nature forays.

SETTING & FACILITIES

Location 4 blocks west of Main St. **Near** Bryce Canyon, Kodachrome Basin, Escalante **Building** 1933 ranch-style bungalow, remodeled & 2d story added in 1989 **Grounds** 0.75 acres w/ large back yard vegetable garden **Public Space** Living room, DR, view decks **Food & Drink** Full breakfast in DR; Seven-Up pancakes a specialty **Recreation** Horse riding, fishing, boating, biking, hiking **Amenities & Services** Laundry, hot tub

ACCOMMODATIONS

Units 5 guest rooms & 1 cottage **All** TV/VCR, ceiling fan, vanity outside bath, sitting area, modem jack (shared line) **Some** Cottage has living room, kitchen, washer & dryer **Bed & Bath** Kings, queens, sleeper beds; all private baths **Favorites** Grandkids Rooms has

Raggedy Ann, teddy bears, Amish granny quilt, large mirrored closet; Lynn & Karen Room has astronaut patches, view of Bryce Canyon & back yard garden **Comfort & Decor** Varies widely, w/ comfortable beds and themes reflecting family interests

RATES, RESERVATIONS, & RESTRICTIONS

Deposit 1 night (7-day cancellation for full refund; if under 7 days, refund only if room re-rented) **Discounts** None **Credit Cards** MC, V **Check-In/Out** 2–5 p.m./ 11 a.m. **Smoking** Designated outside smoking areas **Pets** No **Kids** Yes **No-Nos** N/A **Minimum Stay** None **Open** All year **Hosts** Lamar & Ethel LeFevre, 61 North 400 West, Tropic 84776 **Phone** (435) 679-8629 or toll-free (888) 200-4211 **Fax** (435) 679-8629 **E-mail** N/A **Web** www.brycepointlodging.com

THE BULLBERRY INN BED & BREAKFAST, Tropic

OVERALL ★★★ | QUALITY ★★★½ | VALUE ★★★★ | PRICE RANGE $45–$85

A modern roadside inn built by an entertaining, hard-working local boy who got "tired of punching a time clock," Bullberry Inn is named after a native berry gathered in the wild for Granny Bird, the host's mother, whose orange-colored bullberry jelly is a taste sensation, jazzing up a mundane breakfast served in wood booths. Great Granny Bird's old wood-burning stove, prominently displayed, allegedly warmed the feet and cooked muffins for the family's Circleville neighbor, the young Butch Cassidy, before he went on to outlaw fame. The inn competes quite successfully with the local motels for the drive-by business, being the first building with a large sign when driving into town from Escalante.

SETTING & FACILITIES

Location SE edge of town, corner of Francisco Lane & UT 12 **Near** Bryce Canyon, Kodachrome Basin, Escalante **Building** 1999 2-story colonial English **Grounds** Large parking area & field surrounds main building **Public Space** Sitting room, DR, front porch **Food & Drink** Full breakfast in DR **Recreation** Horse riding, fishing, boating, biking, hiking **Amenities & Services** Satellite TV

ACCOMMODATIONS

Units 5 guest rooms, 4 upstairs **All** Ceiling fan, TV **Some** Porches, private outside entrances **Bed & Bath** Queen; all private baths, tubs **Favorites** Best rooms have porches and private outside entrances **Comfort & Decor** Carpeted rooms with simple pine log furnishings and some good mountain views

RATES, RESERVATIONS, & RESTRICTIONS

Deposit None (pay at time of arrival) **Discounts** None **Credit Cards** None (cash or check only) **Check-In/Out** Flexible (no set times) **Smoking** No **Pets** No **Kids** Yes **No-Nos** N/A **Minimum Stay** None **Open** All year **Hosts** Wally, Nettie, & Steven Bird, 412

S. UT 12, Tropic 84776 **Phone** (435) 679-8820 **Fax** N/A **E-mail** N/A **Web** N/A

THE CANYON LIVERY BED & BREAKFAST, Tropic

OVERALL ★★★★ | QUALITY ★★★½ | VALUE ★★★★ | PRICE RANGE $65–$95

The rooms at Canyon Livery have double French doors and varying views of irrigated pastures, surrounding farms, and the Amphitheater rock formation in Bryce Canyon National Park, which is only 1.5 miles away as the crow flies but a dozen miles by road. Though not as remote as the Stone Canyon Inn and several blocks closer to town than Fox's, Canyon Livery is still a good place to seek solace from the summer crowds. Besides the large lawn, there is a sizable vegetable garden and peach, plum, cherry, apricot, and apple trees—an abundance that finds its way into homemade breads and jams. Afternoon tea by the hot tub gazebo is an unexpected treat.

SETTING & FACILITIES
Location 6 blocks west of Main St. **Near** Bryce Canyon, Kodachrome Basin, Escalante **Building** 1980 2-story ranch house **Grounds** Back yard fruit orchard **Public Space** Living room, DR **Food & Drink** Full breakfast in DR; homemade breads & jellies; afternoon tea by gazebo **Recreation** Horse riding, fishing, boating, biking, hiking **Amenities & Services** Hot tub

ACCOMMODATIONS
Units 5 guest rooms, 3 upstairs **All** AC, hat rack, clock, private outside entrance **Some** TV/VCR (on request), private balcony (3), shared porch (2) **Bed & Bath** Queens; all private baths, tubs **Favorites** Upstairs rooms have private balconies; Western Room has a big eyebrow-shaped window & old wood-framed cowboy prints **Comfort & Decor** White walls, carpets, cast-iron bed frames, handmade quilts, double French doors.

RATES, RESERVATIONS, & RESTRICTIONS
Deposit $30 (7-day cancellation for full refund; if under 7 days, refund only if room re-rented) **Discounts** Winter rates Nov. 1–April 1 **Credit Cards** MC, V (cash or travelers check payment requested on arrival) **Check-In/Out** 4–8 p.m./10 a.m. **Smoking** No **Pets** No (horse boarding available) **Kids** Yes **No-Nos** Food or drink in rooms **Minimum Stay** None **Open** All year **Hosts** Kevin & Jeannie Shakespeare, 50 South 660 West, P.O. Box 24, Tropic 84776 **Phone** (435) 679-8780 or toll-free (888) 889-8910 **Fax** N/A **E-mail** tclbnb@color-country.net **Web** www.canyonlivery.com

FOX'S BRYCE TRAILS BED & BREAKFAST, Tropic

OVERALL ★★★★ | QUALITY ★★★★ | VALUE ★★★★ | PRICE RANGE $65–$105

A redwood staircase at the front of Fox's Bryce Trails provides a private entrance, bypassing the downstairs living room and leading to a second-story deck with a view of what Europeans call a cowboy scene. Painters like to set up their easels here and paint the foreground of cattle grazing next to a weathered shack surrounded by an old wood fence, with Bryce Canyon's renowned sandstone rock formations in the background. In contrast, Fox's interior is a study in white and immaculate housekeeping. The large floral carpeted dining room has rattan-back wood chairs, ferns, green plants, and painterly scenes beckoning from beyond the breakfast-room windows.

SETTING & FACILITIES

Location West From UT 12 on Bryce Way, just past high school & stone fruit orchards **Near** Bryce Canyon, Kodachrome Basin, Escalante **Building** 2-story contemporary ranch house w/ redwood deck **Grounds** Rural back yard **Public Space** Living room, DR **Food & Drink** Full breakfast in DR **Recreation** Hunting, fishing, horse riding, hiking **Amenities & Services** Sundeck

ACCOMMODATIONS

Units 6 **All** AC, ceiling fan, TV, private entrance **Some** N/A **Bed & Bath** Kings, queens; all private baths, tubs **Favorites** Mossy Cave has wicker & wood furnishings w/ green accents **Comfort & Decor** Clean white walls, beige carpets, floral spreads, quilts, sitting areas, big windows, hanger racks,

RATES, RESERVATIONS, & RESTRICTIONS

Deposit 1 night (7-day cancellation for full refund; if under 7 days, refund minus $10 fee only if room re-rented) **Discounts** None **Credit Cards** MC, V **Check-In/Out** 2–8 p.m./11 a.m. **Smoking** No **Pets** No **Kids** Yes **No-Nos** N/A **Minimum Stay** None **Open** All year **Hosts** Richard & LuCine Fox, Elaine Haas, P.O. Box 87, 1001 Bryce Way, Tropic 84776 **Phone** (435) 679-8700 **Fax** (435) 679-8727 **E-mail** foxbrycetrails@yahoo.com **Web** N/A

FRANCISCO'S FARM BED & BREAKFAST, Tropic

OVERALL ★★★★ | QUALITY ★★★★ | VALUE ★★★★ | PRICE RANGE $60–$70

Free-range chickens lay breakfast eggs, and jams and jellies are homemade at this small organic fruit and vegetable farm. Francisco's Farm is a favorite of parents, a traditional family farm providing kids with an old-fashioned country experience with surrogate grandparents who have lived here for seven decades. In the evening, children can go with "Grandpa Francisco" to feed and pet the cats, dogs, hunting hounds, chickens, geese, ducks, and burros or even ride the horse. A mountain lion that was attacking people in the national park is now mounted on a living room ledge near the ceiling. The kitchen and dining room have a log wall and windows looking out on hummingbird feeders.

SETTING & FACILITIES

Location SE edge of town, 1 block from Main St., corner of Francisco Lane & UT 12 **Near** Bryce Canyon, Kodachrome Basin, Escalante **Building** 1980 owner-built 2-story farmhouse **Grounds** 10-acre farm w/ pastures and petting animals **Public Space** DR, kitchen, living room, porch **Food & Drink** Full breakfast in DR; guests can cook in kitchen **Recreation** Horse riding, bird-watching, fishing, boating, biking, hiking **Amenities & Services** Sheltered hot tub holds 8

ACCOMMODATIONS
Units 3 guest rooms, 1 downstairs **All** AC, alarm clock **Some** Handicap-accessible (1) **Bed & Bath** Queens; all private baths **Favorites** Bryce View has slanting ceilings, an alcove, 2 queen beds, & sunset views of Bryce Canyon over a horse pasture; Grandma's Peach Room downstairs has a wood ceiling, large mirrored closet, lucky dude horseshoe, & handicap-accessible walk-in shower **Comfort & Decor** Slanting ceilings, mirrored closets, white walls with floral wallpaper accents, wood furnishings, carpet.

RATES, RESERVATIONS, & RESTRICTIONS
Deposit $30 (7-day cancellation for full refund; if under 7 days, refund only if room re-rented) **Discounts** Winter rates **Credit Cards** MC, V (cash or traveler's check payment requested on arrival) **Check-In/Out** 4–8 p.m./10 a.m. **Smoking** No **Pets** Yes (must stay in shop outside or friend's kennel; horses welcome) **Kids** Yes **No-Nos** Animals inside house **Minimum Stay** None **Open** All year **Hosts** Evadean & Charlie Francisco, 51 Francisco Lane, P.O. Box 3, Tropic 84776 **Phone** (435) 679-8721 or toll-free (800) 642-4136 **Fax** (435) 679-8769 **E-mail** N/A **Web** N/A

STONE CANYON INN, Tropic

OVERALL ★★★★½ | QUALITY ★★★★½ | VALUE ★★★★★ | PRICE RANGE $89–$129

The closest bed-and-breakfast to Bryce Canyon National Park, Stone Canyon has its own stockman's gate for hiking into the park. A tall stone fireplace separates the dining and living rooms, which have sloping 20-foot-high knotty alder beam ceilings and beige faux textured walls. A world map is etched into an old leather trunk that serves as the living room coffee table. To its side are a telescope, an ancient bird cage, and an old European doll cabinet. A carpeted wrought-iron staircase topped with wood leads to the upstairs rooms, all uniquely designed with architectural touches like pentagonal and octagonal windows, purple floral pillows, and comforters.

SETTING & FACILITIES
Location From Main St., go 1 mi. west on Bryce Way and 0.5 mi. west on Fairyland Lane (dirt) **Near** Bryce Canyon, Kodachrome Basin, town of Escalante **Building** Contemporary (2000) rustic 2-story Old World–style wood & stone house **Grounds** 80 acres of pinion & juniper extending to Bryce Canyon National Park boundary **Public Space** Living room, DR, porch **Food & Drink** Full breakfast in DR **Recreation** Horse riding, mountain biking, fly-fishing, snowshoeing, cross-country skiing, hiking **Amenities & Services** Private hiking gate into park

ACCOMMODATIONS

Units 5 guest rooms, 4 uppers and 1 lower **All** Robes, carpeting, TV/VCR, phone, "retro" clock **Some** Partially handicap-accessible (1) **Bed & Bath** King (1), queens (4), roll-aways (3); all private baths, jetted tub (1), two-person jetted tubs (4) **Favorites** Grapevine Room has purple florals, 3D metal floral sink mirror, & welded king bed frame w/ tree trunks, grape leaves, & fruit bunches; Ivy Room has pointed metal bed frame w/ ivy greenery, pentagonal window, & Bryce views from Jacuzzi tub **Comfort & Decor** Creative metalwork, painted hanging herbal wreaths, "mudded" white sheetrock walls, octagonal and pentagonal windows, porcelain Mexican tile baths, granite sinks with modern nickel fixtures.

RATES, RESERVATIONS, & RESTRICTIONS

Deposit None (72-hour cancellation) **Discounts** None **Credit Cards** AE, MC, V, D **Check-In/Out** 3 p.m./11 a.m. **Smoking** No **Pets** No **Kids** Yes (over age 5) **No-Nos** N/A **Minimum Stay** None **Open** All year **Hosts** Mike & Dixie Burbidge, P.O. Box 123, 1220 W. Stone Canyon Lane, Tropic 84776 **Phone** (435) 679-8611 **Fax** (435) 679-8411 **E-mail** stonecanyon@starband.net **Web** www.stonecanyoninn.com

SNOW FAMILY GUEST RANCH BED & BREAKFAST, Virgin

OVERALL ★★★★ | QUALITY ★★★½ | VALUE ★★★★ | PRICE RANGE $109–$149

Alongside the road leading into Zion National Park, a white fence and pasture leased out for cattle grazing front the Snow Family Guest Ranch. The living room of this American quarter horse ranch has a wagon wheel chandelier, branding irons, cowboy hats, and window views of colorful layered sandstone mountains. Rifles and a revolver grace the wall of a smaller room with a big-screen TV, and another room has a piano. The ranch, founded by the current owner's grandfather, is named after surveyor Leo Snow, whose report lead President William Taft to declare the Zion area Mukuntuweap National Monument in 1909. The rooms are relatively austere and clean, a quiet place to sleep after a hard day riding along the creek or into the hills.

SETTING & FACILITIES

Location 12 mi. west of Zion National Park's south entrance on UT 9, across the street from Zion River RV Resort **Near** National parks, Cedar City (Shakespeare Festival) **Building** Ranch house renovated mid-1990s **Grounds** 12 acres facing highway have pond, creek, gazebo, hiking trails **Public Space** Living room, 2 side rooms, DR, library, deck **Food & Drink** Full breakfast in DR **Recreation** Biking, horse riding, winter sports, hiking **Amenities & Services** Big-screen TV, piano, pool, hot tub, florist for special occasions, guided trail rides ($49/2 hours), weddings, reunions, corp. & group retreats

ACCOMMODATIONS

Units 9 guest rooms, 5 upper and 4 lower **All** Ceiling fans **Some** TV (1), window seats (7) **Bed & Bath** Kings (3), queens (5), twins (2); all private baths, tubs (3), jetted tub (1)

Favorites Anniversary Suite has TV, blue comforter, pine headboard, sitting area, jetted tub **Comfort & Decor** Simple ranch style with rustic pine furnishings, clean white walls, wallpaper ceiling border, and light carpets.

RATES, RESERVATIONS, & RESTRICTIONS
Deposit Credit card for 1st night (7-day cancellation for refund minus $20 fee) **Discounts** Groups **Credit Cards** AE, MC, V, D **Check-In/Out** 4–7 p.m./11 a.m. **Smoking** No **Pets** No (3 ranch dogs, 9 horses, ducks, homing pigeons on premises) **Kids** Yes (over age 8, well behaved) **No-Nos** N/A **Minimum Stay** 2 nights **Open** All year **Hosts** Steve & Shelley Penrose, 633 E. UT 9, P.O. Box 790190, Virgin 84779 **Phone** (435) 635-2500 or toll-free (800) 308-7669 **Fax** (435) 635-2758 **E-mail** bandb@redrock.net **Web** N/A

Southeast

Southeastern Utah is tucked into the Four Corners region where Arizona and Utah meet near Colorado's Mesa Verde National Park and Farmington, New Mexico. Southeastern Utah stretches across Monument Valley Navajo Tribal Park and Lake Powell along the Arizona border, and parallels the Colorado border in the east. In a geographical oddity, Big Water's bed-and-breakfast is disconnected from the region's roads on an arm of Lake Powell seven miles from Page, Arizona, in Grand Canyon country.

Monument Valley, a favorite Hollywood Western movie backdrop, straddles the Arizona–Utah border south of Mexican Hat and Goosenecks State Park. The 1,000-foot-deep Goosenecks of the San Juan River are a classic textbook case of an entrenched meander in a river flowing through 300-million-year-old rocks. Steep, curvy, unimproved roads lead to more geologic wonders in the Valley of the Gods. Dust devils, chilly high winds, and summer thunderstorms are the rule.

Bluff, 21 miles northeast of Mexican Hat, has the closest bed-and-breakfasts for exploring these geologic wonders and Hovenweep National Monument to the east. Blanding, 25 miles north of Bluff, is closest to UT 95, which heads west toward Natural Bridges National Monument (loop drive closed in winter) and the Bullfrog Basin and Halls Crossing Marinas on Lake Powell in the Glen Canyon National Recreation Area. Monticello, 21 miles north of Blanding, is closest to UT 212, the road west to Newspaper Rock State Historic Monument and the orange sandstone rock formations, slot canyons, and deep sandy washes of Canyonlands National Park, Needles District.

Moab, the region's tourism center and a mountain biking favorite, is closest to Arches National Park, Dead Horse State Park, and the isolated mesas, buttes, and spires of Canyonlands National Park, Island in the Sky District. March–May and fall are peak seasons, though winter cold, extreme summer heat, and flash floods do not stop tourism. Green River, a truck stop and river rafting favorite on I-70 halfway between Las Vegas and Denver, is within an hour of Arches National Park to the southeast and Goblin Valley State Park to the southwest.

DREAMKATCHERS' BED & BREAKFAST, Big Water

OVERALL ★★★★½ | QUALITY ★★★★½ | VALUE ★★★★★ | PRICE RANGE $65–$95

A custom home designed and built specifically to be a bed-and-breakfast, DreamKatchers' is best known for its outdoor wrought-iron spiral staircase leading above the garage to a rooftop sundeck and hot tub. The rooftop is particularly popular for nighttime stargazing, though the large windows in the library/den and beam-ceiling living room also offer excellent panoramic views across the desert to the mountains behind Lake Powell. Breakfast on the patio overlooking the desert garden may include summer quiches with vegetables from a local organic farm or Swedish lingonberry pancakes. Some guests spend the day reading and relaxing, others head out to explore or play on Lake Powell.

SETTING & FACILITIES
Location 7 mi. east of Page, AZ; from US 89, Mile Marker 5, go to corner of South American & Revolutionary Way **Near** Lake Powell, Glen Canyon Dam, Antelope Canyon, Paria Wilderness, Kanab **Building** 2000 Mediterranean-style house **Grounds** An acre w/ desert garden and small fountain **Public Space** Living room w/ an Egyptian wall, library/den, DR, patio **Food & Drink** Full breakfast on patio; hallway fridge stocked w/ drinks; special diets honored **Recreation** Boating, golf **Amenities & Services** Fridge, ice maker, laundry, TV, rooftop sundeck w/ hot tub, boat parking

ACCOMMODATIONS
Units 3 **All** Ceiling fan, carpeting, hair dryer, dresser, nightstand **Some** N/A **Bed & Bath** Kings (2), queen (1), daybed (1); all private baths, tubs **Favorites** Cherub Room's naked angel babies and candles on walls are popular w/ honeymooners; Asian Room has gold and black fabrics, large fans on wall; Classic Room has queen and daybed, dark woods, hallway

bath, and is best for families **Comfort & Decor** Simplicity is the design goal, with white walls, wood, and marble mixed with large glass windows and antiques in the arched and angled public spaces.

RATES, RESERVATIONS, & RESTRICTIONS
Deposit 1 night; week's notice for cancellation **Discounts** Weekly **Credit Cards** AE, MC, V **Check-In/Out** 2 p.m./11 a.m. **Smoking** No **Pets** No **Kids** Yes (over age 12) **No-Nos** N/A **Minimum Stay** None **Open** All year (closed Thanksgiving & Christmas Days) **Host** Eric Ingvardsen, P.O. Box 5114, Page 86040 **Phone** (435) 675-5828 or toll-free (888) 479-9419 **Fax** N/A **E-mail** jackvan@az.net **Web** www.dreamkatchersbandb.com

GRAYSON COUNTRY INN, Blanding

OVERALL ★★½ | QUALITY ★★★ | VALUE ★★★★ | PRICE RANGE $59–$64

Grayson Country Inn is most popular with groups. Families renting the whole house and using their ingenuity and the living room hide-a-bed sofas have managed to squeeze in as many as 40 people. Families with children like renting individual rooms, as children under age 12 stay free and those over age 12 pay only $5 extra for a full breakfast. Breakfast specialties include homemade cinnamon rolls and granolas, which are served in a carpeted dining room that has light wood paneling and a wall map with pins showing guest points of origin. The family-style living room has gold-embossed felt wallpaper. The new owners live in the gray house next door and also rent out an apartment with a kitchen to longer-term guests.

SETTING & FACILITIES
Location Downtown **Near** National monuments, national parks, state parks, rivers, museums **Building** 1908 Pioneer house **Grounds** 0.5-acre yard w/ picnic tables **Public Space** LR, DR **Food & Drink** Full breakfast in DR **Recreation** Biking, boating, rafting, fishing, horse riding **Amenities & Services** Basketball hoop, playground, weddings, family reunions

ACCOMMODATIONS
Units 8 **All** Cable TV, alarm clock, central heat **Some** Swamp cooler (5), ceiling fan **Bed & Bath** 1–2 queens (7), doubles (1); all private baths, tub (1) **Favorites** Blue Room has 2 queen beds, angled ceiling, lavender carpet, blue walls, shower; Parlor Room, original house parlor, has 1900s-period fixtures, original stained-glass windows & light fixtures **Comfort & Decor** Very basic furnishings, angled walls on uppers, one-color carpets, different color walls.

RATES, RESERVATIONS, & RESTRICTIONS
Deposit Credit card holds (24-hour cancellation policy) **Discounts** Whole house rental, groups **Credit Cards** AE, MC, V **Check-In/Out** After 2 p.m./11 a.m. **Smoking** No **Pets** No **Kids** Yes **No-Nos** N/A **Minimum Stay** None **Open** All year **Hosts** Cliff & Diane Kerbs, 118 East 300 South, Blanding 84511 **Phone** (435) 678-2388 or toll-free (800) 365-0868 **Fax** N/A **E-mail** graysoninn@hotmail.com **Web** N/A

RODGERS HOUSE BED & BREAKFAST INN, Blanding

OVERALL ★★★★★ | QUALITY ★★★★★ | VALUE ★★★★★ | PRICE RANGE $52–$99

Originally the home where the Rodgers family raised their dozen children, Rodgers House was renovated into a bed-and-breakfast in the 1990s. The front porch still has the swing where Old Man Rodgers sat and watched the world go by on Main Street (US 191). The attractive living room has hardwood floors, a marble fireplace, and antique furnishings like a mahogany piano. Rooms are named after local historical figures like Jim Mike, the Paiute Indian who discovered Rainbow Bridge and lived for 105 years, and Bradford, whose decades-long tunnel project between world wars brought Blue Mountain water to Blanding in 1953. Rodgers House has a regular business clientele attracted by the summer walk-in policy and desks with laptop computer connections.

SETTING & FACILITIES
Location Town center **Near** National monuments, national parks, state parks, rivers, museums **Building** 1915 settler's house, renovated in 1993 **Grounds** 0.25 acre **Public Space** LR, DR, porch **Food & Drink** Full breakfast in DR **Recreation** Biking, boating, rafting, fishing **Amenities & Services** Piano, barbecue, wedding receptions

ACCOMMODATIONS
Units 5 **All** TV, phone, alarm clock, ceiling fan, swamp cooler **Some** Desk (2) **Bed & Bath** Queen beds; all private baths, jetted tub (3), tub (1), double shower (1) **Favorites** Cowboy room has pole bed, crocheted bedspread, walnut armoire, easy chair, desk, original house kitchen sink, jetted tub; Jim Mike has Native American Southwest decor, TV that pulls out of armoire **Comfort & Decor** Varying themes with four-poster and brass beds, crocheted bedspreads, TVs hidden in armoires, brass bath fixtures, some early American sinks outside bathrooms, and extra-long jetted tubs.

RATES, RESERVATIONS, & RESTRICTIONS
Deposit None (reservations needed Nov. 1–March 1) **Discounts** Whole house rental, regular corp. customers **Credit Cards** MC, V **Check-In/Out** 4–9 p.m./11 a.m. **Smoking** Yard, porch **Pets** No **Kids** Yes **No-Nos** N/A **Minimum Stay** None **Open** All year **Hosts** Pete & Charlotte Black, 412 S. Main St., Blanding 84511 **Phone** (801) 678-3932 or toll-free (800) 355-3932 **Fax** (801) 678-3276 **E-mail** hosts@rogershouse.com **Web** www.rogershouse.com

PIONEER HOUSE INN, Bluff

OVERALL ★★★½ | QUALITY ★★★★ | VALUE ★★★★ | PRICE RANGE $56–$125

Located 50 miles north of Monument Valley, 35 miles west of Hovenweep National Monument, 55 miles south of Natural Bridges National Monument, and 107 miles south of Arches National Park, Pioneer House was built a century ago by local pioneers James and Anna Decker. The huge family house, which has exterior hints of Victorian style, has five suites ranging in size from one to three bedrooms, as well as small, economical single rooms. Taken as a whole, the house is like a gallery of local art, particularly local landscapes, ranging from oil paintings to black-and-white, infrared, color and artistic Polaroid photography. The old backyard outhouse (sans toilet) is now a phone booth taking calling cards.

SETTING & FACILITIES
Location Town center, corner of Mulberry & 3rd East **Near** National monuments, national parks, state parks, rivers, museums **Building** 1898 renovated Pioneer adobe brick w/ Victorian & buckaroo influences **Grounds** 1 acre w/ cottonwood trees, gourd arbor, multiflora roses, organic salsa garden **Public Space** DR, porches **Food & Drink** Full breakfast in DR **Recreation** Biking, boating, rafting, fishing, horse riding, winter sports **Amenities & Services** Ice machine, phone, day tours, customized tours, meetings, retreats, weddings, sunset cookouts, parties (4+), horseshoes, baseball

ACCOMMODATIONS
Units 9 guest rooms, 5 are suites w/ 1 or more BRs **All** Private entrances, heat **Some** Kitchenette (2) **Bed & Bath** Doubles, twins; all private baths, tub (1) **Favorites** 2-BR suite has a tub, 2 3-BR units have kitchens & sleep the most people; all are basic, no frills, but walls have an interesting mix of paintings and photographs **Comfort & Decor** Basic but clean, mixes old and new architectural elements, metal and concrete, plain walls enlivened by local artists' photos and paintings, carpet or wood floors, flannel quilts, wool blankets.

RATES, RESERVATIONS, & RESTRICTIONS
Deposit 1 night (14-day cancellation policy) **Discounts** Day-trip area archaeology packages, custom guided trips **Credit Cards** MC, V **Check-In/Out** 4–8 p.m./10:30 a.m. **Smoking** Outside **Pets** No **Kids** Yes **No-Nos** N/A **Minimum Stay** None **Open** All year **Hosts** Thomas Rice & Kelly McAndrews, P.O. Box 219, Bluff 84512 **Phone** (435) 672-

2446 or toll-free (888) 637-2582 **Fax** N/A **E-mail** rmcbluff@sanjuan.net **Web** www. pioneerhouseinn.com

BANKURZ HATT, Green River

OVERALL ★★★½ | QUALITY ★★★½ | VALUE ★★★★ | PRICE RANGE $65–$75

The front porch with a watermelon field view in this truck stop town known for its river rafting is less than an hour from Arches and Canyonlands National Parks to the east and Goblin Valley State Park to the west. From the Bankurz Hatt front porch a double quarter-cut oak entry leads into an 1890s parlor with an old Victrola, a fireplace, a grandfather clock, and Queen Anne chairs. Built by the town's first banker and purchased by the hostess's grandfather, Frank Hatt, in the 1930s, this one-time boarding house was originally to be named Bankers Hatt. But the state of Utah feared confusion, so Bankurz became the phonetic equivalent for Bankers. Three upper rooms sharing a shower is the price of maintaining architectural integrity in this masterfully decorated building.

SETTING & FACILITIES
Location Near state park & corner of 250 South & Green River Blvd. **Near** Arches & Canyonlands National Parks, Dead Horse Point & Goblin Valley State Parks **Building** 1896 2-story 4-square Victorian **Grounds** Rural yard w/ gazebo **Public Space** Living room, DR, front porch **Food & Drink** Full breakfast in DR; dinners by special request **Recreation** Rafting, golf, horse riding, hiking **Amenities & Services** Hot tub

ACCOMMODATIONS
Units 4 guest rooms, 3 uppers share shower **All** Ceiling fan **Some** N/A **Bed & Bath** Queens; 1 private bath w/ tub, 1 shared bath (servicing 3 rooms) w/ shower **Favorites** Parlor Room, the downstairs master BR, has carved wood-framed fireplace, chandelier, pastel floral wallpaper, dark wood furnishings, oval tiled tub, & stained glass **Comfort & Decor** 1890s with bronze and crystal Spanish filigree chandeliers, dark wood antiques, old black-and-white photos, pastel floral to purple wallpapers, turquoise carpet.

RATES, RESERVATIONS, & RESTRICTIONS
Deposit Credit card (72-hour cancellation policy) **Discounts** None **Credit Cards** MC, V **Check-In/Out** 3–6 p.m./11 a.m. **Smoking** No **Pets** No **Kids** Over age 12 **No-Nos** N/A **Minimum Stay** None **Open** All year **Hosts** Ben & Lana Coomer, 214 Farrer St., Green River 84525 **Phone** (435) 564-3382 **Fax** N/A **E-mail** benlana@etv.net **Web** bankurzhatt.com

CALI COCHITTA, Moab

OVERALL ★★★½ | QUALITY ★★★★ | VALUE ★★★★ | PRICE RANGE $69–$150

Across the street from Dream Keeper Inn, Cali Cochitta ("House of Dreams" in Aztec) is a compact, two-story brick Victorian reflecting the hosts' restaurant and food industry background and passion for building a dream garden with red rocks, a pond with a small waterfall, and a willow tree weeping under the weight of an idyllic swing. A short walk to all the Moab action on Main Street and bike storage make this a convenient trip-jumping-off or -ending place. Though the house lineage is Victorian, the atmosphere fostered by the hosts and their two daughters is informal, in contrast to the more elegant Sunflower Hill.

SETTING & FACILITIES

Location Downtown, near Main St. **Near** Arches National Park, Canyonlands National Park **Building** 1870s renovated (w/ additions) brick Victorian **Grounds** 0.5 acre red rock garden has patio, willow tree w/ swing, herbs, small pond **Public Space** DR, living room **Food & Drink** Full breakfast in DR or patio; evening snacks; 24-hour hot beverages; box lunch & dinner options **Recreation** Mountain biking, rafting, kayaking, golf **Amenities & Services** Hot tub, laundry, bike storage, weddings & meetings

ACCOMMODATIONS

Units 6 **All** Robes, cable TV **Some** Private entrance (2), French glass doors (1), data ports **Bed & Bath** Queens, extra double (1), twins; all private baths **Favorites** Cemonoque is stand-alone 2-BR cottage w/ twins; Suite Cochitta has two rooms w/ queen and double; Cenca is large, bright upstairs corner w/ mountain view **Comfort & Decor** Cherry and wood furnishings, hardwood or carpeted floors.

RATES, RESERVATIONS, & RESTRICTIONS

Deposit Credit card; full refund minus $10 fee if cancellation within 14 days, 50% refund within 10 days unless room rebooked **Discounts** Whole house rental **Credit Cards** AE, MC, V **Check-In/Out** 3–7 p.m./11 a.m. **Smoking** No **Pets** No (small poodle on premises) **Kids** Yes **No-Nos** N/A **Minimum Stay** None **Open** All year **Hosts** David & Kimberley Boger, 110 South 200 East, Moab 84532 **Phone** (435) 259-4961 or toll-free (888) 429-8112 **Fax** (435) 259-4964 **E-mail** calicochitta@lasal.net **Web** www.moab dreaminn.com

DESERT HILLS BED & BREAKFAST, Moab

OVERALL ★★★★★ | QUALITY ★★★★½ | VALUE ★★★★★ | PRICE RANGE $50–$130

On the outskirts of Moab with a backdrop of red sandstone mountains and neighborhood horse sounds, Desert Hills is indeed in the desert hills. The host, a former international banker from Belgium, fell in love with Moab during long vacations visiting his tour guide daughter who settled here. He eschewed the Euro to develop expertise on the fishing, motor-biking, and jeep trails running through the local deserts, mountains, and Colorado River canyons. There is a sandstone living room fireplace, but the best place to hang out is the wood patio deck with wrought iron and sun and shade sitting areas for taking in the views.

SETTING & FACILITIES

Location 5 mi. south of Moab; from US 191 take Spanish Trail Rd. past stop sign and golf course roundabout to Murphy Lane **Near** Arches National Park, Canyonlands National Park **Building** 1993 contemporary 3-story house **Grounds** 1.2 acres includes patio w/ wood path across lawn to hot tub **Public Space** Living room, DR, patio **Food & Drink** Full breakfast in DR or on patio **Recreation** Golf, mountain biking, fishing, rafting, kayaking, horse riding, jeep touring, hiking **Amenities & Services** Hot tub, barbecue, TV; Dutch, French, & German spoken

ACCOMMODATIONS

Units 4 guest rooms, 1 lower and 3 upstairs **All** Individually controlled AC, ceiling fan, carpeting **Some** TV (1) **Bed & Bath** Queens, additional futon sofas (2); all private baths, tubs and whirlpool (1) **Favorites** Largest unit has 2 downstairs BRs and LR; Sunrise Room has queen and futon sofa bed, large walk-in closet, great Moab Rim views; Sunset Room adds jetted tub to Rim views **Comfort & Decor** Timber furniture, log bed frames, metal-sculpted lamps, and lizard light switches add Southwestern ambience to clean and uncluttered white-walled rooms with drapes.

RATES, RESERVATIONS, & RESTRICTIONS

Deposit 1 night or 50% of stay; cancellations 14 days before arrival get refund minus $10 fee **Discounts** Off-season **Credit Cards** AE, MC, V **Check-In/Out** 3–9 p.m./11 a.m. **Smoking** No **Pets** No (Siamese cat stays outside) **Kids** Yes (if over age 3) **No-Nos** N/A **Minimum Stay** None **Open** All year **Hosts** John & Winni Souvereyns, 1989 S. Desert Hills Lane, Moab 84532 **Phone** (435) 259-3568 **Fax** (435) 259-7530 **E-mail** info@deserthillsbnb.com **Web** www.deserthillsbnb.com

DREAM KEEPER INN, Moab

OVERALL ★★★★★ | QUALITY ★★★★½ | VALUE ★★★★★ | PRICE RANGE
$85–$150

Identified in front only by a brightly painted dream scene mailbox (the city prohibits bed-and-breakfast signage), Dream Keeper can easily be missed in this suburban neighborhood two blocks from Main Street, the Visitors Center, and all the Moab action. Constructed by a uranium millionaire, the living room boasts a stone fireplace, Southwest decor, and a large window looking out over the front lawn and a large willow tree. Many guests like to sit and read in the living room, though others prefer the pool and hot tub in back. The innkeepers live in a separate house next door and are unobtrusive but there to help when needed.

SETTING & FACILITIES

Location 2 blocks from downtown, near intersection of Center & Main Sts. **Near** Arches National Park, Canyonlands National Park, Slick Rock Bike Trail **Building** 1950s suburban California-style brick and wood ranch house w/ rear cottages added in 1998 **Grounds** 1 acre corner lot w backyard pool, rose garden, & large cottonwood & pepper trees **Public Space** Living room, DR **Food & Drink** Full breakfast in DR or breakfast box for early departures; ice & drinks in garage freezer **Recreation** Golf, biking, rafting, kayaking, horse riding, hiking **Amenities & Services** Pool, hot tub, bike storage

ACCOMMODATIONS

Units 6 guest rooms, 4 in main house & 2 in detached cottage **All** AC, small fridge, phone, alarm clock, modem access **Some** Private entrance (5), ceiling fan (5), TV/VCR (2), small steps down from hall into room **Bed & Bath** Kings, queens, daybeds (3); all private baths, tubs (2), whirlpool tubs (2) **Favorites** Ivy and Willow Cottages are detached from main house, have sitting areas, daybeds, TV/VCRs, whirlpool tubs, share pool-facing porch w/ rocking chairs; Tree Room is largest, has twig-framed king & daybed, paisley, and Western prints, but is only room lacking sliding glass door to yard **Comfort & Decor** Mostly light woods, clean white walls, iron or wood bed frames, local photographs, themes varying from ivy in Ivy Room to timber in Tree Room to floral in Garden Room and Navajo in Mesa and Kiva Rooms

RATES, RESERVATIONS, & RESTRICTIONS

Deposit 1 night or 50%; 14-day cancellation for full refund minus $10 fee, otherwise refund only if room rebooked **Discounts** None **Credit Cards** AE, MC, V, D **Check-In/Out** 3–6 p.m./11 a.m. **Smoking** No **Pets** No **Kids** Yes (under age 15 not recommended because of pool) **No-Nos** N/A **Minimum Stay** 2 nights on holidays **Open** All year **Hosts** Jim & Kathy Kempa, 191 South 200 East, Moab 84532 **Phone** (435) 259-5998 or toll-free (888) 230-3247 **Fax** (435) 259-3912 **E-mail** info@dreamkeeperinn.com **Web** www.dreamkeeperinn.com

THE MAYOR'S HOUSE BED & BREAKFAST, Moab

OVERALL ★★★★★ | QUALITY ★★★★½ | VALUE ★★★★★ | PRICE RANGE $80–$130

Begun as a bed-and-breakfast by former mayor Tom Stock, the Mayor's House is renowned around town for its luxurious yet informal ambience. A sumptuous vaulted-ceiling living room with a Texas banana tree and two-story picture windows looks out on extensive gardens and a large lap pool. In the adjacent dining area, antlers hang near a 900-year-old red cedar crafted into a table. Perhaps most unusual is the custom joined timber furniture from Dan Batwinas & Sons' New Covenant Workshop, near Eddie McStiff's microbrewery (great Moab lime beer). Sometimes termed Four Corners Shaker, the bark beetle–damaged wood has haunting bands of gray and black buffed out with linseed oil and beeswax.

SETTING & FACILITIES
Location Central, 4 blocks east from intersection of Main and Center Sts. **Near** Arches National Park, Canyonlands National Park, Slick Rock Bike Trail **Building** 1980s 2-story 6,000-sq.-ft. ranch house **Grounds** 1.2 acres w/ cascading pond, sunken garden, vegetable & melon patch **Public Space** Living room, DR, sunken garden lobby w/ extra bath **Food & Drink** Full breakfast family-style in DR or patio; afternoon baked snacks; special diets w/ advanced arrangement; guest barbecue available for dinners **Recreation** Golf, biking, rafting, kayaking, horse riding, hiking **Amenities & Services** Heated pool w/ lap lane, hot tub, trampoline, Western movie collection, bike storage

ACCOMMODATIONS
Units 6 **All** Robes, TV/VCR, alarm clock, phone hookup **Some** Bar, microwave, fridge **Bed & Bath** King (1), queens (5), daybeds; all private baths, jetted tubs (3), tubs (2) **Favorites** Master Suite is largest on main level, has timber furnishings, king & daybed, jetted tub; Bunk house is 2,000-sq.-ft. downstairs w/ wet bar, large-screen TV, microwave, fridge, queen bed, bunks, queen sofa beds, double showers, has held up to 15 people **Comfort & Decor** Varies, with rustic Southwestern accents and native woods, but also some faux painted walls

RATES, RESERVATIONS, & RESTRICTIONS
Deposit 50% (balance due 14 days prearrival on holidays, festivals only); 14 days (7 days nonholiday/festival) cancellation for refund minus $20 fee, otherwise room must be rebooked for guaranteed refund **Discounts** Groups, extended stays **Credit Cards** MC, V **Check-In/Out** 3–7 p.m./11 a.m. **Smoking** No **Pets** No **Kids** Yes (over age 12 best; must be supervised) **No-Nos** N/A **Minimum Stay** 2 nights weekends Mar.–May, Sept., Oct. **Open** All year **Hosts** David Engals & Cary Cox, 505 E. Rose Tree Lane, Moab 84532 **Phone** (435) 259-6015, (435) 259-3019 or toll-free (888) 791-2345 **Fax** (435) 259-7752 **E-mail** rosetreeln@lasal.net **Web** www.moab.net/mayorshouse/index.shtml

---

SUNFLOWER HILL BED & BREAKFAST INN, Moab

OVERALL ★★★★½ | QUALITY ★★★★½ | VALUE ★★★★ | PRICE RANGE $85–$175

Fronted by tall shade trees on a quiet street within three blocks of the downtown action, Sunflower Hill mixes informal gardens with a more formal interior ambience. The sunken living room, has a beam ceiling, an old plank floor, stone fireplace, floral sofas, an old steamer trunk table and large windows looking out on pine trees. This family enterprise, which derives its name from the founders' former business, the Sunflower Hill Bakery, bakes its own pastries and breads and obtains organic fruits and vegetables from the family's Castle Valley organic farm. The gardens are particularly good for sitting and relaxing, and the feel is more like a small country inn than a traditional bed-and-breakfast.

SETTING & FACILITIES

Location Downtown, 3 blocks from Main St. **Near** Arches National Park, Canyonlands National Park **Building** 100-year-old farmhouse remodeled in 1996, and 2d house next door **Grounds** Over an acre of pathways and garden area **Public Space** Sunken living room, DR, phone room, reception desk, guest pantry **Food & Drink** Full breakfast buffet in DR; picnic lunches; evening refreshments; guest pantry w/ drinks & snacks **Recreation** Golf, biking, rafting, kayaking, hiking **Amenities & Services** Hot tub, barbecue, ice, laundry, phone, bike storage

ACCOMMODATIONS

Units 12 guest rooms, 3 upper & 9 ground floor, 6 per building **All** Robes, AC, TV/VCR, radio alarm clock, green plants **Some** French doors opening onto private balconies (suites), ceiling fans **Bed & Bath** Queens, additional sleeper sofas; all private baths, tubs or jetted tubs (4) **Favorites** Honeymoon Suite has 200-year-old bedroom set, 2-person jetted tub; Garden Suite has garden mural; Apple Cellar has private patio entrance, large picture window facing garden **Comfort & Decor** Country motif combining antiques and modern furniture, some iron frame beds, stencils, faux painted walls.

RATES, RESERVATIONS, & RESTRICTIONS

Deposit 1 night or 50% (full amount for reservations made within 14 days of arrival); 14-day cancellation gets refund minus $10 fee, under 14 days gets refund only if room rebooked **Discounts** None **Credit Cards** AE, MC, V, D **Check-In/Out** 3–6 p.m./11 a.m. **Smoking** No **Pets** No **Kids** Yes (age 10 and older) **No-Nos** N/A **Minimum Stay** 2 nights for holidays, special events **Open** All year **Host** Gregg Stucki, 185 North 300 East, Moab 84532 **Phone** (435) 259-2974 or toll-free (800) 662-2786 **Fax** (435) 259-3065 **E-mail** Innkeeper@sunflowerhill.com **Web** www.sunflowerhill.com

THE GRIST MILL INN BED & BREAKFAST, Monticello

OVERALL ★★★★ | QUALITY ★★★★½ | VALUE ★★★★★ | PRICE RANGE $60–$90

The Grist Mill, formerly a four-story flour mill, has a large living room with a reception desk, TV, stereo, and gas log fireplace surrounded by a solid steel elevator shaft filled with grain bags, a winnowing machine, a flour bagger, a scale with 100-pound weights, and drive shafts. The enclosed porch dining room, which has a continental breakfast for early risers followed by a full breakfast, has brick and adobe walls, a paneled wood ceiling, and views of the mill's old engine shed and two metal silos. Rescued from bankruptcy by new owners in May 2001, this 7,000-foot-elevation property is an hour south of Moab.

SETTING & FACILITIES

Location In town, 3 blocks from US 191 **Near** National monuments, national parks, state parks, rivers, museums **Building** 1933 flour mill restored as B&B, newer 4-BR house

Grounds 1 acre w/ enough parking for RVs **Public Space** LR, 2d-floor TV area, 3d-floor library, DR, gift shop, porch **Food & Drink** Early cont'l breakfast followed by full breakfast in DR; 24-hour hot beverages **Recreation** Biking, boating, rafting, fishing, horse riding **Amenities & Services** TV/VCR, stereo, weddings, receptions (250 people)

ACCOMMODATIONS

Units 11 **All** Cable TV, alarm clock, individual heat control **Some** Ceiling fan (10) **Bed & Bath** King (2), queen (6), queen & twin (1), queen & daybed (1), double (1); all private baths, tub (2) **Favorites** 2d-floor Corbin Suite has high wood ceiling, king bed, leather-like seating, large desk; Keller Room has queen bed, claw-foot tub, shower, best Horsehead Mountain view; Neilson Suite has queen bed, small 2d room w/ twin, circular bath view window; 4th-floor Bailey Suite has raised 2d room w/ twin, sewing machine theme **Comfort & Decor** Varied room layouts and color schemes, mill architecture, slanted ceilings, carpet, quilts.

RATES, RESERVATIONS, & RESTRICTIONS

Deposit None **Discounts** Gov't., corp. **Credit Cards** AE, MC, V, D **Check-In/Out** 4–6 p.m./11 a.m. **Smoking** No **Pets** No **Kids** Yes **No-Nos** N/A **Minimum Stay** None **Open** All year **Hosts** Glen & Phyllis Swank, 64 South 300 East, P.O. Box 488, Monticello 84535 **Phone** (435) 587-2597 or toll-free (800) 645-3762 **Fax** (435) 587-2597 **E-mail** reservations@thegristmillinn.com **Web** www.thegristmillinn.com

Additional Bed-and-Breakfasts and Small Inns

While our 300 profiles give you a fine range of bed-and-breakfasts and small inns, some may be fully booked when you want to visit, or you may want to stay in areas where we have not included a property. So we have included an annotated listing of 300 additional bed-and-breakfasts and small inns, spread geographically throughout the Southwest. All properties meet our basic criteria for this guide: They have about 3–25 guestrooms, a distinct personality and individually decorated guestrooms, are open regularly, and include breakfast in the price (with a few exceptions). Prices are a range from low to high season. Most are highly recommended, but we have not visited all of these properties so we cannot recommend them across the board. We suggest you get a brochure, look on the Internet, or call and ask about some of the categories that are on the profile format to find out more. While some of these supplementals are famed and excellent, others may not be up to the level of the profiled properties.

Arizona

ZONE 1: Old West Country

Aravaipa
Aravaipa Farms, $225–$250
  (520) 357-6901;
  www.aravaipafarms.com
Bisbee
Calumet & Arizona Guest House,
  $50–$77
  (520) 432-4815; timbersj@juno.com
Harvest Home B&B, $55–$60
  (520) 432-3927;

franknroz@theriver.com
Main Street Inn, $75–$175
  (520) 432-1202 or toll-free (800) 467-
  5237; mainstreetinn@theriver.com,
  www.mainstreetinn.net
Mile High Court Travel Lodge, $45–$55
  (520) 432-3472
Oliver House, $55–$93
  (520) 432-4286; olivrhs@c2i2.com

Arizona (continued)

ZONE 1: Old West Country *(continued)*

Bisbee *(continued)*
Park Place, $50–$70
  (602) 432-3054 or toll-free (800) 388-
  4388; www.theriver.com/parkplace/
Cochise Stronghold
Cochise Stronghold B&B, $95–$155
  (520) 826-4141 or toll-free (877) 426-
  4141; njyates@vtc.net, www.cochises-
  strongholdbb.com
Hereford
San Pedro River Inn, $105–$139
  (520) 366-5532; sanpedrorvinn@
  juno.com, www.sanpedroriverinn.com
Madera Canyon
Chuparosa Inn, $95–$105
  (520) 393-7370; info@chuparosa
  inn.com, www.chuparosainn.com
Mount Lemmon
Aspen Trails B&B, $170–$195
  (520) 576-1558; aspntrail1@aol.com,
  www.mt-lemmon.com
Patagonia
Duquesne House Bed & Breakfast, $75
  (520) 394-2732 or (520) 394-0054
Sierra Vista
Gasthaus Mountain View, $80–$120
  (520) 378-2554; gasthausmv@
  earthlink.net, www.gasthausmountain
  view.com
Sonoita
The Vineyard Bed & Breakfast, $85–$95
  (520) 455-4749
Tombstone
Marie's Engaging Bed & Breakfast,
  $55–$85 (520) 457-3831;
  maries@theriver.com,
  www.theriver.com/maries
Victoria's Bed & Breakfast and Wedding
  Chapel, $55–$85 (520) 457-3677;
  victoriac@theriver.com,
  www.victoriasplace.net

Tubac
Tubac Country Inn, $80–$100
  (520) 398-3178
Valle Verde Ranch B&B, $80–$135
  (520) 398-2246
Tucson
Adobe Rose Inn, $65–$125
  (520) 318-4644 or
  toll-free (800) 328-4122
Araibi Place B&B, $76–$98
  (520) 749-3033 or toll-free (800) 749-
  3036; mast3033@aol.com,
  www3.cactus-web.com/oraibi
Casa Tierra Adobe B&B, $135–$300
  (520) 578-3058;
  www.casatierratucson.com
Catalina Park Inn, $84–$144
  (520) 792-4541 or toll-free (800) 792-
  4885; www.catalinaparkinn.com
Copper Bell B&B, $85–$95
  (520) 629-9229
El Adobe Ranch B&B, $110–$175
  (520) 743-3525 or
  toll-free (888) 866-1537 ext. 72009;
  ellen@eladoberanch.com,
  www.arizonaguide.com/el-adobe-ranch
El Presidio B&B Inn, $95–$115
  (520) 623-6151 or toll-free (800) 349-
  6151; www.bbonline.com/az/elpresidio
La Posada del Valle, $105–$145
  (520) 795-3840 or toll-free (888) 404-
  7113; laposadabandbinn@hotmail.com,
  www.bbonline.com/az/laposada
Peppertrees B&B Inn, $98–$185
  (520) 622-7167 or toll-free (800) 348-
  5763; pepperinn@gci-net.com,
  www.peppertreesinn.com
The Suncatcher, $80–$145
  (520) 885-0883 or toll-free (877) 775-
  8355; info@thesuncatcher.com,
  www.thesuncatcher.com

ZONE 3: Grand Canyon Country *(continued)*

Flagstaff

Arizona Mountain Inn Cabin Rentals and
  B&B, $80–$110 (928) 774-8959 or
  toll-free (800) 239-5236;
  www.arizonamountaininn.com
Comfi Cottages of Flagstaff, $105–$250
  (928) 774-0731 or toll-free (888) 774-
  0731; www.comficottages.com
Conifer House, $95–$150
  (928) 774-2438 or
  toll-free (888) 788-3614
Lynn's Inn B&B, $89–$109
  (928) 226-1488; www.lynnsinn.com
Mount Elden B&B, $90–$110
  (928) 526-3901
Tree House B&B, $105
  (928) 214-8664 or
  toll-free (888) 251-9390

Sedona

Angels Inn Sedona, $65–$110
  (928) 284-9680 or
  toll-free (800) 866-5430

The Canyon Wren Cabins for Two,
  $135–$150 (928) 282-6900 or toll-free
  (800) 437-9736;
  www.canyonwrencabins.com
Grace's Hideaway, $95–$105
  (928) 284-2340 or
  toll-free (800) 579-2340
Moestly Wood B&B, $110–$125
  (928) 204-1461 or toll-free (888) 334-
  4141; moestlywood.com
Sunset Chateau B&B Inn, $110–$220
  (928) 282-2644 or
  toll-free (877) 655-BEDS

Williams

Canyon Country Inn B&B, $40–$85
  (928) 635-2349 or
  toll-free (800) 578-1020
Mountain Country Lodge B&B, $49–$119
  (928) 635-4341 or toll-free (800) 973-
  6210; www.stayon66.com;
  www.thegrandcanyon.com/mclodge

ZONE 5: Western Border

Aguila

Robson's Mining World Boarding House,
  $50–$95 (520) 685-2609

Kingman/Hualapi Mountain

Pine Lake Inn, $95
  (928) 757-1884/9754

ZONE 6: Central Territory

Camp Verde

Hacienda de la Mariposa, $175–$225
  (928) 567-1490; lamariposa-az.com

Chino Valley

Little Thumb Butte, $50–$100
  (928) 636-4413

Cornville

J Bar T Ranch, $100–$150
  (520) 634-4084 or
  toll-free (800) 246-7584

Prescott

Dolls & Roses, $89–$139
  (928) 776-9291 or toll-free
  (800) 924-0883; www.fourcorners.
  com/az/inns/dollsroses
Gurley St. Lodge B&B, $79–$179
  (520) 778-6048;
  cableone.net/prescottlodge/
Log Cabin B&B, $85–$125
  toll-free (888) 778-0442;
  prescottlogcabin.com

Arizona (continued)

ZONE 6: Central Territory *(continued)*

Prescott *(continued)*
Pleasant Street Inn B&B, $95–$130
  (520) 445-4774 or
  toll-free (877) 226-7128; www.
  cwdesigners.com/pleasantstreet
Rocamadour B&B, $99–$189
  Toll-free (888) 771-1933;
  rocamadour-inn-arizona.com

Wickenburg
Owl Tree Inn, $50–$150
  (520) 684-1197
Rincon Ranch, $50–$150
  toll-free (888) 684-2328

ZONE High Country

Eagar
Paisley Corner B&B, $75–$95
  (520) 333-4665

Greer
The Red Setter Inn, $135–$220
  (520) 735-7441; www.redsetterinn.com

White Mountain Lodge, $95–$135
  (520) 735-7568 or toll-free (888) 493-
  7568; www.wmlodge.com
Pinetop/Lakeside
Rawhide & Roses B&B, $95–$125
  (520) 537-0216 or
  toll-free (888) 418-5963

Nevada

ZONE 7: Nevada

Carson City
Bliss Mansion, $175
  (775) 887-8988;
  www.site-works.com/blissmansion
Tyson's Canyon Ranch, $125–$165
  (775) 847-7223;
  www.nevadaduderanch.com
Ely
Steptoe Valley Inn, $80–$104
  (775) 289-8697;
  www.nevadaweb.com/steptoe
Genoa
Genoa House Inn, $135–$150
  (775) 782-7075; genoahouseinn@pyra-
  mid.net, www.genoahouseinn.com

Jarbidge
Tsawhawbitts Ranch B&B, $65–$150
  (775) 488-2338
Virginia City
Hardwicke House B&B, $35–$60
  (775) 847-0215
Spargo House, $75–$150 (775) 847-7455
Wellington
Hoye Mansion B&B, $75
  (775) 465-2959; hoye@tele-net.net
Belmont
Monitor Inn, $90   (775) 482-2000
Smith Valley
Smith Valley B&B, $65   (775) 465-2222

New Mexico

ZONE 8: Southeast

Cloudcroft

Burro Street Boarding House, $68
(505) 682-3601 or toll-free (888) 682-
3601; lindalc@tularoso.net

Crofting B&B, $85–$215
(505) 682-2288 or
toll-free (800) 395-6343

Waterfall Lodge, $75–$97
(505) 682-5454; www.waterfalllodge.com

Lincoln

Ellis Store & Co., $79–$139
(505) 653-4609 or toll-free (800) 653-
6460; www.ellisstore.com

Ruidoso

Black Bear Lodge, $109–$159
toll-free (877) 257-1459;
www.ruidoso.net/blackbear

Monjeau Shadows, $81+
(505) 336-4191; shadows@zianet.com,
www.ruidoso.net/shadows

Park Place B&B, $80+
toll-free (800) 687-9050;
www.ruidoso.net/parkplace

ZONE 9: Southwest

Cliff

Duck Creek Inn, $80
(505) 535-2167;
www.nmbedandbreakfast.com

Gila Hot Springs

The Wilderness Lodge, $45–$65
(505) 536-9749;
www.gilanet.com/wildernesslodge

Las Cruces

Hilltop Hacienda, $75–$85
(505) 382-3556

Lodge of the Desert, $65–$100
(505) 523-9605

ZONE 10: Central

Albuquerque

Brittania & W. E. Mauger Estate B&B Inn,
$89–$179 (505) 242-8755 or toll-free
(800) 719-9189; www.maugerbb.com

Canoncito

Apache Canyon Ranch B&B Country Inn,
$88–$265 (505) 836-7220

Cedar Crest

Elaine's, A B&B, $85–$139
(505) 281-1384 or toll-free (800) 821-
3092; www.elainesbnb.com

Corrales

Casa de Koshare B&B, $50–$100
(505) 898-4500 or toll-free (877) 729-
8100; darvinr@att.net,
www.casadekoshare.com

Chocolate Turtle B&B, $65–$135
(505) 898-1800 or
toll-free (800) 898-1842

Nora Dixon Place B&B, $80–$100
(505) 898-3662 or
toll-free (888) 677-2349

Sandhill Crane B&B, $90–$160
(505) 898-2445 or
toll-free (800) 375-2445

Edgewood

Alta Mae's Heritage Inn, $95–$125
(505) 281-5000; www.altamae-nm.com

Placitas

Hacienda de Placitas Inn of the Arts,
$99–$199 (505) 867-0082

New Mexico (continued)

ZONE 11: Northwest

Aztec

Miss Gail's, $60 (505) 334-3452 or toll-
   free (888) 534-3452;
   business.fortunecity.com/vc/829

Thoreau

Zuni Mountain Lodge, $55–$85
   (505) 862-7616; www.cia-g.com/~zuniml

Zuni

The Inn at Halona, $80+
   (505) 782-4547; www.halona.com

ZONE 12: North Central

Angel Fire

Wildflower B&B, $75–$150
   (505) 377-6869;
   www.angelfirenm.com/wildflower

Chama

Gandy Dancer B&B, $65–$125
   (505) 756-2191;
   www.gandydancerbb.com

Chimayo

La Posada de Chimayo, $80
   (505) 351-4605; sue@latierra.com,
   www.laposadadechimayo.com

Rancho Manzana, $85–$120
   (505) 351-2227 or toll-free (888) 505-
   2227; www.taosweb.com/manzana

Cimarron

Casa del Gavilan, $75–$135
   (505) 376-2246 or toll-free (800) GAVI-
   LAN, www.casadelgavilan.com

Espanola

Inn at the Delta, $100–$150
   (505) 753-9466

Rancho de San Juan, $195–$250
   (505) 753-6818 or toll-free (800) 726-
   7121; www.ranchodesanjuan.com

Los Alamos

Adobe Pines, $50–$75
   (505) 662-6761

North Road Inn, $50–$75
   (505) 662-3678; (505) 279-2898

Santa Fe

Adobe Retreat B&B, $100–$125
   (505) 474-7725;
   www.newmex.com/adoberetreat

Casa Pueblo, $149–$229
   (505) 988-4455 or toll-free (800) 955-
   4455; www.eldoradohotel.com

El Farolito, $115–$180
   (505) 988-1631 or toll-free (888) 634-
   8782; www.farolito.com

El Paradero, $70$150
   (505) 988-1177; www.elparadero.com

Four Kachinas Inn, $100–$165
   (505) 982-2550 or toll-free (888) 634-
   8782; www.fourkachinas.com

Inn of the Turquoise Bear, $95–$315
   (505) 983-0798 or toll-free (800) 396-
   4104; bluebear@newmexico.com,
   www.turquoisebear.com

Pueblo Bonito, $80–$160
   (505) 984-8001 or toll-free (800) 461-
   4599; pueblo-bonito@travelbase.com,
   www.pueblobonitoinn.com

Seret's 1001 Nights, $139–$249
   (505) 992-0957

Territorial Inn, $99–$219
   (505) 982-6636 or toll-free (800) 745-
   9910; www.santafehotels.com

ZONE 12: North Central *(continued)*

Taos

Adobe and Stars B&B, $115–$180
(505) 776-2776 or toll-free (800) 211-
7076; www.taosadobe.com

The Brooks Street Inn, $80–$160
(505) 758-1489 or toll-free (800) 758-
1489; www.brooksstreetinn.com

Casa Grande Guest Ranch B&B,
$115–$195 (505) 776-1303 or toll-free
(888) 236-1303; www.guestranch.com

Dreamcatcher B&B, $79–$114
toll-free (888) 758-0613;
www.taosweb.com/dreamcatcher

Inn on La Loma Plaza, $90–$275
toll-free (800) 530-3040

Mountain Light B&B, $45–$75
(505) 776-8474; www.mtnlight.com

Orinda B&B, $80–$130
(505) 758-8581 or toll-free (800) 847-
1837; www.taosnet.com/orinda

Red Cloud Ranch, $110–$130
(505) 751-0015; www.innplace.com

Taos Country Inn, $110–$150
toll-free (800) 866-6548;
www.taoscountryinn.com

Truchas

Truchas Farmhouse B&B and Rooms,
$50–$75 (505) 689-2245

Rancho del Llano B&B, $100–$120
(505) 689-2347; vmarkley@la-tierra.
com, www.la-tierra.com/vmarkley

Texas

ZONE 13: Hill Country

Austin

Adams House B&B, $75–$125
(512) 453-7696 or toll-free (800) 871-
8908; www.theadamshouse.com

Austin's Wildflower Inn, $90–$140
(512) 477-9639;
www.austinswildflowerinn.com

Brava House, $85–$99
(512) 478-5034 or toll-free (888) 545-
8200; reservations@bravahouse.com,
www.bravahouse.com

Fairview, a B&B Establishment, $99–$150
(512) 444-4746 or toll-free (800) 310-
4746; www.fairview-bnb.com

Houston House B&B, $80–$100
(512) 479-0375;
www.houstonhousebnb.com

The Inn at Pearl Street, $110–$200
(512) 477-2233; www.innpearl.com

The Miller-Crockett House, $100–$170
(512) 441-1600;
www.millercrockett.com

Park Lane Guest House, $80–$150
(512) 444-7555;
austin.home.rr.com/supersis/BB/BB.htm

Woodburn House, $70–$100
(512) 458-4335;
www.woodburnhouse.com

Boerne

Ye Kendall Inn, $100–$140
toll-free (800) 364-2138;
www.yekendallinn.com

Burnet

Lakeside Lodge, $50–$100
(512) 756-4935;
www.lakesidelodgetx.com

Verandas, $100–$120
(512) 715-0190;
www.touringtexas.com/verandas

Texas (continued)

ZONE 13: Hill Country *(continued)*

Canyon Lake

Aunt Nora's Countryside Inn, $115–$210 (830) 905-3989 or toll-free (800) 687-2887; auntnoras@compuvision.net, www.texasbedandbreakfast.com/aunt noras.htm

Comfort

Carrington House B&B, $75–$95 (830) 997-0443; www.fredericksburg-lodging.com/carrington-house

The Comfort Common, $70–$125 (830) 995-3030; www.comfortcommon.com

Haven River Inn B&B, $75–$125 (830) 995-3834 or toll-free (888) 995-7200; haven@fbg.net, www.bed-breakfast-comfort.com

Fredericksburg

The Cotton Gin Restaurant and Lodging, $139 toll-free (888) 991-6749; www.fredericksburg-lodging.com/cotton-gin

Creekside Inn, $85–$100 (830) 997-6316, www.fbg.net/creekside

Das College Haus B&B, $110–$125 (830) 997-9047; www.dascollegehaus.com

Hill Country Guest House & Gardens, $80–$110 (830) 997-2689 or toll-free (866) 427-8374 (reservations); gasthaus@ktc.com, bglodging.com/tradtown/hillcog.htm

Kuenemann House Inn, $100–$115 (830) 990-0364 or toll-free (866) 427-8374 (reservations); www.fbglodging.com/tradtown/kuenemann.htm

Main Street Cottages, $95–$119 (830) 997-8396; www.mainstreetcottages.com

Red Stairs Guest Home, $110 toll-free (888) 991-6749; www.fredericksburg-lodging.com/red-stairs

Settlers Crossing, $135–$195 toll-free (800) 874-1020; www.settlerscrossing.com

Georgetown

Inn on the Square Historic B&B, $85–$125 toll-free (888) 718-2221; www.innonthesquare.net

Gruene

Gruene Apple B&B, $100+ (830) 643-1234; www.grueneapple.com

Gruene Homestead Inn, $100–$185 (830) 606-0216 or toll-free (800) 238-5534; www.gruenehomesteadinn.com

Lake Travis

Lake Travis B&B, $165–$250 toll-free (888) 764-5822; www.laketravisbb.com

Lampasas

Markwood Manor, $60–$100 (512) 556-4238

Leander

Trails End B&B, $75–$125 (512) 267-2901 or toll-free (800) 850-2901; trailsendbb.com

Llano

Century Ranch Lodging, $95–$160 (915) 247-4047; www.centuryranchlodging.com

Marble Falls

Liberty Hall Historic Guest Haus, $50–$100 (210) 693-4518

New Braunfels

Acorn Hill B&B, $125–$175 (830) 907-2597 or toll-free (800) 525-4618; www.acornhillbb.com

ZONE 13: Hill Country *(continued)*

New Braunfels *(continued)*

Historic Kuebler Waldrip Haus, $85–$175
(830) 608-9001 or toll-free (800) 299-
8372; www.cruising-america.com/
kuebler-waldrip

Karbach House B&B Inn, $105–$200
(830) 625-2131 or toll-free (800) 972-
5941; www.bbhost.com/karbach

The Old Hunter Road Stagecoach Stop,
$95–$125 (830) 620-9453 or toll-free
(800) 201-2912; stagecoach@satx.rr.com

Uvalde

Casa de Leona B&B, $55–$150
(830) 278-8550,
bednbrek@admin.hilconet.com

Wimberley

Blair House, $145–$225
(512) 847-1111 or toll-free (877) 549-
5450; www.blairhouseinn.com

ZONE 14: Hill Prairies and Lakes

Bastrop

Pecan Street Inn, $65–$100
(512) 321-3315;
www.pecanstreetinn.com

Brenham

Long Point Inn, $80–$130
(979) 289-3171 or toll-free (877) 989-
3171; longpointinn@aol.com

Bryan

Angelsgate B&B, $80–$110
(979) 779-1231 or (979) 775-7024;
stay@angelsgate.com

Denton

The Heritage Inn B&B Cluster, $65–$125
(940) 565-6414 or toll-free (888) 565-
6414; redbudbb@gte.net,
www.bbhost.com/redbudbb

Wildwood Inn, $125–$225
(940) 243-4919;
info@denton-wildwoodinn.com,
www.denton-wildwoodinn.com

Fort Worth

B&B at the Ranch, $85–$125
(817) 232-5522 or toll-free (888) 593-
0352; www.bandbattheranch.com

Miss Molly's Hotel, $55–$110
(817) 626-2723 or toll-free (800) 996-
6559; www.missmollys.com

Gainesville

Alexander Bed and Breakfast Acres,
$60–$125 (903) 564-7440 or toll-free
(800) 887-8794; abba@texoma.net

Glen Rose

Bussey's Something Special B&B,
$80–$125 (254) 897-4843 or toll-free
(877) 426-2233; sbussey@busseys.net,
www.busseys.net

Hill Street Inn, $90–$115
toll-free (888) 256-7535;
www.hillstreetinn.com

Hummingbird Lodge, $92–$112
(254) 897-2787; www.eaze.net/~hbird

Inn on the River, $125–$215
(254) 897-2929 or toll-free (800) 575-
2101; www.innontheriver.com

Lilly House B&B, $110–$175
toll-free (800) 884-1759;
www.lillyhouse.com

Wild Rose Inn, $75–$150
toll-free (888) 346-8066;
www.wildroseglenrose.com

Gonzales

Belle Oaks Inn, $95–$140
(830) 857-8613; www.belleoaksinn.com

Texas *(continued)*

ZONE 14: Hill Prairies and Lakes *(continued)*

Gonzales *(continued)*

Boothe House B&B, $85–$140
(830) 672-7509;
www.bbonline.com/texas/boothehouse

Houston House B&B, $90–$175
toll-free (888) 477-0760; www.houston
house.com

St. James Inn B&B, $75–$125
(830) 672-7066; www.stjamesinn.com

Granbury

Baker St. Harbour B&B on the Lake,
$105–$130 (877) 578-3684;
www.welcome.to/theharbour

Captain's House on the Lake, $80–$158
(817) 579-6664; www.virtualcities.
com/tx/captainshouse.htm

Doyle House on the Lake, $110–$140
(817) 573-6492; www.doylehouse.com

The Iron Horse Inn, $95–$175
(817) 579-5535;
www.theironhorseinn.com

Manor of Time B&B, $95–$120
(877) 437-9110 or toll-free (877) 437-
9110; www.manoroftime.com

Pearl Street Inn, $79–$119
(817) 579-7465 or toll-free (888)
pearlst; www2.itexas.net/~danette

Mineola

English House B&B, $80
(903) 569-0223;
www.bnbenglishhouse.com

Fall Farm B&B Retreat, $110–$250
(903) 768-2449; info@fallfarm.com,
www.fallfarm.com

Munzesheimer Manor, $85–$95
toll-free (888) 569-6634, www.
munzesheimer.com

Round Top

Briarfield at Round Top B&B, $95–$115
(979) 249-3973 or toll-free (800) 472-
1134; stanhope@cvtv.net, www.briarfield
atroundtop.com

Round Top Inn B&B, $95–$140
(409) 249-5294 or toll-free (888) 356-
8946; frank@cvtv.net

The Settlement at Round Top, $110–$225
(979) 249-5015; www.thesettlement.com

Salado

The Baines House, $65–150
(254) 947-5260 or toll-free (866) sala-
dos; info@baineshouse.com,
www.baineshouse.com

Brambley Hedge, $95–$125
(254) 947-1914 or toll-free (800) 407-
2310; www.touringtexas.com/brambley

Country Place, $85–$110 (254) 947-9683
or toll-free (800) 439-3828; www.
bbonline.com/tx/countryplace

Halley House, $65–$140 (254) 947-1000;
www.touringtexas.com/halley

Rose Mansion, $79–$159
(254) 947-8200 or toll-free (800) 948-
1004; www.touringtexas.com/rose

Waco

Brazos House, $65–$120
(254) 754-3565

Colcord House, $65–$110
(254) 753-6856; www.bbchannel.com

Colonial House, $70–$110
(254) 756-1968

Judge Baylor House, $72–$105
(254) 756-0273 or toll-free (888) JBAY-
LOR; jbaylor@iamerica.net,
www.judgebaylorhouse.com

Waxahachie

Chuska House B&B, $125–$165
(972) 937-3390 or toll-free (800) 931-
3390; www.chaskabb.com

The Harrison, $120–$165
(972) 938-1922 or toll-free (888) 354-
5761; www.harrisonbb.com

The Rosemary Mansion on Main Street,
$120–$165 (972) 935-9439; www.
texasguides.com/rosemarymansion.html

ZONE 15: Piney Woods

Canton

Roseland Plantation, $75–$150
(903) 849-5553

Tumble on Inn, $75–$140
(903) 963-7669 or toll-free (888) 707-3992; www.tumbleoninn.com

Jefferson

Captain's Castle B&B, $100–$120
(903) 665-2330 or toll-free (800) 650-2330

Claiborne House, $95–$169
(903) 665-8800 or toll-free (877) 385-9236; www.claibornehousebnb.com

Clarksville St. Inn, $100–$125
(903) 665-6659 or toll-free (800) 665-6659; clarksvilleinn.com

Cottonwood Inn, $65–$105
(903) 665-2080;
www.jeffersontx.com/cottonwoodinn

Falling Leaves, $95–$115
(903) 665-8803;
www.fallingleavesinn.com

Maison-Bayou Waterfront Lodging,
$79–$145
(903) 665-7600; www.maisonbayou.com

Twin Oaks Country Inn, $90–$120
(903) 665-3535 or toll-free (800) 905-7751; www.twinoaksinn.com

Lufkin

Wisteria Hideaway B&B, $80–$105
(936) 875-2914;
www.wisteriahideaway.com

Nacogdoches

The Haden Edwards Inn, $70–$100
(936) 559-5595 or toll-free (877) 559-5009

Llano Grande Plantation B&B, $95–$125
(936) 569-1249; www.llanogrande.com

Texarkana

House of Wadley B&B and Singing Supper
Club, $69–$129
(870) 773-7019;
www.houseofwadley.com

Mansion on Main B&B Inn, $85–$115
(903) 792-1835;
mansiononmain@aol.com,
www.bestinns.net/usa/tx/mansion.html

Tyler

Rosevine Inn, $85–$150
(903) 592-2221; rosevine@iamerica.net,
www.rosevine.com

ZONE 16: Gulf Coast

Corpus Christi

Ocean House, $155–$495
(361) 882-9500; stan@oceansuites.com,
www.oceansuites.com

Galveston

Away at Sea Inn, $85–$200
(409) 762-1668 or toll-free (800) 762-1668; awayatsea@aol.com,
www.awayatseainn.com

Charles Adams House, $99–$219
(409) 763-1577; www.galveston/rosehall

Coppersmith Inn, $94–$170
toll-free (800) 515-7444;
coppersmith@att.net,
www.coppersmithinn.com

Garden Inn, $100–$185
(409) 770-0592 or toll-free (888) 770-7298; www.galveston.com/gardeninn

Inn at 1816 Post Office, $130–$195
(409) 765-9444 or toll-free (888) 558-9444; inn1816@aol.com,
www.bbonline.com/tx/1816

Mermaid & The Dolphin, $99–$359
(409) 762-1561 or toll-free (888) 922-1866; manddlnn@swbell.net,
www.mermaidanddolphin.com

Houston

The Lovett Inn B&B, $75–$175
(713) 522-5224 or toll-free (800) 779-5224; ww.virtualcities.com/ons/tx/h/
txha6020.htm

Texas *(continued)*

ZONE 16: Gulf Coast *(continued)*

Houston *(continued)*

Robin's Nest, $75–$150
   (713) 528-5821 or toll-free (800) 622-
   8343; www.therobin.com

Sara's B&B, $85–$200
   (713) 868-1130 or toll-free (800) 593-
   1130; www.saras.com

Kemah

Captain's Quarters B&B, $40–$145
   (281) 334-4141;
   www.captsquarters.com

Los Fresnos

Inn at Chachalaca Bay, $150–$195
   (956) 233-1180; www.chachalaca.com

Palacios

Moonlight Bay & Paper Moon B&B,
   $95–$200 (361) 972-2232 or toll-free
   (877) 461-7070; grogers@wcnet.net,
   www.bbhost.com/moonlightbaybb

Port Isabel

Historic Queen Isabel Inn, $75–$200
   (956) 943-1468 or toll-free (800) 943-
   1468; www.queenisabelinn.com

Rockport

Hoopes' House, $95–$170
   (361) 729-8424 or toll-free (800) 924-
   1008; www.hoopeshouse.com

Seabrook

Pelican House B&B, $90–$100
   (281) 474-5295; pelicanhouse@usa.net,
   www.pelicanhouse.com

South Padre Island

Brown Pelican Inn, $75–130
   (956) 761-2722; www.brownpelican.com

Historic Queen Isabel Inn, $75–$200
   toll-free (800) 943-1468;
   www. queenisabelinn.com

Moonraker B&B, $75–$130
   (956) 761-2206; islatex@flash.net,
   www.moonrakerbb.com

Spring

McLachlan Farm B&B, $80–$115
   (281) 350-2400 or toll-free (800) 382-
   3988; stay@macfarm.com,
   www.macfarm.com

ZONE 17: South Texas Plains

Del Rio

Villa del Rio, $85–$175
   (830) 768-1100 or toll-free (800) 995-
   1887; www.villadelrio.com

San Antonio

A Yellow Rose B&B, $95–$150
   (210) 229-9903 or toll-free (800) 950-
   9903; www.ayellowrose.com

Academy House B&B, $85–$145
   (210) 731-8393 or toll-free (888) 731-
   8393; www.ahbnd.com

Adams House B&B, $89–$144
   (210) 224-4791 or toll-free (800) 666-
   4810; www.san-antonio-texas.com

Beauregard House B&B, $99–$149
   (210) 222-1198 or toll-free (888) 667-
   0555; www.beauregardhouse.com

Brackenridge House B&B, $95–$200
   (210) 271-3442 or toll-free (800) 221-
   1412; www.brackenridgehouse.com

Christmas House B&B, $75–$150
   (210) 737-2786 or toll-free (800) 268-
   4187; www.christmashousebnb.com

The Columns on Alamo B&B, $92–$255
   (210) 271-3245 or toll-free (800) 233-
   3364; www.bbonline.com/tx/columns

Inn at Craig Place, $100–$125
   (210) 225-6333 or toll-free (877) 730-
   0019; www.craigplace.com

ZONE 17: South Texas Plains *(continued)*

San Antonio *(continued)*
Inn on the River, $99–$175
(210) 225-6333 or toll-free (800) 730-
0019; www.hotx.com/sa/bb

Terrell Castle B&B, $85–$125
(210) 271-9145 or toll-free (800) 481-
9732; www.geocities.com/south
beach/pier/9656

Utah

ZONE 18: North

Midway
Kastle Inn, $76–$125
(435) 657-2755 or toll-free (877) 202-
9868; kastle@shadowlink.net,
www.clegg-kastle.com
Johnson Mill B&B, $85–$275
(435) 654-4466 or toll-free (888) 272-
0030; oldmill@shadowlink.net,
www.johnsonmill.com
Ogden
The Alaskan Inn, $140–$265
(801) 621-8600
Park City
Old Town Guest House, $75–$190
(435) 649-2642 or toll-free (800) 290-
6423 ext. 3710;
dlove@compuserve.com,
www.oldtownguesthouse.com
Woodside Inn B&B, $76–$150
(435) 649-2392 or
toll-free (888) 241-5890
Salt Lake City
Anniversary Inn—Salt City Jail, $99–$249
(801) 363-4900 or toll-free (800) 324-
4152; www.anniversaryinn.com
Ellerbeck Mansion Inn B&B, $119–$149
(801) 355-2500
Grandmother's House B&B, $50–$125
(801) 943-0909 or
toll-free (800) 524-5511

Log Cabin on the Hill B&B, $75–$125
(801) 272-2969 or toll-free (888) 639-
2969
Pine Crest B&B Inn, $85–$195
(801) 583-6663
Red Brick Inn, $60–$120 (801) 322-4917
Wildflowers B&B, $85–$95
(801) 466-0600 or toll-free (800) 569-
0009; www.travelbase.com/
destinations/salt-lake-city/wild-flowers
Willow Creek Inn, $75–$175
(801) 944-1962
Wolfe Crest Inn B&B, $150–$300
(801) 521-8710
Sandy
Castle Creek Inn, $76–$250
(801) 567-9437 or
toll-free (800) 571-2669
1887 Hansen House B&B, $65–$175
(801) 562-2198
Mountain Hollow B&B Inn, $65–$175
(801) 942-3428

Utah (continued)

ZONE 19: Central

Manti
Heritage House, $50–$75
  (435) 835-5050

ZONE 20: Southwest

Alton
Alton John's B&B, $76–$125
  (435) 648-2214 or toll-free (866) 221-
  5123, altonjohn@scinternet.com,
  www.altonjohn.com
Jonathon Heaton B&B, $50–$75
  (435) 648-2164 or toll-free (888) 741-
  7099; sylyoung@color-country.net,
  members.aol.com/galarae/bandbhome.
  html
Cedar City
The Garden Cottage B&B, $80–$90
  (435) 586-4919;
  www.thegardencottagebnb.com
Stratford B&B, $80
  (702) 898-5704 or (435) 867-5280 or
  toll-free (877) 530-5280
Willow Glen Inn B&B, $50–$100
  (801) 586-3275; info@willowgleninn.
  com, www.willowgleninn.com
Glendale
Dream Catcher B&B, $49–$125
  (435) 648-2162 or toll-free (800) 645-
  3003; dcatcher@color-country.net,
  www.dreamcatcherbb.net
Homeplace B&B, $49
  (435) 648-2194; 103230.2721@aol.com,
  www.members.aol.com/hmplaceut/
  homeplace.html
Hatch
Calico Home B&B, $50–$75
  (435) 735-4382
Hurricane
Pah Tempe Mineral Hot Springs, $59–$80
  (435) 635-2879 or toll-free (888) 726-

8367; pahtempe@infowest.com,
  www.infowest.com/pahtempe
Marysvale
Moore's Old Pine Inn, $50–$75
  (435) 326-4565 or toll-free (800) 887-
  4565; oldpine@color-country.net,
  www.marysvale.org/pine-inn.html
Mt. Carmel Junction
Sugar Knoll B&B, $50–$75
  (435) 648-2335; mrogers@lds.net,
  www.sugarknoll.com
Panguitch
L&L B&B, $50–$75
  (435) 676-2228
The William Prince Inn B&B, $49–$69
  (435) 676-2525 or toll-free (888) 676-
  2525, quilts@color-country.net
Rockville
Blue House B&B, $50–$75
  (435) 772-3912
Dream Catcher Inn, $50-$80
  (435) 772-3600 or toll-free (800) 95-
  dream; www.burgoyne.com/pages/dcinn
Serenity House B&B, $45–$75
  (435) 772-3393
Springdale
Canyon Vista Bed & Breakfast, $95
  (435) 772-3801;
  www.canyonvistabandb.com
O'Tooles Under the Eaves, $50–$125
  (435) 772-3457; www.otooles.com
Red Rock Inn, $75–$125
  (435) 772-3139

ZONE 20: Southwest *(continued)*

Teasdale
Cockscomb Inn B&B, $50–$75
(435) 425-3511 or toll-free (800) 530-
1030; coxcomb@color-country.net,
www.go-utah.com/cockscombinn
Toquerville
Springs Creek Gardens, $50–$75
(435) 635-3053

Tropic
Buffalo Sage B&B, $65–$85
(435) 679-8443; buffalosage@
scinternet.net, www.buffalosage.com

ZONE 21: Southeast

Bluff
Calabre B&B, $45
(435) 672-2252; www.calabre.com
Calf Canyon B&B, $65–$85
(435) 672-2470 or toll-free (888) 922-
2470; www.calfcanyon.com
Boulder
Eaglestar Ranch B&B, $35–$50
(435) 335-7438; belnap@color-
country.net, www.eaglestarranch.com
Castle Valley
Castle Valley Inn, $66–$165
(435) 259-6012 or toll-free (888) 466-
6012; www.castlevalleyinn.com
La Sal
Mt. Peale Country Inn & Retreat,
$75–$115 (435) 686-2284
Mexican Hat
Valley of the Gods B&B, $95–$115
(979) 749-1164
Moab
Adobe Abode, $110
(435) 259-7716; adobeabode@lasal.net,
www.adobeabodemoab.com
Aunt Aggie's B&B, $79
(435) 259-4961

Canyon Country B&B, $65–$110
(435) 259-5262 or toll-free (888) 350-
5262; mail@canyoncountrybb.com,
www.canyoncountrybb.com
Desert Chalet, $45–$75
(435) 259-5793 or toll-free (800) 549-
8504; www.moab-utah.com/desertchalet
The Old Peachtree Inn, $75–$100
(435) 259-3453 or toll-free (800) 246-
0824; opeachtree@lasal.net,
www.theoldpeachtreeinn.com
Pioneer Springs B&B, $65–$80
(435) 259-4663; www.
moab-utah.com/pioneerspring
Tomahawk B&B, $90–$125
(435) 259-8125; tomahawk@lasal.net,
www.moab-utah.com/tomahawk
Vernal
Landmark Inn, $50–$175
(435) 781-1800 or toll-free (888) 738-
1800, landmark@easilink.com,
www.landmark-inn.com

Index